15   DATA ANALYSIS–BASIC QUESTIONS 390
     Choice of Analysis Technique: An Example 390
     Basic Considerations 393
     Overview of Statistical Procedures 399
     Summary 400
     Questions 401
     Applications and Problems 401
     Appendix: Quick Stats Review 402
     Null Hypothesis 402
     Types of Errors 404
     Procedure 405
     Power 407
     Summary 412
     Questions 412
     Applications and Problems 412

16   ARE MY GROUPS THE SAME OR DIFFERENT? 413
     Hypotheses about One Mean 413
     Hypotheses about Two Means 416
     Hypotheses about Two Proportions 423
     Summary 426
     Questions 426
     Applications and Problems 426
     Appendix: Analysis of Variance 428
     Randomized Blocks 432
     Summary 438
     Questions 438
     Applications and Problems 439

17   ARE THESE VARIABLES RELATED? 441
     Simple Regression and Correlation Analysis 441
     Simple Regression 442
     Correlation Coefficient 451
     Multiple-Regression Analysis 454
     Summary 460
     Questions 460
     Applications and Problems 460
     Appendix: Conjoint Analysis 463
     Variable Transformations 463
     Dummy Variables 464
     Conjoint Analysis 465
     Summary 475
     Questions 475
     Applications and Problems 475

18   MULTIVARIATE DATA ANALYSIS 477
     Discriminant Analysis 477
     Factor Analysis 491
     Cluster Analysis 506
     Multidimensional Scaling and Perceptual Mapping 524
     Summary 533
     Questions 533
     Applications and Problems 533
     Appendix: More Multivariate Statistical Techniques 537
     Correspondence Analysis 537

Structural Equations Models 539
Neural Networks 540
Social Networks 541
Cases for Part 5
Case 5.1   CTM Productions (B) 544
Case 5.2   E-Food and the Online Grocery Competition (C) 544
Case 5.3   Internet Advertising and Your Brain (B) 545
Case 5.4   A Picture Is Worth a Megabyte of Words:
            Census Data and Trends in Lifestyle Purchases 546
Case 5.5   CountryCable: Customer Satisfaction Survey Data 547
Case 5.6   Teeth-Whitening Conjoint Study 549
Case 5.7   Sports Marketing and Television Programming 549
Case 5.8   Repositioning a Brand 552
Case 5.9   Conjoint—Brand & Pricing 553
Case 5.10   Segmentation Study 554

part 6 The Research Report 557

19   THE RESEARCH REPORT 558
      Criteria of Research Reports 558
      The Oral Report 563
      Graphic Presentation of the Results 566
      Summary 571
      Questions 571
      Applications and Problems 572

      Epilogue 573

      Appendix A: Cumulative Probabilities for the Standard Normal Distribution 576

      Appendix B: Critical Values of χ^2 577

      Appendix C: Critical Values of t 579

      Appendix D: Percentage Points of the F Distribution. $\alpha = .05$ 580

      GLOSSARY 584
      SUBJECT INDEX 594
      AUTHOR INDEX 602

marketing
research

Methodological Foundations 10e

Dawn **Iacobucci**
Owen Graduate School of Management,
Vanderbilt University

Gilbert A. **Churchill**, Jr.
University of Wisconsin—Madison

SOUTH-WESTERN
CENGAGE Learning™

Australia • Brazil • Japan • Korea • Mexico • Singapore • Spain • United Kingdom • United States

SOUTH-WESTERN
CENGAGE Learning™

Marketing Research: Methodological Foundations, Tenth Edition
Dawn Iacobucci, Gilbert A. Churchill, Jr.

Vice President of Editorial, Business:
Jack W. Calhoun

Editor-in-Chief: Melissa Acuña

Executive Editor: Mike Roche

Developmental Editor: Suzanna Bainbridge

Marketing Coordinator: Shanna Shelton

Sr. Content Project Manager:
Martha Conway

Media Editor: John Rich

Frontlist Buyer, Manufacturing:
Miranda Klapper

Sr. Marketing Communications Manager:
Sarah Greber

Production Technology Analyst:
Emily Gross

Sr. Text Permissions Manager:
Margaret Chamberlain-Gaston

Production Service: Macmillan Publishing
Services

Sr. Art Director: Stacy Jenkins Shirley

Cover Designer: Chris Miller

Cover Image: © Shutterstock

Library of Congress Control Number: 2009934717

International Student Edition with Qualtrics ISBN 13: 978-0-538-74377-8

International Student Edition with Qualtrics ISBN 10: 0-538-74377-8

Cengage Learning International Offices

Asia
cengageasia.com
tel: (65) 6410 1200

Australia/New Zealand
cengage.com.au
tel: (61) 3 9685 4111

Brazil
cengage.com.br
tel: (011) 3665 9900

India
cengage.co.in
tel: (91) 11 30484837/38

Latin America
cengage.com.mx
tel: +52 (55) 1500 6000

UK/Europe/Middle East/Africa
cengage.co.uk
tel: (44) 207 067 2500

Represented in Canada by Nelson Education, Ltd.
nelson.com
tel: (416) 752 9100 / (000) 668 0671

For product information: **www.cengage.com/international**
Visit your local office: **www.cengage.com/global**
Visit our corporate website: **www.cengage.com**

Printed in Canada
2 3 4 5 6 7 13 12 11

part 1   Marketing Research and the Research Process 1

   1   Marketing Research: It's Everywhere! 2

   2   Alternative Approaches to Marketing Intelligence 18

   3   The Research Process and Problem Formulation 29

       Cases for Part 1 48

part 2   Determine Research Design 57

   4   Research Design, Exploratory Research, and Qualitative Data 58

   5   Descriptive Research 84

   6   Causal Designs 99

       Cases for Part 2 127

part 3   Design Data-Collection Methods and Forms 141

   7   Data Collection: Secondary Data 142

       Appendix 7: Secondary Data 173

   8   Data Collection: Primary Data 177

   9   Questionnaires and Data-Collection Forms 204

  10   Attitude Measurement 232

       Appendix 10: Psychological Measurement 251

       Cases for Part 3 263

part 4   Sample Design for Data Collection and Sample Size 281

  11   Sampling Procedures 282

  12   Determining Sample Size 312

  13   Field Procedures for Collecting the Data 328

       Cases for Part 4 344

part 5   Data Analysis and Interpretation 349

  14   Preprocessing the Data, and Doing Cross-Tabs 350

       Appendix 14: Chi-Square and Related Indices for Cross-Tabs 378

  15   Data Analysis–Basic Questions 390

       Appendix 15: Quick Stats Review 402

  16   Are My Groups the Same or Different? 413

       Appendix 16: Analysis of Variance 428

  17   Are These Variables Related? 441

       Appendix 17: Conjoint Analysis 463

  18   Multivariate Data Analysis 477

       Appendix 18: More Multivariate Statistical Techniques 537

       Cases for Part 5 544

part 6   The Research Report 557

  19   The Research Report 558

       Epilogue 573

       Appendix A: Cumulative Probabilities for the Standard Normal Distribution 576

       Appendix B: Critical Values of χ^2 577

       Appendix C: Critical Values of t 579

       Appendix D: Percentage Points of the F Distribution. $\alpha = .05$ 580

       Glossary 584

       Subject Index 594

       Author Index 602

part 1 ## Marketing Research and the Research Process 1

1   MARKETING RESEARCH: IT'S EVERYWHERE! 2

Role of Marketing Research 3
Who Does Marketing Research? 7
Organization of Marketing Research 11
Employment Opportunities in Marketing Research 13
Summary 15
Questions 16
Applications and Problems 16

2   ALTERNATIVE APPROACHES TO MARKETING INTELLIGENCE 18

Marketing Information Systems and Decision Support Systems 19
Components of MISs and DSSs 20
Using the Data, Model, and Interface 24
Comparing Marketing Information Technologies and Marketing Research Projects 24
Data Mining 25
Summary 28
Questions 28
Applications and Problems 28

3   THE RESEARCH PROCESS AND PROBLEM FORMULATION 29

Marketing Research—Sequence of Steps 29
Problem Formulation 34
The Decision Maker and the Environment 35
Translating Decision Problem to Research Problem 37
The Research Proposal 38
Is Marketing Research Justified? 42
Choosing and Using a Research Supplier 44
Summary 46
Questions 46
Applications and Problems 46
Cases for Part 1
Case 1.1   Big Brothers of Fairfax County **48**
Case 1.2   Using Loyalty Data at Flowers 4U **48**
Case 1.3   E-Food and the Online Grocery Competition (A) **49**
Case 1.4   Choosing a Brand Name **50**
Case 1.5   Moving Consumers from Awareness to Loyalty **51**
Case 1.6   Qualitative Data from Open-Ended Survey Items: A Service Quality Example **52**
Case 1.7   Extending a Travel Brand **54**

part 2 ## Determine Research Design 57

4   RESEARCH DESIGN, EXPLORATORY RESEARCH, AND QUALITATIVE DATA 58

Plan of Action 58
Types of Research Design 58

Exploratory Research 60
Relationship Between Exploratory Research and Qualitative Data 61
Some Basic Types of Exploratory Research 61
Standard Qualitative Marketing Research Methods 63
Summary 81
Questions 81
Applications and Problems 82

5   DESCRIPTIVE RESEARCH 84
When to Use Descriptive Research 84
Longitudinal Analysis 86
Cross-Sectional Analysis 93
Summary 96
Questions 96
Applications and Problems 96

6   CAUSAL DESIGNS 99
Concept of Causality 99
Role of the Evidence 103
Laboratory and Field Experiments 105
Internal and External Validity 107
Experimental Design 107
Specific Designs 111
Experimentation in Marketing Research 119
Problems of Experimentation 119
Types of Test Markets 120
Summary 123
Questions 124
Applications and Problems 124
Cases for Part 2
Case 2.1   Riverside County Humane Society (A) 127
Case 2.2   HotStuff Computer Software (A) 127
Case 2.3   Advertising Agency's Databank 129
Case 2.4   Bakhill Foods 130
Case 2.5   Internet Advertising and Your Brain (A) 132
Case 2.6   Customer Relationship Management 133
Case 2.7   Ethnography in Practice: The Case of ESPN Zone, Chicago 135
Case 2.8   Brand Association Maps 138

part 3   Design Data-Collection Methods and Forms 141

7   DATA COLLECTION: SECONDARY DATA 142
Using Secondary Data 142
Types of Secondary Data 148
Standardized Marketing Information Services 156
Summary 171
Questions 171
Applications and Problems 171
Appendix: Secondary Data 173

8   DATA COLLECTION: PRIMARY DATA 177
     Types of Primary Data 177
     Basic Means of Obtaining Primary Data 186
     Communication Methods 188
     Questionnaires Classified by Method of Administration 191
     Structured vs. Unstructured and Disguised vs. Undisguised Observation 201
     Summary 202
     Questions 202
     Applications and Problems 202

9   QUESTIONNAIRES AND DATA-COLLECTION FORMS 204
     Questionnaire Design 204
     Observational Forms 224
     Summary 228
     Questions 229
     Applications and Problems 229

10   ATTITUDE MEASUREMENT 232
     Scales of Measurement 233
     Scaling of Psychological Attributes 235
     Which Scale to Use 247
     Summary 248
     Questions 248
     Applications and Problems 248
     Appendix: Psychological Measurement 251
     Variations in Measured Scores 253
     Classification and Assessment of Error 254
     Direct Assessment of Validity 256
     Indirect Assessment Through Reliability 258
     Summary 260
     Questions 261
     Applications and Problems 261
     Cases for Part 3
     Case 3.1   E-Food and the Online Grocery Competition (B) 263
     Case 3.2   Premium Pizza Inc. 264
     Case 3.3   CTM Productions (A) 268
     Case 3.4   Comparing Ads Against a Databank 270
     Case 3.5   Measuring Magazines 271
     Case 3.6   Secondary Data on Health from CDC 273
     Case 3.7   Critiquing Questionnaires 274

part 4   Sample Design for Data Collection and Sample Size 281

11   SAMPLING PROCEDURES 282
     Required Steps 283
     Types of Sampling Plans 285
     Nonprobability Samples 286
     Probability Samples 287
     Summary 308
     Questions 309
     Applications and Problems 309

12   DETERMINING SAMPLE SIZE 312
      Basic Considerations 312
      Sample Size Determination When Estimating Means 313
      Sample Size Determination When Estimating Proportions 319
      Population Size and Sample Size 321
      Other Probability Sampling Plans 321
      Using Anticipated Cross Tabs to Determine Sample Size 322
      Summary 325
      Questions 325
      Applications and Problems 325

13   FIELD PROCEDURES FOR COLLECTING THE DATA 328
      Impact of Nonsampling Errors 328
      Types of Nonsampling Errors 329
      Total Error Is Key 340
      Summary 341
      Questions 342
      Applications and Problems 342
      Cases for Part 4
      Case 4.1   Riverside County Humane Society (B) 344
      Case 4.2   Sampling Lead-Users for New Products 344
      Case 4.3   Sampling from Your Loyalty
                  Database 345
      Case 4.4   International Differences in the
                  Cost of Data 345
      Case 4.5   Online Samples 346
      Case 4.6   Sampling Gambling 347

part 5   Data Analysis and Interpretation 349

14   PREPROCESSING THE DATA, AND DOING CROSS-TABS 350
      Editing 350
      Coding 351
      Tabulation 352
      Goodness-of-Fit Chi-Square Test on One Variable 359
      Kolmogorov-Smirnov Test 362
      Contingent Relationships in Cross-Tabs 364
      Presenting Tabular Data 374
      Summary 375
      Questions 375
      Applications and Problems 376
      Appendix: Chi-Square and Related Indices for Cross-Tabs 378
      Hypotheses and Statistics to Test Them 378
      Log Linear Models 382
      Nonparametric Measures of Association 385
      Summary 388
      Questions 388
      Applications and Problems 388

Intended Market

This book *introduces* marketing research to MBA students, Executive MBA students, and advanced undergraduates. It also serves as a *reference resource* for marketing managers.

Marketing research is complicated—it requires answers to many questions, and tough decisions are made at each step in the process, e.g., techniques to be used to solve the research problem. In this book, we provide an over-arching framework so that students won't become overwhelmed by the bits and pieces, and they'll be able to see the relationship of the parts to the whole. This appreciation is important because decisions made at one stage in the marketing research process have consequences for other stages.

This book attempts to serve both the marketing manager and marketing researchers through its basic organization around the *stages of the research process:*

1. Formulate the problem.
2. Determine the research design.
3. Design the data-collection method and forms.
4. Design the sample and collect the data.
5. Analyze and interpret the data.
6. Prepare the research report.

Each stage is discussed in several chapters. Breaking the steps down allows the reader to see the forest for the trees, and it gives instructors latitude about what is covered. An instructor's decision on what to cover will depend, of course, on the background, interests, and preparation of the students, and on the time provided in the curriculum for marketing research.

Organization

Part 1, on *formulating the problem,* consists of three chapters. Chapter 1 provides an overview of marketing research, including the kinds of problems for which it is used and who is doing research. Chapter 2 provides an overview of the various ways of gathering marketing intelligence. It emphasizes the increasingly important role played by marketing intelligence systems in providing business and competitive information. Chapter 3 overviews the research process in terms of the kinds of decisions to be made at each stage and then discusses in greater detail the problem formulation stage of the research process.

Part 2 consists of three chapters and deals with the nature of the *research design.* It emphasizes ensuring that the research addresses the appropriate questions and treats them in an efficient manner. Chapter 4 presents the varieties of research designs, then proceeds to exploratory research and qualitative data. Chapter 5 presents aspects of descriptive designs. Chapter 6 discusses the role of experiments.

In Part 3, we get into data. We discuss methods of data collection and the design of *data-collection forms.* Chapter 7 focuses on secondary data as an information resource and includes a discussion of commercial marketing information services. The prime sources of secondary data are just a click away on our Web site. Chapter 8 discusses the kinds of information we can gather, e.g., attitudes and behaviors, and the means by which we can gather that information, e.g., via observation or techniques that rely on forms of communication (e.g., interviews, surveys). Chapter 9 covers the construction of questionnaires. Chapter 10 explains the general topic of attitude measurement using scales and discusses some of the more common types of attitude scales. The important topic of developing measures for marketing constructs is discussed in the appendix to Chapter 10.

Part 4, which consists of three chapters, is concerned with the *actual data collection* to answer questions. Chapter 11 discusses the various types of sampling plans that can be used to determine the population elements from which data should be collected. Chapter 12 treats the question of how many of these elements are needed, so that the problem can be answered with the required precision and confidence in the results. Chapter 13 discusses the types of errors that can arise in completing this data-collection task, so that managers can assess the quality of the information they receive from research.

Once data have been collected, emphasis in the research process logically turns to *data analysis,* which amounts to searching for meaning in the collected information. The five chapters and several appendices in Part 5 present an overview of these steps and questions. Chapter 14 reviews the preliminary analysis steps of editing, coding, and tabulating the data. The appendix covers chi-squares and related approaches to analyzing categorical data. Chapter 15 provides a framework of basic questions that must be resolved before statistical examination of the data can begin.

Next, Chapters 16, 17, and 18 review the statistical techniques most useful in the analysis of marketing data. Chapter 16 discusses the procedures appropriate for examining the differences between groups; Chapter 17 covers the assessment of association—namely, correlation and regression, including conjoint analysis; and Chapter 18 examines the multivariate techniques of discriminant analysis, factor analysis, cluster analysis, and multidimensional scaling. The appendix to Chapter 18 introduces correspondence analysis, structural equations modeling, neural network models, and social networks.

Part 6 consists of one chapter and an epilogue. Chapter 19 discusses a critical part of the research process, the *research report,* which often becomes the standard by which the research effort is assessed. Chapter 19 discusses the criteria a research report should satisfy and the form it can follow to contribute positively to the research effort. This chapter also discusses some of the graphical means that can be used to communicate the findings. The epilogue ties together the elements of the research process by demonstrating in overview fashion their interrelationships.

Organizational Flexibility

Given the flexibility in structure of this book, *Marketing Research: Methodological Foundations,* 10th ed., can be used in a variety of marketing research course sequences: one- or two-quarter sequences, semester courses, etc. For example, instructors with only a single, brief introductory course in marketing research who hope their students will develop a basic appreciation might choose to overview the research process at an elementary level. One way to accomplish this would be to omit Chapters 6, 10, and 12, and use only Chapter 14 from among the five analysis chapters. This approach would serve to present the basics.

In contrast, instructors who wish to emphasize, say, data analysis would have ample materials to do so. There are databases online that instructors can have students analyze. Students can perform their own analyses, thereby increasing their comfort level with the statistical techniques discussed.

Each part of the book offers cases to illustrate the issues. The cases present actual situations, although many of them have disguised names and locations to protect the identity of the sponsors. Students can apply what they have learned by critically evaluating what others have done, thereby increasing their analytic skills.

To help students, there are:

- Cases at the end of each section to develop evaluation and analytical skills. The cases are diverse across industries, and raw data are available to let students try various analyses.

- Ethical Dilemmas present students with scenarios that arise when making marketing research choices. Students can be challenged to see the advantages and disadvantages of making certain choice and in their social consequences.

- Research Realities illustrate what is going on in the world of marketing research today, both in general and at specific companies.

- Problems at the end of chapters have students apply the concepts to very focused situations, to develop an understanding of the strengths and weaknesses of various techniques.

- The Thorndike Video Case is structured so that the segments follow the sections of the books, so it can interact with students and simulate a real world research process.

- NFO Coffee Study. The questionnaire, coding form, and raw data from a study on ground coffee conducted by NFO are used to frame a number of application problems. Everything is online and it allows students to work with "live" data in honing their skills in translating research problems into data analysis issues and in interpreting computer output.

For instructors:

- Due to their popularity, we've retained the Thorndike Sports Video Case (it's online, alone with the Avery Sporting Goods materials), the "Ethical Dilemmas" presented in each chapter, and the Research Realities to demonstrate to students "how they do it in the *real world.*"

- There is a lot of support for instructors online (data bases, slides, lecture support, etc.).

  ○ An Instructor's Manual to help the instructor cover the material, depending on their desired emphases and time frames. For each chapter, there are resources: 1) learning objectives, 2) list of key terms, 3) detailed outline, 4) lecture and discussion suggestions, 5) suggested supplementary readings, 6) answers to the application questions and/or problems in the book, 7) more exercises (and answers) for students, and 8) suggested cases for the chapter, from our cases and from HBS.

  ○ New cases, covering these applications:

    ▪ loyalty and RFM

    ▪ brand extensions

- advertising databases
- brand associations
- new products lead-users
- customer satisfaction and CRM
- online marketing research samples
- conjoint: brand equity and pricing
- segmentation study

○ There are slides drawn from the book and others to facilitate classroom discussion.

○ There are 1,100+ test questions (multiple choice) in a computerized test bank. The computerized test bank enables instructors to preview and edit test questions, as well as add their own. The test and answer keys can also be printed in scrambled formats.

○ Data Disk. The raw data for the cases are online, which allows instructors and students to use them for analysis.

○ Video Collection. In addition to the Thorndike Video Case, there are other clips online. Companies ranging from Fossil watches to Hard Candy focus on the ideas and concepts presented throughout the text.

This book is intended to teach, but it is also an extraordinary reference—it's very thorough. In addition, the level of difficulty of material naturally varies within and across the chapters. Some sections are straightforward, while others are more abstract or technical, and more challenging for readers. We do not shy away from topics simply because they can be challenging; that is, we didn't want to produce a marketing research text that is fluff. We also didn't want to provide a book decipherable only by highly motivated techno-geeks. We hope that the reader finds the material clearly presented. You'll also see in *Marketing Research: Methodological Foundations*, 10th ed., sections that professors can teach through, or ask students to skip when reading.

ACKNOWLEDGMENTS

I'd like to thank Gil Churchill, a wonderful coauthor and mentor. I thank Curt Dommeyer (Cal State, Northridge) for an amazing eye. I also thank the Cengage team, Melissa Acuña, Michael Roche, John Abner, Neil Marquardt, Suzanna Bainbridge, Martha Conway, and an astonishingly terrific sales force.

Dawn Iacobucci
Nashville, Tennessee

Writing a book is never the work of a single person, and when attempting to acknowledge the contributions of others, one always runs the risk of omitting some important contributions. Nonetheless, the attempt must be made, because this book has been helped immensely by the many helpful comments I have received along the way from users and interested colleagues. I especially wish to acknowledge those people who reviewed the manuscript for this or for one of the earlier editions of the book. While much of the credit for the strengths of the book is theirs, the blame for any weaknesses is strictly mine. Thank you one and all for your most perceptive and helpful comments.

My colleagues at the University of Wisconsin have my thanks for the intellectual stimulation they have always provided. Dr. B. Venkatesh was particularly instrumental in getting the first edition off the ground. My discussions with him were important in determining the scope and structure of the book.

I wish to thank the many assistants at the University of Wisconsin, especially Janet Christopher, who helped in the preparation of one or more versions of the manuscript. I also wish to thank students Tom Brown, Sara Evans, Margaret Friedman, Diana Haytko, Jacqueline Hitchon, Larry Hogue, Joseph Kuester, Jayashree Mahajan, Jennifer Markanen, Sara Pitterle, Kay Powers, and Frank Wadsworth for their help with many of the miscellaneous tasks on either this edition or one of the earlier editions. I would like to thank the acquisitions editor and the developmental editor, as well as the entire production staff at Cengage for their professional effort. I also want to thank P.J. Ward of NFO for contributing the questionnaire, coding form, database, and the compatible problems and exercises using the database regarding coffee consumption that illustrate so nicely the statistical ideas discussed in the text. I am grateful to the literary executor of the late Sir Ronald A. Fisher, F.R.S., to Dr. Frank Yates, F.R.S., and to the Longman Group Ltd., London, for permission to reprint Table III from their book *Statistical Tables for Biological, Agricultural and Medical Research* (6th edition, 1974).

Finally, I owe a special debt of thanks to my wife, Helen, and our four children, Carol, Elizabeth, David, and Thomas. Their understanding, cooperation, and support through all editions of this book are sincerely appreciated.

Gilbert A. Churchill, Jr.
Madison, Wisconsin

Mark I. Alpert, *University of Texas–Austin*

Robert L. Anderson, *University of South Florida*

Gary M. Armstrong, *University of North Carolina*

Emin Babakus, *University of Memphis*

Sri Beldona, *University of Dallas*

Frank J. Carmone, Jr., *Drexel University*

Joseph Chasin, *St. John's University*

Imran S. Currim, *University of California–Irvine*

Michael R. Czinkota, *Georgetown University*

Albert J. DellaBitta, *University of Rhode Island*

John Dickinson, *University of Windsor*

James F. Engel, *Eastern College*

Peter Faynzilberg, *Carnegie Mellon University*

Claes Fornell, *University of Michigan*

Margot Griffin, *California Lutheran University*

Sachin Gupta, *Northwestern University*

James W. Harvey, *George Mason University*

Vince Howe, *University of North Carolina–Wilmington*

Roy Howell, *Texas Tech University*

G. David Hughes, *University of North Carolina*

Dipak C. Jain, *Northwestern University*

Robert Krapfel, *University of Maryland*

Patrick Kurby, *Rutgers University*

H. Bruce Lammers, *California State University–Northridge*

Peter La Placa, *University of Connecticut*

Charles L. Martin, *Wichita State University*

M. Dean Martin, *Western Carolina University*

David Mick, *University of Virginia*

Carlos W. Moore, *Baylor University*

David J. Moore, *University of Michigan*

Carl Obermiller, *Seattle University*

Christie H. Paksoy, *University of North Carolina–Charlotte*

Kalyan Ramon, *University of Florida*

C. P. Rao, *University of Arkansas*

Arno Rethans, *California State University–Chico*

Kenneth J. Roering, *University of Minnesota*

Abhijit Roy, *Plymouth State College*

William Rudelius, *University of Minnesota*

Alan G. Sawyer, *University of Florida*

Randall L. Schultz, *University of Texas–Dallas*

Subrata K. Sen, *Yale University*

Allan D. Shocker, *University of Minnesota*

Seymour Sudman, *University of Illinois*

David Szymanski, *Texas A&M University*
Sandra Teel, *University of South Carolina*
Robert Thomas, *Georgetown University*
Rex S. Toh, *Seattle University*
David J. Urban, *Virginia Commonwealth University*
Elizabeth J. Wilson, *Boston College*

Dawn Iacobucci is the E. Bronson Ingram Professor of Marketing at the Owen Graduate School of Management, Vanderbilt University. Prior to joining Owen, Iacobucci was Professor of Marketing at Kellogg (1987–2004), Wharton (2004–2007), and The University of Arizona (2001–2002). Her research focuses on social networks and methodological questions. She has published in the *Journal of Consumer Psychology, Journal of Marketing, Journal of Marketing Research, Journal of Service Research, Harvard Business Review, Marketing Science, International Journal of Research in Marketing, Psychometrika, Psychological Bulletin,* and *Social Networks.* Iacobucci teaches Marketing Management, Marketing Research, Marketing Models, Services Marketing, and New Products to MBA and executive MBA students, and multivariate statistics and methodological topics in Ph.D. seminars. She is recent editor of both the *Journal of Consumer Research* and *Journal of Consumer Psychology.* She edited *Networks in Marketing, Handbook of Services Marketing and Management, Kellogg on Marketing, Kellogg on Integrated Marketing,* and she is author of *Mediation Analysis* and of *Marketing Management* (also published by Cengage).

Gilbert A. Churchill, Jr., received his DBA from Indiana University in 1966 and joined the University of Wisconsin faculty in 1966. Professor Churchill was named Distinguished Marketing Educator by the American Marketing Association in 1986—only the second individual so honored. The lifetime achievement award recognizes and honors a living marketing educator for distinguished service and outstanding contributions in the field of marketing education. Professor Churchill was also awarded the Academy of Marketing Science's lifetime achievement award in 1993 for his significant scholarly contributions. In 1996, he received a Paul D. Converse Award, which is given to the most influential marketing scholars, as judged by a national jury drawn from universities, businesses, and government. Also in 1996, the Marketing Research Group of the American Marketing Association established the Gilbert A. Churchill, Jr., lifetime achievement award, which is to be given each year to a person judged to have made significant lifetime contributions to marketing research. In 2002, he received the Charles Coolidge Parlin lifetime achievement award for his substantial contributions to the ongoing advancement of marketing research practice.

Professor Churchill is a past recipient of the William O'Dell Award for the outstanding article appearing in the *Journal of Marketing Research* during the year. He has also been a finalist for the award five other times. He is a coauthor of the most and third-most influential articles of the past century in sales managements as judged by a panel of experts in the field. He was named Marketer of the Year by the South Central Wisconsin Chapter of the American Marketing Association in 1981. He is a member of the American Marketing Association and has served as consultant to a number of companies, including Oscar Mayer, Western Publishing Company, and Parker Pen.

Professor Churchill's articles have appeared in such publications as the *Journal of Marketing Research, Journal of Marketing, Journal of Consumer Research, Journal of Retailing, Journal of Business Research, Decision Sciences, Technometrics,* and *Organizational Behavior and Human Performance,* among others. He is coauthor of several books, including *Basic Marketing Research,* 7th ed. (Mason, OH: Cengage, 2010) *Marketing: Creating Value for Customers,* 2nd ed. (Burr Ridge, IL:

McGraw-Hill, 1998), *Sales Force Management: Planning, Implementation, and Control,* 6th ed. (Burr Ridge, IL: Irwin/McGraw-Hill, 2000), and *Salesforce Performance* (Lexington, MA: Lexington Books, 1984), in addition to his coauthorship of *Marketing Research: Methodological Foundations,* 10th ed. (Mason, OH: Cengage, 2010). He is a former editor of the *Journal of Marketing Research* and has served on the editorial boards of the *Journal of Marketing Research, Journal of Marketing, Journal of Business Research, Journal of Health Care Marketing,* and the *Asian Journal of Marketing.* Professor Churchill is a past recipient of the Lawrence J. Larson Excellence in Teaching Award.

Marketing Research and the Research Process

We begin with two basic questions: What is marketing research? Why is it important?

Chapter 1 illustrates the enormous variety of problems that marketing research can address and the types of business people who require a working knowledge: marketing researchers and marketing managers of course, but also consultants, entrepreneurs, financial analysts—anybody who seeks an edge in understanding customers in competitive market environments.

Chapter 2 discusses alternative ways of providing marketing intelligence, namely, projects designed to investigate specific issues, or information technologies for ongoing data collection and analytical systems.

Chapter 3 presents the research process that forms the backbone of this book and discusses in detail the problem formulation stage of that process.

Marketing Research: It's Everywhere!

1

Questions to Guide Your Learning:

Q1 What is marketing research?

Q2 What kinds of questions can marketing research answer?

Q3 Why is marketing research important?

Q4 What is the relationship among marketing, marketing research, and the rest of the firm?

Q5 Who does marketing research?

Many people think that marketing research is about asking consumers what they think about a brand or ad. That's true, but it's so much more. Consider these examples.

EXAMPLE After watching countless hours of videotapes of consumers entering various retail outlets such as department stores, grocery stores, and banks, marketing researchers have advised against investing in elaborate store displays for the first 30 feet from the entrance—the "decompression zone" in which shoppers are merely getting oriented to the store layout and are not inclined to pick up merchandise for purchase. Similarly, researchers noted that most consumers are likely to veer right as they proceed into the store, not because most are right-handed, but because we drive on the right—British and Australian consumers veer left.[1]

EXAMPLE Social networks are everywhere, and naturally they're affecting marketing research too.[2] User groups support each other, from geeks exchanging tips in troubleshooting electronics to new moms offering suggestions for baby products. Online brand and affinity communities offer efficient samples of highly involved consumers. Thus, new product concepts are easily tested, as are comparisons among competitive product offerings and their attributes.

EXAMPLE Radio Frequency Identification (RFID) tags contain microchips and tiny radio antennas and increasingly are embedded in product labels on anything from skin-care products to frozen foods.[3] RFIDs help manufacturers and retailers with inventory. They provide convenience to customers, from gas station swipe fobs to credit card instant approval. They also help

---

[1] Paco Underhill, *Why We Buy: The Science of Shopping* (Simon & Schuster, 2008).
[2] Mike Cooke and Nick Buckley (2008), "Web 2.0, Social Networks and the Future of Market Research," *International Journal of Market Research* 50, (2), 267–292.
[3] Sam K. Hui, Peter S. Fader, and Eric T. Bradlow, "The Traveling Salesman Goes Shopping," *Marketing Science*.

pharmaceutical companies track prescription drugs to discourage counterfeiters. And they send data to marketing researchers for subsequent number crunching. Marketers can follow the shopping path a customer's grocery cart takes around the store and advise the redesign of the retail layout.

EXAMPLE Marketing researchers are using online chat-rooms as a focus group forum. They cite large savings in travel expenses, because the participants can log in from all over the world. New product concepts and advertisements can be tested online just as easily as in person. Focus group tapes don't need to be transcribed, because the online focus group is conducted in text. Critics say that nonverbal body language is lost online, but supporters respond that they encourage participants to use emoticons, and note that soon video capabilities will be faster, allowing participants to see each other, simulating more closely a traditional focus group.[4]

> Good decisions require good information.

EXAMPLE Marketing research is increasingly being used to determine ROI for various marketing mix tactics, ultimately also justifying its own value to the firm. CEOs understand that marketing research may be useful, but they want it to be "cost-effective." For example, don't start from scratch with each project, but build on existing in-house information; use research to keep existing customers; run field experiments to measure ROI.[5]

These examples begin to illustrate the scope of marketing research. Obtaining customer insights via marketing research is a pervasive activity that takes many forms. The choice of marketing research tools depends on the problem to be solved. The basic purpose of marketing research is to help managers make better decisions. Marketing research gives managers and CEOs an edge—an edge that is particularly useful in competitive markets or tough economic times.[6]

> Marketing Research turns *data* into *information*.

Role of Marketing Research

Every day, marketing managers are called upon to make *decisions*, and whether large or small, every decision is better informed with the intelligent use of marketing research. Effective decision making depends on quality input, and marketing research translates data into useful information. Any business seeking an edge in attracting and retaining customers in competitive market environments turns to marketing. Marketing can create strategies to enhance attraction and retention, if the business understands its customers. This understanding comes through marketing research.

Beyond marketing researchers and marketers, a working knowledge of marketing research helps anybody's business career. For example, much of management consulting is fundamentally marketing research. Entrepreneurs enhance their likelihood of success by understanding their customer base. Financial analysts need to understand the perceptions of their customers to sell their products.

Organizations that are not businesses can also benefit. For example, land developers choose site locations for malls and parks using marketing research. Politicians and trial lawyers use marketing research to test spin strategies. Clergy

---

[4] Marketing Sherpa, reported in "Measure Twice," *Marketing News* (Sept. 1, 2008), p. 26.
[5] Deborah Colby, "Using Marketing Research," *Quirk's Marketing Research Review* (www.quirks.com).
[6] Aberdeen Group says more than half of the "Best in Class" companies are increasing their budgets for customer analytics ("Most Best-in-Class Companies to Raise Analytics Budgets," marketingcharts.com).

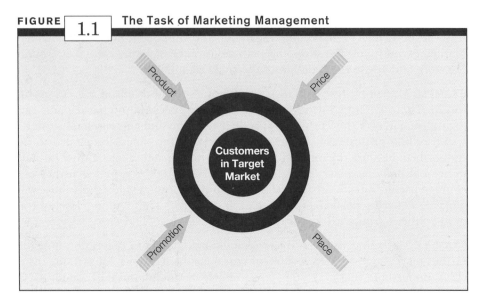

FIGURE 1.1   The Task of Marketing Management

use marketing research to determine what genre of worship music to play at different services.

The principal task of marketing is to create value for customers. Customers will make purchases when (1) the benefits exceed the costs, and (2) the products or services offer superior value compared to alternatives. Marketing managers generally focus their efforts on the elements of the marketing mix, i.e., the four Ps—the product or service, its price, its placement or the channels in which it is distributed, and its promotion or communications mix (see Figure 1.1).

Marketing managers adjust elements of the marketing mix, but the results can be somewhat uncertain because of uncontrollable factors in the environment (see Figure 1.2). Consequently, the marketing manager has a continuous need for information—and marketing research provides it.

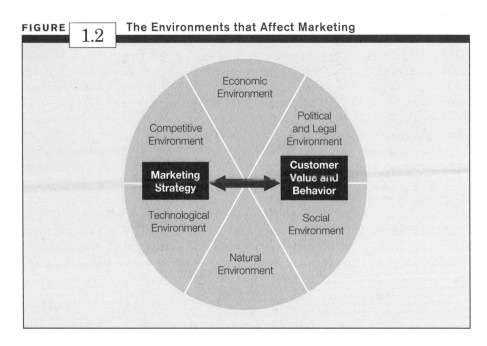

FIGURE 1.2   The Environments that Affect Marketing

The American Marketing Association's (AMA) definition of marketing research emphasizes its role in linking marketing managers to information about their customers (marketingpower.com):

Marketing research is the function which links the consumer, customer, and public to the marketer through information—information used to identify and define marketing opportunities and problems; generate, refine, and evaluate marketing actions; monitor marketing performance; and improve our understanding of marketing as a process.

Note that marketing research is involved with all phases of the information-management process, including: (1) the specification of what information is needed; (2) the collection and analysis of the information; and (3) the interpretation of that information with respect to the objectives that motivated the study in the first place.

Marketing research can be used to assist all aspects of marketing, such as:

- Product (concept testing, brand name development, test markets, packaging designs)
- Pricing (price elasticity, market demand, sales potential, and forecasting)
- Distribution (Web site testing, channel performance, coverage, exports)
- Promotion (media and ad copy effectiveness, sales force compensation, and territories)
- Buyer behavior (segmentation, awareness, satisfaction, preferences, and behavior)
- General corporate research (market trends, diversification opportunities)

Figure 1.3a shows the frequency of different kinds of marketing research applications, in general and Figure 1.3b for online marketing research projects.

Another way of looking at the function of marketing research is to consider how management uses it (see Table 1.1). Some marketing research is used for planning (e.g., which market opportunities are viable?), some for problem

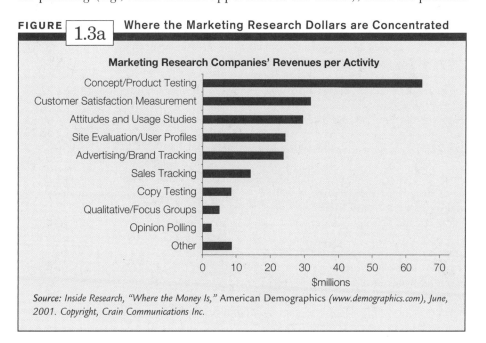

FIGURE 1.3a   Where the Marketing Research Dollars are Concentrated

Marketing Research Companies' Revenues per Activity

Source: Inside Research, "Where the Money Is," American Demographics (www.demographics.com), June, 2001. Copyright, Crain Communications Inc.

FIGURE 1.3b   Online Marketing Research Expenditures (%)

1 Quality/Focus Groups
2 Survey
3 Site Evaluations
4 Copy Testing
5 Advertising/Branding
6 Sales Tracking
7 Concept Testing

Source: insideresearch.com.

TABLE 1.1   Kinds of Questions Marketing Research Can Help Answer

A. Planning
   1. Segmentation: What kinds of people buy our products? Where do they live? How much do they earn? How many of them are there?
   2. Demand estimation: Are the markets for our products increasing or decreasing? Are there promising markets that we have not yet reached?
   3. Environmental assessment: Are the channels of distribution for our products changing? What should our presence on the Internet be?
B. Problem Solving
   1. Product
      a. In testing new products and product-line extensions, which product design is likely to be the most successful? What features do consumers value most?
      b. What kind of packaging should we use?
      c. What are the forecasts for the product? How might we reenergize its life cycle?
   2. Price
      a. What price should we charge for our products?
      b. How sensitive to price changes are our target segments?
      c. Given the life-time value assessments of our segments, should we be discounting or charging a premium to our most valued customers?
   3. Place
      a. Where, and by whom, are our products being sold? Where, and by whom, should our products be sold?
      b. What kinds of incentives should we offer the trade to push our products?
      c. Are our relationships with our suppliers and distributors satisfactory and cooperative?
   4. Promotion
      a. How much should we spend on promotion? How should it be allocated to products and to geographic areas?
      b. Which ad copy should we run in our markets? With what frequency and media expenditures?
      c. What combination of media—newspapers, radio, television, magazines, Internet ad banners—should we use?
      d. What is our consumer coupon redemption rate?
C. Control
   1. What is our market share overall? In each geographic area? By each customer type?
   2. Are customers satisfied with our products? How is our record for service? Are there many returns? Do levels of customer satisfaction vary with market? With segment?
   3. Are our employees satisfied? Do they feel well-trained and empowered to assist our customers?
   4. How does the public perceive our company? What is our reputation with the trade?

TABLE 1.2 Marketing Research Questions About International Markets

- What is the nature of competition in the international markets? Who are the major direct and indirect competitors? What are their characteristics?

- What are our firm's competitive strengths and weaknesses with respect to product quality, product lines, warranties, services, brands, packaging, distribution, sales force, customer service, advertising, prices, experience, technology, capital and human resources, and market share?

- What are the trade incentives and barriers in the countries under consideration? What specific requirements (e.g., import or export licenses) must be met?

- What is their government doing specifically to encourage or discourage international trade?

- How developed are the international mass communication media? Are the print and electronics media abroad efficient and effective?

- Are there adequate transportation and storage or warehouse facilities in this new market? What is the state of its retailing institutions?

solving (e.g., short-term vs. long-term trade-offs), and some for control (e.g., monitoring current operations).

Given its central role in the decision-making process, marketing research is an essential element of marketing. Consider the exhortations offered from industry:[7]

- "Who better to provide advice and counsel to top management than those who are charged with understanding customers, developing brands and evaluating the effectiveness of marketing activities?"

- Ipsos "helps the clients make the right decisions in terms of their business... helping a company have success with their brands and products in the market and make successful launches. [We] bring insight on top of all the research that's done to ensure the client makes the right decisions."

- GfK NOP can "provide clients with a broad picture of the marketplace as well as a drilled-down analysis of trends and issues germane to their industry."

- Marketing research "has increasingly found a role in offering managers insight into the return on marketing expenditures and activities."

In addition, marketing research has become increasingly important as we've moved to a highly competitive global economy (Table 1.2). Globalization of marketing research naturally follows the globalization of large, multinational clients.[8]

Who Does Marketing Research?

The marketing research industry began to grow after World War II, when firms found they could no longer sell all they could produce but rather had to assess

---

[7] Gordon Wyner, "Biz Problems Can Get Solved with Research"; Deborah Vence, "New Train of Thought," both in *Marketing News*, marketingpower.com; David W. *Stewart* (2008), "How Marketing Contributes to the Bottom Line," *Journal of Advertising Research*, 94–105.

[8] And, naturally, managing international research project is even more challenging than smaller-scale, local ones; cf. Robert B. Young and Rajshekhar G. Javalgi, "International Marketing Research: A Global Project Management Perspective," *Business Horizons*, 50, 113–122.

market needs and produce accordingly. Marketing research departments emerged to estimate these needs, and they grew with management sophistication and the data revolution created by computers.

Currently, most large firms have a formal marketing research department, or at least a person in charge of marketing research. Marketing research departments are prevalent among industrial and consumer manufacturing companies. Advertising agencies have research departments devoted to studying the effectiveness of ad copy and optimizing the frequency of exposures of customers to ads. Media companies conduct or buy marketing research to generate audience statistics and demographic profiles so they can sell advertising space and time. Financial service companies use marketing research to forecast market potential and analyze sales.

Marketing research is also conducted by specialized marketing research and consulting firms, government agencies, and universities. Research Realities 1.1 shows the revenues of the largest global marketing research firms. Some firms provide syndicated research—they collect certain information on a regular basis, which they then sell to interested clients. These firms include ACNielsen, which provides product movement data for grocery stores and drugstores, and the NPD Group, which operates a consumer panel. The syndicated services research is not custom designed (except that the firms will perform special analyses for

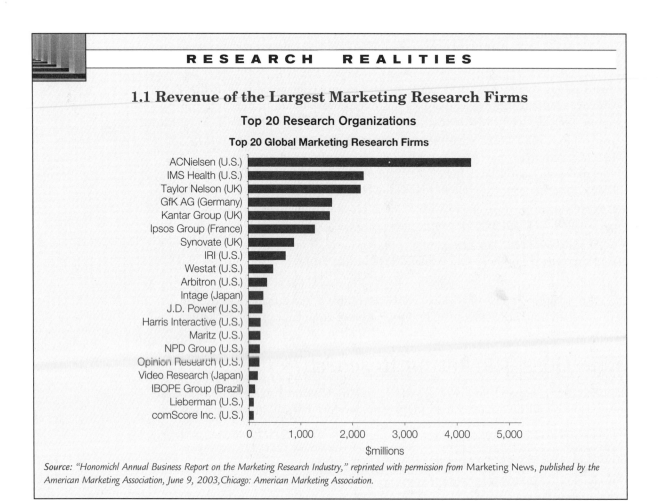

RESEARCH   REALITIES

1.1 Revenue of the Largest Marketing Research Firms

Top 20 Research Organizations

Top 20 Global Marketing Research Firms

Firm	
ACNielsen (U.S.)	
IMS Health (U.S.)	
Taylor Nelson (UK)	
GfK AG (Germany)	
Kantar Group (UK)	
Ipsos Group (France)	
Synovate (UK)	
IRI (U.S.)	
Westat (U.S.)	
Arbitron (U.S.)	
Intage (Japan)	
J.D. Power (U.S.)	
Harris Interactive (U.S.)	
Maritz (U.S.)	
NPD Group (U.S.)	
Opinion Research (U.S.)	
Video Research (Japan)	
IBOPE Group (Brazil)	
Lieberman (U.S.)	
comScore Inc. (U.S.)	

$millions (0, 1,000, 2,000, 3,000, 4,000, 5,000)

Source: "Honomichl Annual Business Report on the Marketing Research Industry," reprinted with permission from Marketing News, *published by the American Marketing Association, June 9, 2003, Chicago: American Marketing Association.*

the client on the data it regularly collects). Other research firms specialize in custom-designed research. Some of these provide only a field service—collecting data for the research sponsor. Some collect the data and also analyze the data for the client. And some are full-service research suppliers, helping the client in the design of the research as well as in collecting and analyzing data.

Other organizations also provide marketing information; e.g., the U.S. federal government is the largest producer of domestic marketing facts through its census data (see Chapter 7). Marketing faculty at business schools report their research in marketing journals, and their counterparts in marketing research firms similarly produce in-house white papers.

Figure 1.4 shows a glimpse of the industry worldwide. The first panel shows the big spenders on marketing research in Europe. The UK dominates, along with

FIGURE 1.4   Who's Conducting Marketing Research?

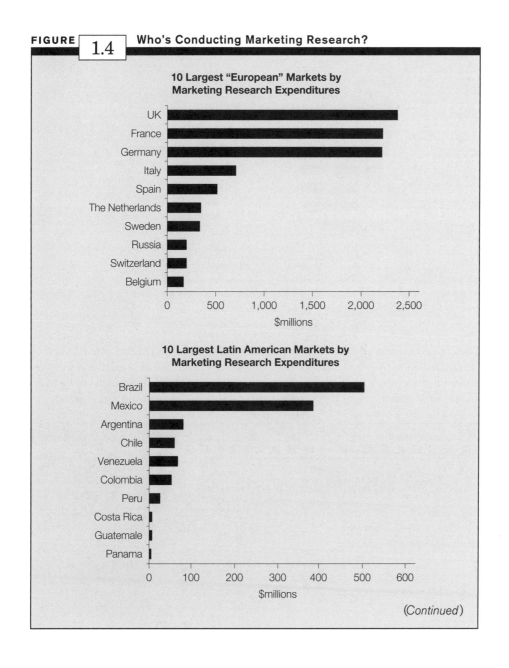

10 Largest "European" Markets by Marketing Research Expenditures

10 Largest Latin American Markets by Marketing Research Expenditures

(Continued)

FIGURE | 1.4 | *Continued*

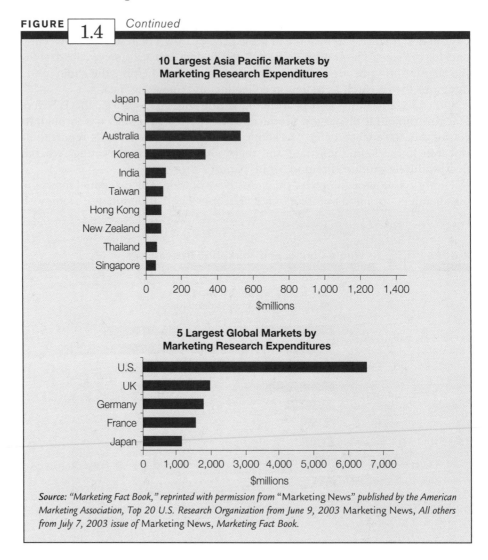

**10 Largest Asia Pacific Markets by
Marketing Research Expenditures**

**5 Largest Global Markets by
Marketing Research Expenditures**

Source: "Marketing Fact Book," reprinted with permission from "Marketing News" published by the American Marketing Association, Top 20 U.S. Research Organization from June 9, 2003 Marketing News, All others from July 7, 2003 issue of Marketing News, Marketing Fact Book.

France and Germany. The second panel illustrates the relatively large marketing research efforts by Brazil and Mexico. In Asia, the volumes of research are largely conducted in Japan (though see Research Realities 1.2 for some facts on China). In the final panel, presumably reflecting trade, the U.S. numbers dominate.

RESEARCH   REALITIES

1.2 Marketing Research in China

- Procter & Gamble is widely acclaimed as the company that single-handedly jump-started marketing research in China. It provided hardware, software, and professional training in sampling and research methodologies. It is still a primary client of Guangzhou Market Research Co., the first professional marketing research company formed in China.

- Where are most of the MR firms? Guangzhou. Why? Closest to Hong Kong (cha-ching$).

Source: Barton Lee, Soumya Saklani and David Tatterson "Top Prospects: State of the MR Industry in China," Marketing News 36, pp. 12–13.

FIGURE | 1.5 | **Marketing Research Spending by Industry**

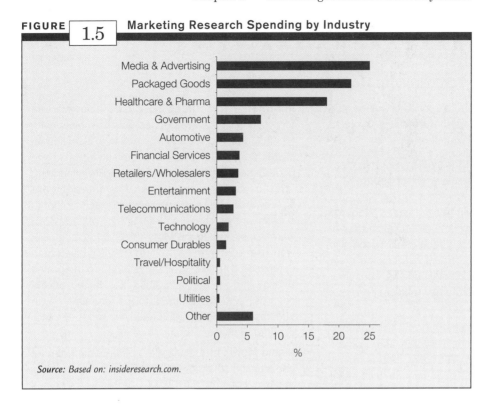

Source: Based on: insideresearch.com.

Figure 1.5 cuts the data differently, representing the amount of research conducted in a variety of industries. Media and advertising, packaged goods, and health care and pharmaceuticals dominate.

Organization of Marketing Research

The organizational form of marketing research depends largely on the size and structure of the individual company. In small firms, one person might handle all the organization's research needs and report to the marketing manager. Larger research units can take a variety of organizational forms:

1. By areas of application, e.g., by product line, brand, market segment, geographic area

2. By marketing function performed, e.g., sales analysis, advertising research, product planning, e-commerce, and electronic forms of research (see Research Realities 1.3)

3. By research technique, e.g., statistical models, interviews, focus groups, surveys

The centralization of the firm also affects the organization of the marketing research function. In decentralized companies, the question is whether each operating unit should have its own marketing research group, or should a single department in central headquarters serve all divisions. The advantages of centralization are greater coordination and control, economy, and greater usefulness to corporate management in planning. The advantage of a group-level location is that it allows research personnel to acquire valuable knowledge about divisional markets, products, practices, and problems. And of course, it's not

RESEARCH   REALITIES

1.3 Marketing Research Companies Online

Marketing research is conducted online by full-service companies and by companies that specialize in online methods and samples. For example:

1. **ACNielsen:** best known for media and retail measurement, formed a subsidiary, eRatings.com as a global service to track audiences, advertising, and user activity online. This group measures Web site traffic, audience exposure and response to banner advertising, and user demographics. ACNielsen also uses the medium in its e-Panel services, an electronic variant of its traditional ongoing consumer panels, to assess reaction to new product concepts and movie previews.

2. **The NPD Group:** traditionally strong in consumer diaries, also has an online research arm. For example, SiteSelect is an NPD tool that randomly samples Web users to invite them to participate in a survey. The ongoing NPD Online Panel is occasionally contacted via e-mail that an online NPD survey awaits them. They conduct audience measurement, chats with Web site visitors, competitor site analysis, online purchase tracking, quick polls, and so on. NPD Online Focus Groups gather international participants in virtual rooms for speedy qualitative consumer insights.

3. **Information Resources Inc. (IRI):** the powerhouse of consumer packaged goods data, combined with Media Metrix Inc. (described next) in e-SCAN, to let clients (e.g., manufacturers of consumer packaged goods) measure the value of their online marketing investments. Clients can track users of their brands to see which Web sites interest them, and tie that to subsequent purchase data (online or offline). Software is installed on the PCs of IRI's panel members, who use a ScanKey to record all their take-home purchases. The two sources of data are integrated to allow the Internet activities (sites visited, ad exposures, surfing patterns) to be correlated with purchase data (volume, purchase cycles, promotional effectiveness, brand loyalty).

4. **Media Metrix Inc.** is a leader in the field of Internet and digital media measurement services. Consisting of a panel of more than 50,000 individuals in homes and in the workplace, they measure which of their computer applications are open, which Web pages are loaded on their browsers, which ads drew clicks, and so on. Results on frequencies of unique visitors can be reported per Internet or media industry, or per consumer usage segment.

unusual in practice to see a mixed arrangement to try to secure the advantages of each.

For example, Kodak has a combination centralized/decentralized marketing research function. The people in the divisions work directly with managers of those business units, whereas the centralized group is responsible for staying on top of industry trends and changing technology, and competitive analysis.

The Japanese are more likely to view research as a "line" function performed by all involved in the decision process rather than as a "staff" function performed by professional marketing researchers. Job rotation is valued in training new hires to understand the entire corporation. Thus, anyone involved in a decision team may play a role in gathering and interpreting information. For example, along with product quality and inventory control, it is still marketing research that is acclaimed as the secret to the success of Japanese car sales. Reliability and perceptions of fair prices matter particularly during tough economies, and when fuel prices rise. These benefits are not all under the purview of, say, engineering or the R&D department, but represent different competitive advantages of the product and consumption experience as a whole. A more integrated organizational structure enhances the overall view of the customer experience, rather than a more focused assessment of some feature in isolation.[9]

The organization of the marketing research function is dynamic. It depends on the scale and complexity of the research activities to be conducted, and the firm's philosophy as to how marketing research should interface with the firm's decision making. Large firms tend to spend a larger proportion of their marketing budgets on research than do small firms. As the firm's size and market position change, the emphasis and organization of the marketing research function must also change so that it continues to suit the firm's information needs.

"CMO is ideal training for CEO!"

Employment Opportunities in Marketing Research

In addition to marketing managers, brand managers, advertising VPs, etc., many types of business people (e.g., consultants, entrepreneurs) frequently find themselves conducting and using marketing research to enhance their business efforts. Thus, if your heart is set on one of these career paths, you must think creatively about how to incorporate marketing research into your corporate responsibilities.

Even if you're not going to be a marketing researcher, or even a marketing manager, it is important to be a knowledgeable and discerning consumer of marketing research. That is, whether you conduct the research or commission it, it is important to be able to evaluate the quality of the research and its implications or caveats.

The best CEOs do not forget that marketing research helps them understand their customers. Marketing research is the premier means to find and sustain competitive advantages. Indeed, some say the CMO role is ideal training for the CEO position.[10]

Marketing research opportunities abound. *Money* magazine ranked marketing research as one of the top 10 careers, with an expected 20% job growth rate for the next decade.[11] Career opportunities depend upon the type, size, organizational structure, and philosophy of the firm. They also depend upon whether the person works for a research supplier or for a consumer of research information. Research Realities 1.4 lists some common job titles and the functions typically performed by people in those positions.

Marketing research: one of top ten careers, 20% job growth rate!

The entry-level position in consumer goods companies (e.g., Kraft, General Motors, Procter & Gamble) is a Brand Analyst. While learning the characteristics and details of the industry, the analyst receives on-the-job training from a research manager. The usual progression is to Senior Analyst and Research Manager for a specific brand, and then a group of brands.

The entry-level position at research suppliers (e.g., ACNielsen, Information Resources, Market Facts, and NPD) is Research Trainee, a position that offers exposure to the types of studies in which the supplier specializes in the procedures that are followed in completing them. Trainees may conduct interviews, code data-collection forms, or assist with analyses. The training provides wide

---

[9] Nicolaos E., Synodinos and Kazuo Kobayashi, (2007) "Marketing Research in Japan," *International Journal of Market Research*, 50 (1), 121–153.

[10] James R. Gregory, "CEO's Heirs Apparent? Clearly, CMOs," *Advertising Age*, (July 21, 2008), p. 14.

[11] Madhav Segal and Edmund Hershberger, "Preparing Research Professionals," *Marketing Research*, marketingpower.com.

RESEARCH REALITIES

1.4 Marketing Research Job Titles and Responsibilities

- Research Director/Vice-President of Marketing Research: The senior position in research. Responsible for the entire research program in the company. Accepts assignments from superiors, clients, and may take initiative to develop research. Employs personnel, supervises research department. Presents findings to clients, company executives.

- Analytically Skilled Methodologists

  ○ Statistician/Data Processing Specialist: expert consultant on theory and application of statistical technique to specific research problems. Responsible for experimental design and data processing.

  ○ Qualitative Specialist: in some firms, the person specifically assigned to oversee interview techniques and focus groups.

- Analysts

  ○ Senior Analyst: helps to plan research projects and directs execution of projects. Minimum supervision. Prepares questionnaires. Selects analytical

techniques. Writes final report. Responsible for budget and meeting time schedules.

  ○ Analyst: handles the bulk of the work of research projects. Assists in survey preparation, pretests questionnaires, and makes preliminary analyses of results.

  ○ Junior Analyst: handles routine assignments, editing and coding of questionnaires, statistical calculations above the clerical level, and library research.

- Data Collection Specialists

  ○ Field Work Director: hires, trains, and supervises field interviewers.

  ○ Full-Time Interviewer: conducts personal interviews. Often outsourced.

- Support Staff

  ○ Clerical Help: tabulates results.

  ○ Clerical Supervisor: central handling and processing of surveys and data.

  ○ Librarian: builds and maintains reference sources.

exposure so that when the trainees become Account Reps, they can be responsive to client needs for information. Research Realities 1.5 presents recent job listings, in both marketing research supplier and buyer firms that give some representation of the variety of employment possibilities.

Increasingly, there is a need for technically skilled marketing researchers—high-level data crunchers. Their skills are crucial to the excellence of a marketing research firm, and they are in short supply. Usually they have training in several of the following areas: statistics, psychometrics, marketing research, buying behavior, microeconomics, marketing management, and business communications. They stay current by subscribing to academic journals and by attending conferences such as the American Marketing Association meetings and the Advanced Research Techniques Forum. Without these talented professionals, many analyses would be implemented by people with no understanding of models or consumers, yielding erroneous results detrimental to the research buyer, and ultimately impacting the research supplier.

A successful marketing researcher needs human relations, communication, conceptual, and analytical skills. Marketing researchers should be able to communicate well both orally and in writing, e.g., to tell colleagues and clients what the results are and what they mean. They need to understand business in general and marketing in particular because they'll deal with brand managers, advertisers, and sales people. Successful marketing researchers realize that marketing research is conducted for one reason—to help make better marketing decisions.

RESEARCH   REALITIES

1.5 A Sampling of Marketing Research Job Advertisements

- *ING Direct*—Marketing Brand Analyst: Manage the identification, development, and refinement of consumer insights. Support marketing strategic initiatives to acquire, retain, and develop profitable customer relationships.

- *Recreational Equipment, Inc.*—Senior Marketing Analyst: One of *FORTUNE* magazine's "100 Best Places to Work," REI is seeking a Senior Marketing Analyst to support Direct Mail Circulation Planning & Analysis. Partnering closely with Marketing leadership, this role is responsible for identifying and delivering reporting, analytical, and forecasting needs related to Direct Mail house file circulation performance.

- *Heinz North America*—Associate Manager of Consumer and Customer Insights: Support the following teams: Brand, Category Development, Research & Development, Consumer Promotions by fully understanding their business, questions or needs and recommending appropriate primary research designs and/or secondary data sources to meet information objectives, plan and execute marketing research projects, and translate research findings into objective, feasible recommendations for consideration. Will manage research budget of approx. <$1 MM annually (w/o syndicated research).

- *Harris Interactive*—Director/VP Research Supplier-Side Marketing Research: With a long and rich history in multimodal research, powered by our science and technology, we assist clients in achieving business results. Design, propose, direct, and analyze results from qualitative and quantitative research, often applying advanced proprietary research tools. Excellent communication skills are essential, along with the ability to interpret research findings so that clients benefit from actionable insights.

- *Saks Fifth Avenue*—Director Database Marketing: Responsible for development, implementation, and delivery of business intelligence that supports marketing, store operations, and merchandise planning. Provide actionable insight based on detailed analysis, suggest customer segmentation and targeting strategy for marketing campaigns, provide data mining to uncover patterns in customer shopping behavior. Prior experience in target modeling, experimental design, clustering, and factor analysis techniques.

- *Publishers Clearing House*—Email Database Analyst: Analyze mailing results by type of email campaign, name group (online paid buyer, offline paid buyer, prospect), quality of name (based on smart keys). Determine which customers should receive which types of email efforts based on segmentation using existing models. Handle "online age/income by product" and "online universe dashboard."

Source: Excerpts taken from jobs.marketingpower.com.

Summary

This chapter presented an overview of marketing research, its usefulness in marketing decision making, a sense of how marketing research gets used, and by what types of companies. Marketing research is *the function that links the consumer, customer, and public to the marketer through information, which is used to identify and define marketing opportunities and problems; to generate, refine, and evaluate marketing actions; to monitor marketing performance; and to improve understanding of marketing as a process.*

Marketing research is a pervasive activity. It is used in every domain of marketing management.

The form of the marketing research function is organized to reflect the specific organization's unique needs. Two factors that are important are the firm's size and the degree of centralization of its operations.

Job opportunities in marketing research are good and getting better. There is great variety in the positions available and in the skills needed for them. Most positions require analytical, communication, and human relations skills.

Questions

1. Who does marketing research? What are the primary kinds of research done by each type of enterprise?
2. How might your responsibilities vary if you conducted marketing research at the following places:
   a. A marketing research firm
   b. An ad agency
   c. A large consumer packaged goods manufacturer
   d. An Internet startup company
3. How is marketing research defined? What are the key elements of this definition?
4. What are the necessary skills for employment in a junior or entry-level marketing research position? Do the skills change as one changes job levels? If so, what new skills are necessary at these higher levels?
5. What is marketing management's task? What is marketing research's task? What is the relation between the two?
6. What factors influence the internal organization of the marketing research department and its reporting location within the company?

Applications and Problems

1. Suppose that you have decided to pursue a career in the field of marketing research, marketing, or marketing and management consulting. In general, what types of courses should you take in order to help achieve your goal? Why? What types of part-time jobs, internships, and volunteer work would look good on your resume? Why?
2. What do the two following research situations have in common?

   Situation I: The sales manager of CanAl, an aluminum can manufacturing company, was wondering whether the company's new cans, which would be on the market in two months, should be priced higher than the traditional products. He confidently commented to the VP of marketing, "Nobody in the market is selling aluminum cans with screw-on tops; we can get a small portion of the market and yet make substantial profits." The product manager disagreed with this strategy. In fact, she was opposed to marketing these new cans. The cans might present problems in preserving the contents. She thought, "Aluminum cans are recycled, so nobody is going to keep them as containers." There was little she could do formally because these cans were the company president's own idea. She strongly recommended to the VP that the cans should be priced in line with the other products. The VP thought a marketing research study would resolve this issue.

   Situation II: A large toy manufacturer was in the process of developing a tool kit for children from 5 to 10 years old. The tool kit included a small saw, screwdriver, hammer, chisel, and drill. This tool kit was different from the competitors', in that it included an instruction manual, "101 Things To Do." The product manager was concerned about the safety of the kit and recommended the inclusion of a separate

booklet for parents. The sales manager recommended that the tool kit be made available in a small case, as this would increase its marketability. The advertising manager recommended a special promotional campaign be launched to distinguish this tool kit from the competition. The vice president thought that all the recommendations were worthwhile but the costs would increase drastically. She consulted the marketing research manager, who further recommended that a study be conducted.

3. Specify some useful sources of marketing research information for the following situation:

   Dissatisfied with the availability of ingredients for his favorite dishes, Albert Lai would like to open his own retail ethnic grocery store. Based on the difficulty of finding many specialty ingredients, Albert realizes the need for a local wholesale distributor specializing in hard-to-find ethnic foodstuffs. He envisions carrying items commonly used in Asian and Middle-Eastern recipes. With the help of a local accountant, Albert prepared a financial proposal that revealed the need for $150,000 in start-up capital for Lai's Asian Foods. The proposal was presented to a local bank for review by its commercial loan committee, and Albert subsequently received the following letter from the bank:

   Dear Mr. Lai:
   We have received and considered your request for start-up financing for your proposed business. The basic idea is sound, but we find that your sales projections are based solely on your own experience and do not include any hard documentation concerning the market potential for the products you propose to carry. Until such information is made available for our consideration,

we have no choice but to reject your loan application.

Albert does not wish to give up on his business idea, because he truly believes that there is a market for these ethnic food products. Given his extremely limited financial resources, what types of information might be useful? Where and how might he obtain the needed information?

4. What do the two following research situations have in common?

   Situation I: The SprayIt Company marketed a successful insect repellent. The product was effective and a leader in the market. The product was available in blue aerosol cans with red caps. The instructions were clearly specified on the container, in addition to a warning to keep the product away from children. Most of the company's products were also produced by competitors in similar containers. The CEO was worried because of declining sales and shrinking profit margins. In addition, companies such as his were being criticized by government and consumer groups for their use of aerosol cans. The CEO contacted the company's advertising agency and asked it to do the necessary research to find out what was happening.

   Situation II: This past April, the directors of a nearby university were considering expanding the business school because of increasing enrollment during the past 10 years. Their plans included constructing a new wing, hiring new faculty members, and increasing the number of scholarships from 100 to 150. The funding for this project was to be provided by private sources, internally generated funds, and the state and federal governments. However, a previous research study completed five years earlier, using a sophisticated forecasting method, indicated that student enrollment would have peaked last year, and that universities could expect gradual declining enrollments for the near future. A decision to conduct another study was made to determine likely student enrollment.

5. Evaluate the research in the following example: The HiFlyer Airline company was interested in altering the interior layout of its aircraft to suit the tastes and needs of business travelers. Management was considering reducing the number of seats and installing small tables to enable people to work during long flights. Prior to the renovation, management decided to do some research to ensure that these changes would suit the needs of the passengers. To keep expenses to a minimum, the following strategy was employed:

   Questionnaires were completed by passengers during a flight. Because they were easy to administer and collect, the questionnaires were distributed only on the short flights (those less than one hour). The study was conducted during the 2nd and 3rd weeks of December, because that was when flights were full. To increase the response rate, each flight attendant was responsible for a certain number of questionnaires. The management thought this was a good time to acquire as much information as possible, so the questionnaire included issues apart from the new seating arrangement. As a result, the questionnaire took 20 minutes to complete. After the study, management decided that the study would not be repeated, because the information was insightful enough.

6. Discuss whether marketing research would be valuable for the types of organizations that follow. If you believe that marketing research would be valuable, describe in detail how it would be used to aid in decision making.

   a. A bank
   b. A multinational oil company
   c. A retail shoe store chain
   d. A Mercedes dealership in LA? In NY?
   e. A candidate for the U.S. Congress, representing a district in Chicago
   f. The L.A. Lakers
   g. A distributor of large-screen televisions operating in Mexico City
   h. The English Department at your university
   i. A wheat farmer in Nebraska with 850 acres

Alternative Approaches to Marketing Intelligence

2

Questions to Guide Your Learning:

Q1 What are the roles of "projects" and "information systems" in marketing research?

Q2 What are Marketing Information Systems (MIS) and Decision Support Systems (DSS)?

Q3 What is data mining?

In Chapter 1, we said that the primary purpose of marketing research is to help marketing managers and other business people make decisions. Marketing managers need to know about changes in customer purchasing patterns, new products, new competitors, etc. As the link with the business environment, marketing research generates, interprets, and transmits feedback regarding the success of the firm's marketing plans and the strategies and tactics used to implement those plans. Marketing research is responsible for this intelligence function.

There are two complementary approaches to marketing research: projects executed to address specific problems, and ongoing marketing intelligence systems. The emphasis in this book is on marketing research projects. The next chapter gives an overview of the steps in a project, and the remainder of the book discusses each step in detail.

In contrast, in a **marketing information system (MIS)** or **decision support system (DSS)**[1] there is a continuous monitoring of consumer and market behavior so that people throughout the organization have the information they need, when they need it, to make good decisions. These systems form the heart of companies' **customer relationships management (CRM)** efforts. Large customer databases (e.g., from loyalty programs) help companies track all purchases (online or at retail outlets), customer inquiries or complaints, promotional extensions and responses, etc. Analyzing these large datasets allows CEOs to improve marketing ROI (see Research Realities 2.1) These streaming systems are the focus of this chapter.

MIS and DSS systems can be designed to be narrow in focus, to address well-defined, predictable issues; e.g., scanner data from groceries may be checked by manufacturers to obtain

---

[1] When discussing corporate information systems, MIS stands for management information system, and DSS refers to the structure of the decision support system for the whole company. Our interest is in marketing intelligence, so we use the term MIS to refer to the marketing information system and DSS to refer to the structure of the information system to support marketing decision making.

RESEARCH   REALITIES

2.1 CRM and Marketing ROI

- Given increased accountability, more companies want more and better marketing data. In fact, the systems pay for themselves: Companies that had improved their ROI capabilities indicated that their marketing was more effective by a margin of 67–95% compared to companies who had not made such system investments.

- American Airlines streamlined its MIS systems and estimated an ROI of 1192% in two months.

- CRM helps marketers more efficiently target new acquisitions (e.g., through direct mailing to local prospects for a retail bank) and customers who are good prospects for cross-selling (e.g., catalog or online merchandise).

- Web analytic services abound: clicktracks.com, visitstat.com, webtrends.com, and others offer customized graphical real-time reporting of users' Web site visits and actions, e-mail activities, and responses to marketing promotions.

- Electronic medical records (EMRs) and electronic health records (EHRs) are improving the efficiency and quality of patient care while reducing cost and errors.

- Enhanced models provide more accurate estimates of customer lifetime values projected five years out.

Source: Deborah L. Vence, "Buckling Down: More Firms are Adding Data Mining Systems to Prove Marketing ROI," Marketing News, *marketingpower.com;* "ROI Case Study: American Airlines," *spss.com;* Herb Edelstein, "Building Profitable Customer Relationships with Data Mining," *spss.com;* Leigh Wells, "Web Keyhole," *SmallBiz.com;* "Analytics in Healthcare," *sas.com;* Peter S. Fader, Bruce G. S. Hardie and Kinshuk Jerath "Estimating CLV using Aggregated Data," *Journal of Interactive Marketing, 21 (3), 55–71.*

hourly market shares. Alternatively, they can be broader in scope, to reflect complex consumer behavior. Information systems are popular because they allow a manager to answer simple questions via a user-friendly interface. The computer takes the input to a model and produces numbers and answers, such as projected sales forecasts for a new product launch.

Marketing Research
Project ➔ Snapshot

Marketing Research
Intelligence Systems ➔
Streaming Video

The philosophical difference between a project approach to marketing research and information systems is analogous to the difference between taking a snapshot vs. getting a continual streaming read on the pulse of the marketplace. Thoughtful marketing managers recognize the value in conducting marketing research and commission projects recurrently. Myopic managers will devise a marketing research project only in times of crisis.

MISs and DSSs represent ongoing efforts to provide pertinent decision-making information to marketing managers on a regular basis. The continuous systems are especially optimal when occasionally blended with data from periodic marketing research projects.

Next, we discuss the nature and components of MISs and DSSs. A critical element is the data set, and because these data sets are becoming huge, we close by discussing issues of "data mining."

Marketing Information Systems and Decision Support Systems

Marketing information systems and decision support systems provide a steady flow of information. They involve procedures for the collection and analysis of information on a recurring rather than periodic basis.

The design of these systems begins with a detailed analysis of the decision-maker roles who will be using the system and the types of decisions to be made, and therefore, the types of information required. Systems designers need to understand the types of information the individual receives regularly as well as the special studies that are needed periodically. They need to know how the input data are obtained, which pieces of data are stored in which databases, which analyses would be helpful, and what report formats would be useful.

The system is then programmed. When the program is debugged and it is operating correctly, it is put online. Once online, managers access the reports through their company's intranet. Finally, the system designers seek feedback from the decision makers for improvements to the current information system.

When first proposed, these information systems were held up as a panacea. Reality, however, fell short of promise, for human and technical reasons. For example, different managers emphasize different things and consequently have different data needs; few report formats can be optimal for different users. Either the developers have to design "compromise" reports that are satisfactory but not ideal for any single user, or they have to engage in the laborious task of programming to meet each user's unique needs.

The costs and time required to establish such systems are substantial, and often underestimated, due to the size of the task, changes in organizational structure or key personnel, and the digital systems they require. By the time these systems are developed, the personnel may have shifted, or the economic and competitive environments changed. Thus, soon after being put online, these systems intended for continual monitoring tend to need continual updating.

Another issue is that it is simply difficult to create a thoughtful, rigorous system that lends itself to solutions for the kinds of problems managers typically face. Many of the activities performed by managers cannot be programmed, nor can they be performed routinely or delegated to someone else, because they involve personal choices. In addition, sometimes a manager's decision making is *ad hoc* to address unexpected events and choices, or exploratory to investigate new opportunities, so it might be difficult to specify in advance what is desired from programmers and model builders.

Components of MISs and DSSs

As depicted in Figure 2.1, an intelligence system comprises data, a model, and dialog systems that can be used interactively by managers. We discuss each system component in turn.

Data. The data system includes the processes used to capture data, as well as the methods used to store data coming from marketing, finance, the sales force, manufacturing, and any other external or internal sources. The typical data system has different modules containing customer information, general economic and demographic information, competitor information, and industry information, including market trends.

The customer information module typically contains information on who buys and who uses the product, where they buy and use it, when, in what situations and quantities, and how often. It could also include information on how the purchase decision is made, the most important factors in making that decision, the influence of advertising or some sales promotion activity on the decision, the price paid, and so on. Marketing research projects would typically supply some of the information input to the customer information module of

FIGURE **2.1**   Components of a Decision Support System

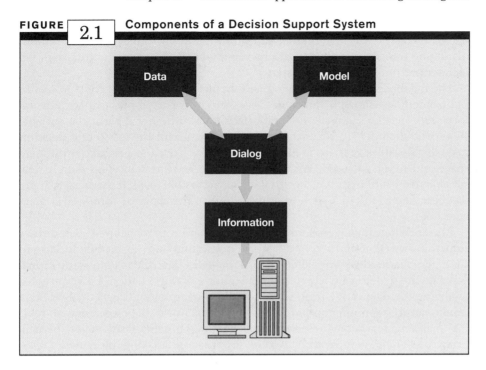

the data system. Other input might come from the purchase of syndicated commercial marketing information.

The data module that contains general economic and demographic information attempts to capture some of the most relevant facts about what is happening in the external environment, such as national or international economic activity and trends, interest rates, unemployment, or changes in GNP. The demographic facts concern changes in population, household composition, or any of the other factors that could potentially affect the future success of the firm. Much of this input comes from government data, primarily from the various censuses.

Another data module could contain information on competitors, addressing questions such as: Who are the competitors and what are their market shares? In which market niches do they operate? What is their percentage of sales by product? What are their distribution methods? Where are their production facilities located? What are their unique capabilities?

The industry information and market trend data module contains general information on what is happening in the industry, including financial information about margins, costs, R&D activities, and capital expenditures. It could also include information on trends in manufacturing or technology, with respect to raw materials or processes.

A popular application of marketing information systems that incorporates these different data modules is the forecasting of sales for new products. Input to these systems includes data on developmental resources (the number of R&D hours behind the prototype), concept testing (percentage of consumers checking "very likely to purchase"), prototype testing (percentages of consumers "very satisfied" with product usage), and marketplace promotion expenditures (advertising budget).

The most important trend in information technology is the explosion in the size of databases that provide information on customers, competitors,

Components of MISs & DSSs:

- *Data* What info do you need?
- *Models* How does the market work?
- *Interface* How does the manager input and extract info?

industries, or general economic and demographic conditions. Thousands of databases can be accessed online, and hundreds apply to business. In addition, marketing information systems are increasingly becoming part of international competitive intelligence data systems.

The databases are mind-boggling, and in fact, managers have come to realize that sometimes, more is not necessarily better. For example, just because information may be available, it is important to ask whether a particular variable should be included in the database—will it be useful for marketing decision making? Variables that are included "just in case" tend to just take up storage space and never get used. We want to capture *relevant* marketing data in reasonable detail and organize those data in an accessible form. It is crucial that the database management system logically organize the data the same way a manager does.

Models. When managers look at data, they have a preconceived idea of how something works and, therefore, what is interesting and worthwhile to have in the data. These ideas are called mental models.[2] Managers then want to manipulate the data to gain a better understanding of the situation. Procedures for analyzing the data range from simple sums, to complex statistical analyses, to a nonlinear programming optimization. In the real world, the most frequent tools for analyzing marketing research data are the simplest: frequencies, percentages, cross-tabs, comparing different groups, and making plots and tables. (We'll cover these techniques and far more throughout the book.)

The explosion in recent years in the number and size of databases has triggered a need for efficient analyses. (Crunching large databases has become known as *data mining,* which we discuss in the next section.) For example, brand managers of consumer packaged goods receive huge quantities of scanner data every week, and even an astute analyst requires a great amount of time to extract simple summaries to see the major trends. In response, a number of firms have been developing artificial intelligence systems that model how experts solve problems. These systems sort through all the data, comparing current results with past results, by brand, category, markets, regions, or key accounts.

The Interface. The dialog system is the interface that permits managers who are not programmers themselves to explore the databases, using the system models to produce reports that satisfy their particular information needs. The reports can be tables or graphs, and the report formats can be specified by the manager. The interfaces are often menu-driven to facilitate user-friendliness, reduce errors, and increase usage. Instead of funneling their data requests through a team of programmers, managers can conduct their analyses themselves, which has the side benefit of allowing them to target the information they want rather than being overwhelmed by irrelevant data. Managers can ask a question and, depending on the answer, follow it with a subsequent question, and thus proceed interactively and quickly.

As the availability of online databases has increased, so too has the need for better dialog systems. The dialog systems are what put data at the managers' fingertips. That sounds simple, but it is a difficult task because of the large amounts of data that are available, the speed with which data hit a company, and the fact that data come from various sources. To compound matters, the geographic boundaries used by the data suppliers differ from each other and most

---

[2] Mark W. Huber et al., *Information Systems: Creating Business Value*, (Wiley, 2006); for more on how managers use marketing data, see Neil A. Morgan, Eugene W. Anderson, and Vikas Mittal, "Understanding Firms' Customer Satisfaction Information Usage," *Journal of Marketing*, 69 (3), 131–151.

often from the firm's own geographic territories. Further, the services typically collect data on different time cycles. Some provide it weekly; others, once or twice a month. The discrepancies must be reconciled if the various data are going to be combined in a way that enables effective decision making.

Increasingly common is distributed network computing online—a user taps into a network of integrated information bases. This decentralization also provides greater protection from hackers. The use of the Web to capture and provide access to information on customers, competitors, industries, or general economic and demographic conditions clearly continues to grow like crazy.

Many companies are exploring graphical interfaces as a means to express more intuitively the core findings in their databases. For example, investment banks use visualization displays for real-time stock updates and mutual funds data, as well as company financial reports and customer profile data. The initial screen pops up with the aggregate picture, and the user can click on an area in the figure to drill down more detailed information about that microcosm of the marketplace.

In particular, these interfaces provide the bases for corporate "dashboards" or "scorecards" (see Figure 2.2). Revenue and market share can be updated in as timely a manner as the scanning systems feed real-time data back to the company. Similarly, customer loyalty can be informed nearly simultaneously with the use of user cards. Customer satisfaction and employee satisfaction are usually measured via periodic surveys, so they might not be refreshed as frequently. Figure 2.2 is just an example, but any subset of metrics that a manager or CEO cares about can be quantified and monitored, to the better management of customer relations and firm performance.

FIGURE 2.2   Dashboard: Visualizing Marketing Metrics

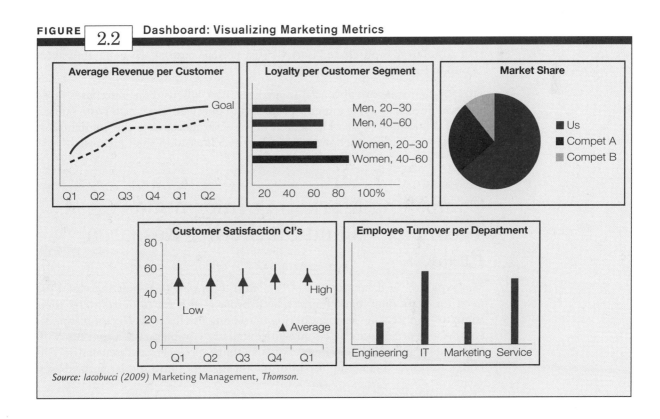

Source: Iacobucci (2009) Marketing Management, Thomson.

Using the Data, Model, and Interface

Information technology systems allow managers to play "what-if" scenarios. Managers can simulate real-world conditions to learn about the relationships among different marketing actions and likely competitive response in a virtual marketplace, without the risk that such experimentation would cause in the real marketplace.

Simulations can be programmed to be as complex and realistic as there are variables, data, experience, and assumptions to help support the interrelationships among the elements of the simulation. Input can include data and estimates on market characteristics (such as seasonality), customer preferences (attributes sought per segment, price sensitivity), customer loyalty (switching costs, trends over time), competitors' positions (consumers' judgments of their known product attributes, their prices and perceived prices), and competitors' access to customers (their distribution channels). Good simulations allow users to modify the input assumptions and parameters to see the range of possible outcomes, to make predictions with some degree of confidence.

For example, banks use decision tree AI tools to analyze a database of loan applicants to predict who is a good credit risk. Such systems begin by making classifications on current customers for whom the outcome is known (that is, whether they paid back a loan or not). The analysis detects which customer characteristics are most diagnostic in distinguishing the good bets from the deadbeats. (In developing the rules, the model iterates toward better prediction, and the iteration gives the appearance that the machine is "learning," hence the label "artificial intelligence.")

Mini AI systems drive the grocery coupons that are generated per customer at point of purchase. The conceptual rules look like this:

- "If customer has purchased Bertollini pasta AND customer is female (known from loyalty card data), then eject coupon for Newman's pesto sauce" OR

- "If customer has purchased Bertollini pasta AND customer is male, then eject coupon for DiGiorno's pizza."

These if-then rules are also used in analyses, e.g., "If customer purchases three pastas in one quarter, customer is predicted to purchase two jars of pasta sauce." The AI is intended to provide benefit to the customer and to the companies—manufacturers in production and retailers deciding upon shelf facings.

Comparing Marketing Information Technologies and Marketing Research Projects

The explosion in databases and information technology has only increased the need for traditional marketing research projects and for understanding their strengths and weaknesses in gathering marketing intelligence. Decision support systems and projects are not competitive, but are complementary and function best if they are well integrated.[3] For one thing, projects (as discussed in this book) are used to generate the information that goes into the large databases.

[3] Ed Crowley, "Market Intelligence versus Marketing Research," quirks.com.

In addition, although a DSS allows managers to stay in tune with their external environments, as a sort of "early warning system," they usually do not provide enough information about what to do in specific instances, e.g., when the firm is faced with a new product, a change in distribution channels, or a new promotion campaign. When actionable information is required to address specific marketing problems or opportunities, the research project continues to play a major role.

In sum, both kinds of marketing research, shorter-term focused projects and longer-term monitoring systems, are important approaches to marketing intelligence. In an increasingly competitive world, information is vital, and a company's ability to obtain and analyze information will largely determine the company's future.

Data Mining

Analyzing large databases has become known as data mining. Businesses hope it will allow them to boost sales and profits by better understanding their customers. The analysis of databases is not new—what is new and challenging is the extraordinary size of these databases.

Huge databases began with scanner data. Estimates suggest that marketers in packaged goods companies are inundated with 100 to 1,000 times more bits of data every few years because of the adoption of scanner technology in their channels of distribution. Some data mining techniques also arose in response to "database marketing" or "direct marketing" (by catalog vendors or coupon distribution providers) in which a company tries to form relationships with its individual customers, as marketing attempts to proceed from "mass" (one media message for all potential buyers), to "segments" (some targeting and positioning differences), to "one-to-one" marketing, e.g., via customized promotions and dynamic pricing. In order to achieve such tailored market offerings, a company has to know a lot about its customers—information provided by marketing research data.

A company's database contains both current business information and historical information. These data warehouses literally dwarf those available even a few years ago. For example, NCR Corporation and Wal-Mart have built the world's largest retailer data warehouse, now into a petabyte[4] of data storage. The system provides information about each of Wal-Mart's over 3,000 stores in multiple countries. Wal-Mart plans to use the information to select products that need replenishment, analyze seasonal buying patterns, examine customer buying trends, select markdowns, and react to merchandise volume and movement.[5]

In response to the increasingly massive data sets, firms have created more sophisticated data mining technologies to analyze the data. Data mining uses massively parallel processing (MPP) and symmetric multiprocessing (SMP) supercomputer technologies.[6] These huge machines support relational database programs that can slice massive amounts of data into dozens of smaller, more manageable pools of information.

[4] 1 petabyte = 1,000 terabytes = 1 quadrillion bytes. 1 terabyte = 1,000 gigabytes = 1,000,000 megabytes. It's big!

[5] Constance L. Hayes, "What Wal-Mart Knows About Customers' Habits," nytimes.com.

[6] In the parallel processing of "supercomputers," multiple data points and subroutines are processed simultaneously, compared with old-fashioned "serial" processing, in which one datum is processed after another.

Sometimes these databases are being analyzed with fairly traditional statistical techniques.

- For example, regression is still a premier analytical tool, because many predictors can be used to capture complex consumer decision-making and market behavior—forecasting sales as a function of season, price, promotions, sales force, and competitor factors.

- Other popular techniques of data mining include cluster analysis for segmentation and neural networks to supplement forecasting.[7]

- Businesses regularly use data mining analytical tools to mathematically model customers who respond to their promotional campaigns versus those who do not. The effects of direct mailing efforts are easily measured and compared as a function of customer information (demographics such as age, household size, income) and purchase behavior (past buying history, cross-sales).

- Data mining can also be used to measure incremental business (additional traffic, sales, profits) that may be directly attributed to a recent promotion by deliberately withholding the promotional mailing from a "control" group (in experiments).

In addition, marketing researchers are creating techniques especially for data mining large data sets. Sales of customer management software are currently growing at five times the rate of the overall software market, as managers struggle to track every encounter with each customer, to facilitate call center interactions between customers and customer service representatives, and to manage internal customers, such as one's sales force. Some of these relational database systems include IBM's Intelligent Miner and SAS's Enterprise Miner. Other software companies offer "content aggregator" services that synthesize multiple databases—company financial information, histories, executive profiles, and the like.

There are analogous techniques being developed for the goal of "text mining," that is, the analysis of large storages of qualitative data. For example, companies such as General Motors need to know whether there are recurrent problems with its products, which can only be determined from studying mechanics' reports of customers' car repairs. These text files are so numerous and unsystematic, that without the assistance of a computer seeking various structures in the data, the task would be impossible. "Pattern recognition" is the class of analytics being developed and explored for the analysis of qualitative data.[8]

As an illustration of a data mining exercise, Farmers Insurance used IBM's DecisionEdge software to look at the 200 pieces of information the company maintained on its database of 10 million automobile insurance policy holders. Think of a sports car owner and "you probably imagine a twenty-something single guy flaming down the highway in his hot rod." This profile fit many of its customers, but the data mining exercise identified another segment of sports car owner—married baby boomers with kids and more than one car. These customers produced fewer claims, yet had been paying the same sports car surcharge. With this information in hand, Farmers could charge them less, providing greater value and customer satisfaction.[9] For additional examples

---

[7] We discuss these techniques in the chapters that follow.

[8] For more, see Ashok Srivastava and Mehran Sahami (2009) *Text Mining,* NY: Chapman & Hall.

[9] Jennifer Lach, "Data Mining Digs In," *American Demographics*, www.demographics.com.

RESEARCH REALITIES

2.2 Consumer Insights Gained from Data Mining

Loyalty programs offer consumers discounted prices and coupon incentives. Companies know that all customers are not equal, and loyalty cards enable one-to-one marketing, customizing the shopping experience for households with different purchasing profiles (sensitivities to price, value, brand, and quality). Due to their success, loyalty programs have expanded to other industries, yielding consumer insights and marketing actions such as these:

- Harrah's loyalty program includes 26 million members, with 6 million active customers who used their cards within the past year. More than 75% of Harrah's gaming revenue is tracked on the cards. Customer service representatives have access to this information and go to greater lengths to satisfy customers who have been identified as more profitable.

- SAS, one of the largest statistical computing suppliers, assists companies in their information management and manipulation needs. SAS helps companies in many phases of marketing:

  - Planning: Which of my 10 million customers are my "best"? What do these customers want?

  - Targeting: Which of my 200+ variables tell me the most important information about my customers? For example, which customers are at risk for leaving vs. which customers show potential for being responsive to attempts at cross-selling?

- SAS created a CRM architecture to address its clients' biggest challenge: coordinating data sets across multiple "customer touch points" (call centers, direct mail, e-mail, trade shows, etc.). SAS integrates internal data, purchased external data, front line records, data analytics, and rules modeling the data.

- For example, in the insurance industry, data mining is used to predict a company's profits, and its expected customers' claims and losses. By studying current customer profiles in profitability, the policies can be targeted more precisely than "potential customer" to "potential customer who: meets policy criteria, is likely to purchase policy, and is likely to retain policy for ten years or more."

- SPSS, the other large statistical computing supplier has its own success stories:

  - A leading telecommunications company analyzed its repairs data, found a frequently occurring glitch, fixed the system, and saved $1 million last year.

  - A bath-and-beauty supplies chain analyzed its data, "found" its customers, and has been reaping the rewards: growing its direct mail response rates by 250%, and its number of retail stores from 18 to 165.

Source: "Harrah's Hits Customer Loyalty Jackpot," sas.com; "Advanced Marketing Automation," and "Taming the CRM Information Explosion," White Paper series, sas.com; "Gain a Competitive Advantage," White Paper series, spss.com.

of the kinds of consumer insights gained from data mining, see Research Realities 2.2.

There is no question that the explosion in databases, computer hardware and software for accessing those databases, and the Internet are changing the way marketing intelligence is obtained. Companies are becoming more sophisticated in using them for general business and competitive intelligence. This, in turn, has produced some changes in the organization of the marketing intelligence function, including the increased importance of the Chief Information Officer (CIO).

The CIO's major role is to run the company's information and computer systems like a business. The CIO serves as the liaison between the firm's top management and its information systems department. Information systems are ideally designed as an electronic library that allows all employees access to the firm's "collective wisdom."

Summary

This book takes a project-based approach to the provision of marketing intelligence. The difference between a project emphasis to research or the alternative Marketing Information System or Decision Support System emphasis is that the latter relies on the continual monitoring of the firm's activities, its competitors, and its environment, whereas the former emphasizes the in-depth study of some specific problem or environmental condition.

An MIS or DSS was defined as a set of procedures for the regular, planned collection, analysis, and presentation of information for use in making marketing decisions. They provide more regular marketing intelligence than periodic, focused marketing research projects.

A DSS is a coordinated collection of data systems, model systems, and dialog systems. The data systems include the processes used to capture and store information useful for marketing decision making. A marketing research project is one input to a data system. The model system includes all the routines that allow users to manipulate data to conduct the kinds of analyses they desire. The dialog systems allow managers to conduct their own analyses by logging onto the company's intranet, even from their cell phones.

Data mining is the term used to describe the analysis of huge consumer databases—scanner purchase data, or investigations in database marketing or direct marketing—tasks for which companies can have hundreds of pieces of information on each of its millions of customers. Large databases require special storage and increasingly sophisticated hardware and software to enable massively parallel processing and symmetric multiprocessing. Traditional statistical techniques (regression, cluster analysis) are used, as is special customer management software.

Questions

1. What is data mining? How does it differ from traditional data analysis?
2. What is a marketing information system? How does a project emphasis to marketing research differ from an information systems emphasis?
3. What is (are) the likely future approaches to marketing intelligence? Will there be a change in the relative importance of traditional research vs. MISs or DSSs?
4. What are the steps in MIS analysis? In developing an MIS system?
5. In a DSS, what is a data system? A model system? A dialog system? Which of these is most important? Why?

Applications and Problems

1. Consider the industries of healthcare management, consulting, or financial investments. What specific capabilities of a DSS would enable greater customer satisfaction and profitability? What kinds of input should the company seek? Who should use the system, and to address what specific needs and questions?
2. Imagine that you are the VP of international marketing for a consumer packaged goods company. In a recent board of directors meeting, it was decided that you would head the development of a competitive information system (CIS) for your organization. You have been asked to write a brief description of the types of data to be stored in the CIS along with possible uses of the data by employees within your company. Write a clear and concise paragraph describing your recommendations.
3. Imagine that you are responsible for deciding whether to adopt a DSS for the following situations. How would you design the system?
   a. Production of profit and loss statements to estimate customer lifetime values for segments of video renters
   b. Introduction of a new product line extension for Smucker's preserves and jellies
   c. Determination of seasonal pricing schedules for Johnson outboard motors
   d. Identification of the amount of time spent on hold by consumers on a toll-free, customer-service assistance telephone line

The Research Process and Problem Formulation

3

Questions to Guide Your Learning:

Q1 What is the difference between a program strategy and a project strategy to research?

Q2 How does the research process unfold? What are the steps and how are they interrelated?

Q3 What is the first stage in the research process: problem formulation?

Q4 What does a research proposal look like and how do I choose among research suppliers?

Different companies use marketing research for different reasons. A company's philosophy of how marketing research fits into its marketing plan determines its program strategy for marketing research. Some companies use marketing research on a continuous basis, to track sales or monitor market share. Other companies use marketing research only when a problem arises or an important decision like the launching of a new product needs to be made.

A program strategy specifies the types of studies to be conducted and their purposes. Research Realities 3.1 outlines the types and purposes of the various studies conducted by Gillette Company in its constant endeavor to maintain its dominant share of the blade and razor market. The design of the individual studies defines the firm's project strategy: these include personal interviews in national consumer studies, mail questionnaires in brand-tracking studies, and telephone interviews when measuring brand awareness. Thus, a **program strategy** addresses the question of what types of studies the firm should conduct and for what purposes, whereas a **project strategy** deals with how a study should be conducted.

Every marketing research problem is unique in some way, requiring some custom tailoring for its own special emphasis. Still, there is a sequence of steps, called the **research process,** that is followed when designing any research project (see Figure 3.1).

Marketing Research—Sequence of Steps

I. Formulate the Problem

The first role marketing research plays is to help define the problem to be solved. When it is defined carefully and precisely, research can be designed to provide pertinent information. This process includes specifying the objectives of the research projects

RESEARCH REALITIES

3.1 Marketing Research at Gillette

Gillette is the global leader in male toiletries products. Its cutting-edge products are offered at premium prices. It is also among the most financially stable of firms. It has achieved these positions through a strong belief in marketing research and innovative products, such as its Fusion razors, which hit the $1b sales mark faster than any other Procter & Gamble brand. In recent years, Gillette has been introducing more than 20 new products per year, and half of its sales come from brands that are no older than five years. Here are some of its marketing research methods:

1. **Annual National Consumer Studies.** These studies determine what brand of razor and blade was used for the respondents' last shave, to collect demographic data, and to examine consumer attitudes toward the various blade and razor manufacturers. These studies rely on personal interviews with national panels of men and women who are selected by using probability sampling methods.

2. **National Brand Tracking Studies.** These studies track the use of razors and blades to monitor brand loyalty and brand switching tendencies over time. Mail questionnaires are issued annually to panels of male and female shavers.

3. **Annual Brand Awareness Studies.** These studies determine the "share of mind" Gillette products have. Telephone surveys employ aided and unaided recall of brand names and advertising campaigns.

4. **Consumer Use Tests.** The use-testing studies ensure that Gillette remains competitive, with products performing up to desired standards, and to substantiate claims in advertising and packaging. At least two consumer use tests are conducted each month by Gillette. In these tests, consumers are asked to use a single variation of a product for an extended period of time, at the end of which their evaluation of the product is obtained.

5. **Laboratory Research Studies.** In Gillette's Center for Clinical and Consumer Testing, they test the performance of existing Gillette products and help design new products. They have people shave with Gillette and competing products and measure the results, as well as determine the number of whiskers on a man's face, how fast whiskers grow, and how many shaves a man can get from a single blade.

Source: "Gillette Fusion Case Study," researchandmarkets.com.

Program Strategy. What studies should we conduct?

Project Strategy. How should we conduct this study?

that might be undertaken. Each project should have one or more clear objectives, and the next step in the process should not be taken until these goals are explicitly stated.

II. Determine the Research Design

The sources of information for a study and the research design go hand in hand. They both depend on how much is known about the problem. If relatively little is known about the phenomenon to be investigated, exploratory research is warranted. Exploratory research begins with a review of **secondary data,** such as published or syndicated data, or trade literature that discusses similar cases. Exploratory research may then involve interviewing knowledgeable people or conducting focus groups. One of the most important characteristics of exploratory research is its flexibility. Researchers know little about the issues at this point, so they must be ready to follow their experience and intuition about possible areas of investigation.

If, on the other hand, the problem is precisely and unambiguously formulated, descriptive or causal research is needed. In these research designs, data collection is not flexible—it is rigidly specified with respect to both the data

FIGURE 3.1   **Stages in the Research Process**

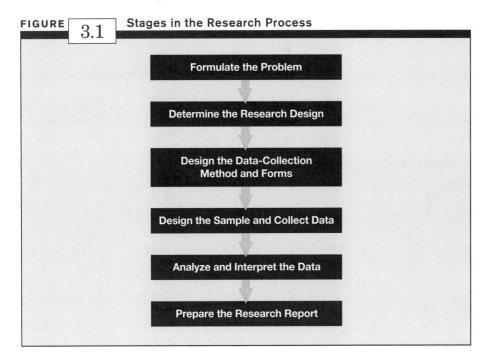

collection and the sample design to obtain precise results and conclusions, with implications that yield actionable results.

III. Design the Data-Collection Method and Forms

Given the dynamic nature of business and customers, it is often the case that the information needed is not found in the firm's own sales data, nor in census reports or industry sales trends. The research then must collect **primary data,** which are gathered specifically for the new research needs. But how? Should the data be collected by observation or questionnaire? Should the form be structured with a fixed set of alternative answers, or should the responses be open-ended? Should the purpose be made clear to the respondent, or should the study objectives be disguised? There are many questions that must be answered in designing research.

IV. Design the Sample and Collect Data

In designing the sample, the researcher must specify: (1) the sampling frame, (2) the sample selection process, and (3) the size of the sample. The **sampling frame** is the list of population elements from which the sample will be drawn. We need to think carefully of whom we (marketers) are targeting and whose opinions we (marketing researchers) are soliciting.

- For example, we may appeal to *pet owners* with advertisements and pricing, but if the product doesn't pass muster with the pets, there will be no repeat purchase.

- Similarly, we might solicit *parents* about buying educational toys, but if their children find the toys boring or uncool, word-of-mouth will ensure no further growth in sales.

Sampling the purchasing agents is clearly important, but so is the testing on the end user.

The sample selection process requires specification about such things as whether it will be a probability or nonprobability sample (these terms are defined in Chapter 11). The decision on sample size (discussed in Chapter 12) involves determining how many people must be studied to get accurate answers to allow a decision to be made.

Once the sample design is specified, data collection can begin. Data-collection methods are dictated by the kinds of information to be obtained and the sampling requirements.

V. Analyze and Interpret the Data

Researchers may amass a mountain of data, but these data are useless unless the findings are analyzed and the results interpreted in light of the problem at hand. Data analysis involves several steps. First, the data-collection forms must be edited—scanned to be sure that they are complete and consistent and that the instructions were followed. Once the forms have been edited, they must be coded. Coding involves assigning numbers to the answers so they can be analyzed. The final step is tabulation, the orderly arrangement of data in a table or other summary format achieved by counting the frequency of responses to each question.

The coding, editing, and tabulation functions are common to most research studies. The statistical tests applied to the data are specific to the sampling procedures and data-collection instruments used in the research.

VI. Prepare the Research Report

The research report is the document submitted to management that summarizes the research results, with conclusions and recommendations. It is all that many executives see of the research effort, and it becomes the standard by which that research is judged. Thus, it is imperative that the research report be clear and accurate, because no matter how well all previous steps have been completed, the project will be no more successful than the report. It is one of the most important factors affecting whether the research will be used to implement change.

Additional Comments

The stages of the research process are linked—choices made at one stage impact another.

Each step is more complex than this overview suggests (see Table 3.1). We will elaborate on these steps throughout the book.

In addition, we have presented the stages rather simply, as if you proceed through them in a lockstep fashion. In fact, the process could loop back if there is a need to rethink and revise the various elements in the process as the study proceeds. For example, the problem might not be specified explicitly enough to allow the development of the research design, in which case the researcher would need to return to stage 1 to delineate the research objectives more clearly.

It is sometimes difficult for beginning marketing researchers to understand, but the steps in the research process are highly interrelated. A decision made at one stage affects decisions at each of the other stages, and a revision of the procedure at any stage often requires modifications of procedures at each of the other stages.

All the steps in the research process are necessary and vital. Errors can arise during any stage, and it is dangerous to worry about one kind of error to the exclusion of others. For example, a large sample size will help reduce statistical sampling error, but some other errors can increase with sample size; e.g., larger samples mean using more interviewers, who need to be trained so they all

TABLE 3.1   **Questions to be Addressed Throughout the Research Process**

Stage	Typical Questions
Formulate the Problem	• What is the purpose of the study: solve a problem, identify an opportunity? • Is additional background information necessary? • What information is needed to make the decision? • How will the information be used? • Should research be conducted?
Determine the Research Design	• How much is already known? • What types of questions need to be answered? • What type of study will best address the research questions?
Design the Data-Collection Method and Forms	• Can existing data be used? • What needs to be measured? How? • What is the source of the data? • Are there cultural factors to be taken into account in the data collection? • Are there any legal restrictions on the collection methods? • Can objective answers be obtained by asking people? • Should the questionnaires be administered in person, over the phone, through the mail, online, or through e-mail? • Should rating scales be used in the questionnaires?
Design the Sample and Collect Data	• What is the target population? • Is a list of population elements available? • Is a probability sample desirable? • How large should the sample be? • How should the sample be selected? • Who will gather the data? • How long will the data gathering take? • What methods will be used to ensure the quality of the data collected?
Analyze and Interpret the Data	• Who will handle the editing of the data? • How will the data be coded? • Who will supervise the coding? • What analysis techniques will be used?
Prepare the Research Report	• Who will read the report? • What is their technical level of sophistication? • Are managerial recommendations called for? • What will the format of the written report be? • How should the oral report be structured?

handle the interviews in a standard way. Otherwise, different responses can be as much a function of the interviewers as the interviewees.

The stages in the research process serve as a structure for this book. The remainder of this chapter deals with stage 1, problem formulation, and each of the remaining stages is addressed in its own section in the book.

Problem Formulation

An old adage says, "A problem well defined is half-solved." This is especially true in marketing research. It's only when the problem has been clearly defined and the objectives of the research precisely stated that research can be designed properly.

"Problem" definition of course refers to real *problems*, but it also applies to situations that might better be described as *opportunities*. Let's look at both.

Marketing research problems or opportunities arise from three fundamental sources: (1) unanticipated change, (2) planned change, and (3) serendipity in the form of new ideas. A large source of **unanticipated change** is the environment in which firms operate. Demographic, economic, technological, competitive, political, and legal changes can have significant effects on the marketing function. How the firm responds to new technology, or a competitor's new product, or changes in the lifestyles of their key customers, determines whether the change turns out to be a problem or an opportunity.

Unanticipated change can also arise from within the firm's internal environment. The firm may be losing market share, or sales might not be as high as forecast. The firm may find itself losing key salespeople or its best distributors to competitors. In situations of unanticipated change, a key issue is finding exactly what is happening and why.

Other change is **planned**. Most firms want business to grow and contemplate marketing actions for facilitating that growth, e.g., with the introduction of new products, improved customer service, and more effective pricing and advertising strategies. Planned change is oriented more toward the future, and the basic question is how the firm may bring about the desired change. Marketing research helps assess the feasibility of alternatives being considered.

A third source of marketing problems or opportunities is **serendipity**, or chance ideas. The new idea might be generated internally, from R&D or one's sales force, or from a customer via a complaint letter. For example, Rubbermaid makes it a practice for its executives to read customer letters to find out how people like the company's products. These letters often lead to new product ideas.

Regardless of how decision problems or opportunities arise, most of them require additional information for resolution. The manager must determine what information is necessary and how it can be obtained. Good communication between the marketing manager (the decision maker) and the marketing researcher is imperative.

- The decision makers need to understand what research can and cannot accomplish.
- The researchers need to understand the nature of the decision that the managers face and what they hope to learn from research—the project objectives.

Researchers must avoid simply responding to requests for information. To do so is akin to allowing a patient who is seeing a doctor to make his or her own diagnosis and prescribe the treatment as well. Instead, the researcher needs to work with the manager to translate symptoms into underlying causal factors. For example, when Xerox became concerned that it was rapidly losing photocopier sales to Japanese competitors, that was the symptom. An investigation revealed that whereas Xerox was focusing on features to add, the problem in the customers' minds was one of product reliability.

Consultants face this issue of clarifying problem definitions all the time; clients think they know what is wrong and they hire consultants to fix it. Often as not, consultants must assess what is "really" wrong before they hope to fix it. Marketing researchers are the consultants in this case—they are the keepers and procurers of useful marketplace information.

Even with a more precisely defined research question and impeccably executed research, both managers and researchers need to recognize that marketing research does not produce answers or strategies. It produces data—data that must be interpreted and converted into action plans by management. To be sure that the research reflects management's needs, managers must play an active role in communicating their information needs to researchers, and they need to stay in touch during the research process itself to ensure that they'll be getting the information they truly need to help them make the decisions they face.

A proper understanding of the basic structure of **decision making** can help researchers interact with management to better specify research issues. Decision situations can be characterized by the following conditions:

1. A decision maker is operating in some environment in which there is a problem.
2. There are at least two courses of action (A_1 and A_2) that the decision maker can follow (e.g., "go" and "no go" on a new product launch).
3. Once the decision maker chooses an action, at least two outcomes of that choice (O_1 and O_2) are possible (product is "successful" or "not"), and one outcome is preferred.
4. There is an unequal chance that each course of action will lead to the desired outcome. (If the chances are equal, the choice does not matter.)

Thus, a person faces a decision situation if he or she (1) has a problem, (2) has several good ways of solving it, and (3) is unsure about which course of action to select. Research can assist in clarifying any of these characteristics of the decision situation. Let's see how.

The Decision Maker and the Environment

A critical element for the researcher in defining the problem is understanding the decision maker and the environment in which that person is operating: What is the background of the business? What factors have led to the manager's concerns? What information would help the decision maker in dealing with these issues? What would the decision maker do with the information?

If the decision maker's original posture will not change regardless of what is found, the research will be wasted. Surprisingly, research is sometimes simply "conscience money"—the results are readily accepted when they are consistent with the decision the individual wants to make, but when the results conflict with the decision maker's original position, the results are questioned or discarded as somehow being inaccurate. The manager's view of the decision problem was so strongly held that research did little to change it. To avoid wasting resources because of the "I know better" or "don't bother me with the facts" traps, researchers need to assess the situation before doing the research, not after. This means determining the decision maker's objectives and finding out how the decision might change if certain results were found.

The researcher also needs to understand the environment in which the decision maker operates. What are the constraints on that person's actions? What are the resources at the decision maker's disposal? What is the time frame in which the manager is operating? It does little good to design a study, however accurate, that costs $50,000 and takes six months to complete when the decision maker needs the results within one month and has only $15,000 for the research. Obviously, some compromises must be made, and it is the researcher's responsibility to anticipate them by carefully examining the decision environment.

Alternative Courses of Action

Research can be properly designed only when the alternative courses of action being considered are known. The options are given to the researcher by the decision maker, and the researcher must determine whether that list exhausts the possibilities. For example, a large consumer packaged goods company saw a decline in sales of one of their lines of ethnic food, and was choosing between strategies of lowering prices and advertising heavily. When the decision maker and researcher discussed the list, they concluded the list was incomplete and added other possibilities, including positioning the food against the market leader.

Researchers must be like detectives to uncover the hidden agendas and alternatives lurking beneath the surface in any decision situation. If a critical piece of information remains undiscovered, even the most sophisticated research techniques cannot solve the problem. A marketing researcher can collect sound data and conduct sophisticated modeling, only to yield results that make no sense to the marketing manager because the model didn't capture the elements the manager thought most important.

Objectives of the Decision Maker

One of the basic facts of decision making is that individuals differ in their attitudes toward risk, and these differences influence their choices. Some people are risk takers, willing to assume a good deal of risk for the chance of a big gain. Others are risk averse, not wanting to assume much risk at all, even when the size of the potential gain is large.

It is also important to determine the decision maker's specific objectives precisely. For example, the decision maker might state that the firm wants customers to perceive their brand as "high quality," without elaborating—what does that *mean*? A clarification of goals is often among the most useful services the marketing researcher provides to the marketing manager.

The researcher must transform the vague platitudes ("high quality") into specific, operational objectives for the research. Once the objectives for the research are finally determined, they should be committed to writing. Doing so often produces additional clarity in communication and thinking. The decision maker and researcher should then agree formally on their written expression to prevent later misunderstandings (we provide a template shortly).

Consequences of Alternative Courses of Action

A lot of marketing research is intended to determine the consequences of various courses of action. The marketing manager wants to know the effect of manipulating an element in the marketing mix to achieve customer satisfaction. It is natural for much of marketing research to seek answers to questions such as: What will be the change in sales produced by a change in the product's package? If we change the sales compensation plan, what will be the effect on the sales representatives' performance and on their attitudes toward the job and company? Which advertisement is likely to generate the most favorable customer response?

Translating Decision Problem to Research Problem

Decision Problem: Wear your marketing manager hat.
Research Problem: Wear your marketing researcher hat.

A detailed understanding of the total decision situation should enable researchers working in consort with managers to translate the decision problem into a research problem. Suppose a new product is introduced and sales are below target. The marketing manager has to decide what to do about the shortfall. Should the target be revised? Should the product be withdrawn? Should an element in the marketing mix, such as advertising, be altered? Suppose the manager suspects that the advertising campaign supporting the new product has been ineffective. The product manager would want evidence that either confirmed or denied that suspicion before changing the advertising program. The research problem would then become the assessment of product awareness among potential customers.

Some of the distinctions between decision problems and research problems are illustrated in Table 3.2. The decision problem involves what needs to be done. Research can provide the necessary information to make an informed choice, and the research problem involves determining what information is needed and how to obtain it.

In making this determination, the researcher must make certain the real decision problem (not just the symptoms) is being addressed. Poor problem definition leads to unfortunate, sometimes dire, consequences. The debacle with Coca-Cola Classic is well known. A less well-known example is that Miller did not invent Lite Beer. It was first developed by Meister Brau and taste tests went well, but when the product was introduced, it failed. Meister Brau sold Lite Beer to Miller. Miller's research suggested that big (er, "frequent") beer drinkers tried to project macho images, and the concept of a diet beer connoted "wimp." Miller's emphasis thus became one of changing the image of the brand through its use of famous sports personalities.

Sometimes the difficulty in problem definition involves cultural differences. A U.S. manager was trying to interest investors in another country in a smoothie franchise. The manager described the entire system, including the corporate support and products. After the long presentation concluded, the investors

TABLE 3.2   Relating Decision Problems and Research Problems

Decision Problems	Research Problems
1. Develop package for a new product	1. Evaluate alternative package designs
2. Increase sales by opening new stores	2. Evaluate prospective locations
3. Increase store traffic	3. Measure current image of the store
4. Increase repeat purchasing behavior	4. Assess current amount of repeat purchasing
5. Develop equitable sales territories	5. Assess current and proposed territories
6. Allocate ad budget geographically	6. Study market penetration in the respective areas
7. Introduce new product	7. Design a test market for assessment
8. Expand into other countries	8. Assess market potential
9. Select overseas distribution channels	9. Evaluate current channel structures and members

politely thanked the presenter and asked, "What is a smoothie?" Oops. The manager had neglected simple marketing research on the investors.

How does one avoid the trap of researching the wrong problem? The primary way is by not responding to requests for information without first developing a proper appreciation for the problem at hand (see Research Realities 3.2). There is an old saying: "If you do not know where you want to go, any road will get you there." The same goes for decision making—if the decision maker doesn't know what he or she wants to achieve, the research study will not accomplish it.

As Figure 3.2 indicates, even marketing managers concur that researchers should take an active role defining the decision problem and in specifying the information that will be useful for solving it. One way to make sure that the true decision problem will be addressed by the research is to use scenarios that anticipate the results. For example, based on his or her understanding of the situation, the researcher tries to anticipate what the final report could look like and asks tough questions, such as, "If I come up with this cross-tabulation with these numbers in it, what would you do?" This communication can clarify the parameters of the study.

For example, a large electronics company wanted to determine the knowledge of and preferences for MP3 components among young consumers. The researchers drew up mock tables with age break downs of 13–16 and 17–20, at which point the company clarified that it meant even younger children, age 10 or older.

The Research Proposal

Once the purpose and scope of the research are agreed on, researchers turn their attention to choosing the techniques to conduct the research. These techniques should also be communicated to the decision maker before the research begins, through a formal research proposal, which allows another opportunity to make sure that the research being planned will provide the information necessary to answer the decision maker's problem.

RESEARCH   REALITIES

3.2 Information Request and Two Responses

Kevin is a research analyst who has been with The Minute Maid Company for a little more than two years. He is well regarded by the marketing team he works with, and is responsive to its research requests.

One morning, Kevin receives a phone call from the marketing manager on Minute Maid Fruit Punches. The marketing manager tells him that R&D has come up with a new, improved flavor. Before authorizing full production of the new formula, it would be prudent to conduct a taste test to determine if consumers will react favorably to the new flavor. He is calling Kevin to find out how much product would be required for such a test. He adds that it is very important that this research be initiated quickly because a competitor, Tropicana, has just come out with a new, improved version of its product.

Kevin says he needs more information. Will this new flavor be available in both chilled and frozen? When will the product be available for the test? After getting those questions answered, Kevin decides to conduct blind taste tests with 600 respondents in a mall. He'll first find out if respondents can detect differences between the products. Then each product will be rated for preference.

You might be thinking this design sounds pretty good—sequential approach so time and money aren't wasted if the new flavor is not as good as everyone thinks; adequate sample sizes for both the chilled and frozen forms, and two parts to the evaluation.

Now let me introduce you to Joan. She has the same credentials as Kevin and is faced with the same initial phone call. The marketing manager asks her how much product she will need in order to conduct a taste test for him.

Joan responds (like Kevin had) that she needs more information. Joan suggests a meeting with the manager to discuss the situation. She reviews the information she has been given by the marketing manager and she develops a list of questions she wants to ask the marketing manager when they get together. First, she goes to her computer and pulls up the most recent Nielsen Scantrack information she has on the Punches segment of the Juice and Juice Drink category. She checks both to see if any change has occurred in the marketplace since the introduction of the new Tropicana Fruit Punch, and to see if Minute Maid Fruit Punch sales have been affected by this introduction. Next, she checks on the Nielsen household scanner panel information to see if any changes have occurred in key household purchase behavior—specifically, household penetration, buying rate, and loyalty rates for both Minute Maid and Tropicana. Finally, she reviews the historical project files to understand the previous research on the brand.

Joan meets with the marketing manager, and asks the following questions:

1. Why are we considering a new formula? Tropicana doesn't seem to have hurt our franchise with the new flavor.

2. If we do use a new formula, what do we hope to accomplish? Do we expect to pull in new users, or do we want to minimize the chances of our consumers shifting over to Tropicana?

3. How will we announce the new flavor? Will it be advertised or will we just use a notice on the package?

4. Does the new formula perform the same in both chilled and frozen forms? Are the sensory profiles identical?

5. Can we obtain product from a regular production location? Often R&D's controls are much more stringent than those of our production plants. We would rather use product for this test that most closely resembles the product that consumers would be buying from grocery stores.

After getting answers to her questions, Joan then works out her research objectives and specific design. She recommends a two-phase study, with objectives to determine Minute Maid users' response to the new flavor in terms of taste and overall preference and to determine competitive users' response to the new flavor versus the new Tropicana flavor.

Joan will also interview 600 respondents who are female heads of household, primary grocery shoppers, between 18 and 60, and who have used Minute Maid Fruit Punch in the past month. Respondents in the first phase of the research must be regular, loyal users of Minute Maid. In the second phase, respondents must be users of the competitive product.

(Continued)

The research will involve in-home placements over a two-week period. In the first phase, 300 respondents will evaluate Minute Maid's new formula versus the current formula to understand how the current franchise will react to the formulation change. In the second phase, 300 respondents will compare the new Minute Maid formula to the new Tropicana formula to determine if the new flavor would attract competitive users. In both phases, half the sample will evaluate the chilled formula, while the other half will evaluate the frozen formula.

There are several clear differences between this research design and the first example, all dependent on the approach used to define the problem.

Kevin is what I would call a "research order taker" or "research technician." He basically responded to the marketing manager's request for a taste test without considering the marketing situation that prompted the request. His research design was sound, at least on the surface, given the information he had. He would have obtained answers to his questionnaire and those answers would probably be correct. Unfortunately, both he and the marketing manager would be wondering why the company was receiving so many consumer calls on the company's 800 number from long-time Minute Maid users complaining about the new flavor.

Joan, on the other hand, is an internal *marketing consultant*—a true *marketing information professional.*

Her approach was to understand the marketplace situation and potential marketing actions that could be taken based on this research. Her research design was more costly and time consuming because she understood the risks involved as well as the potential gains that could accrue to the company based on this formula change.

In both instances, the marketing manager could make a decision based on the data obtained from a research study. The difference is that in one case, the manager might feel suspect about marketing research because it failed to predict some Minute Maid users' negative response to the formula change, whereas in the other case, the manager may be more confident in using marketing research.

Marketing information professionals must strive to go beyond simple problem solving. They must be internal marketing consultants. That is the only way to assure that research designs, techniques, and statistical analyses will be valid. It is the only way that marketing management will become more confident in its use of marketing research. It is the only way senior management can be assured that the company is receiving full value for its investment in resources and spending for marketing research.

Source: Personal correspondence with Larry P. Stanek, Marketing Information, The Minute Maid Company.

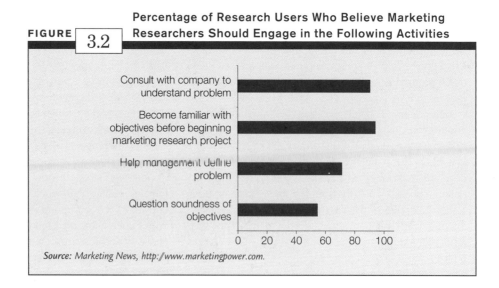

FIGURE 3.2 Percentage of Research Users Who Believe Marketing Researchers Should Engage in the Following Activities

Source: Marketing News, http://www.marketingpower.com.

Research proposals can take many forms. Some are very long and detailed, running 20 pages or more. Others are short and to the point. The length depends on the detail describing each part. Figure 3.3 contains a template that can be followed in preparing a research proposal.

Research Realities 3.3 contains portions of an actual research plan (with some confidential authorization and budget information removed) that was prepared by General Mills. Note the clearly stated criteria that will be used to interpret the results and the carefully crafted action standards, specifying what will be done depending on what the research results indicate.

FIGURE 3.3   Parts of a Research Proposal with an Example

Project Title:
Research on Your Consumers

by bidding Marketing Research Firm

1

Marketing Problem

Brief description of general problem;
    reason for conducting research
Sum up preliminary discussions
    between researcher and manager;
    demonstrate knowledge of situation
    and particular info needs

2

Purpose of Research Project

State goals and objectives, with rationales
Describe scope of project (i.e., what will
    not be investigated)
Spell out specific questions to be answered
Address possible limitations due to time
    or budget constraints (to avoid later
        disagreement)

3

Data Sources and Methodology

Describe secondary data to be used
Describe how primary data will be
    gathered (surveys, experiments)
Keep methods descriptions nontechnical
Describe sample and proposed size
Include draft of questionnaire or focus
    group moderator outline (etc.), if
        applicable

4

Time and Personnel

Provide time estimates for each phase of
    the research
Specify personnel required and their
    rates of pay
Calculate nonpersonnel costs (e.g.,
    supplies, printing, mailing, etc.)

5

(Continued)

FIGURE 3.3 *Continued*

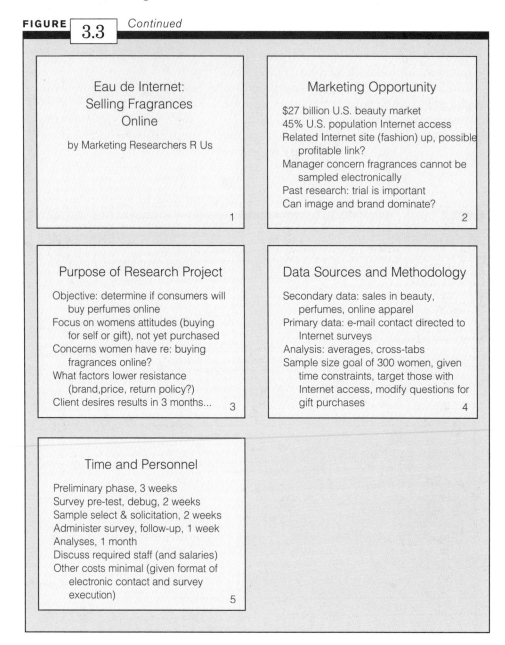

Eau de Internet:
Selling Fragrances
Online

by Marketing Researchers R Us

1

Marketing Opportunity

$27 billion U.S. beauty market
45% U.S. population Internet access
Related Internet site (fashion) up, possible
    profitable link?
Manager concern fragrances cannot be
    sampled electronically
Past research: trial is important
Can image and brand dominate?

2

Purpose of Research Project

Objective: determine if consumers will
    buy perfumes online
Focus on womens attitudes (buying
    for self or gift), not yet purchased
Concerns women have re: buying
    fragrances online?
What factors lower resistance
    (brand,price, return policy?)
Client desires results in 3 months...

3

Data Sources and Methodology

Secondary data: sales in beauty,
    perfumes, online apparel
Primary data: e-mail contact directed to
    Internet surveys
Analysis: averages, cross-tabs
Sample size goal of 300 women, given
    time constraints, target those with
    Internet access, modify questions for
    gift purchases

4

Time and Personnel

Preliminary phase, 3 weeks
Survey pre-test, debug, 2 weeks
Sample select & solicitation, 2 weeks
Administer survey, follow-up, 1 week
Analyses, 1 month
Discuss required staff (and salaries)
Other costs minimal (given format of
    electronic contact and survey
    execution)

5

Is Marketing Research Justified?

The benefits of marketing research are many, but it is not without its drawbacks. The question of whether the research costs are likely to exceed the research benefits always needs to be asked. There is no denying that the research process is often time consuming and expensive. One might first ask, "Is there enough time to conduct a thoughtful research investigation?" In today's fast-paced marketplace, it might seem that the answer is frequently no. However, a negative answer neglects three important resources:

1. Informal queries of in-house experts can be made quickly to yield preliminary insights.

R E S E A R C H   R E A L I T I E S

3.3 General Mills Research Proposal for Protein Plus Cereal

1. **Problem and Background.** Protein Plus has performed below expectation in its test market. New product and copy alternatives are being readied for testing. Three alternative formulations—Honey Graham, Nut, and Cinnamon, which retain the basic identity of current Protein Plus, but which have been judged to be sufficiently different and of sufficient potential—have been developed for testing against the current formula.

2. **Decision Involved.** Which product formulations should be carried into the concept fulfillment test?

3. **Method and Design.** In-home product tests will be conducted. Each of the four test products will be tested by a separate panel of 150 households. Each household will have purchased adult ready-to-eat (RTE) cereal within the past month and will be interested in the test product as measured by the selection of Protein Plus as one or more of their next 10 cereal packages they would like to buy. They will be exposed to Protein Plus in a booklet that also contains an ad for several competitive products, such as Product 19, Special K, Nature Valley, and Grape Nuts. A Protein Plus ad will be constructed for each of the four test products, differing primarily in the kind of taste reassurance provided. Exposure to these various executions will be rotated so that the four test panels are matched on RTE cereal usage.

   The study will be conducted in eight markets. Product will be packaged in current Protein Plus package flagged with the particular flavor reassurance for that product.

   The criterion measure will be the homemakers' post-study brand-share, adjusted to reflect the breadth of interest in the various Protein Plus communications strategies.

   Rather than trust a random sampling procedure to represent the population at large, a quota will be established to ensure that the sample of people initially contacted for each panel will conform as closely as possible to the division of female heads of households under 45 (56%) and over 45 (44%) in the U.S. population.

4. **Criteria for Interpretation.** Each formulation generating a higher weighted homemaker share than standard will be considered for subsequent testing. If more than one formulation beats standard, each will be placed in a concept fulfillment test unless one is better than the other(s) at odds of 21 or more.

5. **Estimated Project Expense.** $25,000 to $125,000.

6. Individual who must finally approve recommended action: _____ .

7. Report to be delivered by _____ if authorized by _____ and test materials shipped by _____ .

Source: Used with permission of General Mills, Inc.

---

2. Secondary data, including free published and relatively inexpensive syndicated databases, may be tapped instantaneously for detailed and comprehensive results.

3. Ongoing, continual data collection and mining efforts, which are increasingly pervasive across companies in the guise of customer relationship databases, can be accessed to understand customers' attitudes and behaviors.

If the manager is pressed for time, therefore, and cannot conduct a new marketing research project, there is likely to be relevant information around the organization already.

   One might then ask, "Is there a budget to conduct the requisite marketing research?" Myopic managers often look to marketing research as a luxury, a budget line some are quick to trim. We may of course be biased, but we would suggest an alternative question: "Will you have any budget to spend in the future if you do not understand your customers?" If conducted and interpreted properly, marketing research is very illuminating and therefore, it is absolutely worth the time and cost.

Choosing and Using a Research Supplier

Ethical **Dilemma**   3.2

The president of a small bank approaches you with plans to launch a special program of financial counseling and support for women and asks you to establish whether sufficient public interest exists to justify starting the program. No other bank in the city caters specifically to women, and you think that professional women might be enthusiastic. If news of the plan leaks out, the president believes that competitors may try to preempt him, so he asks you to keep the bank's identity secret from respondents and to inquire only into general levels of interest in increased financial services for women. However, as you read through the literature that he has left on your desk, you notice that the bank is located in the most depressed area of the city, where women might be harassed and feel unsafe.

- Would it be unethical to research the general problem of how much demand exists for a women's banking program, when the bank in question will interpret the demand as encouragement to launch such a program itself?
- What might be the costs to the researcher in voicing misgivings about the suitability of this particular bank's launching of the program? Would you voice your misgivings?
- Does it violate respondents' rights if you do not reveal the identity of the research sponsor? If so, is it a serious violation in this case? Is there a conflict of interest with respect to respondents' right to be informed versus the client's right to confidentiality?

There are lots of reasons to hire marketing research suppliers. Even large consumer products companies with large marketing research departments occasionally use outside suppliers, e.g., outsourcing to manage workloads, bringing in vendors with special expertise (e.g., in "focus groups" or "youth"), hiring suppliers so the sponsoring company can remain anonymous, and, finally, to avoid internal politics.

Though it is common to buy marketing research, many managers are uncertain as to how to select a research supplier. The first step is to know what you want. Before contacting research suppliers, it is important to identify the most critical areas of uncertainty and the issues that would benefit most from research.

There are thousands of qualified marketing research companies in the U.S. alone. Some are full-service, generalist companies; others specialize in marketing areas like advertising-copy testing or concept testing; while others specialize in research approaches such as interviews, data processing, or statistical analyses. An excellent source is the American Marketing Association Web site (marketingpower.com).

Once you have a short list of candidate suppliers, their capabilities must be evaluated in light of your company's research needs. Experts suggest that managers should seek proposals from at least three companies. Investigate these potential research suppliers, on cost, the firm's expertise, their style, and the attention they would devote to your project.

TABLE 3.3   Criteria Used to Evaluate Research Suppliers

- **General Attitude, Responsiveness:** helpful, prompt replies on cost estimates, proposals
- **Marketing Insight:** understands objectives, able to analyze data, provide recommendations
- **Fundamental Design:** questionnaire is well designed, instructions are clear to consumers
- **Questionnaire Construction:** easy to follow, questions are clear, suited to research questions
- **Tabulation Design:** format is easy to understand, calculations are accurate
- **Day-to-Day Service:** responsive and informative on study progress
- **Analysis:** thorough, accurate, relates to objectives
- **Quality of Report Writing:** concise, clear, accurate, provides executive summary
- **Presentation:** well planned, concise, organized, clear communication, smooth presentation
- **Delivery Time:** topline, tables, report
- **Cost:** over, under, justified

Source: Courtesy of Stephen Lauring, Marketing Research Manager, Land O'Lakes, Inc.

Marketing research is still a bit of an art, not entirely a science. It benefits from heavy involvement of senior research professionals who provide insights that come only from years of experience. A research firm's most important asset is the qualification of the research professionals who are involved in the design, supervision, and interpretation of the research.

The research user's responsibility is to communicate effectively with the prospective vendor and to provide the necessary background and objectives for the study. It is also a good idea to ask about the supplier's quality-control standards. Most research firms are pleased when clients show concern about quality and will gladly explain their quality-control steps in the areas of fieldwork, coding, and data processing.

Useful resource: *American Marketing Association* www. marketingpower.com.

After reading the proposals and meeting key personnel, the manager should perform a comparative analysis. Many firms have formal evaluation systems with specified criteria for evaluating suppliers, especially if they use suppliers on a regular basis. Land O'Lakes uses the criteria shown in Table 3.3. Top suppliers will seem equally competent, so a manager must rely on judgment regarding the soundness of the research design proposed, the supplier's responsiveness to questions, and the vendor's understanding of the subtler aspects of the marketing problem.

An increasingly popular way for firms to work with marketing research suppliers is to form long-term partnering relationships with a few select firms. Doing so helps the research buyer feel that the research supplier is more accountable. In a typical collaborative partnership, the client and research firm work together on an ongoing basis on those projects where the research firm has expertise, instead of the client relying on project-by-project bids to select suppliers for each of those projects. Over time, the research firm becomes more familiar with the client's business and issues, which then allows the client firms to spend more time on managerial functions, including problem definition, interpretation, and recommendations, and less time on the nuts-and-bolts of a typical study.

Summary

A company's philosophy of how marketing research fits into its marketing plan determines its program strategy for marketing research. A program strategy specifies the types of studies that will be conducted and determines their purposes. The design of the individual studies defines the firm's project strategy.

Although each research problem imposes its own special requirements, a marketing research project can be viewed as a sequence of steps—the research process—that includes the following:

1. Formulate the problem.
2. Determine the research design.
3. Design the data-collection method and forms.
4. Design the sample and collect data.
5. Analyze and interpret the data.
6. Prepare the research report.

These steps are highly interrelated and usually performed not simply consecutively, but with a good deal of iteration between the various steps.

The first stage in the research process is problem formulation. In defining the decision problem, the researcher and the manager need to be honest in their communications with each other. It is imperative that the research address the "real" decision problem and not some visible, but incorrect, aspect of it. Once an understanding is achieved, the researcher should prepare a research proposal that describes the techniques that will be used to address the problem. The research proposal should include some perspective on how each stage in the research process will be handled, as well as the time and cost estimates.

Questions

1. What are the fundamental characteristics of decision problems?
2. Why would firms want to use outside suppliers for their research? How should decision makers go about choosing an outside supplier for some research?
3. What are the sources of marketing problems or opportunities? Does a source change typically trigger a change in research emphasis? Explain.
4. What is the purpose of a research proposal? What goes into the various parts?
5. What is the most serious error in research? Explain.
6. What is involved in using scenarios to help define the decision problem?
7. What is the research process?
8. What is involved in a research request? What is included in the written statement?
9. What is the difference between a program strategy for research and a project strategy?

Applications and Problems

1. In the absence of company problems, is there any need to conduct marketing research?
2. Briefly discuss the difference between a decision problem and a research problem.
3. You are the marketing manager of a new entrepreneurial venture. Recently you solicited proposals for an upcoming research project from three outside marketing research suppliers. You have the formal proposals in hand and must choose which supplier to use. In general, what criteria should you use in making your decision?
4. Given the following research problems, identify corresponding decision problems for which they might provide useful information:

a. Design a test market to assess the effect on sales volume of a discount plan.
b. Evaluate inventory for retail and e-tail warehouses.
c. Evaluate the sales and market share of grocery stores in a metropolitan area.
d. Develop sales forecasts for a new product.
e. Assess the level of awareness of the benefits of a new generation of cell phones.
f. Assess attitudes and opinions of customers toward existing theme restaurants.

5. In each of the following situations, identify the fundamental source of the marketing problem or opportunity, a decision problem arising from the marketing

problem or opportunity, and a possible research problem.

a. Cool Pool Supply is a manufacturer of swimming pool maintenance chemicals. Recently, a malfunction of the equipment that mixes anti-algae compound resulted in a batch of the product that not only inhibits algae growth but also causes the pool water to turn a beautiful shade of light blue.

b. The MBA director of a local college recently extended offers to 20 promising students. Only five offers were accepted. In the past, acceptance rates have averaged 90%. A survey of nonacceptors conducted by the director revealed that the primary reason students declined the offer was their perception that the college's course requirements are too "restrictive."

c. Chocoholic Candy Company has enjoyed great success in its small regional market. Management attributes much of this success to Chocoholic's unique distribution system, which ensures twice-weekly delivery of fresh product to retail outlets. The directors of the company have instructed management to expand Chocoholic's geographical market if it can be done without altering the twice-weekly delivery policy.

6. Given the following decision problems, identify the research problems:

a. What pricing strategy to follow for a new product

b. Whether to increase the level of advertising expenditures on print or online

c. Whether to increase in-store promotion of existing products

d. Whether to increase training for frontline service providers

e. Whether to change the sales force compensation package

f. Whether to change the combination of ticket price, entertainers, and security at the Indiana State Fair

g. Whether to revise a bank's electronic payment service

C A S E S

CASE 1.1
Big Brothers of Fairfax County

Big Brothers of America is a social-service program designed to meet the needs of boys ages 6 to 18 who may have needs for more attention. Most of the boys served by the program live with their mothers and rarely see or hear from their fathers. The purpose of the program is to give these boys the chance to establish a friendship with a caring adult male. Big Brothers of America was founded on the belief that an association with a responsible adult can help program participants become more responsible citizens and better adjusted young men.

The program was started in Cincinnati in 1903. Two years later, the organization was granted its first charter in New York state through the efforts of Mrs. Cornelius Vanderbilt. By the end of World War II, there were 30 Big Brothers agencies. Today there are more than 300 agencies across the U.S., and more than 120,000 boys are matched with Big Brothers.

Fairfax County has a chapter of Big Brothers of America, and it relies on United Way for about 85% of its funding. The remaining 15% is raised by the local Big Brothers agency.

Information about the Big Brothers program in Fairfax County reaches the public primarily through local media (local papers, radio, public-service announcements, posters on buses and in windows of local establishments), and word-of-mouth advertising. The need for volunteers is a key message emanating from these sources. The agency phone number is always included so that people who want to know more about the program can call for information. Those calling in are given basic information over the telephone and are invited to attend one of the monthly orientation sessions organized by the Big Brothers program staff. At these meetings, men get the chance to talk to other volunteers and to find out what will be expected of them should they decide to join the program. At the end of the session, prospective volunteers are asked to complete two forms. One is an application form and the other is a questionnaire in which the person is asked to describe the type of boy he would prefer to be matched with, as well as his own interests.

The files on potential Little Brothers are then reviewed in an attempt to match boys with the volunteers. A match is made only if both partners agree. The agency stays in close contact with the pair and monitors its progress. The three counselors for the Big Brothers program serve as resources for the volunteer.

The majority of the inquiry calls received by the Fairfax County agency are from women who are interested in becoming Big Sisters (in the Big Brothers program) or from people desiring information on the Couples Program. Both programs are similar to the Big Brothers program and are administered by it. In fact, of 55 calls concerning a recent orientation meeting, only 5 were from males. Only three of the five callers actually attended the meeting, a typical response.

Although the informational campaigns and personal appeals thus seemed to have some effect, the results were also generally disappointing and did little to alleviate the shortage of volunteer Big Brothers. Currently, 250 boys are waiting to be matched with Big Brothers, and the shortage increases weekly.

Big Brothers of Fairfax County believed that a lack of awareness and accurate knowledge could be the cause of the shortage of volunteers. Are there men who would volunteer if only they were made aware of the program and its needs? Or is the difficulty a negative program image? Do people think of Little Brothers as problem children, boys who have been in trouble with the law or who have severe behavioral problems? Or could there be a misconception of the type of man who would make a good Big Brother? Do people have stereotypes with respect to the volunteers, for example, that the typical volunteer is a young, single, professional male?

QUESTIONS

1. What is (are) the marketing decision problem(s)?

2. What is (are) the marketing research problem(s)?

3. What types of information would be useful to answer these questions?

4. How would you go about securing this information?

CASE 1.2
Using Loyalty Data at Flowers 4U

Flowers 4U is an online flower and plant service. Like 1-800-Flowers, Flowers.com, and FTD(.com), Flowers 4U takes customers' orders by phone or online and executes the order by contacting their preferred local florists nearest the requested delivery site. The local florist partner then fulfills the order and delivers the flowers to the recipient.

Currently, Flowers 4U is much smaller than these other competitors, and it is trying to expand its market share. It knows that it needs to build relationships with more local florists, and it is working on that. But Flowers 4U wants to go beyond that. The marketing manager knows that once their distribution channels are extended, the company will merely be meeting the existing competition. The manager is thinking about how the brand can be perceived as better than the competition. The company has been considering offering a variety of additional services, from a yearly planner with reminder-prompts to buy flowers for birthdays and anniversaries, to the delivery of gourmet foods, to partnering with other retailers to allow customers to pay for a variety of gift certificates to accompany the flower delivery, such as $100 salon treatment, $35 dry-cleaning pick-up, $50 local restaurant coupon, etc.

Flowers 4U knows that it will need to grow by attracting new customers. However, in developing these service expansion efforts, the marketing manager plans to ask current customers to voluntarily complete online surveys. The manager wants to sample the company's "best" customers.

Traditionally, to define "best customer," customer relationship marketing and direct marketing programs look at three dimensions, known popularly as RFM—recency, frequency, and monetary value (see Figure 1.2.1). That is, good customers have probably made purchases recently, they probably purchase frequently, and their orders are probably bigger than other customers. All three dimensions, RFM, are used because they do not provide redundant information (in other words, R, F, and M are not that highly correlated).

The marketing manager is confident that once a sample of best customers are contacted, the company will get good guidance about what additional services Flowers 4U should offer.

QUESTIONS

1. What is the decision problem?

2. What is (are) the research problem(s)?

3. What recommendations would you make to the marketing manager to address the research problem(s)? That is, what data would you collect and how might those data be used to answer the research question(s) posed?

CASE 1.3
E-Food and the Online Grocery Competition (A)

When everybody's busy, something's got to give. The service industry of online groceries (that is, grocery shopping online and the home delivery of the purchased items) has grown to address today's consumer demands of convenience and time savings.

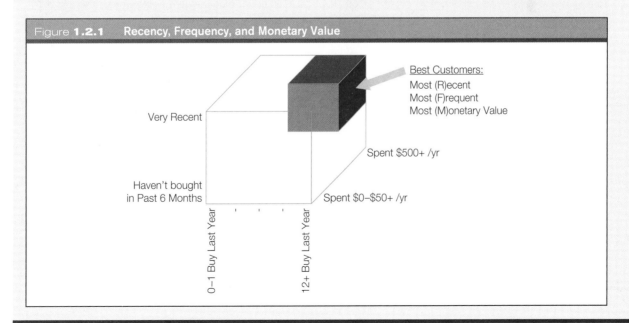

Figure **1.2.1**   **Recency, Frequency, and Monetary Value**

Several competitors serve hundreds of thousands of households, including groceronline.com (which uses UPS and Federal Express rather than local delivery operators), netgrocer.com (which covers towns and rural areas, with no annual fee, and makes available merchandise such as books and CDs), etc., and industry experts predict continued strong growth (anywhere from $5billion to $80 billion in the next three to five years).

These online grocery services provide virtual stores through which the electronic visitor navigates, as if pushing a shopping cart in a traditional grocery store. The user clicks on items to purchase, which are placed in the user's cart. When complete, the user is "checked out," specifying a delivery date and time (paying a premium for narrower windows of delivery time precision, such as from 1 p.m. to 1:30 p.m. compared to 1 p.m. to 4 p.m.). Some services require users to pay annual dues, other recoup delivery costs proportionate to each shopping bill.

The software allows the user to store his or her preferences in a personal shopping list, which may be altered, adding or deleting items as deemed necessary with each e-visit. Across the various providers, the software also usually allows facile consumer comparison; for example, the SKUs in a particular category may be sorted by brand name, by price, by value (price per ounce, for example), by what is on "feature" (sale and point of purchase promotions), by various dietetic goals ("healthy," "low fat"), and so on. The user may write in "notes," to specify in more detail, for example, "Please pick up green (unripe) bananas, not yellow ones," or, "If Fancy Feast is out of beef, please get turkey instead," which instruct the professional shopper as to the user's particular preferences. Categories of items that can be purchased are continually expanding, from foods to drugstore items and other merchandise.

Most users are women, employed full-time, and married, with household incomes that exceed $120,000. Online grocery providers tend to conduct the online business very well, if customers' satisfaction, repeat visits, and word-of-mouth are any indicators. That is, the software provided, the merchandise selected, the delivery reliability, and so on, are valued by the customer, with few complaints. However, home delivery of food is not a particularly profitable industry. One of the major paths to profit is in selling the data that result from the visitors' trips to the Web site.

Ashley Sims is an MBA student, taking her last term of classes, and is thinking about starting up a local competitor online grocer. She's certain that by learning from the templates of the current providers in other markets, she too can run the logistics of the business. However, she hopes that given her computer expert contacts, she can create a competitive advantage in the software setup, if she understands the consumers' mindset as they travel through the e-grocery stores. She wants to know just what a user is thinking from the first click onto the Web site to the last "Done Shopping" click off the site. This knowledge would allow her to offer better advice to her software developers in terms of what features would facilitate the visitors' traversal of the grocery store. Data like these would help improve the system, and it would also lend great insight to the consumers' decision processes.

QUESTIONS

1. What is the decision problem?

2. What is (are) the research problem(s)?

3. Prepare a research proposal to submit to an online grocer on behalf of your research team.

CASE 1.4
Choosing a Brand Name

The choice of a brand name is very important. It is a single word with a great deal of responsibility. The word must convey what the product is, what it is not, why it's great, or at least better than the others, and why you should buy it.

New brand names are required in a number of marketing settings. A new product requires a new name. A line extension for a brand may be created to help stimulate sales.

Oddly enough, one arena that is seeing a frequent need to generate and test a "brand name" is in the health services sector. Increasingly, two or more offices of physicians are merging to meet some mutual goal more effectively (serve more patients, service more needs of their patients, share management and overhead costs, etc.). When this occurs, the groups have a decision to make: Shall they go by the first group's name? The second group's name? Or pick a new name?

Most frequently, the groups choose to pick a new name. The reasons are usually twofold. First, there are politics. Specifically, the management of group 1 (or 2) likes its name better and doesn't want group 2 (or 1) to think they're going to run the show. But the better reason for our purposes is the "marketing" reason. Specifically, given that the groups are combining so as to achieve a new goal, the new brand name is the opportunity to communicate to the new potential customers how the merger could be good for them.

Usually a brand name choice study runs something like this: (1) Many names are generated. These names can come from the marketing research and advertising team, top management, the employees (e.g., in a contest), etc.

(2) All the names are collected and the list is pruned, in-house, by a number of criteria, including, for example, deleting names that are too close to the competition or that are already legally registered, deleting names that are difficult to pronounce or spell, deleting names that have negative or lame connotations, and in international applications, names that don't translate well, etc.

(3) Then the remaining short list of candidate names are pretested with "real" customers. Usually a number of constituencies are polled. Internal customers are asked for their reactions to the list of potential names. In this example, the employees would be the physicians. Multiple external customers would also be queried (by interview or survey). These include business partners, such as representatives of nearby hospitals and medical centers, and the insurance payers. These external customers also include patients of various sorts. "Current" customers would be asked, as would patients who are the kind the new group hopes to serve more often. It would be relatively easy to find members of all but the last of these groups to include in your study.

The results of just this process produced, for one health group merger, the following names:

- Mid-Central Hospital
- Downtown Medical Center
- Airus Group
- Health Protection Facilities
- Wellness Consultants
- Health and Life
- Touchpoint.

The attributes that were tested for each of these proposed names, in each of the constituency samples, included:

- General positivity or negativity toward the name
- Connotations of excellence and quality
- Affiliation with a particular geographic focus
- A traditional vs. contemporary image
- A formal vs. friendly image
- Distinctive
- Easily understood
- Perceptions of convenience and accessibility.

QUESTIONS

1. Which of these attributes do you think are more important than others? With regard to achieving what goals?

2. Which name(s) do you think scored best on which attributes? From which segment's perspective?

3. How would you modify the names? Why?

CASE 1.5
Moving Consumers from Awareness to Loyalty

Marketers talk about the phases that consumers go through in terms of their relationships with products. There needs to be awareness before trial. If there is trial, there can be repeat purchasing. If there is predictable repeat purchasing, we might call that loyalty, etc.

Marketing strategies, such as goals to find segments of customers to target who will be profitable for the firm, are translated into marketing tactics. The marketing tactics involve decisions about the product features, the price level that's right for the product and segment, the promotions used to convey the competitive advantages of this product vs. its competitors, and the place or distribution points of availability for the product's purchase. Sometimes even very simple data can shed light on the successfulness of the marketing campaign at the different stages.

Figure 1.5.1 contains two sets of data, one for the brand offered by firm A (brand A), and one for another firm's offering, brand B. Each brand was tested in the marketplace for awareness, trial, and repeat purchasing.

The data are simple to collect and easy to represent, and they communicate very clearly the marketing challenges at the two companies. Discuss these scenarios either in class or with a group of fellow students.

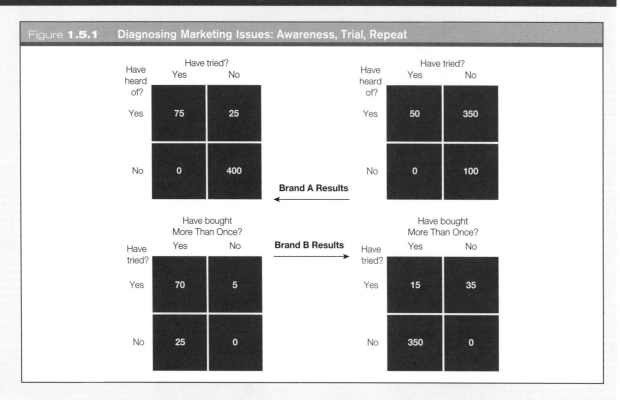

Figure **1.5.1**   Diagnosing Marketing Issues: Awareness, Trial, Repeat

Use the data and the following questions to structure your discussion:

QUESTIONS

1. Which brand is better known in the marketplace?
   a. How can you enhance awareness for the other brand?
   b. If there is low awareness, what is the most likely reason? Product? Price? Promotion? Place?

2. Which brand, once there is awareness, is more likely to induce people to try it?
   a. If there is awareness but not trial, what's the problem? Perception? Price? Availability?
   b. For the brand with lower awareness, how would you entice more people to try the product?
   c. If there is low trial, what is the most likely reason? Product? Price? Promotion? Place?

3. Which brand enjoys the most repeat purchasing?
   a. If the brand with lesser repeat wanted to improve on this aspect, what should it do?
   b. When repeat is strong, what does that mean the company has done well? Product? Price? Promotion? Place?

4. If you could request more marketing research for either of the brands, what would you request and why?

CASE 1.6
Qualitative Data from Open-Ended Survey Items: A Service Quality Example[1]

In order to understand how customers think about service quality, people were asked to reflect on examples from their recent experiences in the marketplace of good service and poor service. We then asked the sample to elaborate and tell us the extended story about the bad service encounters in particular. People are quite willing to do this—it's an opportunity to vent and it feels good, so the marketing researcher can get high response rates.

We asked the following questions of all respondents in an attempt to identify the features of service encounters that make them satisfactory or unsatisfactory:

• Think of a time when, as a customer, you had a particularly dissatisfying interaction with an employee of an airline, hotel, or restaurant, etc.

• When did the incident happen?

• What specific circumstances led up to this situation?

[1] The first few records of the qualitative data set are presented here. The larger data set is available online.

Figure 1.6.1   Service Quality Open-Ended Survey Question

Think back to the last time you had a bad encounter with a service provider (e.g., airlines, hotel, bank, restaurant, retail shop, etc.). Think about what made the experience so dissatisfying, and why you thought the service quality was so poor. Describe the situation and your feelings—what about the situation went wrong?

_____

_____

_____

_____

- Exactly what did the employee say or do?
- What resulted that made you feel the interaction was dissatisfying?

The part of the qualitative data we'll focus on was gathered through the survey item in Figure 1.6.1. People were free to write as little or as much as they wished, about anything they wanted that was related to their disappointing service interaction.

The surveys were collected, and administration assistance was hired to type in the verbatim responses (sometimes online surveys are used, where respondents type in their reactions, so the data are already entered in text form). Pay your staff well, because this work is challenging: It is tedious, it is difficult to decipher many people's handwriting, and finally, you need high quality control on data entry if you're going to be interpreting the data shortly.

Figure 1.6.2 depicts the beginning of the qualitative database. (You can get the rest of these data online.) The first column is simply an arbitrary label for the survey respondent. The second column is the verbatim response from the customer about what upset them about the service encounter.

Figure 1.6.3 offers the beginnings of a coding scheme. These schema are developed iteratively, beginning with the marketing manager's "hunches" about the qualities that people are sensitive to and therefore are likely to mention, integrated with a perusal of the comments themselves.

Figure 1.6.4 shows how the data in Figure 1.6.2 would be coded. So, for example, for survey 002b, the

Figure 1.6.2   Service Quality Open-Ended Survey Verbata A Sampling of the Data

Id#	Typed Verbatim Consumer Response
002b	It was too expensive.
001c	It was slow.
006a	The waitress didn't acknowledge our presence when we sat down.
005f	I felt it was low quality.
007a	The attitude of the employees.
009a	All she did was bring me a grilled cheese.
010a	Timeliness.
011b	Individuals at the service desk appear to not know their jobs.
012b	The service provider completed the process quickly.
013a	They did nothing to calm my anger.
003c	They did not apologize. They made excuses.
004g	I knew they could do better.
014a	The service throughout the flight by the attendants was very good.
015c	I was able to get an omelet that met my vegetarian needs without egg yolk (no fat/low cholesterol).

Figure 1.6.3   Service Quality Open-Ended Survey Coding Scheme

A. Cost, price, value,

B. Speed of service (usually too slow, but note if too fast)

C. (Not) treated like a valuable customer

D. Employee related

E. Equipment or technology failure

F. Fell short of my customer expectations

G. Were they empowered to meet my specific requests

customer's comment was pretty clearly about cost, so the category label of "A" seems appropriate. Note, however, that some survey responses are less easily categorized, making the task of coding overall nontrivial. A number of decisions must always be made.

When coders have difficulty applying the coding scheme to the data, it is always the fault of the coding scheme. For example, there isn't really a code that may be applied to respondent 005f, "I felt it was low quality," so the coding scheme needs to be expanded.

Sometimes a customer can offer a comment that needs multiple codes, and the marketing researcher has to think about how to treat that observation, e.g.,

Figure 1.6.4   Using Coding Scheme

The data file would resemble:

002b	A
001c	B
006a	D
005f	
007a	D
009a	
010a	B
011b	D
012b	B,D
013a	
003c	
004g	F
014a	
015c	G

expand the variable into two variables and allow for multiple thought units? The survey labeled 012b is such an example. The respondent said, "The service provider completed the process quickly." Is this thought predominately about the service provider, hence warranting the code "D" for employee, or is the comment more about speed, for which "B" would be the appropriate code.

QUESTIONS

1. Go online, get the rest of the data.

2. Develop a coding scheme you believe in. What is it based on?

3. Apply the coding scheme to the data. There are almost 70 responses in the database. Try to code at least half. Estimate how long it would take you to do them all!

4. What can you do with the data? An easy quantitative assessment would be to calculate frequencies for the occurrence of the different codes in your database. What do those summary statistics tell you? What don't they tell you? Qualitative marketing researchers wouldn't perform such counts—they'd assess the data by reading through and forming a judgment about what customers are saying. If you were to do this, how could you substantiate your claims to convince others (e.g., your boss)?

CASE 1.7
Extending a Travel Brand

You're sitting in your apartment, staring at the stack of work you've got ahead of you, thinking about the two biggest projects due this term—one you're looking forward to, for your entrepreneurship class; the other sounds like a drag—for your geeky marketing research class. You're wondering, "How can I leverage the one in the other—don't I have to know about customers (like a marketing research project) to launch a new product into the marketplace (for my entrepreneurship class)?"

The entrepreneurship project is coming from a local travel agent who came to class to solicit help. She represents a tentative R&D alliance between two of the biggest travel package service providers—Trafalgar and Globus. (If you're not familiar with them, check them out online so you'll know what you're talking about.)

T&G have been watching the growing trends of men traveling in small groups with their buddies (an "all guys weekend"), and women doing the same thing ("girls weekend out"), and naturally wondering, "Is there a business opportunity here?" T&G both have great brand images. They're known as high quality, though reasonably priced. They provide housing, some meals, and itineraries—places of interest to see, from cultural destinations (e.g., museums, archaeological sites) to popular entertainment (e.g., evening amusements).

T&G's initial thoughts are to offer several trips for the men, such as to Las Vegas (for drinking, cigars, and showgirls), fishing in Montana, or auto racing (in Indiana, Florida, or Germany). The trips for the women would be to spas (San Diego and Miami), or shopping centers (New York or Los Angeles).

While T&G have many decades of experience between them, they're just guessing which trip combinations would be in great demand. Can you help them?

QUESTIONS

1. What is the decision problem?

2. What is (are) the research problem(s)?

3. Sketch out a draft of a research proposal to submit to Trafalgar or Globus (1–3 slides, 4–5 bullet points per slide, big font).

4. To really impress T&G, go online and try to get some initial, rough estimates of numbers of tourists, travel destinations, etc.

Determine Research Design

Part 2 deals with designing research so that it addresses the appropriate questions effectively.

Chapter 4 provides an overview of various research designs: exploratory, descriptive, and causal research designs. The chapter continues with a discussion of exploratory research and qualitative data.

Chapter 5 discusses descriptive research, the most popular kind of marketing research.

Chapter 6 discusses the role of causal experiments in marketing research.

Research Design, Exploratory Research, and Qualitative Data

4

Questions to Guide Your Learning:

Q1 What is *exploratory research*? How does it relate to *qualitative data*?

Q2 What can a literature search, experience survey, or case study do for me?

Q3 What makes for a good *focus group* or *interview*?

Q4 What is a *projective test*?

Q5 What kinds of *observational methods* are there?

Q6 What is an *ethnography*?

The preceding chapters presented some of the kinds of problems that marketing research can help solve. Some marketing research questions can be very specific: "If we change the advertising mix, what might happen to sales?" Others are more general: "Why have sales fallen below target?" Or, "How do customers feel about the product?" Different formulations of a problem lead to different research approaches to finding answers.

This chapter introduces types of research designs. We then proceed to the topics of exploratory designs and qualitative data.

Plan of Action

A **research design** is the framework or plan for a study, used as a guide to collect and analyze data. It is the blueprint that is followed to complete a study.

Research can be conducted without a detailed blueprint, but the findings will probably differ greatly from what the user of the research wanted, e.g., "These results are interesting, but they do not solve the basic problem," is a common lament. Further, just as a house built without a blueprint is likely to cost more because of midstream alterations, research conducted without a design is likely to cost more than that executed using a proper design.

Thus, a research design ensures that the study (1) will be relevant to the problem and (2) will use economical procedures. There are many research design frameworks, but they can be classified into three basic types: *exploratory*, *descriptive*, or *causal*.

Types of Research Design

The major emphasis in **exploratory research** is on the discovery of *ideas and insights*. For example, a soft-drink manufacturer faced with decreased sales might conduct an exploratory study to generate possible explanations. An electronics firm looking to launch a new-to-the-world product needs to begin with exploratory research to assess consumers' reactions.

The **descriptive research** study is typically concerned with determining the *frequency* with which something occurs or the *relationship* between two variables. An investigation of trends in the consumption of soft drinks with respect to such characteristics as age, gender, and geographic location would be a descriptive study. A segmentation study that tied propensity to try the new technology to user characteristics, such as average daily time spent online, would be a descriptive study.

A **causal research** design is concerned with determining *cause-and-effect* relationships, and these are studied via experiments. For instance, an advertising experiment would ascertain the effectiveness of different ad appeals—different ads would be used in different geographic areas to investigate which ad generated the highest sales. If the experiment is designed properly, the company can conclude that one specific appeal caused the higher rate of sales. Experiments are also frequently used with different price points in different markets to assess price sensitivity.

It is important to note that the three types of research design are interrelated as stages in a continuous process (see Figure 4.1). Exploratory studies are usually the initial step. When researchers begin an investigation, naturally they lack a great deal of knowledge about the problem. The question, "Why is our brand share slipping?" is very broad, but exploratory research will help narrow and refine the question. The possible explanations, or hypotheses, for the sales decrease then serve as specific guides for the subsequent descriptive or causal studies.

Suppose the tentative explanation emerged that "Brand X is economy-priced, originally designed to compete with low-cost store brands. Families have more money today than when the brand was first introduced and are willing to pay more for higher quality products. It stands to reason that our market share would decrease." The hypotheses that families have more real income to spend and that a larger proportion of that money is going toward products in this category could be examined in a descriptive study of trends in the industry.

Suppose that the descriptive study did support the hypotheses. The company might then want to determine whether parents were, in fact, willing to pay more for higher-quality products and, if so, what features were most important to them. This might be accomplished partially through a test-marketing study, a causal design.

Research Designs:

- Exploratory
- Descriptive
- Causal

FIGURE 4.1   Relationship among Research Designs

FIGURE 4.2   Types of Research Designs

Figure 4.2 provides an overview of the three kinds of research—exploratory, descriptive, and causal. In this chapter, we continue with exploratory research. Descriptive and causal designs are treated in more detail in the next two chapters.

Exploratory Research

The general objective in exploratory research is to gain insights and ideas. The exploratory study is particularly helpful in breaking large, vague problem statements into smaller, more precise subproblem statements, ideally in the form of specific hypotheses. A **hypothesis** is a statement that specifies how two or more measurable variables are related. A good hypothesis also carries clear implications for testing stated relationships.

In the early stages of research, we usually lack sufficient understanding of the problem to formulate a specific hypothesis. Further, there are often several tentative explanations for a given marketing phenomenon. For example: Sales are off because our price is too high, our dealers or sales representatives are not doing the job they should, our advertising is weak, and so on.

Exploratory research can be used to establish priorities in studying these competing explanations. The priorities would be established because a particular hypothesis discovered in the exploratory study appears to be promising. They might also arise because the exploratory study generates information about the practical possibilities of researching specific conjectures.

The exploratory study may be used to clarify concepts. Say management is considering a change in a service policy that should result in improved dealer satisfaction. An exploratory study could be used to clarify the notion of "dealer satisfaction" and to develop such a measure.

Exploratory studies are characterized by *flexibility* with respect to the research methods used. They rarely use detailed questionnaires or complex sampling plans. Rather, investigators frequently change the research procedure as the vaguely defined initial problem is transformed into one with more precise meaning. Researchers follow where their noses lead them in an exploratory study. Ingenuity, judgment, and good luck inevitably play a part in leading to the one or two key hypotheses that may ultimately account for the phenomenon.

In general, exploratory research is appropriate for any problem about which little is known. Exploratory research is the foundation for a good study.

We now consider the relationship between exploratory research and qualitative data. We then present a number of key marketing research techniques that may be characterized as exploratory and qualitative.

Relationship Between Exploratory Research and Qualitative Data

The different kinds of research are frequently tied to a product's life cycle. For example, in a new product launch, exploratory research is conducted (some focus groups are run), followed by some descriptive research to "get the numbers" (surveys are conducted), perhaps followed up with some causal research as the product and category matures (experiments are run to tweak pricing issues).

Thus, in long-standing tradition, qualitative research methods are said to be exploratory in nature. Yet that does not mean that the techniques or their findings are somehow of lesser importance. In fact, one might argue that research conducted at the earliest stages is the most critical, because if it is not executed well, the entire marketing research program goes down the wrong path, eventually to answer irrelevant questions.

And indeed, in some sense the results of a focus group are somewhat tentative. While focus groups are interesting and a customer verbatim compelling, it wouldn't be smart to proceed to spend vast resources launching a new product or rolling out a new ad campaign. After all, the results of even three focus groups (say $24,000–$45,000) yields the opinions of a maximum of 24–30 persons. Given that product launches and advertising campaigns are expensive ($mm), and jobs rest on such decisions, the decisions usually require the additional steps of gathering even more intelligence.

In addition, sometimes qualitative techniques are used later in the research process, where their role is more "confirmatory" than exploratory. For example, in a study of a national retailer, overall customer satisfaction scores seemed to be correlated with a factor called "pleasantness of store layout." Follow-up interviews were required to understand just what about a retail layout makes it pleasant. Hence in this case, exploratory research (the interviews) was used to clarify the descriptive research. Still, these caveats aside, usually when someone in industry (marketing or marketing research) says "qualitative" they usually mean "exploratory," and vice versa.

Some Basic Types of Exploratory Research

Initial tools for exploratory research include literature searches, experience surveys, and the analysis of selected cases. We'll discuss each in turn. When people speak of qualitative marketing research methods, however, they're usually referring to focus groups, interviews, or ethnographies, and we'll discuss these techniques later in the chapter.

Literature Search

**Basic Explorations
(Qualitative Data That
Already Exist)**

• Literature search

• Experience surveys

• Case analyses

One of the quickest and cheapest ways to discover hypotheses is in the work of others, through a literature search. The search may involve *conceptual literature, trade literature,* or *published statistics,* depending on the problem being addressed. *Conceptual literature* would pop up from a search engine (e.g., Web of Science or Google Scholar for articles in marketing, psychology, sociology, or economics journals). Most industries have *trade publications* to keep track of competition and common customer concerns. The information in these databases is usually extensive and may be accessed with membership to affiliated associations. *Published data* on many industries are so vast that we devote a large section to them in Chapter 7 on secondary data, and link them on our Web site.

When these sources of information are combined, a firm's problem might be diagnosed fairly clearly. For example, if "sales are down," we need to know whether the problem was an industry problem or a firm problem. Different research is in order if the firm's sales are down but (1) the company's market share is up, because industry sales are down farther; (2) the company's market share has remained stable; or (3) the company's market share has declined. The last situation would trigger an investigation of the firm's marketing-mix variables, whereas the first condition would suggest an analysis to determine why industry sales are off.

Experience Survey

The experience survey, sometimes called the key informant survey, taps the knowledge of those familiar with the general subject being investigated. In studies concerned with the marketing of a product, anyone who has any association with the marketing effort is a potential source of information. This would include the top executives of the company, the sales manager, the product manager, and sales representatives.

Usually, a great many people know something about the general subject of any given problem. It is important to include people with differing points of view, e.g., company executives, key people in the product group, sales representatives, managers of retail outlets, etc. One does not interview people who have little experience or competence in the area.

Analysis of Cases

The analysis of selected cases involves the intensive study of selected cases of the phenomenon under investigation (e.g., business school cases). In the analysis of a case, the researcher records all relevant data, not just those that support initial hypotheses. In exploratory research, the goal is to gain insights, not to test explanations. By remaining neutral, it is easier for the researcher to be flexible as new information emerges. The researcher must also be able to sort through all the data and see the "big picture," insights that should apply across multiple cases, not just details that apply only to individual cases.

A frequently used example of the use of selected cases to develop insights is **benchmarking**. One or more organizations are identified that excel at some function, and those companies' best practices are used as a source of ideas for improvement. Xerox is synonymous with benchmarking, beginning the practice in the U.S. 30 years ago. Xerox studied Japanese competitors to learn how they could sell midsized copiers for less than what it cost Xerox to make them. Today many companies use benchmarking as a standard research tool, and it's not unusual for a company to look to a leader in a different industry, e.g., a consumer packaged goods company may study the efficiency of a catalog retailer to redesign its call center.

Standard Qualitative Marketing Research Methods

Literature searches, experience surveys, and the analysis of cases are important in exploratory research, but when people talk about "qualitative" methods, they usually mean one or more of the following techniques:

King of the Qualitative: Focus Groups

- Focus group
- Depth interview
- Projective technique
- Ethnography
- Observational techniques, including those assisted by mechanical devices (e.g., galvanometers, fMRIs, eye cameras, EEGs, voice pitch analyses)

We'll discuss each in turn.

Focus Groups

Focus groups are one of the most popular tools in marketing research, and the most frequently used qualitative technique.[1] In a focus group, a small number of individuals are brought together in a room to sit and talk about some topic of interest to the focus group sponsor. The discussion is directed by a moderator. The **moderator** attempts to follow a rough outline of the issues under consideration, while at the same time making sure that the comments made by each person present are included in the group's discussion. The group discussion should be dynamic, much like a conversation. Each individual hears the ideas of the others and also voices his or her own opinions to the group for consideration.

Focus groups are an extremely useful method for gathering ideas and insights. They are used for a variety of purposes, including the following:

- Generate hypotheses that can be further tested quantitatively
- Generate information helpful in structuring consumer questionnaires
- Provide background information on a product category
- Obtain customer impressions on new product concepts or ad copy

As an example, BMW conducted focus groups in which it asked for customer feedback to some 25 different sounds and pitches, to select just the right sounds and noises for the instrument warning panel. BMW wants its customers to say that a BMW even sounds like a BMW. Instead of some harsh buzz, the BMW managers sought a polite-sounding signal that fit the luxurious brand essence of a "Bimmer." For more examples, see Research Realities 4.1.

[1] David W. Stewart, Prem Shandasani, and Dennis Rook, *Focus Groups: Theory and Practice* (2nd ed., Sage, 2006); also see *Supplement to Quirk's Marketing Research Review: Focus Group Facilities Directory,* quirks.com.

RESEARCH REALITIES

4.1 Focus Groups Examples

- To attract tourists, researchers studying perceptions of Scotland found that the country's core industries were incorrectly perceived to be whisky, wool, and salmon, when in fact, information technology (IT) is its greatest export. Ad copies were tested for consumer reaction: themes of tenacity played well, and an ad that emphasized Scotland's spirit with bright and dramatic tartan colors played especially well to younger consumers. (The project's name, "Galore," comes from the fact that galore is supposedly one of only two words to come out of Gaelic to enter into the English language. The other word is whisky.)

- Health care management has found the magic of focus groups: segments of users have been asked to discuss their experiences during recent hospital stays and outpatient services, to discuss possible facility upgrades and improvements; others have been asked why parents are driving so far for their pediatric services.

- An experienced focus group moderator tells tales of needing to bite her lip when a participant said he practiced mahogany (meaning monogamy), another said she didn't like genetic brands (meaning generic brands), or when a male dancer said he liked control top pantyhose because 'it holds up my stuff.'

Sources: Kate Hamilton, "Project Galore," Journal of Advertising Research 40, 107–111; David Marlowe, "Table Manners," Marketing Health Services, marketingpower.com; Naomi R. Henderson, "Learn to Expect and Embrace Change," Marketing Research, marketingpower.com.

Focus Group Golden Rules:

- 8–12 participants
- Each compensated $60–$75
- Tues., Wed., Thurs. best
- Small, cool room
- Comfortable chairs
- Soft drinks, cookies
- Approx. 4 groups
- 1½ hours
- One-way mirror (observers)
- Taped
- ~6 week turnaround (from planning to report)

Number of Participants?

Although focus groups vary in size, most consist of 8 to 12 members. Smaller groups are too easily dominated by one or two members; and with larger groups, frustration and boredom can set in, because members have to wait their turn to respond or get involved. Respondents are generally screened in selection so that the groups are relatively homogeneous, minimizing differences in experience in the category, as well as conflicts among group members on irrelevant attributes. Differences can intimidate some participants and stifle discussion.

Screening interviews determine who will be allowed to participate in a focus group. One type of person usually screened out is the individual who has participated in focus groups before, since these people tend to behave as "experts." Their presence can cause the group to behave in dysfunctional ways as they continually try to make their presence felt. Participants are also screened to be sure friends or relatives aren't already included in the group, because this tends to inhibit spontaneity in the discussion as the acquaintances talk to each other.

Number of Groups?

Given that the participants in a group are reasonably homogeneous, a firm ensures that it gets a wide spectrum of insights by having multiple groups. The characteristics of the participants can vary across groups, as can the moderator's guide regarding the issues to be covered in each group. For example, ideas discovered in one group can certainly be followed up in a subsequent group for reaction.

A typical project runs 4 groups, but some may have up to 12. The guiding criterion is whether the later groups are generating additional insight into the phenomenon under study. When they show diminishing returns, the groups are stopped.

The typical focus group session lasts about 1½ hours. Most focus groups are held at specially designed focus group facilities:[2] they are centrally located for easy access by the participants (e.g., focus group facilities are often near airports or large hotel clusters); they have one-way mirrors with room behind the mirror to accommodate 6–10 observers (e.g., the marketing research and brand management team); they have audio- and videotaping technologies, etc. Increasingly, there are also video-conferencing capabilities and Internet chat-room set-ups to facilitate participants at different locations to interact with one another.

Qualities of Moderators

The moderator in the focus group has a key role. A good moderator begins the job long before the actual focus group. The moderator needs to understand the marketing problem and the most important information the client hopes to obtain from the research. The moderator takes this background information and translates the study objectives into a discussion guide that serves as an outline for the focus group session. In the focus group itself, the moderator must lead the discussion so that all objectives of the study are met, encouraging interaction among the group members. In successful focus groups, participants talk to each other, rather than to the moderator, about the issues raised.

The moderator's role is extremely delicate. It requires someone who is familiar with the objectives of the research and someone who possesses good interpersonal communication skills (see Table 4.1).[3] Prepping a moderator for a focus group on consumer products is fairly straightforward, but business-to-business and technical topics usually require more extensive briefings. For some topics, the group participants know more about the product than the moderator, and it's fine for a moderator to ask for more information, e.g., "Well, what is the problem when you use that company's drill bit in your patient's mouth?"

Responsibilities of Focus Group Moderators:

- Prior to session:
  - Plan, learn about topic
  - Prepare moderator guide, with points to cover
- During session:
  - Warm up group, establish rapport
  - Cover topics, but don't rush
  - Probe topics (follow the "energy" of the discussion), but re-direct (know when to return to the guide)
  - Encourage all to participate
  - Be neutral, objective, not judgmental
- After session:
  - Oversee tapes and transcriptions
  - Prepare analysis, report, caveats

TABLE 4.1	**Traits of Effective Focus Group Moderators**

- **Personable**—A moderator must put people at ease quickly, develop rapport with participants, so they will "open up" during the discussion. Must not be overbearing or pretend to know it all.

- **Superior Listening Ability**—A moderator must pay close attention to what the participants are saying. Comments cannot be missed due to lack of attention or misunderstanding. Is often silent so as to encourage others to speak. Doesn't answer the question "What do you think?" but turns the question around to get the focus group participants to do so.

- **A Quick Learner**—An effective moderator learns about a topic quickly to be effective in guiding successful group sessions. Knows topic so well, moderator outline is rarely consulted.

- **High Energy Level**—When a group gets laid back and lifeless, it dramatically lowers the quality of the information that the participants generate. The best moderators find a way to inject enthusiasm into the group so the participants are energized throughout the session. The moderator must be able to keep his or her own energy level high so the discussion can continue to be very productive to the end.

[2] See the annual (March) issues of *Marketing News*, available from the American Marketing Association (www.marketingpower.com) "Directory of Focus Group Facilities and Moderators."
[3] Occasionally to cut costs, marketing managers think they can run a focus group. This is not smart. First, they will not be objective. Second, there are real skills that moderators have. Pay for that expertise!

Many benefits can accrue from properly conducted focus groups. Often as not, ideas simply drop "out of the blue" during a discussion. This serendipity is often a result of the group dynamics—the comment by one individual can trigger a chain of responses from the others until the discussion has snowballed into something unanticipated.

A Typical Session

Usually focus groups start with a brief introductory warm-up period (5–10 minutes covering background material and setting a context), to simply begin building rapport and trust. Participants often begin by writing their first names on placards to be placed in front of them, to facilitate reference from the moderator and the other participants, all strangers. The moderator begins by saying a few introductory words. For example, if the focus group is about vitamins, the moderator might say, "As you're probably aware from the questions you were asked when you were invited to come here, we're going to talk about health-related behaviors— eating, drinking, exercising, vitamin supplements, etc. So tonight we're going to talk about all those kinds of things. There are no right or wrong answers here, so please just talk freely about your opinions. Just so you know, I have some colleagues observing us and taking notes in that room behind the mirror, and we're taping the session so that we can remember all the issues that you folks raise. You'll see on the other side of the room there are soft drinks and snacks—feel free to help yourself at any time during the evening." To get the participants warmed up and get them all to talk, the moderator continues by asking a general question, such as, "What sorts of things do you do to try to stay healthy?"

After this initial roundtable, the moderator, participants, and observers already have a sense of the group—Joe is a bodybuilder, uh-oh watch out that he doesn't dominate the discussion, Jerry is a beer and pizza-nut, uh-oh watch that he doesn't slip out of a conversation on vitamins, etc. Then the moderator poses another, slightly more specific question, but calls upon a few participants in a mixed-up order. The moderator begins to studiously not look at the speaker, so the speaker must look to the other group members for affirmation. The participants soon begin speaking to each other and the moderator knows to fade into the background.

Usually, that's all it takes. At this point, the group is going. Soon respondents become sufficiently involved that they want to express their ideas and feelings. Many people actually feel more secure in a group environment than if they were being interviewed alone, in part because it is nearly inevitable that someone else in the group will feel the same way they do about something. Consequently, responses are often more spontaneous than they might be in an interview. The moderator's job as the discussion progresses is to know when to allow the discussion to follow some unanticipated path vs. when to reign the members back in and move on to the next talking point on the moderator's guide (see Table 4.2).

After the Focus Group

Finally, moderators' responsibilities do not end when the group sessions end. They supervise the preparation of a transcript of each session and use the transcripts to develop a report for the client detailing the key insights the focus groups generated. They've also seen zillions more focus groups than the shiny new marketing VP who was an observer behind the one-way mirror, who might attach undue weight to a single comment when the moderator knows to wait until all the groups have been run to determine whether such a comment was a theme, even by a minority-sized segment, or just a random idiosyncrasy.

TABLE 4.2	Tips for Successful Focus Groups

- **Keep the Moderator Guide Simple**—In an attempt to "get their money's worth," sometimes clients put too many topics and discussion points on the moderator's guide. Unfortunately, then the topics are covered superficially. Prioritize "need to know" items from "nice to know" ones.
- **Begin by Bonding**—A simple, nonthreatening warm-up exercise is a great icebreaker.
- **Behind the Scenes**—Clients often watch the focus group sessions in the room behind the one-way mirror at focus group facilities. These rooms are difficult to soundproof entirely, so turn off cell phones, and don't laugh too loudly.
- **Don't Look to Project Findings**—These data are small samples, not representative, the data are qualitative, gathered in an artificial environment. Findings are more suited to "suggesting" (e.g., lines of follow-up research), than predicting (e.g., sales or market shares).
- **Do a Focus Group When**—you want feedback on new product concepts, advertising copy or proposed marketing promotions, product and service positioning, and product usability tests.
- **Don't Conduct a Focus Group When**—you want answers to numerical questions ("How many customers...?" "What percentage...?"), you cannot afford a survey, you're trying to set prices, or you need to make a "go/no go" decision.

It is important to remember that the focus group results are a direct function of the group dynamics, including the directions the moderator provided as well as the unpredictable, creative process of the group interactions. Accordingly, the results are not "representative" of what would be found in the general population, and thus are not projectable. Further, the unstructured nature of the responses makes coding, tabulation, and analysis difficult; thus, focus groups shouldn't be used to develop head counts of the proportion of people who feel a particular way. Focus groups are better for generating ideas and insights than for systematically examining them.

Focus groups have many benefits, but they are not without their weaknesses. For example, the results can be difficult to interpret—it's easy to find evidence in one or more of the group discussions that supports almost any position. And, because executives can observe the discussions through one-way mirrors or watch tapes of the sessions, focus groups are even more susceptible to executive biases than other data-collection techniques.

What's New in Focus Groups?

Increasingly, focus groups are being run via chat-rooms online.[4] The advantages include: 1) convenience for participants (no travel required, flexibility in scheduling), 2) transcripts are immediately available, since participants are typing in their responses; and as a result of both of these, 3) costs are lower. But there are disadvantages also: 1) Expressions are completely verbal—there are no cues to body language or emotions. 2) Conversation is more stilted when participants are writing and the posting is sequential, than when people are excited and interrupting each other with a good free-flowing conversation. Still, as bandwidth and video capabilities continue to increase, these issues might be resolved.

[4] Willemijn van Dolen, Ko de Ruyter, and James Carman, "The Role of Self- and Group-Efficacy in Moderated Group Chat," *Journal of Economic Psychology*, 27, 324–343; Donna J. Reid and Fraser J. M. Reid, "Online Focus Groups," *International Journal of Market Research*, 47 (2), 131–162.

Depth Interviews

Figure 4.3 shows the commonalities and differences between interviews and focus groups. Focus groups used to be called "group interviews." In a one-on-one interview, the interviewer also tries to build rapport quickly and then proceeds through a set of questions, from the general to the more specific, with the list of questions intended more as a guide than a structured survey.

Any given respondent will answer some questions in greater depth and others in a more perfunctory manner. The former usually indicate greater knowledge and involvement, and are worth pursuing. The latter usually indicate lack of

FIGURE 4.3   Focus Groups and Depth Interviews

interest or expertise and may be worth pursuing only to be sure the interviewer is communicating clearly with the interviewee.

This flexibility is of course the critical quality of exploratory research methods. Thus, after presenting a few initial questions, an interview becomes unstructured as the interviewer probes more deeply asking follow-up questions. Hence, interviews are often termed (the rather redundant) "depth interviews." The respondent's answers determine the direction the interviewer takes next. The interviewer may attempt to follow a rough outline, but the order and the specific framing of the questions will vary from interview to interview, as will the specific content resulting from each interview.

The freedom permitted the interviewer in conducting interviews reveals the major advantages and disadvantages of the method. Proponents of interviews say these methods enable the researcher to obtain deeper, richer, "thicker" descriptions than, say, surveys with fixed-alternative responses. By careful probing and by not constraining the respondent to a fixed set of replies, an experienced interviewer derives a fairly accurate picture of the respondent's true position on some issue.

Note the caveats "careful probing" and "experienced interviewer." Depth interviews require highly skilled interviewers. Good interviewers are hard to find and expensive to hire. Further, the lack of structure allows the interviewer to influence the result; that is, the interviewer's judgment about when to probe and how to word the probes affects the response.

Good depth interviews can take a long time to complete (an hour or more), which makes it difficult (and expensive) to obtain the cooperation of respondents. Studies using depth interviews tend to involve fewer respondents.

The interview can also be problematic to analyze. The services of a skilled psychologist are typically required to interpret the responses. These consultants are expensive, and their own background will affect the interpretation. This subjectivity raises questions about both the reliability and validity of interview results. It also causes difficulty in determining what the correct interpretation is and presents problems when tabulating the replies.

However, with these caveats in mind, the depth interview is well suited to exploratory research. It allows the flexibility to pursue whatever the consumers wish to talk about—topics that the marketing researcher is unlikely to anticipate fully enough to write questions for a survey.

A currently popular use of the depth interview is called "laddering," which seeks to discover the relationship between product attributes and consumer benefits. The ladder metaphor implies that the researcher is going from specific attributes up to more abstract values.

For example, in one study, consumers were asked whether they recycle or not, and if so why. Some respondents answered "to reduce waste." This specific goal was pursued: "Why is that important?" to which respondents answered, "to keep the environment clean." This intermediary goal was further pursued: "And why is that important?" to which the response was given, "to save the planet for future generations." Thus, the ladder was built from specific features to abstract goals, and the nonprofit researcher gained a clearer understanding of this segments' motivations.

Qualitative Techniques:

- Focus Groups
- Depth Interviews
- Projective Tasks
- Ethnographies

Projective Techniques

A projective technique involves the use of an ambiguous stimulus (the proverbial inkblot) that an individual is asked to describe, expand on, or build a story around. Three common types of projective methods are: word association, sentence completion, and storytelling.[5]

Word Association

With word association projective methods, consumers respond to a list of words, reacting to them with the first word that comes to mind. The test words are interspersed throughout the list with some neutral words to conceal the purpose of the study. In a study on pollution, the list of keywords might be traffic, lakes, smokestacks, and city, mixed in with words such as margarine, blue jeans, and government.

The responses to each of the keywords are recorded verbatim and analyzed. The key analysis is the examination of the content of the responses to see what themes may be derived from these respondents' word choices.

Although the analysis of the responses is subjective, some common responses usually emerge. These responses are classified and grouped, and reveal patterns of underlying motivations. It is often possible to categorize the associations as favorable–unfavorable, pleasant–unpleasant, modern–old-fashioned, etc., depending on the research question.

For example, for each of the following words, very often only two or three common descriptor words emerge (try it among your friends!): McDonald's, Exxon, Microsoft, Nordstrom's, Sears, Verizon, Britney Spears, Miley Cyrus, Tom Brady, New York, Los Angeles, Mexico, Japan, lawyers, accountants, marketers, and consultants. This list also illustrates the flexibility of the method—one can obtain consumer perceptions of firms and brand equity, celebrity endorsers, tourist destinations, career objectives, or anything else. When a word elicits a greater variety of associations across respondents, it is thought that the stimulus may be less familiar (e.g., lacrosse, Swedish royal family) or more complex (e.g., California, carbohydrates, Supreme Court), or for other reasons yields greater individual differences.

The word association responses are also judged in three objective, easily measured ways:

- By the frequency with which any word is given as a response

- By the amount of time that elapses before a response is given (easily measured in milliseconds if the words are administered via computer)

- By the number of respondents who do not respond at all to a test word after a reasonable period of time

Sentence Completion

This method is much like the word association task. As the name implies, the method requires the respondent to complete a number of sentences. Respondents are instructed to reply with the first thoughts that come to mind. The responses are recorded verbatim and then analyzed.

Once again, though the analysis of qualitative responses is subjective, the results are nevertheless often clear and there would be good agreement in their interpretation. For example, imagine one person completing sentences about the environment as follows:

- People who are concerned about ecology *care about the future.*

- A person who does not use our lakes for recreation is *being thoughtful about the ecosystem.*

[5] Clive Boddy, "Projective Techniques in Market Research," *International Journal of Market Research*, 47 (3), 239–254, Gregory J. Boyle et al. *Sage Handbook of Personality Theory and Assessment: Vol.2* (Sage 2008).

• When I think of living in a city, I *can't help but think of smog.*

Compare those data to the responses of another person:

• People who are concerned about ecology *are just tree-huggers who want to run up my taxes.*

• A person who does not use our lakes for recreation is *a person who doesn't enjoy water sports.*

• When I think of living in a city, I *think about cruising my car downtown on Saturday night!*

Presumably, these two respondents could easily be characterized as belonging to segments of consumers who are more and less ecologically concerned.

Sometimes the disguised nature of sentence completion questions can shed light on a topic that a more direct rating scale might not. For example, when consumers are asked, "Do you think it is important to give blood?" most say yes, due to pressures for social desirability and conformity. And we might indeed be convinced that a person regularly gives blood who completes sentences like:

• "I always give blood during blood drives at work, unless . . . *I'm sick,*" and

• "People who don't give blood . . . *are pretty selfish, in my opinion.*"

Contrast the values of that person with someone who completed the sentences as follows:

• "I always give blood during blood drives at work, unless . . . *I'm in a hurry,*" and

• "People who don't give blood . . . *just don't like needles.*"

From this second person's sentences, a picture emerges of someone who will resist donating blood in the presence of only minor hurdles, suggesting that their actual compliance will be low.

A particular form of association tests that is gaining some popularity is to have consumers draw metaphors and analogies in the sentence completions, "An X is like a Y." For example, in a health care study in a major U.S. city, participants were asked to talk about their health care insurance and their perceptions of the other brands. Then they were asked to draw comparisons between them and brands of cars. Weird, yes? But watch this: One consumer said, "[Plan A] is a Cadillac…If I were to get into an accident, the car would absorb most of my injuries, [Plan A] would absorb my financial aspects. [Plan B] is a GMC or Chevy truck…it has the cushion in case I ever did need it…a truck might be pretty big but…it's got a lot of metal to take care of you. You can be injured a lot worse."

Again, the responses are open, and it may seem that the interpretation would be subjective, but the consumers help interpret their own metaphors when they say, "Plan A is like a Lincoln Town Car *in that it is* comfortable, nice, all-American," or "Plan A is like a Lexus or Infiniti *in providing* a very good product, and very good service." In comparison, in this study, Plan B was likened to a station wagon (low-key transportation, not flashy), Ford Escort (comparably small and inexpensive), and Hyundai (unproven, unfamiliar, comparably small). These researchers didn't care about cars *per se,* but that the cars metaphor allowed consumers to talk about their plans in unrestricted and creative ways.[6]

---

[6] Russell Lacey, "Dimensions of the Ideal HMO Brand," *Marketing Health Services,* marketingpower.com; also see Gerald Zaltman and Lindsay H. Zaltman (2008), *Marketing Metaphoria: What Deep Metaphors Reveal About the Minds of Consumers,* Harvard Business School Press. For related research, see Jennifer E. Escalas, "Self-Referencing and Persuasion: Narrative Transportation versus Analytical Elaboration," *Journal of Consumer Research,* 33 (1), 421–429.

Storytelling

The storytelling approach often relies on pictorial material, such as cartoons, photographs, or drawings. These pictorial devices are descendants of the psychologists' Thematic Apperception Test (TAT), which in turn descended from the famous Rorschach ink blot tests. Respondents are shown a picture and asked to tell a story about the picture. The responses are used to assess attitudes toward the consumer behavior phenomenon.

For the environmental pollution example, the stimulus might be a picture of a city, and the respondent might be asked to describe what it would be like to live there. The analysis of the individual's response would then focus on the emphasis given to pollution in its various forms. If no mention were made of traffic congestion, dirty air, noise, and so on, the person would be classified as displaying little concern for pollution and its control.

Sometimes the participants are asked to do some homework—prior to coming to the research gathering, they're asked to create a collage of photos cut out of magazines that remind them of a brand. During the session, the interviewer probes the respondent about the meaning of the selected pictures, e.g., "What does that picture say about you? About the brand?"

Research Realities 4.2 describes a study in which participants were interviewed about flowers, and they were asked to draw pictures of flowers. Even though both pictures and stories are subjective, you can see that their pictures and stories are remarkably consistent. The first woman remarks on themes of beauty and thoughtfulness, and she drew soft, fluffy looking flowers. The second woman associates flowers with love, and her flower petals are drawn in the shape of hearts. The third respondent was a man who reports a common male theme, that flowers are associated with ambivalence. The man describes a dream and draws flowers that also express his mix of positive and negative feelings.

Focus groups, interviews, and projective tests share a reliance on communication with the researcher. There are also research methods that simply require the researcher to observe the respondents' behaviors. We discuss those methods next.

Observational Methods

Ethical **Dilemma** 4.2

A national department store chain with a relatively sophisticated image is planning to open a store in an area inhabited by wealthy professionals. The marketing research director of the company wants a detailed profile of the residents' characteristics and lifestyles to tailor the new store to the tastes of this lucrative new market. He suggests that you, a member of his staff, contribute to the research effort by spending a month observing the residents going about their daily affairs, such as eating in restaurants, attending church, shopping in other stores, socializing with one another, and so on. You are then expected to prepare a report on what types of expenditures support their lifestyles.

- Are there ethical problems involved in observing people in public places?
- Are there ethical problems if you socialize with your informants?
- Who has ethical responsibility for your behavior: The marketing research director? You? Both?

R E S E A R C H   R E A L I T I E S

4.2 Customers Drawing Pictures for a Study Sponsored by a Large Florist Retail Chain*

Interviewee #1:

Woman, 30–39 years old.

Describe yourself:

I am a quiet person, I keep mostly to myself and keep out of trouble that way.

When do you buy flowers?

I love flowers because they beautify the surroundings. They give me a special calm feeling of enjoyment. I give flowers to let someone know you are thinking about them.

Describe a dream involving flowers:

I would send flowers to the ladies at work with a note attached and they would all start crying at one time.

How are flowers and funerals related?

All the funerals I've been to have flowers. I guess when you die, you will be in paradise and paradise is full of flowers.

Her drawing:

Interviewee #2:

Woman, 20–29 years old.

Husband sends her flowers because:

I am sweet.

Three words associated to flowers:

I love you.

Compared to other gifts, flowers are:

Warmest, most romantic, highest class, sexiest, most fun.

Flowers remind me of:

Love!

Describe a dream involving flowers:

Someone gets married, they are happy and I am pleased for them and I send flowers to congratulate them. Everyone likes it and they live happily ever after.

How are flowers and funerals related?

I'm opposed to the idea of flowers at funeral. Flowers at funeral are sad. The tradition of sending flowers to a funeral may have come about in order to cover the smell of the body.

Her drawing:

Interviewee #3:

Man, 40–49 years old.

Describes himself as:

…a loving and generous man. He celebrates all occasions with lavish and often costly gifts. He is enthusiastic about giving flowers and says they make him think about happiness and warmth.

He also says:

The main reason to send flowers is to apologize for having a fight. They lift the spirits, women would be happy about the flowers.

Describe a dream involving flowers:

I had a dream that I send some flowers and as the person bent down to smell the flowers, a thorn cut her lips. Even though she was bleeding she called to thank me for sending her the lovely roses.

His drawing:

*A million thank you's to Sidney Levy for sharing these stories and pictures.

Here are some examples of observations on consumer behaviors that have been used over the years:

- Researchers watched senior citizens buy dog treats. Unfortunately for these no-longer-flexible adults, the treats were usually stocked on the top-most shelf. These researchers' cameras "witnessed one elderly woman using a box of aluminum foil to knock down her brand of dog biscuits." When the retail grocer moved the treats to where older people could reach more easily, sales soared overnight.[7]

- A car dealer in a large metro market checked the position of the radio dial of each car brought in for service. The dealer then used this as a proxy for share of listening audience in deciding upon the stations on which to advertise.

- The number of different fingerprints on a page has been used to assess the readership of various ads in a magazine, and the age and condition of the cars in the parking lot has been used to gauge the affluence of the group patronizing the outlet.

- Scuff marks on museum floor tile have long been used as a means of measuring the popularity of the display.

- Consumers have been watched through one-way mirrors trying to assemble kids' toys right out of the box (no, we don't tend to read the instructions).

- By peering from catwalks built above the stores, researchers for a large supermarket chain discovered that people shopped heavily the periphery of the store—the produce, dairy, and meat sections—often bypassing the central dry-goods section that accounts for the bulk of the store space.

Observations may be made either in the field or in the lab. The field study may be a completely natural setting, or we may induce an experimental manipulation. For example, if we want to understand customers' brand choices for soups, we might simply snoop around the soup aisle of a grocery store, watching shoppers as they deliberate before they toss a can of soup into their carts. Alternatively, we may introduce a point-of-purchase display and measure its effectiveness, by noting how much more frequently the focal brand get chosen in the stores in which we've set up the display compared with the stores whose shelf facings we left alone. Both of these studies would take place in a supermarket, which would be the natural setting. Alternatively, we could bring consumers into a controlled lab environment, where they could engage in some simulated shopping behavior.

Why Observational Techniques?

Observation is often more useful than surveys in sorting fact from fiction with respect to behaviors, particularly "desirable" behaviors. For example, most people would not want to acknowledge that they spend more on cat food than on baby food, but consumers can be observed doing so. In another study, asking parents whether the color of a new toy would matter, the parents uniformly said no, yet at the end of the study, as a token of their participation, the parents were offered a toy to take home to their child, and all the parents clamored for the purple and blue toys.

Observation can help us see consumer behaviors that the consumers themselves probably aren't aware of or couldn't articulate. For example, to

[7] Paco Underhill, *Why We Buy: The Science of Shopping* (Simon & Schuster, 2008).

understand why a new frozen baby food was underperforming relative to expectations, a researcher hung out where that product was sold and noticed that children got fidgety in the frozen-food sections because they were cold, so mothers would rush down that aisle. The researcher was able to persuade managers to place smaller freezer units in the regular (warmer climate) baby food aisles. Sales were then quite successful.[8]

Observational data comprise the heart of a popular form of research, the "mystery shopper." In this technique, firms use paid observers disguised as shoppers to evaluate sales service and the courtesy of employees. Hotels use reports from secret shoppers to decide which features of the customer experience at the hotel (e.g., the check-in process or the cleanliness of the bathrooms) should be highest priority for redesign and improvement.

In this multicultural world, observation methods are useful for marketers to learn about tastes and preferences of different ethnic groups. Rather than creating a survey that might not be in the respondent's first language, or worrying about translations and back-translations, researchers can simply watch what consumers do.

For the same reason, observational techniques can also be useful in studying children as consumers. The appeal of new toy offerings can be assessed in a natural play setting, rather than struggling with surveys and 9-point scales.

Observations in the Field

A popular form of field consumer study is the simple **audit**. Instead of asking people, "What's your favorite brand?" with the question's inherent subjectivity in recollection and reporting, the researcher can conduct a pantry audit. With permission, the marketer visits respondents' homes and opens cupboards. For example, part of understanding how consumers use a particular product (e.g., peanut butter) can be determined by the other products they buy and use with it (e.g., jelly, chocolate, bananas, crackers). The inventory of kitchen cabinets and refrigerators would demonstrate the co-ownership of complementary products.

Researchers have inventoried or photographed the contents of consumers' medicine cabinets, closets, garages, students' school lockers, etc. Photos of a medicine cabinet indicate not only what products it contains, and what brands and sizes, but also their arrangement—what is stored front and center is probably used most frequently.

Another popular form of field consumer study is the **ethnography**.[9] Ethnographic methods are increasingly being used by marketers as another example of an in-depth case approach to develop insights (see Research Realities 4.3). These procedures, which have been adapted from anthropology, involve the prolonged observation of consumers' behaviors, emotional responses, and cognitions during their ordinary daily lives. Unlike anthropologists, though, who might live in an exotic culture for a year, marketing researcher ethnographers use a combination of direct observations, interviews, and video and audio recordings to make their observations on consumers far more quickly, as business demands.

Ethnographic research can employ a number of methods, but a hallmark of the technique is a combination of observation and interviews. The marketing

Short excursions into the field have been termed "ethno-dunking."

---

[8] Bill Abrams, *The Observational Research Handbook* (marketing power.org).

[9] Paul A. Atkinson et al., *Handbook of Ethnography* (Sage, 2007). For a great example, see John F. Sherry, Nina Diamond, Mary Ann McGrath, Albert Muniz, Stefania Borghini, and Robert Kozinets, "American Girl and the Brand Gestalt: Closing the Loop on Sociocultural Branding Research," *Journal of Marketing*, to appear.

RESEARCH   REALITIES

4.3 Ethnography Examples

1. Researchers for MTV regularly reconnaissance young teen consumers' MP3 music collections, their closets, and the places they hang out. All these venues give the adult researchers insights into youth values, enabling them to design more relevant programming and to advertise in a way that communicates more authentically to these rather affluent young people. (Teens are a substantial segment, spending a good $150 billion annually.)

2. Barilla watched consumers during dinner preparation and meal consumption to get a handle on what makes a meal Italian and why. Italianness was multitextured: the hyper-masculinity of The Sopranos and Godfather, the gastronomic experience of pizza and spaghetti, the arts and culture of Verdi, Dante, Raphael, Leonardo da Vinci, and Michelangelo. They found Italian food connoted comfort:

"An Italian experience is laidback, easygoing and full of life." It was also considered universal: "I don't know a single person who doesn't like Italian food. With Italian food you can never go wrong."

3. A pharmaceutical manufacturer followed sales reps in the field to observe some 150 interactions between sales reps and physicians and support staff. They watched sales reps approach the docs, how they got around their gatekeepers, how they delivered their brands' messages, and so forth. These observations led to improvements in training new reps.

Sources: Lisa Holton, *"The Surfer in the Family,"* American Demographics, *adage.com;* Hy Mariampolski and Sharon Wolf, *"What Does Italian Mean to You?"* quirks.com; Richard Durante and Michael Feehan, *"Watch and Learn: Leverage Ethnography to Improve Strategic Decision Making,"* Marketing Research, *marketingpower.com.*

researcher observes consumers in their natural settings. This direct observation offers a number of advantages, e.g., actual consumer behavior is observed, so there is no need to rely on self-reported intentions of future behavior or faulty recollections of past behaviors. In addition, this holistic approach to research gives the ethnographer an environment and context that helps explain the observations they make, the consumers' behaviors, and the consumers' comments offered in their interviews.

In the field, researchers take notes on the observations they make and the interviews they conduct. One or more individuals are trained to systematically observe a phenomenon and record specific events. Methods include the written field notes, wherein researchers make their initial on-site observational impressions. Audio and video recorders assist the capture of observations, and they're surprisingly unobtrusive during the research and interactions with the consumers at the field site. Increasingly, field researchers bring laptops with them to take notes, supplementing their observations, to minimize memory error later.

Researchers also interview consumers and may ask them to provide tangible artifacts. For example, to understand the context of consumers and their uses of brands, consumers might be asked to show favorite possessions to express their individualities ("This tie is special to me because I wore it at my first job interview," or "I know this vase is chipped, but it was my grandmother's, from the old country, and it always adds warmth to the flowers I pick up at the market," or "This picture shows me and my kid brother on our trip to Vegas—our first trip without our parents"). Later, off-site, all these sources of data are integrated by the researcher, who provides a conceptual and managerial summary.

Although the marketing manager's observations can be valuable for self-edification, for the serious data-collection effort, as with any marketing research, it is best to hire an expert (e.g., a marketing researcher trained in

R E S E A R C H   R E A L I T I E S

4.4 What's New in Ethnography

The Internet is changing everything, even marketing research techniques that rely upon observation. Can it be done? Sure. Consider what a "cookie" does—it is a file that contains information about where you've been online, what you've viewed, done, searched, purchased, and so forth. Ethnographers are also exploring the power of this medium that has made so many things faster, more plentiful, sometimes simpler, and usually less expensive in our world.

Some segments of consumers are naturally online, such as Star Trek fans (in all the generational forms) or Apple's Macintosh cult. In such cases, the frequent concern that samples of data obtained online may be biased seems less applicable when studying digital consumers who are present online in large number.

Prof. Kozinets suggests guidelines for budding netnographers, which include (p. 281):

a. Investigating possible online field sites, initiating and making cultural entrée

b. Collecting and analyzing data

c. Ensuring trustworthy interpretations

d. Conducting ethical research, and

e. Providing opportunities for the feedback of culture members

So, for example, a marketing researcher might scout out blogs relevant to their brands and product category. They might simply observe the communications among the posting members, or they might introduce themselves into the dialogue. If they are lurking, the observations, and scientific summaries made, are not different from watching shoppers at a mall or grocery store. If they insert themselves into the community, they are expected to present themselves as a researcher, and they gain credibility if they are also an authentic member of the "tribe" (e.g., a new mom, a biker, a SAS user, etc.).

As with any qualitative data-collection effort, the quant jocks in the office will try to turn these observations into a coding exercise. The ethnographer will resist, saying that the gestalt understanding of the observations in their cultural context is essential and cannot be reduced to histograms.

Source: Robert V. Kozinets, (2006) "Click to Connect: Netnography and Tribal Advertising," Journal of Advertising Research, *46 (3), 279–288.*

anthropology), to minimize the biases that a brand manager is likely to have that the objective, neutral party would not. Most of what you pay for in hiring marketing research experts is neither their time nor even the logistics of sending them to the field to observe. Their added value comes from their training, their experience, and their ability to yield insights from observational data. For what's new in ethnography, see Research Realities 4.4.

Observations in the Lab

An increasingly popular method for assessing customer reactions in a controlled environment is for marketers to use computer simulations and virtual reality to display potential new products or product displays without going to the expense of physically building them. For example, automobile manufacturers use virtual reality technology to test consumers' reactions to the view from the front seat of a new car without having to go through the expense of building even a single prototype car.

The technology has also been used in consumer shopping experiments. The computer screen simulates the retail environment, beginning with a picture of a grocery store shelf facing, and including an ability to "lift" an icon of a box of cereal, rotate it to see the side of the box and list of nutrients, etc., and then put it into a virtual cart. The customer can comment on the appearance of the displays as well as the merchandise itself. This technique can also be used in concept testing prototypes, such as interactive accounting or tax preparation software.

These interactive interviews are vivid and often intrinsically interesting and fun for the respondent—it feels like a video game. Thus, data quality is thought to be good and response rates can be relatively high. These multimedia interviews often strike clients of marketing researchers as having high face validity (they seem "believable"), which should therefore enhance forecasting consumer reactions to new product concepts.

In addition, you can see how easy it would be to program an experiment. The system could have both test and control conditions simulated for different marketing mix variables; e.g., change the price points to gauge customers' levels of interest.

The advantage of the laboratory environment over the field is that we are better able to control extraneous influences that might affect the interpretation of what happened, thus creating greater internal validity.[10] The disadvantage of the laboratory setting is that the contrived setting itself may cause differences in behavior and thus raise real questions about the external validity (generalizability) of the findings. Yet the vividness of these virtual reality shopping "games" makes progress toward a testing scenario that is high on both internal validity (due to the lab control) and external validity (due to the seeming realness of the simulation).

Observations via Hi-Tech Mechanical Measures

Technology carries with it the advantage of precision in measurement, but the drawback of the contrived nature of the process. A **galvanometer** records changes in the electrical resistance of the skin associated with the (slight) sweating that accompanies emotional arousal. A consumer is fitted with small electrodes to monitor electrical resistance and then is shown some ad copy. The instrument measures autonomic reactions, that is, reactions not under an individual's voluntary control. Because these responses are not controlled, consumers cannot hide their "true" reactions to a stimulus. The strength of the current induced is used to infer a person's interest or attitude toward the copy.

The **eye camera** is used to study eye movements while a respondent views some stimulus, again, often reading ad copy online. Tiny cameras are positioned to strike the cornea of the respondent's eye, and eye movements are traced on videotape and analyzed by computer. Watching where people look allows the marketer to answer questions such as: Where do people look first? How long did they linger on any particular place? Did they read the whole ad or just part of it? Similar technology measures pupil dilation, which is assumed to indicate a person's interest in the stimulus being viewed. **Pupilometrics** have been used to evaluate color schemes in packaging and optimal advertisement placement in magazines.

Two measures, response latency and voice pitch analysis, began to be implemented as the industry of telephone surveying matured. Response latency is also easily measured during Web surveys. **Response latency** is the amount of time a respondent deliberates before answering a question. Response time is assumed to be related to a consumer's uncertainty, thereby indicating the consumer's strength of preference when choosing among alternatives. Once a survey question appears on the computer screen, a stopwatch function internal to

---

[10] We say more about extraneous factors, and internal and external validity in the chapter on causal research.

the computer gets reset to zero and counts time (in milliseconds!) until a response is entered into the keyboard. The method provides an accurate measure without respondents even being aware that this aspect of their behavior is being recorded.

Voice pitch analysis relies on the same premise as the galvanometer in that involuntary physiological reactions, such as changes in blood pressure, rate of perspiration, or heart rate, accompany emotional arousal by external or internal stimuli. Voice pitch analysis examines changes in the relative vibration frequency of the human voice. A baseline is established by recording the respondent during an unemotional conversation. Deviations from the baseline indicate that the respondent has reacted to the stimulus question (whether or not the changes were discernible to the human ear). (It's like a lie-detector.)

Perhaps most exotic of all are EEGs and fMRIs. Marketing researchers are exploring the use of high-tech headsets based on electroencephalogram (**EEG**) technology developed at NASA to monitor astronauts' alertness. Five times per second, electrodes monitor the electrical impulses emitted by the brain as the consumer is exposed to various stimuli (e.g., again, often advertising). The two hemispheres of the brain respond to different stimuli, with the right hemisphere responding more to emotional stimuli and the left to rational stimuli.[11] The technique of functional magnetic resonance imaging (**fMRI**) is a brain scan—researchers are finding increasing evidence of mapping of certain cognitive and affective functions and marketers are using these scans to supplement product evaluations.[12] Critics argue that the techniques are too new to have benchmarking data to interpret results. Supporters argue that these measures indicate many phenomena more objectively than consumers' self-reported data.

Coding

We close this chapter by discussing **coding**. Coding is the task of translating qualitative observations into quantitative measures.

Should We Code?

Qualitative marketing research methodologists vary in their regard for, or disdain of, numbers. Coding is actually an anathema to some qualitative researchers. They argue that the "analysis" of qualitative data (whether interview transcripts, focus group interactions, observations in the field or lab) needs to be done holistically and verbally—that the inferences about consumer behavior come from identifying the themes elicited from the respondents and the manner in which they are interwoven in the context of the consumers' lives.

They would argue that if even only one consumer informant talked about, say, how taking the family car in for an oil change is a way to express care for his family, then there is a segment, however large, of consumers who feel similarly, and whose sentiments this informant represents. Indeed, many urge that reports from focus group studies not include numbers, such as "2 of the 8 focus group members liked the new drink flavor, but 4 of the 8 did not," because it is too tempting to generalize (i.e., to 25% and 50% of the population). Instead, reports include cautious language, such as "some respondents" or "a few participants" mentioned the flavor.

[11] Rebecca Gardyn, "What's on Your Mind?" *American Demographics* (April 2000), pp.31–33; Jennifer Gilbert, "Capita Taps Brain Waves to Study Web Ads' Potency," *Advertising Age* (Feb. 14, 2000), p.55.

[12] See Carolyn Yoon, Angela H. Gutchess, Fred Fienberg, and Thad A. Polk, "A Functional Magnetic Resonance Imaging Study of Neural Dissociations between Brand and Person Judgments," *Journal of Consumer Research*, 33 (2), 31–40.

Yet, fair or not, there is a perception that summaries of qualitative studies are soft and somehow not as rigorous as numbers, so there is a desire to quantify the qualitative data.[13] Hence, there is often coding.

As an example of coding, let's return to our "spying on soup purchasers" example. Say you've posted yourself midway down the grocery's soup aisle, pretending to be shopping for the nearby Ragu, but instead are surreptitiously studying the consumer who is checking out Campbell's and Progresso. A coding form looks like an Excel spreadsheet, where each new shopper is a row, and the columns might be structured for you to enter:

length of time standing in front of soups, number of cans picked up, number of can labels read, number of cans placed in cart, brands of cans (picked up, read, placed in cart), whether any brands were on sale, gender of shopper, approximate age, shopping alone or with children, was shopper reading from a grocery list or not (i.e., did this appear to be a planned purchase), day of week, time of day, etc.

The number of categories of information requested of each observation can be extensive, and if the coding form is too elaborate, mistakes are more easily made.

In this example, the structured observational form (i.e., specific things to look for) implies that the marketing manager and researcher decided precisely what was to be observed and the specific categories and units that would be used to record the observations. These decisions presuppose specific hypotheses (e.g., based on secondary data, account manager experience, or intelligent guesswork). Thus, the odd thing is that such structured coding forms require the research to be more descriptive or causal in nature. For exploratory research, it would be difficult to create a coding scheme with such precision. Exploratory research, as this chapter has been illustrating, is ideally suited to generating insights into the relevant dimensions of the soup purchaser's deliberation and search behavior.

How to Code

Coding open-ended questions can be challenging, and it is nearly always more time-consuming than entering rating scale data and computing means. However, the information obtained from consumers "in their own words" through interviews and open-ended questions on surveys can also be extremely rewarding and insightful. Further, some of the problems with coding open-ended questions may be changing with new technology. Researchers are increasingly feeding respondents' answers into computers programmed to recognize a large vocabulary of words in their search for regularities in the replies.[14]

Consumers' responses are usually first broken into **thought units**. For example, if a consumer is asked, "Tell me about the last time you had poor service at a restaurant," and answers, "Well, the service was slow and the waiter was rude," the sentence would be parsed into "service was slow" and "waiter was rude," because they express different characteristics of the encounter and would need to be coded differently. Each word is ranked by the frequency of usage across respondents so researchers can see recurring themes. These systems automate the coding, but they still leave the interpretation to the analyst.

---

[13] There are, of course, errors of measurement in survey numbers!

[14] A popular program for content analysis goes by the acronym NUD*IST (for Non-numerical Unstructured Data Indexing Searching and Theorizing) and is easily found online (www.qsr.com.au). There are computing programs to help with "text mining," e.g., streams of documents, customer complaint e-mails, virtual community discussion groups, open-ended questions on customer satisfaction surveys, call center staff notes, etc. (SAS Text Miner, sas.com; SPSS Ascribe, spss.com). A document taxonomy or dictionary searches for common themes, and these themes are then easily tabulated and clustered.

Nevertheless, the software systems achieve in hours what would take a person weeks to accomplish.

Once the codes are obtained, remember again that this is not a numbers game. If "service is slow" is clearly the most popular complaint, then subsequent research (descriptive surveys) would be required to obtain more precise estimates as to this attitude's prevalence relative to the other issues that customers raised. For example, a rough coding scheme might not have differentiated "it was difficult to get a reservation" (i.e., "service" prior to entering the premises) vs. "service at the bar was slow" vs. "food came slowly," etc.[15] One way to develop consistency in coding is to train multiple coders and judge inter-rater agreement in the ratings of the interview verbata.

Summary

A research design is the blueprint for a study that guides the collection and analysis of data. The three classes of research designs are: exploratory research, descriptive research, and causal research.

Exploratory research is basically "general picture" research. It is very useful for becoming familiar with a phenomenon, for clarifying concepts, for developing but not testing "if-then" statements of causality, and for establishing priorities for further research. Exploratory methods are characterized by their flexibility. Literature searches, experience surveys, and case studies are all useful means for gaining insight into a phenomenon.

Qualitative techniques also include the popular methods of focus groups, depth interviews, projective testing, and observational ethnographic studies. A focus group is the most popular qualitative marketing research tool. They are thought to be creative in generating ideas to follow up in subsequent research because the group members interact dynamically, playing off each other's remarks. Interviews are more labor intensive, given that they are conducted one-on-one, but have the advantage that the researcher understands this particular consumer's attitudes in their idiosyncratic life context richly and in depth. Projective tests are indirect means

of getting at consumers' underlying motivations and wants and needs. They can include word association tasks, sentence completions, storytelling, and picture drawing.

While most observations in marketing research are conducted in a completely natural setting, some observational studies are conducted in the lab using computers and other mechanical equipment. The lab allows greater control of extraneous influences and thus may be more internally valid, although less externally valid. Electrical and mechanical measuring instruments permit more objective, reliable measurements by eliminating possible human observers' biases such as selective attention. However, the human researcher must still provide the overall interpretation and understanding of the data.

Ethnographies are typically a combination of observations and interviews in which the researcher is embedded in the natural setting. Observations of the field site are made, and interactions with the other participants in the setting form the basis of these qualitative studies. Finally, the coding of qualitative data is somewhat controversial, and is difficult to do well until the researchers have some basic questions to form the structure of the coding schema.

Questions

1. What principle underlies the use of a galvanometer? What is an eye camera? What does response latency assess? What is voice pitch analysis?
2. What is the key characteristic of exploratory research?
3. What is an ethnography?
4. What are the basic uses for exploratory research?
5. What is a word association test? A sentence completion test? A storytelling test?
6. What is the crucial tenet of research?

[15] To be fair, a survey might also have just a single item "speed of service," which would be equally non-diagnostic for the restaurateur in suggesting means of improvement. The point of exploratory research is to break down what "speed of service" means to inform the survey design, to include items about reservations, bar, food, etc.

7. What is the difference between an observational study conducted in the field vs. in the lab?

8. What are the different types of research designs? What is the basic purpose of each?

9. What are some of the more productive types of exploratory research? What are the characteristics of each type?

10. What is a research design? Is a research design necessary to conduct a study?

Applications and Problems

1. Investment Services, Inc. (IS) is a real estate developer headquartered in Florida but operating throughout the southeastern U.S. One of the military bases located in one of the cities within IS's market area recently closed, and the 40 housing units for military people located at the base were put up for public sale. The housing units, which were all duplexes, were somewhat rundown. IS's management thinks that these units will command only a very low price at the public sale because of their dilapidated condition. The developers believe that because of this low price, the units could be repaired and sold at a nice profit. Before bidding on the contract, though, IS's management is interested in determining what kind of demand there might be for these units. It has asked you to assist in determining this reaction. What kind of research design would you suggest? Why?

2. Greg Martin is the owner of a pizza restaurant that caters to college students. Through informal conversations with his customers, Greg has begun to consider how to expand his menu. While there are many things the restaurant could do, he's not sure what would be most attractive to his customers. Thinking back to a marketing research course he took in school, Greg has decided that focus group research would be an appropriate method to gather information that might be useful in deciding whether to pursue further development of his idea (developing a formal business plan, store policies, etc.).

　a. What is the decision problem and resulting research problem in this situation?

　b. Who should Greg select as participants in the focus group?

　c. Where should the focus group session be conducted?

　d. Who should be the moderator of the focus group?

　e. Develop a discussion outline for the focus group.

3. Fred Spears, director of advertising for ScubaYou, is responsible for selling advertising space in the magazine. The magazine deals primarily with vacation spots and the marketing of the hospitality industry, and is distributed solely by subscription.

The size and composition of the target audience for ScubaYou are key concerns for prospective advertisers, so Mr. Spears wants more detailed data on the magazine's readership. He has total circulation figures, but these typically understate the real readership and thereby the potential exposure of an ad in ScubaYou. In particular, he thinks that for every subscriber, the magazine is read by several friends. Fred wishes to determine how large this secondary audience is, and also wishes to develop more detailed data on readers.

　a. Does Fred have a specific hypothesis? If yes, state the hypothesis.

　b. What type of research design would you recommend? Justify your answer.

4. Gettings & Gettings, a father-and-son insurance agency in Lafayette, Indiana, was concerned with improving its service. In particular, the firm wanted to assess whether customers were dissatisfied with current service and, if so, the nature of this dissatisfaction. What research design would you recommend? Justify your choice.

5. Airways Luggage is a producer of lightweight, cloth-covered luggage. The company distributes its luggage through major department stores, mail-order houses, clothing retailers, and other retail outlets, such as stationery stores and leather-goods stores. The company advertises rather heavily, and supplements this promotional effort with a large field staff of sales reps, numbering around 400. There is a large turnover in sales reps (10%–20% per year). Because the cost of training a new person is estimated at $15,000 to $20,000, not including the lost sales that might result because of a personnel switch, Ms. Brooks has been conducting exit interviews with each departing sales rep. On the basis of these interviews, she has formed the opinion that the major reason is dissatisfaction with promotional opportunities and pay. But top management has not been sympathetic to Ms. Brooks' pleas regarding the changes needed in these areas of corporate policy, saying her suggestions are based on intuition and little hard data.

Ms. Brooks has decided to call on their in-house Marketing Research Department.

   a. Identify the general hypothesis that would guide your research efforts.

   b. What type of research design would you recommend to Ms. Brooks? Why?

6. Industrial Health Technologies, Ltd. (IHT), located on the East Coast, is a manufacturer of industrial respirators. The R&D department designed a prototype respirator that is battery powered and would extend the operating life of current models from 8 to 30 hours without recharging. A similar model introduced by Deep Mine Safety Apparatus (DMSA) four months earlier was marginally successful. However, both IHT's and DMSA's models suffered from a technical flaw (using the respirators for 30 hours without recharging required 18 hours of recharging the batteries). Still, IHT's management team, headed by Chuck Montford, was excited about the product's potential. He, with Carl Corydon, IHT's marketing manager, decided to do a sample survey to gauge customer reactions. A random sample of 100 firms was chosen from a list of East Coast firms. Mail questionnaires were designed to determine respondents' attitudes and opinions toward this new respirator. In this situation, is the research design appropriate? If yes, why? If no, why not?

Descriptive Research

5

Questions to Guide Your Learning:

Q1 What is *descriptive research*?

Q2 When is it used? When in the product life cycle? When in the research program?

Q3 What *hypotheses* may be tested using descriptive techniques?

Q4 What marketing questions would require a *longitudinal* study vs. a *cross-sectional* one?

Q5 What are: dummy tables? marketing research panels? brand-switching tables?

This chapter covers descriptive research. The vast majority of marketing research studies are descriptive in nature. In descriptive research, the marketing manager has moved beyond the "What's going on?" stage of exploratory research but isn't ready for the "If I tweak this marketing mix variable, what will happen to sales?" sort of question that is answered using causal designs described in the next chapter.

When to Use Descriptive Research

Descriptive research is used when the purpose is to:

- Describe characteristics of certain groups, e.g., we might attempt to *profile users* of our brand with respect to income, gender, age, educational level, etc.

- Estimate the proportion of people who behave in a certain way, e.g., the proportion of *people who live or work within a specified radius* of a proposed shopping complex.

- Make specific predictions, e.g., if we could *predict the level of sales* we should expect over the next five years, we could plan for the hiring and training of new sales reps.

Descriptive research encompasses an array of research objectives. The fact that a study is descriptive study doesn't mean that it is simply a fact-gathering expedition. There are tons of facts out there—just surf the net. What makes facts useful is a theory or conceptual understanding, an explanation of those facts and how they relate to each other.

A good descriptive study presupposes much prior knowledge about the phenomenon studied. We shouldn't submit to the temptation of designing a descriptive research study with the vague thought that the data collected should be interesting. Hypotheses, or conjectural statements, guide the research in specific directions. Thus, a descriptive study design is very different from an exploratory study design—whereas an exploratory study is characterized by its flexibility, descriptive studies are more rigid.

Consider a chain of convenience stores planning to open a new outlet. The company wants to determine how people would patronize the new outlet. Sounds easy, but consider these questions:

Descriptive studies: who, what, when, where, why, and how.

Who is to be considered a patron? Anyone who enters the store? What if they do not buy anything but just participate in the grand-opening prize giveaway? Perhaps a patron should be defined as anyone who purchases anything from the store. Should patrons be defined on the basis of the family unit, or should they be defined as individuals, even if they are in the same family? What characteristics of these patrons should be measured? Are we interested in their age and gender, or perhaps in where they live and how they came to know about our store? When shall we measure them—while they are shopping, or later? Should the study take place during the first weeks of operation of the store, or should the study be delayed until the situation has stabilized somewhat and word-of-mouth has had a chance to operate? Where shall we measure the patrons? Should it be in the store, or immediately outside of the store, or should we attempt to contact them at home? Why do we want to measure them? Are we going to use these measurements to plan promotional strategy? In that case the emphasis might be on measuring how people become aware of the store. Or are we going to use them as a basis for locating other stores? In that case the emphasis might shift more to determining the trading area of the store. How shall we measure them? Shall we use a questionnaire, or shall we observe their purchasing behavior? If we use a questionnaire, what form will it take? Will it be highly structured? Will it be in the form of a scale? How will it be administered? By telephone? By mail? Perhaps by personal interview?

Yikes!

Sometimes we can answer a few of these questions after a small exploratory study. It's best to delay the fuller data collection until we know what hypotheses we'll examine and how the data will be analyzed. Ideally, we would mock up a set of "dummy tables" before beginning the collection process to make explicit how the data will be analyzed. The dummy tables would be complete in that they contain titles, headings, and specific categories for the variables making up the tables. They just don't have any data in them yet.

Table 5.1 illustrates a table used by a women's specialty store investigating whether it is serving a particular age segment better than its competitors. The table lists the particular age segments. The variables and categories are specified before data collection begins. The tables help us see which statistical tests should be used to study the relationship between age and store preference, again, determined prior to data collection. Inexperienced researchers often question the need for such detailed decisions before collecting the data. They assume that

TABLE 5.1   Dummy Table—Store Preference by Age

Age	Prefer A	Prefer B	Prefer C
<30 yrs			
30–39			
40+			

FIGURE | 5.1 | **Classification of Descriptive Studies**

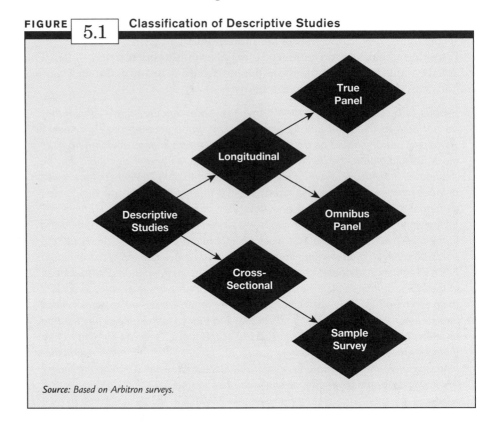

Source: Based on Arbitron surveys.

delaying these decisions until after the data are collected will somehow make the decisions easier. They'll only make that mistake once.

Once the data have been collected and analysis is begun, it is too late to lament, "If only we had collected information on X" or "If only we had measured Y using a finer scale." Rectifying such mistakes at this time is impossible. Rather, we must account for such contingencies when planning the study. Structuring the tables used to analyze the data makes such planning easier. To ensure that we'll be getting the data we need, we should specify in advance the objective each question addresses, the reason it's included, and the analysis in which it will be used.

One of the decisions we'll make in planning is whether to conduct a longitudinal or cross-sectional study (see Figure 5.1). The cross-sectional study is the most common kind of study run. We measure various characteristics on a sample from the population of interest. The measures are taken one time only. Longitudinal studies, on the other hand, involve panels—a sample (of stores, individuals, etc.) that remains relatively constant over time and is measured repeatedly.

Longitudinal Analysis

Longitudinal or sequential data are common—stock market performance is plotted against time to study trends, agencies track consumer confidence to predict holiday sales and inventory needs, political groups continually measure the liberal vs. conservative sentiments in the populace, and so on. Research Realities 5.1 illustrates several more examples: (a) market shares may be compared within a category over time; (b) the content and photos uses in print ads have been examined over decades to show the developments of consumer attitudes and industry trends; (c) the increase or decrease in sales for a new or established product is frequently pored over by a brand manager; and (d)

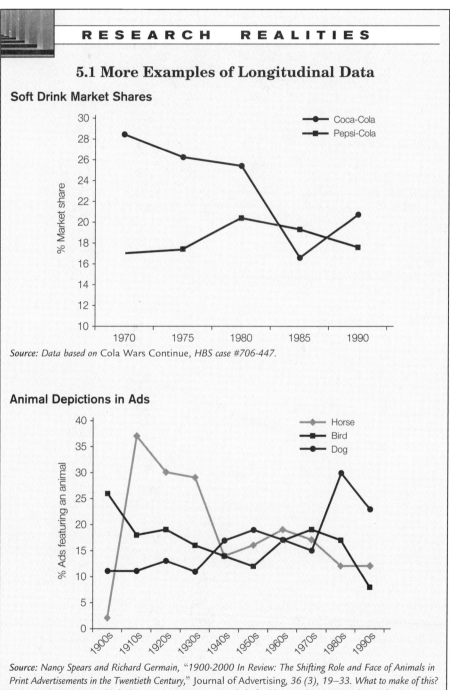

RESEARCH   REALITIES

5.1 More Examples of Longitudinal Data

Soft Drink Market Shares

Source: Data based on Cola Wars Continue, *HBS case #706-447.*

Animal Depictions in Ads

Source: Nancy Spears and Richard Germain, "1900-2000 In Review: The Shifting Role and Face of Animals in Print Advertisements in the Twentieth Century," Journal of Advertising, *36 (3), 19–33. What to make of this? Spears and Germain say birds dominate in 1900s as a symbol of wildness and unrestraint, horses dominate in 1910s to convey themes of power, strength, and war. Dogs dominate in the 1980s to express themes of relationships and conservativeness, nostalgia, taming the land and machismo.*

(Continued)

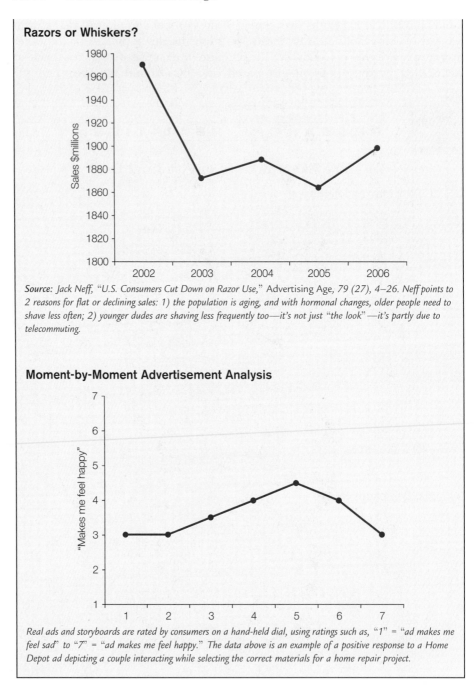

Razors or Whiskers?

Source: Jack Neff, "U.S. Consumers Cut Down on Razor Use," Advertising Age, 79 (27), 4–26. Neff points to 2 reasons for flat or declining sales: 1) the population is aging, and with hormonal changes, older people need to shave less often; 2) younger dudes are shaving less frequently too—it's not just "the look"—it's partly due to telecommuting.

Moment-by-Moment Advertisement Analysis

Real ads and storyboards are rated by consumers on a hand-held dial, using ratings such as, "1" = "ad makes me feel sad" to "7" = "ad makes me feel happy." The data above is an example of a positive response to a Home Depot ad depicting a couple interacting while selecting the correct materials for a home repair project.

advertisements are tested before they are aired, and one means of doing so is to obtain moment-by-moment consumer reactions. In each case, the marketer is trying to understand the meanings of the fluctuations of the data over time.[1]

---

[1] For more ideas, see Anita Elberse, "The Power of Stars: Do Star Actors Drive the Success of Movies," *Journal of Marketing*, 71 (3), 102–120; Raghuram Iyengar, Asim Ansari, and Sunil Gupta, "Leveraging Information Across Categories," *Quantitative Marketing and Economics*," 1, 425–465; Alan L. Montgomery, Shibo Li, Kanna Srinivasan, and John C. Leichty, "Modeling Online Browsing and Path Analysis Using Clickstream Data," *Marketing Science*, 23 (4), 579–595; Vincent R. Nijs, Shuba Srinivasan, and Koen Pauwels, "Retail-Price Drivers and Retailer Profits," *Marketing Science*, 26 (4), 473–487.

In addition, longitudinal data can result from a panel. There are two types of panels: true panels and omnibus panels. **True panels** rely on repeated measurements of the same variables. Nielsen and National Purchase Diary (NPD) maintain international panels of households who use a hand-held scanner to record every UPC-coded item they purchase. They scan the items they've purchased when they return from shopping (from groceries and clothing to office supplies and furniture) and then answer a programmed set of questions (e.g., store where purchased, price paid) by responding to a series of prompts from the machine. These panels yield one source of secondary data that we'll discuss later in the book.

Measuring the same variables over time allows the marketer to ask questions such as:[2]

- What is the long-term effect of the price promotions that occur in our category?

- Do consumers stockpile and only purchase again when another sale is in effect? That is, have we in essence taught our consumers to be price sensitive?

- What products in a customer's basket yield the most brand loyalty?

If the same variables were not measured at multiple points in time, data patterns might vary simply due to different households providing the data, or because the data represented a different selection of brands in the category, etc.

There are many methods for collecting panel data—not just scanners. For example, see Research Realities 5.2 to learn how Arbitron captures radio listening data. Online panels are also clearly important and we'll discuss them shortly.

In contrast, in an **omnibus panel**, a sample is maintained, but the information collected from the members varies over time. At one time, we might ask the sample about attitudes toward a new product. At another time, we might ask the panel to choose between ads. In each case, a sample is selected from the panel.

- A panel sample might be drawn randomly; for example, Nickelodeon, the children's cable television network, might draw a random sample from its existing panel of kids to evaluate some new programming (see Research Realities 5.3).

- Alternatively, participants may be chosen who meet some criterion; i.e., they have been screened and we know they have some desired characteristics. For example, the Parker Pen Company can go to its panel of 1000 individuals who had expressed interest in writing instruments to ask them to test a new fountain pen.

The distinction between the true panel and the omnibus panel is important. True longitudinal analysis, or time series analysis, can be performed only on the first type of data, with repeated measurements of the same variables and the same respondents over time. Omnibus panels mostly offer the advantage of easy access—the panelists are a relatively random sample who is readily available to participate in research. But the studies are usually very different.

---

[2] Rebecca Slotegraaf and Koen Pauwels, "The Impact of Brand Equity and Innovation on the Long-Term Effectiveness of Promotions," *Journal of Marketing Research* 45 (2008), 293–306. Also see S. Siddarth, Randolph E. Bucklin, and Donald G. Morrison, "Marking the Cut: Modeling and Analyzing Choice Set Restrictions in Scanner Panel Data," *Journal of Marketing Research*, 32, 255–266.

RESEARCH   REALITIES

5.2 Arbitron Radio Listening Diary

	Time		Station		Place				
	Start	Stop	Call letters or station name. Don't know? Use program name or dial setting.	Check one		Check one			
				AM	FM	at home	in car	at work	other

THURSDAY heading spans the table. Data rows labeled:

→ Early morning from 5AM

→ Midday

→ Late afternoon

→ Night to 5AM Friday

If you didn't hear a radio today, please check here: _____

Brand Loyalty and Brand Switching

One of the most important longitudinal questions that true panel data can address is the question of brand loyalty and brand switching. Suppose we have consumer purchase data from a panel of 1000 families. We are interested in determining the effect of a recent package design for our Brand A. We have two main competitors, B and C, and a number of other smaller competitors we'll lump into a single miscellaneous category, labeled Brand D. We'll look at our brand at time t_1, before the change, and time t_2, after the package change.

We could perform several types of analyses on these data.[3] We could look at the proportion of those in the panel who bought our brand in period t_1 and period t_2. Table 5.2 shows a scenario where the package change was successful. Brand A's market share increased from 20% to 25%, and it seemed to make its gains at the expense of its two major competitors, whose market shares decreased.

[3] Hans Baumgartner and Jan Benedict Steenkamp, "An Extended Paradigm for Measurement Analysis of Marketing Constructs Applicable to Panel Data," *Journal of Marketing Research*, 43 (3), 431–442; Edward W. Frees, *Longitudinal and Panel Data* (Cambridge University Press, 2004); Thomas P. Novak, "Log-Linear Trees: Models of Market Structure in Brand Switching Data," *Journal of Marketing Research* 30 (3), 267–287; Aric Rindfleisch, Alan J. Malter, Shankar Ganesan, and Christine Moorman, "Cross-Sectional Versus Longitudinal Survey Research," *Journal of Marketing Research* 45 (2), 261–279.

RESEARCH   REALITIES

5.3 Nickelodeon Marketing Research

Nickelodeon has been the highest-rated basic cable television network in the U.S. for the past 15 years. Critics complain that even poor shows get good ratings just due to the popularity and brand equity of the network.

Nickelodeon has a lock on the 2-to-11-year-old market, and it is attributable to their "obsession with research." They run 300 focus groups a year to test shows and identify trends among kids. They also set up one of the first online consumer product testing panels. They argue that the kids' market is notoriously fickle and hence must be continually monitored. The focus groups show the children in action, and the online panel allows convenient access, both due to the immediacy of the online technology as well as the availability of the established panel.

The children in the panel are in households that are wired and that have cable. They try to represent diverse ethnic groups and have equal gender representation. Household income is also wide ranging, to further enhance the likely generalizability of the findings to the eventual market placements of shows, ads, and products.

Online isn't perfect for the youngest among this target, who are expected to type in answers, or point to a face that says "cool" or "ick," so the online panel is supplemented with traditional research, including the focus groups or interviews at schools.

Source: For more info, see Susan Linn, Consuming Kids *(Anchor, 2005); Juliet B. Schor,* Born to Buy *(Simon & Schuster, 2005).*

But that is not the whole story. Given that we have repeated measures of the same households, we can create a **brand-switching matrix** (or a "turnover table") as in Table 5.3. Note that it contains the same basic information as Table 5.2 (e.g., we see that 20% of the families bought Brand A in period t_1). In addition, Table 5.3 shows that Brand A in fact did not make its market share gains at the expense of Brands B and C, as originally suggested, but rather captured some of the families who previously bought one of the brands in D: 75 families switched from D in t_1 to Brand A in period t_2. In addition, Brand A lost some of its previous users to Brand B: 25 families switched from A at t_1 to B at t_2.

Table 5.3 also allows the calculation of brand loyalty. For Brand A, 175, or 87.5% of the 200 who bought Brand A in period t_1, remained "loyal" to it (bought it again) in period t_2. Table 5.4 contains the row percentages, which suggest that among the three major brands, Brand A elicited the greatest loyalty and Brand D the least.[4] (Whether those who switched from Brand D to Brand A

TABLE 5.2   # Families in Panel Purchasing Each Brand

Brand Purchased	During First Time Period, t_1	During Second Time Period, t_2
A	200	250
B	300	270
C	350	330
D	150	150
Total	1000	1000

[4] The table is also called a "transition matrix," because it depicts the brand-buying changes or transitions occurring from period to period. Knowing the proportion of switching allows early prediction of the ultimate success of a new product or a change in market strategy.

TABLE 5.3   # Families in Panel Buying Each Brand in Each Period

		During Second Time Period t_2				
		Bought A	**Bought B**	**Bought C**	**Bought D**	**Total**
During	Bought A	175	25	0	0	200
First	Bought B	0	225	50	25	300
Time	Bought C	0	0	280	70	350
Period, t_1	Bought D	75	20	0	55	150
	Total	250	270	330	150	1000

TABLE 5.4   Brand Loyalty and Brand-Switching Probabilities among Families in Panel

		During Second Time Period t_2				
		Bought A	**Bought B**	**Bought C**	**Bought D**	**Total**
During	Bought A	.875	.125	.000	.000	1.000
First	Bought B	.000	.750	.167	.083	1.000
Time	Bought C	.000	.000	.800	.200	1.000
Period, t_1	Bought D	.500	.133	.000	.367	1.000

did so because of the package change is open to question, for reasons that we discuss in the next chapter.)

These tables enable us to look at changes in consumers' behavior and relate those changes to our marketing tactics—advertising copy, package, price changes, etc. Further, because the same respondents are measured before and after changes in marketing variables, small changes in the criterion variable are more easily identified than if separate studies were made using two or more independent samples. The turnover table is the heart of panel analysis.

Panels have other advantages as well. For example, the fairly frequent contact between a panelist and the research company creates rapport, which encourages honest answers. In addition, because the panelists have opted in, they tend to be cooperative, and participation rates can be much higher than a random sample of regular (non-panelist) people.

On the other hand, the main concern about panels is that they are probably somewhat nonrepresentative. The fact that the panelists have agreed to participate in answering surveys from time to time (usually for only a token benefit or payment) means they might not quite be like other people who don't want to be bothered. In addition, panel samples often underrepresent minorities, people with poor English-language skills, and those at the extremes of the socioeconomic spectrum.[5] Whether these characteristics of the panel are problematic depends on the purpose of the study and the particular variables of interest.

Marketing research firms understand this concern and try to make their panels as "representative" as possible for their clients. To investigate the

---

[5] "Mail Panels vs. General Samples," *Research on Research* (synovate.com); Seymour Sudman and Brian Wansink, *Consumer Panels* (2nd ed.) American Marketing Association.

RESEARCH   REALITIES

5.4 Comparison of Responses of the Market Facts

Mail Panel and a Randomly Selected Telephone Sample

Source: "*Mail Panels vs. General Samples,*" Research on Research *(Synovate.com).*

"representativeness" of a panel, a marketing research company compared data that were gathered using their panel to random telephone samples. Research Realities 5.4 shows that with respect to a product ownership, lifestyle, and leisure activity characteristics, the samples were pretty similar.

Cross-Sectional Analysis

The cross-sectional study is the best known, most frequently used, and therefore most important type of descriptive design. The cross-sectional study has two distinguishing features. First, it provides a snapshot of the variables of interest at a single point in time. Second, the sample is typically selected to be representative of some known universe. Accordingly, a great deal of emphasis is placed on selecting sample members, usually with a probability sampling plan. That is one reason that the technique is often called a sample survey (we'll talk more about sampling in Chapter 11).

Sample surveys usually yield a large number of cases, which allows for cross-classification of the variables. The objective of cross-classification is to learn how variables relate to each other. We detail the methods later, in Chapter 14, but for the moment, simply note that it involves counting the simultaneous occurrence of some variables of interest.

For example, suppose you're a brand manager and you believe that a consumer's occupation is an important factor in determining the consumption of your product: say you expect white-collar workers to be more likely to use the product than blue-collar workers. In a cross-sectional study, you'd measure a representative sample of the population with respect to occupation and use of the product. In a cross-tab, you'd count the number of cases that fell in each of the following classes:

Cross-sectional studies are the bread & butter of marketing research.

• White-collar and use of the product

• Blue-collar and use of the product

- White-collar and do not use the product
- Blue-collar and do not use the product

That is, the emphasis would be on the relative frequency of occurrence of the joint phenomenon—white-collar occupation *and* user of the product. According to your hypothesis, the proportion of white-collar workers using the product should exceed the proportion of blue-collar workers using the product.

You'll see in the chapters that follow that cross-classification analysis is an important technique that marketing researchers use to make sense out of all survey data. One particular type of cross-tabs arises when there is a series of "properly spaced" surveys, because this allows cohort analysis of the data. A **cohort** is the group of individuals who experience the same event within the same time interval, and it serves as the basic comparison unit of analysis. A common analysis is on birth cohorts, i.e., groups of people born within the same time interval.

In Table 5.5 we see such a cohort structure. Note that the table is constructed so that the interval between any two survey periods corresponds approximately to the age-class interval that is used to define the age cohorts used in the study (10 years in this case). Because of this, the age cohorts can be tracked over time by reading down the diagonal. For example, in 1990, cohort 5 (C5) comprised people born between 1971 and 1980, that is, they were between 10 and 19 years old. In 2000, they had matured to 20–29 years old, by 2010 they will be 30–39 years of age, etc. We might ask marketing questions about cohorts' changing needs, e.g., comparing the data of the C5 group from 1990 to 2000. Alternatively, we can compare cohorts, such as looking at C4 when they were in their 20s (i.e., data collected in 1990) to data collected in 2000 on C5.

Table 5.6 illustrates one use of cohort analysis. Life insurance is a product that we tend to buy as we get older, when we carry financial obligations that might burden loved ones, have discretionary money to buy the product, etc. Table 5.6 indicates fairly stable percentages in purchasing over the lifecycle. As people hit the 30–39 year old bracket, more purchase, and that percentage increases in the 40s and levels off in the 50s.[6]

TABLE 5.5   Set-up of Cohorts

Age	1990	2000	2010	2020
10–19	C5	C6	C7	C8
20–29	C4	C5	C6	C7
30–39	C3	C4	C5	C6
40–49	C2	C3	C4	C5
50+	C1	C2	C3	C4

C1-cohort born before 1940   C5-born 1971–1980
C2-born 1941–1950   C6-born 1981–1990
C3-born 1951–1960   C7-born 1991–2000
C4-born 1961–1970   C8-born 2001–2010

[6] For more examples, see Rex Y. Du and Wagner Kamakura, "Household Life Cycles and Lifestyles in the U.S.," *Journal of Marketing Research*, 43 (2), 121–132; David A. Schweidel, Peter S. Fader, and Eric T. Bradlow, "Understanding Service Retention Within and Across Cohorts Using Limited Information," *Journal of Marketing* 72 (1), 82–94.

TABLE 5.6   Percentage Purchasing Life Insurance

Age	1980	1990	2000	2010
10–19	.0	.5	1.0	.5
20–29	2.5	3.7	4.0	4.5
30–39	25.0	26.5	32.0	27.0
40–49	35.5	41.0	42.0	45.0
50+	37.0	40.5	45.0	49.0

Cohort analysts note the events that shape people's lives (e.g., good economies or bad, which wars and what political events they lived through), as well as consumption items (e.g., what music and television shows were popular). Understanding the mindset of a cohort group can help the marketer communicate through advertising with more resonance.

Marketing research studies don't have to be cohort designs in order to examine age differences. Figure 5.2 depicts television viewing habits of children for three age groups, 6–8, 9–11, and 12–14 years of age. For many genres of television entertainment, there are discernible maturing patterns. Cartoon shows are popular with both boys and girls, especially among the youngest viewers, but this preference falls off with age, declining at a faster rate for girls than boys. Preferences for comedies and sitcoms show the reverse trends, increasing with age, faster for girls than for boys. There are predictable gender differences as well. Action shows and sports programs are preferred by boys, at any age. (We'll talk more later in the book about how to test where all these differences are significant.)

FIGURE 5.2   Television Viewing Habits of Children

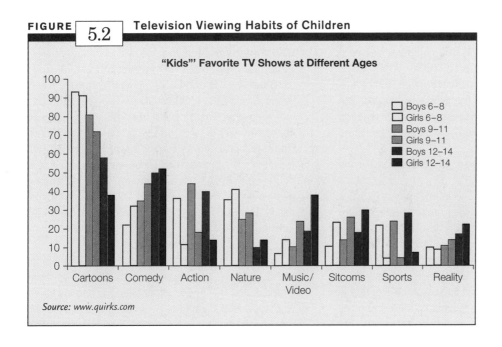

Source: www.quirks.com

Summary

Descriptive studies are systematic, and fixed in format and structure. Descriptive studies are used when the research is intended to describe the characteristics of certain groups, to estimate the proportion of people who behave in a certain way, or to make predictions.

Descriptive studies are of two types: longitudinal and cross-sectional. Longitudinal studies rely on panel data. A panel is a fixed sample of individuals from whom repeated measurements are taken. Panels in which the same measurements are taken in each measurement period are called true panels, and those in which different measurements are taken in each measurement period are called omnibus panels.

Cross-sectional studies, or sample surveys, rely on a sample of elements from the population of interest that are measured at a single point in time. The sample is generated scientifically so that the members are representative of the population of interest. The analysis of sample survey results rests heavily on the cross-classification table, which is used to report the joint occurrence of the variables of interest.

Questions

1. What are the basic types of panels, and how important are the differences?
2. What is a cohort? What is cohort analysis?
3. What is the key characteristic of descriptive research?
4. What are the advantages and disadvantages of a sample survey?
5. What are the main types of descriptive studies, and what do their differences mean?
6. How do you read a cross-tab? What kinds of analyses can be done?
7. What are the basic uses of descriptive research?

Applications and Problems

1. The LoCalor Company is a medium-sized manufacturer of highly nutritional food products. The products have been marketed as diet foods with high nutritional content. Recently, the company was considering marketing these products as snack foods but was concerned about their present customers' reaction to the change in the products' images. The company has decided to assess customers' reaction by conducting a study using one of the established consumer panels.

    What type of panel would you recommend in the preceding situation? Why?

2. The leadership of the Boy Scouts of America (BSA) is concerned about several issues related to their membership. These issues include low retention rates among members (many scouts quit after only one or two years), high turnover rates among leaders, and declining membership in some regions (such as in large urban areas). Design a marketing research program to assist BSA in assessing and reversing these trends.

3. Peppy Pet Company, a large manufacturer of pet food products, conducted a study in this past spring in order to assess how its brand of dog food was faring in the market. Questionnaires were mailed to a panel of 1260 families with a dog. The Peppy Pet brand had three major competitors: Brand A, Brand B, and Brand C. A similar study conducted the year before had indicated the following market shares: Peppy Pet, 31.75% (400 families); Brand A, 25% (315 families); Brand B, 32.54% (410 families); and Brand C, 10.71% (135 families). The present study indicated that Peppy Pet's market share had not changed during the one-year period. However, Brand B increased its market share to 36.5% (460 families). This increase could be accounted for by a decrease in Brand A's and Brand C's market shares (Brand A now had a share of 22.23%, or 280 families; Brand C now had a share of 9.52%, or 120 families). The management of the Peppy Pet Company decided it had little to worry about.

    The new study also revealed some additional facts. Over the one-year period, 70 families from Brand A and 30 families from Brand C had switched to Peppy Pet. Five families from Brand B and 30 families from Brand C had switched to Brand A, while none of the Peppy Pet users had switched to Brand A. These facts further reassured management. Finally, 45 families switched from Brand B to

Brand C, but none of the families using Peppy Pet or Brand A had switched to Brand C. Brand C's loyalty was estimated to be .556.

a. Do you think that the management of the Peppy Pet Company was accurate in its analysis of the situation? Justify your answer.

b. You are called upon to do some analysis. From the preceding data, construct the brand-switching matrix.

c. Indicate what this matrix reveals for each of the brands over the one-year period.

d. Complete the following table and compute brand loyalties.

e. What can be said about the degree of brand loyalty for each of the four products?

		At Time t_2				
		Bought Peppy Pet	**Bought A**	**Bought B**	**Bought C**	**Total**
At	Bought Peppy Pet					
	Bought A					
Time	Bought B					
t_1	Bought C					
	Total					

4. The U.S. Treasury has been considering some changes in currency design. One change involves paper money, changing the colors and shapes, e.g., $1 on green paper, $5 on blue paper, $10 on red, etc., and a five-dollar bill would be larger than the one, the ten would be larger than the five, and so on. Before making these changes, the Department of the Treasury believes that it might be useful to conduct some marketing research. Thus, LJ Marketing Research Inc. (LJMR) is contacted by the Department of the Treasury and asked to collect some information to help forecast whether these changes will be successful and popular with consumers. What research should LJMR propose? Be specific when describing alternative research designs.

5. The Wisconsin Ice Cream Co. of Mount Horeb, Wisconsin, a regional manufacturer of gourmet ice cream and frozen novelties, conducted a study this past summer to assess how its brand of gourmet ice cream was faring in the market. Mail questionnaires were sent to a panel of 1575 households. Wisconsin Ice Cream has three major competitors: Baumgardt's Food Co. of State College, Pennsylvania; Doug's Ice Cream of Michigan City, Indiana; and Guyer Foods of Charlevoix, Michigan. A similar study conducted a year before had indicated the following market shares: Wisconsin, 29.84% (470 families); Baumgardt's, 22.54% (355 families); Doug's, 26.03% (410 families); and Guyer's, 21.59% (340 families). The current study indicated that Wisconsin's market share had not changed, Baumgardt's market share had decreased to 20% (315 families), Doug's market share had decreased to 20.32% (320 families), and Guyer's market share had increased to 29.84% (470 families). Wisconsin Ice Cream Co. managers decided that they had little to worry about.

The new study revealed some additional facts. Over the one-year period, 80 families had switched from Doug's and 50 families had switched from Guyer's to Wisconsin Ice Cream. Ten families had switched from Wisconsin and 15 families had switched from Doug's to Baumgardt's Ice Cream. Results also indicated that although none of Baumgardt's families had switched to Doug's Ice Cream, 40 of the Wisconsin and 5 of Guyer's families now purchased Doug's Ice Cream. It was revealed that Guyer's current customers comprise 80 families formerly purchasing Wisconsin Ice Cream, 65 families formerly purchasing Baumgardt's Ice Cream, and 40 families formerly purchasing Doug's Ice Cream.

a. Do you think that Wisconsin's management team is accurate in analyzing the situation? Justify your answer.

b. You are called on to do some analysis. From the preceding data, construct the brand-switching matrix. (Hint: Begin by filling in the row and column totals.)

c. Indicate what this matrix reveals for each of the brands over the one-year period.

d. Complete the brand loyalty and switching possibilities matrix on the next page.

e. What can be said about the degree of brand loyalty for each of the four products?

		At Time t_2				
		Bought Wisconsin	Bought Baumgardt's	Bought Doug's	Bought Guyer's	Total
At Time t_1	Bought Wisconsin					
	Bought Baumgardt's					
	Bought Doug's					
	Bought Guyer's					
	Total					

6. A medium-sized manufacturer of high-speed copiers was introducing a new desktop model with a small footprint. The vice president of communications had to decide between two advertising programs for this product. He preferred advertising program gamma and was sure it would generate more sales than its counterpart, advertising program beta. The next day he was to meet with the senior vice president of marketing and planning to decide on an appropriate research design for a study that would aid in the final decision about which advertising program to implement. What research design would you recommend? Justify your choice.

7. The Pen-Lite Company is a manufacturer of writing instruments such as fountain pens, ballpoint pens, soft-top pens, and mechanical pencils. Typically, these products have been retailed through small and large chains, drugstores, and grocery stores. The company recently diversified into the manufacture of small perfumes and aftershaves. Distribution of this product was to be restricted to drugstores and grocery stores because management believed that its target market of low- and middle-income consumers would use

these outlets. Your expertise is required to decide on an appropriate research design to determine if this would indeed be the case. What research design would you recommend? Justify your choice.

8. Emilie Malti, president of Jamaican Specialties, a specialty food marketing firm, was convinced that the target audience for her line of Caribbean conserves in mango, lime, passion fruit, and papaya consisted of women, ages 25 to 44, with household incomes of $30,000 and up. Jamaican Specialties' major competitor's (Pacific Flavor) market segment appeared to be more widely dispersed with respect to both age and income. Emilie and her marketing vice president, Ruth Marion, attributed this difference to the type of magazines in which Pacific Flavor advertised. Emilie and Ruth decided to conduct a study to determine the socioeconomic characteristics of their firm's market segment. They formed a panel of 800 women ages 18 and up. Mail questionnaires would be sent to all panel members. One month after receiving all questionnaires, the company would send similar questionnaires to all panel members again. In this situation, is the research design appropriate? If yes, why? If no, why not?

Causal Designs

6

Questions to Guide Your Learning:

Q1 What is *causality*?

Q2 What are the *types of evidence* necessary to infer causal relationships?

Q3 What is an experiment, and what's the difference between *lab* and *field* experiments?

Q4 What are the *extraneous factors* that can affect the interpretation of research results?

Q5 What are standard test markets, electronic test markets, and simulated test marketing?

Marketing managers frequently wish to answer the question "Does X cause Y?" For example, "Will a 5% increase in price hurt customer demand?" "Will a cereal package that has been redesigned for kids improve families' attitudes toward the product?" These research questions are best answered via experimentation and causal analysis.

Concept of Causality

The scientific concept of causality is different from the everyday notion. The everyday interpretation of the statement "X causes Y" suggests that X is the only cause, whereas the scientific statement holds that X is only one of a number of determining conditions. In addition, whereas the everyday interpretation implies a completely deterministic relationship (i.e., X must always lead to Y), the scientific understanding of causality implies a probabilistic relationship (i.e., the occurrence of X makes Y more likely). Finally, the scientific concept implies that we can never *prove* that X is a cause of Y. We *infer* that a relationship exists—an inference based on data, perhaps acquired in a controlled experimental setting—but the scientific approach recognizes the fallibility of any procedure.

Thus, the question becomes, "What kinds of evidence can be used to support scientific inferences?" There are three basic kinds of evidence: concomitant variation, time order of the variables, and elimination of other possible causal factors.

Concomitant Variation

Consider the statement "X is a cause of Y." Evidence of **concomitant variation** is the extent to which X and Y occur together (or vary together) in the way predicted by the hypothesis. There are two cases—the qualitative and the quantitative.

Consider the qualitative case first. Suppose we were interested in testing the statement "The quality of our dealers (X) drives

Evidence supporting causality:

- concomitant variation
- time order of variables
- eliminate alternative explanations

our company's market share (Y)." We believe that where we have good dealers, we have good market penetration, and where we have poor dealers, we have less of the market. If X is to be considered a cause of Y, we should expect to find the following: In those territories with good dealers, we would expect to have satisfactory market shares, and in those territories where poor dealers are located, we would expect to have unsatisfactory market shares. However, if we found that the proportion of territories with unsatisfactory market shares was higher where the good dealers were located, we would conclude that the hypothesis was untenable.

In Table 6.1, the 100 dealers in each of the company's sales territories have been classified as good or poor, and the firm's market penetration in each sales territory has been categorized by management as either satisfactory or unsatisfactory. This table provides evidence of concomitant variation. Where we find the presence of X, a good dealer, we also find the presence of Y, good market share.

In fact, 67% of the good dealers are found in territories where our market share is satisfactory. A perfect relationship would yield data in which all good dealers were located in territories with satisfactory market shares and all poor dealers were located in territories with unsatisfactory market shares. The "pure" case will rarely be found in practice, because other causal factors will produce some deviation from this one-to-one correspondence between X and Y. So we search for the proportion of cases having X that also possess Y.

With continuous variables, the approach is similar, e.g., a firm's advertising dollar expenditure is logically considered a cause (X), and sales, the effect (Y). If we believe that "the higher the level of advertising expenditure, the greater the sales," then we would expect to find a positive relationship between the variables.

If we analyze the relationship between X and Y and find supporting evidence of concomitant variation, we can say that the association makes the hypothesis "X causes Y" more tenable, but it does not "prove" it.[1] Similarly, the absence of an association between X and Y cannot be taken in and of itself as evidence that there is no causal relationship between X and Y, because we are always inferring, rather than proving, that a causal relationship exists.

Consider first the case in which there is positive evidence of concomitant variation. Table 6.2 suggests that candy consumption is affected by marital status.[2] Single people are more likely than married people to eat candy regularly: 75% of the single people in the sample ate candy regularly, whereas only 63% of the married people were regular consumers. The evidence is strong, based on a rather large sample of 3,009 cases. Thus, can we safely conclude that marriage causes a decrease in candy consumption, or are there other possible explanations?

What about the effects of age? Married people are usually older than single people, and perhaps older people eat less candy. Table 6.3 shows the

TABLE 6.1   Evidence of Concomitant Variation: Qualitative Case

Dealer Quality—X	Market Share—Y		Total
	Satisfactory	Unsatisfactory	
Good	40 (67%)	20 (33%)	60 (100%)
Poor	10 (25%)	30 (75%)	40 (100%)

[1] We'll discuss in subsequent chapters how to test for concomitant variation. Note that association or correlation between X and Y does not mean there is causality between X and Y.

[2] Adapted from Hans Zeisel, *Say It with Figures*, 5th ed., Harper & Row, pp. 137–139.

TABLE 6.2 Evidence of Concomitant Variation Between Marital Status and Candy Consumption

| | Candy Consumption—Y | | |
Marital Status—X	Eat Candy Regularly	Do Not Eat Candy Regularly	Total
Single	750 (75%)	249 (25%)	999 (100%)
Married	1265 (63%)	745 (37%)	2010 (100%)

TABLE 6.3 Candy Consumption by Age and Marital Status

| | <25 Yrs | | | 25 Years + | | |
	Eat Candy Regularly	Do Not Eat Candy Regularly	Total	Eat Candy Regularly	Do Not	Total
Single	632 (79%)	167 (21%)	799 (100%)	120 (60%)	80 (40%)	200 (100%)
Married	407 (81%)	96 (19%)	503 (100%)	873 (58%)	634 (42%)	1507 (100%)

relationship between candy consumption and marital status for different age segments of the population—younger than vs. older than 25 years. In this table, we are holding the effect of age constant, and now we see there is little difference in the candy-eating habits of married and single people: Up to 25 years of age, 79% of the singles and 81% of the marrieds eat candy regularly. For those over 25, 60% of the singles and 58% of the marrieds eat candy regularly. Thus, the data indicate that candy consumption is unaffected by one's marital status. The original association suggested by Table 6.2 was spurious.

Consider now the absence of initial evidence of concomitant variation and let's see why that does not imply that there is no causation between X and Y. Table 6.4 implies that there is no relationship between a person's listening to classical music and the individual's age: In a sample of 1,279, 64% of those under 40 and 64% of those over 40 listen to classical music.[3] Is that result what you'd have expected?

Consider what happens when educational level is introduced as another explanatory variable. Table 6.5 reveals that an association exists between age and

TABLE 6.4 Lack of Evidence of Concomitant Variation Between Age and Listening to Classical Music

| | Listening to Classical Music—Y | | |
Age—X	Listen	Do Not Listen	Total
Below 40	390 (64%)	213 (36%)	603 (100%)
40+	433 (64%)	243 (36%)	676 (100%)

[3] Also Zeisel, *Say It with Figures*, pp. 123–125.

TABLE 6.5	Listening to Classical Music by Age and Education					
	College			Less than College		
Age	Listen	Do Not Listen	Total	Listen	Do Not Listen	Total
<40	162 (73%)	62 (27%)	224 (100%)	228 (61%)	151 (39%)	379 (100%)
40+	195 (78%)	56 (22%)	251 (100%)	238 (56%)	187 (44%)	425 (100%)

listening to classical music. As college-educated people get older, they display a higher propensity to listen to classical music: 78% of those 40 and over listen, whereas only 73% of the under-40 listen. The reverse occurs among those who do not have a college education: 61% of the under-40 age group listen to classical music, and only 56% of the 40-plus age group do so. The relationship between age and listening to classical music was originally obscured by the effect of education. When education was held constant, the relationship became visible.

Though the concept of concomitant variation may seem straightforward, you can see it's actually somewhat complex. Further evidence of the existence of a causal relationship can be provided by looking at both the order of occurrence of variables and also by eliminating other possible sources of explanation. See Research Realities 6.1 for the lesson: correlation does not imply causation.

Time Order of Occurrence of Variables

The **sequential ordering** of the occurrence of variables X and Y helps provide evidence of a causal relationship between the two. If X causes Y, typically X precedes Y. X and Y may occur nearly simultaneously, but we cannot claim X to be a cause of Y if Y precedes X.

Although conceptually simple, this type of evidence requires an intimate understanding of the time sequence governing the phenomenon. For example, we usually think of X (advertising) causing Y (sales), but a portion of this year's sales (Y) is usually budgeted for the subsequent year's advertising (X). So, which way does the relationship run: Does advertising lead to higher sales, or do

RESEARCH   REALITIES

6.1 Correlation Does Not Imply Causation

"Fox News recently reported that a 'healthy love life leads to well-being.' The news piece was based on research conducted by the Centers for Disease Control and Prevention, which stated, 'Married people were healthier than those who were single, divorced, widowed, or separated.' As reported by the Washington, D.C.-based Statistical Assessment Service, 'The problem is that marriage may not be the cause of the good health experience by married people. Marriage may simply be correlated with health. Perhaps healthy people are more likely to get married. Perhaps failing health contributes to being divorced or separated. Perhaps married people are more likely to have health insurance to meet their health needs.'"

Source: Anon. *"Healthy Relationships,"* Marketing Research, marketingpower.com and stats.org.

higher sales lead to an increased ad budget? Again we see the lesson that we need to understand something about the phenomenon before we can interpret the data.

Elimination of Other Possible Causal Factors

The **elimination of other possible causal factors** is very much like playing Sherlock Holmes: "When you have eliminated the impossible, whatever remains, however improbable, must be the truth."[4] To eliminate other possible explanations, we might physically hold other factors constant, or we might need to "adjust" our results to remove the effects of other factors.

Suppose you're advising the divisional manager of a chain of supermarkets who is interested in the effects of end-of-aisle displays on munchy apple sales. Suppose the per-store sales increased during the past week and that a number of stores were using the displays. To reasonably conclude that the displays (X) were responsible for the sales increase (Y), we'd need to eliminate other explanations such as price, size of store, apple type and quality, etc. We'd need to compare apple sales for stores of approximately the same size. We'd check to see if the prices were the same in stores having an increase in sales and stores with no increase, and we'd check to determine if the type and quality of apples were consistent with those of the previous week.

Or consider the testing of new products, where manufacturers want to determine whether the new product has any differential advantages in consumers' minds (e.g., superior quality, better features, etc.). Yet when consumers are given a product to test, their responses can be affected by awareness of the brand or manufacturer. Respondents might rate the product higher or lower because of their attitudes toward the manufacturer, which makes it difficult to determine whether respondents liked the product itself. To overcome such bias, letters rather than brand names are often used to label the products. Yet you can see in Research Realities 6.2 that respondents systematically favor particular letters (letters near the beginning of the alphabet and M and S).[5]

Role of the Evidence

Experiments provide all three types of evidence of causality. It allows us to check for concomitant variation and time order of occurrence, and, if the experiment has been designed correctly, many alternative explanations will have been eliminated. However, even in an experiment, it's difficult to eliminate all other explanations. For example, we might conclude that X caused Y, when in fact we had neglected another factor that is associated with X but was the true cause of Y. Or, we might conclude that X did not cause Y, but be wrong because we neglected some condition under which X is indeed a determiner of Y.

The correct philosophy toward these three types of evidence is that they provide a reasonable basis for believing that X is (or is not) a cause of Y. We can never be absolutely sure that the relationship has been conclusively demonstrated. But we gain confidence in the result as an accumulation of studies point to the same conclusion. Further, an intimate knowledge of the phenomenon helps us interpret research results with more clarity than would a person untrained in the subject matter.

[4] Arthur Conan Doyle's Sherlock Holmes: *The Sign of the Four.*
[5] "Using Letters to Identify Products or Brands," *Research on Research* (synovate.com).

RESEARCH   REALITIES

6.2 Using Letters to Identify Products or Brands

To determine if some letters are perceived more favorably than others, questionnaires were sent to 4,000 households in a consumer mail panel. The sample was nationally representative with respect to geographic region, population density, age, and income. Approximately 3,000 questionnaires were returned. The instructions given to the respondents were as follows:

When some people look at different letters of the alphabet, they may feel that certain letters have a more favorable meaning than other letters. For each letter shown below, please check the response that best describes how you feel about any meaning of the letter.

The 26 letters were then listed in one of four sequences:

1. Alphabetical order

2. Reverse alphabetical order

3. Random order: TJENXBFHZOGPACRWLQKDSI VYMU

4. Reverse random order

The responses available to the respondents were as follows:

    Very Favorable (200)

    Somewhat Favorable (100)

    No Meaning (0)

    Somewhat Unfavorable (−100)

    Very Unfavorable (−200)

The numbers in parentheses are the values assigned to the responses for the analysis of the data (and were not shown to the respondents).

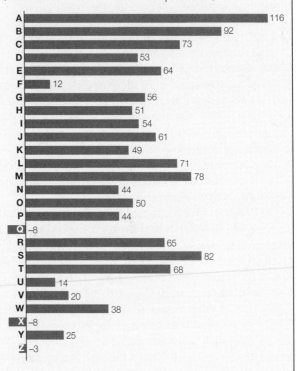

Source: "Using Letters to Identify Products or Brands," Research on Research 16 *(synovate.com).*

Experimentation

> In experiments, we *manipulate* at least one *independent variable* and *measure* at least one *dependent variable.*

An **experiment** can provide more convincing evidence of causal relationships than exploratory or descriptive designs. In fact, experiments are often called "causal research." An experiment can provide evidence of causality because of the *control* it affords researchers. A marketing researcher manipulates and controls one or more factors (the "independent variables") and measures the effects on another (the "dependent variable").[6]

---

[6] Both exploratory and descriptive designs are distinguished from experimental designs in that they are examples of *ex post facto* research, which literally means "from what is done afterward." In *ex post facto* research, the criterion variable Y is observed and we try to find one or more causal variables, Xs, that offer plausible explanations as to why Y occurred. This kind of retrospective analysis allows little control of the Xs and therefore contains great potential for error—the occurrence of Y may be attributable to some other Xs than the ones being investigated.

Figure 6.1a displays the design of a classic scientific study. Participants are randomly sampled (to enhance external validity, discussed shortly) and then randomly assigned (to enhance internal validity, discussed shortly) to get a new drug vs. a placebo. The measure of success of the new treatment is whether there are fewer sick people among the group that received the new drug, compared to the group that didn't get medical treatment. Marketing research experiments are run similarly. Figure 6.1b shows the same design for a market test of two package designs for perfume boxes (e.g., "contemporary and abstract" or "flowering and romantic"). The consumers are randomly sampled (so they should resemble all our potential customers) and randomly assigned to see one package design, and then we measure estimates of the two groups' preferences between the abstract vs. flowering packages.

Laboratory and Field Experiments

There are two types of experiments—the laboratory experiment and the field experiment. Each has its own advantages and disadvantages.

A **laboratory experiment** is one in which the researcher creates a situation with the desired conditions and then manipulates some variables while controlling others. The investigator is thus able to observe and measure the effect of the manipulation of the independent variables on the dependent variable while holding the other variables constant (or at least minimizing their effect). A **field experiment** is a research study in a realistic or natural situation, and involves the manipulation of independent variables under conditions that are as carefully controlled as the field situation will permit.

FIGURE 6.1a   Example of a Classic Scientific Experiment

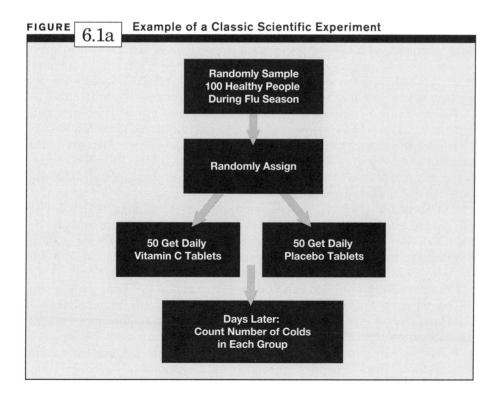

FIGURE 6.1b   Example of a Marketing Research Experiment

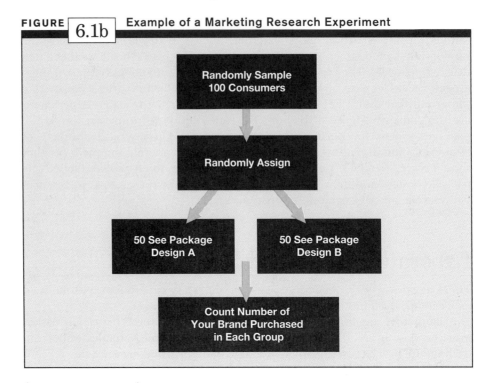

The laboratory experiment is distinguished from the field experiment primarily in terms of environment. The researcher creates a setting for a lab experiment, whereas a field experiment is conducted in a natural setting.

For example, a popular economic-driven marketing question is to study the relationship between price and demand. We might wonder how close the price-demand estimates from a lab experiment correspond to those generated from a field experiment. First, a lab experiment was run to simulate shopping trips. Respondents chose the brand they wished to purchase from a full assortment of pre-priced brands of cola and coffee. The relative prices of the different brands were changed for each of the simulated purchase trips. This study was administered in a systematic sample of 135 homes in a small town in Illinois.

The prices of brands of cola and coffee were also manipulated in a field experiment. The field experiment was conducted in two small towns in Florida, 10 miles apart. Four supermarkets were used in all, two from each town. The stores in one town were designated as control stores, where the price of each brand was maintained at its regular level throughout the experiment. In the experimental town, the prices were systematically varied during the experiment. The effect of the price changes was monitored by recording weekly sales for each brand so that brand market shares for each price condition could be determined. All other controllable factors were also held as constant as possible (no displays, special packaging, etc., were used to draw consumer attention to the fact that the relative prices of the brands had been altered).

Note the distinction between the two studies. In the field experiment, no attempt was made to set up special conditions. The manipulation of the experimental variable—price—was imposed in the natural environment. The laboratory experiment, on the other hand, was contrived. People were told to behave *as if* they were actively shopping for the product. Though the simulated shopping trips generated reasonably valid estimates of consumers' reactions to "real life" (field study) price changes for cola, they produced relatively

---

Ethical Dilemma 6.1

The promotions manager of a soft-drink company asks you to help her run an experiment to determine whether she should start advertising in cinemas showing X-rated movies. She explains that she has read a journal article indicating that viewers' responses to upbeat commercials are more favorable if the commercials follow arousing film clips, so she believes that her soft-drink commercial will stimulate more sales of the drink in the cinema if it follows previews of very violent or erotic films.

- If you ran a laboratory experiment for this client, what kinds of manipulations would you use, and what are the ethical issues involved in their use?
- Is it feasible to run a field experiment, and would the ethical issues change if a field experiment were run rather than a laboratory experiment?
- If you found that increasing viewers' arousal levels did indeed make them more favorably disposed toward products advertised through upbeat commercials, what are the ultimate ethical implications for influencing television programming?

---

invalid estimates for brands of coffee (the lab study overstated the effects of the price changes). Is there something about cola vs. coffee (e.g., frequency of purchasing)? Possibly. Do we have to be careful in drawing conclusive statements from the lab *or* the field (for different reasons)? Of course.

Internal and External Validity

The two types of experiments have different advantages and disadvantages. The lab experiment typically has greater internal validity. **Internal validity** is the ability to attribute the effect that was observed to the experimental variable, and not to other factors. In the pricing experiment, the question is whether demand is due to price, rather than other factors, e.g., advertising, display space, store traffic. In the study, we couldn't have attributed demand differences to, say, advertising, because this factor didn't exist in the simulated shopping trip. We were better able to eliminate the effects of other factors that may obscure or confound the relationships, either by physically holding the factors constant or by controlling for them statistically. Thus, we may conclude that the observed effect was due to the manipulation of the experimental variable.

The field experiment is considered to exhibit greater external validity. **External validity** is the extent to which the effect can be generalized. Lab experiments are more artificial than field experiments, so it's questionable whether the results can be generalized to other populations and settings. In the simulated shopping trip, no real purchase takes place. Further, the experimenter called attention to the price, which may induce people to be more price conscious than they would be in a supermarket. Further, people who agreed to participate in the lab study may not be representative of the larger population of shoppers, and this too would jeopardize the external validity, or generalizability, of the findings.

Internal validity.
Is the effect due to our hypothesized cause?
External validity.
Can we generalize to other samples/stimuli?

Experimental Design

There are a number of types of experimental design.[7] Let "X" refer to the exposure of an individual or group to an experimental treatment, the effects of which are to be measured and compared. The marketing mix elements are all frequently used as

---

[7] Thomoas P. Ryan, *Modern Experimental Design* (Wiley, 2007).

experimental treatments (e.g., alternative prices, package designs, advertising themes). We'll let "O" refer to the process of observation or measurement of the test units. The test units could be individuals, groups, stores, sales reps, etc.

Time is represented by a horizontal arrangement of Xs and Os. Thus:

$$X \quad O_1 \quad O_2$$

indicates that a test unit was exposed to an experimental variable and then its response was measured at two different points in time. Different test units are arranged vertically. Within a "column," different groups are simultaneously treated. The symbolic arrangement

$$X_1 \quad O_1$$
$$X_2 \quad O_2$$

indicates there are two different groups of test units (one per row); and each group was exposed to a different experimental treatment at the first point in time (and at the same time); and then the responses of the two groups were subsequently measured (again, simultaneously).

Extraneous Variables

Extraneous variables are alternative explanations.

We need to design experiments carefully, because we want to be able to conclude that the observed response was due to our experimental manipulations. In particular, we need to rule out extraneous factors as possible causes. Extraneous factors fall into several categories.

History refers to the specific events, external to the experiment but occurring at the same time, that may affect the dependent variable. Suppose a major appliance manufacturer was interested in consumers' price sensitivity for refrigerators. Suppose they proposed the following experiment to take place in Detroit. Sales (at regular prices) would be monitored for a 4-week period, then prices would be cut 10%, and sales monitored for 4 more weeks. We'd compare weekly sales at the lower price with those at the higher price. The experiment is a pre-test, intervention, post-test design:

$$O_1 \quad X \quad O_2$$

What if, soon after the price reduction, the union contract with the auto industry expired and there was a strike? The purchase of refrigerators and other major appliances would likely be postponed, so we might see fewer sales at the lower price than at the higher one. Would we therefore conclude that higher prices induce the sales of more units? No, because we know there were extenuating circumstances that caused the aberration.

Unfortunately, the effects of history on a research conclusion are rarely so obvious. There are always many variables that can affect what we observe and whose effect is subtle or hidden. We need to isolate the effect, given that we're rarely in a position to physically control it.

Seasonality is a related phenomenon. Literal seasons are obvious (e.g., sales of snow shovels in the north will be greater in the late fall and winter). But many products have purchasing cycles, so whether you're testing price changes, in-store ads, product placement, etc., seasonality can confound your results. The best solution is to be sure to run the experiment (particularly in a field vs. lab study) for a sufficient duration so as to give the "season" a chance to cycle through.

Maturation specifically refers to changes occurring within the test units (e.g., consumers) that are not due to the effect of the experimental variable but result from the passage of time. For example, people get older, become tired, or grow hungry and distracted. Measured changes in attitude toward a product may occur simply because people have become bored and disinterested while using the product, and not because of the product or ad. Similarly, individuals in a consumer panel may change brands over time, not because of any changes in marketing strategies, but perhaps their marital or family status changed.

Maturation effects can occur in test units other than people. Organizations also change. Dealers grow, become more successful, diversify, etc. Stores change—traffic increases, its composition changes, the store's physical makeup decays and then is renovated, etc.

Of course, the type of maturation depends on the duration of the experiment. We wouldn't worry about maturation of people in an experiment that lasted only a week. On the other hand, if they were participating in an interview, and the questioning lasted a couple of hours, they could very well grow tired or feel pressed for time. Thus, responses to later questions may be affected because their personal situation has changed, and for no other reason.

Testing is concerned with the fact that the experiment itself may affect the responses. There are two kinds: the main testing effect and the interactive testing effect.

The *main testing effect* is the effect of a prior observation O_t on a later observation O_{t+1}. The first administration in and of itself is responsible for the change. In many situations, the main testing effect is a result of respondents' desire to be consistent. Thus, in successive administrations of an attitude questionnaire, respondents reply in a consistent manner even though there has been some change in their attitudes. Even in a single survey administration, responses to the latter part of the questionnaire are somewhat conditioned by responses to the early questions.

The main testing effect may also be *reactive;* there are very few things in social science that can be measured so that the process of measurement itself doesn't change what's being measured. For example, people asked about their attitude toward Honda at time t may begin to think about Honda somewhat and their attitude might even change slightly by time t + 1.

There is also an *interactive testing effect*, which means that a prior measurement affects perceptions of the experimental variable. For example, people who are asked to indicate their attitudes toward Chevrolet may become more aware of the Chevrolet ads than those who are not queried. Yet if we are interested in the attitude impact of the ads, we are interested in their effect on the population as a whole and not simply on those individuals in our sample.

The results of the two testing effects are different. In the {O_1 X O_2} study, the main testing effect has an effect from O_1 to O_2. The interactive testing effect, on the other hand, has an effect from O_1 to X.

Instrument variation includes any changes in measuring instruments that might account for differences. The change may occur in the instrument itself, or it may result from variations in its administration. When many interviewers are used, it is difficult to ensure that they will all ask the same questions with the same voice inflections, use the same probes, develop the same rapport, and so on. As a result, the recorded differences between, say, the awareness level of two respondents may not reflect a true difference but rather a difference that arose because each interviewer handled the interview slightly differently. The same thing can occur with interviews conducted by the same interviewer—it's unlikely

Extraneous factors:

- History
- Maturation
- Testing
  - main
  - interactive
- Instrument variation
- Statistical regression
- Selection bias
- Experimental mortality

that each situation will be handled in exactly the same way. Interviewers may become more adept at eliciting the desired responses, or they may become bored with the project and tired of interviewing.

We might modify the measuring instrument during the course of the research project. If the changes are big (e.g., a new set of attitude statements), the responses would probably be analyzed separately. Sometimes, though, a minor modification is needed, such as a slight change in wording to make a specific question more understandable. Although slight, this kind of change should be checked for variations in the reported answers.

Statistical regression is the tendency of "extreme" cases to move closer to the average during the course of an experiment. For example, if people are chosen for the study because they are frequent drinkers, then over the next couple of surveys, the reported alcohol intake for those people would appear closer to the average.

Alternatively, a study investigating the use of a brand of orange juice might reveal several families who consumed 10 cartons in a week. If they had had house guests, it wouldn't be surprising if subsequent consumption would be less.

Selection bias arises from the way in which test units are selected and assigned in an experiment. It is said to be present when there is no way of certifying that groups of test units were equivalent before being tested.

Consider the standard news reaction to a presidential address, "Many say the president has convinced them that the X (pick your topic) crisis is real. In a CNN poll last week, 60% of those who heard the president's speech agreed that there is a worldwide crisis, while 40% of those who didn't hear the speech believe the crisis is real." The results, 60:40, make it appear that the president is persuasive, but the fallacy is that there is no way of knowing their attitudes before the speech. Watching the speech is voluntary, and thus the exposed and unexposed groups inevitably possess a systematic difference on the factors determining the choice. Republicans listen to the speeches of Republican candidates, Democrats listen to Democrats, people with a favorable attitude toward a product pay more attention to the product's ads, and so on. If we are to conclude that exposure to the experimental stimulus (TV special, speech, ad, whatever) was responsible for the observed effect, we must ensure that the groups were equal prior to exposure.

Ethical **Dilemma** 6.2

The regional sales manager for a large chain of men's clothing stores asks you to establish whether increasing his salespeople's commission will result in better sales performance. Specifically, he wants to know whether increasing the commission on limited lines of clothing will result in better sales on those lines, along with the penalty of fewer sales on the remaining lines, or even whether raising the commission on all lines will produce greater sales on all lines. Suppose that you think that the best way to investigate the issue is through a field experiment in which some salespeople receive increased commission on a single line, others receive increased commission across the board, and still others make up a control group whose members receive no increase in commission.

• Are there ethical problems inherent in such a design?
• Is the control group being deprived any benefits?

The equality of groups is established in two ways: matching or randomization. Suppose we have 20 stores, 10 of which will comprise an experimental group, and the other 10, a control. Sales of anything in the stores are likely to be correlated with the store's traffic, so to make the groups as similar as possible before introducing an intervention into the experimental group, we would match the stores according to some external criterion, such as annual sales or square feet of floor space. Then we'd assign one store from each matched pair to the experimental group and one to the control.

Matching isn't perfect. It's hard to match test units on any but a few characteristics, so the test units may be equal in terms of the variables chosen but unequal in terms of others. In addition, if the matched characteristic turns out not to be an important determinant of the response, the researcher has wasted time and money in matching the test units.

Randomization doesn't have these problems and is generally the preferred procedure. We would assign the 20 stores at random to each of the groups, using a table of random digits. Randomization produces groups that are "equal on the average" when the sample is large enough to allow the positive and negative deviations about the average to balance.

Experimental mortality is the loss of test units during the course of an experiment. The problem is that there is no way of knowing if the people who have dropped out would have responded to the experiment in the same way as those that were retained. In the example of testing a special display in a grocery store, suppose that in the middle of the experiment, the managers of two of the stores in the experimental group got nervous—they thought the display wasn't working, so they used the display for another product. This would reduce the number of experimental stores to eight. Our interest is in the average store sales in the experimental group vs. those in the control group, and we'd have no way of knowing if the experimental group average would have been higher or lower if the two dropout stores had continued participating. We can't simply assume that the sales would have been like those in the other experimental stores. They might have been, but maybe not. We need to design studies so that this issue is eliminated.

Specific Designs

Three types of experimental designs are commonly distinguished: *pre-experimental designs, true experimental designs,* and *quasi-experimental designs.* True experimental designs provide the most control over extraneous factors, so they are the most effective in helping us confidently interpret research results. Not all marketing problems allow the use of true experimental designs, but knowledge of their features allows a more rigorous scientific interpretation of results. Then we can better understand the necessary caveats when pre-experimental or quasi-experimental designs are used.

Pre-experimental Designs

In a **pre-experimental design**, the researcher has very little control over when participants are exposed to the experimental stimuli, or even who the participants are. Similarly, there is little control of the measurement, the timing, or the respondents.

The One-Shot Case Study

Let's start simply. The one-shot case study is diagrammed:

$$X \quad O$$

A single group of test units is exposed to an experimental variable, and then that group's response is observed. There is no random allocation of test units; rather, the group is self-selected or is selected arbitrarily by the experimenter. For example, we might interview (O) a convenience sample of readers of a particular trade journal (X) for their reaction to our ad.

The one-shot case study is of little value in establishing the validity of hypothesized causal relationships because it provides too little control over extraneous influences. It provides no basis for comparing what happened in the presence of X with what happened when X was absent. The minimum demands of scientific inquiry require that such comparisons be made. Thus, the one-shot case study is more appropriate for exploratory than conclusive research, that is, suggesting hypotheses, but not testing their validity.

The One-Group Pre-test–Post-test Design

The one-group pre-test–post-test design is diagrammed as follows:

$$O_1 \quad X \quad O_2$$

It adds a pre-test to the one-shot case study design; e.g., the convenience sample of respondents is interviewed for their attitudes toward our product before the ad is placed. They are also interviewed after the ad is run, and the effectiveness of the ad is taken as the difference (d) in their attitudes before and after exposure to the ad: $d = O_2 - O_1$.

This design is widely used to argue the effectiveness of marketing strategies, but the design's failure to control extraneous error nullifies its conclusions. Consider some of the factors that might be responsible for the $O_2 - O_1$ difference, aside from the experimental variable X. First, other factors may have occurred simultaneously with the experiment that caused the attitude change (history). The respondents may have been more responsive to the product at O_2 than at O_1 (maturation). Respondents were interviewed at O_1, which might make them pay more attention to the ad than the normal reader (interactive testing effect). Respondents might attempt to appear consistent with their O_1 score (main testing effect). Perhaps the respondents' initial responses created an extreme attitude score in either a positive or negative direction; then statistical regression is likely to have occurred with the O_2 scores. Further, the sample was a convenience sample, and the result probably could not be generalized to the larger population. What a mess!

The Static-Group Comparison

The static-group comparison is a design using two groups, one that has experienced X and another that has not. A key feature is that the groups have not been created by randomization. The static-group comparison is diagrammed:

$$\text{EG}: \quad X \quad O_1$$
$$\text{CG}: \qquad\quad O_2$$

To continue with our previous example, this design would be conducted as follows: After the ad is run, interviews would be conducted among a sample of readers. Those who remembered seeing the ad would be labeled the "experimental group," EG. Those who did not recall seeing the ad would be the "control group," CG. The attitudes of each group toward the product would be measured, and the effectiveness of the ad would be taken to be $d = O_1 - O_2$. The equation states the difference in attitudes between those who saw the ad and those who didn't.

Thus, it is a better design, but there are sources of extraneous error in this design. For example, there is no way of ensuring that the groups were equivalent prior to the comparison, e.g., people with favorable attitudes toward a product often pay more attention to ads for the product than people with unfavorable attitudes. The $O_1 - O_2$ difference may reflect a difference in the initial attitude of the two groups, and maybe not attributable to the ad.

True Experimental Designs

Randomization makes the data from true experimental designs more valid than data from any pre-experimental design. The true experimental design is distinguished by the fact that the experimenter **randomly assigns** treatments to randomly selected test units. The experimenter can control who gets the experimental condition and who doesn't, and when the intervention (X) and measurement (O) occur. To distinguish the true experiment, we denote a random assignment of test units to treatments by (R).

Before–After with Control Group Design

The before–after with control group design was considered ideal for a number of years. The design is:

$$EG : (R)\ O_1\ X\ O_2$$
$$CG : (R)\ O_3\ \ \ \ O_4$$

This design diagrams simply, but it requires that the researcher decide which test units will receive the experimental stimulus and which will not. (It is not up to the test units to self-select whether they will be members of the control or experimental groups, as they did in the pre-experimental designs.)

Consider the problem faced by an in-house credit union in promoting the credit union idea among the company's workers. Suppose that the company is considering the effectiveness of a rather expensive brochure, "Know Your Credit Union," in creating awareness and understanding of the functioning of the credit union. The brochure is the experimental stimulus, X. The use of the "before–after with control group" design to investigate the effectiveness of the brochure would proceed along the following lines:

1. A sample of the firm's employees would be selected at random.

2. Half of these employees would be randomly assigned to the experimental group (to receive the brochure), and the other half would form the control group.

3. Each respondent would fill out a questionnaire to assess their knowledge of the credit union.

4. The brochure would be distributed to the respondents in the experimental group.

5. After the lapse of some appropriate time interval (say, 1–2 weeks), the questionnaire would again be administered to the sample to assess their current knowledge.

Now consider this design in terms of possible error. The difference $O_4 - O_3$ reflects effects of extraneous influences. For instance, it's possible that during the course of the experiment there may be a change in the bank prime lending rate and credit might become more expensive. This history effect would be partially responsible for any differences in O_4 and O_3. However, it would also exert a similar influence on those belonging to the experimental group. Thus, if we were to consider the effect of the experimental variable to be E and the effect of these extraneous or uncontrolled sources of variation to be U, the impact of the experimental stimulus X could be:

$$
\begin{aligned}
O_2 - O_1 &= E + U \\
O_4 - O_3 &= \phantom{E + {}} U \\
\hline
(O_2 - O_1) - (O_4 - O_3) &= E
\end{aligned}
$$

More notation! *Excellent!*

But note that this calculation applies to the following sources of extraneous variation: history, maturation, main testing effect, statistical regression, and instrument variation. All these influences should affect both groups approximately equally. Selection bias was eliminated by random assignment.

This design is nearly ideal! Still, nothing's perfect, and for example, this design may not control for the interactive testing effect. The pre-test can make the experimental subjects respond to X partly because they have been sensitized. If there is an interactive testing effect, the situation becomes:

$$
\begin{aligned}
O_2 - O_1 &= E + U + I \\
O_4 - O_3 &= \phantom{E + {}} U \\
\hline
(O_2 - O_1) - (O_4 - O_3) &= E + I
\end{aligned}
$$

where "I" measures the interactive effect of testing. We're basically unable to determine the impact of the experimental stimulus because it's confounded with the interactive testing effect. Our calculation of the net difference among the Os provides a result, but the result has two components—one due to the E and another due to I.

Four-Group Six-Study Design

When an interactive testing effect is likely to be present, the four-group six-study design is a good choice:

EG#1 :	(R)	O_1	X	O_2
CG#1 :	(R)	O_3		O_4
EG#2 :	(R)		X	O_5
CG#2 :	(R)			O_6

Let's use this design to make the credit union brochure example more elaborate. We'd first select a random sample of the firm's employees. Then, we'd randomly divide the sample into four groups. Those designated for the first experimental and control groups would be measured for their knowledge of the credit union. The brochure would then be mailed to those designated as belonging to the first and second experimental groups. Finally, all four groups would be measured on their knowledge of the credit union. Six measurements are made in all, per the name of the design.

This design offers the researcher a lot of control. Selection bias is handled by the random assignment of test units to groups. The other extraneous sources of error are handled as they were in the previous design, i.e., by making the logical assumption that factors such as history or maturation should affect all groups. By looking at the "difference in differences," the impact of these extraneous factors should be netted out. Further, whereas there might be an interactive testing effect with the first experimental group, there couldn't be any with the second experimental group, because there is no prior measurement to sensitize the respondents.

Let's see how to calculate the effect of X. When we randomly assign test units to groups, we can assume that, except for sampling variation, the four groups were equal *a priori* in their knowledge of the credit union. Thus, the best estimate of the "before measurement" for EG#2 and CG#2 (where there hadn't been pre-test measures) would be the average of the before measurements that were taken: $\frac{1}{2}(O_1 + O_3)$. Substituting in this estimate, the differences between before and after measurements are as follows:

$$
\begin{aligned}
\text{EG\#1}: O_2 - O_1 &= E + U + I \\
\text{CG\#1}: O_4 - O_3 &= U \\
\text{EG\#2}: O_5 - \tfrac{1}{2}(O_1 + O_3) &= E + U \\
\text{CG\#2}: O_6 - \tfrac{1}{2}(O_1 + O_3) &= U
\end{aligned}
$$

What is the impact of the experimental stimulus? It is determined by comparing the second experimental and control groups and is given specifically by the following calculation:

$$[O_5 - \tfrac{1}{2}(O_1 + O_3)] - [O_6 - \tfrac{1}{2}(O_1 + O_3)] = [E + U] - [U] = E$$

This design also allows us to estimate the effect of the uncontrolled extraneous factors, U, by looking at each of the control groups. In addition, an estimate of the interactive testing effect is provided by comparing Experimental Groups I and II through the calculation

$$[O_2 - O_1] - [O_5 - \tfrac{1}{2}(O_1 + O_3)] = [E + U + I] - [E + U] = I$$

Given that this design allows us to estimate the experimental effect so cleanly, it's become a conceptual ideal. Its practical application in marketing is somewhat limited, though, because the design is expensive; marketing samples aren't always so large that we have the luxury of dividing the sample into four groups. Nevertheless, this design enables the isolation of various effects, which makes it a standard against which other designs may be compared.

After-Only with Control Group Design

You might have noticed that we can estimate the impact of the experimental stimulus in the four-group six-study design simply by comparing Experimental Group #2 to Control Group #2, which raises the question of why Experimental Group #1 and Control Group #1 are included. They aren't needed to estimate a "before" measure for Experimental Group #2 and Control Group #2, because regardless of what this measurement is, it cancels in the basic calculation of the effect of the experimental variable:

$$[O_5 - \tfrac{1}{2}(O_1 + O_3)] - [O_6 - \tfrac{1}{2}(O_1 + O_3)] = O_5 - O_6$$

The before measurements are helpful if we wish to study individual cases of change, but if the sole interest is in estimating the impact of the experimental variable, as is often the case, this estimate can be provided by studying the last two groups of the four-group six-study design in an after-only with control group design:

$$
\begin{aligned}
\text{EG}: \quad &(R) \quad X \quad O_5 \\
\text{CG}: \quad &(R) \qquad\;\; O_6
\end{aligned}
$$

The observations have been subscripted with a 5 and 6 to indicate that these groups have not been pre-tested in the four-group six-study design. In the "Know Your Credit Union" brochure example, the researcher would again begin by selecting a random sample of employees. One-half would be randomly assigned to the experimental group, and the other half would form the control group. Neither group would be premeasured, and the brochure would be mailed to all those in the experimental group. After some appropriate time lapse, both groups would be measured for their knowledge, and the estimated effect of the brochure would be provided by the difference $O_5 - O_6$.

Many extraneous sources of error are eliminated even in this fairly simply designed experiment. The main extraneous factors are assumed to affect both groups, so their influence is eliminated by calculating the difference between O_5 and O_6. No interactive testing effect occurs since no pre-test has taken place. The experimental test units should behave much like the larger population of employees, in that some might read the brochure carefully, some might read it casually, and some might simply throw it away without reading it. This is as it should be, so the results can be generalized to the population of employees. For all these reasons, this design is frequently used in marketing research. With only two groups and two measures, it offers sample-size, cost, and time advantages.

There are two very important caveats, though, with respect to this design. First, it is sensitive to problems of selection bias. The prior equality of the groups is assumed because of the random assignment of test units to groups. No pre-measure is made, so this assumption cannot be checked. Further, the design is sensitive to experimental mortality. There is no way of determining whether those who refuse to cooperate or who drop out of the experimental group are similar to those dropping out of the control group.

Quasi-Experimental Designs

We have just seen that the true experimental design is distinguished by the control it imposes in the research. The researcher is able to determine who will be exposed to the experimental stimulus, when the exposure will occur, who will be measured, and where that measurement will take place. In a **quasi-experimental design**, the investigator is not able to schedule the experimental stimuli, and perhaps more problematic is that the researcher isn't able to randomly assign test units to groups.

Time-Series Experiment

There are a number of quasi-experimental designs, though we discuss only the time-series experiment, a methodology well-suited to some types of routine marketing data.[8] The time-series experiment can be diagrammed as:

$$O_1 \quad O_2 \quad O_3 \quad O_4 \quad X \quad O_5 \quad O_6 \quad O_7 \quad O_8$$

This diagram indicates that a group of test units is observed over time, that an experimental stimulus is introduced, and that the test units are again observed

---

[8] See Donald T. Campbell and Julian Stanley, *Experimental and Quasi-Experimental Designs for Research*, Houghton Mifflin, 36–64. For a nice example, see Markus Christen and Miklos Sarvary, "Competitive Pricing of Information: A Longitudinal Experiment," *Journal of Marketing Research* 44 (1), 42–56. Also see Neeraj Arora and Ty Henderson, "Embedded Premium Promotion," *Marketing Science*, 26, 514–531; Fusun F. Gonul and Frenkel Ter Hofstede, "How to Compute Optimal Catalog Mailing Decisions," *Marketing Science*, 25 (1), 65–74; and Prokriti Mukherji, Shantanu Dutta, and Surendra Rajiv, "Estimating the Effects of Direct-to-Consumer Advertising for Prescription Drugs: A Natural Experiment," research in process. Also see Devon DelVecchio, Cheryl Burke Jarvis, Richard R. Klink, and Brian R. Dineen, "Leveraging Brand Equity to Attract Human Capital," *Marketing Letters*, 18 (3), 149–164.

for their reaction. A change in the previous pattern of observations is taken as the effect of the experimental stimulus.

The time-series experiment requires that researchers have repeated access to the same test units. Further, though researchers cannot schedule the exposure of the experimental stimulus, they can control when the respondents are surveyed. Panel data are a popular sort of marketing research time-series experiment.

The goal of establishing that the observed effect is due to the experimental variable requires that we eliminate other plausible hypotheses for the occurrence of the phenomenon. Consider some of the possible patterns of responses that may result, as illustrated in Figure 6.2.

Note first of all that the *pattern* of responses, rather than any single observation, is key in interpreting the data from a time-series experiment. Consider the impact of a package change, X, on the firm's market share. On the basis of the plot of the data points in Figure 6.2, it would seem logical to conclude that the package change:

1. Exerted a positive impact in situation A (it raised the firm's market share)
2. Had a positive impact in situation B (it halted a decline in market share)
3. Had no long-run impact in situation C (sales in Period 5 seem to be borrowed from sales in Periods 6 and 7)
4. Had no impact in situation D (the firm's market share growth remained steady)
5. Had no impact in situation E (the observed fluctuation after the introduction of the experimental variable is no greater than what was previously observed)

And, naturally, we would be interested in testing the statistical significance of these changes.

In the time-series experiment, maturation can be partially ruled out as causing the difference in O_5 and O_4 because it is unlikely that it would operate only

FIGURE 6.2   Some Possible Outcomes in a Time-Series Experiment when Introducing an Experimental Variable X

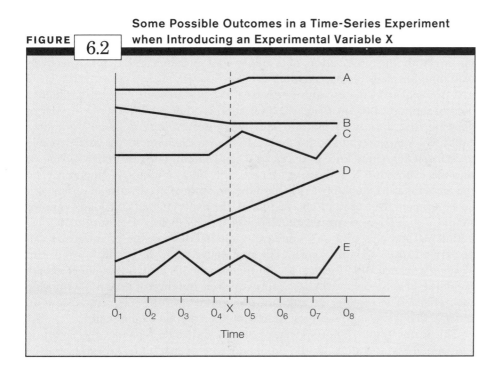

in this one instance. Rather, it would logically have an effect on a number of other observations. Instrument variation, statistical regression, and the main testing effect would be similarly avoided. Selection bias can be reduced by the random selection of test units. Experimental mortality can be controlled by paying some premium to maintain cooperation.

The failure to control for history is the critical weakness of the time-series experiment. Despite this, a carefully executed time-series experiment can provide some useful insight. If the careful examination of consumer panel data before, during, and after introducing the experimental variable fails to turn up any unusual competitive reaction, and if researchers also record other environmental changes as they occur, the researchers are in a position to make a valid assessment of the effect of the experimental stimulus. Of course, researchers can never be as sure that the impact of history has been ruled out entirely in a quasi-experimental design as they can in a true experimental design. However, a repeatable stimulus, such as a cents-off coupon program, allows greater certainty, because the history wouldn't be the same each time.

Experimental versus Nonexperimental Designs

By now you should appreciate that exploratory and descriptive designs are not particularly useful in establishing the existence of causal relationships. They don't provide the control necessary to infer that a causal relationship does indeed exist. Exploratory studies are less of a problem in this regard, since they are rarely used to make causal statements. Unfortunately, the same cannot be said about descriptive studies. Frequently, the evidence of a cross-sectional survey is used to argue that X caused Y or the evidence from some time-series data is analyzed using, say, regression analysis to establish X as causing Y.

The error in such logic can be appreciated by dissecting the typical descriptive study: A random sample of respondents is selected. The respondents are measured with respect to some response variable Y. Next, they are queried about the hypothesized causal factor X. If it is found that those who possess X also possess Y and those who lack X also lack Y, the truth of the assertion that "X causes Y" is established. The research is *ex post facto,* because the researcher is starting with the observation of a dependent variable and is retrospectively searching for plausible explanations.

Internal validity.
Need random assignment
External validity.
Need random sampling

A problem arises in descriptive studies with respect to all three types of evidence used to support causality. *Concomitant* variation is observed, but there is no way of knowing that those who did and did not possess Y were at some prior time equivalent with respect to both Y and X. In the experiment, the researcher is able to establish this equivalence by the random assignment. The researcher also knows who was exposed to X and doesn't have to rely on a respondent's memory. The researcher is also better able to establish the *time order* of occurrence of variables in an experiment. Due to random assignment, the experimental and control groups should not differ in terms of the response variable before exposure to the experimental stimulus, and with some experimental designs, the pre-measures can be verified to be roughly similar. The descriptive study affords little control in *eliminating other possible explanations.* All the extraneous factors that affect experimental results also operate in descriptive research, but there is no way of removing their effects. The result is the awkward position of asserting it is "this X" and no other X that is causing Y—an assertion resting on a great deal of faith.

This is not to deny the important role descriptive designs play in marketing research. They are, after all, the dominant type of marketing research. But be aware of the dangers of using descriptive designs to establish causal linkages between variables.

Experimentation in Marketing Research

The growth of experiments in marketing has been steady over the past 40 years. One of the most important growth areas has been in market testing, or test marketing. Some marketers make a distinction between the terms, but the essential feature of the **market test** is that it is an experiment, done in a small section of the marketplace, with the goal of predicting the sales results of some proposed marketing action.[9] Test markets aren't infallible, but they are helpful. For example, it's better to find out about possible problems in a test market than after a product is introduced nationally. Test marketing is often done for new products, but it is also used to examine the sales impact of almost every element of marketing. Consider these examples:

- To compete with Quiznos' heated sub sandwiches, Togo's launched tests in 45 Chicago and New York locations, including testing the effectiveness of the small toasters, given the typically constrained Togo's retail square footage.[10]

- Kodak tested photo-developing kiosks in Atlanta, found positive results, and soon began plans for 500 such photo-developing stations.[11]

- Pfizer has used Canada as a test for the U.S. (sorry northern neighbor!) to test Viagra ads, Listerine Pocket Paks, and medicated freezer pops for children.[12]

Problems of Experimentation

Marketing experiments have many strengths, particularly in determining the precise effect of a marketing intervention. Still, no methodology is perfect. Three of the more critical problems with test marketing are cost, time, and control.

A major consideration in test marketing has always been cost. There are the normal research costs (designing the data-collection instruments, wages paid to the data-collection field staff, etc.). Moreover, if the test market is to reflect the marketing strategy intended for rollout, the test also includes marketing costs (advertising, personal selling, etc.). With new-product introductions, there are also the costs associated with producing the merchandise. To produce the product on a small scale is typically inefficient. Yet to gear up immediately for large-scale production can be wasteful if the test market indicates that the product is a failure.

The time required for an adequate test market can be substantial. The accuracy of a test market increases with its duration; experiments conducted over short periods do not allow for the cumulative effect of the marketing actions. Consequently, a year is often recommended as a minimum period before any kind of go/no-go decision is made, to account for seasonal sales variations and repeat-purchasing behavior. And yet, let's face it: Time is of the essence in today's fast-paced global environment, where competitive reaction can be so swift that many firms have committed themselves to speeding product introductions worldwide.

[9] See "Some Methodological Issues in Product Testing," *Research on Research*, p.41 (synovate.com).
[10] Lori Lohmeyer, "Sub Shops Launch Toasted Sandwich in Bid to Warm Up Sales," *Nation's Restaurant News* 37, 4,115.
[11] Todd Wasserman, "Moms in Kodak's Focus," *Brandweek* 44, 10.
[12] Jim McElgunn, "The Ultimate Test Market," *Marketing Magazine* 108, 30.

Lastly, the problems associated with control manifest themselves in several ways. In the experiment itself, the issues include choice of specific test markets, product distribution in those markets, soliciting cooperation from wholesalers and retailers, etc. Often, simply because the product is being test-marketed, it receives more attention in-house than it would as a regular product on a national scale, e.g., in the test market, store shelves may be better stocked, the sales force more diligent, and the advertising more prominent than would normally be the case.

Control problems are associated with competitive reaction too. The test-marketing firm can control its own marketing actions, but competitors can, and do, sabotage experiments by cutting the prices of their own products, gobbling up quantities of the test marketer's product (thereby creating false results for the test marketer), etc.

Types of Test Markets

Figure 6.3 shows some of the most commonly used **standard test markets**.[13] A standard test market is one in which companies sell the product through their normal distribution channels. The results are typically monitored by a standard distribution service (discussed in the next chapter). Research Realities 6.3 walks you through other logical questions for choosing markets to compare.

In an **electronic test market**, a panel of households in the test market area is recruited, and we get their demographic information. People in these house-

Types of *test markets*:

- Standard
- Electronic
- Simulated

FIGURE 6.3   Standard Test Markets

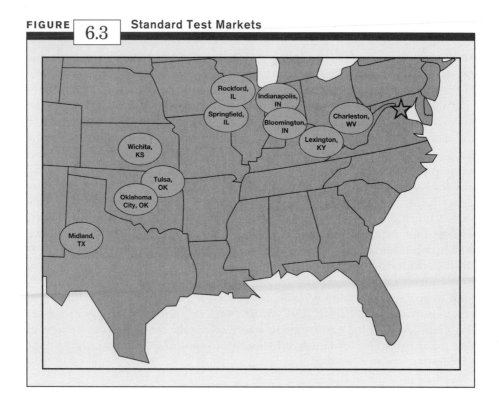

---

[13] These locations are generally "Middle America," chosen to be representative.

RESEARCH   REALITIES

6.3 Factors to Consider when Choosing Test Cities

You don't have to use only the tried-and-true test markets, known for being "average America." Other cities could be used, providing knowledge of those marketplaces is available and sensible for the particular test. Figure A shows data that were used to argue that Portland has managed its metropolitan growth more effectively than Atlanta has, as indicated by property taxes, and commuting factors like number of miles and time spent in the commute, as well as environmentally related effects like measures of ozone and energy consumption. Depending on the product category or service sector you were studying, you might say the cities were similar (e.g., both urban areas are enjoying strong growth rates, job growths, incomes) so one market could serve as a control for the other. Or you could argue the cities were so different (e.g., the commute) that comparing data on them would be apples-to-oranges; that is, you wouldn't know whether differences in sales were due to the different products you've made available to those markets' consumers, or to the natural differences among those markets.

You don't have to worry only about matching cities. If you were conducting advertising tests where the experiment involved showing one version of the ad during one television show and another version of the ad during another time slot or show, you better be confident the time slots or shows are comparable, to defend your conclusion that a difference in the memorability of the ads was due to the ads themselves, rather than some by-product of one show being more popular, or a better context in which to show one of the versions of the ads.

Figure B gives you a sense of the media coverage for some of the highest rated shows, by category of music or acting awards shows, and the top sports programming.

Could you compare the Grammys to the Golden Globes—even with similar ratings, might those audiences differ? Could you compare performances of ads run during the AFC and NFC championships?

Ad testing requires ratings information!

Increases for 2 Cities during Last Decade

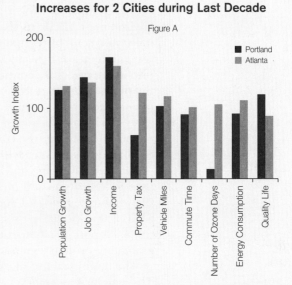

Source: From American Demographics, *January 2001. Copyright 2001 Crain Communications Inc.*

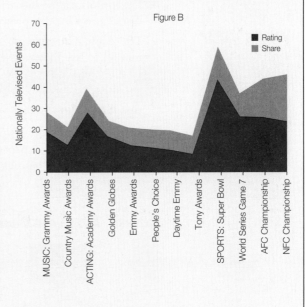

Source: Nielsen Media Research.

holds are given ID cards, which they show when checking out at grocery stores. Everything they purchase is automatically recorded and associated with the household through scanners found in all supermarkets in the area. Suppliers of these services also monitor each household's television-viewing behavior. They then correlate exposure to commercials with purchase behavior, which in turn allows testing of the consumer acceptance of a new or modified product and other marketing elements.

A **simulated test market** (STM) is frequently used as a prelude to a full-scale market test. STMs operate like this: Consumers are interviewed in shopping malls, exposed to the new product, and asked to rate its features. They are then shown commercials for it and for competitors' products. In a simulated store environment, they are given the opportunity to buy the product using seed money or cents-off coupons to make the purchase. Those not purchasing the test product are typically given free samples. After a usage period, follow-up phone interviews are conducted with the participants to assess their reactions to the product and their repeat-purchase intentions. All the information is fed into a computer model, which has equations for the repeat purchase and market share likely to be achieved by the test model. The key to the simulation is the equations built into the computer model. Validation studies indicate that most STM models can come within ±3% of actual sales in two-thirds of the cases.[14]

A prime advantage of STMs is the protection from competitors. They can be used to assess trial- and repeat-purchasing behavior. They're faster and cheaper than full-scale tests and good for spotting weak products. The Achilles' heel of STMs is that given their simulated nature, they don't provide information about trade support or competitive reaction. Thus, they're often better suited for evaluating product extensions than for new-to-the-world products.

The traditional test market provides a more natural environment than STMs. The standard test market plays a more vital role when the following situations apply:

1. It is important for the firm to test its ability to actually sell to the trade and get distribution for the product.

2. The capital investment is substantial, and the firm needs a prolonged test market to accurately assess its capital needs or its technical ability to manufacture the product.

3. The firm is entering new territory and needs to build its experience base so that it can play for real, but it wants to learn how to do so on a limited scale.

In the choice among types of test market, it's useful to look at the alternatives as stages in a sequential process, with STMs preceding test markets (see Figure 6.4). See Research Realities 6.4 for more.

FIGURE 6.4   A Perspective on Various Types of Test Markets

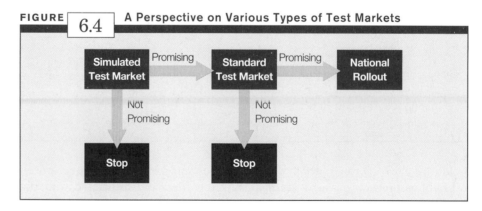

[14] Kevin J. Clancy, Peter Krieg, and Marianne Wolf, *Market New Products Successfully: Using Simulated Test Market Technology* (Lexington Books, 2005).

RESEARCH   REALITIES

6.4 Experiments in Marketing Research

- Plaxo used marketing research to identify product features that customers cared about and were more likely to talk about, and in doing so, supported their viral campaign to spur growth of adoption and sales and diffusion in the marketplace.

- A longitudinal study on physician prescription rates for different types and brands of antidepressants was conducted to assess the effectiveness of direct-to-consumer (DTC) advertising. Over the three-year period, researchers found that while DTC spending didn't influence drug choice for depression, it did affect their use for the treatment of anxiety.

- An experiment was run to measure the effectiveness of different fund-raising appeals. The results showed one approach was more appealing than the others,

and it was used in the subsequent direct mail marketing program.

- An insurance company used a quasi-experiment to assess the effectiveness of a key account management approach on customer profitability.

- An IT vendor ran a field experiment to study the effectiveness of their account managers on employee and customer satisfaction.

Source: Kirthi Kalyanam, Shelby McIntyre, and J. Todd Masonis, "Adaptive Experimentation in Interactive Marketing: The Case of Viral Marketing at Plaxo," Journal of Interactive Marketing, *21 (3), 72–85; Julie M. Donohue and Ernst R. Berndt, "Being Direct,"* Marketing Health Services, *30–36, marketingpower.com; Margaret Faulkner and Rachel Kennedy, "A New Tool for Pre-testing Direct Mail,"* International Journal of Market Research, *50 (4), 469–490; Lynette Ryals and Hugh Wilson, "Experimental Methods in Market Research,"* International Journal of Market Research, *47 (4), 347–366.*

Summary

The emphasis in this chapter was on the third basic type of research design—causal design. The notion of causality was reviewed, and, according to the scientific interpretation of the statement "X causes Y," it was found that (1) we could never prove that X caused Y, and (2) if the inference that it did was supported by the evidence, X was one factor that made the occurrence of Y more probable, but it did not make it certain.

Three types of evidence support the establishment of causal linkages. Concomitant variation implies that X and Y must vary together in the way predicted by the hypothesis. The time order of occurrence of variables suggests that X must precede Y. The elimination of other factors requires the analyst to design the investigation so that the results do not lend themselves to a number of conflicting interpretations.

Experiments provide the most convincing evidence of causal linkages. An experiment is a scientific study in which an investigator manipulates and controls one or more predictor variables and observes the response of a criterion variable. There are two general types of experiments: the laboratory experiment, in which an investigator creates an artificial situation for the manipulation of the predictor variables, and the field experiment, which allows these manipulations to take place in a natural setting. The greater control of a lab experiment allows more precise determination of the effect of the experimental stimulus, but there is a greater danger of generalizing the results because of its artificial nature.

In either type of experiment, we must be on guard against extraneous sources of error that may confound interpretation: history, maturation, testing (main and interactive), instrument variation, statistical regression, selection bias, and experimental mortality. True experimental designs are useful in minimizing the impact of these errors. They are distinguished from pre-experimental and quasi-experimental designs by the fact that the researcher decides who is to be exposed to the experimental stimulus and when the exposure is to occur.

The growth of experiments in marketing has been steady. The market test has become standard practice for some companies to establish the sales potential of new products, and increasingly to determine the effectiveness of contemplated changes of any elements of the marketing mix.

Questions

1. How does a simulated test market (STM) work? What are its main advantages and disadvantages compared to full market tests?
2. How is the effect of the experimental stimulus determined in a before–after with control group design? In a four-group six-study design? In an after-only with control group design?
3. How does an electronic test market work? What are its advantages compared to a traditional test market?
4. What are extraneous variables that can affect the outcome of a research investigation?
5. What is a test market? For what kinds of investigations can test markets be used? What are the problems associated with test markets?
6. What are the main ways of establishing the prior equality of groups?
7. How would you explain marketing's infrequent use of experimental research before 1960 and its steadily increasing use since then?
8. What is the difference between internal and external validity?
9. Compare descriptive research and true experimental design with respect to the ability of each to control or allow for extraneous factors.
10. What is the distinction between a laboratory experiment and a field experiment?
11. What is the nature of the time-series experiment? How does the time-series experiment differ from the pre-experimental, one-group pre-test–post-test design? What is the importance of this difference?
12. What is an experiment?
13. When would one want to employ a before–after with control group design or a four-group six-study design in lieu of an after-only with control group design, and vice versa?
14. What types of evidence can be employed to support an inference of causality?
15. When would one want to employ a four-group six-study design instead of a before–after with control group design, and vice versa?
16. How do the scientific notions and commonsense notions of causality differ?
17. How does the true experimental, after-only with control group design differ from the pre-experimental, static-group comparison research design?

Applications and Problems

1. The product development team at Flameglo Log Company has been working on several modifications of Flameglo's highly successful line of fireplace logs. The most promising development is a new log that burns in several different colors. Based on favorable feedback from a few employees who have tested the product in their homes, management feels that the new log has the potential to become a major seller.

   At a recent strategy meeting, the vice president of marketing suggested a test-marketing program before committing to introduction of the new log. He pointed out that a test market would be a good way to evaluate the effectiveness of two alternative advertising and promotional campaigns that have been proposed by Flameglo's ad agency. He feels that effectiveness should be evaluated in terms of the trial- and repeat-purchasing behavior engendered by each program. He also wants to gauge Flameglo's current distributors' acceptance of the new product.

   The CEO of Flameglo, however, is not very enthusiastic about the idea of test marketing. She is concerned that Flameglo's competitors could easily duplicate the new log, that the company is nearing the limit of its budgeted costs for developing the new log, and that the seasonal nature of log sales makes it imperative to reach a "go/no-go" decision on the new log by early April, only four months away.

   The director of marketing research stated that she felt a test-marketing plan could be devised that would satisfy both the vice president of marketing and the CEO. She was instructed to submit a preliminary proposal at the next strategy meeting.
   a. What information should be obtained from the test market in order to satisfy the vice president of marketing?
   b. Under what constraints must the test-marketing plan operate in order to satisfy the CEO?
   c. Given your answers to the questions above, what method of test marketing should the director recommend? Why?
2. The research department of the company in Question 3 investigated the change in repeat-purchase frequency for each store location. Using criteria

supplied by management, the department categorized repeat-purchase frequency changes as increased substantially, increased marginally, or no increase. Consider the following table, in which 624 store locations have been classified as old or gourmet:

Repeat-Purchase Frequency

In-Store Location	Increased Substantially	Increased Marginally	No Increase	Total
Gourmet	180	72	12	264
Old	120	96	144	360

a. Does this table provide evidence of concomitant variation? Justify your answer.

b. What conclusions can be drawn about the relationship between X and Y on the basis of the preceding table?

3. Milbar Corporation, a specialty hand-tool company located in Chagrin Falls, Ohio, was considering introducing a new style of snap ring pliers. Before it went ahead with production of the pliers, Jack Bares, CEO, decided that the company should test the effectiveness of its sales promotion campaign. Jack chose four disparate cities in which to run the experiment. In two of the randomly chosen cities, Binghamton, New York, and Manderville, Louisiana, Milbar first questioned mechanics and parts people on their attitudes toward snap ring pliers. Next, Milbar ran the new pliers sales promotion campaign in the randomly chosen Binghamton and Medford, Oregon. Then Milbar went back to all four cities—Binghamton, Manderville, Medford, and Omaha, Nebraska—and measured mechanics' and parts people's attitudes toward the new and old snap ring pliers.

4. Consider the following statement: "The increase in repeat-purchase frequency is due to retailers' decisions to stock our product in the gourmet food section of supermarkets during the last nine months. Repeat purchases from the gourmet section are up as much as 50% from our previous store location." Identify the causal factor X and the effect factor Y in the preceding statement.

5. A leading manufacturer of frozen food products decided to test the effectiveness of an in-store display. Four large supermarkets, located near the company's main office, were selected for the experiment. The display was set up in two of the stores, and sales were monitored for a period of two weeks. The sales of the other two stores were also recorded, but no displays were used. Sales volume for the frozen food products increased 2% more in the stores

that used the in-store displays than in the stores that did not use the displays.

6. To gather support for his conclusion, Charlie asked the research department of Hitech to investigate the sales of each of the company's salespeople. Using criteria supplied by management, the department categorized territory sales changes as increased substantially, increased marginally, or no increase. Consider the following table, in which 260 sales personnel have been classified as old or new:

Territory Sales Change

Salesperson Assigned	Increased Substantially	Increased Marginally	No Increase	Total
New	75	30	5	110
Old	50	40	60	150

a. Does this table provide evidence of concomitant variation? Justify your answer.

b. What conclusions can be drawn about the relationship between X and Y on the basis of the table?

7. Six months later, the research department in the previous question investigated the situation once again. However, a new variable was considered in the analysis—namely, the size of the package. More specifically, it considered if repeat-purchase frequency was affected depending on whether the package was a 14- or 18-ounce size. The following table summarizes the research department's findings:

14-ounce Package

Salesperson Assigned	Increased Substantially	Increased Marginally	No Increase	Total
New	84	24	–	108
Old	65	19	–	84

18-ounce Package

Salesperson Assigned	Increased Substantially	Increased Marginally	No Increase	Total
New	6	12	6	24
Old	24	48	24	96

a. If the size of package is ignored, does this table provide evidence of concomitant variation between a change in repeat purchases and in-store location? Justify your answer.

b. If the size of package is considered, does the table provide evidence of concomitant variation between repeat purchases and in-store location? Justify your answer.

Several experimental designs are described in the questions that follow. For each design, complete the following tasks:

a. Determine what type of design is being used. Explain.

b. Diagrammatically represent the design.

c. Discuss the threats to internal and external validity for the design.

8. Charlie Sharp is the national sales manager of Hitech Inc. Charlie recently hypothesized that "Hitech's increase in sales is due to the new sales personnel that we recruited from the vocational school over the last several years. Sales of the new salespeople are up substantially, whereas sales for longer-term salespeople have not increased." Identify the causal factor X and the effect factor Y in the preceding statement.

9. A new manufacturer of women's cosmetics was planning to retail the firm's products through mail order. The firm's management was considering the use of direct-mail advertisements to stimulate sales of their products. Prior to committing themselves to advertising through direct mail, management conducted an experiment. A random sample of 1,000 consumers was selected from Memphis, Tennessee. The sample was divided into two groups, with each subject being randomly assigned to one of the two groups. Direct-mail advertisements were sent twice over a period of one month to respondents of one of the groups. Two weeks later, respondents of both groups were mailed the company's catalog of cosmetics. Sales to each group were monitored.

CASES

CASE 2.1
Riverside County Humane Society (A)

The demands on the Riverside County Humane Society (RCHS) had increased dramatically over the past several years, while the tax dollars the society received to provide services had remained relatively unchanged. In an effort to halt further decline in the quality of its services and to provide better care for the pets at the center, the membership committee of the board of directors began making plans for a member/contributor drive. The organized drive was to be the first of its kind for the local chapter, and the committee members wanted it to be as productive as possible.

As the plans began to evolve, the committee realized that the organization had only scattered bits and pieces of information about its current members. It did have a list of members and contributors for the last five years that had been compiled by the RCHS staff. In addition, it had access to the results of a survey done by a staff member several years earlier that focused on member usage of shelter facilities and their opinions of shelter services and programs. However, the organization had only sparse knowledge of the profile of its typical member and contributor, why they belonged or contributed, how long they had been associated with the Humane Society, how the services of the Humane Society could be improved, and so on. The committee members believed information on these issues was important to the conduct of a successful membership drive, and thus they commissioned some research to secure it.

One of the first things the researchers did was to contact other Humane Society chapters to determine what kinds of research they had done, particularly with respect to identifying the characteristics of their members. The researchers also interviewed key Riverside County Humane Society staff members and several board members for their thoughts and ideas regarding RCHS membership. The researchers held a focus group among members of the membership committee. These research activities produced the following general ideas about membership and contributions:

1. The people who use the center's facilities are not necessarily the same people who would become members. Members love their own pets, take good care of them, and want other animals to be treated humanely.

2. Most contributors do not care about being a "member" because membership does not confer any rights or privileges, except a newsletter. Members are very different from contributors.

3. The female member of the household is probably making the decision regarding membership or contribution to the RCHS.

4. The majority of members in the RCHS are female and are at least 35 years old.

5. Many retired or elderly people contribute to or are members of the RCHS.

6. The average contribution is about $15 to $25.

7. People in the community have a generally positive perception of the RCHS.

8. An emotional appeal in a membership drive is likely to have the best chance for success.

9. Most people have heard about the RCHS primarily through education programs conducted by the society.

10. The greatest benefit associated with membership is the warm feeling that people get from belonging to the RCHS.

The research firm planned to select a sample of names from the current lists of members and contributors and to send them mail questionnaires to explore these ideas further.

QUESTIONS
1. What kind of research design is being used?
2. Is it a good choice?
3. Design a questionnaire that addresses the issues raised and that also gathers helpful demographic information on members and contributors.

CASE 2.2
HotStuff Computer Software (A)[1]

Simpson, Edwards and Associates has had considerable success with a computer software package that it designed to enable government agencies to manage their database systems. The firm is currently developing

[1] The contributions of Jacqueline C. Hitchon to the development of this case are gratefully acknowledged.

a second product, a more specialized version of its first endeavor. Called HotStuff, its latest computer software concept targets the firefighting industry. Researchers at Simpson, Edwards and Associates have a hunch that fire departments are a prime market for database software because of their extensive information-handling responsibilities—equipment inventories, building layouts, hazardous materials data, budget records, personnel files, and so on.

At this embryonic stage in the new product's development, the company is following the same game plan that helped it launch its previous success. Responsibilities have been broadly divided: Jean Edwards has assumed command of the production side and Craig Simpson has taken charge of marketing and promotion. Craig's first move was to reassemble the original team of staff members who had researched the market for government agency software. At their first orientation meeting, he submitted the following objectives for their deliberation:

1. Determine market potential.
2. Identify important product attributes.
3. Develop an effective promotional strategy.
4. Identify competitors in the market.

By the close of discussion, the group had decided that its first task would be exploratory research. Specifically, it decided to conduct experience surveys involving local fire chiefs, informal telephone interviews with state and national fire officials, and a literature search. Based on findings from the exploratory research effort, the group hoped to pursue descriptive research to fulfill the four objectives.

Exploratory Research

The first finding to emerge from the exploratory research affected the target market for HotStuff. Fire departments are made up of two broad categories: municipal departments with full staffs of paid firefighters, and volunteer departments consisting of a paid chief and remaining members, who may or may not be paid firefighters. The team quickly discovered that the two kinds of departments differ in two important ways. First, from the point of view of funding, municipal departments receive the majority of their funds from taxes, so the money is tightly controlled and tends to be earmarked for specific uses. Volunteer fire departments, on the other hand, rely heavily on donors and special events as sources of income, to the extent that

fund-raising may account for more than 50% of their total receipts. Since money obtained through fund-raising is not technically part of the budget, it is not subject to budgetary controls *per se*.

The second key difference between municipal and volunteer departments concerned purchasing procedures. Local municipal departments tended to route all purchases through a central purchasing agent, who would then apply for approval from the data-processing center at city hall before acquiring computer hardware and software. Fire chiefs interviewed in volunteer departments, however, reported that they had sole authority to purchase any hardware or software required.

Telephone calls to out-of-state fire officials indicated that these differences were consistent across the nation. As a result, Simpson, Edwards and Associates decided to restrict its target market to volunteer fire departments.

A second finding uncovered in the exploratory research concerned the extent to which the needs of the target market were already being met. Inquiries within the state revealed that only a few volunteer departments had already purchased computers. Further, those with computers had not possessed them for long and were still in the process of automating manual databases. The general feeling among fire officials was that computerization would be an inevitable development in the industry in the near future. Indeed, four specialized software packages were already being advertised in fire prevention journals: Chief's Helper, Fire Organizer, Spread Systems, and JLT Software. Spread Systems differed from the others in that it consisted of separate programs, each of which sold individually and covered a particular information type, such as inventory records or hazardous materials. The strategy followed by Spread Systems allowed fire departments to reduce their expenditure on software because they could select only those programs that they needed. It was conjectured at Simpson, Edwards and Associates that specific programs for specific functions may help overcome initial consumer caution toward spending several thousand dollars for computer software, because the expenditure would not be made all at one time. It was also believed that some makers of generic software packages that perform spreadsheet or database management analysis should be included in the list of competitors, although users of generic software packages needed some proficiency with computers to tailor these basic packages to their specific applications.

A third finding of interest from the exploratory research was that the term volunteer was offensive to departments officially classified as volunteer because they thought that it implied a lack of professionalism. In fact, their staffs were as well trained as members of municipal departments. This sentiment led the researchers to conclude that the label volunteer should not be used in the future promotion of HotStuff.

Based on what it learned from the exploratory research, Simpson, Edwards and Associates decided to conduct a more formal investigation to address the following objectives:

1. Determine the market potential for its new software by
   a. establishing the incidence of computer use and planned computer purchases in volunteer fire departments, and
   b. obtaining more information about volunteer fire departments' funding and authority structures.

2. Identify important product attributes—that is, the types of information that need to be handled by volunteer fire departments and that therefore need to be incorporated into the software.

3. Secure ideas for promotional strategy by
   a. determining which fire publications are read by the target market, and
   b. determining which association conventions are most well attended by the target market.

4. Identify competitors in the market by
   a. establishing which brands of software are currently used in volunteer fire departments, and
   b. establishing how satisfactory existing software packages are perceived to be.

Study Design

Simpson, Edwards and Associates' researchers believed that the best way to address these objectives was through a national survey of volunteer fire departments. They decided on a structured-disguised telephone survey using team members as interviewers. The state fire marshal informed the group that most volunteer fire departments were located in communities with populations under 25,000. Consequently, it was decided to sample towns with populations under 25,000 that were situated within a 20-mile radius of cities of at least 100,000 people. Volunteer fire departments within those towns could then be contacted by

telephone by means of directory assistance. Two large cities were randomly selected from each state in the United States, excluding Alaska and Hawaii, and then a town located near each city was randomly selected. An atlas and the most recent Current Population Reports were used to identify cities and towns of the right specification.

A questionnaire was devised and pre-tested twice. The first pre-test was conducted through personal interviews and was meant to test the questionnaire; the second pre-test was performed by telephone and was meant to test the mode of administration.

In each case, inquiries were directed to the fire chiefs as representatives of the departments. The actual survey was conducted between April 13 and April 24. It would have taken less time to administer the survey had there not been a national fire convention the week that the phone survey began. Because the national fire convention coincided with Easter week, many fire chiefs were not at their departments; because their children were not in school, they attended the convention with their families. Nonetheless, the interviewer team was able to increase the response rate to 85% by numerous callbacks.

QUESTIONS

1. Evaluate Simpson, Edwards and Associates' decision to focus on volunteer fire departments as its target market, based on the exploratory research.

2. Do you think the exploratory research was productive in this case? Could further useful insights have been gained without significantly greater expenditure of resources? If so, what and how?

3. Comment on the differences among the four objectives as originally formulated and as reformulated after exploratory research.

4. Was the choice of phone interviews a good one?

CASE 2.3
Advertising Agency's Databank

Anna, the EVP of Client Interactions at the Burbank, CA, branch of a large New York advertising agency, is excited that her branch just landed a new client (in the hospitality industry; i.e., hotels). She's got her team assembled to do some planning. They want to do a great first project for the hotelier, to come out strong, so to speak. Anna and her team are contemplating three approaches, trying to decide how to move forward.

- In the first approach, Anna and her team had advocated exploratory research to the hotel chain. They had argued that they didn't know enough about the hotel sector, nor consumers' perceptions of this particular hotel brand, so it would not be useful to go out and execute some large-scale survey.

- The 2nd and 3rd proposals had come from the client. For the 2nd, the hotel CEO had pointed out that one of the reasons they brought their account to Anna's particular ad agency was the ad agency's extensive history of testing ads, and the database they maintain of which ads test well and which ads go on to induce greatest sales. The hotel CEO wants the ad agency to show him data that their ads will bring in a lot of business.

- The 3rd proposal was also recommended by the CEO, who said he was aware of a friend whose CPG firm had used this ad agency for a test market to really get a clear answer to the ROI question of "Was my advertising dollar worth it?"

QUESTIONS

1. What are the trade-offs among the research designs being proposed? What information can each technique obtain that the others cannot?

2. Imagine role-playing one of Anna's team members and defending one of the three proposals. What strengths does your approach offer? What shortcomings must you acknowledge? What action could be taken as a result of obtaining the information in the form you seek it?

CASE 2.4
Bakhill Foods

Michelle Gill, the marketing manager for Bakhill Foods, was discussing the future advertising strategy for Bakhill Coffee with the firm's advertising agency when the discussion turned to magazine ads and the copy for those ads.

Gill had recently been to a conference on psychological perception. At that conference, it was pointed out that in spite of the old adage "you can't judge a book by its cover," we do just that in our interpersonal relations; an individual's initial perception of and reaction to another individual is affected by the physical attractiveness of the other person. Further, a fair summary statement of that research is "what is beautiful is good." The evidence cited at the conference supporting this proposition was impressive. What particularly impressed Gill, though, was that the positive attributes one associates with a physically attractive person do not depend on actual contact with that person. They arise when the judge is simply shown photographs of physically attractive and unattractive individuals but is otherwise unaware of the subjects' traits.

Gill thought that this knowledge could be used to advantage in the advertising copy for Bakhill Coffee. She proposed that the product be shown with a physically attractive female. The advertising agency countered with the argument that it would be better to employ physically unattractive people in the ads to make the ads more believable and effective by making them less "romantic," since coffee is not a romantic product. Further, the agency suggested it might be better to employ males in the ads rather than females. After considerable discussion, the advertising agency proposed and conducted the following research to answer two questions: Should physically attractive or unattractive individuals be used in the ads? Should male or female models be employed?

The Design

Four different advertisements were prepared. The copy was the same in each ad; only the person holding the coffee was changed. The four ads included an attractive male, an attractive female, an unattractive male, and an unattractive female. The attractiveness of each model was determined by having a convenience sample of subjects view photographs of 20 different models (10 men and 10 women) and rate each model on a seven-point scale where "1" was unattractive and "7" was attractive. The male and female models with the highest and the lowest mean scores were then selected as the stimulus persons for the experiment.

A color ad with each of the four models and the planned copy was then developed. A sample of subjects for the experiment was developed by random sampling from the New York City telephone book. Contacted subjects were asked to participate in a marketing research experiment. The subjects were paid for their participation, and they were also reimbursed for their travel to the agency's headquarters.

On their arrival at the ad agency, the 96 recruits who had agreed to participate were randomly assigned to one of the advertisements. The 48 men and 48 women were first divided randomly into 12 groups of four persons each. One member of each group was then assigned to one of the four ads. Each saw one, and only one, test ad. However, three other "filler" ads were also used to disguise the particular ad of interest. The "fillers" were the same for each participant. Each participant was introduced to the experiment with the following instructions:

> We are interested in obtaining your opinions concerning particular test advertisements. You will be shown four ads, one at a time, and after each showing, you will be asked several questions about your reaction to the ad and the particular product depicted in the ad. You should note that this is not a contest to see which ad is better, so please do not compare the four ads in making your evaluations. Each ad should be judged by itself, without reference to the other ads.

After answering any questions, the experimenter presented the first ad. When the respondent had read the advertisement, it was taken away, and the experimenter then handed the respondent a copy of the data-collection sheet (see the figure). After completion of this form, the experimenter presented the second ad, and the process was repeated. At no time were the participants allowed to look back at the advertisements once they had surrendered them to the researcher. To allow the respondents time to warm up to the task, the experimenter always placed the test ad third in the sequence of four.

The Scale

The items in the scale were chosen in order to tap all three components (cognitive, affective, and conative) of attitude. *A priori*, it was thought that the cognitive component would be measured by the terms believable, informative, and clear; that the affective or liking component would be effectively tapped by the terms

---

Figure 2.4.1   The Bakhill Survey

On each of the scales below, please check the space that you feel best describes the advertisement you just read

Interesting	⌷⌷⌷⌷⌷⌷⌷⌷⌷	Dull
Unappealing	⌷⌷⌷⌷⌷⌷⌷⌷⌷	Appealing
Unbelievable	⌷⌷⌷⌷⌷⌷⌷⌷⌷	Believable
Impressive	⌷⌷⌷⌷⌷⌷⌷⌷⌷	Unimpressive
Attractive	⌷⌷⌷⌷⌷⌷⌷⌷⌷	Unattractive
Uninformative	⌷⌷⌷⌷⌷⌷⌷⌷⌷	Informative
Clear	⌷⌷⌷⌷⌷⌷⌷⌷⌷	Confusing
Not eye-catching	⌷⌷⌷⌷⌷⌷⌷⌷⌷	Eye-catching

What is your overall reaction to this ad?

Unfavorable ⌷⌷⌷⌷⌷⌷⌷⌷⌷ Favorable

With regard to the product itself, how do you feel this product compares to similar products put out by other manufacturers?

Distinctive ⌷⌷⌷⌷⌷⌷⌷⌷⌷ Ordinary

Would you like to try this product?

No, Definitely Not ⌷⌷⌷⌷⌷⌷⌷⌷⌷ Yes, Definitely

Would you buy this product if you happened to see it in a store?

Yes, Definitely ⌷⌷⌷⌷⌷⌷⌷⌷⌷ No, Definitely Not

Would you actively seek out this product in a store in order to purchase it?

No, Definitely Not ⌷⌷⌷⌷⌷⌷⌷⌷⌷ Yes, Definitely

interesting, appealing, impressive, attractive, and eye-catching; and that the conative component would be captured by the three behavioral-intention items at the bottom of the questionnaire.

These *a priori* expectations were not strictly confirmed. A basic item analysis suggested that the term "interesting" was not related to any of the three components, and it was dropped from the analysis. Responses to the remaining items in each component were summed to produce a total score for each component. The analysis of these scale scores indicated the following:

1. The attractive male model produced the highest cognition scores for the ad among females and males.

2. The attractive male model produced the highest affective scores among female subjects, whereas the attractive female model produced the highest affective scores among males.

3. The attractive male model produced the highest conative scores toward the product for female subjects, whereas the unattractive male model produced the highest conative scores among male subjects.

On the basis of these results, the advertising agency suggested that the attractive male model be employed in the advertisement.

QUESTIONS

1. What kind of design is being employed in this investigation?

2. Evaluate the design.

CASE 2.5
Internet Advertising and Your Brain (A)

Imagine that your first job after business school is as the main marketing person for a fairly young company (started by the usual, a friend of a friend…). This company supports a travel Web site that specializes in "extreme sports" (e.g., skiing off cliffs, riding mountain bikes from great heights into large air bags, as well as the more "traditional" bungee jumping and skydiving). The target audience is the current profile of users, that is, men in their 20s (though the percentages of women and older thrill-seekers are growing). This group of customers is coincidentally also highly likely to be "wired"; thus, advertising online is expected to be effective at reaching this audience.

It is your responsibility as the Extreme Marketer to conduct tests to assess the ROI effectiveness of your company's online advertisements. At the moment, you've created two variations of a banner ad inviting browsers to your Web site and you're trying to choose between the two—which is most likely to attract these guys to click onto your site to learn more about your vacation packages and then possibly purchase one?

One of the ad banners your creative staff has developed is depicted in vivid colors, with captivating graphics that attempt to illustrate the possible thrills, such as a photo with a view of skiers at the top of a mountain shot from their delivery helicopter, or a photo of a skydiver in midair taken by a skydiving photographer. This ad format offers very little by way of informative content, such as details about the logistics of the trips, locations, lengths of stay, price, and so on. This ad is analogous to what is traditionally called the "beauty" shot in advertising production (a televised or still photo shot that shows the car or the jar of peanut butter without mentioning miles per gallon or caloric content). Thus, let's call this version of the possible banner ad "beauty."

Another banner ad has been prepared that appears somewhat less colorful and less pictorial in style, but which contains more detailed information about the extreme sports outings you are hoping to encourage the viewers to purchase. Given its greater information content, let's call this version of the banner ad "info."

You could just run a little study at this point. You could purchase banner ad space on your usual business relationship Web sites, randomly assigning half of those sites your beauty ad, and half your info ad. Then you would sit back and count over some duration (such as the next two weeks) the number of click-throughs you achieved with the one ad format versus the other, and conclude that the banner ad with the greater draw should be the one with which your firm proceeds.

However, you have done your homework and are aware of some secondary data from eye-tracking studies. These studies insert small cameras into PC screens that monitor where the PC user is looking. The results suggest that placing the banner ad on some locations on the screen may be more effective than others. For example, one theory is that the brain processes whatever is in the right of a person's visual field in the left half of the brain, and stimuli in the left part of a person's visual field is processed in the right-brain hemisphere. Research conducted by physiological psychologists suggests that the left brain processes analytical features and verbal descriptions most effectively, whereas the right brain processes pictures and holistic impressions better.

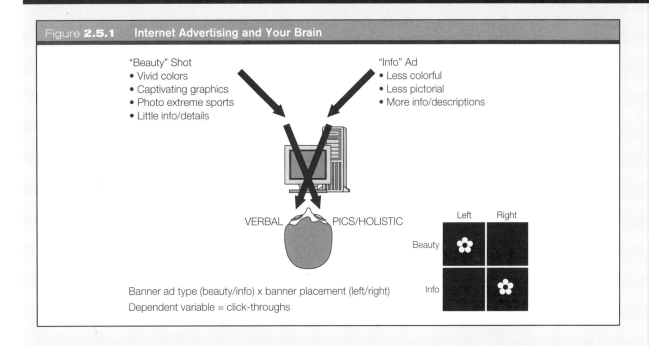

Figure **2.5.1**   Internet Advertising and Your Brain

"Beauty" Shot
• Vivid colors
• Captivating graphics
• Photo extreme sports
• Little info/details

"Info" Ad
• Less colorful
• Less pictorial
• More info/descriptions

VERBAL   PICS/HOLISTIC

Banner ad type (beauty/info) x banner placement (left/right)
Dependent variable = click-throughs

The info ad is verbal and offers many facts that readers could use to analyze and assess their interest, and the beauty ad is mostly graphics and leaves a holistic impression of the thrill-seeking vacation. Thus, you're beginning to think that perhaps the info ad would be best understood and most persuasive if it were processed by a viewer's left brain, which would dictate placing it on the right side of a Web page. In contrast, the beauty ad might be better understood and more persuasive if it were processed by a viewer's right brain, which means placing the banner ad on the left side of the viewer's screen. See Figure 2.5.1

So now the Internet advertising study you've created is somewhat more complicated. There are two factors, rather than just one: the advertising type (beauty or info) and the banner placement (left or right). Your expectations are that the ad is most likely to be effective (measured for the moment by the number of click-throughs it achieves) if the beauty ad is placed to the left or the info ad is placed to the right. However, you create all possible combinations because, after all, your hypothesis about "which ad should do better where" is in fact just a hypothesis. Thus, although each Web traveler sees only one ad, there are four ad variations: beauty on the left, beauty on the right, info on the left, and info on the right. You buy your ad space at your usual supplier Web sites, and you randomly assign one of the four ads to each of those locations. You

determine how long you will wait (for example, two weeks) before counting the results.

QUESTIONS

1. What kind of design has been described?

2. How might you improve upon what has been proposed?

3. What are the (null) hypotheses that will be tested using this design?

4. What method(s) will you use to analyze the resulting data that you obtain?

5. What strategic questions might supplement your approach to investigating these issues?

CASE 2.6
Customer Relationship Management

A long time ago, when a customer thought of a "relationship" in the marketplace, he or she might have thought of the neighborhood butcher, baker, tailor, grocer, newspaper boy, milkman, door-to-door encyclopedia salesman (ask your grandparents), etc. Now of course, the word is used a little more loosely to mean, a company has some data on your past purchases and knows some of your preferences, and it tries to use that information to figure out how to get you

Table **2.6.1** Customer Relationship Management (CRM) Data				
contact email	**on page**	**#past**	**bought now**	**$**
jack@v.com	10.15:08:15:34	0	0	0
bert@x.gov	10.12:14:35:22	3	0	0
elena@swim.com	09.01:22:23:09	1	1	49.99
chris@ggk.net	10.14:03:46:13	1	0	0
craig@ledg.com	08.04:10:13:19	1	0	0
nanc@wash.gov	09.29:13:09:54	0	0	0
marina@agon.com	10.14:09:04:44	2	1	12.99
more1@erb.edu	09.15:16:40:11	0	0	0
...				
Etc.				

to buy some of their other products. This knowledge is stored in huge databases, and marketing researchers and direct marketing managers try to "mine" the data to find nuggets of insight that they can implement to get you to buy more.

Table 2.6.1 shows the beginning of what an example database looks like. This particular data set is captured from Web visits, but catalog data look similar. You'd have access to the household/customer's electronic contact information, which is important, of course, because once you understand the data, you want to take advantage of the newfound marketing knowledge by sending more announcements, ads, pdf

catalogs, etc., to the people in your database who you think are the best prospects for more purchases.

The variables in this data set are as follows. First, the company has captured the time of the most recent Web visit (the units are "month.day:hour:minutes:second"), the total number of purchases this customer has made from the company's Web site in the past (since the beginning of the Web site database), and a 0/1 variable indicating whether they bought during this particular Web visit. Finally, the last variable is the information about the purchase, if they made one, and what the dollar value was of purchases they made this time.

Customer Relationship Management databases (and direct marketing databases) have several distinctive properties: (1) they have gobs of observations, in our example, tens of thousands of Web visiting potential customers; (2) yet they often have very few variables; and (3) even stranger, these databases are mostly full of zeroes (this property of these large databases would be more obvious if you saw the entire data set, but it is clearer in the table that follows). But this makes sense. Think about your own Web site visits—what proportion of them translate into sales for the company? Some do, but we "browse" a lot too, or we might look several times before actually buying, etc.

Table 2.6.2 gives a picture of the aggregated data. Use the information in the tables to answer the following.

Table **2.6.2** CRM Aggregated Data		
Most Recent Week of Visit	**Bought before**	**Bought this time**
T=0 (this week)	693	22
T-1 (last week)	772	31
T-2 (2 weeks ago)	501	62
T-3 (3 weeks ago)	596	109
T-4 (last month of previous)	7438	233

	Bought before?	
Of those who bought this time, value of purchase:	**Yes** ("Loyals")	**No** ("Acquisitions")
$5–$25	5	5
$26–$50	50	23
$51–$100	45	54
$101–$200	36	36
$200–$350	99	15
$351+	74	15

QUESTIONS

1. How many people are in this database? How is the database defined, i.e., what single criterion is required, that, once the customer does it, the customer is entered into the database?

2. Is there any way to test whether the 80:20 rule, where 20% of your customers are responsible for 80% of the purchases, applies here? If so, what's the answer? If not, what's an analogous question that might be answered?

3. Is there a marketing problem with the products being sold? If you were showing these numbers to your company's CEO, the CEO might say that the response rates look low, but how do you know what's low? Go online and search for statistics on direct marketing rates of conversion to make comparisons and evaluate these proportions.

4. What are some of the descriptive questions the marketing manager could pose that the marketing research could answer? What additional variables do you think the database manager should begin capturing? What new marketing questions would that information allow you to address?

5. What are some questions that a marketer might pose that could be answered if you designed an experiment? What would your experimental group be? Who would comprise your control group? What would you do to the experimental group? What response would you measure in the experimental and control groups to make comparisons?

6. In general, how could you use databases like these to think about segmentation studies? How could you study price sensitivities? How could you compute lifetime customer values? How might you pretest an ad? How would you select the segments you would target?

7. If you were to implement any of the marketing research procedures you've just proposed, how would you measure the effectiveness of the marketing change? How would you demonstrate the value of the marketing information in leading to that marketing decision?

CASE 2.7
Ethnography in Practice: The Case of ESPN Zone, Chicago[2]

ESPN—The Brand
ESPN was founded in 1979 and bought by Disney in 1996. It is the first network to own the rights to broadcast all major pro sports leagues (NFL, MLB, NBA, NHL) as well as college basketball and college football. ESPN is a highly successful brand: awareness is strong (97% among Americans, comparable to Coca-Cola); 87 million Americans rely on ESPN for their sports—the channel is #1 in local cable advertising sales ($500 million last year). ESPN Zone is essentially an elaborate sports bar brand extension.

Field Site Background and Project Mission
ESPN Zone, Chicago embodies recent retail trends toward enhancing brand image through the creation of flagship brand stores. The site inhabits a stretch of E. Ohio St. in Chicago's Magnificent Mile retail corridor, with neighboring stores for Sony, Nike, Disney, and Harley-Davidson. ESPN Zone, Chicago is a 35,000 square-foot retail complex that includes a 10,000 square-foot sports video and skill game arena, as well as a large sports screening room and two separate dining areas (see Figure 2.7.1).

The Research
The research team, consisting of two faculty and four doctoral students, set out to understand this retail servicescape, extracting themes emergent from consumers' experiences at ESPN Zone and meanings consumers associate with the ESPN brand. To illustrate the evolutionary nature of ethnography, the discussion proceeds chronologically. We divide the research into three, six-week stages and discuss critical aspects associated with each stage.

Stage 1 (Weeks 1–6)
First, permission to conduct the observations and interviews on-site was procured from the store's managers. This took several meetings with several managers requesting additional detail.

The research team then organized a plan for on-site coverage, for each day of the week, all times of the day. The team also convened biweekly strategy meetings to share field notes, compare observations and preliminary interpretations, and adjust field immersion and interviewing strategies as necessary.

Very early on it became clear that the highly brand-loyal ESPN customers considered the heart of ESPN Zone to be the "Screening Room." This room houses dozens of TV screens at various points in the room such that multiple screens are plainly visible no matter one's position in the room. The focal point of the room is an electronic monolith consisting of digital boards reminiscent of a Las Vegas sportsbook displaying

[2] The authors are grateful to Adam Duhachek for writing this case.

Figure **2.7.1**   Topographic Map of ESPN Zone, Chicago

sports statistics, and 12 medium-sized TV screens outlining an enormous 16' × 12' television.

In this room, we were struck by the ways in which gender was made salient. For instance, the best seats in the room, a row of leather recliners (called the "Throne Zone") equipped with stereo sound speakers, a tray table for food and drink, and remote controls to tune in particular games, were disproportionately occupied by men. Women in this room rarely sat in these highly visible chairs. In preliminary on-site interviews, we elicited widely contrasting views from men and women about their experiences "in the chair." Women referred to their experience in the chair as one marked by sensations of conspicuousness and discomfort, and isolation stemming from the difficulty in maintaining conversation with friends directly to their right or left in adjacent recliners.

Men, however, seemed to relish this sense of isolation. Men consistently remarked that their experience in the chair was sports nirvana, a transcendental couch potato episode of extreme comfort and luxury that allowed them to experience games without distraction.

Stage 2 (Weeks 7–12)

In this stage of the research, we began to delve deeper into the emerging themes. For example, consumer experiences throughout the Zone seem to be distinguished by varying levels of personal control and interactions with technology (see Table 2.7.1). To test or validate these thematic interpretations, the focus of the research tools turn to interviews, conducted to see if the resulting consumer verbatim responses would concur or refute our initial impressions.

Table **2.7.1**	Games and Arenas Catalogued by Perceptions of Control and Technology/Media	
	Low Technology	**High Technology / Interactive Media**
High Perceived Control:	*Example Games:* • Armchair Quarterback • 3-Point Basketball Game	*Example Games:* • Car racing
	Representative Activity: • Walking around Game Arena Floor • Watching others participate in games	*Representative Activity:* • Sitting in Throne Zone • Tacking across multiple sound and television feeds
	Consumer Sensations/Themes: • Competition • Skill • Athleticism • Confidence	*Consumer Sensations/Themes:* • Mind/Body Dissociation • Unaware of Passage of time
Low Perceived Control:	*Example Games:* • Skeet Shooting	*Example Games:* • 3-D Bowling • 3-D Boxing
	Representative Activity: • Standing in lower level bar when Screening Room is closed (for private parties or at capacity)	*Representative Activity:* • Standing in rear of Screening Room, reacting viscerally to large screen in front
	Consumer Sensations/Themes: • Frustration • Envy • Isolation	*Consumer Sensations/Themes:* • Passivity • Increased Effort • Embarrassment

At this point, we began to encounter an unanticipated methodological difficulty. The site often prohibited elaborate conversations with consumers because the atmosphere is noisy and the people we wished to interview were engaged in sports games as participants (we couldn't interrupt their video game) or as spectators (they were watching a game and we were distracting them). Thus, we ran print ads in the *Trib* to recruit informants for longer interviews off-site that allowed us to probe deeper in an interview session ($50 for two hours).

From these longer interviews, we began to converge on another critical Zone consumer theme, one related to consumers' sense of reality in different areas within ESPN Zone. For example, in the game arena, consumers formulated strong opinions about which games were "really real." The entertainment ranged from sophisticated virtual reality games (like the virtual reality boxing game where players actually don gloves to battle digitally created foes, or the skydiver game where virtual reality headsets cast the illusion that consumers were "really" falling toward a target landing site), to more traditional, "real" skill games such as the armchair quarterback game where consumers must throw "real" footballs through "real" cardboard cutout receivers to earn points before the time clock expires.

Consumer interpretations of these experiences ran counter to our team's preconceived notions. Many consumers told us that the computer-mediated reality games felt more "real" than those where there was no digital interface. In probing deeper, we found that consumers thought the computers enhanced the feelings that they were "really playing the game."

Stage 3 (Weeks 13–18)

In the final stages of the research, the focus of the field immersion became more precise. We sought further consumer insight into such themes as the meaning and importance of sport, consumers' associations and images of the ESPN brand, consumer fantasy, the phenomenology of television viewing, etc. These themes were explored in greater depth by asking consumers specific questions around these topics, rather than conducting completely consumer-driven, unstructured interviews as was done earlier in the project. At this point in the research, we also employed projective techniques by having consumers view photographs and other artifacts collected on-site to improve the sharpness of their expositions.

Conclusion

Although this brief synopsis omits a number of insights emergent from this extended field research project, the sampling of ethnographic findings and summary of the research trajectory taken were meant to illustrate ethnographic techniques. Market researchers are frequently asked to procure relevant, consumer-driven insights to guide managerial practice. Ever increasingly, researchers are finding that such insights are practically obtained via ethnography.

QUESTIONS

1. What kind of information have these researchers discovered?

2. How is the nature of this information related to the research methodology?

3. How might these findings be communicated back to "management"?

4. What kinds of marketing decisions can be made on the basis of this kind of study?

CASE 2.8
Brand Association Maps

There's a man, let's call him Joe, who inherited millions, but he has worked hard to turn his family wealth into some real money. He's now hitting that 50ish age, which means he is overdue for a serious midlife crisis. He actually likes his first wife, and he's had convertibles on and off over the years, so what he's done is bought a sports team. He's friends with the dean of a business school, and the dean tells him that one of his faculty members creates brand studies that are called brand maps. He recommends that Joe have the professor run a branding study for his new sports team. Joe looks at the example that the dean had (this was for laptops, in Figure 2.8.1), and Joe thought it looked foolish. The dean said, "What do you have to lose? Why not give one a try?"

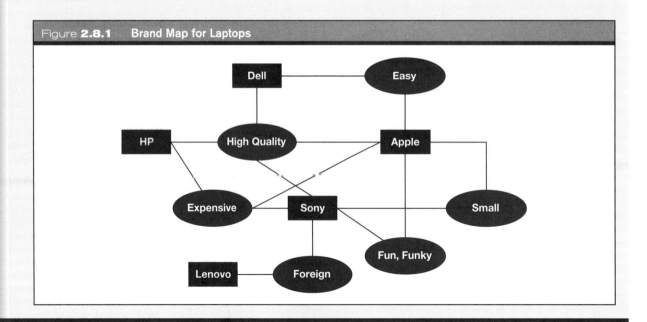

Figure 2.8.1   Brand Map for Laptops

QUESTIONS

1. What kind of information can this research approach unveil?

2. Can Joe, or anyone, look at a research approach and dismiss it completely out of hand?

3. What kinds of marketing decisions can be made on the basis of this kind of study?

4. Help the dean show Joe that this technique, and the information you can obtain, can be very valuable:

   a. If you like sports, choose one league (e.g., pro or college football, soccer, women's basketball, minor league baseball, whatever). If you don't like sports, choose (i) sports cars, (ii) brands of handbags, or (iii) clothing designers.

   b. Pick a willing friend (okay, so this is a "convenience sample," not one that will be representative...) and have them list the top 5 sports teams (or cars, bags, designers) that come to mind, right off the top of their head.

   c. Ask them about the ones they listed as #1, 3, and 4. What do these have in common and how are they different. The attribute that links two of the three, and the attribute that makes one of them different might be different attributes (e.g.,

New York and Boston are both northeast whereas as Cubs are on WGN, yields two attributes: location and access).

   d. Ask how do #2, 4, and 6 compare. Then #1, 2, and 7. Then #3, 5, and 6. Finally, #5, 6, and 7.

   e. Brand mapping studies are a little more complicated than this, but you sort of have the basics. Thank your poor friend. Then go create a spreadsheet with the 5–7 brands forming 5–7 columns, and collect all the attributes and make them rows of this table. Put a "1" in the cell if the attribute describes the column/brand, and a "0" if it does not. You might need to ask your friend to fill in the rest of the table with you.

   f. Repeat (b)–(e) for two more friends. Hey, research is hard work. Go do it.

   g. Now you have three tables. Make a map like Figure 2.8.1 for each of your friends. In the map, write down every brand/column label and every attribute/row label. Connect any two that have a "1" in the table.

   h. How do the maps look for your friends? Are there similarities? Do the differences make sense, knowing your friends? How would you combine the three friends' maps?

Design Data-Collection Methods and Forms

Part 3 covers the third stage in the research process—designing the methods of data collection and the data-collection forms.

Chapter 7 focuses on secondary data as an information resource. The Appendix to this chapter offers a very thorough list of secondary data sources.

Chapter 8 presents the main methods of data collection.

In **Chapter 9**, you learn how to construct questionnaires.

Chapter 10 discusses the general topic of attitude measurement and reviews the many types of attitude scales. The Appendix to Chapter 10 presents the criteria for assessing the quality of questionnaires–reliability and validity.

Data Collection: Secondary Data

7

Questions to Guide Your Learning:

Q1 What are *secondary data?* What are the advantages and disadvantages of these sources?

Q2 What are some of the key sources of *internal* and *external* secondary data?

Q3 What kind of free data does the *government* compile?

Q4 What kinds of data are available from *commercial* providers?

Once a marketing research problem is defined and clearly specified, the research effort logically turns to data collection. The natural temptation for inexperienced researchers is to advocate some sort of survey among appropriate respondent groups. However, surveys shouldn't be conducted until other possibilities have been exhausted. First attempts at data collection should logically focus on secondary data. We'll show you why.

Secondary data are statistics that already exist; they had been gathered for a previous purpose, not your particular study. **Primary data**, in contrast, are originated by the researcher for the purpose of the immediate investigation at hand. It is clear in Figure 7.1 that most marketing research professionals use both kinds of data.

The purpose of the research defines the distinction of the data. For example, if GE collected information on the demographic characteristics of refrigerator purchasers to determine who buys their brand, this information would be primary data. If the company looked up this same information from internal records gathered previously for other purposes (e.g., warranty information) or from published statistics, the information would be considered secondary data.

Using Secondary Data

Inexperienced researchers usually underestimate the amount of secondary data available. Table 7.1 lists just some of the information on people and households that is available, even down to the refined level of small geographic areas, due to the government's population census. Secondary data possess important advantages over primary data, so the researcher should always start with secondary data, particularly given the "information explosion" and the enormous volume of existing data. If you go online and conclude, "There are no data on this out there," you haven't looked hard enough.

FIGURE 7.1   Marketing Research Methods in Practice: Information Sources

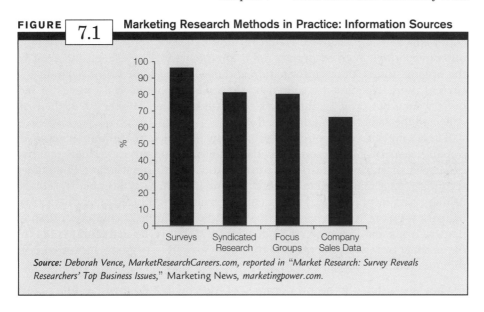

Source: Deborah Vence, MarketResearchCareers.com, reported in "Market Research: Survey Reveals Researchers' Top Business Issues," Marketing News, *marketingpower.com.*

Advantages of Secondary Data

The most significant advantages of secondary data are the *cost* and *time* economies they offer. If the required information is available as secondary data, the researcher simply needs to get online or go to the library, locate the appropriate sources, and extract and record the information desired. Doing so takes little time and involves little cost. In contrast, if the information had to be collected in a field survey, the following steps would have to be executed: 1) data-collection form designed and pre-tested, 2) field interview staff selected and trained, 3) sampling plan devised, 4) data gathered and checked for accuracy and omissions, and 5) data coded and tabulated.

TABLE 7.1   Information You Can Get from the Population Census

	Population	Housing
All households report on:	• Household relationships • Gender • Race • Age • Marital status • Hispanic origin	• Number of units in structure • Number of rooms in unit • Tenure owned or rented • Value of owned unit, or rent paid
Some households report on:	• Education • Place of birth, citizenship • Language spoken at home • Disability • Veteran status • Occupation • Commute	• Source of water • Autos, light trucks, vans • Year structure built • Year moved into residence

As a conservative estimate, the survey process would take 2–3 months and could cost $1000s, because it would include expenses and wages for field and office personnel. With secondary data, these expenses have been incurred by the original source of the information and don't need to be borne again by the current user. Expenses are shared by the users of commercial sources of secondary data, but even so, the user's costs will be much less than had the firm collected the same information itself.

A good marketing research study should *always* start with secondary data!

These time and cost economies prompt the general admonition: *Do not bypass secondary data.* Begin with secondary data, and only when the secondary data are exhausted or show diminishing returns, proceed to primary data. Sometimes secondary data may provide enough insight that there is no need to collect primary data on the topic. This scenario is true when all the analyst needs is a ballpark estimate (which is often the case). For example, a common question that confronts marketing research analysts is, "What is the market potential for the product or service?" Secondary data may be used to begin to answer parts of the question, such as:

- What are estimates of proportions of potential customers in the target markets?
- How might the marketplace be segmented?
- What are the recent sales histories in the industry?
- Who are the major competitors, and what are their approximate relative market shares?
- What are the existing environmental influences that will impact this venture?

To use secondary data effectively, it is often necessary to make some assumptions. One practical way to do this is to vary your assumptions in "what-if" scenarios to determine how much the conclusion changes. If you alter an assumption and your forecasts don't change much, additional information on this aspect of the marketing problem probably isn't that beneficial.

Rarely do secondary data completely answer all your questions, but they typically will:

1. Help to clarify the problem under investigation
2. Suggest improved methods or data for investigating the problem
3. Provide comparative benchmarks against which primary data can be more insightfully interpreted

Thus, *any good marketing research study should begin with secondary data!*

Disadvantages of Secondary Data

Two problems commonly arise when secondary data are used: (1) They typically do not completely fit the problem, and (2) there may be problems with their accuracy.

Problems of Fit

Because secondary data were collected for someone else's purposes, it is rare when they fit your problem perfectly. In some cases, the fit is so poor as to render the data completely inappropriate. Secondary data may be ill-suited to problems for three reasons: (1) units of measurement, (2) class definitions, or (3) publication currency.

It is common for secondary data to be expressed in units different from those required for the project. Size of retail establishment, for instance, can be expressed in terms of gross sales, profits, square feet, and number of employees. You might want sales, but the data might be reported in terms of labor. Consumer income can be expressed by individual, family, or household spending unit. So it is with many variables, and it is a recurring source of frustration in using secondary data.

Even if the units are consistent, the classification boundaries are often different from those needed. For example, the census data aggregates people by age into the following categories: <18 years old, 18 to 24, 25 to 34, 35 to 44, and so on. If FirstMortgage.com sought to learn more about potential home buyers who were "30-something" to tailor its services and position its Internet banners, it would not be able to identify this age group cleanly. The firm could access data on people who were 25 to 34 and 35 to 44 years old. That imprecision may be acceptable for some purposes, but not others. See Research Realities 7.1 for an example of ethnicity and Research Realities 7.2 for an example with international youth numbers.

RESEARCH   REALITIES

7.1 Categorizing Ethnicity in the Census

The most recent census survey was modified with regard to categories for reporting race or ethnicity. To recognize the increasing diversity of the U.S. population, citizens were offered the opportunity to check multiple affiliations to identify their ethnic origin more precisely. In addition, the ethnicity categories were refined, offering more distinct options.

Of particular interest was the attempt to clarify the meaning of the "Latino" or "Hispanic" category. This concern was addressed by providing more subcategories.

Take a look at the form. One person in the household answers this question for everyone in the household, hence the odd wording:

---

5) **Is this person Spanish / Hispanic / Latino?** Mark the **"No"** box if **not** Spanish / Hispanic / Latino:

☐ No, not Spanish / Hispanic / Latino   ☐ Yes, Puerto Rican

☐ Yes, Mexican, Mexican American, Chicano   ☐ Yes, Cuban

☐ Yes, other Spanish / Hispanic / Latino—print group:

— —

6) **What is this person's race? Mark one or more races** to indicate what this person considers himself/herself to be:

☐ White

☐ Black, African American, or Negro

☐ American Indian or Alaska Native—print name of principal tribe:

— —

☐ Asian Indian   ☐ Japanese   ☐ Native Hawaiian

☐ Chinese   ☐ Korean   ☐ Guamanian or Chamorro

☐ Filipino   ☐ Vietnamese   ☐ Samoan

☐ Other Asian—print race: ☐ Other Pacific Islander—print race:

— —

☐ Some other race—print race:

— —

(Continued)

Regardless of the good intentions (for political correctness and greater measurement accuracy), census administrators were disappointed with the "confusion of the results," and are working to clarify the categories and instructions for the next census. They said the results were confusing because 43% of the Hispanic/Latino citizens marked "Some other race" in question 6. The instructions said to complete both questions 5 and 6, so if you were Hispanic, what would you have marked? (Who's writing these surveys anyway? Not someone who has read this book! Election results anyone?)

Fun census facts:

1. U.S. population is estimated at 281,421,906 (906? Sure not 907?)

2. 97.6% of us claimed "one race" (marked only one box); 2.3% claimed 2 races, .1% claimed 3

3. About 43% of Hispanics / Latinos classified themselves as "Some other race," and 97% of the people reporting themselves as "Some other race" were Hispanic or Latino

4. Hispanic or Latino is considered an ethnicity; people may be of any race (e.g., Mexican, Cuban, Puerto Rican)

5. There were 28 Hispanic or Latino categories: Mexican, Puerto Rican, Cuban, Dominican Republic, Central American (Costa Rican, Guatemalan, Honduran, Nicaraguan, Panamanian, Salvadoran, Other Central American), South American (Argentinean, Bolivian, Chilean, Colombian, Ecuadorian, Paraguayan, Peruvian, Uruguayan, Venezuelan, Other South American), Other Hispanic or Latino (Spaniard, Spanish, Spanish American, All other Hispanic or Latino)

6. 66.1% of the U.S. Hispanic population is composed of people of Mexican origin; 14.5% from Central and South America, 9.0% Puerto Rican, 4.0% Cuban, 6.4% all other

7. Five Alaska Native categories: Alaska Athabaskan, Aleut, Eskimo, Tlingit-Haida, All other tribes

8. 36 American Indian categories: Apache, Blackfeet, Cherokee, Cheyenne, Chickaswa, Chippewa, Choctaw, Colville, Comanche, Cree, Creek, Crow, Delaware, Houma, Iroquois, Kiowa, Latin American (Aztec, Inca, Mayan, etc.), Lumbee, Menominee, Navajo, Osage, Ottawa, Paiute, Pima, Potawatomi, Pueblo, Puget Sound Salish, Seminole, Sioux, Tohomo O'Odham, Ute, Yakama, Yaqui, Yuman, All other categories

9. 17 Asian categories: Asian Indian, Bangladeshi, Cambodian, Chinese except Taiwanese, Filipino, Hmong, Indonesian, Japanese, Korean, Laotian, Malaysian, Pakistani, Sri Lankan, Taiwanese, Thai, Vietnamese, Other Asian

10. 12 Hawaiian and Pacific Islanders: Polynesian (Native Hawaiian, Samoan, Tongan, Other Polynesian), Micronesian (Guamanian or Chamorro, Other Micronesian), Melanesian (Fijian, Other Melanesian), Other Pacific Islander

An important direct use of shifting populations is the allocation of the number of seats each state is entitled to in the House of Representatives according to the Constitution. Federal programs that address Affirmative Action, Community Reinvestments, and Public Health Services also use this information. Beyond politics and civics, there are commercial implications; e.g., the multicultural Hispanic market comprises 13% of the U.S. population, resulting from a 58% growth in the previous decade. Clearly these numbers represent huge opportunities. Companies as varied as Hanes, Enterprise Rent-a-Car, Sears, H&R Block, and ESPN are paying attention, introducing tailored market offerings, and bilingual ad appeals.

Source: John Kavaliunas, "Get Ready to Use Census Data" Marketing Research 12 (3), 4–43; census.gov. Also see Laurel Wentz, "Hispanic Fact Book," advertisingage.com.

Finally, secondary data quite often lack publication currency. The time from data collection to dissemination is often long, e.g., 2–3 years with government census data. Census data have great value while they're current, but this value diminishes with time, given that many marketing decisions require current, rather than historical, information.

Problems of Accuracy

The accuracy of much secondary data is also questionable. As we discuss throughout this book, numerous sources of error are possible in the collection,

RESEARCH   REALITIES

7.2 Global Youth

If you're a brand manager for anything trendy, such as music, fast foods, blue jeans, funky fashion accessories, or other elements of pop culture, one of your most important target markets is teens and young adults. Yet getting this group to adopt any product is nearly impossible, and even once you've got their attention, the group is known to have an attention span of a fruit fly, so loyalty and extensive repeat purchasing is iffy.

So, if you come upon a successful product, how might you leverage it while it's still hot? Go global!

Turns out that pre-teens, teens, and 20-somethings are surprisingly homogeneous globally, due to satellite television, the Internet, and other media. Thus, once you have the recipe for success with the youth of one country, find the youth in another!

- Kids become brand-conscious at about 2 years of age, and by 3 years old, they're evaluating brands as "cool" or not.

- Kids in the U.S. between 4-12 years of age spent about $50billion of their own money and request another $500 billion from mom and dad. Don't ignore these powerful rugrat consumers!

- Fisher-Price's Play Lab is the only full-time, on-site facility of its kind at an American toy company.

- For 50 years, children have tested toy concepts and prototypes, and product reliability.

- For more, read Juliet Schor's *Born to Buy* (NY: Scribner, 2005).

Percentage Population Aged 14 Years or Younger

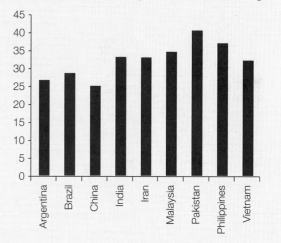

analysis, and presentation of marketing information. Researchers collecting the information can assess its accuracy better than subsequent users of that information. The following criteria, though, should help the marketer judge the accuracy of any secondary data: 1) the *source*, 2) the *purpose of publication,* and 3) *general evidence regarding quality.*

Secondary data can be obtained from either a *primary source* or a *secondary source.* A primary source is the source that originated the data. A secondary source is a source that, in turn, obtained the data from the original source. *The Statistical Abstract of the United States,* which is published each year, contains a great deal of useful information for many research projects. The *Statistical Abstract* is a secondary source (of secondary data), because none of what is published in the *Statistical Abstract* originates there. Rather, all of it is compiled from other government and trade sources.

Whenever possible, use the primary source of secondary data. Why? First, it's usually only the primary source that describes the methods of data collection and analysis. Secondary sources typically do not include the caveats and qualifications included as disclaimers by the primary source. Second, the primary source is usually more accurate and complete. Errors in transcription can occur in copying the data from a primary source, for example.

A second criterion by which the accuracy of secondary data can be assessed is the purpose of publication. If CNN announced, "Studies show that pizza can be the mainstay in a healthy diet," wouldn't it matter if the research were sponsored by the American Heart Association versus a pizza restaurant franchise? In which case might you believe the claims? In which case might you have confidence in the objectivity of the results? The objectivity of data is generally suspect when the findings are used as propaganda to promote sales or to advance the causes of a political party or special industry.

You can be most confident in a source that has no ax to grind but, rather, publishes secondary data as its primary business function. If data publication is a source's *raison d'être*, high quality must be maintained to ensure its own long-term sustenance. Inaccurate data offer a firm no competitive advantage, and poor-quality data would eventually lead to its demise. The success of any organization supplying data as its primary purpose depends on the long-term satisfaction of its users that the information supplied is indeed accurate.[1]

The third criterion by which the accuracy of secondary data can be assessed is the general evidence of quality. One item of evidence here is the ability of the supplying organization to collect the data. The Internal Revenue Service, for example, has greater leverage in securing income data than does an independent marketing research firm. In addition, the user needs to ascertain how the data were collected. A primary source should provide a detailed description of the methodology, including definitions, data-collection forms, methods of sampling, and so forth. If it does not, researcher beware! Such omissions are usually indicative of sloppy methods.

When the details of data collection are provided, the user of secondary data should examine them thoroughly. Was the sampling plan sound? Was this type of data best collected through questionnaire or by observational methods? What about the quality of the field force—what kind of training was provided, what kinds of checks of the fieldwork were employed? What was the extent of nonresponse due to refusals, to respondents not at home, and by item? Is the information presented in a well-organized manner? Are the tables properly labeled, and are the data within them internally consistent? Are the conclusions supported by the data? As these questions suggest, the user of secondary data must be familiar with the research process and the potential sources of error, and we address all these elements throughout the book.

Types of Secondary Data

Secondary data can be classified in several ways. One of the most useful is by source: **internal** data are those found within one's own organization, whereas **external** data are those obtained from outside sources. The external sources can be further classified into those that regularly publish statistics and make them available to the user at no charge (such as by the U.S. government) and the commercial organizations that sell their services to various users (e.g., Information Resources Inc., ACNielsen). Together they represent the most commonly used sources of secondary data, the places where researchers begin (see Figure 7.2).

Internal Secondary Data

Data that originate within the firm are internal data. The sales and cost data compiled in the normal accounting cycle can help address many research

---

[1] See the National Council on Public Polls' "Who Paid for the Poll and Why Was It Done?" (ncpp.org).

FIGURE 7.2   Types of Secondary Data

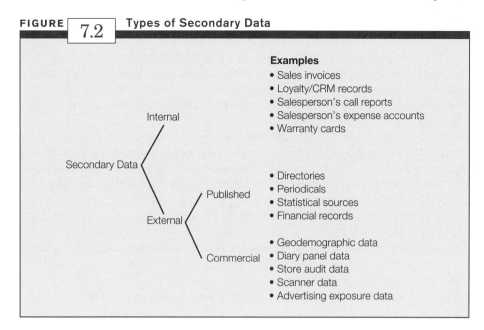

problems, such as evaluating past marketing strategy or assessing the firm's competitive position in the industry. In future-directed decisions, such as evaluating a new product or a new advertising campaign, internal sales data are more helpful simply as a foundation for planning the research.

From a sales invoice alone, information can be extracted such as:

• Customer name and location

• Products and services sold

• Volume and dollar amount of the transaction

• Salesperson or agent responsible for the sale

• Location of customer facility where product is to be shipped and/or used

• Customer's industry, class of trade, and/or channel of distribution

• Applicable discount

• Transportation used in shipment, etc.

Loyalty programs, membership clubs, and online shopping allow companies to accumulate the details of each sale for each transaction over time with each customer.[2] Relational databases store and continually update sequence of sales transactions. Ideally, such detailed data enable the firm to offer customized market offerings to the consumer, with the presumed goal of greater customer satisfaction. In reality, many companies are overwhelmed with the enormous

For answers and data, start in-house!

---

[2] Chris Forman, Anindya Ghose and Avi Goldfarb, "Competition between Local and Electronic Markets," *Management Science*, to appear; Ran Kivetz, Oleg Urminsky, and Yuhuang Zheng, "The Goal-Gradient Hypothesis Resurrected: Purchase Acceleration, Illusionary Goal Progress and Customer Retention," *Journal of Marketing Research* 43 (1), 39–58; Michael Lewis, "The Influence of Loyalty Programs and Short-Term Promotions on Customer Retention," *Journal of Marketing Research*, 41 (3), 281–292; Mike Lewis, "Customer Acquisition Promotions and Customer Asset Value," *Journal of Marketing Research*, 43 (2), 195–203; Gail McGovern and Youngme Moon, "Companies and the Customers Who Hate Them," *Harvard Business Review*, hbrreprints.org; Oded Netzer, James Lattin, and V. Srinivasan, "A Hidden Markov Model of Customer Relationship Dynamics," *Marketing Science*, 27 (2), 185–204; Preethika Seshasainam, "Consumer Options and Forward Pricing," research in process.

size of the databases, and are only beginning to learn how to sort through the masses of information (see Research Realities 7.3).

Other internal documents provide more specialized input (see Table 7.2). Most companies are likely to use only two or three of these sources of sales information in addition to the sales invoice. The selections depend on the company and the types of analyses used to plan and evaluate the marketing effort.

Another useful but often overlooked source of internal secondary data is previous marketing research studies on related topics. Even though each study typically addresses a number of specific questions, great synergy can result when the key learnings are studied and combined. Many marketing research and consulting firms have built internal video libraries in which key personnel describe a study they had recently executed for a client. These video clips are cross-referenced by keywords such as industry, segment, marketing issue, the study's purpose, etc., and they can be accessed over the firm's intranet. Managers at these firms are convinced that such aggregations of knowledge are yielding a competitive advantage as their researchers collectively move further and more quickly up the learning curve, compared to their counterparts at competitor firms.

Two of the most important advantages associated with internal secondary data are their ready availability and low cost. Internal secondary data are the

RESEARCH   REALITIES

7.3 Data Mining

Data mining is the term applied to the exercise of digging through a lot of "coal"—seemingly uninteresting data—to find the golden nugget of useful marketing information. The analogy is continued when researchers speak of "drilling down" into the data. Database technology, statistics, and business acumen are all brought to bear in data mining. Data analysis is not new, but what is new is the enormous size of the databases on which the analytics are applied, due in part to the reduction in the expense of data-storage technology. In particular, loyalty programs capture consumer-purchase histories and expenditures, preferences, and demographics and result in huge databases.

Data mining provides a benefit to the company—the discovery and understanding of one's most profitable customers, and an ability to track customers' sales responses to various promotions. The benefit to business customers can be direct store delivery (e.g., the replenishment of inventory as stock is electronically counted down) and the coordination of invoices and vendors. The benefit to end-user consumers is usually a product tailored more specifically to their particular needs.

For quantitative analyses, sample sizes are typically huge, so most inferential statistics (e.g., t-tests) are generally significant. Thus, analysts often rely on simple descriptive statistics, such as means and correlations. Regressions are common, as are cluster analyses to form customer segments.

For qualitative data such as click-stream data, analysts use "text mining" techniques. These methods are comparable to standard descriptive statistics, but are applied to alphabetic strings rather than numeric strings of data.

Recommendation technologies (RTs) such as those on books and CD e-tail vendors can be applied to the large quantitative or qualitative databases. These algorithms are the fastest-growing models among data mining tools. The models use "collaborative filtering," which is a form of cluster analysis to identify similar users, who, due to their similarity, help (collaborate) in creating overlapping lists of products that form the basis of the recommendations. (We say more in Chapter 18 in the section on cluster analysis.)

TABLE 7.2   Useful Sources of *Internal* Secondary Data

Document	Info Provided
Cash register receipts	• Type (cash or credit) and dollar amount of transaction by department by salesperson
Salesperson's call reports	• Customers and prospects called on (company and individual seen; planned or unplanned calls)
	• Products discussed
	• Orders obtained
	• Customers' product needs and usage
	• Other significant information about customers
	• Distribution of time spent on customer calls, travel, and office work
	• Sales-related activities: meetings, conventions
Salesperson's expense	• Expenses by day, by item (hotel, meals, travel, accounts)
Individual customer (and prospect) records	• Name and location and customer
	• Number of calls by company salesperson (agents)
	• Sales by company (in dollars and/or units, by product or service, by location of customer facility)
	• Customer's industry, class of trade, and/or trade channel
	• Estimated total annual usage of each product sold by the company
	• Estimated annual purchases from the company of each product
	• Location (in terms of company sales territory)
Financial records	• Sales revenue (by product, geographic market, customer, class of trade, unit of sales organization)
	• Direct sales expenses (similarly classified)
	• Overhead sales costs (similarly classified)
	• Profits (similarly classified)
Credit memos	• Returns and allowances
Warranty cards	• Indirect measures of dealer sales
	• Customer service

least costly of any type of marketing research. Internal sales data can be used to analyze the company's sales performance by product, geographic location, customer, channel of distribution, and so on.

Searching for Published External Secondary Data

A huge wealth of external data exists. Some relevant external secondary data are available on almost any problem a marketer might confront. The fundamental problem is not availability; it is identifying and accessing what is there. See Figure 7.3 for some guidelines to get started on a search of secondary data.

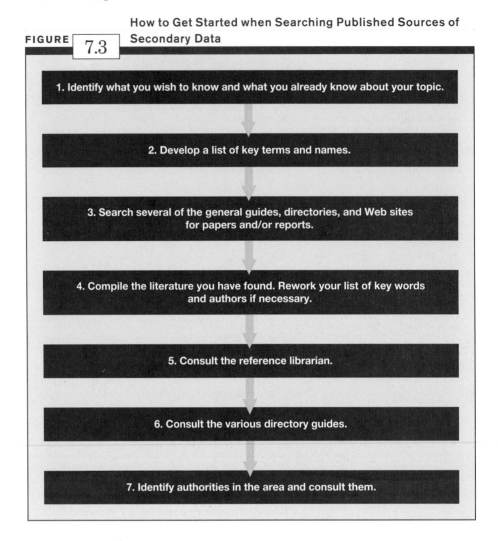

FIGURE 7.3   How to Get Started when Searching Published Sources of Secondary Data

1. Identify what you wish to know and what you already know about your topic.

2. Develop a list of key terms and names.

3. Search several of the general guides, directories, and Web sites for papers and/or reports.

4. Compile the literature you have found. Rework your list of key words and authors if necessary.

5. Consult the reference librarian.

6. Consult the various directory guides.

7. Identify authorities in the area and consult them.

Step 1

Identify what you already know and what you wish to know about your topic, including relevant facts, names of researchers or organizations associated with the topic, and key papers and other familiar publications.

Step 2

Develop a list of keywords and names. These terms will provide access to secondary sources. Unless you have a very specific topic of interest, it is better to keep this initial list long and general.

Step 3

You are ready to go online or to the library. Begin with the directories listed throughout this chapter and on our Web site. Look at only the previous 2–3 years of work in the area, using 3–4 general guides. Some directories and indexes use a specialized list of keywords or descriptors. Such indexes often have thesauri that can help you map your keywords onto the directory's terms.

Step 4

Compile the literature you have found. Is it relevant to your needs? You may be overwhelmed by information, or you may have found little that is relevant (if so, rework your list of keywords and expand the search to include a few more years and a few additional sources). By the end of step 4, you should have a clear idea of the nature of the information you are seeking and sufficient background to use more specialized sources.

Step 5

One very useful specialized source is a reference librarian. These people are specialists who have been trained to know the contents of many of the key information sources in a library and on the Web, as well as how to search those sources most effectively. (Don't think that just because you know Google that these people can't help you.)

Step 6

If you have had little success or your topic is highly specialized, consult more general guides to information. These are really directories of directories, which means the search will be very general. You first need to identify potentially useful primary directories, which will then lead you to other sources.

Step 7

If you are still unhappy with what you have found, use an authority. Identify some individual or organization that might know something about the topic. The *Consultants and Consulting Organizations Directory, Encyclopedia of Associations,* or *Research Centers Directory* should help you identify sources. The Bureau of the Census puts out a list of department specialists whom users can contact for information on any of the bureau's studies. These people are knowledgeable about related studies in their areas of expertise. Faculty at universities, government officials, and business executives can also be useful sources of information.

> Some sources of *secondary data* are free. Others, you have to pay for, but it's still usually *less expensive* and *faster* than collecting primary data.

Key General Sources of External Secondary Data

Additional important sources of external secondary data are associations, general guides to useful marketing information, and online computer searches.

Associations

Most associations gather detailed information on such matters as industry sales, growth patterns, environmental factors affecting the industry, etc. Trade associations are often able to get information from members that other research organizations cannot because of the working relationships that exist between the association and its member firms. Two useful sources for locating associations serving a particular industry are *Directories in Print* and the *Encyclopedia of Associations* (described online).

General Guides to Business Information

There are many useful sources for locating information on any given topic. Table 7.3 lists what the *Encyclopedia of Business Information Sources* has to say about data sources on just one single industry. It is important also to acquaint yourself with the general sources of marketing information so that you know what statistics are available and where they can be found.

TABLE 7.3   Sources of Data on the Music Industry

Abstracts and Indexes

- *Music Index:* Subject-Author Guide to 300+ International Periodicals. Harmonic Park Press. Monthly.

Bibliographies

- *Information Sources in Music.* Lewis Foreman, ed. Bowker-Saur. Evaluates information on range of topics, including copyright, music publishing, reprographics, and the use of computers in music publishing.

- *Mix Bookshelf: Information Resources for Music Professionals.* Cardinal Business Media, Inc. Annotated catalog of about 600 publications relating to music, electronic music technology, musical instruments, and the music business.

Biographical Sources

- *Celebrity Register.* The Gale Group. Profiles 1,500 famous individuals in the performing arts, sports, politics, business, and other fields.

Directories

- *Billboard's International Buyer's Guide of the Music Industry.* BPI Communications. Recording companies; music publishers; wholesalers; services and supplies for the music industry; U.S. and over 65 countries.

- *Recording Industry Sourcebook.* Cardinal Business Media, Inc. More than 12,000 listings in 57 categories of labels, producers, distributors, managers, equipment suppliers.

Handbooks and Manuals

- *All You Need to Know About the Music Business.* Donald S. Passman. Simon & Schuster. Covers the practical and legal aspects of recording contracts, music publishing, management agreements, touring, and other music business topics.

- *Entertainment Law.* Howard Siegel, ed. New York State Bar Assn. Covers legal aspects of television, motion pictures, theatre, music, and related topics.

Trade/Professional Associations

- *American Society of Composers, Authors and Publishers.* One Lincoln Plaza, New York, NY 10023.

Source: Adapted from Encyclopedia of Business Information Sources, *24th ed. (Gale/Cengage, 2009).*

Online Computer Searches

Online computer searches are the state of the art, having become increasingly popular, more comprehensive, and user-friendly for locating published information and data via computer-readable storage systems and databases. Many public and university libraries have invested in the equipment and personnel necessary to make database searching available to their patrons. There are several thousand databases to pick from, with several hundred of them applying to business.

One huge, free, accessible database that should never be overlooked is the census data. The census data contain information on population characteristics as well as economic and business conditions. The directory begins at www.census.gov. See Research Realities 7.4 for an overview of this amazing resource.

An online service involves three main components: a database producer, a database vendor, and a data user. The database producer collects the information and edits it according to the organization's criteria, compiles it, and sells it to the vendor. The vendor mounts the data onto a computer or, e.g., sells the information on a CD. The vendor might combine or split the information to fit

RESEARCH REALITIES

7.4 Data Available from www.census.gov

The Bureau of the Census of the U.S. Department of Commerce is the largest gatherer of statistical information in the country. There are some two dozen population and economic industry censuses, all of which can interest to the marketing researcher. Here are a few:

- **Census of Finance, Insurance, and Real Estate:** Collects statistics on commercial banks, savings institutions, credit unions, life insurance providers, hospital and medical service planners, fire, marine and casualty insurance providers, and real estate land developers. Information includes location, revenue, and payroll.

- **Census of Government:** Presents information on state and local governments, including employment, size of payroll, amount of indebtedness, and operating revenues and costs.

- **Census of Housing:** Lists type of structure, size, building condition, occupancy, water and sewage facilities, monthly rent, average value, and equipment, including stoves, dishwashers, air conditioners. For large metropolitan areas, it provides detailed statistics by city block.

- **Census of Manufacturers:** Categorizes 450 types of manufacturing establishments and contains detailed industry and geographic statistics for such items as the number of establishments, quantity of output, value added in manufacture, capital expenditures, employment, wages, inventories, sales by customer class, and energy consumption.

- **Census of Population:** Reports population by geographic region. Provides detailed breakdowns on characteristics such as gender, marital status, age, education, race, national origin, family size, income, and employment and unemployment.

- **Census of Retail Trade:** Classifies retail stores by type of business, presenting statistics on the number of stores, total sales, employment, and payroll. The statistics are broken down by small geographic areas, such as counties, cities, and standard metropolitan statistical areas.

- **Census of Service Industries:** Provides data on receipts, employment, type of business (e.g., hotels), and number of units by small geographic areas.

- **Census of Transportation, Communications, and Utilities:** Covers passenger travel, truck and bus inventory and use, and the transport of commodities by the various classes of carriers, telephone and telegraph communications, and electric, gas, steam, water, and sanitary services. Indices cover expenses, revenues, and output measures per state.

its own needs, thus, the same database from different vendors might have different subsets of information. The vendor pays a fee every time the database is used online and pays a fee for all citations from it. Access at public and university libraries is often free, but some sources charge for accessing the database, and sometimes for printing charges. Some useful databases for marketers contain the following information:

Go to our Web site for these links!

- *Specific company or industry information:* This information comes primarily from reports filed with the Securities and Exchange Commission, stockholder reports, and stock market information. The databases cover financial, marketing, and product information, some company profiles, and the usual directory information, such as the name of the organization and its address and phone number. For example, both Moody's and Standard and Poor's provide both U.S. and international corporate profiles (moodys.com, standardandpoors. com). And of course, Internet search engines (e.g., the business category at Yahoo) are extremely useful in locating information about companies.

- *Mergers, affiliations, ownership information:* These databases list the institutions and people that own a stock by name, ownership changes, including the mergers and acquisitions that have taken place in the recent past or are pending (see dialogweb.com, library.dialog.com, and worldtraderesources. com).

- *Company directory information:* Numerous directories are available that differ in the types of companies they cover (such as public or private), the size of the companies covered, and their geographic coverage. In addition to the name, address, and telephone number, many directories list the NAICS (formerly SIC) codes for the business (e.g., Dun's Business Locator, dnb.com).

- *U.S. government contract information:* These databases are particularly useful to businesses dealing with the government. They contain information on whether a specific company has any government contracts and any recent contract awards; an example is Commerce Business Daily (cbd.savvy.com).

- *Economic information:* These databases contain general economic and demographic information from U.S. census materials and from the private sector. Many even contain forecasts of future economic activity; an example is Cendata (agnic.org).

- *General business information:* These databases cover companies, industries, people, and products. Increasingly these sources locate global, not just U.S., information. The sources are primarily trade and business-oriented journals, selected newspapers, and various reports. Examples are ABI/Inform and LexisNexis.

- *Brand name/trade name information:* These databases contain information on specific products, including what competitors might be doing with respect to new-product introductions or expenditures on advertising, and which company owns a specific trademark; e.g., Thomas Register Online (thomasregister. com).

As this list indicates, companies use online databases to search for marketing data, economic trends, legislation, inventions, reports, speeches, journal articles, and many other types of information on a particular topic.

Standardized Marketing Information Services

Many standardized marketing information services provide another important source of secondary data. These services are available at some cost to the user and thus are more expensive than published secondary data. However, they are still typically much less expensive than primary data, because purchasers share the costs incurred in collecting, editing, coding, and tabulating these data. Here are some of the types of these data.

Customer Profiles

Market segmentation demands that firms classify their customers into relatively homogeneous groups, to tailor marketing programs for each group. A common segmentation base starts with the industry designations of its customers, by means of the North American Industry Classification System (NAICS) codes. Figure 7.4 displays an example, the categorization for marketing consultants.

One of the popular commercial services is Dun's Business Locator, an index that provides data on over 10 million U.S. businesses, including the industry

FIGURE | 7.4 | **Excerpts of Naics Codes for *Marketing Consultant***

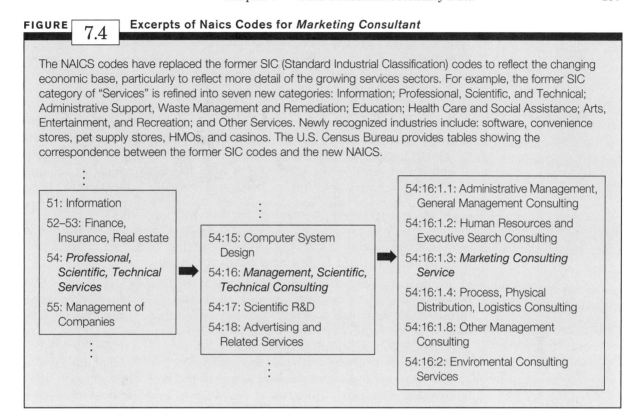

The NAICS codes have replaced the former SIC (Standard Industrial Classification) codes to reflect the changing economic base, particularly to reflect more detail of the growing services sectors. For example, the former SIC category of "Services" is refined into seven new categories: Information; Professional, Scientific, and Technical; Administrative Support, Waste Management and Remediation; Education; Health Care and Social Assistance; Arts, Entertainment, and Recreation; and Other Services. Newly recognized industries include: software, convenience stores, pet supply stores, HMOs, and casinos. The U.S. Census Bureau provides tables showing the correspondence between the former SIC codes and the new NAICS.

51: Information

52–53: Finance, Insurance, Real estate

54: *Professional, Scientific, Technical Services*

55: Management of Companies

54:15: Computer System Design

54:16: *Management, Scientific, Technical Consulting*

54:17: Scientific R&D

54:18: Advertising and Related Services

54:16:1.1: Administrative Management, General Management Consulting

54:16:1.2: Human Resources and Executive Search Consulting

54:16:1.3: *Marketing Consulting Service*

54:16:1.4: Process, Physical Distribution, Logistics Consulting

54:16:1.8: Other Management Consulting

54:16:2: Enviromental Consulting Services

code of each establishment (see dnb.com). These records allow sales management to construct B-to-B sales prospect files, define sales territories and measure territory potentials, and isolate potential new customers with particular characteristics. They allow advertising management to select prospects by size and location; to analyze market prospects and select the media to reach them; to build, maintain, and structure current mailing lists; to generate sales leads qualified by size, location, and quality; and to locate new markets for testing. They allow marketing researchers to assess market potential by territory, to measure market penetration in terms of numbers of prospects and numbers of customers, and to make comparative analyses of overall performance by districts and sales territories and in individual industries.

Analogously, firms selling consumer goods target groups of customers. Their ability to do this has increased substantially with the census, which allows tabulation by geographic boundaries, and other cuts of the data. "Geodemographers" combine census data with survey data or other data (e.g., motor vehicle registrations, credit transactions) to produce customized products for their clients.[3]

For example, R. L. Polk has a product for retailers called the Vehicle Origin Survey (stratmap.com and polk.com). Polk gathers license-plate numbers from

---

[3] For more, see Marc Farr, Jessica Wardlaw, and Catherine Jones, "Tackling Health Inequalities Using Geodemographics: A Social Marketing Approach," *International Journal of Market Research*, 50 (4), 449–467; Oscar Gonzalez-Benito and Javier Gonzalez-Benito, "The Role of Geodemographic Segmentation in Retail Location Strategy," *International Journal of Market Research*, 47 (3), 295–316; Wolfgang Jank and P. K. Kannan, "Understanding Geographical Markets of Online Firms Using Spatial Models of Customer Choice," *Marketing Science*, 24 (4), 623–634; Randolph E. Bucklin, S. Siddarth, and Jorge M. Silva-Risso, "Distribution Intensity and New Car Choice," *Journal of Marketing Research*, 45 (3), 473–486.

cars parked in shopping centers and matches them against their National Vehicle Registration Database to find out where these retail customers live.[4] The shopping center can then use plots of its customers' residences to determine its trading area. Moreover, the locations can be matched with the Census Bureau's data, thereby providing a demographic profile of the people who shop there.

Claritas Inc., the pioneer and a leader in the industry, used over 500 demographic variables in its PRIZM (Potential Ratings for Zip Markets) system to classify residential neighborhoods. This system breaks the 250,000 neighborhood areas in the U.S. into 40 types based on consumer behavior and lifestyle. Each type has a label that describes the people living there, such as *Urban Gold Coast, Shotguns and Pickups, Pools and Patios,* etc. (see Figure 7.5).

Measuring Product Sales and Market Share

Firms use market share to assess their status in the marketplace. Firms selling B-to-B goods or services typically track their own sales and market shares through analyses of their sales invoices. They also obtain feedback from the sales force in terms of how they did in various system competitions. Often, online data sources publish market share statistics.

Manufacturers of consumer packaged goods (CPGs) also monitor sales by account through the examination of sales invoices. For CPGs, though, more information is required. Using factory shipments as a sales barometer neglects the filling or depleting of distribution pipelines that may be occurring. The other part of the equation involves the measurement of sales to final consumers. Historically, such measurements have been handled several ways, including the use of diary panels of households and the measurement of sales scanned at the store level.

Diary Panels

The NPD Group, a market research company that has the largest national consumer diary panel in the U.S., samples continually from its panel of more than half a million households. These panelists use a preprinted diary to document their monthly purchases in a product category—Figure 7.6 shows the diary for food. Note that the diary asks for considerable detail about the food consumed at each meal; e.g., Was the food bought fresh or frozen? Was the packaging glass, plastic, cardboard? How much of the food item was served? What was served with it? Were toppings or side orders added? How much of the food remained after the meal?

The households composing NPD panels are geographically dispersed and balanced with respect to size, age of female head of household, household income, etc., so they can be projected to total U.S. purchasing. Panel members are recruited quarterly and added to the active panel after they have satisfactorily met NPD's reporting standards. Panel members are compensated for their participation with small gifts, and households are dropped from the panel at their request or if they fail to return three of their last six diaries.

[4] The U.S. Department of Motor Vehicles is also directly involved as a supplier of data to marketing researchers, providing driver information (e.g., age, gender, marital status, household income, number of children, home-ownership, etc.), automobile information (e.g., car make, model, year, purchase date, engine size, fuel type, bought new or used, etc.), along with the geographic details (state, county, zip, area code, etc.), to research suppliers such as Survey Sampling International (see ssi.com and worldopinion.com/the_frame).

FIGURE 7.5 Sample Cluster Profile from the Potential Ratings for Zip Marketing Systems

The **Towns and Gowns** cluster describes most of our college towns and university campus neighborhoods. With a typical mix of half locals (Towns) and half students (Gowns), it is wholly unique, with thousands of penniless 18-to-24 year-olds, plus highly educated professionals, all with a taste for prestige products beyond their evident means.

Predominant Characteristics:

- 1,293,200 (1.4% of U.S. Households)
- College Town Singles
- Ethnicities: Dominant White, High Asian
- Single marital status
- Age ranges: under 24, 25–34
- Education: College Grads
- Employment level: White-collar/Service
- Housing: Renters/Multi-Unit 10+

Descriptors: More Likely To:

Lifestyle	*Products and Services*
• Go to college football games	• Have student loans
• Go skiing	• Use ATM cards
• Play pool	• Own a Honda
• Use cigarette rolling paper	• Buy 3+ pairs jeans annually
TV/Radio	• Drink Coca-Cola Classic
• Listen to rock	• Eat Kraft Macaroni and Cheese
• Watch MTV, VH1	*Prints*
• Watch *Jeopardy*	• Read newspaper comics section
• Watch The *Simpsons*	• Read *Rolling Stone*
	• Read *GQ, Cosmo*

Source: http://Claritas.com.

The diaries are returned to NPD monthly, the purchase histories are aggregated, and reports are prepared. Using these reports, the subscribing company can assess the following:

- Size of the market, % of households buying over time, and amount purchased per buyer
- Manufacturer and brand shares over time
- Brand loyalty and brand-switching behavior
- Frequency of purchase and amount purchased per transaction
- Influence of price and special price deals, as well as average price paid
- Characteristics of heavy buyers

FIGURE 7.6   Sample Food Diary

DAILY MEAL DIARY

QUESTIONS OR PROBLEMS?

If you have any questions or problems concerning this diary, give us a call at our toll-free number 800-645-1900 Monday through Friday between 9:15AM and 4PM Eastern Time. In New York State call 800-632-1911.

Ethical **Dilemma**   7.1

An independent marketing research firm was hired by a Los Angeles clothing designer to study the Denver ski resort market for upscale, *après* ski-wear. The manufacturer wanted to determine (1) whether sufficient market potential existed to warrant opening a retail store there, and (2) if so, where precisely the store should be located in the metropolitan area. The research firm went about the task by examining secondary data on the Denver market, particularly statistics published by the Census Bureau. In less than two months, the research firm was able to develop a well-documented recommendation as to what the clothing designer should do.

Approximately six months after completing this study, the firm was approached by an outdoor sporting goods designer and manufacturer to do a similar study concerning the location of a store through which it could more effectively serve its Denver customers.

- Is it ethical for the research firm to use the information it had collected in the first study to reduce its cost quote to the client in the second?
- Does it make any difference if the sporting goods firm also designs and distributes ski-wear?
- Would your answers change if some of the data were collected through personal interviews that the first client paid for?

- Impact of a new manufacturer or brand on the established brands
- Effect of a change in advertising or distribution strategy

If you see the media reporting trends in food consumption, the data probably originated with NPD. Its food guru, Mr. Harry Balzer, points to trends such as the growth in take-out foods, or the concern by the industry—but not consumers—of healthy meals.[5] Regarding the latter, the beauty of the NPD diaries is that actual behaviors are recorded rather than attitudes, which are likely biased in the direction of social desirability (e.g., "Yes, I would like to eat more healthily... Say, are you going to finish your fries?").

Store Audits

Sales can also be compiled at the store level, using store audits or inventories. The research firm sends field workers to a select group of retail stores at fixed intervals. On each visit, the auditor takes a complete inventory of all designated products. The auditor also notes the merchandise moving into the store by checking wholesale invoices, warehouse withdrawal records, and direct shipments from manufacturers.

Scanners

ACNielsen's pioneering SCANTRACK service was made possible by the grocery industry's installation of scanning equipment to read Universal Product Codes (UPCs), the 11-digit numbers imprinted on each product sold in a supermarket (see Figure 7.7). As each product is pulled across the scanner, the scanner identifies its 11-digit number, looks up the price in the attached computer, and immediately prints the description and price of the item on the cash register receipt.

[5] See npd.com/press/releases.

FIGURE | 7.7 | **Universal Product Codes (UPCs)**

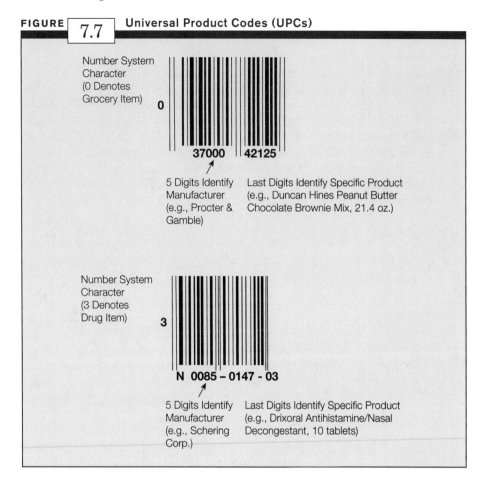

Scanners were initially useful for inventories, but scanners' effects on the collection of sales and market share data have been profound. Scanners are so pervasive that the majority of information supplied today is based on scanning data. Using either a sample of stores to represent a channel or a census of all stores to represent a retail organization, scanning data are available across multiple outlets, including grocery, mass merchant, drug, selected warehouse club, and selected convenience store.

By combining the retail sales and marketing mix factors (e.g., TV and local newspaper ad exposure data, coupon usage), the effectiveness of various marketing actions can be assessed (see Table 7.4). Several firms have further linked these purchase behavior data with household demographic information. When these large marketing research suppliers (e.g., Information Resources Inc. (IRI) and ACNielsen) link household demographics, TV-viewing behavior, and product-purchasing behavior, the results are called **single-source data**.[6]

The basics of single-source research are straightforward. In IRI's BehaviorScan system, their panel of more than 55,000 households presents an ID card every time they make a purchase at the supermarket or drugstore. Almost all the supermarkets and drugstores in each area are provided scanners by IRI.

[6] Hugh Cannon, J. Alexander Smith, and David Williams, "A Data-Overlay Approach to Synthesizing Single-Source Data," *Journal of Advertising*, 36 (4), 7–18. For similar marketing questions, see Jean-Pierre Dube and Sachin Gupta, "Cross-Brand Pass-Through in Supermarket Pricing," *Marketing Science*, 27 (3), 324–333; Jie Zhang and Aradhna Krishna, "Brand-Level Effects of Stockkeeping Unit Reductions," *Journal of Marketing Research*, 44 (4), 545–559.

TABLE 7.4   Sample Scanner Data

Scanner data are the grocery- and retail-scanned purchases made by consumers. Variables include store number, brand purchased, quantity purchased, number of ounces or size purchased, whether any of the brands in the category were on sale or otherwise featured (e.g., end-of-aisle displays), whether a coupon was used, etc. Any random grocery shopper's purchases are captured in scanner data. Scanner panel data are those that further integrate a household's purchases with information on its family's demographics, TV viewing behavior, etc. These additional data are known only for the participating panel members (families agree to participate, presenting their membership card to be scanned to flag their data in the database for later analyses, in exchange for moderate compensation). In this data set, the variables are interpreted as follows:

X_1 = observation number

X_2 = household identification number

X_3 = brand bought during this purchase

X_4 = brand bought during last purchase

X_5 = price per ounce of brand A, X_6 = price per ounce of brand B

X_7 = price per ounce of brand C, X_8 = price per ounce of brand D

X_9 = 1 if brand bought was advertised on television last week

X_{10} = 1 if brand bought was on display or otherwise featured in the grocer

X_{11} = 1 if a coupon was used to buy the brand

X_{12} = number of total purchases by this household through the duration of this data set

X_1	X_2	X_3	X_4	X_5	X_6	X_7	X_8	X_9	X_{10}	X_{11}	X_{12}
109	2212251	A	--	.53	.59	.62	.51	1	0	0	5
110	2212251	C	A	.63	.51	.66	.50	0	0	0	5
111	2212251	B	C	.57	.60	.56	.45	0	1	0	5
112	2212251	A	B	.55	.54	.42	.41	1	0	0	5
113	2212251	A	A	.56	.54	.56	.49	0	0	0	5
114	4412319	D	--	.55	.53	.51	.48	0	0	0	9
115	4412319	B	D	.53	.55	.52	.50	0	1	0	9
116	4412319	C	B	.44	.50	.46	.51	0	0	0	9
117	4412319	B	C	.61	.40	.65	.50	0	1	0	9
118	4412319	C	B	.54	.59	.60	.51	0	1	0	9
119	4412319	C	C	.56	.56	.46	.50	0	0	0	9
120	4412319	B	C	.56	.54	.41	.49	0	1	0	9
121	4412319	A	B	.55	.55	.52	.48	1	0	0	9
122	4412319	C	A	.55	.54	.71	.50	0	0	0	9
123	4142957	C	--	.55	.53	.45	.50	0	1	1	4
124	4142957	B	C	.53	.53	.52	.50	0	1	0	4
125	4142957	C	B	.54	.50	.55	.51	0	0	1	4
126	4142957	B	C	.51	.51	.53	.49	0	1	1	4
127	5281115	B	--	.55	.50	.64	.48	0	1	0	5
128	5281115	A	B	.49	.54	.46	.45	1	0	0	5
129	5281115	B	A	.60	.48	.61	.52	0	1	0	5
130	5281115	B	B	.56	.52	.42	.50	0	1	1	5
131	5281115	B	B	.55	.52	.56	.50	0	0	0	5
132	2143377	A	--	.53	.52	.51	.51	1	0	1	7
133	2143377	C	A	.52	.51	.42	.52	0	1	1	7
134	2143377	B	C	.55	.50	.46	.48	0	0	0	7
135	2143377	C	B	.50	.54	.51	.47	0	1	0	7
136	2143377	B	C	.51	.50	.62	.44	0	1	1	7
137	2143377	A	B	.55	.50	.56	.45	0	0	1	7
138	2143377	A	A	.56	.50	.61	.48	0	0	1	7
139	3301329	A	--	.56	.55	.62	.51	1	0	0	3
140	3301329	A	A	.54	.54	.66	.50	0	0	1	3
141	3301329	A	A	.55	.53	.61	.51	1	0	0	3

The household member presents the family's ID card when checking out. The card is scanned along with the purchases, allowing IRI to relate that family's purchases (by brand, size, and price, etc.) to the family's demographics and its known exposure to coupons, newspaper ads, free samples, and point-of-purchase displays. (Cool, huh?)

IRI also is able to direct different TV advertising spots to different households through the "black boxes" that have been attached to the television sets in each test household, in cooperation with the cable television systems serving the markets. Doing so allows IRI to monitor the buying reactions to different ads or to the same ad in different types of households (e.g., whether the buying reactions to a particular ad are the same or different among past users and nonusers of the product).

ACNielsen's Homescan Service maintains a panel of 55,000 participating households whose purchases are measured through an electronic wand they manually pass over the UPCs on products they've bought. The Homescan Panel does not depend on retailer cooperation or retailer scanning abilities, so it is not outlet-dependent and provides a total market perspective regarding sales of a product. The electronic unit then queries panel members with respect to where the purchase was made, age and gender of the shopper, price paid, deal type, etc. (see Table 7.5).[7]

As you might imagine, a different kind of integrated data source is on the horizon through TiVo and other DVRs. Television service is becoming personalized, and marketers are exploring the utility of experimenting with long-form advertising (TV ads that run for four minutes). The consumer is completely in charge and can end the ad with a button click, or can request more information on the products featured (e.g., a Web address, or information on a local dealership).

Measuring Advertising Exposure and Effectiveness

A great deal of commercial information is available for marketers that relates to the assessment of exposure to and effectiveness of advertising. Most suppliers of B-to-B goods advertise most heavily in trade publications. To sell space more effectively, the various trade publications typically sponsor readership studies, which they then make available to potential advertisers. Suppliers of consumer goods and services also have access to media-sponsored readership studies. In addition, a number of services have evolved to measure consumer exposure to the various media.

Television and Radio

The Nielsen Television Index is probably the most generally familiar commercial information service. Even the most casual television watcher has probably heard of the Nielsen ratings and the impact they have on which TV shows are canceled by the networks and which are allowed to continue. The index itself is designed to provide estimates of the size and nature of the audience for individual television programs. For a long time, the data were gathered through the use of electronic devices attached to the TV sets in Nielsen households. For 30 years now, Nielsen has relied on "people meters." These devices measure not only the TV channel, but who in the household is watching. Each member of the family has his or her own viewing number. Whoever turns on the set, sits down to watch, or changes the channel is supposed to enter his or her number into the people meter. All this information is transmitted immediately to Nielsen for processing.

[7] See acnielsen.com.

TABLE 7.5   Analyses Possible Using ACNielsen's Homescan Service, Scantrack

Type	Purpose	Key Measures
Market Overview, Trend Analysis	To provide a general overview of consumer purchasing for a particular product category, its major segments, and major brands. Measures are compared between brands and over time to identify changes in the marketplace.	Volume and market share % households purchasing category (penetration) Volume per buyer (buying rate) Pricing (total, deal, nondeal) % volume on deal (coupon vs. store special) Distribution of volume by outlet (e.g., grocery, drug, club warehouse)
Demographic Analysis	To target advertising and promotional efforts most effectively by determining the demographic profile of particular buyer groups (e.g., brand buyers, heavy buyers, frequent commercial viewers).	Distribution of buyers across segments Distribution of volume across segments Market share % volume on deal
Loyalty, Combination Purchase	To understand the extent to which buyers are loyal to a brand or store; to determine the competitive set in which brands or stores operate; and to identify size, flavor, form preference, and looks at the importance of price when buyers purchase competitive items.	% brand buyers purchasing competitive items % brand volume by buyers who purchase competitive brands % competitive brand volume purchased on deal
Brand-Shifting	To identify the sources of growth or decline in a brand's sales.	Brand-shifting volume New or lost category buyers % shifting gains and losses
Trial and Repeat	Trial measures consumer interest in a new product by counting households making at least one purchase. Repeat evaluates product satisfaction by determining percentage triers repurchasing.	Cumulative trial and repeat Package rate (volume on trial, on repeat) % volume on deal (total on trial, on repeat) Market share (total from trial vs. repeat)

Source: ACNielsen.

Ethical Dilemma 7.2

In early March, a marketing manager for a tax consultancy stumbled onto an important piece of competitive intelligence while visiting a local printer near the company's plant. While waiting to speak with the salesperson who handled the company's account, the manager noticed some glossy advertising proofs for one of its competitor's products. The ad highlighted a new customer satisfaction guarantee. When he mentioned the guarantee to the printer, he was told that it was part of a new advertising campaign. The marketing manager called a meeting of the company's own management on his return to headquarters. As a result of that meeting, the company initiated a preemptive customer satisfaction guarantee campaign of its own that effectively neutralized the competitor's strategy.

- Did the marketing manager act ethically in reporting the information back to his own company?
- Would your judgment be different if the proofs were in a folder and the marketing manager somewhat casually but inadvertently opened the folder while standing there? What if he did so on purpose after noticing that the folder pertained to the competitor?
- Should information like this be entered into the firm's DSS?

Nielsen estimates the number and percentage of all TV households viewing a given TV show. Ratings are tabulated per 10 socioeconomic and demographic characteristics, including location, education and occupation of head of household, time zones, household income, age of female head of house, Internet service subscription, number of children, and household size. These classifications assist the network in selling advertising on particular programs, while they assist the advertiser in choosing programs to sponsor that reach households with the desired characteristics.

Advertisers buying radio time are also interested in the size and demographic composition of the audiences they will be reaching. Radio-listening statistics are typically gathered using household panel diaries. Arbitron, for example, calls households (telephone numbers generated randomly, to ensure reaching households with unlisted numbers). Those household members who agree to participate are sent diaries, in which they record their radio-listening behavior for a short period. Most radio markets are rated only once or twice a year, although some of the larger ones are rated four times a year. The April/May survey is conducted in every Arbitron market and consequently is known as the "sweeps" period. Radio ratings are broken down by audience age and gender, and focus more on individual than household behavior, in contrast to television ratings.

Print Media

Several services measure exposure and readership to print media. For example, the Roper Starch Readership Service measures the reading of ads in magazines and newspapers. They maintain the world's largest database of some 10,000s of print ads in more than 1,000 issues of consumer magazines, business publications, and newspapers, which are assessed each year, using over 50,000 personal interviews in more than 35 countries. Starch measures recognition—with the magazine open, the respondent is asked to indicate whether he or she has read each ad. Three degrees of reading are recorded:

1. Noted—a person who remembered seeing any part of the ad in that particular issue

2. Associated—a person who not only "noted" the ad but also saw or read some part of it that clearly indicates the brand or advertiser

3. Read most—a person who read 50% or more of the written material in the ad[8]

During the course of the interview, data are also collected on the observation and reading of the component parts of each ad, such as the headlines, subheadings, pictures, copy blocks, etc.

Interviewing begins a short time after the issue of the magazine is placed on sale. For weekly and biweekly consumer magazines, interviewing begins 3–6 days after the on-sale date and continues for 1–2 weeks. For monthly magazines, interviewing begins two weeks after the on-sale date and continues for two weeks. The size of the sample varies by publication. Most Starch studies are based on a minimum of 100 issue readers.

Starch readership reports are compiled issue by issue and include three features: (1) labeled issue, (2) summary report, and (3) adnorm tables. The target ads in each issue are labeled to indicate overall readership level as well as the noting or reading of the major components of the ads. The summary report lists all the ads that were measured in the issue. The ads are arranged by product category and show the percentages for the three degrees of ad

[8] See the Starch Readership Report: Methodology and Use (www.roper.com).

readership—noted, associated, and read most—allowing the comparison of the readership of each ad versus the other target ads in the issue. The adnorm tables enable one to compare the readership of an ad in a given issue with the norm for ads of the same size and color that are for the same product category for that publication.

Starch readership data allow advertisers to compare their ads with competitors' ads, current ads with previous ads, current ads against competitors' previous ads, and current ads against Starch adnorm tables. This process can be effective in assessing changes in theme, copy, layout, use of color, etc.

Multimedia Services

The Simmons Media/Marketing Service uses a national probability sample of more than 20,000 respondents and serves as a comprehensive data source allowing the cross-referencing of product usage and media exposure. Four different interviews are conducted with each respondent so that magazine, TV, newspaper, and radio can all be covered by the Simmons Service (smrb.com).

Interviewers obtain measures of readership of individual magazines and newspapers. Questionnaires are used to gather product purchase and usage information for over 800 product categories. Television-viewing behavior is ascertained by means of a personal viewing diary, and radio-listening behavior is gathered through telephone and personal interviews. Table 7.6 displays a small portion of the information provided by Simmons.

Simmons measures magazine readership "through-the-book"—respondents are screened to determine which magazines they have read during the past six months. They are shown actual issues of magazines stripped of advertising pages and recurring columns and features. Nine feature articles unique to the issue are exhibited, and respondents are asked to select the articles they personally find especially interesting. At the end, a qualifying question is asked: "Now that you have been through this magazine, could you tell me whether this is the first time you happened to look into this particular issue, or have you looked into it before?" Respondents must affirm prior exposure to the issue to qualify as readers. Simmons provides databases of usage and preference for some 865 product lines, but its focus is on media, covering 150 variables on magazine readership, cable-viewing habits, radio-listening patterns, etc.

Mediamark Research also makes available information on exposure to various media and household consumption of a number of products and services. Its annual survey of 20,000 adult respondents covers more than 250 magazines, newspapers, radio stations, and television channels and over 450 products and services (mediamark.com). Information is gathered from respondents through personal interviews (for demographics and media exposure data) and a sorting of a deck of cards with magazine logos on them—the respondent sorts the deck according to whether they (1) are sure they have read, (2) are not sure they have read, and (3) are sure they have not read the magazine within the previous six months.

Newspaper readership is measured using a "yesterday reading" technique in which respondents are asked which of the daily newspapers on the list of papers that circulate in the area were read or looked into within the previous seven days. For Sunday and weekend papers, a four-week time span is used. Radio listening is determined through a "yesterday" recall technique in which respondents are shown a list of five time periods and are asked how much time was spent listening to a radio during each time period on the previous day. They are then asked what stations they listened to. TV audience data are collected in a similar manner.

TABLE 7.6 Sample Output from Simmons Media/Marketing Service

	TOTAL U.S. '000	Interactive Computer Services Use or Subscribe				Personal Computer: Total Own at Home/Use at Work				Own At Home				Personally Use at Work			
		A '000	B DOWN	C %	D INDX	A '000	B DOWN	C %	D INDX	A '000	B DOWN	C %	D INDX	A '000	B DOWN	C %	D INDX
TOTAL ADULTS	187747	9973	100.0	5.3	100	58794	100.0	31.3	100	41392	100.0	22.0	100	35896	100.0	19.1	100
MALES	90070	5178	51.9	5.7	108	28652	48.7	31.8	102	20931	50.6	23.2	105	16917	47.1	18.8	98
FEMALES	97676	4795	48.1	4.9	92	30142	51.3	30.9	99	20462	49.4	20.9	95	18980	52.9	19.4	102
# SHOPPERS	115901	5596	56.1	4.8	91	33828	57.5	29.2	93	22997	55.6	19.8	90	21535	60.0	18.6	97
18-24	23951	1407	14.1	5.9	111	7535	12.8	31.5	100	5652	13.7	23.6	107	3680	10.3	15.4	80
25-34	41492	2466	24.7	5.9	112	13864	23.6	33.4	107	7931	19.2	19.1	87	9545	26.6	23.0	120
35-44	40678	3112	31.2	7.6	144	16372	27.8	40.2	129	11910	28.8	29.3	133	10649	29.7	26.2	137
45-54	29045	2124	21.3	7.3	138	11628	19.8	40.0	128	8691	21.0	29.9	136	7395	20.6	25.5	133
55-64	21263	656	6.6	3.1	58	5684	9.7	26.7	85	4041	9.8	19.0	86	3281	9.1	15.4	81
65 OR OLDER	31318	208	2.1	.7	13	3712	6.3	11.9	38	3168	7.7	10.1	46	1347	3.8	4.3	22
18-34	65443	3873	38.8	5.9	111	21399	36.4	32.7	104	13582	32.8	20.8	94	13225	36.8	20.2	106
18-49	122143	8176	82.0	6.7	126	44653	75.9	36.6	117	30601	73.9	25.1	114	28109	78.3	23.0	120
25-54	111215	7702	77.2	6.9	130	41864	71.2	37.6	120	28532	68.9	25.7	116	27589	76.9	24.8	130
35-49	56701	4304	43.2	7.6	143	23254	39.6	41.0	131	17019	41.1	30.0	136	14884	41.5	26.3	137
50 OR OLDER	65603	1797	18.0	2.7	52	14141	24.1	21.6	69	10791	26.1	16.4	75	7787	21.7	11.9	62
COLLEGE GRAD	37353	4261	42.7	11.4	215	19396	33.0	51.9	166	14460	34.9	38.7	176	12998	36.2	34.8	182
SOME COLLEGE	39301	3243	32.5	8.3	155	15170	25.8	38.6	123	10506	25.4	26.7	121	9358	26.1	23.8	125
H.S.	73139	2112	21.2	2.9	54	18834	32.0	25.8	82	12486	30.2	17.1	77	11037	30.7	15.1	79
SOME H.S.	37954	357	3.6	.9	18	5395	9.2	14.2	45	3940	9.5	10.4	47	2504	7.0	6.6	35
EMPLOYED MALES	62041	4359	43.7	7.0	132	22896	38.9	36.9	118	16191	39.1	26.1	118	14722	41.0	23.7	124
EMP FEMALES	53100	4197	42.1	7.9	149	22405	38.1	42.2	135	13920	33.6	26.2	119	16125	44.9	30.4	159
EMP FULL-TIME	99735	7571	75.9	7.6	143	39145	66.6	39.2	125	25452	61.5	25.5	116	27601	76.9	27.7	145
EMP PART-TIME	15406	985	9.9	6.4	120	6156	10.5	40.0	128	4659	11.3	30.2	137	3247	9.0	21.1	110
NOT EMPLOYED	72606	1417	14.2	2.0	37	13494	23.0	18.6	59	11281	27.3	15.5	70	5049	14.1	7.0	36
PROF'L/MANAGER	32308	3716	37.3	11.5	217	17275	29.4	53.5	171	12245	29.6	37.9	172	12575	35.0	38.9	204
TECH/CLERK/SALE	35568	3752	37.6	10.5	199	15754	26.8	44.3	141	9646	23.3	27.1	123	11142	31.0	31.3	164
PRECISION/CRAFT	12562	430	4.3	3.4	65	3640	6.2	29.0	93	2537	6.1	20.2	92	2156	6.0	17.2	90
OTHER EMPLOYED	34704	658	6.6	1.9	36	8631	14.7	24.9	79	5684	13.7	16.4	74	4974	13.9	14.3	75
SINGLE	41125	2448	24.5	6.0	112	12533	21.3	30.5	97	8489	20.5	20.6	94	6954	19.4	16.9	88
MARRIED	111354	6208	62.3	5.6	105	39317	66.9	35.3	113	28638	69.2	25.7	117	24221	67.5	21.8	114
DIV/SEP/WDW	35268	1317	13.2	3.7	70	6944	11.8	19.7	63	4266	10.3	12.1	55	4721	13.2	13.4	70
PARENTS	61860	4511	45.2	7.3	137	23819	40.5	38.5	123	16839	40.7	27.2	123	14792	41.2	23.9	125
WHITE	159985	8666	86.9	5.4	102	52721	89.7	33.0	105	37324	90.2	23.3	106	32329	90.1	20.2	106
BLACK	21570	882	8.8	4.1	77	4266	7.3	19.8	63	2605	6.3	12.1	55	2732	7.6	12.7	66

OTHER	6191	1426[1]	4.3	6.9	130	1808	3.1	29.2	93	1463	3.5	23.6	107	836	2.3	13.5	71
NE-CENSUS	38611	1966	19.7	5.1	96	11922	20.3	30.9	99	8163	19.7	21.1	96	7272	20.3	18.8	99
MIDWEST	45021	2576	25.8	5.7	108	15610	26.6	34.7	111	10468	25.3	23.3	105	9944	27.7	22.1	116
SOUTH	65246	3721	37.3	5.7	107	18893	32.1	29.0	92	13309	32.2	20.4	93	11449	31.9	17.5	92
WEST	38869	1710	17.2	4.4	83	12368	21.0	31.8	102	9453	22.8	24.3	110	7231	20.1	18.6	97
COUNTY SIZE A	76945	4369	43.8	5.7	107	24542	41.7	31.9	102	17476	42.2	22.7	103	14688	40.9	19.1	100
COUNTY SIZE B	55516	3229	32.4	5.8	110	18012	30.6	32.4	104	12638	30.5	22.8	103	11308	31.5	20.4	107
COUNTY SIZE C	27293	1190	11.9	4.4	82	8752	14.9	32.1	102	6254	15.1	22.9	104	5303	14.8	19.4	102
COUNTY SIZE D	27993	1184	11.9	4.2	80	7488	12.7	26.7	85	5025	12.1	17.9	81	4597	12.8	16.4	86
METRO CITY	58084	2824	28.3	4.9	92	17115	29.1	29.5	94	12005	29.0	20.7	94	10374	28.9	17.9	93
METRO SUBURB	88940	5638	56.5	6.3	119	30126	51.2	33.9	108	21543	52.0	24.2	110	18334	51.1	20.6	108
NON-METRO	40722	1512	15.2	3.7	70	11553	19.6	28.4	91	7845	19.0	19.3	87	7188	20.0	17.7	92
TOP 5 ADI'S	42410	2098	21.0	4.9	93	13209	22.5	31.1	99	9165	22.1	21.6	98	7848	21.9	18.5	97
TOP 10 ADI'S	59256	3183	31.9	5.4	101	18943	32.2	32.0	102	13219	31.9	22.3	101	11365	31.7	19.2	100
TOP 20 ADI'S	81977	4730	47.4	5.8	109	26089	44.4	31.8	102	18500	44.7	22.6	102	15985	44.5	19.5	102
HSHLD. INC. $75K+	26297	2967	29.7	11.3	212	12811	21.8	48.7	156	10029	24.2	38.1	173	7919	22.1	30.1	157
$60,000 OR MORE	43694	4393	44.1	10.1	189	20680	35.2	47.3	151	15855	38.3	36.3	165	13037	36.3	29.8	156
$50,000 OR MORE	61638	5922	59.4	9.6	181	28313	48.2	45.9	147	21123	51.0	34.3	155	17876	49.8	29.0	152
$40,000 OR MORE	83714	7345	73.6	8.8	165	36288	61.7	43.3	138	26594	64.2	31.8	144	22835	63.6	27.3	143
$30,000 OR MORE	110173	8431	84.5	7.7	144	45042	76.6	40.9	131	32011	77.3	29.1	132	28400	79.1	25.8	135
$30,000–$39,999	26459	1087	10.9	4.1	77	8753	14.9	33.1	106	5417	13.1	20.5	93	5565	15.5	21.0	110
$20,000–$29,999	28910	841	8.4	2.9	55	6755	11.5	23.4	75	4530	10.9	15.7	71	3770	10.5	13.0	68
$10,000–$19,999	29666	424	4.3	1.4	27	4575	7.8	15.4	49	3052	7.4	10.3	47	2555	7.1	8.6	45
UNDER $10,000	18998	277[2]	2.8	1.5	27	2423	4.1	12.8	41	1800	4.3	9.5	43	1171	3.3	6.2	32
HHOLD =1 PERSON	23989	626	6.3	2.6	49	4499	7.7	18.8	60	2458	5.9	10.2	46	3083	8.6	12.9	67
2 PEOPLE	61625	2525	25.3	4.1	77	17399	29.6	28.2	90	11972	28.9	19.4	88	11261	31.4	18.3	96
3 OR 4 PEOPLE	75459	5268	52.8	7.0	131	27736	47.2	36.8	117	20306	49.1	26.9	122	16349	45.5	21.7	113
5+	26674	1554	15.6	5.8	110	9161	15.6	34.3	110	6657	16.1	25.0	113	5203	14.5	19.5	102
#CHILDREN	113318	4693	47.1	4.1	78	31278	53.2	27.6	88	21714	52.5	19.2	87	19495	54.3	17.2	90
#<2 YEARS	13676	657	6.6	4.8	90	4461	7.6	32.6	104	2760	6.7	20.2	92	2659	7.4	19.4	102
2–5 YEARS	27475	1493	15.0	5.4	102	8887	15.1	32.3	103	5954	14.4	21.7	98	5544	15.4	20.2	106
6–11 YEARS	35656	2595	26.0	7.3	137	12916	22.0	36.2	116	9451	22.8	26.5	120	7798	21.7	21.9	114
12–17 YEARS	34050	2769	27.8	8.1	153	13431	22.8	39.4	126	10183	24.6	29.9	136	7627	21.2	22.4	117
OWN RESIDENCE	129490	7682	77.0	5.9	112	44189	75.2	34.1	109	31867	77.0	24.6	112	27007	75.2	20.9	109
VALUE: $70,000+	80885	6351	63.7	7.9	148	32555	55.4	40.2	129	24353	58.8	30.1	137	19684	54.8	24.3	127
VALUE: <$70,000	48605	1331	13.3	2.7	52	11633	19.8	23.9	76	7515	18.2	15.5	70	7323	20.4	15.1	79
RENT	52590	1781	17.9	3.4	64	12694	21.6	24.1	77	8111	19.6	15.4	70	7786	21.7	14.8	77

[1] Projection relatively unstable because of sample base—use with caution

[2] # cases too small for reliability—shown for consistency only

Source: Simmons Market Research Bureau, Inc., smrb.com.

On completion of the interview, interviewers leave a questionnaire booklet with respondents. The booklet covers personal and household usage of approximately 3,500 product categories and services and 5,700 brands.

Customized Measurements

It is true that some industries are more likely than others to compile databases on their vendors and customers. For example, consumer packaged goods have access to scanner data, which yield information about one's own product and one's competitors, and the marketing mix environment for both. Similarly, data are plentiful in the pharmaceuticals industry, e.g., physicians' scripts. In contrast, for many business and services marketing questions, secondary data are minimal, and primary marketing research dominates.

Mail Panels

To discuss all the suppliers of customized, primary marketing information would take us far afield, but we do want to discuss mail panels to give readers a sense of their operation. Although they are not a true source of secondary data (because the data collected using them are specifically designed to meet the client's needs), the studies are standardized.

NFO Research Inc. is one of the major independent research firms specializing in custom-designed consumer surveys using mail panels. NFO maintains representative panels drawn from a sampling frame of more than 550,000 U.S. households and more than 100,000 in Europe. These panels represent over one million consumers who have agreed to cooperate without compensation in completing self-administered questionnaires on a variety of topics, including product usage, reaction to a product or its ads, reaction to a product package, attitude toward or awareness of some issue, product, service, or ad, etc.

Parts of the national panel are continually dissolved and rebuilt (for complete turnover every two years) so that the panel is fresh and still matches current family population characteristics with respect to income, population density, age of homemaker, and family size for each of the nine geographic divisions in the census.

A demographic profile is maintained for each family in the data bank (e.g., size of family, education, age of family members, presence and number of children by gender, occupation of the principal wage earner, race). This information is used to generate highly refined population segments. If the user's needs require it, NFO can offer the client panels composed exclusively of mothers of infants, teenagers, elderly people, dog- and cat-owning segments, etc. Each of these panels can be balanced to match specific quotas requested by the client (nfow.com).

The Consumer Mail Panel (CMP), operated as part of Synovate, also represents a sample of households that have agreed to respond to mail questionnaires and product tests. Samples of persons for each product test or use are drawn from over 750,000 households in the CMP pool. The pool is representative of the geographical divisions in the U.S. and Canada, and is broken down according to total household income, population density and degree of urbanization, and age of panel member. It also includes place of residence (state, county, metropolitan area), marital status, occupation and employment status, household size, age, gender, home ownership, and ownership of pets, dishwashers, washing machines, dryers, PCs, and automobiles.

Summary

When confronted by a new problem, the marketer should first seek secondary data. Secondary data are statistics that already exist, in contrast to primary data, which are collected for the purpose at hand. Secondary data possess significant cost and time advantages, and it is only when their pursuit shows diminishing returns and the problem is not yet resolved that the researcher should proceed to primary data.

Secondary data can be found in either primary or secondary sources. A primary source is the source that originated the data, whereas a secondary source is a source that secured the data from an original source. The primary source should always be used. Further, the researcher should make some judgment about the quality and accuracy of secondary data by examining the purpose of publication, the ability of the organization to collect the data, and general evidence of careful work in its presentation and collection.

Secondary data include internal company data, published external secondary data, and data supplied by commercial marketing information services. Internal sales and cost data are the least expensive source of marketing information and can be used to gain perspective on research problems. A wealth of published external secondary data is available.

Standardized marketing information services can be an important adjunct to the researcher's data-collection efforts. These services offer economies of scale because they serve a number of clients for a variety of purposes, and thus they are able to spread their costs of operation among clients. If they are suitable for the clients' needs, they offer substantial time and cost advantages in the collection of primary data. Some common uses of the standardized marketing databases are to profile customers, to measure product sales and market share, and to measure advertising exposure and effectiveness.

Questions

1. For what types of studies would you use mail panels?
2. What is the difference between a primary source and a secondary source of secondary data? Which is preferred? Why?
3. How do the multimedia services operate?
4. What criteria can be employed to judge the accuracy of secondary data?
5. Describe how a type of business can be more successfully identified using Dun's Business Locator.
6. What are the advantages and disadvantages of secondary data?
7. What distinguishes internal secondary data from external secondary data?
8. What is the difference between primary and secondary data?

Applications and Problems

1. Assume that you are interested in opening a fast-food Mexican restaurant in St. Louis, Missouri. You are unsure of its acceptance by consumers and are considering doing a marketing research study to evaluate their attitudes and opinions. In your search for information you find the following studies:
   - Study A was recently conducted by a research agency for a well-known fast-food chain. To secure a copy of this study, you would be required to pay the agency $350. The study evaluated consumers' attitudes toward fast food in general based on a sample of 500 stay-at-home moms for the cities of Springfield, Illinois; St. Louis and Kansas City, Missouri; and Topeka, Kansas. The findings indicated that respondents did not view fast food favorably. The major reason for the unfavorable attitude was the low nutritional value of the food.
   - Study B was completed by a group of students as a requirement for an MBA marketing course. This study would not cost anything; it is available in your university library. The study evaluated consumers' attitudes toward various ethnic fast foods. The respondents consisted of a convenience sample of 200 students from St. Louis. The findings indicated a favorable attitude toward two ethnic fast foods, Italian and Mexican. Based on these results, one of the students planned to open a pizza parlor, but instead accepted a job as sales representative for General Foods Corporation.

   a. Critically evaluate the two sources of data.
   b. Which do you consider to be better? Why?

c. Assume that you decide it will be profitable to become a fast-food franchisee. Identify five specific secondary sources of data and evaluate the data.

2. Several scenarios follow. In each case, a need exists for standardized marketing information. Recommend a service that could provide the required information. Explain your choices.

a. As part of its advertising-sales strategy, radio station KMJC wants to stress that its programming appeals to young adults between the ages of 19 and 25. The advertising salespeople need "numbers" to back up this claim.

b. Fresh Express brand managers have developed a unique coupon and TV campaign for its self-contained bags of salads. The company needs to know the following in order to evaluate the campaign:

i. Are people more likely to use the coupon if they have also seen the TV ad?

ii. What is the median size of the household using the coupon?

iii. What is the proportion of new purchasers to past purchasers among the users of the coupon?

c. DLH Advertising Agency assured one of its clients that, despite the $300,000 cost of placing a half-page ad in one issue of a national magazine, the actual cost of the ad per reader would be less than two cents. DLH is preparing a report to the client and needs data to back its assurance.

d. WestTowne Shopping Center wants to know the demographic characteristics of its patrons. However, the mall's retail tenants recently voted to ban marketing research interviews in or around the mall area, due to numerous customer complaints about harassment by interviewers. Where might the mall obtain the desired information?

3. List some major secondary sources of information for the following situations:

a. The marketing research manager of a national soft-drink manufacturer has to prepare a comprehensive report on the soft-drink industry.

b. Mr. Baker has several ideas for instant cake mixes and is considering entering this industry. He needs to find the necessary background information to assess its potential.

c. Ms. Smith wishes to make the tee-off times at the golf course she manages available to schedule online. She needs to collect information on the golf business and Internet penetration in her city.

d. Mr. Wabit has heard that the profit margins in the fur business are high. The fur industry has always intrigued him, and he decides to do some research to determine if the claim is true.

e. A recent graduate hears that condominiums are once again a good investment. She decides to collect some information on the condominium market.

4. Assume that your school is interested in developing a marketing plan to boost sagging attendance at major athletic events, particularly home football games. As an initial step in developing the new marketing plan, the athletic department has decided that it needs demographic and lifestyle profiles of people who currently attend games on a regular (season ticket) basis. Fortunately, the ticket office maintains a listing of all season-ticket purchasers (including names and addresses) from year to year. What potential sources of internal secondary data might the athletic department first investigate before considering the collection of primary data?

Appendix:
Secondary Data[1]

7

T ons of secondary data are available. Here is a list to get you started.

Census Data

The Bureau of the Census of the U.S. Department of Commerce is the largest gatherer of statistical information in the country. The first "Census of Population" was a head count required by the Constitution to apportion representatives in Congress. Now dozens of different population and economic industry censuses exist which are of interest to the marketing researcher. Several were listed in Research Realities 7.4. For more, go to www.census.gov.

In addition, for Industry Information, see sources such as these:

Commodity Yearbook (Knight-Ridder Financial/Commodity Research Bureau, www.investorsoftware.com): This annual publication contains data on prices, production, exports, stocks, and other aspects for approximately 100 individual commodities.

Industry Norms and Key Business Ratios (Dun & Bradstreet, www.dnb.com): This annual publication provides industry norm statistics for over 800 types of businesses.

Inside U.S. Business: A Concise Encyclopedia of Leading Industries (McGraw Hill): Includes major industries, description of top companies, recent trends, and key issues.

Manufacturing USA: Industry Analyses, Statistics, and Leading Companies (Gale Research): Provides comprehensive information on more than 450 manufacturing industries. (Also see Service Industries USA, listed later.)

[1] For more information about these sources, and for even more sources, please go to our Web site.

Moody's Industry Review (www.moodys.com): Provides financial information on more than 135 industry groups and compares the performance of top companies within each industry.

North American Industry Classification System Manual (at census.gov): Provides the basic system used for classifying industries into 20 major divisions. The system is used for federal economic statistics classified by industry. Replaced SIC codes.

Predicast's Basebook (Foster City, CA: Information Access Co.): Arranged by industry, this publication provides a wide array of statistical information on U.S. business sectors.

RMA Annual Statement Studies (Robert Morris Associates, www.rmahq.org): This volume provides composite financial data on over 400 manufacturers, wholesalersers, retailers, service providers, and agricultural endeavors.

Service Industries USA: Industry Analyses, Statistics, and Leading Organizations (Gale Research): Provides comprehensive information on 150 service industries.

Standard & Poor's Industry Surveys (standardpoor.com): Organized by industry, consists of detailed articles as well as charts and graphs depicting trends in 52 areas.

Worldcasts (Foster City, CA: Information Access Co.): Provides worldwide forecast information for regions and products. Forecast data are drawn from over 800 publications.

Company Information

Fortune Directory (fortune.com): Published annually by the editors of *Fortune* magazine, this directory provides information on sales, assets, profits, invested capital, and employees for the 500 largest industrial corporations in the United States.

Hoover's Handbook of American Business (Austin, TX: Hoover's Business Press): Profiles over 700 of the largest and fastest-growing companies in the United States. A useful "List-Lover's Compendium" is also included.

Million Dollar Directory (Dun & Bradstreet): Lists the offices, products, sales, and number of employees for United States companies with assets of at least $500,000.

Moody's Manuals (moodys.com): Published annually, these manuals contain balance sheets and income statements for individual companies and governmental units.

Standard & Poor's Corporate Records (www.standardandpoors.com): Provides current financial statistics, news items, and background information on 12,000 publicly traded companies.

Standard & Poor's Register of Corporations, Directors and Executives (standardandpoors.com): Lists officers, products, sales, addresses, telephone numbers, and employees for more than 56,000 U.S. and Canadian public companies.

Market and Consumer Information

A Guide to Consumer Markets (New York: The Conference Board): Issued annually, this publication contains data on the behavior of consumers in the marketplace. It includes statistics on population, employment, income, expenditure, and prices.

Aging America—Trends and Projections (U.S. Senate Special Committee on Aging and the American Association of Retired Persons, Washington, DC: Government Printing Office): This chartbook describes the sustained growth in

America's elderly population expected during the next 30 years. Includes graphs and tables on demographics, employment, health, and income.

Marketing Economics Guide (New York: Marketing Economics Institute): This annual publication provides detailed operating information on 1,500 retailing centers throughout the country on a regional, state, county, and city basis; includes information on population, percentage of households by income class, disposable income, total retail sales, and retail sales by store group.

Rand McNally Commercial Atlas and Marketing Guide (Rand McNally Company): This annual atlas contains marketing data and maps for some 100,000 cities and towns in the United States. Included is information on such matters as population, auto registrations, and retail trade.

Sales and Marketing Management Survey of Buying Power (New York: Sales and Marketing Management): Contains market data for states, a number of counties, cities, and standard metropolitan statistical areas. Included are statistics on population, retail sales, and household income, as well as a combined index of buying power for each reported geographic area.

General Economic and Statistical Information

Economic Indicators (Council of Economic Advisers, Washington, DC: Government Printing Office): This monthly publication contains charts and tables of general economic data, such as gross national product, personal consumption expenditures, and other series important in measuring general economic activity. An annual supplement presenting historical and descriptive material on the sources, uses, and limitations of the data is also issued.

The Economic Policy Institute (epinet.org): A nonprofit, nonpartisan think tank that conducts research and provides its findings and observations on the economy, including labor markets and globalization, the government, and public policy.

Federal Reserve Bulletin (Washington, DC: Federal Reserve System Board of Governors): Published monthly, this publication is an important source of financial data, including statistics on banking activity, interest rates, savings, the index of industrial production, an index of department store sales, prices, and international trade and finance.

The Handbook of Basic Economic Statistics (Washington, DC: Economic Statistics Bureau of Washington, DC): Compiles some 1,800 statistical series related to the national economy condensed from the volumes of information released by the federal government.

Handbook of Cyclical Indicators (Washington, DC: U.S. Department of Commerce): This monthly publication contains at least 70 indicators of business activity designed to serve as a key to general economic conditions.

Statistical Abstract of the United States (U.S. Bureau of the Census, Washington, DC: Government Printing Office): This annual publication reproduces more than 1,500 tables originally published elsewhere that cover such areas as the economic, demographic, social, and political structure of the United States.

International and Cross-Cultural Information

Business America: This biweekly publication of the Department of Commerce (doc.gov) contains marketing reports and economic analyses per country.

Business Organizations, Agencies, and Publications Directory (Detroit: Gale Research): This directory serves as a guide to approximately 30,000 organizations, agencies, and publications related to foreign and domestic business, trade, and industry.

Country Information Kits (Washington, DC: Overseas Private Investment Corporation, opic.gov): Provides information on developing and emerging countries and worldwide regions.

EuroMonitor's Global Market (euromonitor.com): A database that provides information on countries and their people and markets, and statistics on market analyses and company profiles.

Hispanic and Asian Marketing Communication Research, Inc. (hamcr.com): This publication presents studies that profile the Latin American and Asian consumer.

Greenbook: International Directory of Marketing Research Companies and Services (New York: American Marketing Association, New York Chapter): Lists domestic and international marketing research companies.

International Financial Statistics (Washington, DC: International Monetary Fund, imf.org): Provides exchange and interest rates, and banking and government financial indexes.

Profit Impact of Market Strategy (pimsonline.com): The PIMS data, as they are known, represent business strategic efforts and results of 3,000 firms in North America and Europe.

Stat-USA.gov: Department of Commerce: Tracks export statistics.

United Nations Statistical Yearbook (New York: United Nations): This annual United Nations publication contains statistics on a wide range of foreign and domestic activities, including forestry, transportation, manufacturing, consumption, and education.

World Almanac and Book of Facts (New York: Newspaper Enterprise Association): Issued annually, this publication serves as a well-indexed handbook on a wide variety of subjects. Included are industrial, financial, religious, social, and political statistics.

World Association of Research Professionals (esomar.nl): Provides detailed information on marketing research firms worldwide—perfect if you need to partner abroad, for example, for global studies of customer satisfaction.

World Factbook (Washington, DC: Government Printing Office): This annual CIA publication provides data on demography, economy, and so on, per country.

Finally, generally helpful company and association sites:

American Marketing Association: marketingpower.com
American Demographics: adage.com
The Gallup Organization: gallup.com

Data Collection: Primary Data

8

Questions to Guide Your Learning:

Q1 What are the kinds of data that marketers want (e.g., demographic, psychographic)?

Q2 What can surveys do for me? What are their limitations?

Q3 How do I write a questionnaire?

Q4 What options are there for administering a survey (e.g., online, mail, phone)?

In the previous chapter, we saw that secondary data represent fast and inexpensive research information. But primary data have strengths also. In the next two chapters, we describe data-collection forms used to obtain primary data, and we talk about how to measure consumer attitudes and behaviors. The current chapter is divided into three parts: (a) types of primary data generally obtained from customers, (2) communication and observation techniques, and (3) modes of administering these methods.

Types of Primary Data

The varieties of primary data to be collected are nearly endless. We present the most popular categories used in marketing research.

Demographic and Socioeconomic Characteristics

One type of primary data of great interest to marketers is a consumer's demographic and socioeconomic characteristics, such as age, education, occupation, marital status, gender, income, or social class. These variables are used to cross-classify data to help make sense of consumers' responses. For example, suppose we are interested in people's attitudes about the environment. We might suspect, test, and find that attitudes toward green marketing are related to the respondents' level of education. Similarly, marketers frequently ask whether the consumption of particular products (e.g., SUVs, disposable diapers, vacation golf packages) are related to a person's (or family's) age, education, income, and so on.

Demographic variables may seem simple (that is, they would not capture nuances of consumer preferences), so it may seem risky to make such generalizations about people. However, consider two stable examples of the usefulness of demographics in predicting consumer preferences and behaviors: (1) 18- to 49-year-old men tend to be interested in sports, and it is this segment that makes sports TV programming highly profitable; (2) most of the disposable income in the U.S. comes from people 40 years old and older. Such demographic information (e.g., age and gender) and socioeconomic characteristics (wealth and discretionary funds) are often used to delineate market segments.

Demographic and socioeconomic characteristics represent attributes of people. Some of these attributes, such as a respondent's age, gender, and level of formal education, can be readily verified. Some, such as social class or cultural traditions can only be approximated because they are relative and not absolute measures of a person's standing in society. Income represents an intermediate degree of difficulty in verifiability—even though a person's income is an actual quantity, ascertaining the amount sometimes proves to be difficult.

Psychological and Lifestyle Characteristics

Another type of primary data of interest to marketers is the customer's psychological and lifestyle characteristics in the form of personality traits, activities, interests, and values. Personality refers to the typical patterns of behavior that an individual exhibits—the attributes, traits, and mannerisms that distinguish one person from another. We often characterize people by the personality traits they display, e.g., aggressiveness, dominance, friendliness, or sociability.[1] The argument is that personality affects a consumer's choice of stores or products (e.g., a consumer concerned with animal testing may purchase body lotions only at the Body Shop) or an individual's response to an in-store ad or point-of-purchase display (e.g., appealing to consumers who are "impulsive" or "variety seekers"), just as it is believed, say, that extroverts are successful salespeople.

Lifestyle or psychographic analysis rests on the premise that the firm can plan more effective strategies to reach its target market if it knows more about those customers in terms of how they live, what interests them, and what they like. For example, the financial services market uses demographics (e.g., income, age) and comfort-level with risk to understand potential investors. It's easy to imagine pitching different investment portfolios to different segments of people. It's also easy to see why just knowing a client's income isn't sufficient—just because two households share an income in the bracket "50,000 to 100,000" doesn't mean they are similar in their lifestyles or psychographic profiles, and so they would find different investment packages attractive.

Much psychographic research has been focused on developing a number of statements that reflect a person's activities, interests, and opinions (AIO) and consumption behavior (see Table 8.1). The statements include such things as, "I like to watch football games on television," "I like stamp collecting," "I am very interested in national politics." Marketing research firms collect large samples of data on purchases as well as omnibus lifestyle patterns. The goal is to identify groups of consumers who have similar lifestyles and therefore are likely to behave similarly toward the product or service. For example, Research Realities 8.1 provides descriptions of travelers who share the goal of visiting friends or relatives, but who differ in family composition (children or not), length of trip (short or long), and the activities they seek (visiting beaches or

Types of primary data:

- Demographics & socioeconomic
- Psychographic & lifestyle
- Attitudes & opinions
- Awareness & knowledge
- Intentions
- Motivation
- Behavior

---

[1] Two helpful collections for marketers are Gordon C. Bruner, Karen James, Paul Hensel (eds.), *Marketing Scales Handbook* (marketingpower.com) and Richard Netemeyer, William Bearden, and Subhash Sharma, *Scaling Procedures* (Sage, 2003).

TABLE 8.1   **Lifestyle Dimensions**

Activities	Interests	Opinions
Work	Family	Themselves
Hobbies	Home	Social issues
Social events	Job	Politics
Vacation	Community	Business
Entertainment	Recreation	Economics
Club membership	Fashion	Education
Community	Food	Products
Shopping	Media	Future
Sports	Achievements	Culture

theme parks). Segment descriptions help the marketer determine which groups to target, and how to formulate their advertising.

It is inefficient for marketers to develop new psychographics or AIO inventories for every different category, each product requiring new data collection and analysis. As an alternative, "Value and Lifestyles" research (VALS) avoids these problems by creating a more general psychographic framework that can be used for a variety of products.[2] Research Realities 8.2 shows the basic framework of VALS, and Table 8.2 illustrates an example of six international segments that have been identified by applying values surveys to teenagers.

RESEARCH   REALITIES

8.1 Lifestyle Descriptions and Qualities Sought by People Traveling to Visit Friends and Family in Australia

Beach Relaxation (38%) Major reason for trip is pleasure travel. Visiting friends and family is important along with taking advantage of warm weather and beaches. Tend to be repeat visitors, staying with friends and relatives, or in recreation vehicle parks.

Active Beach Resort (15%) Tend to be younger, traveling with children, coming longer distances. Seek weather as dominant feature. They'll visit theme parks, beaches, and other family attractions. These young families stay in suites or apartments, or with friends and relatives. This group incurs the greatest overall expenditures.

Active Nature Lovers (16%) Seek good weather, then visiting friends and family and the Great Barrier Reef. Likely to have traveled greater distances (e.g., from Europe), and therefore spend the most on transportation. They stay the longest, often with friends and relatives.

Inactives (31%) Visiting friends and relatives is the only major activity planned; likely to have traveled shorter distances, staying the shortest duration. They spend the least.

Source: Gianna Moscardo et al., "Developing a Typology for Understanding Visiting Friends and Relatives Markets," Journal of Travel Research, *38 (3), 251–259.*

---

[2] Another value-based classification scheme is the List of Values (LOV); for an application, see Julie Anne Lee, Geoffrey N. Soutar, and Jordan Louviere, "Measuring Values Using Best-Worst Scaling: The LOV Example" *Psychology and Marketing* 24 (12), 1043–1058.

R E S E A R C H   R E A L I T I E S

8.2 The Structure of the VALS Inventory

VALS is basically a questionnaire about different aspects of consumers' lives and value systems. The survey asks the consumer to indicate the extent to which they agree or disagree with items on numerous issues, such as:

- "I like a lot of variety in my life."
- "I love to make things I can use everyday."
- "I like being in charge of a group."
- "I like trying new things."
- "I like to dress in the latest fashions."
- "I like my life to be pretty much the same from week to week."
- "I would like to spend a year or more in a foreign country."

Consumers who provide similar patterns of responses are segmented into one of eight groups, as described shortly. These values-based segments have been used in a wide variety of marketing applications, including:

- Concept formation in new product development
- Development of ads and media selection to communicate targeted messages about features and benefits of new and improved products
- Selection of the most suitable business alliance partners and distribution channel relationships

The eight segments of consumers are formed as follows. First, people are classified according to their *primary motivation.* That is, people are thought to be primarily driven by one of the following (which are you?):

- Ideals-people (people guided by knowledge and principles)
- Achievement-Oriented (consumers look for products as signs of their success)

- Self-Expression (people seeking social or physical activity, variety and risk)

People may also be classified according to their level of resources and innovativeness. People with greater incomes and education levels have more resources to bring to expressing themselves in the marketplace, but resources are not just about money. People with high energy and self-confidence, and people who are intelligent, seek novelty, are leaders, and are somewhat vain have greater cognitive and emotional resources to bring to their expression.

The three primary motivations and a person's level of resources determine their membership in one of six segments:

- **Thinkers:** people with many resources motivated by ideals
- **Believers:** people with fewer resources for whom ideals are very important
- **Achievers:** people who care about achievement and have the resources to go after goals
- **Strivers:** people with fewer resources but who are trying to achieve
- **Experiencers:** people who care about self-expression and have the resources to do so
- **Makers:** people who care about self-expression but have few resources at their disposal.

We said "eight" and, yes, you've counted only six segments. *Innovators* are purely high on the resources/innovativeness scale, but are not distinguishable on the ideals/achievement/expression dimension. At the other extreme, the *Survivors* are doing just that—they have minimal resources and are motivated more simply by survival than more abstract motivations.

Attitudes and Opinions

The term attitude is used to refer to an individual's "preference, inclination, views, or feelings toward some phenomenon," and opinions are "verbal expressions" of those attitudes. We treat the terms interchangeably as representing a person's ideas, convictions, or liking with respect to a specific object or idea.

TABLE 8.2   Segments Identified Using Values Surveys Among Teens Worldwide

Segment	%	Key Countries	Enjoy	Worry About	Own/Wear/Do
Thrills & chills (sensations)	18	Germany, U.K., Lithuania, Greece, Netherlands, South Africa, U.S.	Going out to eat, to a bar, drinking, smoking, going to a party, going on a date, dancing; have most online access	Finding love, unplanned pregnancy, own attractiveness	Fast food, acne medication, perfume, would dye hair, would like tattoo or nose ring; do not have a job or attend church
Upholders (family, tradition)	16	Vietnam, Indonesia, Taiwan, China, Italy, Peru, Venezuela, Puerto Rico, India, Philippines, Singapore	Reading books, spending time with family and visiting relatives; have least online access	Not living up to others' expectations; believe the world will improve in their lifetime	Do not have jobs to earn money, eat fast food, wear deodorant, wear tattoos or nose rings, carry guns; girls do not wear makeup
Quiet achievers (success, anonymity)	15	Thailand, China, Hong Kong, Ukraine, Korea, Lithuania, Russia, Peru	Studying, listening to music, visiting museums; do not enjoy going to parties or drinking wine/beer	Not living up to others' expectations; do not worry about finishing education, pregnancy, AIDS, drugs	Do not have jobs, or backpacks, blue jeans or athletic shoes; girls do not wear makeup
Resigned (low expectations)	14	Denmark, Sweden, Korea, Japan, U.K., Norway, Germany, Belgium, France, Netherlands, Spain, Argentina, Canada, Turkey, Taiwan	Do not enjoy doing something artistic/creative, attending opera, play or ballet, or visiting relatives	Do not worry about going to college, the economy, rain forest, global warming, living up to others' expectations	Have dyed hair or would dye hair; do not care about access to new technology
Boot-strappers (achievement, individualism)	14	Nigeria, Mexico, U.S., India, Chile, Puerto Rico, South Africa, Venezuela, Colombia	Spending time with family and visiting relatives	Do not worry about not having friends; believe education is good prep for future, expect to have a good life	Attend religious services; do not receive allowances

(Continued)

TABLE 8.2   Continued

Segment	%	Key Countries	Enjoy	Worry About	Own/ Wear/Do
World savers (environment)	12	Hungary, Brazil, Philippines, Venezuela, Spain, Colombia, Belgium, Argentina, Russia, Singapore, France, Poland, Ukraine, Italy, South Africa, Mexico, U.K.	Attending opera, plays, and ballet, doing something artistic/creative (such as taking photos), going camping/hiking, going to a bar, dancing	Racism, poverty for others, environment, AIDS, war, terrorism, being able to have children, finding love	Would not carry gun

Source: For more information, see Elissa Moses, The $100 *Billion Allowance: Accessing the Global Teen Market* (Wiley, pp. 80–103).

Attitudes are pervasive because it is generally thought that they are related to behavior—when consumers like a product, they are more inclined to buy it than when they do not like it, and when they like one brand more than another, they tend to buy the preferred brand. Attitudes thus are said to be the forerunners of behavior.

Accordingly, marketers are interested in people's attitudes toward a product (e.g., "Do you like soft drinks?"), their attitudes with respect to specific brands ("Coke, Pepsi, or 7-Up?"), and their attitudes toward specific features of the brands ("diet, caffeine-free, cherry?"). Attitude is so important in marketing that we devote an entire chapter shortly to various attitude measures.

Awareness and Knowledge

Awareness and knowledge refer to what respondents know about some object. For instance, an important problem in marketing is determining the effectiveness of ads in such media as TV, radio, magazine, billboard, and Web banners. One measure of effectiveness is the product awareness generated by the ad, using one of the three approaches described in Table 8.3. All three tests of memory—unaided recall, aided recall, and recognition—are aimed at assessing the respondent's awareness and knowledge. The three measures reflect differences in the extent to which consumers have cognitively processed (in depth and detail or just superficially) the ad. It is thought that consumers have retained more knowledge from the ad when they state the brand in an *unaided recall* test ("What products and brands do you remember seeing ads for?") compared to a *recall* test where they have been given hints ("Do you remember recently seeing ads for PCs?"), and that both of these show superior knowledge and retention over simple *recognition* ("Do you remember seeing this ad for Dell?").

One of the common indices used to measure the short-term success and impact of an ad is day-after recall (or DAR), which is a phone survey made the day following the airing of a new ad (e.g., the day after the Super Bowl). The DAR scores are compared to the ad agency's database of such indices to project sales, by using other recent ads that had achieved similar DAR scores as benchmarks.

Increasingly, advertising researchers are exploring the idea that consumers do not have to explicitly remember an ad for that ad to nevertheless have an impact on their behavior. For example, after airing an ad for Reebok, the researcher might choose to use "implicit" or indirect tests of memory. Rather than

TABLE 8.3	Approaches Used to Measure Awareness

Unaided recall: Without being given any clues, consumers are asked to recall what advertisements they have seen recently. Prompting is not used because, presumably, even if prompting for the general category were used (such as for soups), respondents would have a tendency to remember more advertisements in that product category.

Aided recall: Consumers are prompted, typically in the form of questions about advertisements in a specific product category. Alternatively, respondents might be given a list showing the names or trademarks of advertisers that appeared recently (in the ad format being tested, such as on radio or Web), along with names or trademarks that did not appear, and would be asked to check those to which they were exposed.

Recognition: Actual advertisements are shown or described to consumers, who are asked whether or not they remember seeing each one.

asking, "Do you remember any recent ads for athletic shoes or Reeboks?" the researcher might instead ask consumers to list brand names of sneakers, their first choice set of sporting shoes, shoes affiliated with athletes, and so on, to assess the number of times the Reebok brand name appears. Researchers have even asked questions as oblique as, "Name all the brands of any kind of product that start with R" to see how often Reebok would appear, along with names such as Reese's, Rolex, and Ramada. The assumption in these tests is that if Reebok appears disproportionately more than it should (based on market shares), the ad was successful in bringing the Reebok brand name to mind.

Ethical Dilemma 8.1

Pharmaceutical Supply Company derives its major source of revenue from physician-prescribed drugs. Until recently, Pharmaceutical Supply had maintained a dominant position in the market. A new competitor had entered the market, however, and was quickly gaining market share.

In response to competitive pressure, Pharmaceutical Supply's management decided that it needed to conduct an extensive study concerning physician decision making with regard to selection of drugs. Janice Rowland, the marketing research director, decided that the best way to gather this information was through the use of personal and telephone interviews. Ms. Rowland directed the interviewers to represent themselves as employees of a fictitious marketing research agency, as she believed that a biased response would result if the physicians were aware that Pharmaceutical Supply was conducting the study. In addition, the interviewers were instructed to tell the physicians that the research was being conducted for their own purpose and not for a particular client.

Was Ms. Rowland's decision to withhold the sponsor's true name and purpose a good one?

- Do the physicians have a right to know who is conducting the research?
- It has been argued that using deception prevents a respondent from making a rational choice about whether or not she or he wishes to participate in a study. Comment.
- What results might have been obtained if the physicians knew the true sponsor?
- What are the consequences for the research profession of using this form of deception?

Intentions

A person's intentions refer to the individual's anticipated or planned future behavior. Marketers are primarily interested in people's intentions with regard to purchasing behavior. The Survey Research Center at the University of Michigan (see isr.umich.edu/src) regularly conducts surveys for the Federal Reserve Board to determine the financial condition of consumers. The center phones a sample of 500 households monthly, asking 50 core questions about consumer confidence and buying intentions for big-ticket items such as appliances, automobiles, and homes during the next few months.

In marketing, intentions are often gathered by asking respondents to indicate which of the following best describes their plans with respect to a new product or service:

- Definitely would buy
- Probably would buy
- Undecided
- Probably would not buy
- Definitely would not buy

The number of people who answer that they "definitely would buy" or "probably would buy" are often combined into a "top 2 box" to indicate likely reaction to the new product or service.

It is true that behavioral intentions do not predict behavior perfectly; a disparity often exists between what people say they are going to do and what they actually do. However, they are fairly correlated. See Research Realities 8.3 for a demonstration.

The prediction of behaviors by intentions is not perfect, but sometimes behavioral data are too expensive, difficult, or even impossible to obtain. For example, if Doritos were to create a new spicy salsa-flavor chip as a line extension, by definition no purchase data would exist because the snack food would not have been available yet for purchase. In the absence of purchase data, consumer intentions are as close to actual behaviors as marketers can get. To help compensate for the imperfect prediction, firms that collect purchase intentions data often adjust the data for the bias that intentions data are likely to contain (based on their past experience).

Purchase intentions are most often used when studying the purchase of commodities requiring large outlays, such as an automobile for a family or plant and equipment for a business. The general assumption is that the larger the dollar expenditure, the more planning necessary, and the greater the correlation between anticipated and actual behavior.

Motivation

Consumers have motives and drives (hunger, thirst, shelter, and sex) and wants (e.g., hunger *needs* give rise to *wanting* a good steak dinner). A marketing researcher's interest in motives typically involves determining why people behave as they do. If we understand the motives behind a person's behavior, we understand the behavior better and, in turn, are in a better position to influence future behavior.

Behavior

Behavior concerns what customers have done or are doing. Usually in marketing, this means purchase and usage behavior. Behavior is a physical activity that

R E S E A R C H   R E A L I T I E S

8.3 What Is the Relationship Between Stated Purchase Intentions and Subsequent Purchase?

A large marketing research firm conducted a study in which they asked consumers for their *purchase intentions,* "How likely is it you will be buying a microwave oven in the next six months?" The responses are provided in the left-most column of data (in the table below). Most people didn't expect to buy this product in the near future.

The consumers were tracked to study their subsequent actual *purchase behaviors.* The results were not veridical (not all of the 7% of those stating they'd be buying a microwave oven in fact did so), but the results were indeed correlated. More people bought who said they'd buy, and fewer people bought who said they wouldn't.

Stated purchase intentions give us information about likely future purchase behaviors.

Microwave ovens:		% of each who:	
	Initial response	**Bought**	**Did not buy**
Intend to buy	7%	20%	56%
Do not intend to buy	78%	3%	70%

Source: "Measuring Buying Intentions: How Valid is the Estimate?"
www.synovate.com/insights/research-on-research/

In an analogous investigation, Burke, Inc. conducted a study in which they asked consumers to rate front-line sales representatives in a services marketing sector on a 10-point scale, measuring a number of attributes, including their rep's knowledge and friendliness.

The customers were also asked about their likelihood of repeat purchasing, that is, the probability that would stay customers of the firm.

Plotting the means on the attributes against the means of the customer retention figures is a helpful diagnostic for the firm. In the plot of the service rep's knowledge, you can see that barely exceeding the mid-point on a 10-point scale (i.e., 5 or more) translates into a customer's likelihood of staying loyal (at least for the short term) of 75% or greater. If the service rep's level of knowledge is truly poor (a rating of 4 or less), the customer retention levels are much lower, e.g., the customers stop purchasing in the category, or they take their dollars to a competitor.

The relationship between a service rep's helpfulness and customer retention is slightly different. Here, a rating of "5" is much worse news than a "5" on the knowledge dimension because customer retention deteriorates more quickly. For a knowledge rating of 5, the retention was 75%; for a helpfulness rating of 5, retention is about 55%. At least for this particular industry, customers are less willing to tolerate front-line service people who don't try to be helpful. You can imagine this translating into employee training—"Even if you don't know the answer to a customer's question, try to be helpful, for example, go find out." Customers won't punish the firm for a service rep's lack of knowledge, but they will for their unhelpfulness.

Source: "Customer Retention as a Function of Customer Service Metrics"
White Paper series *(burke.com).*

TABLE 8.4	Behavior Checklist	
	Purchase Behavior	**Use Behavior**
What and how much		
Who		
When		
Where		
How		

takes place under specific circumstances, at a particular time, and involves one or more participants. Table 8.4 is a checklist of the key dimensions of behavior. There are many facets to each dimension. For example, the "where of purchase" may be specified according to the kind of store, the location of the store by broad geographic area or specific address, the size of the store, etc.

Behavior data are becoming increasingly available through various technologies and are very important to marketers in customer relationship management. The most prevalent behavioral data are scanner data, as described in Chapter 7. A different source of behavior data is online click-streams, which capture personal profile data, click-stream trails, and records of ads and responses. Many marketers feel more confident predicting customers' future behavior as a function of their past behavior, rather than from surveys of likely future behavioral intentions; others point out that attitudinal and motivational data supplement behavioral data, giving the marketer an understanding of *why* consumers behave the way they do. Clearly this information is complementary and it would enrich the marketer's understanding to have both.

Basic Means of Obtaining Primary Data

Primary data can be collected in several ways (see Figure 8.1). The primary decision is whether to use communication or observation techniques. The first involves a questionnaire or survey, oral or written. Observation does not involve questioning. Rather, facts or behaviors are recorded. The observer may be a person (e.g., a researcher conducting a pantry audit) or some mechanical device (namely scanners or the Web).

Communication and observation each has its own advantages and disadvantages that can be classified according to several dimensions:

1. Versatility: "What can you do with the technique?"

2. Business logistics: "How much will a study cost, how quickly will we see the results, and what do response rates look like?"

Communication: Ask people
Observation: Watch them

3. Data quality: "Are the responses objective and accurate?"

The communication method of data collection has the general advantages of versatility, speed, and lower cost, whereas observational data are typically more objective and accurate.

Versatility

Versatility refers to a technique's ability to collect information on the different types of primary data of interest to marketers. A respondent's demographic and socioeconomic characteristics and lifestyle, attitudes and opinions, awareness and knowledge, intentions, motivations underlying actions, and even behaviors

FIGURE 8.1   Choices when Collecting Primary Data

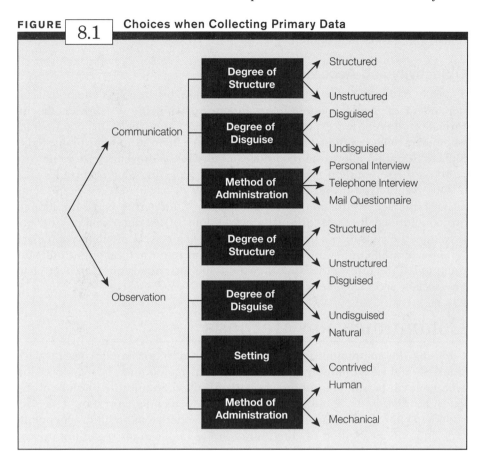

may all be obtained by the communication method (e.g., interview or survey). All we need to do is ask (problems of accuracy may result, and we discuss this issue later).

Observation is more limited. It is best suited for obtaining information about behavior and certain demographic or socioeconomic characteristics. Among behaviors, note that we are limited to observing present behavior; we cannot observe past behavior, nor intentions for future behavior. Among demographic or socioeconomic characteristics, some can be readily observed (e.g., gender). Others can be observed but with less accuracy. A person's age and income, for example, might be inferred by closely examining a person's clothing and purchasing behavior.

Speed and Cost

The speed and cost advantages of the communication method are closely intertwined (time is money!). Communication is often a faster means of data collection, because researchers are not forced to wait for events to occur as they are with the observation method. For example, an observer checking for the brand purchased most frequently in one of several appliance categories might have to wait a long time to make any observations at all. Much of the time the observer would be idle. Such idleness is expensive, given that the worker is probably compensated on an hourly rather than a per-contact basis.

There are always exceptions. Observation is faster and costs less than communication in the purchase of consumer packaged goods. Scanners allow many more purchases to be recorded and at less cost than if purchasers were questioned about what they bought.

Objectivity and Accuracy

Typically data are more accurate by observation because this method is independent of the respondent's unwillingness or inability to provide the information desired. For example, respondents are often reluctant to cooperate when their replies would be embarrassing or place them in an unfavorable light. Since observation allows the recording of behavior as it occurs, it does not depend on the respondent's memory or mood in reporting what occurred.

Observation typically produces more objective data. The interview represents a social interaction situation. Thus, the replies of the person being questioned are conditioned by the individual's perceptions of the interviewer. With observation, the consumer's perceptions play less of a role. Sometimes people are not even aware that they are being observed, thus removing the opportunity for them to tell the interviewer what they think the interviewer wants to hear or to give socially acceptable responses.

Communication Methods

Choosing the communication method of data collection implies several decisions. Should we administer questionnaires by e-mail, online, by mail, over the telephone, in person at a shopping mall, or via fax? Should the purpose of the study be disguised? Should the answers be open-ended, or should the respondent choose from a set of alternatives? These decisions are interdependent; a decision about method of administration has implications regarding the degree of structure that must be imposed on the questionnaire.

Figure 8.1 summarizes the decisions that a researcher must make when collecting data, including issues of structure and disguise. **Structure** is the degree of standardization imposed on the questionnaire. In a highly structured questionnaire, the questions to be asked and the responses permitted the respondents are predetermined (e.g., "Circle a number from 1 to 7"). In an unstructured questionnaire, the questions to be asked are only loosely determined, and respondents are free to answer in their own words (e.g., "Tell me how your family feels about ice cream").

Disguise is the amount of knowledge about the purpose of a study communicated to a respondent. An undisguised questionnaire makes the purpose of the research obvious by the questions posed, whereas a disguised questionnaire attempts to hide the purpose of the study. For example, if Ford wished to determine its customers' satisfaction, they might worry that a cover letter from Ford and questions all about Ford cars and trucks would bias the respondents' answers favorably toward Ford, since the survey's purpose is clear. If Ford wanted more objective data, it might go through an outside marketing research agency, and ask its drivers about Ford, GM, and Honda cars. In this scenario, the target of the research is less clear, and it would be expected that the customer would answer more truthfully.

Structured–Undisguised Questionnaires

Structured–undisguised questionnaires are most commonly used in marketing research. Questions are presented with exactly the same wording, in the same order, to all respondents. The reason for standardizing questions is to ensure that all respondents are replying to the same question. If one interviewer asks, "Do you drink orange juice?" and another asks, "Does your family use frozen orange juice?" the replies would not be comparable.

Typically the responses are also standardized. Consider the following question regarding a person's attitude toward legislation about pollution, and note the fixed-alternative responses.

Do you feel the United States needs more or less environmental legislation?

☐ Needs more

☐ Needs less

☐ Neither more nor less

☐ No opinion

This question is an example of a structured–undisguised question: The question's purpose is clear and respondents are limited to one of four replies.

Structured–undisguised questions are simple to administer and easy to tabulate and analyze. Respondents have little difficulty replying. Their responses should be reliable in that if they were asked the question again, they would respond in a similar fashion.

The fixed-alternative question is reliable for several reasons. First, the frame of reference is apparent from the alternatives. For example, if a respondent is asked, "How much do you watch television?" one person might say "every day," another might say "regularly," and still another might respond, "five hours per day." These responses would be difficult to interpret and compare.

Providing responses also often helps make the question clear. The question, "What is your marital status?" is more confusing than is the question, "Are you married, single, widowed, or divorced?" The alternatives frame the reply and help ensure the reliability of the question.

Fixed-alternative questions are best when possible replies are well known, clear-cut, and limited in number. Thus, they seem to work best when securing factual information (age, education, home ownership) and when eliciting expressions of opinion about issues on which people hold clear-cut opinions (strongly agree to strongly disagree).

Consumer research can be structured in ways other than rating scales. New technology is being explored in testing advertisements, whereby consumers watch ads and turn knobs and dials continuously through the ad to depict moments during which the ad made them feel happy or sad. Usually the ad is then replayed and the consumers are asked to explain their highest and lowest dial registers. Researchers find that an overall rating of an ad tends to correlate with the peak emotional experience during the ad, and the final moments in the ad.

Unstructured–Undisguised Questionnaires

In unstructured–undisguised questionnaires, the purpose of the study is clear but responses to the questions are open-ended. Interviews are the primary method. For example, the question, "How do you feel about environmental issues and the need for more legislation?" is delivered the same to every respondent, but the interviewer gets the respondent to talk freely about their attitudes. After the initial question, the interview becomes very unstructured as the interviewer probes more deeply, following whatever direction the respondent leads. Figure 8.2 classifies a number of communication-based marketing

FIGURE 8.2   Structure and Disguise in Communication Methods

	Structured	Unstructured
Undisguised	**Typical Questionnaire (very frequently used)**	**Interviews Open-Ended Questions**
Disguised	**Least Used**	**Motivation Research Word Association Sentence Completion Story Telling**

research techniques by their degree of structure and disguise. Interviews and open-ended questions on surveys are popular methods.

Unstructured–Disguised Questionnaires

Unstructured–disguised questionnaires lie at the heart of what has become known as motivation research. Some areas of inquiry are not easily amenable to direct questioning. Many important motives and reasons for choice are of a kind that consumers will not describe, because a truthful description would be embarrassing. Other motives are difficult to describe or the motives exist below their level of awareness. Direct questions yield replies that are either useless or misleading. Yet such motives are often of paramount importance in consumer behavior.

Projective techniques (see Chapter 4) were developed by researchers to circumvent respondents' reluctance to discuss their feelings. These techniques are largely independent of the respondents' self-awareness and willingness to reveal themselves. The assumption in projective methods is that an individual's reaction to a relatively unstructured stimulus is indicative of the person's basic perceptions of the phenomenon. Reactions to an ambiguous stimulus (e.g., a picture of a man seated at an office desk) allow, even require, respondents to project their needs, motives, and values; the respondent chooses his or her own interpretation, description, and evaluation of the ambiguous stimulus.

The next research challenge in using these methods is in the analysis, or making sense of the replies. The final interpretation of what was said often reflects the interpreter's frame of reference as much as it does the respondent's. Different interpreters can reach different conclusions about the same response, which raises havoc with the coding of replies. Projective methods are thus more suited for exploratory research than for descriptive or causal research.

Structured–Disguised Questionnaires

Structured–disguised questionnaires are the least used in marketing research. They were developed in an attempt to reveal subconscious motives and attitudes yet to do so in a structured manner to facilitate coding.

One proposition holds that consumers' knowledge and memory are conditioned by their attitudes. Individuals selectively perceive and retain ideas that are consistent with their own beliefs. Thus, if we want information about people's attitudes when a direct question might produce a biased answer, we can simply ask them what they know. For example, Democratic voters would be expected to know more about Democratic candidates than those intending to vote Republican. This argument is consistent with what we know about the operation of selective cognitive processes. Thus, if we want to know someone's attitude about the environment, but we don't want them to simply respond in a socially acceptable way, we could ask people what they know rather than how they feel.

However, one question is whether a high level of awareness is indicative of a favorable or an unfavorable attitude. That is, whether this measure of knowledge can also be interpreted as a measure of the person's attitude relies on an assumption about the consumer's cognitive system.

Questionnaires Classified by Method of Administration

Questionnaires can also be classified by the method used to administer them. The main methods are personal interview, telephone, mail, fax, and e-mail and online surveys.

A personal interview is a direct, face-to-face conversation between the interviewer and the respondent or interviewee. The interviewer asks the questions and records the respondent's answers, either while the interview is in progress or immediately afterward. The interview can take place in a home or an office, but it usually is in a central location like a shopping mall, where shoppers are stopped (or intercepted, hence the term "mall intercept") and asked to participate.

Means of Communication: online, e-mail, mail, phone, in person, fax…

The telephone interview is usually a cold call with a few questions (no longer than 2–3 minutes). A mail questionnaire involves mailing the questionnaires to designated respondents with an accompanying cover letter. The respondents complete the questionnaire at their leisure and mail their replies back to the research organization. Faxed surveys operate like mail surveys (except of course that they are faxed) and work well for business-to-business research.

E-mail surveys are one of two types:

• The questions of the market research study are embedded in the text of the e-mail itself.

• The e-mail directs the recipient to a Web site to take the survey.

Each has its pros and cons: Replying to embedded e-mail surveys is extremely quick, but Web surveys can look sharp—very professional in that hypertext and graphics can improve both the appearance and quality control of the survey.

A number of variations and combinations are possible. Questionnaires for a "mail" administration may be attached to products or printed in magazines. Questionnaires in a personal interview may be self-administered, perhaps in the interviewer's presence, in case the respondents seek clarification from the interviewer. Alternatively, the respondents might complete the questionnaire in private and drop it in the mail to return to the research organization.

Often the different modalities are mixed to enhance sample cooperation. For example, marketing researchers seeking the opinions of busy business managers or physicians typically employ an introductory letter, e-mail, or phone call asking for their help in the study, and after this pre-notification, the survey is sent (e.g., faxed) to their place of business.[3]

---

[3] Andrea Michaud, "Multiple Methods for Multiple Specialties," quirks.com.

Each of these methods of communication possesses some advantages and disadvantages. These include sampling control, information control, and administrative control.

Sampling Control

Sampling control concerns the researcher's ability to find a designated respondent and to get the desired cooperation from that respondent. A sampling frame is the list of population elements from which the sample is drawn. With the telephone method, online phone books serve as the sampling frame, from which respondents are selected randomly, but they are inadequate because they do not include households with unlisted numbers or those without phones. For example, about a third of the 90 million U.S. telephone households have unlisted numbers. Unlisted households tend to be younger, urban, nonwhite, more mobile, and either very high or very low income, with the majority residing in Californian cities. "Do not call" registries have also wreaked havoc, with nearly 75% of Americans blocking telemarketing calls, even though marketing research calls serve a different purpose.[4]

Some researchers attempt to overcome the sampling bias of unlisted numbers by using random digit dialing (RDD). Numbers are randomly generated and called through automatic dialing at a central interviewing facility. This procedure allows geographically wide coverage. In plus-one sampling, a probability sample of phone numbers is selected from the telephone directory and a single, randomly determined digit is added to each selected number.

For mail questionnaires, one or more mailing lists serve as the sampling frame. Again, the quality of these lists determines the sampling biases. Some firms have established panels of consumers that can be used to answer mail questionnaires and that are representative of the population. Business marketing research is usually easier in that contact information is more stable than those for consumers, and target businesses are fewer in number.

Beyond a good working list, it is also critical to target well. Response rates are greater for surveys on topics that the recipient cares about. Targeting is more efficient than simply increasing the sample size. Fewer complete surveys are obtained from a mass, uncustomized effort. It is estimated that the average U.S. consumer receives some 550 unsolicited mailings per year (compared with 50 to 100 for Germany, the UK, and France); direct mailing is a $1.5 trillion market in the U.S., employing 9 million people.[5]

Regarding newer technologies, fax surveys operate like phone surveys in their sampling frames. E-mail-administered questionnaires are similar to mail questionnaires when it comes to sampling control. The sample, of course, is limited to those who own or have access to a computer and an e-mail account (who tend to be more affluent and better educated). However, if an accurate, applicable, and readily available list of e-mail addresses exists, e-mail allows a geographically dispersed sample to be used.

It is conceptually difficult, but practically possible, to achieve sampling control for the administration of questions using personal interviews. For some select populations (e.g., doctors, architects, businesses), a list of members may be available in trade directories. Consumer studies frequently use mall intercepts, in which interviewers stop shoppers in a mall and ask if they would be willing to

---

[4] See ssisamples.com for statistics on unlisted phone numbers and solutions.

[5] All those who think unsolicited mail is a bother can contact the Direct Marketing Association (www.the-dma. org), a trade group of over 4,600 direct-mail marketing firms (commercial and nonprofit, U.S. and 53 nations abroad), and that organization will remove the name from every member's list.

participate in a research study. Those who agree are taken to the firm's interviewing facility in the mall (a small, rented office), where the interview is conducted. Mall intercepts pose two issues: 1) Most people shop at malls, but some do not. 2) A person's chances of being asked to participate depend on the frequency with which he or she shops there and the time spent in the mall.

Getting Cooperation

Directing the survey to a specific respondent is one thing; getting a response from that individual is another. In this respect, the personal interview affords the most sample control, e.g., the respondent's identity is known and there is little opportunity for anyone else to reply. The rate of refusal-to-participate is also typically lower than with phone interviews or mail questionnaires.

Usually the principle holds that the more personal the appeal, the more difficult it is for a respondent to say no: Malls are face-to-face and phone solicitations are person-to-person. Mail is the least personal, most anonymous channel, and many mail surveys end up in recycling bins, unless the topic is inherently interesting to the consumer, or perhaps if some incentive is offered to complete the survey. We say more about these factors later.

Telephone methods suffer from "not-at-homes"; one-third of calls result in a no-answer, but this number is surprisingly stable even in the face of the growth of answering machines and caller ID. Research firms generally can still get through to talk to a live consumer, by being persistent (by making more contacts).[6] See Research Realities 8.4 for key ingredients to enhancing participation in phone surveys.

For mail questionnaires, the researcher has little control over whether the intended respondent is really the person who completes the survey, if anybody completes the survey at all.[7] Many persons refuse to respond. Often only those most interested in the survey topic respond. Some people are functionally illiterate (e.g., they have difficulty reading job notices or getting a driver's license).

E-mail- or Web-administered questionnaires are somewhat better in these respects. For one thing, literacy is not a problem because those owning and using computers are typically better educated. Moreover, there is much less likelihood that someone other than the intended respondents will reply, given that the questionnaires reside in personal e-mail accounts.

Generally, regardless of the method of survey administration, marketing researchers have noted the steady decline in sample cooperation. It has been suggested that higher compensations may be required to obtain responses. Greater incentives would drive up costs of research or tempt researchers to be frugal on sample size.

Yet one consistent finding is that potential respondents are more likely to participate in the study if the research topic is inherently interesting to them—intrinsic interest exceeds extrinsic incentives in raising response rates. Enhanced databases should facilitate greater tailoring so that consumers are contacted only on topics relevant to them.

Other solutions will continue to evolve. For example, it has been suggested that for e-commerce, filling out a survey may become part of the cost of an online service provider.

---

[6] James M. Lepkowski et al., *Advances in Telephone Methodology* (Wiley, 2007).
[7] Robert Clark and David Steel, "Sampling Within Households in Household Surveys," *Journal of the Royal Statistical Association A*, 170 (1), 63–82, and see Floyd J. Fowler, *Survey Research Methods* (4th ed., Sage, 2008) for ways to overcome respondent resistance.

RESEARCH   REALITIES

8.4 Telephone Survey Practices

The Council for Marketing and Opinion Research (CMOR) is comprised of several partners:

- American Marketing Association (AMA)
- Advertising Research Foundation (ARF)
- Council of American Survey Research Organizations (CASRO)
- Marketing Research Association (MRA)

CMOR conducted a study of phone survey participation. The key ingredients in a telephone interviewer's introduction that help provide the perception of a professionally conducted marketing research survey, which in turn enhanced participant cooperation, included:

- Stating the sponsoring company's name
- Giving a brief overview about the general topic of the survey
- Providing the participant with the interviewer's first name
- Assuring the interviewee that there will be no attempt to "sell anything"
- Assuring the interviewee that their responses will be held confidential

- Providing an accurate estimate as to the approximate length of the interview

When you hire a marketing research firm to, in turn, hire a service to conduct phone interviews, it may help to understand a profile of the telephoning personnel:

- The telephone interviewers are usually working on more than one study at a time.
- Most have more than six months experience with the particular call center facility that now employs them.
- 25% of the employees are full-time (thus, 75% are part-timers—think about that).
- In terms of compensation, the median starting hourly wages are $6.90; the top pay is around $10. Half (only!) of these employees get an annual bonus or pay raise. Half (only) get benefits (vacation time, holiday pay, health insurance, sick leave pay).
- The training received before being put into place to begin interviewing is one day.

Moral of the story: Keep your survey clear and simple.

Source: cmor.org.

Information Control

The different methods of data collection also vary in the type of questions that can be asked, and in the amount and accuracy of the information that can be obtained from respondents. The personal interview can be conducted using almost any form of questionnaire: structured or unstructured, disguised or undisguised. The interaction allows the interviewer to present pictures or examples of ads, lists of words, scales, and so on. The consumer can taste new flavors of cookies or smell new colognes. Visual aids can be used with mail questionnaires, but not with telephone surveys.

Personal interviews allow the use of open-ended questions that require extensive probes. Written questionnaires do not lend themselves to such questions. Telephone interviews can incorporate open-ended questions, but not nearly to the same extent as in-person interviews, mostly because phone surveys need to be brief so as not to be discontinued by an increasingly bored or irritated respondent midway through the survey.

Personal interviews also allow the automatic, contingent sequencing of questions; for example, if the answer to question 4 is positive, the interviewer may be instructed to proceed to ask questions 5 and 6, whereas if the answer had been negative, the interviewer asks questions 7 and 8. Automatic sequencing is also possible with telephone interviews, especially when the interviewer is reading from a computer screen and the question skipping is preprogrammed. Skipping questions is not advised for mail questionnaires, because respondents will get confused and make errors. Web surveys can easily be programmed to contain skip patterns.

There is also a greater danger of "sequence bias" with hard-copy questionnaires; respondents can see the whole questionnaire, so their replies to any question may be conditioned by their previous responses. For example, if you present a print ad on page 1, and on page 3 ask memory questions about the ad, the respondent could, and likely would, flip back to page 1 and fill in your questions dutifully, but doing so would destroy the validity of those questions for recall. On the other hand, mail, e-mail, Web, or fax questionnaires allow respondents to work at their own pace, so their responses may be more thoughtful.

Mail questionnaires are more anonymous, so people can be more frank on sensitive issues. Replies to e-mail can be traced to the sender, so there is less anonymity. Respondents tend to feel anonymous online, and so they may answer questions there more truthfully.

Personal and telephone interviews can reflect interviewer bias because of the respondent's perception of the interviewer, or because different interviewers ask questions and probe in different ways. This kind of bias does not occur for mail, e-mail, or faxed questionnaires.

With regard to length of questionnaire or amount of information to be collected, the rule of thumb is that long questionnaires can be handled best by personal interview, next best by written formats (mail, online), and least well by telephone interview. In particular, the still-experimental technique of sending surveys to cell phones and asking for text responses can only be 2–3 questions long.[8] Much depends on the topic of inquiry and the form of the questionnaire.

Computers are helpful aids in conducting surveys. Phone interviews are linked to computers—interviewers read aloud questions as they come up on the screen and enter respondents' answers directly into the system. Partly because of the advantages that accrue with computer administration of questionnaires (quick and less expensive), telephone interviews have become the most popular data-collection technique (as you're probably aware, from the number of times you've been disturbed by such a call during dinner).

Currently, there are two applications of computer-aided interviewing (CAI) software:

- Telephone surveys, in which each interviewer has a personal computer from which to ask questions (see Table 8.5 for Computerized Adaptive Telephone Interviewing, or CATI)

- In-person interviews, such as mall intercepts, in which the interviewer transports a laptop computer to the interview site and uses it to interview the respondent, or places the computer in front of the respondent and lets the respondent answer questions as they appear on the screen

One of the most important advantages of computer-assisted interviewing is its level of information control. The computer displays each question exactly as the researcher intended (and programmed). It shows only the questions and

---

[8] Shintaro Okazaki, "Assessing Mobile-Based Online Surveys," *International Journal of Market Research*, 49 (5), 651–675.

TABLE 8.5	Common Features in Computerized Adaptive Telephone Interviewing (CATI) Software

Questionnaire writing system: Helps the researcher create a computer-administered questionnaire. The software aids the construction of complex, contingent skip patterns and logic branches, in which different answers direct interviewer to different parts of the questionnaire; randomization of questions; insertion of previous answers into the text of the current question.

Call management system: (1) Builds sample database by manually typing in the sample or by transferring from an existing database; (2) controls the flow to interviewing stations. Ensures that: call backs are made when scheduled, busy numbers are redialed after a preset delay, time zones are recognized.

Call disposition monitoring system: Tracks each call attempt by its disposition (no answer, busy, immediate refusal, failed to qualify, call back, complete). Also calculates incidence of qualified respondents to compare with incidence assumed in the cost quote for study.

Interviewer system: Displays the questionnaire for the interviewer, dials the number, automatically reschedules a "no answer" for another attempt, determines when "busy" numbers are to be redialed, aids in scheduling call backs.

Reporting system: Generates accurate and timely reports, including call disposition reports, incidence reports, top-line reports of respondent data, and interviewer productivity reports. Increases supervisor productivity and overall quality of the data collection.

Analysis capabilities: Integrated cross-tabulation and statistical analyses.

The latest: MCAPI: "Mobile computer-assisted personal interviewing"; the interviewer sets up a table in a mall, intercepts a sample respondent, then either walks them through questions prompted by a laptop or has the respondent sit down in front of the computer to complete the survey at their own pace.

Source: See quirks.com and *"Computer-Assisted Telephone Interviewing"* at sawtoothsoftware.com.

information that the respondent should see and it displays the next question only when an acceptable answer to the current one is entered. In addition, you get:

- Personalization of the questions. During the course of the interview, the computer can use answers to previous responses (name of spouse, cars owned, favorite brands) to customize the wording of subsequent questions, e.g., "When your wife, Ann, goes shopping, does she usually use the Toyota or the Buick?" Such personalized questions are thought to enhance rapport and provide for higher-quality interviews.

- Customized questionnaires. Key information elicited early in the interview can be used to tailor the questionnaire for each respondent. For example, if it's clear the respondent is a novice, they won't be asked about certain technical product attributes.

After the data are collected, preliminary results are available at a moment's notice, because the data are already stored. The marketing manager does not have the 2–3 week delay caused by coding and data entry that happens when questionnaires are completed and entered by hand.

However, even computers have limitations. They cannot win over respondents with social chitchat or explain questions that are misunderstood. Computers are incapable of recognizing fuzzy or superficial answers, and they cannot prod respondents to elaborate on their answers.[9]

Administrative Control

One of the greatest advantages of Web surveys is that they provide the marketing researcher the quickest turnaround. Half of e-mail surveys are typically completed and returned the same day they were sent (see Research Realities 8.5). For phone surveys, a number of calls can be made from a central exchange in a short period, perhaps 15 to 20 per hour per interviewer if the questionnaire is short. It can take two weeks to achieve that same response rate using the postal service.

After a couple of weeks, during which the bulk of the replies come in, a follow-up mailing is begun. The response rates will increase, but so does the overall time required to complete the study.

In-home personal interviews are the most expensive per completed contact (followed by phone surveys); the e-mail and Web questionnaires tend to be the cheapest (followed by mail interviews). The per-contact cost of a mail questionnaire is low, but if nonresponse is substantial, the cost per return may be high. Faxing can be expensive if the destinations are long-distance. Telephone, mall, and in-home personal interview methods require large field staffs. The larger the field staff, the greater the problems of control. Labor and particularly good quality control cost money, so these methods are the most expensive data-collection techniques.

Table 8.6 presents the results of several studies that compared the turn-around times, response rates, and costs of a variety of methods of administering questionnaires. The table shows response rates for traditional research methods (mail, phone, mall, door-to-door) as well as newer techniques (fax, e-mail, Web), along with turnaround times and cost.

Each method of data collection has its uses, and none is superior in all situations. For example, a trial product may be sent by regular mail or picked up at a mall, with a phone or Web survey follow-up to assess consumers' reaction.

Many researchers worry that Internet samples are still peculiar, in part due to differential access to e-mail and the Web (see Table 8.7).[10] Worse, the novelty of an e-mail or Web survey is starting to wear off, and response rates are beginning to drop. Nevertheless, because e-mail surveys and Web surveys are so quick and so cheap (no real costs other than labor), and the quality of the data seems roughly comparable to standard techniques, clearly e-mail and Web surveys are here to stay.

Figure 8.3 summarizes the logistics comparisons between these major methods of administering questionnaires. Table 8.8 elaborates on the overall strengths and weaknesses of these methods and Figure 8.4 illustrates their frequency in practice.

---

[9] Fred Bronner and Ton Kuijlen, "The Live of Digital Interviewer," *International Journal of Market Research*, 49 (2), 167–190.

[10] The situation is further complicated if international samples are sought: Different countries have different levels of internet penetration, and cross-cultural differences in surveys, and responses, are often subtle (Elisabeth Deutskens, Ad de Jong, Ko de Ruyter, and Martin Wetzels, "Comparing the Generalizability of Online and Mail Surveys in Cross-National Service Quality Research," *Marketing Letters*, 17, 119–136).

RESEARCH   REALITIES

8.5 Online, Pros and Cons

No question: Online marketing research is very cool. But if it were perfect, suppliers would have closed down focus group facilities, canceled subscriptions to scanner databases, and moth-balled their call centers. So, what are the techniques' strengths, and what are the issues to watch out for?

- **Fast.** Definitely. It's easy to program and post a survey on the Web. Turnaround times are quick. (We'll say more about "methods of administering surveys" in later chapters.)

- **Cheap.** Not free, but definitely inexpensive relative to many other forms of research.

- **Flexible, Convenient.** The mantra is *"at my own pace, in my own place."* Online surveys, via e-mail or the Web, may be done at the respondent's convenience, more like a hard copy mail survey.

- **Accurate**? There are concerns of **samples** being not representative. Some 50% of the U.S. households are still not wired, and they are likely different from those who do have Internet access. Does this matter? Depends on the product category you're investigating. (We'll say more about sampling later in the book.)

- As an example, Owen Graduate School of Management runs an e-panel with Research Subject pool, with 100,000 active panelists, refreshed with 2,000 new members each month, representing 200 countries. eLab is run by Sean Rhea and James Robbins—thanks guys!

TABLE 8.6   Comparing Methods of Administering Questionnaires

The following table compares traditional techniques (door-to-door, mall, phone, mail) to electronic techniques (fax, e-mail, Web) in terms of response notes, completion times, and costs.

	Technique						
	Door-to-Door	Mall	Phone	Mail	Fax	E-mail[1]	Web
Response rates	15%	29%	75%	35–63%	25%	8–37%	26%
% bad addresses				0–19%	41%	19–20%	24%
Response time in days (mean)				13–18	9	4–6	7
Days (median)				12	12	2	5
# Days to receive 45% responses				13		1	
# Days to receive 80% responses				28		9	
Fixed costs				$59	$57	$57	$57
Unit cost				$1.56	$.56	$.01	$.01
Variable costs (200 surveys sent)				$312	$112	$2	$2
Total cost				$371	$169	$59	$59

[1] Response rates for e-mail surveys that are embedded in the text of the e-mail tend to run 20 to 25%. When the recipient must open an attached file, response rates dropped to 8%. No differences were found in the content of the responses, but attached surveys were considered more attractive and easier to fill out.

Source: The indices in this table were compiled from the following sources: Respondent Cooperation and Industry Image Survey *(The Council for Marketing and Opinion Research, cmor.org); Duane P. Bachmann, John Elfrink, and Gary Vazzana, "E-mail and Snail Mail Face Off in Rematch,"* Marketing Research 11, *marketingpower.com; Curt J. Dommeyer and Eleanor Moriarty, "Comparing Two Forms of an E-mail Survey: Embedded vs. Attached,"* International Journal of Market Research 42, 39–50.

TABLE 8.7   Comparing Mall and E-Panels

		Mall Tests	Internet Tests	Panel Members
Demographics are starting to look similar:	Household size	2.8	2.9	3.0
	Average age	40.5	39.2	37.2
	Employed	71%	72%	69%
	White	86%	88%	89%
	Male	20%	21%	15%
	College	40%	43%	46%

Responses to marketing questions show correlations between sample methodologies and suggest modality is not critical and should not create bias →

Correlation Between Responses:

	Mall vs. Internet
Purchase intent	.86
Frequency	.94
Liking	.85
Price/value	.90

Other Comparative Observation

	Internet	Phone
Time survey took to administer	12.5	19.4 minutes
Upon completion, would respondent participate in future studies?	35% yes	26% yes
More experienced Internet users	x	
Used rating scale extreme "endpoints" more frequently		x

Source: Jeff Miller and Alan Hogg "Internet vs. Telephone Data Collection" White paper *(burke.com).*

FIGURE 8.3   Comparing Methods of Survey Administration

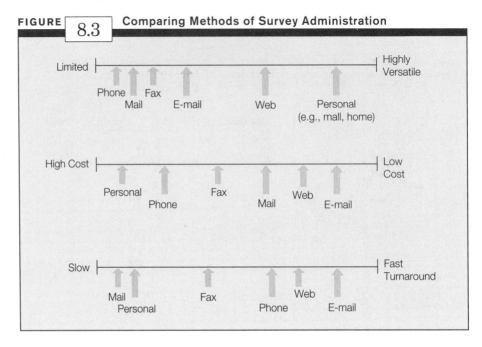

TABLE 8.8   Primary Communication Methods of Data Collection: Advantages (+) and Disadvantages (−)

	Sampling Control	Information Control	Administrative Control
Personal Interview (e.g., Mall)	+ high response rates; best for getting response from specific person	+ any type of question; allows probing via open-ended questions; clarification of ambiguous questions; easy use of visuals and other sensory stimuli	− generally most expensive method; relatively slow
	− narrow distribution, difficult to identify sampling frame	− interviewer bias	
Written Formats (Mail, Fax, Web, E-mail)	+ only method to reach certain people; sampling frame easy via mailing lists	+ not subject to interviewer bias; respondents work at their own pace; ensures anonymity; best for personal, sensitive questions	+ generally least expensive; very short response time for e-mail
	− low response rates; little control in who completes survey; cannot control speed of survey completion	− researcher cannot explain ambiguous questions; no probing	− longer response time for mail
Telephone	+ relatively strong response rates; wide distribution possible	+ less interviewer bias than in person, interviewer supervision is stronger	+ relatively low cost; quick turnaround; little difficulty and cost in handling call backs; allows easy use of computer support
	− difficult to establish representative sampling frame due to unlisted numbers	− cannot use visual aids; more difficult to establish rapport over the phone than in person	− must be brief

FIGURE 8.4   **Frequency of Marketing Research Methods in Practice**

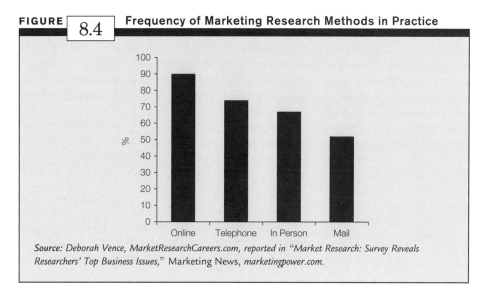

Source: *Deborah Vence, MarketResearchCareers.com, reported in "Market Research: Survey Reveals Researchers' Top Business Issues,"* Marketing News, *marketingpower.com.*

Structured vs. Unstructured and Disguised vs. Undisguised Observation

Like communication methods, observational data may be gathered using structured or unstructured methods that are either disguised or undisguised. Unstructured observation is used for studies in which the formulation of the problem is not specific; more flexibility is allowed the observers in terms of what they note and record. Unstructured observation is well-suited for exploratory research—just what does the customer do?[11]

Structured observation is applicable when the problem is defined precisely enough to clearly specify the behaviors that will be observed and the categories that will be used to record and analyze the observations. Structured observation can be quite precise. For example, traffic counters capture speed and accidents, which inform local governments and insurance agencies.

Disguise in observational methods refers to whether the consumers know they are being observed. A researcher acting as a mystery shopper is an example disguised observation. When a researcher interacts with the targets of their observations, e.g., "Why did you pause at the display of cashmere sweaters?" the purpose of the research becomes undisguised.

When companies capture your Web site visits unbeknownst to you, this is an example of structured, disguised recording of observations. Your behavioral data are logged in a structured manner (e.g., Web addresses), and since you didn't know your behavior was being observed, the purpose of the research is disguised.

[11] Michael Angrosino, *Doing Ethnographic and Observational Research* (Sage, 2007).

Summary

After marketing researchers study secondary data to find answers to their marketing questions, they then turn to primary data collection. The types of primary data of interest to marketing researchers include demographic and socioeconomic characteristics, psychological and lifestyle characteristics, attitudes and opinions, awareness and knowledge, intentions, motivation, and behavior of individuals and groups.

Communication and observation are the two basic means of obtaining primary data. Communication involves the direct questioning of respondents, whereas observation entails the systematic checking of appropriate facts or actions. Observation can be used to secure behavioral data and has the advantage of objectivity over communication methods. However, communication methods must be used to measure things that are not directly observable, such as attitudes, awareness, knowledge, intentions, or motivation.

Communication methods may be classified by their degree of structure, disguise, and method of administration. A structured questionnaire has a well-defined sequence and standardized response categories and can be used in descriptive or causal research. The disguised questionnaire attempts to hide the purpose of the research from the respondent.

Questionnaires can be administered by personal interviews, over the phone, using paper-and-pencil questionnaires by mail or fax, or by using computer-administered surveys via e-mail or on the Web. Each approach has advantages and disadvantages, and the approaches vary in terms of the control they offer the researcher with respect to sample, information, and administration. The methods are not mutually exclusive and can often be used in combination.

Questions

1. How do personally administered questionnaires, telephone surveys, mail, fax, e-mail, or Web surveys differ with respect to the following?
   a. Sampling control
   b. Information control
   c. Administrative control
2. What is a disguised questionnaire? What is a structured questionnaire?
3. What is the rationale for employing unstructured–disguised stimuli?
4. What are the general advantages and disadvantages associated with obtaining information by questioning or by observation?
5. What are the advantages and disadvantages of structured–undisguised questionnaires? Of unstructured–undisguised questionnaires?
6. What types of primary data interest marketing researchers most?

Applications and Problems

1. Which survey method (mail, telephone, personal interview in the home or in a mall, fax, e-mail, or Web) would you use for the following situations? Justify your choice.
   a. Administration of a questionnaire to determine the number of people who listened to the "100 Top Country Tunes of the Year!" a program that aired on December 31.
   b. Administration of a questionnaire to determine the number of households having an individual with mental health problems and a history of such problems in the family.
   c. Administration of a questionnaire by a national manufacturer of microwave ovens to test people's attitudes and opinions toward a new model.
   d. Administration of a questionnaire by a local dry cleaner who wants to determine customers' satisfaction with a recent discount scheme.
   e. Administration of a questionnaire by the management of a small hotel that wants to assess customers' opinions of its service.
2. Consider each of the following research projects. In each case, identify weak areas and describe how the research might have been improved to better attain its objectives.

a. A local bank was interested in determining how it might better serve the needs of low-income households. It inserted a four-page survey into the monthly statement-of-account mailings of all account holders with less than $500 in their accounts. The survey was structured and undisguised; 1,200 surveys were mailed and 98 were completed and returned.

b. A new business clothing shop is planning to open in a few months. The owners are unsure whether the new shop should be located in a shopping mall or at a downtown location. Since they think it would be best to simply ask shoppers for their location preferences, the owners contracted a local marketing research company to conduct a study. Using a structured- undisguised questionnaire format and the mall intercept method of administration, the research company was able to report that most people prefer to shop for clothes in a shopping mall.

c. Quick-Stop Inc. recently opened a new convenience store in Northglenn, Colorado. The store is open every day from 7:00 A.M. to 11:00 P.M. In order to better plan the location of other units in the Denver metro area, management is interested in determining the trading area from which this store draws its customers. How would you determine this information by questionnaire? By observation method? Which method would be preferred? Be sure to specify how you would define "trading area."

3. Should the communication or observational method be used in the following situations? Justify your choice. Also, specify the degree of structure and disguise for each.

a. The Metal Products Division of Geni Ltd. devised a special metal container to store plastic garbage bags. Plastic bags posed household problems, as they gave off unpleasant odors, looked disorderly, and provided a breeding place for insects. The container overcame these problems, as it had a bag-support apparatus that held the bag open for filling and sealed the bag when the lid was closed. In addition, the storage area held at least four full bags. The product was priced at $59.99 and was sold through hardware stores. The company has done little advertising and has relied on in-store promotion and displays. The divisional manager was wondering about the effectiveness of these displays and has called on you to do the necessary research.

b. Cardworth is a national manufacturer and distributor of greeting cards. The company recently began distributing a lower-priced line of cards using recycled paper. Quality differences between the higher- and lower-priced cards did not seem to be noticeable to laypeople. The company followed a policy of printing its name and the price on the back of each card. The initial acceptance of the new line of cards convinced the vice president of production that the company should use recycled paper for all its cards and increase its profit margin from 12.3% to 14.9%. The sales manager has strongly opposed this move and commented, "You know, consumers are concerned about the quality of greeting cards; a price difference of five cents on a card does not matter." The VP has called on you to undertake the study.

4. Several objectives for marketing research projects follow. For each objective, specify the type(s) of primary data that would be of use along with a possible method of data collection.

a. Assess "people flow" patterns inside a shopping mall.

b. Gauge the effectiveness of a new advertisement.

c. Gauge a salesperson's potential for success.

d. Segment a market.

e. Identify the shopper types that patronize a particular store.

f. Discover how people feel about a new package design.

Questionnaires and Data-Collection Forms

9

Questions to Guide Your Learning:

Q1 How do I create a questionnaire?

Q2 How do I avoid ambiguous questions, leading questions, double-barreled questions?

Q3 What's an open-ended question?

Q4 How do I implement branching?

I n the previous chapter, we discussed types of questionnaires and observation forms and their methods of administration. Now we get down to specifics—once you decide you want a survey, how do you create one? This chapter presents the procedures to follow to develop a questionnaire or observational data-collection form.

Questionnaire Design

Much progress has been made, but designing questionnaires is still an art, not a science. It is easier to embrace admonitions such as "avoid leading questions" or "avoid ambiguous questions" than it is to develop questions that are neither leading nor ambiguous.

Figure 9.1 is a procedural template to develop questionnaires. The stages are presented here in sequence, but in reality, this step-by-step procedure is often modified via some iteration and looping. For example, you may read a nearly completed draft of a survey only to find that some items are worded badly and need changing. A pre-test (Step 9) can tell us whether the typical respondent will understand each question and is able and willing to supply the information.

Specify What Information Will Be Sought

Deciding what information you want is easy to the extent that researchers have been precise at earlier stages in the research process. Both descriptive and causal research demand sufficient prior knowledge to allow the framing of specific hypotheses for investigation, which then guide the research, which in turn helps guide writing the questionnaire. The hypotheses determine what information will be sought and from whom, because they specify what relationships will be investigated.

It is certainly true that the preparation of the questionnaire itself may suggest further hypotheses and other relationships that might be investigated at slight additional effort and cost. If the

FIGURE | **9.1** | **Procedure for Developing a Questionnaire**

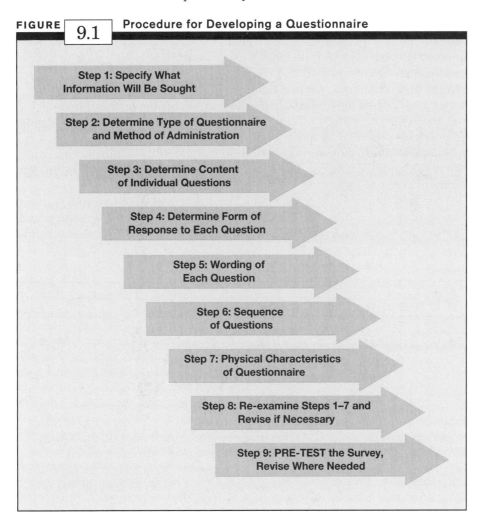

Step 1: Specify What Information Will Be Sought

Step 2: Determine Type of Questionnaire and Method of Administration

Step 3: Determine Content of Individual Questions

Step 4: Determine Form of Response to Each Question

Step 5: Wording of Each Question

Step 6: Sequence of Questions

Step 7: Physical Characteristics of Questionnaire

Step 8: Re-examine Steps 1–7 and Revise if Necessary

Step 9: PRE-TEST the Survey, Revise Where Needed

new hypothesis is indeed vital, by all means include it. But if it simply represents one of those potentially "interesting findings," forget it—those items simply lengthen the questionnaire, in turn lowering response rates.

What information do you want from the survey?

Exploratory research is, of course, aimed at the discovery of ideas and insights and so a questionnaire for an exploratory study is loosely structured, with only a rough idea of the kind of information that might be sought. The research is intended to shed clarity for future research.

Type of Questionnaire and Method of Administration

After specifying the basic information that will be sought, the researcher needs to specify *how* it will be gathered. This stage requires decisions about the *structure* and *disguise* to be used in the questionnaire and whether it will be administered by *mail, telephone, personal interviews, fax, e-mail,* or *Web.* These decisions are not independent—e.g., a disguised–unstructured questionnaire using a storytelling format precludes phone and probably mail administration. Similarly, mail is not recommended for unstructured–undisguised questionnaires with open-ended questions, particularly if they should have probes.

The type of data to be collected will have an important effect on the method of data collection. For example, a San Francisco research firm had a client that wanted to know what proportion of Internet users had various multimedia plug-ins. From experience, the researchers knew that most users don't actually know which plug-ins or versions they have. It would have been a waste of time to call them and ask. So instead, the researchers created an online survey in which plug-in files of different formats were used to display images. For each image, survey respondents were asked whether they could see the image. If they clicked yes, the researchers knew what plug-in they were using. The methodology let respondents provide data without knowing the technical details.[1]

Another influence on the data-collection method is the culture of the country where the study is being done (see Research Realities 9.1). Different norms and different access to technology modify global research projects.

Figure 9.2 offers another example. The research is about attitudes toward various brands of coffee. The questions are all very structured and undisguised. The survey is administered by mail, using part of the NFO (National Family

---

RESEARCH   REALITIES

9.1 Marketing Research in Different Countries

Willingness to Cooperate. Compared with people around the world, Americans tend to be unusually open, which is reflected in their general willingness to cooperate in marketing research surveys. Quite often, Americans will answer the questions of a total stranger (e.g., interviewers) about almost any subject—including their sex life. And Americans will agree to be interviewed anywhere: over the telephone, in a shopping mall, or at their place of business.

This climate of assumed cooperation can spoil Americans for doing research elsewhere in the world. Individual consumers in many other countries are less ready to answer any questions from an interviewer, let alone personal ones.

In Korea, for example, business people are reluctant to answer any survey questions about their company—it is considered disloyal to divulge any type of information to "outsiders." And most Japanese business people are hesitant to take part in surveys during business hours—taking time away from your work for a survey is like "stealing" from your employer.

Differences in Research Costs. The cost of doing exactly the same research can vary dramatically from country to country. Japan is generally regarded as the most expensive research market;

projects there usually cost several times what the same study would cost in the U.S.

But even within a single region, such as the European community, costs can vary dramatically from country to country. ESOMAR, the European Society for Opinion and Marketing Research (the European equivalent of a combined American Marketing Association and Advertising Research Foundation), periodically studies differences in research costs from country to country within Europe.

Differences in Administration Methods. Telephone interviews are common in the U.S., and frequent in the Netherlands, Germany, and the UK. They are rare in Japan, where it is not culturally acceptable to answer questions from strangers over the telephone. For different reasons (the unreliability of the communications networks), phone surveys are rare in Mexico, Argentina, and Hungary. Door-to-door interviewing is illegal in Saudi Arabia, legal but prohibitively expensive in the U.S., and more common in Switzerland and the UK. Finally, good mailing lists are available for mail surveys in the U.S. and also in Sweden, where the government routinely publishes lists of every Swedish household, making mail studies feasible there.

Source: For more on cultural research differences, see esomar.org.

---

[1] Chris Grecco and Hal King, "Of Browsers and Plug-Ins," quirks.com.

FIGURE 9.2   Mail Questionnaire for Caffeinated Ground Coffee Study

1. a. Check all the brands of regular ground coffee that you have ever used at home. (Check ALL that apply):
   b. Check the one brand you use most often. (Check ONE):
   c. Check all the brands you currently have on hand. (Check ALL that apply):
   d. Check the one brand you will probably buy next. (Check ONE):
   e. For each brand please indicate how much you like the brand overall on a scale of 1 to 10 with "1" meaning "dislike it extremely" and "10" meaning "like it extremely." Rate each brand, whether you have used the brand or not.

	A Ever Used	B Use Most Often	C Have On Hand	D Will Buy Next	"1" ← Dislike It Extremely								→ "10" Like It Extremely	
Folgers	1☐	1☐	1☐	1☐	1☐	2☐	3☐	4☐	5☐	6☐	7☐	8☐	9☐	10☐
Hills Brothers	1☐	1☐	1☐	1☐	1☐	2☐	3☐	4☐	5☐	6☐	7☐	8☐	9☐	10☐
Maxwell Regular	1☐	1☐	1☐	1☐	1☐	2☐	3☐	4☐	5☐	6☐	7☐	8☐	9☐	10☐
Maxwell House Master	1☐	1☐	1☐	1☐	1☐	2☐	3☐	4☐	5☐	6☐	7☐	8☐	9☐	10☐
Yuban	1☐	1☐	1☐	1☐	1☐	2☐	3☐	4☐	5☐	6☐	7☐	8☐	9☐	10☐
Other	1☐	1☐	1☐	1☐	1☐	2☐	3☐	4☐	5☐	6☐	7☐	8☐	9☐	10☐

(please specify): _____

2. What do you usually add to the coffee you drink? (Check ALL that apply):
   1. ☐ Nothing (I drink it black)
   2. ☐ A dairy creamer, like milk, cream, or half-and-half
   3. ☐ A non-dairy creamer, powdered or liquid
   4. ☐ Sugar
   5. ☐ Artificial sweetener
      ☐ Something else (please specify): _____

3. Are you the principal coffee purchaser for your household?
   1. ☐ Yes
   2. ☐ No

4. Please indicate how important it is to you that a ground coffee have each of the following characteristics. (Check ONE box for EACH characteristic):

	Not at All Important					Extremely Important				
Rich taste	1☐	2☐	3☐	4☐	5☐	6☐	7☐	8☐	9☐	10☐
Always fresh	1☐	2☐	3☐	4☐	5☐	6☐	7☐	8☐	9☐	10☐
Gets the day off to a good start	1☐	2☐	3☐	4☐	5☐	6☐	7☐	8☐	9☐	10☐
Full-bodied taste	1☐	2☐	3☐	4☐	5☐	6☐	7☐	8☐	9☐	10☐
Rich aroma in the cup	1☐	2☐	3☐	4☐	5☐	6☐	7☐	8☐	9☐	10☐
Good value for the money	1☐	2☐	3☐	4☐	5☐	6☐	7☐	8☐	9☐	10☐
The best coffee to drink in morning	1☐	2☐	3☐	4☐	5☐	6☐	7☐	8☐	9☐	10☐
Rich aroma in the can/bag	1☐	2☐	3☐	4☐	5☐	6☐	7☐	8☐	9☐	10☐
Smooth taste	1☐	2☐	3☐	4☐	5☐	6☐	7☐	8☐	9☐	10☐
Highest quality coffee	1☐	2☐	3☐	4☐	5☐	6☐	7☐	8☐	9☐	10☐
Premium brand	1☐	2☐	3☐	4☐	5☐	6☐	7☐	8☐	9☐	10☐
Not bitter	1☐	2☐	3☐	4☐	5☐	6☐	7☐	8☐	9☐	10☐
The coffee that brightens my day	1☐	2☐	3☐	4☐	5☐	6☐	7☐	8☐	9☐	10☐
Costs more than the other brands	1☐	2☐	3☐	4☐	5☐	6☐	7☐	8☐	9☐	10☐
Strong taste	1☐	2☐	3☐	4☐	5☐	6☐	7☐	8☐	9☐	10☐
Has no aftertaste	1☐	2☐	3☐	4☐	5☐	6☐	7☐	8☐	9☐	10☐
Economy brand	1☐	2☐	3☐	4☐	5☐	6☐	7☐	8☐	9☐	10☐
Rich aroma while brewing	1☐	2☐	3☐	4☐	5☐	6☐	7☐	8☐	9☐	10☐
Best ground coffee available	1☐	2☐	3☐	4☐	5☐	6☐	7☐	8☐	9☐	10☐

(Continued)

	Not at All Important					Extremely Important				
Enjoy drinking with a meal	1☐	2☐	3☐	4☐	5☐	6☐	7☐	8☐	9☐	10☐
Costs less than other brands	1☐	2☐	3☐	4☐	5☐	6☐	7☐	8☐	9☐	10☐

5. On a scale of 0 to 10 with "0" meaning "does not describe at all" and "10" meaning "describes completely," please indicate how well the following statements describe each of the coffee brands listed below. Rate each brand. Please write in the number that indicates your answer on the lines provided:

	Folgers	Hills Brothers	Maxwell Regular	Maxwell Master	Yuban
Rich taste	_____	_____	_____	_____	_____
Always fresh	_____	_____	_____	_____	_____
Gets the day off to a good start	_____	_____	_____	_____	_____
Full-bodied taste	_____	_____	_____	_____	_____
Rich aroma in the cup	_____	_____	_____	_____	_____
Good value for the money	_____	_____	_____	_____	_____
The best coffee to drink in morning	_____	_____	_____	_____	_____
Rich aroma in the can/bag	_____	_____	_____	_____	_____
Smooth taste	_____	_____	_____	_____	_____
Highest quality coffee	_____	_____	_____	_____	_____
Premium brand	_____	_____	_____	_____	_____
Not bitter	_____	_____	_____	_____	_____
The coffee that brightens my day	_____	_____	_____	_____	_____
Costs more than the other brands	_____	_____	_____	_____	_____
Strong taste	_____	_____	_____	_____	_____
Has no aftertaste	_____	_____	_____	_____	_____
Economy brand	_____	_____	_____	_____	_____
Rich aroma while brewing	_____	_____	_____	_____	_____
Best ground coffee available	_____	_____	_____	_____	_____
Enjoy drinking with a meal	_____	_____	_____	_____	_____
Costs less than other brands	_____	_____	_____	_____	_____

6. Please indicate your gender and age: 1 ☐ Male   2 ☐ Female   Age: _____

Opinion, Inc.) panel. Given the structure, note how easily most of the responses could be tabulated.

Individual Question Content

The researcher's previous decisions (information needed, structure and disguise, method of administration) largely control the decisions regarding individual question content. But in editing the survey, the researcher should ask some additional questions.

Is the Question Necessary?

If an issue is important and it's not been adequately covered by other questions, a new question is in order. It should be framed to yield an answer with the required detail, but not more than needed. For example, family consumption behavior is often explained by "stage in the life cycle," a concept captured by variables such as marital status, presence of children, and ages of the children. The presence of children indicates a dependency relationship, particularly if the youngest child is under 6. Thus, there would be no need to ask the age of each child, but only the age of the youngest child.

Are Several Questions Needed Instead of One?

There are often situations in which several questions are needed instead of one. Consider the question, "Why do you use Crest?" One respondent may reply, "To reduce cavities." Another may reply, "Because our dentist recommends it." Obviously two different frames of reference are being employed to answer this question. The first respondent is replying in terms of current usage, whereas the second is replying in terms of initial brand choice. It would be better to break this one question down into separate questions that reflect the possible frames of reference that could be used:

• How did you first happen to use Crest?

• What is your primary reason for using it?

Do Respondents Have the Necessary Information?

Each item should be carefully examined to see whether the typical respondent is likely to know the answer. Respondents will give answers, but whether the answers mean anything is another matter. Sometimes we just don't want to be embarrassed to admit we don't know something in a public opinion survey, and sometimes the question is so plausible and the interviewer so credible that we assume the question has validity. For example, you could survey people about the Consumers' Rights Act on Privacy of Internet Information, say, and, 50% or more people will report a familiarity with the Act, when in fact such an act does not exist (but it sounds plausible that it might, doesn't it?). If you ask people whether they've tried SmileBrite toothpaste, some will say they have, when the brand doesn't exist. If you ask, "When is the last time you saw the Jolly Green Giant (or any of a number of brand icons) on TV?" they'll say "within the past year" when in fact the tall fellow hasn't appeared in years.[2]

From a different perspective, consider the question, "How much does your family spend on groceries in a typical week?" Unless the respondent does the grocery shopping, he or she is unlikely to know. It might be helpful to begin with "filter questions" to determine if the individual is indeed likely to know, e.g., "Who does the grocery shopping in your family?"

Your respondents need to have the information, and they need to remember it. Some things are salient and memorable, e.g., most of us remember the first car we ever owned, but many of us are unable to recall the particular TV shows we watched last night. We need to put ourselves in the shoes of the respondent, not the product manager, when deciding what information is important enough for the individual to remember.

Can the respondent answer?

We also need to recognize that a person's ability to remember an event is influenced by how long ago it happened. Even if we could recall the TV programs we watched last night, we would have more difficulty remembering what we watched last week. If an event is likely to be considered relatively unimportant to most individuals, we should ask about only very recent occurrences of it.

For more important events, two effects operating in opposite directions affect a respondent's ability to provide accurate answers. **Telescoping error** refers to the fact that most people remember an event as having occurred more recently

---

[2] Also see A. Peter McGraw, Barbara A. Mellers, and Ilana Ritov, "The Affective Costs of Overconfidence," *Journal of Behavioral Decision Making*, 17, 281–295; John G. Lynch Jr. and Gal Zauberman, "Construing Consumer Decision Making," *Journal of Consumer Psychology*, 17 (2), 107–112; and Drazen Prelec, "Rebuilding the Boat While Staying Afloat: The Modeling Challenge for Behavioral Economics," *Journal of Marketing Research*, 43, 332–336.

Ethical **Dilemma** 9.1

As a new consultant, you are told to design an attitude and usage questionnaire for an appliance manufacturer. Before starting this project, your supervisor mentions that a similar study was completed 12 months ago and may provide some useful background information. Because you have no experience in durable consumer goods, you decide to use this previous report as a good source of secondary information.

After finding a copy of the previous study's final report, you discover that the report was completed for a competing appliance company. However, the report provides valuable background and competitive information. Because a questionnaire was developed and used successfully for this project, you decide to take a copy of the survey and update it for the current client.

- Is it ethical for researchers to use questionnaires developed and paid for by prior clients on competitive client projects?
- Would it be legitimate to use the previous report as a source of secondary information to provide background information for the current project?
- Would the preceding situation be different if the prior research had been completed for a long-term, contract client?

---

than it had. **Recall loss** means that they forget an event happened at all. For long periods, the telescoping effect is smaller whereas the recall loss effect is larger. For short periods, the reverse is true. The appropriate reference period to frame questions depend on factors such as the purchase cycle of the product category.

Will Respondents Give the Information?

Will the respondent answer?

Even though respondents have the information, there is always a question of whether they will share it. Often respondents are flattered that they are being asked for their opinions. For example, participation in Nielsen television panels makes one believe that one is influencing programming choices.

Sometimes the concern is that the survey question is rather sensitive, and the respondent might not wish to divulge private information. When an issue is embarrassing or otherwise threatening to respondents, they are likely to refuse to cooperate. If the issue is essential to the study, pay close attention to the question phrasing.

As we develop the questionnaire, we also need to be mindful of the amount of effort it might take respondents to give the information we seek. When the effort is excessive, we may have to settle for approximate answers, or we may be better off omitting the issue completely, since these types of questions tend to irritate respondents and damage their cooperation with the rest of the survey.

In general, it is better to address sensitive issues later rather than earlier in the survey.[3] Rapport gets established as respondents answer nonthreatening questions early in the interview, particularly when those questions that establish the legitimacy of the project.

When sensitive questions must be asked, it helps to consider ways to make them less threatening. Some helpful techniques include:

---

[3] Question sequence is discussed more fully later in the chapter.

1. Hide the question among other, more innocuous, questions.

2. State that the behavior or attitude is *not unusual* before asking the specific questions of the respondent (e.g., "Recent studies show that one of every four households has trouble meeting monthly financial obligations"). This makes it easier for the respondent to admit the potentially embarrassing behavior.

3. Phrase the question in terms of *others* and how they might feel or act ("Do you think most people cheat on their income tax? Why?"). Respondents might readily reveal their attitudes toward cheating when preparing income tax forms when asked about other people, but they might be very reluctant to do so if they were asked outright if they ever cheat on their taxes.

4. Use the **randomized response model**, a now fairly standard approach in which the respondent answers one of several paired questions.[4] The particular question is selected at random—for example, by having the respondent flip a coin. The respondent is instructed to answer Question A if the coin comes up "heads," and Question B if the coin is "tails." The interviewer is unaware of the question being answered by the respondent, because he or she never sees the outcome of the coin flip. Under these conditions, respondents are less likely to refuse to answer or to distort their answer.

A study to investigate the incidence of shoplifting might pair the sensitive question, "Have you ever shoplifted?" with the innocuous question, "Is your birthday in January?" The incidence of shoplifting can still be estimated by using an appropriate statistical model, because the percentage of respondents answering each question is controlled by the coin flips.

← Check this out. Very cool!

For a fair coin, the probability that the respondent will answer Question A, "Have you ever shoplifted?" is .5. The proportion of people whose birthdays fall in January is known to be .05 from census data. Suppose that the proportion who answered "yes" to either Question A or B is .20. Using the standard laws of probability, we could then estimate the proportion of the people in the sample who were responding "yes" to the sensitive question by using the formula:

$$\lambda = p\pi_s + (1 - p)\pi_A$$

where

λ = the total proportion of "yes" responses to both questions

p = the probability that the sensitive question is selected

$1-p$ = the probability that the innocuous question is selected

π_s = the proportion of "yes" responses to the sensitive question

π_A = the proportion of "yes" responses to the innocuous question

Substituting the appropriate quantities indicates that

$$.20 = .50\ \pi_s + .50\ (.05)$$

yielding $\pi_s = .35$.

That is, 35% of the respondents had shoplifted. Note, though, that we do not know specifically which respondents have shoplifted. Thus, we cannot determine, for example, if shoplifting behavior was associated with any particular demographic characteristics.

---

[4] For more info, see Gerty J. L. M. Lensvelt-Mulders, Joop J. Hox, Peter G. M. van der Heijden, and Cora J. M. Maas, "Meta-Analysis of Randomized Response Research: 35 Years of Validation," *Sociological Methods & Research*, 33 (3), 31–38.

Form of Response

Once the content of the individual questions is determined, the researcher needs to decide on the particular form of the response. Will the question be open-ended or fixed-alternative? If fixed-alternative, will it be a multichotomy, a dichotomy, or perhaps a scale?

Open-Ended Questions

Respondents are free to reply to open-ended questions in their own words rather than being limited to choosing from a set of alternatives, such as:

> How old are you?
>
> Do you think laws are needed to limit the amount of interest businesses can charge?
>
> Can you name three sponsors of the Monday night football games?
>
> What commercials do you remember seeing on TV last night?
>
> Do you intend to purchase an automobile this year?
>
> Why did you purchase a Sony brand color TV?
>
> Do you own a DVD player?
>
> How many call minutes do you use on your cell phone in a typical week?

Open-ended questions are extremely versatile—we can ask questions about demographic characteristics, attitudes, intentions, and behavior.

Open-ended questions can be used to begin a questionnaire. It's thought best to proceed from general to specific topics in constructing questionnaires, so an opening question like, "When you think of TV sets, which brands come to mind?" gives a sense of the respondent's frame of reference. The open-ended question is also often used to probe for additional information. The probes "Why?" "Why do you feel that way?" and "Please explain" are often used to seek elaboration of a respondent's reply.

Multichotomous Questions

The multichotomous question is a fixed-alternative question; respondents are asked to choose the alternative that most closely corresponds to their position on the subject. Table 9.1, for example, contains some of the preceding open-ended questions rewritten as multichotomous questions.

Note some of the limitations when using multiple-choice questions. In the interest-ceiling legislation question, the respondent's true opinion may be more complex; e.g., he or she may believe that legislation is needed, if businesses won't reduce the amount of credit available to customers or shorten the repayment period. If the conditions can't be satisfied, the respondent may feel just the opposite. The multiple-choice question doesn't permit individuals to elaborate but requires them to condense their complex attitude into a single statement.

Most researchers believe that 4-point or 5-point scales provide more fine-tuned information from customers. However, even simple 2-point, binary responses allow customers to say "yay" or "nay" (see Research Realities 9.2).

The TV-purchase question (Table 9.1) illustrates other problems associated with multiple-choice questions. First, the list of reasons cited for purchasing a Sony color TV may not be *exhaustive*. The "other" response category attempts to solve this problem. However, if many respondents check the "other" category,

TABLE 9.1   Examples of Multichotomous Questions

Age

How old are you?

☐ Less than 20

☐ 20–29

☐ 30–39

☐ 40–49

☐ 50–59

☐ 60 or over

Television Purchase

Why did you purchase a Sony brand color TV?

☐ Price was lower than other alternatives

☐ Feel it represents the highest quality

☐ Availability of local service

☐ Availability of a service contract

☐ Picture is better

☐ Warranty was better

☐ Other

Interest-Ceiling Legislation

Do you think laws limiting the amount of interest businesses can charge consumers are needed?

☐ Definitely needed

☐ Probably needed

☐ Probably not needed

☐ Definitely not needed

☐ No opinion

Telephone-Use Behavior

How many long-distance telephone calls do you make in a typical week?

☐ Less than 5

☐ 5–10

☐ More than 10

the study will be useless. Thus, the burden is on the researcher to make the list of alternatives comprehensive.

Unless the respondent is instructed to check all alternatives that apply, or is to rank the alternatives in order of importance, the multiple-choice question also demands that the alternatives be *mutually exclusive.* The income categories shown below violate this principle:

☐ $10,000–$20,000

☐ $20,000–$30,000

A respondent with an income of $20,000 would not know which alternative to check. When questions are about a product's features (e.g., a TV's picture, warranty, price, etc.), you often see instructions such as, "Check the most important reason," "Check all those reasons that apply," or "Rank all the reasons that apply from most important to least important."

The list of alternative responses should be exhaus*tive,* but a long list will be exhaus*ting* to respondents! So, when designing multiple-choice questions, the researcher should remain cognizant of human beings' limited data-processing capabilities.

The fourth weakness of the TV-purchase question is that it may be susceptible to order bias. The recommended procedure for combating this order bias is to prepare several forms of the questionnaire, with several different orders. If each alternative appears early, late, and in the middle across the different forms, the researcher can feel reasonably comfortable that position bias has been neutralized.

The long-distance telephone call example in Table 9.1 illustrates a problem with questions designed to get at the frequency of behaviors. The range of the categories used in the question seems to cue respondents about how they should reply. A scale with the following categories would likely produce a different picture than the one shown in Table 9.1:

☐ Fewer than 10
☐ 10–20
☐ More than 20

Respondents seem reluctant to report behaviors that are unusual in the context of the response scale—e.g., extreme behaviors. It's thought better to just use an open-ended question to get data on behavioral frequencies.

Dichotomous Questions

The dichotomous question is also a fixed-alternative question but one in which there are only two alternatives:

RESEARCH   REALITIES

9.2 Information in Binary Scales

A large marketing research firm compared consumers' responses on 5-point scales, vs. 2-point checklists (yes/no) for several product categories.

Figure A shows the results for pain relievers. Some consumers were asked:

> "<Branded Aspirin> lasts longer than others."
>
> | 1 | 2 | 3 | 4 | 5 |
> |---|---|---|---|---|
> | disagree strongly | disagree somewhat | neither agree/disagree | agree somewhat | agree strongly |

The % of these respondents who answered "4" or "5" (agree somewhat or strongly) is charted in Figure A.

Other consumers were asked to simply check:

> "<Branded Aspirin> lasts longer than others."
>
> | 1 | 2 |
> |---|---|
> | disagree | agree |

The % of these respondents who marked "2" (agree) is charted in Figure A.

There is some consistency in the overall favorability and perceived strengths and weaknesses of thse products over the different attributes rated. Whether comparing branded aspirin to branded ibuprofen, or branded aspirin to unbranded aspiring, results are often strikingly comparable. For example, the two branded products are thought to "last longer"; the ibuprofen is thought to "not irritate the stomach" as much as the aspirins, etc.

Analogously for the beer category, some consumers were asked:

> "<Branded Beer> is a good thirst quencher."
>
> | 1 | 2 | 3 | 4 | 5 | 6 | 7 |
> |---|---|---|---|---|---|---|
> | disagree strongly | | | neither agree/disagree | | | agree strongly |

The % of these respondents who answered "6" or "7" is charted in Figure B.

Other consumers were asked to:

> "Please check the beers listed below that you think are good thirst quenchers."
>
> _____ Budweiser
> _____ Coors
> _____ Heineken
> _____ Miller

The % of the respondents who checked each brand is charted in Figure B.

Again, there is some consistency. Bud and Coors are largely comparable, except on perceptions of "value" where Coors' profiles resemble Miller's more. Heineken is perceived as the "premium quality" beer, not a good value, and not terribly thirst-quenching.

Thus, perhaps surprisingly, 2-point scales can deliver basic customer reactions that are largely consistent with the finer 7-point scale information.

(Continued)

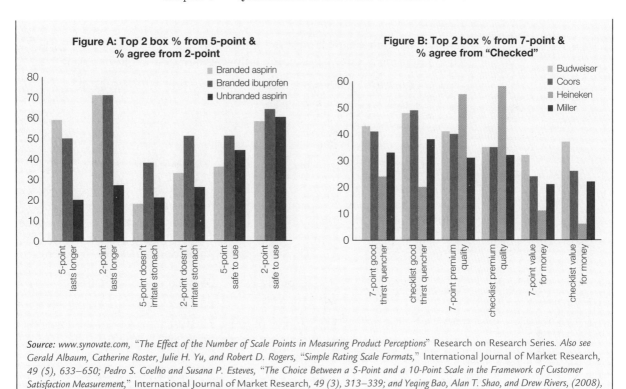

Figure A: Top 2 box % from 5-point & % agree from 2-point

Legend: Branded aspirin, Branded ibuprofen, Unbranded aspirin

Categories: 5-point lasts longer, 2-point lasts longer, 5-point doesn't irritate stomach, 2-point doesn't irritate stomach, 5-point safe to use, 2-point safe to use

Figure B: Top 2 box % from 7-point & % agree from "Checked"

Legend: Budweiser, Coors, Heineken, Miller

Categories: 7-point good thirst quencher, checklist good thirst quencher, 7-point premium quality, checklist premium quality, 7-point value for money, checklist value for money

Source: www.synovate.com, "The Effect of the Number of Scale Points in Measuring Product Perceptions" Research on Research Series. Also see Gerald Albaum, Catherine Roster, Julie H. Yu, and Robert D. Rogers, "Simple Rating Scale Formats," International Journal of Market Research, 49 (5), 633–650; Pedro S. Coelho and Susana P. Esteves, "The Choice Between a 5-Point and a 10-Point Scale in the Framework of Customer Satisfaction Measurement," International Journal of Market Research, 49 (3), 313–339; and Yeqing Bao, Alan T. Shao, and Drew Rivers, (2008), "Creating New Brand Names," Journal of Advertising Research, 148–162.

Do you think laws limiting the amount of interest businesses can charge consumers are needed?

☐ Yes

☐ No

Do you intend to purchase an automobile this year?

☐ Yes

☐ No

Dichotomous questions are easy for respondents to answer and they're easy to code and tabulate. Not surprisingly, they're the most popular kind of survey question.

Question framing is critical for the dichotomous question; e.g., consider:

Do you think that gasoline will be *more* expensive or *less* expensive next year than it is now?

☐ More expensive

☐ Less expensive

Do you think that gasoline will be *less* expensive or *more* expensive next year than it is now?

☐ Less expensive

☐ More expensive

The questions appear identical, but they will elicit different responses. Which, then, is the correct wording? One generally accepted "fix" is to use a "split ballot"—each order is used on half of the questionnaires. The averaged percentages from the two forms should cancel out any biases.

Scales

Another fixed-alternative question is the kind that uses a scale. For instance, when inquiring about DVR use, the following question might be asked:

How often do you tape programs for later viewing with your DVR?

☐ Never

☐ Occasionally

☐ Sometimes

☐ Often

In this form, the question is multichotomous. However, the responses also represent a scale, which is perhaps more obvious in a different form, such as:

In this format, the descriptors are usually presented at the top of the page, and types of programs could be listed along the left margin (e.g., films, sporting events, network specials). The respondent then designates the frequency of

Never	Occasionally	Sometimes	Often

DVR usage for recording each type of show. The instruction would only need to be given once at the beginning, and a great deal of information could be obtained from the respondent in a short period of time.

Decide on Question Wording

Step 5 in the questionnaire development process involves the phrasing of each question. This task is critical—poor phrasing of a question will cause respondents to skip over the question and not answer it, or they'll answer the question incorrectly. The first condition, **item nonresponse**, can create problems during data analysis. The second condition produces **measurement error**, in that the recorded score does not equal the respondent's true opinion.

Experienced researchers know that the phrasing of a question can directly affect the responses:

> *A Dominican priest and a Jesuit priest are discussing whether it is a sin to smoke and pray at the same time. "After failing to reach a conclusion, each goes off to consult his respective superior. The next week they meet again. The Dominican says, 'Well, what did your superior say?' The Jesuit responds, 'He said it was all right.' 'That's funny,' the Dominican replied, 'my superior said it was a sin.' Jesuit: 'What did you ask him?' Reply: 'I asked him if it was all right to smoke while praying.' 'Oh,' says the Jesuit, 'I asked my superior if it was all right to pray while smoking.'"*

Here are several rules of thumb that are useful for enhancing the wording of questions.

Use Simple Words

Most researchers are more highly educated than the typical respondent, so it's easy to make the mistake of writing questions with vocabulary that may be unfamiliar to the respondents. The average person in the U.S. has a high school education, and many people have difficulty in coping with tasks like completing a job application form. So, keep the words simple (see Research Realities 9.3).

R E S E A R C H   R E A L I T I E S

9.3 Ambiguous Words to Avoid

about "About" sometimes means "somewhere near" in the sense that both 48% and 52% are "about" half. It also sometimes means nearly or almost, in that 48% is "about" half whereas 52% is "over" half. This small difference in interpretation would yield different responses.

all This is a "dead giveaway" word. Your own experience with true-false tests has probably demonstrated to you that it is safe to count almost every all-inclusive statement as false.

Would you say that all cats have four legs?

Is the mayor doing all he can for the city?

An all-inclusive word usually produces an overstatement. Most people may go along with the idea, accepting it as a form of literary license, but the purists and quibblers may either refuse to give an opinion or may even choose the other side in protest.

always Another dead-giveaway word.

Do you always observe traffic signs?

Is your boss always friendly?

and This simple conjunction in some contexts may be taken either as separating or connecting two alternatives.

Is there much rivalry among the baseball park vendors who sell beer and soft drinks?

Some people will answer in terms of rivalry between two groups—those who sell beer and those who sell soft drinks. Others will take it as rivalry within the single group comprising both beer and soft drinks vendors.

any The trouble with "any" is that it may mean "every," "some," or "one only" in the same sentence or question, depending on the way you look at it. See whether you can get both the "every" and "only one" illusions from this question and notice the difference in meaning:

Do you think any word is better than the one we are discussing?

You could think, "Yes, I think just any old word (every word) is better." On the other hand, you might think, "Yes, I believe it would be possible to find a better word."

bad In itself the word "bad" is not at all bad for question wording. It conveys the meaning desired and is satisfactory as an alternative in a "good or bad" two-way question.

Sometimes a criticism needs to be softened. For example, after asking, "What things are good about your job?" it might seem perfectly natural to ask, "What things are bad about it?" But if we want to lean over backward to get as many criticisms as we can, we may be wise not to apply the "bad" stigma but to ask, "What things are *not so good* about it?"

ever This word tends to be a dead giveaway in a very special sense. "Ever" is such a long time and so inclusive that it makes it seem plausible that anything may have happened.

Have you ever listened to the Song Plugger radio program?

"Yes, I suppose I must have at some time or other."

go "Go" is given more space in the index of The American Thesaurus of Slang than any other word—a total of about 12½ columns.

When did you last go to town?

If the respondent takes this literally, it is a good question, but the "go to town" phrase has more than a dozen different slang meanings, including a couple that might get your face slapped.

less This word is usually used as an alternative to "more," where it may cause a minor problem. The phrase "more or less" has a special meaning all its own in which some respondents do not see an alternative. Thus, they may simply answer "yes, more or less" to a question like:

Compared with a year ago, are you more or less happy in your job?

(Continued)

The easy solution to this problem is to break up the "more or less" expression by introducing an extra word or so to reverse the two:

Compared with a year ago, are you more happy or less happy in your job?

Compared with a year ago, are you less happy or more happy in your job?

like This word is sometimes used to introduce an example. The problem with bringing an example into a question is that the respondent's attention may be directed toward the particular example and away from the general issue that it is meant only to illustrate. The choice of an example can affect the answers to the question—in fact, it may materially change the question, as in these two examples:

Do you think that leafy vegetables like spinach should be in the daily diet?

Do you think that leafy vegetables like lettuce should be in the daily diet?

you The dictionary distinguishes only two or three meanings of "you"—the second person singular and plural and the substitution for the impersonal "one"—"How do you get there?" in place of "How does one get there?" In most questions "you" gives no trouble whatever, it being clear that we are asking the opinion of the second person singular. However, the word sometimes may have a collective meaning as in a question asked of radio repairmen:

How many radio sets did you repair last month?

This question seemed to work all right until one repairman in a large shop countered with, "Who do you mean, me or the whole shop?"

Much as we might want to, therefore, we can't give "you" an unqualified recommendation. Sometimes "you" needs the emphasis of "you yourself" and sometimes it just isn't the word to use, as in the above situation where the entire shop was meant.

Source: See the classic Stanley L. Payne, The Art of Asking Questions (Princeton University Press), pp. 158–176. Also see Norman M. Bradburn, Seymour Sudman, and Brian Wansink, Asking Questions (Wiley).

Avoid Ambiguous Words and Questions

The words used should also be unambiguous. Consider again the multichotomous question:

How often do you tape programs for later viewing with your DVR?

- ☐ Never
- ☐ Occasionally
- ☐ Sometimes
- ☐ Often

For all practical purposes, the replies to this question would be worthless. The words "occasionally," "sometimes," and "often" are ambiguous. To one respondent, the word "often" might mean "almost every day." To another it might mean, "once a week." Thus, the question would generate little understanding of DVR usage.

A better strategy would be to provide concrete alternatives for the respondent, for example:

- ☐ Never use
- ☐ Use approximately once a month
- ☐ Use approximately once a week
- ☐ Use almost every day

The question provides a consistent frame of reference for each respondent. Respondents are no longer free to superimpose their own definitions on the response categories.

An alternative way to avoid ambiguity in response categories when asking about the frequency of some behavior is to ask about the most recent instance. For example:

Did you tape any programs with your DVR in the last two days?

☐ Yes

☐ No

☐ Can't recall

The proportion responding "yes" would then be used to infer the frequency with which the DVR was used, and the follow-up question, "For what purpose?" (among those responding yes) would give insight as to how respondents are using it. Some respondents who normally use their DVR might not have used it the last two days, but the opposite would be true for others. There might be some variation compared to what they normally do, but the variation should cancel out if a large enough sample were used. Thus, the aggregate sample should provide a good indication of the DVR usage.

Avoid Leading Questions

A leading question is one framed to give the respondent a clue about how he or she 'should' answer. Consider the question:

Do you feel that limiting taxes by law is an effective way to stop the government from picking your pocket every payday?

☐ Yes

☐ No

☐ Undecided

You can see instances every day in the newspaper. Without seeing the questionnaire, the public is treated to a discussion of the results of studies concerning how people feel on issues. Yet the wording of a question makes a difference, and it is important for researchers to realize that. If you want accurate data, you need to avoid leading the respondent.

Avoid Implicit Assumptions

Questions are frequently framed so that there is an implied assumption about what will happen as a consequence. The question, "Are you in favor of placing price controls on crude oil?" will elicit different responses from individuals, depending on their views of what that might produce in the way of rationing, long lines at the pumps, and so forth. A better way to state the question is to make explicit the consequence(s). Thus, "Are you in favor of placing price controls on crude oil if it would produce gas rationing?"

Avoid Generalizations and Estimates

Questions should always be asked in specific rather than general terms. The question, "How many salespeople did you see last year?" might be asked of a purchasing agent. To answer the question, the agent would probably estimate how many salespeople call in a typical week and then multiply this estimate by 52. This burden should not be placed on the agent. Rather, ask, "How many representatives called last week?" and the *researcher* multiplies the answer provided by 52.

Avoid Double-Barreled Questions.

A double-barreled question is one that calls for two responses and thereby creates confusion for the respondent. The question, "What is your evaluation of the price and convenience offered by catalog showrooms?" is asking respondents to react to two separate attributes by which such showrooms could be described. The respondent might think that the prices are attractive but the location is not, and thereby has a dilemma about how to respond. One can avoid double-barreled questions by splitting the question into two.

Decide on Question Sequence

Now the items are put together into the questionnaire. The order of the questions can be crucial. Here are some useful rules of thumb.

- Open with interesting questions
- Move from general to specific
- Demographics and sensitive questions go last

Use Simple, Interesting Opening Questions

The first questions are key. If respondents cannot answer them easily, find them uninteresting, or find them threatening, they may refuse to complete the remainder of the questionnaire. Thus, it is essential that the first few questions be simple, interesting, and in no way threatening. Questions that ask respondents for their opinion on some issue are often good openers, as most people like to think that their opinion is important. Sometimes it is helpful to use such an opener even when those responses will not be analyzed, simply to relax the respondents and get them to talk freely.[5]

Use the Funnel Approach

The funnel approach to question sequencing gets its name from its shape: We start with broad questions and progressively narrow the scope. If respondents are to be asked, "What improvements are needed in the company's service policy?" and also, "How do you like the quality of service?" the first question needs to be asked before the second. Otherwise, quality of service will be emphasized disproportionately in the responses simply because it is fresh in the respondents' minds. There should also be some logical order to the questions. Avoid making sudden changes and jumping around, from topic to topic.

Ethical **Dilemma** 9.2

A candy manufacturer tells you that he wants to raise the price of his gourmet chocolates and he needs you to establish the maximum price increase that shoppers will stand. He suggests that you interview patrons of gourmet candy shops without informing them of the sponsor or purpose of the research, describe the candy to them in general terms, and suggest prices that they might find acceptable, starting with the highest price.

- Is it ethical to ask people questions when their answer may be detrimental to their self-interest?
- Is it ethical not to reveal the purpose or sponsor of the research? If you did reveal the purpose of the research, would survey respondents give the same answer as otherwise?

---

[5] Sometimes you're lucky in that the topic of the survey is fun, such as when Paramount Parks surveys its theme park visitors; Joseph Rydholm, "The Theme is Fun," quirks.com.

Design Branching Questions with Care

Branching questions are used to direct respondents to different places in the questionnaire, based on their response to the question at hand. A respondent replying "yes" to the question of whether he or she bought a new car within the last six months would be asked for specific details about the purchase, whereas someone responding "no" would be asked other questions. Branching questions and directions are easy to program via "if-then" statements in computer-assisted interviewing for surveys administered by telephone or in person. With mail questionnaires, branching can be used (e.g., "If Yes, please go to question 37"), but it needs to be kept to a minimum and the directions need to be crystal clear.

Ask for Classification Information Last

The typical questionnaire contains two types of information: basic information and classification information. Basic information refers to the subject of the study (e.g., intentions or attitudes of respondents). Classification information refers to the other data that we collect to classify respondents, e.g., demographic variables.

The proper questionnaire sequence is to ask questions about the basic information first and the classification information last. Why? The basic information is most critical—without it, there is no study. We cannot risk alienating the respondent by asking personal questions before getting to the heart of the study. Respondents who readily offer their attitudes toward the energy crisis may balk when asked for their income. An early question aimed at determining their income may affect the whole tenor of the interview or other communication. It is best to avoid this possibility by placing the classification information at the end.

Place Difficult or Sensitive Questions Late in the Questionnaire

The basic information itself can also present some sequence problems. If respondents feel threatened, they will leave the interview or stop filling out the questionnaire. Thus, the sensitive questions should be relegated to the body of the questionnaire, intertwined and hidden among some not-so-sensitive ones. Once respondents have become involved in the study, they are less likely to react negatively or be turned off completely when delicate questions are posed.

Determine Physical Characteristics

The physical characteristics of the questionnaire can affect the accuracy of the replies, respondents' reactions, and the ease of processing. Here are some tips.[6]

Appearance of the Questionnaire

The physical appearance of the questionnaire can influence respondents' cooperation. If the questionnaire looks sloppy, respondents are likely to think that the study is unimportant and not bother to cooperate. If the study is important (and why conduct it if it is not?), make the questionnaire look as sharp as your résumé.

The introduction is also important. With mail questionnaires, the cover letter introduces the study. It must convince the designated respondent to cooperate (see Research Realities 9.4). With personal and telephone interviews, the introduction is quick, but it still needs to convince respondents about the importance of the research and their participation. The basics include describing

---

[6] Also see Pamela W. Henderson, "Just My Type," *Harvard Business Review*, F0504, 22–23.

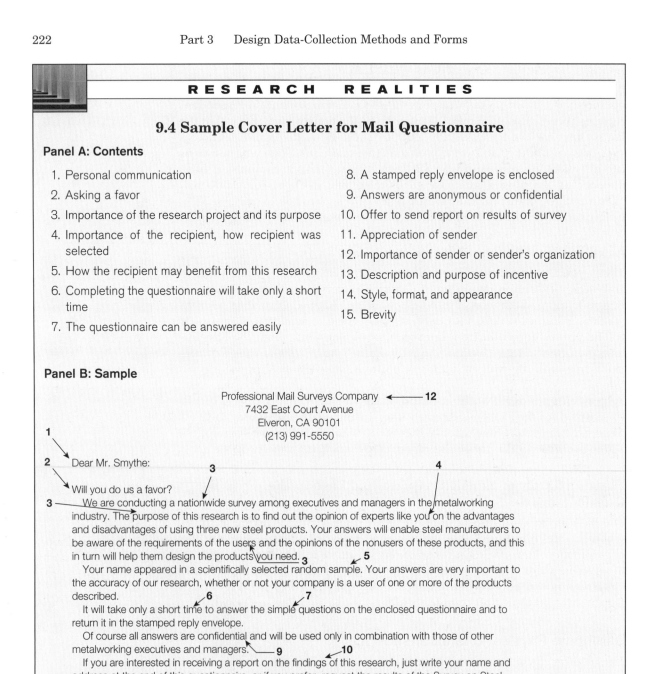

RESEARCH REALITIES

9.4 Sample Cover Letter for Mail Questionnaire

Panel A: Contents

1. Personal communication
2. Asking a favor
3. Importance of the research project and its purpose
4. Importance of the recipient, how recipient was selected
5. How the recipient may benefit from this research
6. Completing the questionnaire will take only a short time
7. The questionnaire can be answered easily

8. A stamped reply envelope is enclosed
9. Answers are anonymous or confidential
10. Offer to send report on results of survey
11. Appreciation of sender
12. Importance of sender or sender's organization
13. Description and purpose of incentive
14. Style, format, and appearance
15. Brevity

Panel B: Sample

Professional Mail Surveys Company ← 12
7432 East Court Avenue
Elveron, CA 90101
(213) 991-5550

1

2   Dear Mr. Smythe: 3   4

Will you do us a favor?

3 —— We are conducting a nationwide survey among executives and managers in the metalworking industry. The purpose of this research is to find out the opinion of experts like you on the advantages and disadvantages of using three new steel products. Your answers will enable steel manufacturers to be aware of the requirements of the users and the opinions of the nonusers of these products, and this in turn will help them design the products you need. 3

Your name appeared in a scientifically selected random sample. Your answers are very important to the accuracy of our research, whether or not your company is a user of one or more of the products described.   6   7

It will take only a short time to answer the simple questions on the enclosed questionnaire and to return it in the stamped reply envelope.

Of course all answers are confidential and will be used only in combination with those of other metalworking executives and managers.   9   10

If you are interested in receiving a report on the findings of this research, just write your name and address at the end of this questionnaire, or if you prefer, request the results of the Survey on Steel Products in a separate letter. We will be glad to send you a complimentary report when it is ready.

Please return the completed questionnaire at your earliest convenience. Thank you for your help!

Sincerely,

James D. Jones   11

James B. Jones

12 → Director

8

13

P.S. The enclosed dollar bill is just a token of appreciation.

how the respondents can benefit, the fact that their replies will be confidential, and the incentive, if any, that they will receive for participating.

It is a good idea to include the name of the sponsoring organization and the name of the project on the first page. Both of these lend credibility to the study.

At the same time, awareness of the sponsoring firm can induce bias in respondents' answers, so many firms use fictitious names for the sponsoring organization.

Facilitate Handling and Control

Questionnaire length is important. Smaller questionnaires are better than larger ones if they do not appear crowded. Shorter questionnaires seem easier to complete; they appear to take less time and are less likely to cause respondents to refuse to participate. Numbering the questions makes it easier to edit, code, and tabulate the responses (see Research Realities 9.5).

Re-examination and Revision of the Questionnaire

First drafts usually don't result in usable questionnaires. Rather, each question should be reviewed to ensure that it isn't confusing or ambiguous, offensive, leading, etc. Be extremely critical of the survey at this stage—it will save you grief later on.

Pre-Testing the Questionnaire

The real test of a questionnaire is how it performs under actual conditions of data collection. For this assessment, the questionnaire **pre-test** is vital (much like test marketing in new-product development).

The most important step in survey development? PRE-TEST it!

Consider these examples. In one lifestyle study, the question was asked: "How would you like to be living two years from now?" Though the question was intended to get at desired lifestyles, a large group of the respondents simply replied "yes." In another study, a question about "house cleaners" made some

R E S E A R C H   R E A L I T I E S

9.5 Guidelines for Web Surveys

Here are suggestions for enhancing Web survey response rates:

1. In the "subject line," include the sponsor, the topic, and the word "survey."

2. In the first sentence, you have a split second to capture the reader's attention. A suggestion: "This is an invitation to take part in a survey project. It's not a sales solicitation."

3. Key drivers to participation:

   a. Is research topic interesting?

   b. How much will I be compensated?

   c. Who is the sponsor?

   d. How much time/effort will this take? (Don't mess around—be truthful!)

4. Have a screener to identify relevant respondents. If a user is bounced out after answering just a few questions that makes it clear they're not the tattooed-Harley-rider-with-a-teenage-daughter-who-needs-a-prom-dress that you were looking for, be

sure to thank them anyway, e.g., "I'm sorry, but you do not qualify to participate in the rest of our survey, but we thank you for your time thus far, and we will enter you into a drawing to win $100 just for trying."

5. Make it clear how the user could contact you for help or more information.

6. Make your privacy statement clear!

   a. For example, "We are a marketing research firm that values your privacy. All of your responses will be kept strictly confidential. Your personal information will not be sold or traded to anyone." (And then don't!)

   b. It couldn't hurt to also have a link to a more elaborate statement of your privacy policy...these are paranoid times.

   c. Ditto for an opt-out opportunity (via e-mail or an 800 number).

Source: Bill MacElroy, "Persuasive E-mail Invitations," Online Research *(www.quirks.com).*

people respond with brands like "Comet" or "Ajax" and others answered, "Yes, we have a service that comes once a week." Data collection should *never* begin without an adequate pre-test of the instrument.

The pre-test should be done by personal interview (regardless of the actual mode of administration that will be used), so the interviewer can watch to see how people answer the questions, where they get confused, etc. Next, the responses that result from the pre-test should be coded and tabulated. The tabulation into dummy tables can help us verify whether we've conceptualized the problem correctly, and see if we'll be getting the data to answer our questions.

The researcher who avoids a questionnaire pre-test and tabulation of replies is naïve. The pre-test is the most inexpensive insurance the researcher can buy to ensure the success of the questionnaire and the research project.

Table 9.2 provides a checklist of steps to take and decisions to make in creating a questionnaire. The steps in the process are those in Figure 9.1, and we've just reviewed the main points, but the checklist can be a quick, handy reference when you're called to write a survey.[7]

Observational Forms

As Yogi Berra has said, "You can observe a lot by watching."

Generally, fewer problems occur in constructing observational forms than questionnaires, because the researcher is no longer concerned with whether the question will affect the response. The observers will be properly trained, and their expertise means the data-collection instrument will be used consistently. Figure 9.3 is an example.

What do you want to observe? Almost any event can be described in a number of ways. When we watch someone making a cigarette purchase, we might report that (1) the person purchased one package of cigarettes; (2) the woman purchased one package of cigarettes; (3) the woman purchased a package of Tareyton cigarettes; (4) the woman purchased a package of Tareyton 100's; (5) the woman, after asking for and finding that the store was out of Virginia Slims, purchased a package of Tareyton 100's; and so on.

The decision about what to observe requires that the researcher specify the following:

- *Who* should be observed? Anyone entering the store? Anyone making a purchase?

- *What* aspects of the purchase should be reported? Which brand they purchased? What about the purchaser? Is the person's gender to be recorded? Is the individual's age to be estimated? Does it make any difference if the person was alone or in a group?

- *When* should the observation be made? On what day of the week? At what time of the day? Should day and time be reported? Should the observation be recorded only after a purchase occurs or should a customer approaching a salesclerk also be recorded, even if it does not result in a sale?

- *Where* should the observation be made? In what kind of store? How should the store be selected? How should it be noted on the observational form—by type, by location, by name? Should vending-machine purchases also be noted?

---

[7] The first commandment in writing surveys is to keep them short. If you must include many questions, consider creating multiple forms to be administered to separate samples and compiled later (for more, see Feray Adiguzel and Michel Wedel, "Split Questionnaire Design for Massive Surveys," *Journal of Marketing Research* 45 (3), 608–617).

TABLE 9.2	**Some Do's and Don'ts When Preparing Questionnaires**

Step 1: Specify What Information Will Be Sought

1. Make sure that you have a clear understanding of the issue and what you want to know.

2. Make a list of your research questions. Review them as you prepare the questionnaire.

3. Use "dummy tables" to guide the data analysis to suggest questions.

Step 2: Determine Type of Questionnaire and Method of Administration

1. Use the degree of structure, disguise, and cost to determine the method of administration.

2. Compare the capabilities and limitations of each method of administration and the value of the data collected from each, with the needs of the survey.

Step 3: Determine Content of Individual Questions

1. For each research question, ask yourself, "Why do I want to know this?" Answer it in terms of how it will help your research. "It would be interesting to know" means the question is superfluous and should be dropped.

2. Make sure each question is specific and addresses only one important issue.

3. Does the question apply to all respondents, if not, make provision for skipping it.

4. Make sure the time period of the question is related to the importance of the topic.

5. Avoid questions that require excessive effort, that have hard-to-articulate answers, and that deal with embarrassing or threatening issues.

6. If threatening questions are necessary:
   a. Hide the questions among more innocuous ones.
   b. Make use of a counterbiasing statement.
   c. Phrase the question in terms of others and how they might feel or act.
   d. Ask respondents if they have ever engaged in the undesirable activity, and then ask if they are presently engaging in such an activity.
   e. Use categories or ranges rather than specific numbers.
   f. Use the randomized response model.

Step 4: Determine Form of Response to Each Question

1. Determine which type of question—open-ended, dichotomous, or multichotomous—provides data that fit the information needs of the project.

2. Use structured questions whenever possible.

3. Use open-ended questions that require short answers to begin a questionnaire.

4. Try to convert open-ended questions to closed (fixed) response questions to reduce respondent workload and coding effort for descriptive and causal studies.

5. If open-ended questions are necessary, make the questions sufficiently directed to give respondents a frame of reference when answering.

6. When using dichotomous questions, state the negative or alternative side in detail.

7. Provide for "don't know," "no opinion," and "both" answers.

8. Be aware that there may be a middle ground.

9. Be sensitive to the mildness or harshness of the alternatives.

10. When using multichotomous questions, be sure that the choices are exhaustive and mutually exclusive, and if combinations are possible, include them.

11. Be sure that the range of alternatives is clear and that all reasonable alternative answers are included.

12. If the possible responses are numerous, consider using more than one question to reduce the potential for information overload.

13. Clearly indicate if items are to be ranked or if only one item on the list is to be chosen.

(Continued)

Step 5: Determine Wording of Each Question

1. Use simple words.

2. Avoid ambiguous words and questions.

3. Avoid leading questions.

4. Avoid implicit assumptions.

5. Avoid generalizations and estimates.

6. Use simple sentences, and avoid compound sentences.

7. Change long, dependent clauses to words or short phrases.

8. Avoid double-barreled questions.

9. Make sure each question is as specific as possible.

Step 6: Determine Question Sequence

1. Use simple, interesting questions for openers.

2. Use the funnel approach, first asking broad questions and then narrowing them down.

3. Ask difficult or sensitive questions late in the questionnaire when rapport is better.

4. Follow chronological order when collecting historical information.

5. Complete questions about one topic before moving on to the next.

6. Prepare a flow chart whenever filter questions are being considered.

7. Ask demographic questions last; if respondent refuses, the other data are still usable.

Step 7: Determine Physical Characteristics of Questionnaire

1. Make sure that the questionnaire looks professional and is relatively easy to answer.

2. Make the questionnaire as short as possible, but avoid a crowded appearance.

3. List the name of the organization conducting the survey on the first page.

4. Number the questions to ease data processing.

5. If the respondent must skip more than one question, use a "go to."

6. If the respondent must skip an entire section, consider color coding the sections.

7. State how the responses are to be reported, e.g., check mark, number, circle, etc.

Step 8: Re-examine Steps 1–7 and Revise If Necessary

1. Examine each word of every question to ensure the question is not confusing, ambiguous, offensive, or leading.

2. Get peer evaluations of the draft questionnaire.

Step 9: Pre-test Questionnaire and Revise If Necessary

1. Pre-test the questionnaire first by personal interviews among respondents similar to those to be used in the actual study.

2. Obtain comments from the interviewers and respondents to discover any problems with the questionnaire, and revise it if necessary. When the revisions are substantial, repeat Steps 1 and 2 of the pre-test.

3. Pre-test the questionnaire to uncover problems unique to the mode of administration.

4. Code and tabulate the Pre-test responses in dummy tables to determine if questions are providing adequate information.

5. Eliminate questions that do not provide adequate information, and revise questions that cause problems.

These are the same kinds of who, what, when, and where decisions that need to be made in selecting the research design. The "why" and "how" are also implicit. The research problem should dictate the why of the observation, whereas the how involves choosing the observation device or form to use. A paper-and-pencil form should be very simple to use. It should permit the recording of observations by a simple check mark if possible.

FIGURE 9.3   **Form Used by Observer Acting as a Shopper to Evaluate Service Provided by Bank Employees**

Bank _____

Date _____ Time _____ Shopper's Name_____

Nature of Transaction: _____In Person   _____ Telephone

Details: _____

_____

_____

_____

A. For In Person Transaction, what was Bank Employee's Name? _____

  How did you obtain that information?

  ☐ employee had name tag

  ☐ name plate on counter or desk

  ☐ I had to ask for name

  ☐ name provided by another employee

  ☐ other: _____

B. For Telephone Transaction, what was Bank Employee's Name? _____

  How did you obtain that information?

  ☐ employee gave name upon answering the telephone

  ☐ name provided by another employee

  ☐ I had to ask for name

  ☐ employee gave name during conversation

  ☐ other: _____

C. Customer Relations Skills	Yes	No	Does not apply
1. Did the employee notice and greet you immediately?	☐	☐	☐
2. Did the employee speak pleasantly and smile?	☐	☐	☐
3. Did the employee answer the phone within 2 rings?	☐	☐	☐
4. Did the employee find out your name?	☐	☐	☐
5. Did the employee use your name during the transaction?	☐	☐	☐
6. Did the employee ask you to be seated?	☐	☐	☐
7. Was the employee helpful?	☐	☐	☐
8. Was the employee's desk or work area neat and uncluttered?	☐	☐	☐
9. Did the employee show a genuine interest in you as a customer?	☐	☐	☐
10. Did the employee thank you for coming in?	☐	☐	☐
11. Did the employee enthusiastically support the bank and its services?	☐	☐	☐
12. Did the employee handle any interruptions effectively (phone calls, etc.)?	☐	☐	☐

Comment on any positive or negative details of the transaction that you found particularly noticeable:

_____

_____

_____

_____

(Continued)

D. Sales Skills	Yes	No	Does not apply
1. Did the employee determine if you had any accounts with this bank?	☐	☐	☐
2. Did the employee use "open-ended" questions to obtain info about you?	☐	☐	☐
3. Did the employee listen to what you had to say?	☐	☐	☐
4. Did the employee sell you on bank services by showing you what the service could do for you?	☐	☐	☐
5. Did the employee ask you to open the service which you inquired about?	☐	☐	☐
6. Did the employee ask you to bank with this particular bank?	☐	☐	☐
7. Did the employee ask you to contact him/her when visiting the bank?	☐	☐	☐
8. Did the employee ask if you had any questions or if you understood the service at the end of the transaction?	☐	☐	☐
9. Did the employee give you brochures about other services?	☐	☐	☐
10. Did the employee give you his/her business card?	☐	☐	☐
11. Did the employee indicate you might be contacted by phone or letter as a means of follow-up?	☐	☐	☐
12. Did the employee ask you to open or use other services?	☐	☐	☐

Check the following if they were mentioned:

☐ savings account	☐ checking account	☐ automatic savings
☐ Mastercharge	☐ Master Checking	☐ safe deposit box
☐ loans	☐ trust services	☐ automatic loan payment
☐ bank hours	☐ other: _____	

Comment on the overall effectiveness of the employee's sales skills:

_____

_____

_____

_____

Summary

A researcher wishing to collect primary data needs to design the data-collection form. Typically this means designing a questionnaire.

Questionnaire design is still very much of an art rather than a science, and there are many admonitions of things to avoid when doing the designing. A nine-step procedure (Figure 9.1) was offered as a guide: What information will be sought? What type of questionnaire will be used? How will that questionnaire be administered? What will be the content of the individual questions? What will be the form of response (e.g., dichotomous, multichotomous, or open-ended) to each question? How will each question be phrased? How will the questions be sequenced? What will the questionnaire look like physically?

Researchers should not be surprised to find themselves repeating the various steps when designing a questionnaire. Further, in our daily rush, the temptation is sometimes great, but one should never omit a pre-test of the questionnaire.

Observational forms are typically easier to construct because the researcher does not need to be concerned with how a question might affect a response. Observational forms do, however, require a precise statement of who or what is to be observed.

Questions

1. How do research hypotheses help determine the information that will be sought?

2. Suppose you were interested in determining the proportion of men in a geographic area who use hair spray. How would you ask this through an open-ended question, a multiple-choice question, or dichotomous question? Which would be preferable?

3. How does the method of administration affect the questions to be used?

4. What criteria determine whether a specific question should be included in a survey?

5. What are some recommended ways by which one can ask for sensitive information?

6. What is an open-ended question? A multichotomous question? A dichotomous question?

7. What is an ambiguous question? A leading question? A question with implicit alternatives? A question with implied assumptions? A double-barreled question?

8. What is the proper sequence when asking for basic information and demographics?

9. What is the funnel approach to question sequencing?

10. What is a branching question? Why are such questions used?

11. Where should one ask for sensitive information in the questionnaire?

12. How can the physical features of a questionnaire affect its acceptance by respondents?

Applications and Problems

1. Evaluate the following questions:
   a. Which of the following magazines do you read regularly?
      - ☐ Time
      - ☐ Newsweek
      - ☐ Business Week
   b. Are you a frequent purchaser of Birds Eye frozen vegetables?
      - ☐ Yes
      - ☐ No
   c. Do you agree that the government should impose import restrictions?
      - ☐ Strongly agree
      - ☐ Agree
      - ☐ Neither agree nor disagree
      - ☐ Disagree
      - ☐ Strongly disagree
   d. How often do you buy detergent?
      - ☐ Once a week
      - ☐ Once in two weeks
      - ☐ Once in three weeks
      - ☐ Once a month
   e. Rank the following in order of preference:
      - ☐ Kellogg's Corn Flakes
      - ☐ Quaker's Life
      - ☐ Post Bran Flakes
      - ☐ Kellogg's Bran Flakes
      - ☐ Quaker Instant Oatmeal
      - ☐ Post Rice Krispies
   f. Where do you usually purchase your office supplies?
   g. When you are watching television, do you also watch most of the advertisements?
   h. Which of the following brands of tea are most similar?
      - ☐ Lipton's Orange Pekoe
      - ☐ Turnings Orange Pekoe
      - ☐ Bigelow Orange Pekoe
      - ☐ Salada Orange Pekoe
   i. Do you think that the present policy of cutting taxes and reducing government spending should be continued?
      - ☐ Yes ☐ No
   j. In a seven-day week, how often do you eat breakfast?
      - ☐ Every day of the week
      - ☐ 5–6 times a week
      - ☐ 2–4 times a week
      - ☐ Once a week
      - ☐ Never

2. Make the necessary corrections to the preceding questions.

3. Evaluate the following multichotomous questions. Would dichotomous or open-ended questions be more appropriate?

a. Which one of the following reasons is most important in your choice of stereo equipment?
☐ Price
☐ In-store service
☐ Brand name
☐ Level of distortion
☐ Guarantee/warranty

b. Please indicate your education level.
☐ Less than high school
☐ Some high school
☐ High school graduate
☐ Technical or vocational school
☐ Some college
☐ College graduate
☐ Some graduate or professional school

c. Which of the following reflects your views toward the issues raised by ecologists?
☐ Have received attention
☐ Have not received attention
☐ Should receive more attention
☐ Should receive less attention

d. Which of the following statements do you most strongly agree with?
☐ American Airlines has better service than Northwest Airlines
☐ Northwest Airlines has better service than United Airlines
☐ United Airlines has better service than American Airlines
☐ United Airlines has better service than Northwest Airlines
☐ Northwest Airlines has better service than American Airlines
☐ American Airlines has better service than United Airlines

4. Evaluate the following open-ended questions. Rephrase them as multichotomous or dichotomous questions if you think it would be appropriate.

a. Do you go to the movies often?
b. Approximately how much do you spend per week on groceries?
c. What brands of cheese did you purchase during the last week?

5. Discuss how each of the following respondent groups would influence the development of the questionnaire form.

a. Medical doctors
b. Welfare recipients
c. Air Force commanders
d. Cuban refugees

6. Campus Cookery, the local burger spot, has asked you to comment on some of the questions that have been developed for a survey they are conducting on a new sandwich offering. What is wrong (if anything) with each of the following questions?

a. Why haven't you tried our new sandwich at Campus Cookery?
b. Don't you think that Campus Cookery's products are of the highest quality?
c. Would you say that our new sandwich tastes good, is priced correctly, is attractive, and is healthy?
☐ Yes ☐ No
d. Have you tried our new sandwich at Campus Cookery?

Very Infrequently	Infrequently	Average	Very Frequently
___	___	___	___

7. Analyze the following questions. What (if anything) is wrong with each question?

a. How do you like the flavor of this high-quality, top-bean coffee?
b. What do you think of the taste and texture of this Danish Treat coffee cake?
c. We are conducting a study for Guess watches. What do you think of the quality of Guess watches?
d. How far do you live from the closest mall?
e. Who in your family shops for clothes?
f. Where do you buy most of your clothes?

8. A small brokerage firm was concerned with the declining number of customers and decided to do a quick survey. The major objective was to find out the reasons for patronizing a particular brokerage firm and to find out the importance of customer service. The following questionnaire was to be administered by telephone. Evaluate the questionnaire.

Good Afternoon Sir/Madam:
We are doing a survey on attitudes toward brokerage firms. Could you please answer the following questions? Thank you.

1. Have you invested any money in the stock market?
___ Yes ___ No
If respondent replies yes, continue; otherwise terminate interview.

2. Do you manage your own investments or do you go to a brokerage firm?
___ Manage own investments
___ Go to a brokerage firm
If respondent replies "go to a brokerage firm," continue; otherwise, terminate interview.

3. How satisfied are you with your brokerage firm?

Very Satisfied	Satisfied	Neither Satisfied nor Dissatisfied	Dissatisfied	Very Dissatisfied
____	____	____	____	____

4. How important is personal service to you?

Very Important	Important	Not Particularly Important	Not at All Important
____	____	____	____

5. Which of the following reasons is the most important in patronizing a particular firm?
   ___ The commission charged by the firm
   ___ The personal service
   ___ The return on investment
   ___ The investment counseling

6. Approximately how long have you been investing through the brokerage firm you are currently using?
   ___ About 3 months   ___ About 9 months
   ___ About 6 months   ___ About 1 year or more

7. How much capital do you have invested?

   ___ $500–$750   ___ $1,000–$1,500
   ___ $750–$1,000   ___ $1,500 or more

Good-bye and thank you for your cooperation.

Attitude Measurement

10

Questions to Guide Your Learning:

Q1 What precisely is an "attitude" and what are the psychological components of an attitude?

Q2 What are "levels of measurement" and why do they matter?

Q3 What are Likert scales, semantic differential scales, and constant sum scales?

Attitude is one of the most pervasive notions in all of marketing. It plays a pivotal role in the major models describing consumer behavior, and it is included, in one form or another, in most marketing investigations. Attitude plays this central role mainly because it is believed to strongly influence behavior. Many marketers believe that attitudes directly affect purchase decisions and that purchase and usage experiences, in turn, directly affect consumers' subsequent attitudes toward the product or service.

People hold attitudes about virtually everything, and marketers study many of them. For example, Research Realities 10.1 reports on an annual poll—the *Fortune* rankings of most admired companies. The companies with the best overall reputations are listed, as are those high on particular qualities, like strengths in social responsibility, innovation, management quality, etc.

Attitude is one of the most widely used ideas in all of consumer behavior, but it is also difficult to pin down a definition. However, there seems to be agreement about the following:

1. Attitude represents a *predisposition* to respond to an object (not yet the actual behavior toward the object). Attitude thus possesses the quality of readiness.

2. Attitude is *persistent* over time, and changing a strongly held attitude is difficult.

3. Attitude is a latent variable that produces consistency in verbal and physical behavior.

4. Attitude has a directional quality. It connotes a preference the object, evaluations of the object, or positive/neutral/negative feelings for the object.

These consistencies lead to our *definition of attitude* as *representing a person's ideas, convictions, or liking with regard to a specific object or idea.*

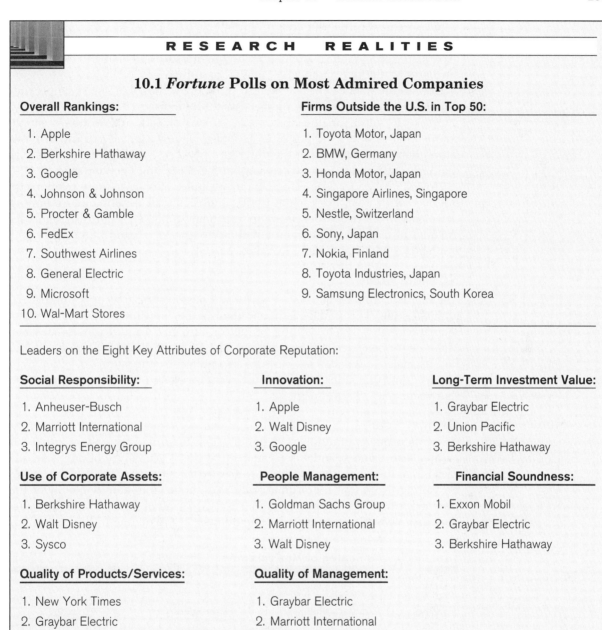

RESEARCH   REALITIES

10.1 *Fortune* Polls on Most Admired Companies

Overall Rankings:

1. Apple
2. Berkshire Hathaway
3. Google
4. Johnson & Johnson
5. Procter & Gamble
6. FedEx
7. Southwest Airlines
8. General Electric
9. Microsoft
10. Wal-Mart Stores

Firms Outside the U.S. in Top 50:

1. Toyota Motor, Japan
2. BMW, Germany
3. Honda Motor, Japan
4. Singapore Airlines, Singapore
5. Nestle, Switzerland
6. Sony, Japan
7. Nokia, Finland
8. Toyota Industries, Japan
9. Samsung Electronics, South Korea

Leaders on the Eight Key Attributes of Corporate Reputation:

Social Responsibility:

1. Anheuser-Busch
2. Marriott International
3. Integrys Energy Group

Innovation:

1. Apple
2. Walt Disney
3. Google

Long-Term Investment Value:

1. Graybar Electric
2. Union Pacific
3. Berkshire Hathaway

Use of Corporate Assets:

1. Berkshire Hathaway
2. Walt Disney
3. Sysco

People Management:

1. Goldman Sachs Group
2. Marriott International
3. Walt Disney

Financial Soundness:

1. Exxon Mobil
2. Graybar Electric
3. Berkshire Hathaway

Quality of Products/Services:

1. New York Times
2. Graybar Electric
3. Anheuser-Busch

Quality of Management:

1. Graybar Electric
2. Marriott International
3. Walt Disney

Source: money.cnn.com/magazines/fortune/mostadmired © 2009 Time Inc. All rights reserved.

Scales of Measurement

If we're hoping to understand "attitude measurement," we have a beginning of an understanding of "attitude," but we also need to define measurement. Then we'll be ready to present the types of **scales** that can be used to measure attitudes. The term "scale" refers to the "level of measurement" (e.g., an ordinal scale) or to a particular scale or type of instrument used (e.g., a scale of customer satisfaction). We take up the level of measurement issues first.

Measurement is the assignment of numbers to objects (e.g., consumers) in a way that reflects the quantity of the attribute that the object possesses (e.g., preference for a brand). Note that we do not measure a person, but we measure attributes of that person: income, height, or attitudes.

How are numbers to be assigned to those properties? Let's start simply with thinking about properties of numbers. With the numbers 1, 2, 3, and 4, let the number "1" stand for one object, "2" for two objects, and so on—a simple count. That simple scale possesses several qualities; e.g., we can say that 2 is larger than 1, we can say that the difference between 1 and 2 is the same size as that between 3 and 4, and we can say that 3 is three times greater than 1.

However, when we assign numbers to attributes of objects, these relations do not necessarily hold. For each attribute, and each scale assignment, we have to determine which properties of numbers actually apply. The four different types of scales of measurement are nominal, ordinal, interval, and ratio. Table 10.1 summarizes important features of these scales.

Nominal Scale

The simplest property of a scale is identity. A person's social security number is a **nominal scale**. The numbers simply identify the individual. In a market segmentation study, if we're coding gender or ethnicity, we have a nominal scale. Males might be coded "1" and females "2." Each individual is uniquely identified as male or female, but nothing is implied by the numbers other than identification of gender. We could just as easily reverse our coding procedure so that women are "1" and men, "2."

Ordinal Scale

A second property of numbers is that of order. We can say that the number 3 is greater than 2 and 1, and 4 is greater still. If this is the nature of our scale, the idea is that the larger the number, the greater the amount of the attribute we're measuring. Note that the **ordinal scale** also implies the identity quality of the nominal scale, since the same number is used for all objects that are the same. For example, suppose we assigned the number "1" to denote freshmen, "2" for

Nominal
Ordinal
Interval
Ratio

TABLE 10.1   Scales of Measurement

Scale	Basic Comparisons[1]	Examples	Measures of Average[2]
Nominal	Identity	Male–female, User–nonuser, Occupations, Uniform numbers	Mode
Ordinal	Order	Preference for brands, Social class, Hardness of minerals, Graded quality of lumber	Median
Interval	Compare intervals	Temperature scale, Grade point average, Attitude toward brands	Mean
Ratio	Compare absolute magnitudes	Units sold, Number of purchasers, Probability of purchase, Weight	Geometric mean, Harmonic mean

[1] The scales are hierarchical, so all comparisons applicable to a given scale are permissible with all scales *above it* in the table. For example, the ratio scale allows the comparison of intervals and the investigation of order and identity, in addition to the comparison of absolute magnitudes.
[2] The measures of average applicable to a given scale are also appropriate for all scales below it in the table; i.e., the mode is also a meaningful measure of the average when measurement is on an ordinal, interval, or ratio scale.

sophomores, "3" for juniors, and "4" for seniors. We could have used the numbers "10" for freshmen, "20" for sophomores, "25" for juniors, and "32.3" for seniors. Either set of scores would indicate the class level of each student.

Note also that we cannot interpret the differences between ranks. If we take the three top people in a graduating class, the fact that one person was ranked number one while the second was ranked number two tells us nothing about the difference in academic achievement between the two.

One reason that ranks are used in marketing is to force customers to distinguish among choices. For example, if a customer is asked, "Which of these attributes are important to you," many customers simply rate every attribute as fairly important. This is not great information for a company—how do you take these data and decide what features to include or improve if all are deemed important? Instead, if customers are asked to rank the attributes, the customer has to make a decision about one feature being more important than another.

Interval Scale

A third property of numbers is that the intervals between numbers are meaningful. That is, the numbers tell us how far apart the objects are with respect to the attribute being measured. The difference between "1" and "2" is equal to the difference between "2" and "3," and the difference between "2" and "4" is twice the difference that exists between "1" and "2."

A classic example of an **interval scale** is the temperature scale. If the low temperature for the day was 40°F and the high was 80°F, can we say that the high temperature was twice as hot (i.e., represented twice the heat) as the low temperature? No. If we convert these temperatures to Celsius (where C = (5F − 160)/9), then the low was 4.4°C and the high 26.6°C, a much different ratio. Thus, we cannot compare the absolute magnitude of interval scales.

What can we say about data from an interval scale? We can say that 80°F is warmer than 40°F. We can say the difference in heat (the attribute being measured) between 80°F and 120°F is the same as the difference between 40°F and 80°F, and that the difference between 40°F and 120°F is twice the difference between 40°F and 80°F.

Ratio Scale

The **ratio scale** possesses a natural or absolute zero. Height and weight are examples. With a real zero, the comparison of the absolute magnitude of the numbers is legitimate. Thus, a person weighing 200 pounds is said to be twice as heavy as one weighing 100 pounds.

We say more about these scales—nominal, ordinal, interval, and ratio—when we begin to talk about data analysis. The statistics we can compute depend on these levels of measurement. For example, we'll see that we can only compute a mode on nominal data, but we could compute a mean on interval level data.

Scaling of Psychological Attributes

The attribute we're trying to measure is itself the key determinant to the level of scale that we can use to measure the characteristic. If the attribute is naturally "ordinal," the best we can do is get an "ordinal" level variable from a survey. We could end up writing a survey item that yields only a "nominal" variable, but we could not write a question that yielded a "ratio" variable. Thus, scale construction partly determines the type of scale generated, so we have to be careful in conceptualizing

FIGURE 10.1

Assessing a Respondent's Liking of Soft Drinks with Nominal, Ordinal, Interval, and Ratio Scales

Nominal
Which of the soft drinks in the following list do you like? (Check ALL that apply):

___ Coke

___ Dr Pepper

___ Mountain Dew

___ Pepsi

___ 7UP

___ Sprite

Ordinal
Rank the soft drinks according to how much you like each (most preferred drink = 1, and least preferred drink = 6):

___ Coke

___ Dr Pepper

___ Mountain Dew

___ Pepsi

___ 7UP

___ Sprite

Interval
Please indicate how much you like each soft drink by checking the appropriate position on the scale:

	Dislike a Lot	Dislike	Like	Like a Lot
Coke	—	—	—	—
Dr pepper	—	—	—	—
Mountain Dew	—	—	—	—
Pepsi	—	—	—	—
7UP	—	—	—	—
Sprite	—	—	—	—

Ratio
Please divide 100 points among these soft drinks to represent how much you like each:

___ Coke

___ Dr pepper

___ Mountain Dew

___ Pepsi

___ 7UP

___ Sprite

100

the attribute. The more powerful scales (ratio, interval) allow stronger comparisons and conclusions than simpler levels of measurement (ordinal or nominal).

Figure 10.1 shows four ways of asking about consumer preferences for soft drinks. The items represent examples of a nominal, ordinal, interval, and ratio scale.

Attitude-Scaling Procedures

By far the most common approach to measuring attitudes is self-reports, in which people are asked directly for their beliefs or feelings toward something, e.g., ads, brands, etc. **Self-report scales** are so prevalent that we'll spend the next section discussing them and the forms they take. But note that attitudes can also be measured in other ways, including: the observation of overt behavior, performance of "objective" tasks, and physiological reactions. These other measures lend complementary insights and can help validate the self-report measure. Multiple measures are useful to establish the convergent and discriminant validity of a measure.[1]

Observation of Behavior

The observation approach assumes that we can infer attitudes from observing behavior. Thus, observers inferred that consumers are *not* looking for a low-fat

[1] Convergent and discriminant validity are discussed in the chapter appendix. Convergent validity (of a measure) is the extent to which it correlates highly with other measures designed to assess the same construct. Discriminant validity is indicated by low correlations between measures that are not supposed to be capturing the same construct.

meal when they enter McDonald's from the fact that the McLean hamburger was a marketing flop in spite of the $50 million product launch.[2]

Performance of an "Objective" Task

These approaches presume that people's performance of objective tasks depends on their attitude. To assess a person's opinion about green marketing, we might ask him or her to memorize some facts about pollution, recycling, and pending legislation. This material would reflect both sides of the issue. The researcher would then attempt to determine what facts the person assimilated. The assumption is that they are more likely to remember the arguments most consistent with their own position.

Physiological Reactions

The physiological reaction approach to attitude measurement uses electrical or mechanical means, such as the galvanic skin response technique, to monitor a person's response to some stimulus. These measures provide an indication of the intensity of the individual's feelings but not an assessment of positive or negative valence.

Self-Report Attitude Scales

In this section, we review types of self-report scales, focusing particularly on those that have novel features or have been used extensively in marketing. We describe what each scale looks like, how it is constructed and how it is used.

Equal-Appearing Intervals

Suppose that one of the banks in town is interested in comparing its image to its competitors' and has developed a list of statements that could be used to describe each bank. Suppose a respondent describes Bank A as having "convenient hours" and "a convenient location" but "generally discourteous service" and "higher service charges on personal checking accounts." Does this customer have a favorable or unfavorable attitude toward Bank A? And suppose that the respondent describes Bank B as just the opposite. Which bank does this person like more? "Equal-appearing interval scaling" develops values for these statements so we can assess the person's attitude toward these banks.

Scale Construction

We first generate a large number of statements about the object of interest (e.g., the banks). The statements are edited to remove ones that are ambiguous, irrelevant, and awkward, as well as those that are simply factual rather than opinion-based. A relatively large sample of judges then sorts the statements by how favorable they are, and a scale value is determined for each statement by noting how many judges consider the statement most favorable, next most favorable, etc. The statements are then screened on the basis of two criteria: the scale values and the dispersion in judgments exhibited by a pre-test of participants. A final scale is formed from those statements that span the range of scale values and that display relatively good interjudge reliability.

For example, in the first phase, generating a large number of statements, we draw from a search of the literature, discussions with knowledgeable people, personal experience, etc., trying to be exhaustive. We create these statements:

---

[2] Hugh Graham, "Annals of Marketing: Don't Go Changin'," *Dow Jones Publications Library*, dowjones.com.

1. The bank offers courteous service.

2. The bank has a convenient location.

3. The bank has convenient hours.

4. The bank offers low interest rates on loans.

5. The bank pays low interest on its savings accounts.

… etc., through to the last:

"m." The bank's service is friendly.

Ideally, "m" (the number of items we've generated) would be in the neighborhood of 100 to 200, and each statement would be presented on a separate card.

After editing the statements, we recruit a large number of respondents to serve as judges. Each judge is instructed to sort the statements into one of 11 piles based on the "degree of favorableness" of the statement. The judges are not asked whether they agree or disagree with a statement, but simply to evaluate how positive it is. They place the most unfavorable statements in the "A" pile of Figure 10.2, the most favorable statements in K, and the neutral statements into the F pile. The presumption is that each judge will perceive the categories A through K as representing equal increments of favorableness, hence the name, "equal-appearing intervals."

Suppose that 200 judges sorted the m statements according to their favorableness and that Table 10.2 contains the resulting distribution for the first four statements. The right-hand columns of the table contain the scale and Q values for each statement (hence a name for this technique, the "Q sort"). The scale value represents the "average" (median) value of the statement, which places each statement on the favorability continuum seen in Figure 10.2. The Q value is the interquartile range, which provides a measure of dispersion.

Both the scale values and the measures of dispersion are used to select a subset of statements to serve as the final survey instrument. Typically, we'd select about 20 statements that span the scale of favorableness; some with low scale values, some intermediate, and some high. Ideally, the scale values would be equally spaced. You can see even from this small example that several of the initial statements have approximately equal scale values. We don't need all of them, so how do we choose among them? This is where the interquartile range enters. We would like to have items that will be interpreted consistently, not statements that could be seen as both positive and negative. Large values of Q indicate wider disagreement among the judges as to the favorableness of the statement, and, therefore, the statement is ambiguous. For two statements with approximately equal values, we choose the one that has the smaller Q. In sum, both the scale and Q values serve as filters for reducing the total stimuli to a more manageable number.

FIGURE 10.2   Equal-Appearing Interval Continuum

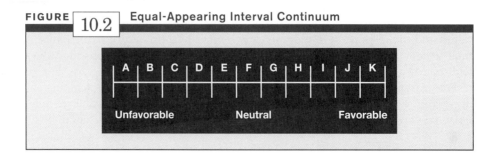

	Sorting Categories												
Statement	A 1	B 2	C 3	D 4	E 5	F 6	G 7	H 8	I 9	J 10	K 11	Scale Value	Q Value
1	0	8	10	30	60	60	14	12	6	0	0	5.4	1.7
2	0	0	0	0	0	6	16	28	44	66	40	9.6	1.8
3	0	0	0	0	10	10	14	32	84	34	16	8.9	1.5
4	0	0	8	16	36	58	48	24	10	0	0	6.2	2.0

TABLE 10.2 Equal-Appearing Interval Sort of Statements into Categories

Scale Use

Assume that some 20 to 22 statements have been selected from the larger list. The statements are placed randomly in the survey so that there is no detectable order to the scale values. The instrument is then ready to be administered to another sample of respondents.

When the instrument is administered, people are asked to indicate those statements with which they agree, e.g., "Which statements from this list best reflect your feelings toward Bank A?" The person's attitude score is computed as the average of the scale scores for the statements with which the person agrees. Thus, if someone agreed with three statements with the scale scores 8.2, 8.7, and 9.8, that person's attitude score would be 8.9. Since a 6 represents a neutral attitude, we'd conclude that this person had a favorable attitude toward Bank A.

One concern is that this method doesn't allow respondents to express the intensity of their feelings. People might "agree" with the statement, "The bank has convenient hours," when they really think that "the bank hours are *really* convenient" or that "the bank hours are *okay*, but could be improved." In either case, the respondent would have agreed with the statement, yet the two attitudes are different.

The equal-appearing interval scale is time consuming to construct, but once it's been constructed, it is easy to administer and is easy for respondents to complete. It can be used to assess attitudes toward a variety of objects (e.g., each bank in town) and other characteristics (e.g., the amount of exaggeration perceived in a series of advertising claims).

Different kinds of self-report scales:

- Equal-appearing intervals
- Likert ratings
- Semantic differential
- Stapel scale

What are they? How to create them?

Summated Ratings

The Likert method of summated ratings allows an expression of intensity of feeling.[3] The method is both constructed and used in a slightly different way than equal-appearing intervals.

Scale Construction

The basic format is that respondents are asked to indicate how much they agree or disagree with every statement in the list. Figure 10.3 serves as an example.

The researcher begins, again, by developing many statements that reflect qualities about the object that might influence a person's attitude toward it. We classify each statement *a priori* as favorable or unfavorable. A screening sample,

---

[3] Trivia for you: What's Likert's first name? The Likert scale was first proposed, in the 1932 paper "A Technique for the Measurement of Attitudes," *Archives of Psychology*, 140, by, drumroll please, Rensis Likert. For research on the technique, see Scott Swain, Danny Weathers, and Ronald W. Niedrich, "Assessing Three Sources of Misresponse to Negated Likert Items," *Journal of Marketing Research*, 45 (1), 116–131.

FIGURE 10.3   Example of Likert Summated Rating Form

	Strongly Disagree	Disagree	Neither Agree nor Disagree	Agree	Strongly Agree
1. The bank offers courteous service.	—	—	—	—	—
2. The bank has a convenient location.	—	—	—	—	—
3. The bank has convenient hours	—	—	—	—	—
4. The bank offers low interest rate loans.	—	—	—	—	—

of, say, 200 people (representative of the subsequent target population) reduces the set of statements to a smaller, more refined instrument. They're asked to indicate how much they agree or disagree with each statement regarding the bank by checking the appropriate category. The levels of agreement are assigned scale values, e.g., -2, -1, 0, 1, 2, or 1, 2, 3, 4, 5 (either is fine). Suppose that we decide to use the values 1 through 5. These scales give us valence and strength information—a person can agree or strongly agree, for example. Further, a person's attitude might be positive if he or she either *agreed* with a *favorable* statement or *disagreed* with an *unfavorable* statement. We "reverse" the scaling with negative statements so that a "strongly agree" response to a favorable statement and a "strongly disagree" response to an unfavorable statement would both receive scores of 5.

A total attitude score is calculated for each respondent, and the distribution of total scores is used to refine the list of m statements. This procedure is known as item analysis, and it assumes that there should be consistency in the response pattern of any individual. If the individual has a very favorable attitude toward the object, he or she should basically agree with the favorable statements and disagree with the unfavorable ones, and vice versa. If we have a statement that generates a very mixed response, we would question the statement on the grounds that it must be somewhat ambiguous.

We develop the scale by assuming that the total score (on all m statements) is a proxy for the person's true attitude. We then relate each statement in turn to this total score to ascertain which statements discriminate clearly between people with positive vs. negative attitudes.

We can relate individual statement scores to total scores by several methods. One approach calculates the correlation of each item with the total score. Those items that have the highest correlation with the total are the best. Those with correlations near zero should be eliminated. We then select those 25, 50, or however many statements having the highest correlations with the total score.

An alternative way of performing an item analysis involves dividing the raters into groups; e.g., those with totals in the top 25% would be considered to have the most favorable attitudes, vs. those with the lowest 25% scores, who would be considered to have the least favorable attitudes. If the item is a good one, it would seem reasonable that (after correcting for the scoring direction), the mean score for each statement for the favorable attitude group should exceed the mean score for the unfavorable attitude group. The statements with mean differences near zero are poor statements and should be eliminated. Table 10.3 displays a comparison of means for a sample statement, "The bank has a convenient location," and responses for the 50 people with the most favorable and the 50 with the least favorable attitudes. The calculation indicates that the statement is a discriminating one, because the difference in mean scores is positive.

TABLE 10.3 Difference in Means for Two Groups with the Most and Least Favorable Attitudes

	Scale Value	High Group		Low Group	
Response Category	X	f	fx	f	fx
Strongly agree	5	28	140	2	10
Agree	4	14	56	6	24
Neither agree nor disagree	3	6	18	18	54
Disagree	2	2	4	20	40
Strongly disagree	1	0	0	4	4
Sums		50	218	50	132

$$\bar{x}_H = \frac{218}{50} = 4.36, \ \bar{x}_L = \frac{132}{50} = 2.64, \ d = \bar{x}_H - \bar{x}_L = 4.36 - 2.64 = 1.72$$

Scale Use

The statements remaining after purification of the original list are randomly ordered on the survey to mix positive and negative ones, and people indicate their degree of agreement with each statement. One advantage of the Likert scale is that people generally find the scales easy to use, and the response categories allow the expression of the intensity of the feeling. The respondent's total score is generated as the sum (or mean) of the scores across the statements.

Interpretation can be somewhat ambiguous; e.g., what does a score of 78 on a 20-item Likert scale indicate? The maximum is $20 \times 5 = 100$, so is it safe to assume that the person's attitude toward the bank is favorable? Only when compared to a standard. On the other hand, we make judgments like these every day; e.g., when we say "The man is tall," we are in effect saying that on the basis of the experience we have, the man is taller than average. In psychological scaling, this comparison is formalized somewhat by clearly specifying the standard, usually simply the average score in our sample (or averages computed for segments within the sample), i.e., the process of developing norms.

Semantic Differential

The semantic differential scale began with many bipolar adjectives, used to get people's reactions to various objects of interest.[4] It was found that ratings tend to be correlated and that three basic dimensions accounted for most of the variation in ratings: an *evaluation* dimension represented by adjective pairs such as good–bad, helpful–unhelpful; a *potency* dimension (powerful–powerless, strong–weak); and an *activity* dimension (fast–slow, alive–dead, noisy–quiet). The same three dimensions tended to emerge regardless of the object being evaluated.

Semantic differentials have been adapted for marketing. First, marketers generate their own items, but they're often still antonyms or bipolar phrases. Second, instead of worrying about scores for evaluation, potency, and activity, marketers have been more interested in developing profiles (e.g., for brands, stores, companies, etc.) to compare competitors.

Using the bank example, we'd begin by generating a large list of bipolar adjectives or phrases. Figure 10.4 lists attributes in a semantic differential format. Note that the negative phrase sometimes appears at the left side of the scale and other times at the right. This is done to prevent respondents from simply checking either the right- or left-hand sides without reading the descriptions.

[4] Charles E. Osgood, George J. Suci, and Percy H. Tannenbaum, *The Measurement of Meaning* (U of Illinois Press).

FIGURE | 10.4 | **Example of Semantic Differential Scaling Form**

Service is discourteous	__:__:__:__:__:__	Service is courteous
Location is convenient	__:__:__:__:__:__	Location is inconvenient
Hours are convenient	__:__:__:__:__:__	Hours are inconvenient
Loan interest rates are high	__:__:__:__:__:__	Loan interest rates are low

The scale would then be administered to a sample. Respondents would be asked to read the set of bipolar phrases and to check the cell that best described their feelings. The end positions are usually defined in the instructions as being very closely descriptive of the object, the center position as being neutral, and the intermediate positions as slightly descriptive. For example, if someone thought that Bank A's service was courteous but only moderately so, that person would check the 6th position reading from left to right.

Respondents could be asked to evaluate two or more banks using the same scale. When several banks are rated, the different profiles can be compared. Figure 10.5 (a "snake diagram"), illustrates that Bank A is perceived as having more courteous service, a more convenient location, and lower interest rates on loans, but also as having less convenient hours than Bank B. Note the customary practice in constructing these profiles is to place all positive descriptors on the right. The plotted values simply represent the average score of all respondents on each descriptor. The plotted profiles represent the positioning—comparative strengths and weaknesses—of Banks A and B as perceived by the sample.

When we want to compare objects, we need a total score. We compute the score by summing (or averaging) the scores, aggregating over the sample of respondents and over items. The items may be scored $-3, -2, -1, 0, 1, 2, 3$, or $1, 2, 3, 4, 5, 6, 7$, like the Likert scale.

Semantic differential scales are very popular in marketing, perhaps because the scales are easy to create and communicate, or perhaps because marketing managers have accumulated a lot of experience of the scales' usefulness. The technique is also clearly versatile, allowing people to express the intensity of their feelings toward company, product, package, advertisement, etc.

Stapel Scale

A modification of the semantic differential scale that is used in marketing is the Stapel scale. It differs from the semantic differential scale in several respects:

FIGURE | 10.5 | **Contrasting Profiles of Banks A and B**

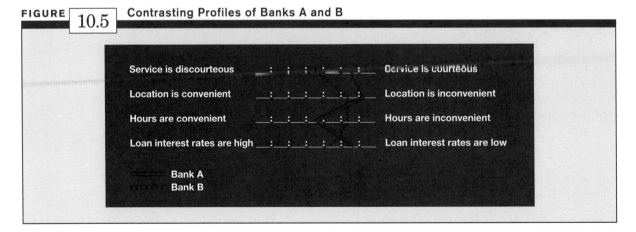

Service is discourteous	__:__:__:__:__:__	Service is courteous
Location is convenient	__:__:__:__:__:__	Location is inconvenient
Hours are convenient	__:__:__:__:__:__	Hours are inconvenient
Loan interest rates are high	__:__:__:__:__:__	Loan interest rates are low

—— Bank A
‑‑‑‑ Bank B

FIGURE 10.6   **Example of a Stapel Scale**

	−5	−4	−3	−2	−1	1	2	3	4	5
Service is courteous	☐	☐	☐	☐	☐	☐	☐	☐	☐	☐
Location is convenient	☐	☐	☐	☐	☐	☐	☐	☐	☐	☐
Hours are convenient	☐	☐	☐	☐	☐	☐	☐	☐	☐	☐
Loan interest rates are high	☐	☐	☐	☐	☐	☐	☐	☐	☐	☐

1. Adjectives or descriptive phrases are tested separately instead of simultaneously as bipolar pairs.

2. Points on the scale are identified by number.

3. There are 10 scale positions rather than 7.

Figure 10.6 shows our four bank attributes in a Stapel scale format. Respondents are asked to rate how accurately each statement describes the object of interest (e.g., Bank A). Instructions such as the following are given to respondents:

> "*Select a plus number for words that you think describe Bank A accurately. The more accurately you think the word describes it, the larger the plus number you would choose. Select a minus number for words you think do not describe it accurately. The less accurately you think a word describes it, the larger the minus number you would choose. Therefore, you can select any number from +5, for words that you think are very accurate, all the way to −5, for words that you think are very inaccurate.*"

The advantage claimed for the Stapel scale is that it frees the researcher from the need to develop so many bipolar adjectives, which can be a formidable task.

We've talked about a number of scales, including the semantic differential, Stapel, and Likert scales. There is some controversy about whether their total scores represent interval or ordinal scaling. Marketers have been inclined to assume interval scaling of their constructs, not because they believe that they

---

Ethical Dilemma 10.1

An independent researcher was hired by a national chain of department stores to develop a scale by which the chain could measure the image of each of its stores. The researcher thought that the best way to do this was through a semantic differential scale. Since she was interested in establishing her credentials as an expert on store-image research, however, she decided to also develop items for a Likert scale and to administer both of the scales to designated participants. She realized that this might induce greater respondent fatigue and perhaps lower-quality responses, but she was willing to take the chance because she knew that the client would not sanction or pay for administering the second survey to an independent sample of respondents.

- Is it ethical for the researcher to accept the risk of lowering the quality of the data addressing the client's issue so that she can further her own goals and career?
- What if the data collected by the two instruments provided stronger evidence that store image had indeed been measured adequately than that collected through the sole use of the semantic differential scale?
- Would it make any difference if there was a reasonable chance that the Likert format would produce a better instrument for measuring retail image than a semantic differential format?

have necessarily measured them on an interval scale, but because interval scaling allows more powerful methods of statistical analysis. If this assumption is wrong, the error would result in the attenuation of relations among variables (e.g., weakening the strength of a correlation between such a scale and some other variable). So, the assumption of interval measurement (when the variable may be ordinal) is at least "statistically conservative," in that it will not lead to the spurious overestimation of results.

Importance Judgments

In addition to determining a person's perceptions of a bank, we might wish to assess how *important* each attribute is to that person. For example, even though someone believes that a bank has convenient hours, if "convenience" isn't valued by that person, then it wouldn't affect his or her overall attitude toward the bank. Researchers have tried a number of ways to capture the differing emphases people place on specific attributes.

A simple measurement problem is that when we ask people directly to rate importance, we often get data that basically say "everything" is important.[5] Such information isn't useful if we're trying to diagnose which features of our bank need improvement most urgently, or which attributes have the greatest impact on loyalty. A popular assessment tool is described in Research Realities 10.2— the importance ratings and the performance are used in a perceptual map.

Graphic

Graphic rating scales are becoming more important with online surveys. Individuals indicate their rating by marking the appropriate point on a line that

---

R E S E A R C H   R E A L I T I E S

10.2 Quadrant Analysis

A quadrant analysis combines customers' ratings of "how important" are a number of attributes with their ratings of "how well are we doing?" on those attributes. Computing means yields two coordinates for each attribute—the perceived excellence in performance of that attribute, and the importance of that attribute. These two judgments (performance and importance) become axes in a two-dimensional space, or the rows and columns of a two-way matrix. These simple data yield surprisingly impactful diagnostics for strategic competitive analysis, e.g., answering questions such as, "What are our product's strengths and weaknesses?" "What is our marketplace position vis-à-vis the competition?" "Where should we focus our attention and resources for improvement?" and so forth.

This first panel shows the basic structure. One dimension charts excellence/performance, and the other dimension represents the importance of an attribute. Attributes of a product, or firm, that are in the upper right quadrant are those that are important to customers, and the company is perceived to be doing a good job on these features. The lower right maps the attributes where the company is also doing well, perhaps too well, considering customers don't care that much about these qualities. The upper left are places to focus on improving, because customers care about these features, yet the company is not perceived as excelling in these areas.

Here is an example, set in the financial services sector, with the corresponding relevant attributes. Note, e.g., that "flexible payment plans" are important to customers, yet this firm is not seen as providing such terrific flexibility.

(Continued)

---

[5] We can also determine attribute importance through conjoint analysis, as we'll demonstrate later in the book.

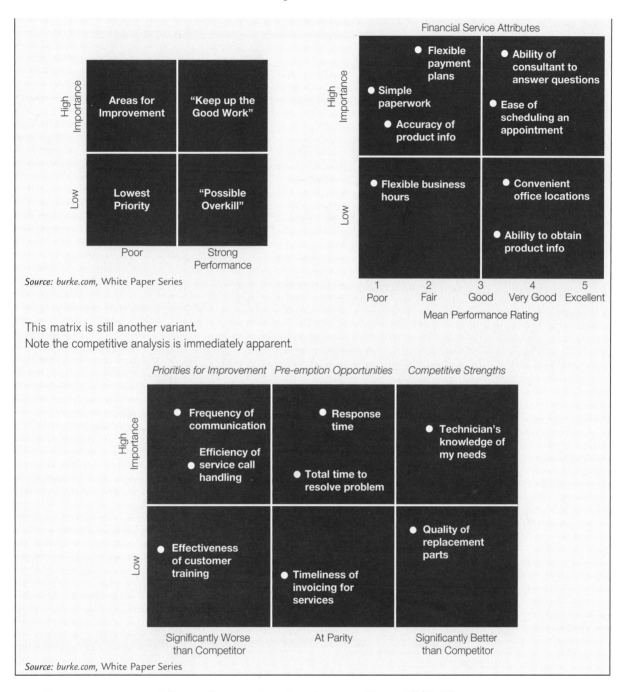

Source: *burke.com*, White Paper Series

This matrix is still another variant.
Note the competitive analysis is immediately apparent.

Source: *burke.com*, White Paper Series

runs from one extreme of the attribute to the other (e.g., see Figure 10.7). The line may be vertical or horizontal, ticked, or unmarked.[6] Respondents mark the line, e.g., using a mouse click somewhere along the line (or just marking with an "X" if the survey is hardcopy), and we infer the importance value by measuring the length of the line from the left origin to the marked position.

One of the advantages of graphic rating scales is that they are easy to construct and use. They provide an opportunity to make fine distinctions, though

---

[6] If the graphic scale is marked, the divisions may be few or many, as in the case of a "thermometer" scale, so called because it looks like a thermometer.

Please evaluate each quality in terms of how important it is to you personally by clicking the cursor at the position on the horizontal line that best reflects your feelings.

	Not Important	**Very Important**
Courteous service	_____	
Convenient location	_____	
Convenient hours	_____	
Low interest rate loans	_____	

we wouldn't want to overinterpret the difference in someone's mouse click being at the 387th pixel vs. the 389th pixel, for example.

Comparative

Comparative rating scales involve relative judgments. Raters judge each attribute with direct reference to the other attributes being evaluated.

An example of a comparative rating scale used for securing importance values is the **constant sum scaling method**. In the constant sum method, we instruct respondents to divide some given sum, e.g., 100 points, among two or more attributes on the basis of their importance. Thus, in Figure 10.8, if the respondent assigned 50 points to courteous service and 50 points to convenient location, the attributes would be judged to be equally important; if the points were 80:20, courteous service would be considered to be four times as important.[7]

Comparative scales require fairly complicated judgments from the rater (e.g., if you program this in an online survey, you can build in a check that the points indeed sum to 100). But here are two strengths of the scales: First, it is not unusual for respondents to want to claim that "all" attributes are important. Yet research indicates that we tend to simplify our decision-making by first reducing the number of alternatives (e.g., brands) by deciding which attributes matter—the same kind of process that these scales are trying to capture. Second, when constant sum scales are used to get judgments other than attribute importance (e.g., say, the performance of brands), these scales tend to eliminate "halo effects." Halo effects occur when there is carryover from one judgment to another, e.g., if a consumer rates a movie, overall, as "7 = great!" they're likely to also rate

Please divide 100 points among the following bank services in terms of relatively how important each is to you:

_____ Courteous service

_____ Convenient hours

_____ Convenient location

_____ Low interest rates

100

---

[7] If we consider all possible pairs of attributes, we can construct unidimensional scale values. In "magnitude estimation," respondents are asked to judge directly each stimulus vs. a referent.

the "storyline," "acting," "music," etc., as "7 = great!" with little or no distinction. The points assigned in these scales could be evenly distributed, but they
tend not to be; evidence that raters try to choose which attributes matter more.

Which Scale to Use

It might seem overwhelming to think about choosing among all these scale
types, number of scale points to use, whether to reverse some of the items, etc.,
but much methodological research (e.g., see Table 10.4) seems to conclude that
the choices do not seem to affect the quality of the measures; thus, you can think
of all these options as just that—choices. All of these scales belong in the marketing researcher's measurement tool kit, and you're free to choose among
them, whichever suits your research needs and interests.

The nature of the marketing problem and the mode of administration (e.g.,
online vs. phone) will affect the final choices. So will the characteristics of the
respondents, their commitment to the task, and their experience and ability to
respond. For example, the simple "happy-to-sad faces" scale in Figure 10.9 is
frequently used for consumer research on children.

TABLE 10.4   Reliability Affected by Scale Characteristics?

Measure Characteristic	Hypothesis	Conclusion
#Items in final scale	Hypothesis: Positive relationship between #items in scale and reliability?	Yes
Difficulty of items	H: Negative relationship between item difficulty and reliability?	No
Reverse scoring	H: Scales with reverse-scored items have lower reliability than scales without them?	No
Type of scale	H: Any type of scale show superior reliability?	No
Number of scale points	H: Positive relationship between # of scale points and reliability?	Yes
Type of labels	H: Numerical or verbal labels superior in yielding more reliability?	No
Extent of scale points description	H: Scales with all points labeled more reliable than scales with only end-points labeled?	No
Respondent uncertainty or ignorance	H: Scales with neutral points more reliable than forced-choice scales?	No

*Source: Adapted from Gilbert A. Churchill, Jr. and J. Paul Peter, "Research Design Effects on the Reliability of
Rating Scales: A Meta-Analysis,"* Journal of Marketing Research *21 (3), 365–366.*

FIGURE 10.9   Happy-to-Sad Faces that Work with Children (and Adults!)

Summary

This chapter reviewed methods for measuring attitudes, which were defined as representations of the person's ideas of, or liking for, a specific object or idea. Typically, marketers are concerned with objects like companies, brands, advertisements, Web sites, and packages.

Measurement was defined as the assignment of numbers to objects (e.g., consumers) to represent quantities of attributes (e.g., their brand preferences). Measurement can be done using a nominal, ordinal, interval, or ratio scale. Attitudes are measured by observing behavior, performing objective tasks, and measuring physiological reactions, but direct assessment by self-report devices is the most common. The main self-report techniques were reviewed, including the methods of equal-appearing intervals, summated ratings, semantic differential, Stapel scale, and Q sorts. These scales are intended to measure what individuals believe and like about specific objects (e.g., brands, companies, etc.). In addition, we might ascertain the importance of the attributes of the objects.

Questions

1. What is an attitude?
2. What are the scales of measurement, and what information is provided by each?
3. What is an equal-appearing interval scale?
4. How are subjects scaled with a Likert scale?
5. What is a semantic differential scale?

Applications and Problems

1. Identify the type of scale (nominal, ordinal, interval, or ratio) being used in each of the following questions. Justify your answer.
   a. During which season of the year were you born?
      ___Winter ___Spring ___Summer ___Fall
   b. What is your total household income?
   c. Which are your three most preferred candy bars? Rank them from 1 to 3 according to your preference, with 1 as most preferred.
      ___M&Ms plain ___M&Ms peanut ___Reese's
      ___Almond Joy ___Good & Plenty
   d. How much time do you spend traveling to school every day?
      ___Under 5 minutes
      ___5–10 mins
      ___11–15 mins
      ___16–20 mins
      ___20 minutes or more
   e. How satisfied are you with *Newsweek* magazine?
      ___ Very satisfied
      ___ Satisfied
      ___ Neither satisfied nor dissatisfied
      ___ Dissatisfied
      ___ Very dissatisfied
   f. On an average, how many beers do you drink in a day?
      ___more than 3
      ___2 to 3
      ___Less than 2

   g. Which one of the following courses have you taken?
      ___Marketing research
      ___Sales management
      ___Advertising management
      ___Consumer behavior
   h. What is the level of education for the head of the household?
      ___Some high school
      ___High school graduate
      ___Some college
      ___College graduate and/or graduate work

2. The analysis for each of the preceding questions is given below. Is the analysis appropriate for the scale used? Is the conclusion appropriate?
   a. About 50% of the sample were born in the fall, 25% of the sample were born in the spring, and the remaining 25% were born in the winter. It can be concluded that the fall is twice as popular as the spring and the summer seasons.
   b. The average income is $25,000. There are twice as many individuals with an income of less than $9,999 than individuals with an income of $40,000 and over.
   c. M&Ms plain is the most preferred brand. The mean preference is 3.52.
   d. The median time spent traveling to school is 8.5 minutes. Three times as many respondents travel

fewer than 5 minutes than respondents traveling 16–20 minutes.

e. The average satisfaction score is 4.5, which seems to indicate a high level of satisfaction with *Newsweek* magazine.

f. 10% of the respondents drink less than two bottles of beer a day, whereas three times as many respondents drink over three bottles a day.

g. Sales management is the most frequently taken course because the median is 3.2.

h. The responses indicate that 40% of the sample has some high school education, 25% of the sample are high school graduates, 20% have some college education, and 10% are college graduates. The mean education level is 2.6.

3. a. Assume that a manufacturer of a line of packaged meat products wanted to evaluate customer attitudes toward the brand. A panel of 500 regular consumers of the brand responded to a questionnaire that was sent to them and that included several attitude scales. The questionnaire produced the following results:

 i. The average score for the sample on a 20-item Likert scale was 105.

 ii. The average score for the sample on a 20-item semantic differential scale was 106.

 iii. The average score for the sample on a 15-item Stapel scale was 52.

The vice president has asked you to indicate whether these customers have a favorable or unfavorable attitude toward the brand. What would you tell him? Please be specific.

b. Following your initial report, the vice president has provided you with more information. The following memo is given to you: "The company has been using the same attitude measures over the past eight years. The results of the previous studies are as follows:

	Likert	Semantic Differential	Stapel
2002	86	95	43
2003	93	95	48
2004	97	98	51
2005	104	101	55
2006	110	122	62
2007	106	112	57
2008	104	106	53
2009	105	106	52

We realize that there may not be any connection between attitude and behavior, but it must be pointed out that sales peaked in 2006 and since then have been gradually declining." With this information, do your results change? Can anything more be said about customer attitudes?

4. A leading manufacturer of electric guitars routinely attempts to measure consumer attitudes toward its products, generally by asking a consumer to examine a product and then to complete a brief questionnaire about several of the product's attributes. Over the years, the research manager for the company has decided that scale items related to five attributes have high correlations with total scale scores. The attributes are tone quality, appearance, durability, price, and ease of playing. The following scale is thus used to assess attitudes toward a product:

	Strongly Disagree	Disagree	Neither Agree nor Disagree	Agree	Strongly Agree
1. Tone quality is good.	—	—	—	—	X
2. The guitar is attractive.	—	—	—	X	—
3. The design is durable.	—	—	—	X	—
4. The price is appropriate.	—	X	—	—	—
5. The guitar is easy to play.	—	—	—	—	X
	(1)	(2)	(3)	(4)	(5)

a. Suppose that a consumer has examined a guitar and provided the responses shown in the preceding table. Determine the total score. Would you say that the consumer has a favorable attitude toward the guitar?

b. The particular model of guitar that the respondent examined has been available for five years. The average total scores using this scale for each of these years are as follows:

1st year	18
2nd year	17
3rd year	18
4th year	16
5th year	17

Would you conclude that the consumer has a favorable attitude toward the guitar?

c. Assume that the respondent had also completed a comparative rating scale by dividing 100 points among the five attributes according to their importance to her. How could this information be useful in assessing the respondent's attitude toward the electric guitar?

d. Following are the results of the comparative rating task completed by the respondent:

Tone quality	10
Appearance	25
Durability	10
Price	40
Ease of playing	15

What can you now conclude about the respondent's attitude toward the guitar?

Appendix: Psychological Measurement

10

Questions to Guide Your Learning:

Q1 What kinds of errors arise when measuring customers' attitudes?

Q2 What is reliability? How do I write a survey to enhance reliability?

Q3 What are content, construct, and predictive validity? How do I maximize validity?

A problem that marketers have in common with scientists is how to measure the variables they want to understand. For example, marketers know that consumer spending can be affected by consumers' general feelings as to "how good things are." But how do you measure a sense of "well-being," or psychological attitudes in general?

The measurement problem is depicted in Figure 10A.1. The researcher uses theories to explain phenomena. These theories or models consist of constructs (denoted by the circles), linkages among the constructs (single line connections), and data that connect the constructs with the empirical world (double lines).

The single lines in Figure 10A.1 represent conceptual definitions; i.e., one construct is defined in terms of its relationship to other constructs in the theorizing. The definition may take the form of a precise equation that expresses the relationship, such as the equation in mechanics that suggests that force equals mass times acceleration, i.e., $F = MA$. Alternatively, the relationship may be only imprecisely stated, which is typically the case in the social sciences, e.g., brand choice = function (preference, price, availability, etc.).

The double lines in Figure 10A.1 represent operational definitions, i.e., a mapping of how the constructs will be measured. The mapping specifies what the researcher must do in order to assign a value to the construct (e.g., sum the scores on the 10 Likert-type statements to generate a total score). Table 10A.1 lists some items used to assess different facets of consumer sentiment toward marketing. The measure comprises respondents' reactions to product quality, prices, advertising, and retailing and personal selling support. Conceptual definitions logically precede operational definitions and guide their development—we have to specify what a construct is before we can measure it.

We hope to establish the relationships that exist among the constructs of the model. Some of the constructs must be related to observable data so the model is testable. Otherwise, the model

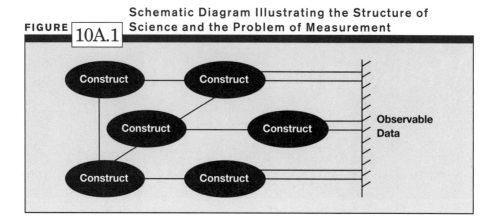

FIGURE 10A.1 Schematic Diagram Illustrating the Structure of Science and the Problem of Measurement

TABLE 10A.1 Illustration of Operational Definitions

Concept	Measurement
Product Quality	Sum of responses to these items, each measured on 5-point disagree-agree scale:
	The quality of most products I buy today is as good as can be expected.
	I am satisfied with most of the products I buy.
	Most products I buy wear out too quickly. (R)
	Products are not made as well as they used to be. (R)
	Too many of the products I buy are defective in some way. (R)
	The companies that make products I buy don't care enough about how well they perform.(R)
	The quality of products I buy has consistently improved over the years.
Price of Products	Most products I buy are overpriced. (R)
	Business could charge lower prices and still be profitable. (R)
	Most prices are reasonable considering the high cost of doing business.
	Competition between companies keeps prices reasonable.
	Companies are unjustified in charging the prices they charge. (R)
	Most prices are fair.
	In general, I am satisfied with the prices I pay.
Ads for Products	Most advertising provides consumers with essential information.
	Most advertising is annoying. (R)
	Most advertising makes false claims. (R)
	If most advertising were eliminated, consumers would be better off. (R)
	I enjoy most ads.
	Advertising should be more closely regulated.
	Most advertising is intended to deceive rather than to inform consumers. (R)
Retailing or Selling	Most retail stores serve their customers well.
	Because of the way retailers treat me, most of my shopping is unpleasant. (R)
	I find most retail salespeople to be very helpful.
	Most retail stores provide an adequate selection of merchandise.
	In general, most middlemen make excessive profits. (R)
	When I need assistance in a store, I am usually not able to get it. (R)
	Most retailers provide adequate service.

Source: An (R) indicates scoring of the item needs to be reversed so that higher scores indicate more positive attitudes. Developed from John F. Gaski and Michael J. Etzel, "The Index of Consumer Sentiment Toward Marketing," in Gordon C. Bruner, Karen James, Paul Hensel (eds.), Marketing Scales Handbook *(marketingpower.com).*

will be circular—with unobservable constructs being defined in terms of other unobservable constructs. A circular model cannot be supported or refuted by empirical data, so it is not legitimately considered a theory. A theory or system of explanation rests on the condition that at least some of the constructs can be operationalized sufficiently to allow measurement.

The challenge with measuring customer attitudes is that we cannot rely on visual comparisons to confirm or refute a measure. We cannot see an attitude, a personality characteristic, a person's knowledge about or awareness of a particular product, or other psychological characteristics, such as intelligence, anxiety, etc. These characteristics must be inferred from our measurements.

We need to understand measurement, measurement error, and the concepts of reliability and validity. So, here we go!

Variations in Measured Scores

Psychological measurement usually takes place in complex situations in which many factors affect the characteristic being measured, including the process of measurement itself. For example, whenever energy prices suddenly soar, a public outcry arises, accompanied by accusations that the oil companies are deliberately creating strategies to manipulate prices. Suppose we develop an attitude scale to measure those feelings and administer the scale to a sample of respondents. A high score means that the respondent believed the oil companies had little to do with precipitating the crisis (a positive attitude), whereas a low score indicates the opposite, therefore reflecting a more negative attitude. Suppose that Heather had a score of 75 and Sofia had a score of 40 (where the minimum and maximum scores were 25 and 100). Conclusion: "Heather has a much more favorable attitude toward the oil companies than does Sofia." Ideally, yes; practically, maybe. It depends on the quality of the measurement. Consider some of the potential sources of differences in the scores of 75 and 40:

1. *True differences in the characteristic we're attempting to measure.* In the ideal situation, the difference in scores would reflect true differences in the attitudes of Heather and Sofia and nothing else. Usually the difference also reflects the factors that follow.

2. *True differences in other relatively stable characteristics of the individuals.* Perhaps the difference between Heather's and Sofia's scores is because Sofia is more willing to express her negative feelings, whereas Heather follows the adage, "If you can't say something nice, don't say anything at all." Her cooperation in the study has been requested and so she responds, but not truthfully.

3. *Differences caused by transient personal factors.* A person's mood, state of health, fatigue, and so on, may all affect the individual's responses. These factors are all temporary and can vary, e.g., Sofia's mood would be different if she had just returned from an IRS audit, vs. she had just received a sizable tax refund.

4. *Differences caused by situational factors.* The situation can affect the score. For example, researchers studying family purchase decisions find that a person's score often changes when the survey is completed in the presence of the spouse.

5. *Differences because of variations in administration.* Marketing surveys can be conducted in person, over the phone, online, etc., and interviewers can vary in the way they ask questions.

6. *Differences resulting from sampling of items.* When we measure any construct, we tap only a sample of items relevant to the characteristic being measured. If we varied the items on the survey, e.g., by adding, deleting, or changing the wording, we would likely change the absolute scores of Heather and Sofia, and possibly even their relative scores so that Sofia seemed more positive. Thus, we must constantly be aware that our measurement represents a narrow conception of the construct. A person's height can serve as an indicator of "size," but so can weight, thigh circumference, length of forearm, and so on. We'd expect to have a better measure of size if we included all these items. The same is true with psychological measurements—other things being equal, a 1-item scale is less adequate than a 25-item scale.

7. *Differences caused by lack of clarity of the measuring instrument.* Sometimes a difference in response to a questionnaire may represent differences in interpretation of an ambiguous or complex question. The researcher must generate items that mean the same thing to all respondents so that the observed differences in scores are real.

8. *Differences caused by mechanical factors.* Scores can also be affected by online surveys with bugs, inadequate space to record responses, inadvertent check marks in the wrong box (like circling the wrong "bubble" in your GMAT test), etc.

9. *Finally, differences in international respondents.* Increasingly, as multinationals seek to satisfy global customer bases, they're comparing numbers that may be a bit "apples to oranges." For example, customer satisfaction scores in Brazilian segments might differ from those in German, Irish, Japanese, and Canadian segments (see Research Realities 10A.1).

Classification and Assessment of Error

Survey researchers talk about a measure reflecting both the true attitude as well as the kinds of errors we've just described. We'll call the measured variable, X_O, ("O" for observed), and write it as a function of several components:

$$X_O = X_T + X_S + X_R$$

where

X_T represents the *true* score of the characteristic being measured

X_S represents *systematic* error

X_R represents *random* error

The total error of a measurement has two components, $X_S + X_R$. **Systematic error** affects the measurement in a predictable way, e.g., measuring a person's height with a poorly calibrated wooden yardstick. Other stable characteristics of the individual are another source of systematic error. **Random error** is not systematic. It's due to transient aspects of the person or measurement situation. A random error produces inconsistency in repeated measurements. An example is the use of an elastic ruler to measure a person's height—it is unlikely that on two successive measures, the person using the elastic ruler would stretch it to the same degree of tautness, so the two measures wouldn't agree even though the person's height hadn't changed.

The distinction between systematic error and random error is critical because of the way the validity of a measure is assessed. **Validity** is synonymous with accuracy or correctness. The validity of a measure is defined as the extent to

RESEARCH   REALITIES

10A.1 Cross-Cultural Differences in Response Styles

When marketing researchers investigate "response styles," they're talking about two kinds of measurement issues. One has to do with *means,* and the other has to do with *variances.*

More positive *means,* e.g., higher ratings of customer satisfaction, tend to come from Asian and Latin American cultures. Why? These cultures are said to value acquiescence or getting along with the community. As a result, these respondents tend to yield more socially desirable responses as a simple "courtesy bias." (All of this research admittedly relies upon stereotypes and generalizations, but the idea is to start with big patterns in the data, and then make more subtle refinements as the research investigation progresses.) Americans and Western Europeans tend to be more individualistic, a crabbier lot, so their ratings appear more negative, even when they're relatively satisfied with the purchase they're evaluating.

So, if your customer satisfaction ratings in Japan exceed those in the UK, do you have a "real" customer difference (e.g., is the product better received in Japan?) or is it a rating scale usage difference? Take the mean difference with a grain of salt, unless you learn there are marketing structural differences, such as better pricing in Japan, better service, easier access, etc., some "real" reason for the apparent satisfaction differences.

In addition, response styles also differ in terms of *variances.* Respondents from cultures labeled "enthusiastic" (including the U.S., France, Italy, Ireland, Australia) tend to select extreme scale values more often than those from cultures expecting more reserved, conservative behavior (e.g., Japan, Germany, England). Imagine a nine-point rating scale for customer satisfaction, where 1 means "extremely dissatisfied" and a 9 means "extremely satisfied." The reported consistent cultural differences would have us predict that the Italian would more frequently say, "Oo! I *love* it!" (a rating of 9) or "Oh, how *awful*!" (a rating of 1), whereas an English respondent says, "Well, perhaps ..." (a rating of 6) or "Goodness, I'm not sure" (a rating of 4).

If the differences in means and standard deviations intimidates you to think that numbers could never be compared across countries, consider your friend the correlation coefficient (which we discuss in greater detail in the chapter investigating associations among variables):

$$r = \frac{\sum_{i=1}^{n}(X_i - \bar{x})(Y_i - \bar{y})}{ns_x s_y}.$$

Suppose X represents respondents' ratings on a customer satisfaction measure, and Y represents their ratings on their perception of quality (or value, or price, or pleasantness of packaging, whatever). When we correlate satisfaction with quality, note that the means come out—i.e., in the numerator of that equation, we take each person's X and subtract the group's $\bar{x}$, and we subtract $\bar{y}$ from each person's Y score. Similarly, note that whether s_x is large or small, ditto for s_y, we divide out those numbers in the equation. The correlation coefficient r captures the relationship between X and Y when we've taken these issues into account.

So! According to the observations stated above, we'd expect a sample from Japan to yield both higher means and lower variances than data on customers from the U.S. But the correlation coefficient is standardized across means and variances. That is, in any data set, regardless of whether one group's means are higher than another's and/or one group's variance is bigger than another's, we're testing whether the relationship between satisfaction and quality is strong or weak. If the correlation between satisfaction and quality is high in the Japanese data, but lower in the U.S. data, you'd know that for Japan, quality is a clear driver of satisfaction, whereas the American customers are satisfied, or not, by other features (e.g., price, service, whatever, you'd have to look into the data). In sum, if you're dealing with international data frequently, you might make correlations your focus, given the ambiguities in interpreting mean differences or differences in standard deviations.

If you want to learn more, you also need to know that equating means is sometimes referred to as "equivalence in origins" and that a difference in standard deviations is alternatively referred to as a "scaling" difference or a difference in "measurement units."

(Continued)

For more information, including suggestions regarding "correcting" for these response style differences, see these papers:

- de Jong, Martijn G., Jan-Benedict E. M. Steenkamp, Jean-Paul Fox, and Hans Baumgartner (2008), "Using Item Response Theory to Measure Extreme Response Style in Marketing Research: A Global Investigation," *Journal of Marketing Research* 45 (1), 104–115.
- Greenleaf, Eric, "Improving Rating Scale Measures by Detecting and Correcting Bias Components in Response Styles," *Journal of Marketing Research* 29 (2), 176–188.
- Johnson, Timothy, Patrick Kulesa, Isr Llc, Young Ik Cho, and Sharon Shavitt, "The Relationship Between Culture and Response Styles: Evidence from 19 Countries," *Journal of Cross-Cultural Psychology* 36 (2), 264–277.
- Strizhakova, Yuliya, Robin A. Coulter, and Linda L. Price (2008), "The Meanings of Branded Products: A Cross-National Scale Development and Meaning Assessment," *International Journal of Research in Marketing*, 25, 82–93.

which scores reflect true characteristics, not systematic biases nor random errors. When a measure is valid, $X_O = X_T$ (there is no error). Our goal is to develop measures in which the score we observe actually represents the true score of the object on the characteristic we are attempting to measure. Easier said than done! This relationship between measured score and true score is inferred, based on (1) direct assessment of validity and (2) indirect assessment via reliability. We'll consider each.

Direct Assessment of Validity

As mentioned, a measure is valid to the extent that variability in scores among objects reflects the true differences of the characteristic being measured. We don't usually know the true score—if we did, we wouldn't need a measure. But we infer the accuracy of the measure by looking for evidence of three types of validity: predictive, content, and construct.

Predictive Validity

In **predictive** or **criterion-related validity**, we assess the usefulness of the measure as a predictor of some other characteristic of the individual. For example, the GMAT is required by many business schools, in part because it is somewhat useful in predicting how well a student will do in an MBA program. The test score is used to predict the criterion of performance.

For some tests, we're not as interested in predicting something in the future as we are in assessing **concurrent validity**, or the relationship between the measure and the criterion variable that occurs at the same point in time. For example, the validity of a pregnancy test is about determining whether she is pregnant now.

This type of validity is determined by the correlation between the measure and criterion—if the correlation is high, the measure is said to have predictive validity. It is easy to assess, though it requires a good criterion (e.g., grades in an MBA program).

Content Validity

Content validity focuses on the adequacy with which the domain of the characteristic is captured by the measure. Say we wished to measure spelling ability, and we used the following words: strike, shortstop, foul, inning, catcher, pitcher, ball, umpire, bullpen, dugout. You can see the nature of the objection has to do with the fact that all the words relate to the sport of baseball. Someone who is a poor speller might do well on this test simply because he or she is a baseball enthusiast. A person who is pretty good at spelling but has little interest in baseball might do poorly. We'd conclude that the test lacks content validity—it doesn't properly sample the domain of all possible words that could be used— it's too selective in emphasis.

Content validity is sometimes known as "face validity" because it is assessed by looking at the measure to ascertain the domain being sampled. If the actual items look different from the possible domain, the measure is said to lack content validity.

Content validity is clearly partly a matter of judgment. We may think our items provide good coverage, but a critic may argue that we have failed to sample some aspect of the characteristic. So, how can we diminish the critics' objections?

Validity:

1. Predictive
2. Content
3. Construct

One of the most critical elements in generating a content-valid instrument is conceptually defining the domain. The researcher has to specify what the variable is, and what it is not. The definition is expedited by examining the literature to determine how the variable has been defined and used previously. Next, a large collection of items is written that broadly represents the variable as defined. Items must be included to represent all the relevant dimensions of the variable. The number of items must be large so that after scale refinement (pre-testing) the measure still contains enough items to adequately sample each of the variable's dimensions.

Construct Validity

Construct validity is concerned with the question of "Does the instrument, in fact, measure what we purport it to measure?" What construct, concept, or trait underlies the score achieved on that test? Does the measure of attitude actually measure attitude or some other characteristic of the individual? Construct validity lies at the very heart of scientific and pragmatic progress. In marketing, we speak of people's socioeconomic class, personality, attitudes, and so on. These are all constructs that we use to explain marketing behavior. They are constructs that are not directly observable, only inferred, e.g., from related behaviors. We operationally define the constructs in terms of a set of observables (measured variables).

Construct validity is difficult to establish. It requires adequately sampling the domain of the construct and internal consistency among the items. This assumption means that the attitude that we're trying to measure is the underlying cause of the correlations among the items. As the correlations increase, we have greater confidence that they're measuring the same construct. A measure said to be strong on construct validity must be consistent internally, but a consistent measure isn't necessarily one that has construct-validity. For example, the items might indeed be measuring the same thing, but they might be measuring something other than what you hoped they measured.[1]

So far, we've specified the domain of the construct, generated a set of items relevant to the breadth of that domain, refined the items, and shown the

[1] For a nice example of scale development, see Frank Pons, Mehdi Mourali, and Simon Nyeck, "Consumer Orientation Toward Sporting Events: Scale Development and Validation," *Journal of Service Research*, 8 (3), 276–287; and for a good overall discussion of construct validity, see Qimei Chen, Shelly Rodgers, and William D. Wells, "Better than Sex, *Marketing Research*, pp. 17–21, marketingpower.org, and Madhu Viswanathan, *Measurement Error and Research Design*, Sage 2005.

FIGURE 10A.2 The Relationship between the Construct "Customer Satisfaction" and its Determinants and Consequences

remaining items are internally consistent. The remaining step is to see how well the measure relates to measures of other constructs that we expect to be theoretically related. Does it behave as expected? Does it fit the theory or model relating the constructs? The diagram showing the relationships among a set of constructs is often referred to as the "nomological net." Determining if the relationships among constructs are as expected is consequently referred to as establishing nomological validity.

For example, Figure 10A.2 depicts the relationship between the constructs "customer satisfaction" and "repeat purchasing." If we've developed the measure X to assess customer satisfaction, construct validity could be assessed by examining the relationship between the measure and customer turnover, measured by Y. Companies where X scores are low have less customer satisfaction, and they should experience more turnover than those with high X scores. If they do not, we'd question the construct validity of the customer satisfaction measure.

Thus, the construct validity of a measure is assessed by whether the measure confirms or denies the hypothesized relationships predicted among the constructs. The difficulty, of course, is that the failure to obtain the hypothesized relationships among the observed variables may be due to a lack of construct validity, or due to incorrect theory. To prevent this ambiguity, we usually try to relate a construct to several other constructs, not just one, and we also try to use theories that are well founded, tried and true, to inspire confidence in their probable correctness.

A construct should also be measurable by several different methods, otherwise it could be considered nothing more than an artifact of the measurement procedure. In attempting to triangulate, the methods should be independent if possible. Given that the different methods are all measuring the same construct, the measures should be highly correlated, and this would provide evidence of **convergent validity**. **Discriminant validity** requires that a measure doesn't correlate too highly with measures that aren't supposed to be related.

Indirect Assessment Through Reliability

The similarity of results provided by independent but comparable measures of the same object or construct is called **reliability**. Reliability is an index of consistency—we should see correlations between two measures of the same concept when we use the same measure. (For validity, we should see correlations between two measures of the same concept even when the methods are different.) If we want the goal to be consistency in comparable measures of the same concept, then we wouldn't want a measure to be one that was influenced by transitory factors. In other words, the more reliable the measure, the lower is X_R.

A measure could be reliable and still not be valid, since even if X_R equals zero, $X_O = X_T + X_S$ (i.e., the X_S can still throw off the validity). The converse is not true—if the measure is valid, $X_O = X_T$ (the measure is reflecting true scores without error). Thus, it is often said that (1) if a measure is valid, it is reliable; (2) if it is not reliable, it cannot be valid;[2] and (3) if it is reliable, then it may or may not be valid, because reliability does not account for systematic error.

In sum, reliability is a necessary, but not sufficient, condition for validity. Reliability is easier to measure than validity, which is probably why researchers emphasize its measurement.

> Reliability is necessary for validity.

Stability

One of the more popular ways of establishing the reliability of a measure is to measure the same objects or individuals at two different points in time and to correlate the scores. If the objects or individuals have not changed in the interim, the two scores should correlate perfectly. To the extent that they do not, random disturbances were operating in either one or both of the test situations to produce less reliable measurement. The procedure is known as test–retest reliability assessment.

A critical decision is determining how long to wait between successive administrations of the measure. If we're looking at attitudes and we wait too long, attitudes may change, producing a low correlation between the two scores. On the other hand, a short wait means people may well remember how they responded the first time and be more consistent in their responses. Two weeks seems to be the interim norm. Further, instead of administering the exact same set of items, many researchers use alternate forms with items that are not identical, but very similar.

Equivalence

The basic assumption in constructing an attitude scale is that when several items are summed into a single score, the items are measuring the same underlying attitude. Each item can be considered a measure of the attitude, and the items should be consistent (or equivalent) in what they indicate about the attitude. The equivalence measure of reliability focuses on the internal consistency or internal homogeneity of the set of items forming the scale.

The earliest measure of the internal consistency of a set of items was the "split-half" reliability of the scale. In assessing split-half reliability, the total set of items is divided into two equivalent halves and the total scores for the two halves are correlated to estimate the reliability. For example, the "even" numbered items form one-half and the "odd" the other half, and their scores correlated.

An even better way to assess the internal homogeneity of a set of items is to use coefficient alpha. This index uses all items simultaneously, not just half; furthermore, coefficient alpha reflects the method of domain sampling. The idea is that items tapping the domain of a construct should be correlated, and if some item is not highly correlated with the others, it is probably drawn from a different domain and its inclusion produces error and unreliability.

[2] How can we claim validity (i.e., "this test measures X") if we don't have reliability (i.e., the items measure something different each time)!

Alpha is calculated as:

$$\alpha = \left(\frac{k}{k-1} \right) \left(1 - \frac{\sum_{i=1}^{k} \sigma_i^2}{\sigma_t^2} \right)$$

where

k = number of items in the scale

σ_i^2 = the variance of scores on item i across respondents

σ_t^2 = the variance of total scores across subjects where the total for each respondent represents the sum of the k item scores. This term includes the sum of the σ_i^2 terms (the numerator), but also includes the covariances between the pairs of items, i.e., the extent to which the items are correlated.

If all k items are measuring different concepts, the correlations among the items will be near zero, so the σ_t^2 will be close in size to σ_i^2, and the term $\sum_{i=1}^{k} \sigma_i^2/\sigma_t^2$ will be close to 1. The term in the parentheses goes to $(1 - 1)$, or zero, and alpha is low (e.g., 0). When the items are all highly correlated, σ_t^2 will be larger than σ_i^2, so $\sum_{i=1}^{k} \sigma_i^2/\sigma_t^2$ will be small, close to zero. Then the parenthetical terms go to $(1 - 0)$, or 1, and alpha is much higher (e.g., 1).

Coefficient alpha should be calculated routinely to assess the quality of measure.[3] If alpha is low, what should the analyst do? If the item pool is large, the poor items should be eliminated. Poor items are easy to identify—we calculate the correlation of each item with the total score and plot the correlations by decreasing order of magnitude. Items with correlations near zero are then deleted.[4]

We've been talking about assessing the reliability of a measure. On occasion, we're also interested in "inter-rater reliability." For example, you might be interested in rating entertainment media for themes like product placement, actors swearing, etc. If so, you would have several viewers code the content of an ad, TV pilot, or movie pretest for those themes. Inter-rater reliability is greater when the raters agree and produce consistent results.

Summary

So, altogether, how does one contend with reliability and validity? Figure 10A.3 diagrams a sequence of steps that can be followed to develop valid measures of marketing constructs.

Step 1 involves *specifying the domain* of the construct to be measured. If you're interested in measuring customer satisfaction with recently purchased space heaters, what attributes of the product should be measured to assess the family's satisfaction? We'd create an exhaustive list of product features, e.g., cost,

durability, quality, performance, and aesthetic features. But how far should the domain extend? Satisfaction is also affected by service and sales assistance and price. You have to draw the line somewhere, of course, but it's clear that we need to be very careful about specifying what is to be included in the domain of the construct being measured and what is to be excluded.

Step 2 is to *generate items* that capture the domain. Exploratory research techniques, including literature

---

[3] The square root of the reliability is the estimated correlation of the k-item test with the true scores.
[4] If the construct had, say, five identifiable dimensions, coefficient alpha would be calculated for each dimension.

Procedure for Measurement Development

FIGURE 10A.3

Step 1: **Specify Domain of the Construct**

Step 2: **Generate Sample of Items**

Step 3: **Collect Data**

Step 4: **Purify Measure**

Step 5: **Assess Validity**

searches are productive here. The literature indicates how the variable has been defined and how many dimensions it has. For the customer satisfaction example, we'd examine product brochures, trade magazines, results of product tests like those in *Consumer Reports*. An experience survey might include discussions with people in the product group responsible for the product, sales reps, dealers, marketing researchers, consumers, and outsiders who have a special expertise in heating equipment.

Step 3 involves *collecting data* from a sample of the target population, e.g., all those who have purchased a space heater within the last six months.

Step 4 uses the data collected in Step 3 to *purify the original set of items*. We eliminate items that are not highly correlated with the others.

Step 5 involves *determining the validity* of the purified measure. We assess the convergent, discriminant, and construct validity. (Content validity will have been addressed in Steps 1 through 4.)

Questions

1. How is measuring an attitude more difficult than measuring a person's height?
2. What is a true score? A systematic error? A random error?
3. How is the quality of a measurement instrument assessed?
4. What is validity? What are the types of validity?
5. What is reliability? The types?
6. What steps should you go through to develop a measure?

Applications and Problems

1. Discuss the idea that a particular measure could be reliable and still not be valid.
2. Discuss the use of IQ tests (or similar tests, such as the GMAT) in measuring intelligence. Do you believe that these tests adequately measure a person's abilities? If not, what traits, abilities, or types of intelligence do the tests fail to measure?
3. You have developed a questionnaire designed to measure attitudes toward a set of TV ads for a new snack-food product. The respondents, as a group, will view the ads on a TV set and then complete the questionnaire. Due to logistical circumstances

beyond your control, you must split your sample of respondents into three groups and collect data on three separate days. What steps might you take in an effort to minimize possible variance in scores caused by the three separate administrations?
4. Many areas of marketing research rely heavily on measures of psychological constructs, e.g., compulsive shopping, motivation to search for information, etc. What characteristics inherent in these constructs make them so difficult to measure? What tools can the marketing researcher bring to bear when evaluating the goodness of the measure? In

other words, what things can we do that allow us to state with some degree of confidence that we are indeed measuring the construct of interest?

5. You are the national sales manager for Perry Pharmaceutical, Inc. You have been concerned with trying to determine the most important characteristics a salesperson must possess to be successful. Much of the current research suggests that salesperson adaptiveness is a key component of success. You would like to determine if this is indeed the case. To assess this, you need to develop a scale to measure salesperson adaptiveness, collect data with your sales force, and then compare the results to each individual's sales record. What kinds of questions would you include? Are there general areas that you think must be measured with a number of different questions?

CASES

CASE 3.1
E-Food and the Online Grocery Competition (B)

Ashley Sims is the MBA student who is considering starting her own online grocery service. Two weeks ago, she ran a focus group consisting of 12 of her class-mates, some of whom use an online grocer, and some of whom do not. She kept the moderator questions broad, just trying to get a sense of what e-visitors are looking for in their online grocery trips. Figure 3.1.1 contains a sampling of the verbata from that focus group.

Those data indicate variance on satisfaction with the current system, and even for loyal users, different levels of satisfaction with different features of the system. Though people seem generally happy, there is clearly room for improvement in elements of online grocery shopping.

In addition, Sims is trying to think long-term, know-ing that she wants one arm of her business to focus on grocery delivery, and one arm of her business to grow into a profitable consumer research business, offering in-depth insight into the consumer-decision processes for grocery shopping and online shopping more gen-erally. Sims figures additional research will be required to understand how to set priorities in potentially im-proving the software, and the broader questions of how to understand the consumer's behavior and infer the thought processes underlying that behavior.

Sims used this textbook in her own marketing re-search class, so she knows there are many research methodologies to choose from. She is fresh off of her experience running the focus group that yielded the data in Figure 3.1.1. Although it was fun and she thinks she learned a lot, she doubts that she could run another focus group that could be shaped to address these fairly specific concerns. She's thought about doing a survey—just asking people, "Do you care about brands?" or "Are you price sensitive?" and so on. However, she doubts that people would admit to being overly influenced by brand or price, even though their purchases may indicate that they are. She's also rejected an observational technique—a friend had suggested that she sit down next to a person who is about to do an online grocery run and just watch what they do and take notes. She's afraid that her presence would be off-putting and the person doing the grocery shopping might behave differently from how they nor-mally would (for example, maybe buy asparagus rather than M&M's).

Ashley's computer-geeky friend tells her that every mouse click gets stored into a user file and that she should look at what people actually do rather than what they say. Sims is intrigued by this but understandably is having difficulty in obtaining such data from current online grocery providers. She decides to invest in having a programmer create a smaller-scale simulation of an online grocer. She will ask participants to pretend they are grocery shopping online. She'll strip off each user file and analyze the click-stream data. She might run a

---

Figure 3.1.1   Sampling of Verbatim Accounts from Focus Group on Online Grocery Trips

- "It's great! I don't need a car!" (Current user)

- "It's difficult to just browse, like if I'm not sure what I'm in the mood for." (Had tried online shopping but is no longer a user)

- "I can't touch the fruits. I can't read the side of the box on cereals." (Current user)

- "They chose my vegetables better than I would have!" (Current user)

- "I wish they could pick up my dry cleaning too." (Not a user, intends to begin)

- "It's kind of expensive. There's a big annual fee, a delivery charge each time, and you know you've got to tip the delivery guy." (Current user)

- "This is terrific—I don't like to shop for food even if I had the time, which I certainly do not." (Current user)

- "I guess it's okay. Thing is, there's a <name of local grocery> on my way home from work, so that's just as convenient. For me." (Non user, does not intend to begin)

- "Don't I get any, you know, frequent flyer points things?" (Non user, getting used to the concept) survey, too, but with the click-streams, she'll know just what people did, not just what they say they would do.

QUESTIONS

1. Sims has considered a number of marketing research approaches. Do you agree with her general assessment or do you feel she was hasty in dismissing any of the techniques? Which of the methods would you recommend and why? How would you modify the technique from what she has been considering?

2. What did you learn from the focus group verbatim accounts? Was the sample suitable? When would it be important to run two different focus groups, one for users, one for nonusers?

CASE 3.2
Premium Pizza Inc.[1]

For 30 years now, promotions have been big business. Promotions include coupons, cents-off deals marked on the package, free gifts, and so on. They're big because they're successful at increasing short-term purchase behavior. In fact, sales promotion is now estimated to account for over one-half of the typical promotion budget, more than advertising. In many industries, however, the initial benefit of increased sales has resulted in long-term escalation of competition. As firms are forced to "fight fire with fire," special offer follows special offer in a never-ending spiral of promotional deals.

The fast-food industry has been one of the most strongly affected by this trend. Pizzas come two for the price of one; burgers are promoted in the context of a double-deal involving cuddly toys for the kids; tacos are reduced in price some days, but not others. It is within this fiercely competitive, erratic environment that Premium Pizza Corporation has grown from a small local chain into an extensive midwestern network with national aspirations. Over the past few years, Jim Battaglia, vice president of marketing, has introduced a number of promotional offers, and Premium Pizza parlors have continued to flourish. Nevertheless, as the company contemplates further expansion, Jim is concerned that he knows very little about how his customers respond to his promotional deals. He believes that he needs a long-term strategy aimed at maximizing the effectiveness of dollars spent on promotions. And, as a first step, he thinks that it is important to assess the effectiveness of his existing offers.

[1] The contributions of Jacqueline C. Hitchon to this case are gratefully acknowledged.

Specific Objectives

In the past, Jim has favored the use of five types of coupons, and he now wishes to determine their independent appeal, together with their relation to several identifiable characteristics of fast-food consumers. The five promotional concepts are listed in Table 3.2.1. The consumer characteristics that Jim's experience tells him warrant investigation include number of children living at home, age of youngest child, propensity to eat fast food, propensity to eat Premium Pizza in particular, preference for slices over pies, propensity to use coupons, and occupation.

The specific objectives of the research study can therefore be summarized as follows:

1. To evaluate the independent appeal of the five promotional deals to determine which deals are most preferred

2. To gain insight into the reasons that certain deals are preferred

3. To examine the relationships between the appeal of each promotional concept and various consumer characteristics

Proposed Methodology

After much discussion, Jim's research team finally decided that the desired information could best be gathered by means of personal interviews, using a combination of open-ended and closed questions. A medium-sized shopping mall on the outskirts of a metropolitan area in the Midwest was selected as the research site. Shoppers were intercepted by professional interviewers while walking in the mall and asked to participate in a survey requiring five minutes of their time.

Table **3.2.1**	**Five Promotional Concepts**
Coupon A	Get a medium soft drink for 5 cents with the purchase of any slice.
Coupon B	Buy a slice and get a second slice of comparable value free.
Coupon C	Save 50 cents on the purchase of any slice and receive one free trip to the salad bar.
Coupon D	Buy a slice and a large soft drink and get a second slice free.
Coupon E	Get a single-topping slice for only 99 cents.

The sampling procedure employed a convenience sample in which interviewers were instructed to approach anyone passing by, providing that they met certain criteria (see Figure 3.2.1). In sum, the sample of respondents was restricted to adult men and women between the ages of 18 and 49 who had both

Figure 3.2.1 Interviewer Instructions

Below are suggestions for addressing each question. Please read all the instructions before you begin questioning people.

Interviewer Instructions
Approach shoppers who appear to be between 18 and 49 years of age. Since we would like equal numbers of respondents in each age category and a 50% male–female ratio, please do not select respondents based on their appeal to you. The interview should take approximately five minutes. When reading questions, read answer choices if indicated.

- Question 1: Terminate any respondent who has not eaten lunch or dinner from any fast-food restaurant in the last seven days.

- Question 2: Terminate any respondent who has not eaten pizza within the last 30 days. This includes carry-out, drive-thru, or dining in.

- Question 3: Terminate respondent if not between 18 and 49 years of age. If between 18 and 49, circle the appropriate number answer. For this question, please read the question and the answer choices.

After completing questions 1 through 3, hand respondent the coupon booklet. Make sure that the booklet and the response sheets are the same color. Also check to see that the coupon booklet number indicated on the upper right-hand corner of the response sheet matches the coupon book number.

- Question 4: Ask the respondent to open the coupon booklet and read the first coupon concept. Read the first section of Question 4 showing the respondent that the scales are provided on the page above the coupon concept. Enter his or her answer in the box provided.

- Read the second section of the question and enter respondent's answer in the second box provided.

- When asking the respondent, "Why did you respond as you did for use," please record the first reason mentioned and use the lines provided to probe and clarify the reasons.

This set of instructions applies to Questions 5 through 8. Periodically remind the respondent to look at the scales provided on the page above the coupon concept that he or she is looking at.

- Question 9: Enter number of children living at home. If none, enter the number zero and proceed to Question 11.

- Question 10: Enter age of youngest child living at home in the box provided.

- Question 11: Read the question and each answer slowly. Circle the number corresponding to the appropriate answer.

- Question 12: Read the question and each answer slowly. Circle the number corresponding to the appropriate answer. If answer is never, proceed to Question 14. Otherwise, continue to Question 13.

- Question 13: Circle the number corresponding to the appropriate answer. Do not read answer choices.

- Question 14: Circle the number corresponding to the appropriate answer. Do not read answer choices.

- Question 15: Read the question and each answer slowly. Circle the number corresponding to the appropriate answer.

- Question 16: Read the question and each answer slowly. Circle the number corresponding to the appropriate answer.

- Question 17: If an explanation is requested for occupation, please tell respondent that we are looking for a broad category or title. "No occupation" is not an acceptable answer. If this should happen, please probe to see if the person is a student, homemaker, retired, unemployed, etc.

At the end of the questionnaire, you are asked to indicate whether the respondent was male or female. Please circle the appropriate answer. This is not a question for the respondent.

purchased lunch, dinner, or carryout food at a fast-food restaurant in the past seven days and had eaten restaurant pizza within the last 30 days, either at a restaurant or delivered to the home. In addition, interviewers were warned not to exercise any bias during the selection process, as they would do, for example, if they approached only those people who looked particularly agreeable or attractive. Finally, interviewers were asked to obtain as close as possible to a 50–50 split of male and female participants.

The questionnaire was organized into three sections (see Figure 3.2.2). The first section contained the screening questions aimed at ensuring that respondents qualified for the sample. In the second section, respondents were asked to evaluate on 10-point scales the appeal of each of the five promotional

---

Figure 3.2.2   Premium Pizza Inc. Questionnaire

Response Number _____

Coupon Book # _____

(Approach shoppers who appear to be between the ages of 18 and 49 and say . . .)

Hi, I'm _____ from Midwest Research Services. Many companies like to know your preferences and opinions about new products and promotions. If you have about 5 minutes, I'd like to have your opinions in this marketing research study.

(If refused, terminate)

1. *Have you eaten lunch or dinner in, or carried food away from, a fast-food restaurant in the last seven days?*
   . . . (must answer yes to continue)

2. *Have you eaten restaurant pizza within the last 30 days, either at the restaurant or by having it delivered?*
   . . . (must answer yes to continue)

3. *Which age group are you in?* (read answers, circle number)

   <u>1:</u> 18–24   <u>2:</u> 25–34   <u>3:</u> 35–49   <u>4:</u> other—terminate interview

I'm now going to show you five different coupon concepts and ask you three questions for each. Please respond to each coupon independently of the others. Look at the next coupon only when I ask you to.

4. *Please read the first coupon concept. Using a 10-point scale as shown on the page above, how would you rate this concept if 1 represents very poor value and 10 represents very good value?* (enter value): _____

Looking at the second scale, how would you rate this concept if 1 represents "definitely would not use" and 10 represents "definitely would use"? (enter value): _____

Why did you respond as you did for use? _____
_____
_____

5. *Please turn the page and read the next coupon concept.*

Ignoring the last coupon and using the same scale, how would you rate this concept in terms of value? (enter value): _____

Referring to the second scale, how would you rate this concept in terms of your level of use? (enter value): _____

Why did you respond as you did for use? _____
_____
_____

6. *Please turn the page and read the next coupon concept. Ignoring the last coupon and using the same scale, how would you rate this concept in terms of value?* (enter value): _____

Referring to the second scale, how would you rate this concept in terms of your level of use? (enter value): _____

Why did you respond as you did for use? _____
_____
_____

(Continued)

Figure **3.2.2**   Continued

7. *Please turn the page and read the next coupon concept. Ignoring the last coupon and using the same scale, how would you rate this concept in terms of value?*   (enter value): _____

Referring to the second scale, how would you rate this concept in terms of your level of use? (enter value): _____

Why did you respond as you did for use? _____

_____

_____

8. *Please turn the page and read the next coupon concept. Ignoring the last coupon and using the same scale, how would you rate this concept in terms of value?*   (enter value): _____

Referring to the second scale, how would you rate this concept in terms of your level of use? (enter value): _____

Why did you respond as you did for use? _____

_____

_____

Thank you. The following questions will help us classify the preceding information.

9. *How many children do you have living at home?*   (enter value): _____
   (if answer is none, proceed to question 11)

10. *What is the age of your youngest child?*   (enter age): _____

11. *How often do you eat fast food for lunch or dinner?*
   (read answers, circle number):   1) Once per month or less
                                      2) 2–3 times per month
                                      3) Once or twice a week
                                      4) More than twice a week

12. *How often do you eat at Premium Pizza?*
   (read answers, circle number)   1) Never visited Premium Pizza
                                     2) Once per month or less
                                     3) 2–3 times per month
                                     4) Once a week or more
   (if answer is never, proceed to question 14)

13. *Do you yourself usually buy whole pies or slices at Premium Pizza?*
   (circle one):   1) Whole pies
                                     2) Slices

14. *Have you used fast-food or restaurant coupons in the last 30 days?*
   (circle one):   1) Yes
                                     2) No

15. *Have you ever used coupons for Premium Pizzas?*
   (read answers, circle number)   1) Never
                                     2) I sometimes use them when I have them.
                                     3) I always use them when I have them.

16. *What is your marital status?*
   (read answers, circle number)   1) Single
                                     2) Married
                                     3) Divorced, Separated, Widowed

17. *What is your occupation?* _____

This is not a question for the respondent.
Respondent was (circle one): 1) Male   2) Female

Thank you for your participation. (Terminate interview at this time.)

---

concepts based on two factors: perceived value and likelihood of use. After they had evaluated a concept, interviewees were asked to give reasons for their likelihood-of-use rating. The third and final section consisted of the questions on consumer characteristics that Jim believed to be pertinent.

The questionnaire was to be completed by the interviewer based on the respondent's comments. In other words, the interviewer read the questions aloud and wrote down the answer given in each case by the interviewee. It was decided to show respondents an example of each coupon before they rated it. For this purpose, enlarged photographs of each coupon were produced. It was also thought necessary to depict the 10-point scales that consumers should use to evaluate the promotional offer. Coupons and scales were therefore assembled in a booklet so that, as the interviewer showed each double-page spread, the respondent would see the scales on the top page and the coupon in question on the bottom page (see Figure 3.2.3).

Figure **3.2.3**   **Respondent Reference to Scale and Coupon Offer**

Because the researcher wished to counterbalance the order in which the coupons were viewed and rated, the five coupons were organized into booklets of six different sequences. Each sequence was subsequently bound in one of six distinctly colored binders. A total of 96 questionnaires were then printed in six different colors to match the binder. In this way, there were 16 questionnaires of each color, and the color of the respondent's questionnaire indicated the sequence that he or she had seen.

The questionnaire and procedure were pre-tested at a mall similar to the target mall and were found to be satisfactory.

QUESTIONS

1. Is the choice of mall intercept interviews an appropriate data-collection method given the research objectives?

2. Do you think that there are any specific criteria that the choice of shopping mall should satisfy?

3. Evaluate the instructions to interviewers (Figure 3.2.1).

4. Evaluate the questionnaire (Figure 3.2.2).

5. Do you think that it is worthwhile to present the coupons in a binder, separate from the questionnaire? Why or why not?

6. Do you consider it advisable to rotate the order of presentation of coupons? Why or why not?

CASE 3.3
CTM Productions (A)[2]

CTM Productions, formerly Children's Theatre of Madison, was formed in 1965 to "produce theater of the highest quality." CTM's mission is to "ensure that our [CTM's] efforts are inclusive of all the human family, rather than parts of it." In order to measure its present and future achievement of this goal, CTM must learn who its audience actually is.

CTM's research team decided to study the audience of CTM's production *To Kill a Mockingbird.* The study had three major objectives: (1) to develop an audience profile, including demographic and media exposure data, (2) to provide a framework and data-collection instrument for future marketing research, and (3) to supply a list of potential season subscribers. CTM had never undertaken any marketing research before this study, so internal secondary information did not exist. External secondary information provided guidance as to the types of questions to be asked on this type of questionnaire and the appropriate phrasing for such questions. The questionnaire is shown in Figure 3.3.1.

CTM's volunteer ushers distributed the survey at each performance of *To Kill a Mockingbird.* The volunteers gave the survey and a pencil to all adults attending the performances (for the purpose of this survey, adults were defined as anyone 16 years or older). Respondents were instructed to complete the questionnaire and hand it back to the ushers during the intermission. In addition, collection boxes were placed next to all the exits. Although the survey was intended for all adult members of the audience, it is unclear as to whether these instructions were followed at every performance.

CTM Productions held five shows each weekend for three weekends. Surveys were distributed at each of the 15 performances; however, the number of completed surveys varied with the size of the audience for each show. A total of 1,016 usable surveys were collected during the course of the study.

Figure 3.3.1   CTM Questionnaire

Introduce Yourself to CTM

Welcome to CTM's production of *To Kill a Mockingbird*. CTM Productions has been around for a long time—since 1965. And in this time we have had over 33,000 people in our audience. People to whom we have never been introduced. Real people like you that presently exist as numbers in our records. Now you have a chance to change your status. Introduce yourself to us by taking two minutes to answer the following questions to help us understand who you really are.

Let's start out with the basics. Your name is ————————————————— *and you live at (please including mailing address with ZIP Code)* ——

How many CTM productions have you attended? [ ] this is my first CTM production

2002–2003 Season	2001–2002 Season	2000–2001 Season
[ ] season subscriber	[ ] season subscriber	[ ] season subscriber
[ ] *Wind in the Willows*	[ ] *Red Shoes*	[ ] *Beauty and the Beast*
[ ] *A Christmas Carol*	[ ] *A Christmas Carol*	[ ] *A Christmas Carol*
[X] *To Kill a Mockingbird*	[ ] *Anne of Green Gables*	[ ] *I Remember Mama*
[ ] *Babar II* (plan to attend)	[ ] *Narnia*	[ ] *Babar the Elephant*

Who is with you today? (check all that apply)
[ ] myself	[ ] my spouse/partner	[ ] my kids
[ ] adult friend(s)	[ ] unrelated kids	[ ] other families

Who have you attended with in the past? (again, check all that apply)
[ ] myself	[ ] my spouse/partner	[ ] my kids
[ ] adult friend(s)	[ ] unrelated kids	[ ] other families

Have you or any of your family participated in any of these CTM activities? (check all that apply)
[ ] after-school drama classes	[ ] auditions	[ ] have not participated
[ ] summer school	[ ] performances	[ ] did not know I could

How did you find out about our production of To Kill a Mockingbird? (again, check all that apply)
[ ] season brochure	[ ] poster

Read story in:
[ ] *State Journal*	[ ] *Capitol Times*	[ ] *Ishtmus*	[ ] other

Saw ad in:
[ ] *State Journal*	[ ] *Capitol Times*	[ ] *Ishtmus*	[ ] other
[ ] radio (which station?) ———————————		[ ] television (which station?) ———————	
[ ] magazine (which one?) ———————————		[ ] word of mouth	

Did you come to this performance because you knew someone in the cast?
    [ ] yes   [ ] no

What other events have you attended in the last six months? (check all that apply)
With your family or friends:
[ ] sports	[ ] movies	[ ] live musical performances
[ ] museums	[ ] lectures	[ ] other live theatrical performance

Alone:
[ ] sports	[ ] movies	[ ] live musical performances
[ ] museums	[ ] lectures	[ ] other live theatrical performance

Your answers to the following demographic questions will help us understand who you are.

Are you female or male?   [ ] female   [ ] male

Which age category do you belong to?
[ ] 16–20	[ ] 31–40	[ ] 51–60	[ ] 71–80
[ ] 21–30	[ ] 41–50	[ ] 61–70	[ ] 81–100

(Continued)

Figure **3.3.1**   Continued

How did you get here today?
[ ] walked   [ ] car   [ ] bus   [ ] other

From how far away did you come?
[ ] within Madison   [ ] less than 5 miles [ ] 6–10 miles   [ ] over 10 miles

How long have you live in the Madison/south-central Wisconsin area?
[ ] do not live here   [ ] just arrived   [ ] 1–3 years   [ ] 4–7 years   [ ] more

What is your highest level of education?
[ ] some high school   [ ] some college   [ ] some graduate school   [ ] more
[ ] high school graduate [ ] college graduate   [ ] graduate school degree

What is your annual household income?
[ ] below $20,000   [ ] $31–40,000   [ ] more than $50,000   [ ] do not wish to reply
[ ] $21–30,000   [ ] $41–50,000   [ ] not sure

Does this represent a dual income?
[ ] yes   [ ] no

How many people live in your household? (circle only one, include yourself)
        1   2   3   4   5   6   more

If you have children, how many are in each grade category?
[ ] not in school yet   [ ] 4th – 5th grade   [ ] high school   [ ] other
[ ] kindergarten–3rd grade [ ] 6th – 8th grade   [ ] college

Would you like to be on our mailing list to keep informed of CTM activities? [ ] yes   [ ] no

Are you a CTM member? [ ] yes   [ ] no

Now here's your chance to share your thoughts with us.

I wish I had known that CTM ——————————————————————————————

I'm glad CTM ——————————————————————————

I wish CTM would ———————————————————————————

I want CTM to know ———————————————————————————

It was a real pleasure meeting you. CTM looks forward to seeing you again very soon.

QUESTIONS

1. The CTM research term used secondary data for question types and wording of specific questions. Did the research team use secondary information effectively in this study?

2. Read through the questionnaire shown in Figure 3.3.1. Does the questionnaire provide CTM with the information necessary to meet the stated objectives? Explain.

3. Considering CTM's objectives, does the sampling plan used for the study provide the necessary information? Does the sampling plan bias the results?

CASE 3.4
Comparing Ads Against a Databank

An advertising agency has a new client, a large hotel chain. The ad agency has never had a hotel chain as a client before, so they're a little concerned that their vast experience in consumer packaged goods (CPGs) and such may not serve them particularly well in this case. Still, to try to serve the client, they are operating as business-as-usual. The agency mocked up an ad to the usual point of pre-production, and tested it on consumers, using the agency's usual sampling methods and using its standard rating scales to keep the method as comparable as possible with their past studies. That way, they can compare how this ad tests against the huge database they already have on how ads have tested in the past for different clients as well as how sales fared for the ads that were used.

Figure 3.4.1 shows the results that the advertising manager, Anna, showed the client. Anna couldn't just show the hotel data alone, because they're hard to interpret without some comparison point for contrast.

Given that they're an ad agency, they first pull (or edit) any ads that don't make viewers feel happy, so all three ads rate pretty well on the "happy" scale. It's also not good for an ad to make a viewer feel sad. The shampoo (for a different client) did the best (the ratings were the least sad), and the hotel didn't do that well. The three ads score comparably in both the "like ad" and "like brand" categories. And the divergent "will buy" scores make sense to Anna because she figures the poor "sad" ratings pulls the hotel estimates down from the shampoo scores.

The client is wondering why he's looking at the shampoo and airline data. He's wondering why their hotel ad scored badly on "sad." He's wondering why the "will buy" data aren't better, like the shampoo data.

QUESTION

1. What do you think is going on here? How would you begin to answer the client's questions, or reassure him that you had good data?

CASE 3.5
Measuring Magazines

When companies decide to advertise, they have many decisions to make: how much to spend, in which media,

how frequently should the ads appear, etc. Each component question is difficult.

Suppose your company sells pharmaceutical drugs. Magazines are a perfect fit for drug advertisements because the outlet allows the company to express in detailed ad copy the side effects and other precautions and disclaimers. The FTC prohibits explicit claims of success on television, which makes most TV ads for drugs ambiguous. For example, you've seen the types of ads in which people are moving through meadows in slow motion ... what ailment does the drug purport to cure? Magazines are a popular medium for many industries, not just pharmaceuticals (see Figure 3.5.1).

So, suppose your firm decides, "Okay, we're going to run a magazine print ad." Now what? "In which magazine should we run an ad?" Well, a "good one." *Good,* as a construct, means what?

Companies decide the magazines in which they will advertise based on the successfulness of the magazine. Magazines earn their money through circulation and advertising, hence, a magazine's "success" may be measured in two ways. One is advertising revenue, depicted in Figure 3.5.2. According to this monetary index, *People, Sports Illustrated,* and *Parade* are the top magazines.

The second, equally valid means of measuring a magazine's success is readership circulation. Figure 3.5.3 shows that *People* and *Sports Illustrated* are still in the top 12, but nowhere near as prominent as their expenditure data had suggested. That is, the ranking of

Source: adweek.com

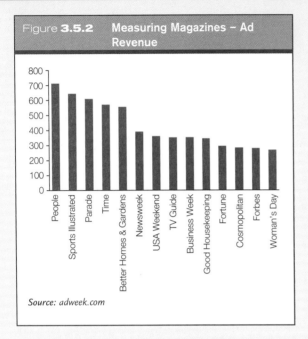

Figure **3.5.2**   **Measuring Magazines – Ad Revenue**

Source: adweek.com

the magazines varies depending on how you measure the success of the magazine.

Note that we're not even trying to measure some subjective, intangible consumer attitude on some customer survey. We're simply trying to get a useful index for the success of a magazine. Yet even something as seemingly simple as the "success" of a magazine is a

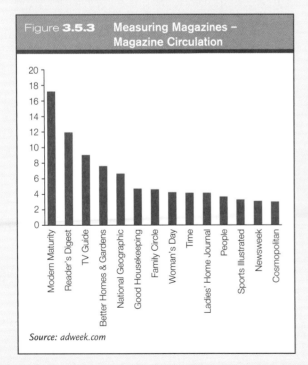

Figure **3.5.3**   **Measuring Magazines – Magazine Circulation**

Source: adweek.com

construct that can usually be measured in more than one manner. In this case, the measure of success that is adopted probably depends on the point of view taken, i.e., the magazine (ad space seller) vs. the manufacturer (buyer).

QUESTIONS

1. Which of these definitions do you think the magazine industry thinks is most important, and on which index do you think the survival of any particular magazine depends?

2. Which of these indices would matter most to your firm? If you want your ad to appear before the most people, do you go after *People* magazine, or do you go for the older population (*Modern Maturity*) and Middle America (*Reader's Digest*)?

3. Where do segmentation, targeting, and positioning enter in the decision making? Which kinds of drugs (or products more generally) fit best with each of these outlets? Your choice of measure of success depends on what marketing and marketing research question you want to answer. You've got to think through how you will use the index to determine which scores are most reflective of your current marketing questions.

If you think the measure of "success" was an isolated example, consider another (there are many!). A different kind of question might be, "Who are the 'big spenders' in magazine advertising?" Instead of playing the role of a pharmaceuticals company looking to place an ad, what if you were the marketing manager in charge of soliciting ads for a magazine? Advertising expenditures per company can be measured not just in how much money is spent, but in how many pages the money buys. Thus, you could approach your quest in one of two ways: You could try to increase the ad revenue for the magazine, or you could increase the number of ads placed in the magazine. Once again, these lead to different results.

Figure 3.5.4 lists the companies who spend a lot on magazine advertising, as measured by cash-ola. Figure 3.5.5 lists the same companies, in the same order for ease of comparison, but note the change in the height of the histograms from Figure 3.5.4 to Figure 3.5.5.

QUESTIONS

1. Which companies spend the most if the expenditure is measured in dollars? If measured in number of pages?

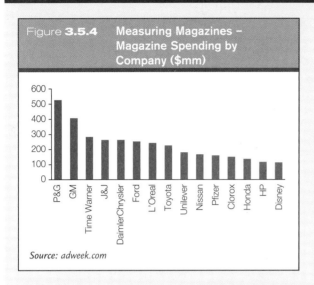

Figure **3.5.4** Measuring Magazines – Magazine Spending by Company ($mm)

Source: adweek.com

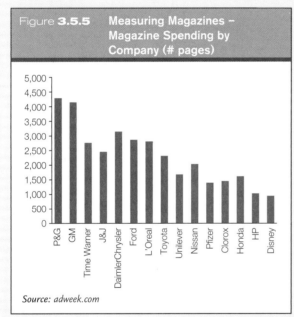

Figure **3.5.5** Measuring Magazines – Magazine Spending by Company (# pages)

Source: adweek.com

2. Why do these profiles differ? When is either measure most relevant?

3. Which is most relevant to show your boss that you've been successful?

Each of these illustrations offered two items that shared similarly strong "face validity" yet were rival indices. Your understanding of the marketing and managerial concerns has to distinguish which measure to use.

CASE 3.6
Secondary Data on Health from CDC[3]

Monstrous amounts of secondary data exist online, for free. The government is easily the largest source of population-related and economic and business-related data (census.gov). You can also get absorbed for hours (okay, we're geeks) at cdc.org if you're interested in health data.

Figure 3.6.1 presents a partial listing, by state and year, of the percentage of citizens who self-report that they have engaged in binge drinking (five drinks for men, four for women, at one sitting) within the last 30 days prior to being surveyed.

Secondary data are free and "quick," but finding all the bits and pieces of these numbers is rather tedious and time consuming (you'll be glad to have a marketing research staff). It's also easy to make copying mistakes, so be sure to factor in quality control before using the data and basing decisions on them.

QUESTIONS

What questions do you want to answer with these masses of data?

1. You can focus on current data, e.g., find the answer to the question, "For the most recent year, which are the top 10 states with binge drinking problems?"

2. You can make comparisons with older data, e.g., answer the question, "Were the states you just listed always the biggest bingers?"

3. Pick *your* state and graph the trend (e.g., in Excel). Is the increase constant and steady, or is there a jump between any years? To what might the jump(s) be attributable? As a social marketer, how might you slow or reverse the trend? Have we (as a country) been successful at changing any such behaviors? (Don't be pessimistic, the answer is yes—think about smoking, condom use for AIDS prevention, etc.)

4. Do you think the trend that you just plotted for your state is typical or unusual? How would you defend your point of view? Plot the trends for additional states—which states would be the best comparisons? Others in your immediate area? Others with comparable population statistics (go to census.gov to find those numbers!)?

[3] The whole data set is available at the text companion Web site.

Figure **3.6.1** CDC Data (cdc.org) on Binge Drinking (%)					
STATE, YEAR:	**2003**	**2004**	**2005**	**2006**	**2007**
Alabama	12.1	12.7	10.4	11.2	11
Alaska	18.4	16.4	17.5	17	19.2
Arizona	16.6	15.5	14.5	15.2	15
Arkansas	12.5	11.2	10.4	12.4	10.4
California	15.9	14.7	14	15.4	16.9
Colorado	18.3	17.3	16.2	16.4	17.3
Connecticut	16.5	14.9	14.8	14.5	17.8
Delaware	18.6	17.4	15.6	19	18.6
D.C.	18.6	16.7	16.8	15.9	16.1
Florida	15.5	12.5	14.1	13.8	14.2
Georgia	13	12.1	12.1	12.1	12.6

…
(See companion Web site for more of this graph)

5. In these data, pick either a year and select all states, or pick your state and select all years. Then return to cdc.org and pick up more data. There are tons of lifestyle-related indices. For example, there are statistics on percentage of people who are obese, who smoke, percentage of people covered by health insurance, etc. Correlate these figures with some of these other measures. Before you conduct the analyses, write down the (social) marketing and (health) managerial questions you think you want to answer.

6. After you play with the data a bit, write down the answers you've arrived at and compare them to the questions you had posed. Have you answered all the questions you set out to answer? If not, why not? Were they harder to answer than you thought, or did you get distracted? How many new questions arose as you began your exploration in the data? If this latter number exceeds five, there's good news and bad news. The good news is that you're now a *bona fide* "data miner." The bad news is that you're a hopeless geek. (Wear that label with pride—it will get you far in life!)

CASE 3.7
Critiquing Questionnaires

Be forewarned! These exercises usually make "monsters" out of otherwise meek business school students. Once you learn to critique a questionnaire, you'll never be able to look at another survey in quite the same way.

Instead of answering the marketing researcher's questions, you'll be looking at the question thinking, "I could have worded that better!" That's okay with us—it's a good measure of your knowledge!

So, to get you started, take a look at the following real surveys (these are all "real," but we've changed the brand names to protect the incompetent).

Figure 3.7.1 was a postcard-sized survey. You see the front. On the back was the address of the office for ease of the customer return (though it was not stamped).

What are the survey's strengths? It's short, and obviously so, so consumers know immediately that filling out the survey won't take too much of their time.

→ Short surveys enhance response rates.

→ Better response rates mean more representative samples.

In addition, a number of different attributes are assessed, to enhance the multidimensionality of the service assessment. There is an open-ended section so that the consumer may say whatever is on his/her mind, whether anticipated by the rating scales of quality, timeliness, etc., or not.

What are the survey's weaknesses? The trade-off on length is that the survey will yield little information. Further, if any of the features is deemed weak, are any of the scales precise enough to diagnose how to remedy the service? A complaint about marketing research that you always want to avoid is, "We can't do anything on the basis of these data."

Figure **3.7.1**	Questionnaires to Critique—A Campus Admin Office

Dear Valued Customer,

To assist us in maintaining the highest possible quality service to your department, please complete and return this card, rating performance on the services performed for you. Please feel free to make any other comments or suggestions. Thank you.

	Excellent	Good	Adequate	Inadequate	Unacceptable
Quality	☐	☐	☐	☐	☐
Timeliness	☐	☐	☐	☐	☐
Price	☐	☐	☐	☐	☐
Convenience	☐	☐	☐	☐	☐
Overall service	☐	☐	☐	☐	☐

Comments/Suggestions: _____

_____

Job Number: _____ Date: _____ Name (optional): _____

Figure 3.7.2 also has strengths and weaknesses (as does any real survey—nothing is perfect). For example, there are again ratings and an open-ended space providing the opportunity to vent or rave about anything the consumer cares about. At the bottom of the survey, there is a means of communication should the

Figure **3.7.2**	A Big Drug Store

	Excellent	Average	Poor
Overall how would you grade this store?	☐	☐	☐
Please check one:			
Our pharmacy	☐	☐	☐
Our check-out service	☐	☐	☐
Our variety & selection	☐	☐	☐
Our everyday prices	☐	☐	☐
Our ad in stock	☐	☐	☐
Our cleanliness	☐	☐	☐
Our film processing	☐	☐	☐
Our everyday in stock	☐	☐	☐
Our people are friendly & helpful	☐	☐	☐

Date of visit: _____

Time of day: _____

Your comments and concerns: _____

_____

_____

_____

_____

☐ I would like a reply   ☐ I don't need a reply

Name _____

Address _____

City _____

State _____ Zip _____ Phone _____

customer wish feedback. Nice touch. On the other hand, what the heck do "Our everyday in stock" and our "Ad in stock" mean? We're marketers, we're smart, we can figure this out. But if it takes us a moment to interpret the jargon, how much longer will it take the average consumer? In the meantime, do we lose that respondent?

Figure 3.7.3 is a survey from a large network of travel agencies. Many of the questions could be improved, but if you want a chuckle, look at the last question.

Enough hints. Now you're on your own. Identify the strengths and weaknesses in the remaining surveys, depicted in Figures 3.7.4 through 3.7.7.

Figure 3.7.3   A Travel Agency

Please help us maintain our high standards of quality by answering the following questions.

On this trip did we:

Provide lowest applicable airfare?	Yes	No	NA/DK
Enter frequent flyer # w reservation?	Yes	No	NA/DK
Book the hotel you requested?	Yes	No	NA/DK
Reserve the type of car requested?	Yes	No	NA/DK
Provide confirmation numbers?	Yes	No	NA/DK
Provide travel documents on time?	Yes	No	NA/DK
Handle special requests and note on tix?	Yes	No	NA/DK
Provide accurate destination information?	Yes	No	NA/DK

How would you rate each of the following?	**Excellent**	**Good**	**Fair**	**Poor**	**NA**
Courtesy of service?	E	G	F	P	NA
Extent to which your questions were answered?	E	G	F	P	NA
Manner in which our staff resolved any problems?	E	G	F	P	NA
Our *overall* service to you?	E	G	F	P	NA

On a scale of 0 to 100, if most travel agencies get an overall quality score of 80, what score would you give to our WorldZoom Travel Network? _____

Figure 3.7.4 A Big Hotel Chain

Please take a moment to share your thoughts with us. We value your business and thank you for your confidence in the *ComfyStay* Brand. Your feedback is greatly encouraged and appreciated.

Overall satisfaction with this ComfyStay	Low	1 2 3 4 5 6 7	High n/a
Likelihood you would recommend this ComfyStay	Low	1 2 3 4 5 6 7	High n/a
Likelihood, *if returning to the area,* you would return to this ComfyStay	Low	1 2 3 4 5 6 7	High n/a
Overall value for the price paid	Low	1 2 3 4 5 6 7	High n/a

Primary purpose of visit
    ☐ Individual business
    ☐ Convention/Meeting
    ☐ Pleasure

How many times have you been a guest at this ComfyStay?   1   2   3   4   5+

Did you have a problem during your stay? Y   N
If yes, did you report it to the staff?   Y   N
Was the problem resolved?   Y   N

If yes, how did our staff measure against your expectations? ☐ Exceeded   ☐ Met   ☐ Fell Below

What was the nature of the problem?_____
_____
_____
_____
_____

Room Number _____   Your name _____
Hotel Name _____   Day phone _____
Date of Stay _____

Figure 3.7.5 A Fancy Pen Online/Catalog Company

Dear Customer,
This order comes with a string attached: your satisfaction.
    Our goal is to ensure that you're 100% satisfied every time you shop with us. Would you mind taking a couple of minutes to tell us how we did? If there's additional assistance we can offer, please call or e-mail us anytime.
    Thank you for your business. We hope we met (or exceeded) your expectations.
        Sincerely,
        Moi
        Director of Customer Service [phone, e-mail address listed here]

Customer Satisfaction Survey

1. Was the merchandise what you expected? _____ Yes _____ No Here's why:_____
_____

2. Did you buy it as a gift? _____ Yes, for this occasion _____ _____ No

3. Will you order from FancyPen again? _____ Yes _____ No Here's why: _____
_____

4. What are your three favorite stores or catalogs?
_____   _____   _____

5. Overall, how would you grade us on customer service?
    ☐ A   ☐ B   ☐ C   ☐ D   ☐ F

How can we make your experience with FancyPen more satisfying?_____
_____

Thank you. Just drop this card in the mail—we'll pay the postage.

Figure **3.7.6**   **YuppieHouseWares**

Customer Service

If you ordered by phone

The Phone Representative's courtesy and
professionalism   ☐ excellent   ☐ very good   ☐ satisfactory   ☐ needs improvement

The ease and efficiency of the ordering
process   ☐ excellent   ☐ very good   ☐ satisfactory   ☐ needs improvement

If you spoke with a Product Specialist

The Product Specialist's courtesy and   ☐ excellent   ☐ very good   ☐ satisfactory   ☐ needs improvement
professionalism

The Product Specialist's promptness in   ☐ excellent   ☐ very good   ☐ satisfactory   ☐ needs improvement
answering your inquiry

The value of the Product Specialist's   ☐ excellent   ☐ very good   ☐ satisfactory   ☐ needs improvement
assistance to you

The ease and efficiency of ordering from   ☐ excellent   ☐ very good   ☐ satisfactory   ☐ needs improvement
the Product Specialist

If you ordered by mail or fax, the ease of ☐ excellent   ☐ very good   ☐ satisfactory   ☐ needs improvement
following the instructions on the Order Form

Delivery

The arrival of your order compared with   ☐ excellent   ☐ very good   ☐ satisfactory   ☐ needs improvement
anticipated time of delivery

The appearance and condition of the   ☐ excellent   ☐ very good   ☐ satisfactory   ☐ needs improvement
packaging

The condition of the merchandise upon   ☐ excellent   ☐ very good   ☐ satisfactory   ☐ needs improvement
receipt

Merchandise

Your initial reaction to the quality of the   ☐ excellent   ☐ very good   ☐ satisfactory   ☐ needs improvement
products you ordered

Your initial perception of the value received ☐ excellent   ☐ very good   ☐ satisfactory   ☐ needs improvement
for the money spent

Just a few more questions

Are you likely to purchase from YuppieHouseWares again?

_____

What additional services may we provide?

_____

If you could implement one change at YuppieHouseWares, what would it be?

_____

May we send our catalog to a friend? Please provide name and address:

_____

If you have a concern or question about your order, please call our Product Specialist at 1-800-etc.

Figure 3.7.7 A Car Dealership

I know you had a choice of where to service your vehicle and I would like to thank you for the opportunity to earn your business. I also know that if I expect to build a strong customer base, I need to make sure that you are completely satisfied with your service experience here today.

Below is a list of questions that may appear on a questionnaire from my dealership. Although some of them seem to rate our entire operation, in fact they all rate my personal performance and the scores become part of my permanent record. If you feel I have not earned all "5" or "Yes" ratings, please call and allow me the opportunity to correct any of my failures.

F A I L I N G !

	Highest				Lowest
	5	4	3	2	1
Promptness, courtesy writing your order:	☐ ←	☐	☐	☐	☐
Communication with service consultant	☐ ←	☐	☐	☐	☐
Knowledge and expertise	☐ ←	☐	☐	☐	☐
Treated in honest, straightforward manner	☐ ←	☐	☐	☐	☐
Amount of time spent with you	☐ ←	☐	☐	☐	☐
Understanding your service, repair request	☐ ←	☐	☐	☐	☐

	Yes	No
Were service items requested completed?	☐ ←	☐
Able to schedule appointment?	☐ ←	☐
Vehicle available when promised?	☐ ←	☐
Car washed, clean when you picked it up?	☐ ←	☐
Was the work explained to your satisfaction?	☐ ←	☐

Sample Design for Data Collection and Sample Size

part 4

In this section, we get into the actual collection of the data needed to answer a problem:

Chapter 11 discusses sampling plans.

Chapter 12 answers the question, "How many respondents do I need in my sample?"

Chapter 13 presents the kinds of errors that can arise in collecting data.

Sampling Procedures

11

Questions to Guide Your Learning:

Q1 How do you get a sample?

Q2 What is a probability sample (vs. a nonprobability sample)?

Q3 How does sampling relate to some basic statistical concepts?

Q4 What is stratified sampling and cluster sampling?

At this point in the research process: (1) We have specified the marketing research problem, (2) developed an appropriate research design, and (3) developed a data-collection instrument. Next, we select those elements from which the information will be collected. One way to do this is to survey every member of the population by a complete canvas, or **census**. Another way is to collect information from a portion of the population by taking a **sample**, on the basis of that subset, infer something about the larger group. The ability to make this inference depends on the sampling method used.

We are often sampling consumers, but an "element" in a population can refer to manufacturing and retail firms, organizations, markets, countries, or inanimate objects (e.g., ads to be sampled, manufactured parts to be tested for quality control), etc. The **target population** is defined as the totality of cases that conform to some designated specifications. For example, a study aimed at establishing a demographic profile of frozen-pizza eaters requires specifying who is to be considered a frozen-pizza eater. Anyone who has ever eaten a frozen pizza? Those who eat at least one a month? A week? Researchers need to be explicit and very precise in defining the target group, and careful to actually sample the target population rather than some other population due to an inappropriate sampling strategy.

We take samples rather than canvas the entire population for several reasons: (1) Complete counts on populations are very costly. (2) A census would take so much time that the information would be obsolete by the time it was completed. (3) Sometimes a census is impossible. For example, in TQM studies, imagine testing the life of electric light bulbs. A 100% inspection using all bulbs until they burned out would reveal the average bulb life but would leave no product to sell. (4) A sample can be more accurate. Censuses involve large field staffs, which can introduce more nonsampling error.[1]

---

[1] Even the Bureau of the Census uses sample surveys to check the accuracy of various censuses.

Required Steps

Figure 11.1 outlines a six-step procedure that researchers can follow when drawing a sample of a population. First, **define the target population** about which you want to make an inference. You must decide whether the target population consists of individuals, households, business firms, other organizations, credit-card transactions, Web pages, or some other unit. In making this specification, you are also specifying what units are to be excluded, e.g., geographic boundaries, time periods, etc. For example, a target population may be defined as all consumers over 18, or women only, or those with a high school education only. A combination of respondent characteristics (age, gender, education, ethnicity, etc.) can also be used.[2]

In general, the simpler the definition of the target population, the higher the incidence and the easier and less costly it is to find the sample. Incidence refers to the percentage of the general population that satisfies the criteria defining the target population. When incidence is high (i.e., most people qualify for the study because only one, or very few, easily satisfied criteria are used to screen

FIGURE 11.1   Six-Step Procedure for Drawing a Sample

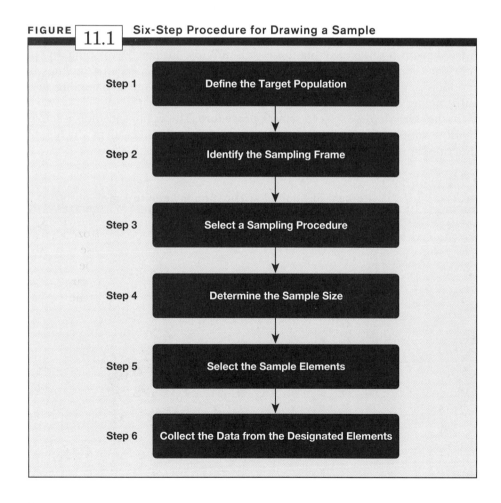

Step 1 Define the Target Population

Step 2 Identify the Sampling Frame

Step 3 Select a Sampling Procedure

Step 4 Determine the Sample Size

Step 5 Select the Sample Elements

Step 6 Collect the Data from the Designated Elements

[2] Specifying geographic boundaries is particularly difficult in international marketing research studies. The composition of the population can vary depending on the location within the country, e.g., northern Chile has a highly centralized Indian population, whereas the south has many individuals of European descent.

potential respondents), the cost and time to collect data are minimized. However, as the number of criteria used to describe what constitutes eligible respondents increases, so does the cost and time necessary to find them.

For example, Figure 11.2 shows the percentage of adults who participate in various sports. The data suggest that it would be more difficult and costly to focus a study on people who motorcycle (only 9% of all adults) than people who walk for health (59%).

Common sense helps. A large restaurant chain was puzzling over whether their customers wanted 60:40 health:taste or 60:40 taste:health in their product offerings. They'll never know whether they solved the problem because they messed up the sampling. They conducted surveys in urban environments, concentrating on young, high-income, white-collar professionals. They then located many of their retail units in low-income, blue-collar areas. Not surprisingly, the results didn't generalize, and sales didn't take off.

The second step in sampling is identifying the **sampling frame**, which is the list of elements from which the sample is drawn. A telephone book is an example of a sampling frame, which also illustrates the condition that there is rarely a perfect correspondence between the sampling frame and the target population of interest. Even though the target population may be all households in a particular metropolitan area, the telephone directory provides a somewhat inaccurate listing, because it omits those without phones or unlisted numbers and it double counts those with multiple listings. Developing an appropriate sampling frame can take some creativity—it may mean sampling via random-digit dialing in telephone surveys. Or it might mean sampling and subsampling to get the target population just right.

In the third step, we select a **sample procedure**. The options include a simple random sample, stratified samples, cluster samples, and others, all of which we'll describe shortly.

Population

→ Target population

→ Sampling frame

→ Sample

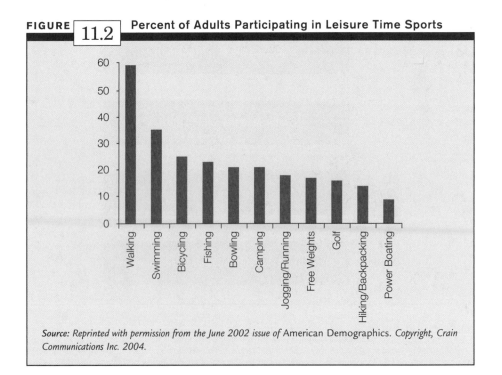

FIGURE 11.2   Percent of Adults Participating in Leisure Time Sports

Source: Reprinted with permission from the June 2002 issue of American Demographics. *Copyright, Crain Communications Inc. 2004.*

Step 4 in the sample selection process requires the **sample size** to be determined, an issue covered in the next chapter. Step 5 indicates that the researcher needs to **do the sampling**, i.e., choose the elements that will be included in the study. Finally, the researcher needs to actually **collect data** from the designated respondents.

Types of Sampling Plans

Sampling techniques can be divided into probability and nonprobability samples. For **probability samples**, each population element has a known, nonzero chance of being included in the sample. It is not necessary that the probabilities of selection be equal, only that one can specify the probabilities. With **nonprobability samples**, in contrast, there is no way of estimating the probability that any population element will be included in the sample, and thus there is no way of ensuring that the sample is representative of the population. All nonprobability samples rely on personal judgment somewhere in the process, and although these judgment samples may indeed yield good estimates of a population characteristic, they do not permit an objective evaluation of the adequacy of the sample. It is only when the elements have been selected with known probabilities that one can evaluate the precision of a sample result.[3]

Samples can be fixed or sequential. **Fixed samples** imply *a priori* determination of sample size and they are the most common (e.g., budget proposals are contingent on sample size). Just so you know, **sequential samples** aim at answering the research question on the basis of accumulated evidence. If the evidence is not conclusive after a small sample is taken, more observations are made; if still inconclusive, a larger sample is drawn; and so on.

Both probability and nonprobability sampling plans can be further divided by type. Nonprobability samples, for instance, can be classified as convenience, judgment, or quota, whereas probability samples can be simple random, stratified, or cluster samples (see Figure 11.3).

FIGURE 11.3   Classification of Sampling Techniques

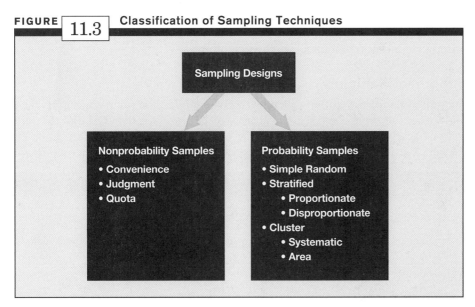

[3] The National Council on Public Polls distinguishes probability-based "scientific" polls from nonprobability-based "pseudo" polls wherein, e.g., respondents volunteer their opinions, e.g., via call-ins to 800 numbers (ncpp.org). Gallup Polls' experts concur, saying you can't have confidence in results without a random sample (gallup.com).

Nonprobability Samples

Nonprobability samples should be used with caution for two reasons: (1) They involve personal judgment somewhere in the selection process. Sometimes this judgment is imposed by the researcher, and sometimes it is left to individual field workers. (2) Sampling error cannot be assessed, which means we cannot place bounds on the precision of our estimates.

Convenience Samples

Examples of convenience samples abound:

- We talk to a few friends, and on the basis of their reactions, we infer the political sentiment of the country.
- A local radio station asks people to call in and express their reactions to some controversial issue, and the opinions expressed are interpreted as prevailing sentiment.
- We ask for volunteers and use those who come forward.

The problem with convenience samples, of course, is that we have no way of knowing if they are representative of the target population.

For example, it is not unusual for political parties or various rights groups to encourage their members to call in, frequently, to voice their opinions. Polls reported on the basis of volunteers calling one 900 phone number for "pro" and another number for "con" are another example of likely nonrepresentative samples. Who are the callers?

When a sample is not representative, increasing its size would not make it so. What is unfortunate is that many people believe the results of these polls are accurate.

An all-too-common use of convenience samples in international marketing research is to use transplanted expats from the countries being studied who are currently residing in the country where the study is being conducted (e.g., Mainland Chinese currently residing in the U.S.). These individuals typically represent the elite class, often already "westernized," and may not be in touch with current developments in their own country.

Judgment Samples

Judgment samples are often called purposive samples; the sample is handpicked because it can serve the research purpose or because it is believed that they are representative. For example, every four years at presidential election time, TV viewers see in-depth analyses of swing communities. These communities are

---

Ethical **Dilemma** 11.1

You are designing an experiment to compare the effectiveness of different types of commercials and need to recruit a large group of participants of varying ages to watch TV for an hour every night for a week. You approach your local church minister and tell her that you will make a donation to the church restoration fund for every member of the congregation who agrees to participate.

- When might incentives be coercive?
- Is it ethical to coerce people to participate in research?
- Will the quality of the data suffer from the coercive recruitment of participants?

handpicked because they are "representative" in that historically the winner there has been the next president. By monitoring these pivotal communities, election analysts are able to offer an early prediction of the eventual winner.

Purposive judgment samples may be useful in exploratory designs. When searching for ideas and insights, the researcher is not interested in sampling a cross section of opinion but rather in sampling those who can offer some perspective on the research question.

The **snowball sample** is a judgment sample that is sometimes used to sample special populations.[4] The researcher locates an initial set of respondents with the characteristics of the target population. These individuals then identify others with the desired characteristics. The sample "snowballs" by getting larger as participants identify still other possible respondents.

Judgment samples cannot be extrapolated to the population. For example, most people believe the Consumer Price Index (CPI) reflects prices everywhere in the U.S. Actually, the CPI is called the Consumer Price Index for Urban Wage Earners and Clerical Workers, and it samples a little over 50 cities, selected on the bases of judgment and political pressure.

Quota Samples

A third type of nonprobability sample is the quota sample. Quota samples attempt to ensure representativeness by selecting the sample to look like the population.

For example, if we wanted a representative sample of a business school's students and the sample contained no marketing majors, we would have serious reservations about the representativeness of the sample. We wouldn't be able to generalize any conclusions beyond the immediate sample. With a quota sample, the researcher could ensure that marketing majors would be included in about the same proportion as they occur in the entire business school.

Even if a quota sample looks like the target population with respect to major, gender, or other attributes, it could be far off with respect to some other important characteristic that may influence results. For example, if the study is concerned with images of domestic brands, it may matter whether field workers interview U.S. or international students. If a quota on country of origin is not specified, the sample is unlikely to just naturally reflect this characteristic.

Probability Samples

In probability samples, you could calculate the likelihood that any given population element will be included in the sample because the final sample elements are selected objectively by a specific process, not according to the whims of the researcher or field worker. Probability samples allow us to assess the amount of "sampling error" likely to occur.

Simple Random Sampling

You are probably already familiar with simple random samples, because they are used in statistics courses. In a simple random sample, each population element has not only a *known* but an *equal* chance of being selected, and every combination of n population elements is a sample possibility just as likely to occur as any other combination of n units.

---

[4] Snowball sampling is related to word-of-mouth, opinion leaders, and network and buzz marketing; e.g., Procter & Gamble finds influentials among their "mommy bloggers" to diffuse information about new products (Jack Neff, "P&G Relies on Power of Mommy Bloggers," *Advertising Age*, 79 (27), 4–24. See Julian Villanueva, Shijin Yoo, and Dominique M. Hanssens, "The Impact of Marketing-Induced Versus Word-of-Mouth Customer Acquisition on Customer Equity Growth," *Journal of Marketing Research*, 45 (1), 48–59.

Parent Population

To discuss probability sampling plans and sampling error, it's important to understand the notion of a sampling distribution.[5] Consider the population of 20 individuals shown in Table 11.1. This population can be described by certain parameters. A **parameter** is a characteristic or measure of a parent population; it is a fixed quantity that distinguishes one population from another. We can calculate a number of parameters to describe this population (e.g., average income, dispersion in educational levels, proportion of newspaper subscribers, etc.). The quantities are fixed in value and would be known perfectly if we could conduct an entire census on the population. However, we will select a sample and use its values to estimate the population parameters.

Suppose we wanted to estimate the average income in this population. First, on this small database, let's see what the true parameters are. (We'll use samples shortly.) Let μ denote the mean population income (a measure of central tendency) and σ^2 the variance of incomes (a measure of spread), defined as

$$\mu = \frac{\sum_{i=1}^{N} X_i}{N} = \frac{28,000 + 30,000 + \ldots + 66,000}{20} = 47,000$$

$$\sigma^2 = \frac{\sum_{i=1}^{N} (X_i - \mu)^2}{N} = \frac{(28,000 - 47,000)^2 + (30,000 - 47,000)^2 + \ldots + (66,000 - 47,000)^2}{20} = 133,000,000$$

where X_i is the value of the ith observation and N is the number of population elements. Thus, to compute the actual population mean, we divide the sum of all the values by the number of values making up the sum. To compute the population variance, we calculate the deviation of each value from the mean, square these deviations, sum them, and divide by N.

Derived Population

Estimates of the population parameters rest on similar calculations. A **statistic** is a characteristic or measure of a sample. We use the statistic to estimate the parameter.

Consider the derived population of all possible unique samples that can be drawn from the parent population. Say we're interested in a sample of size $n = 2$ (drawn by simple random sampling without replacement). Imagine the lottery machines that blow plastic balls around in a machine, and imagine that there are 20 balls, each with one of the incomes printed on it. Table 11.2 displays the derived population of all possible samples from following this procedure. There are 190 possible combinations of pairs of the 20 balls. For each combination, we calculate the sample mean. Thus, for the sample AB, the sample mean income $\bar{x}_1 = (28,000 + 30,000)/2 = 29,000$, and, in general,

$$\bar{x}_k = \frac{1}{n}\left(\sum_{i=1}^{n} X_i\right)$$

where k refers to the sample number, $\bar{x}$ to the sample average, and n to the sample size. Figure 11.4 displays the estimates of population mean income and

#	Element	Income (Dollars)	Education (Years)	Newspaper Subscription
1	A	28,000	8	X
2	B	30,000	9	Y
3	C	32,000	11	X
4	D	34,000	11	Y
5	E	36,000	11	X
6	F	38,000	12	Y
7	G	40,000	12	X
8	H	42,000	12	Y
9	I	44,000	12	X
10	J	46,000	12	Y
11	K	48,000	13	X
12	L	50,000	13	Y
13	M	52,000	14	X
14	N	54,000	14	Y
15	O	56,000	15	X
16	P	58,000	16	Y
17	Q	60,000	16	X
18	R	62,000	17	Y
19	S	64,000	18	X
20	T	66,000	18	Y

TABLE 11.1   Hypothetical Population

the amount of error in each estimate when samples $k = 25, 62, 108, 147,$ and 189 are drawn.

Note that in practice, we do not actually generate the derived population. All the practitioner does is draw one sample of size n. But the researcher makes use of the "derived population" concept in making inferences. (We show how shortly.) Also note that the derived population is defined as the population of all possible distinguishable samples that can be drawn via the sampling plan. Change any part of the sampling plan, and the derived population also changes. For example, with samples of size 3, ABC is a sample possibility, and there are 1,140 possibilities (not just 190). If the researcher samples with replacement, the samples could include AA, BB, and so on.

Sample Mean versus Population Mean

Now consider the relationship between the sample means and the population mean. Note three things. First, if we add the sample means in Table 11.2 and divide by the number of samples—in other words, average the averages—this yields:

$$\frac{29,000 + 30,000 + \ldots + 65,000}{190} = 47,000$$

which is the mean of the population. This is what is meant by an unbiased statistic. A statistic is **unbiased** when its average value equals the population parameter it is supposed to estimate. Note that even though the statistic overall is unbiased, a particular estimate may be far from the true population value (e.g., look at samples AB or ST).

Second, consider the spread of these sample estimates. We saw that the population variance $\sigma^2 = 133,000,000$. The variance of mean incomes is computed

Derived Population of All Possible Samples of Size $n = 2$ with Simple Random Selection

TABLE 11.2

k	Identity	Mean	k	Identity	Mean	k	Identity	Mean	k	Identity	Mean
1	AB	29,000	51	CQ	46,000	101	GI	42,000	151	KQ	54,000
2	AC	30,000	52	CR	47,000	102	GJ	43,000	152	KR	55,000
3	AD	31,000	53	CS	48,000	103	GK	44,000	153	KS	56,000
4	AE	32,000	54	CT	49,000	104	GL	45,000	154	KT	57,000
5	AF	33,000	55	DE	35,000	105	GM	46,000	155	LM	51,000
6	AG	34,000	56	DF	36,000	106	GN	47,000	156	LN	52,000
7	AH	35,000	57	DG	37,000	107	GO	48,000	157	LO	53,000
8	AI	36,000	58	DH	38,000	108	GP	49,000	158	LP	54,000
9	AJ	37,000	59	DI	39,000	109	GQ	50,000	159	LQ	55,000
10	AK	38,000	60	DJ	40,000	110	GR	51,000	160	LR	56,000
11	AL	39,000	61	DK	41,000	111	GS	52,000	161	LS	57,000
12	AM	40,000	62	DL	42,000	112	GT	53,000	162	LT	58,000
13	AN	41,000	63	DM	43,000	113	HI	43,000	163	MN	53,000
14	AO	42,000	64	DN	44,000	114	HJ	44,000	164	MO	54,000
15	AP	43,000	65	DO	45,000	115	HK	45,000	165	MP	55,000
16	AQ	44,000	66	DP	46,000	116	HL	46,000	166	MQ	56,000
17	AR	45,000	67	DQ	47,000	117	HM	47,000	167	MR	57,000
18	AS	46,000	68	DR	48,000	118	HN	48,000	168	MS	58,000
19	AT	47,000	69	DS	49,000	119	HO	49,000	169	MT	59,000
20	BC	31,000	70	DT	50,000	120	HP	50,000	170	NO	55,000
21	BD	32,000	71	EF	37,000	121	HQ	51,000	171	NP	56,000
22	BE	33,000	72	EG	38,000	122	HR	52,000	172	NQ	57,000
23	BF	34,000	73	EH	39,000	123	HS	53,000	173	NR	58,000
24	BG	35,000	74	EI	40,000	124	HT	54,000	174	NS	59,000
25	BH	36,000	75	EJ	41,000	125	IJ	45,000	175	NT	60,000
26	BI	37,000	76	EK	42,000	126	IK	46,000	176	OP	57,000
27	BJ	38,000	77	EL	43,000	127	IL	47,000	177	OQ	58,000
28	BK	39,000	78	EM	44,000	128	IM	48,000	178	OR	59,000
29	BL	40,000	79	EN	45,000	129	IN	49,000	179	OS	60,000
30	BM	41,000	80	EO	46,000	130	IO	50,000	180	OT	61,000
31	BN	42,000	81	EP	47,000	131	IP	51,000	181	PQ	59,000
32	BO	43,000	82	EQ	48,000	132	IQ	52,000	182	PR	60,000
33	BP	44,000	83	ER	49,000	133	IR	53,000	183	PS	61,000
34	BQ	45,000	84	ES	50,000	134	IS	54,000	184	PT	62,000
35	BR	46,000	85	ET	51,000	135	IT	55,000	185	QR	61,000
36	BS	47,000	86	FG	39,000	136	JK	47,000	186	QS	62,000
37	BT	48,000	87	FH	40,000	137	JL	48,000	187	QT	63,000
38	CD	33,000	88	FI	41,000	138	JM	49,000	188	RS	63,000
39	CE	34,000	89	FJ	42,000	139	JN	50,000	189	RT	64,000
40	CF	35,000	90	FK	43,000	140	JO	51,000	190	ST	65,000
41	CG	36,000	91	FL	44,000	141	JP	52,000			
42	CH	37,000	92	FM	45,000	142	JQ	53,000			
43	CI	38,000	93	FN	46,000	143	JR	10,800			
44	CJ	39,000	94	FO	47,000	144	JS	11,000			
45	CK	40,000	95	FP	48,000	145	JT	11,200			
46	CL	41,000	96	FQ	49,000	146	KL	9,800			
47	CM	42,000	97	FR	50,000	147	KM	10,000			
48	CN	43,000	98	FS	51,000	148	KN	10,200			
49	CO	44,000	99	FT	52,000	149	KO	10,400			
50	CP	45,000	100	GH	41,000	150	KP	10,600			

FIGURE 11.4 Possible Samples and Their Respective Errors when Estimating the Population Means

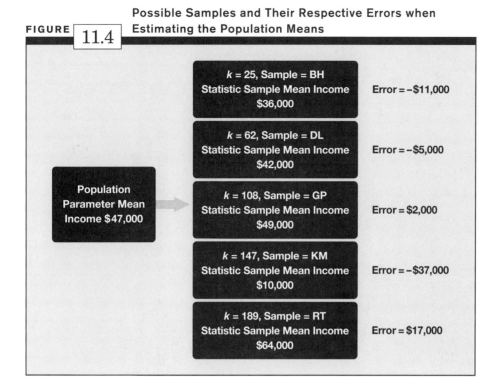

similarly—that is, by taking the deviation of each mean around its overall mean, squaring and summing these deviations, and then dividing by the number of cases:

$$\frac{(29,000 - 47,000)^2 + (30,000 - 47,000)^2 + ... + (65,000 - 47,000)^2}{190} = 63,000,000$$

Note the relationship between σ^2 (the variance of the variable in the original population) and the spread of the estimates in the derived population (called $\sigma_{\bar{x}}^2$ to denote the variance of means). Instead of direct calculations using the 190 sample estimates, $\sigma_{\bar{x}}^2$ could have also been calculated by the following expression:[6]

$$\sigma_{\bar{x}}^2 = \frac{(N - n)\sigma^2}{(N - 1)n} = \frac{(20 - 2)133,000,000}{(20 - 1)2} = 63,000,000$$

Third, consider the distributions. Figure 11.5 is the histogram representing the sampling distribution of the statistic. It is symmetrical about the population mean value of 47,000. The frequencies are those in Table 11.3.

The notion of **sampling distribution** is the cornerstone of statistical inference. If you know the sampling distribution for a statistic, you can make an inference about the corresponding population parameter. Researchers then rely on these distributions—whether they are for a sample mean, sample proportion, etc.—in making their inferences from single samples to population values. Note that the distribution of sample means is mound shaped and symmetrical about the population mean with samples of size 2.

---

[6] The expression $(N - n)/(N - 1)$ is known as the finite population correction factor. Whenever the sample size is less than 10% of the population size, the finite population correction factor is ignored, since $(N - n)/(N - 1)$ is very close to 1 and the more complex form $\sigma_{\bar{x}}^2 = (\sigma^2/n)(N - n)/(N - 1)$ reduces to $\sigma_{\bar{x}}^2 = \sigma^2/n$.

FIGURE 11.5   Distribution of Mean Estimates in Derived Population

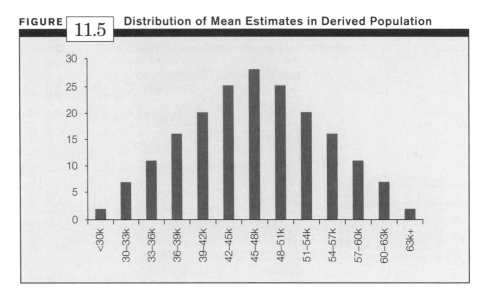

Recapitulating, we have shown that:

1. The mean of all possible sample means is equal to the population mean.

2. The variance of sample means is related to the population variance:

$$\sigma_{\bar{x}}^2 = \frac{(N - n)\sigma^2}{(N - 1)n}$$

3. The distribution of sample means is mound shaped, whereas the population is spiked.

This first result is true in general for simple random sampling (with or without replacement, from a finite or infinite parent population). The second result is true only when sampling is from a finite population without replacement. If sampling from an infinite population or when sampling from a finite population with replacement, the simpler expression $\sigma_{\bar{x}}^2 = \sigma^2/n$ holds. (For many, if not most, problems in marketing, this simpler expression is used.)

TABLE 11.3   Classification of Estimates by Size

Sample Mean	#Samples
≤$30,000	2
$30,500–33,000	7
$33,500–36,000	11
$36,500–39,000	16
$39,500–42,000	20
$42,500–45,000	25
$45,500–48,000	28
$48,500–51,000	25
$51,500–54,000	20
$54,500–57,000	16
$57,500–60,000	11
$60,500–63,000	7
$63,500+	2

Central-Limit Theorem

The third result of a mound-shaped distribution of estimates provides preliminary evidence of the operation of the Central-Limit Theorem, which holds that if simple random samples of size n are drawn from a parent population with mean μ and variance σ^2, then when n is large, the sample mean will be approximately normally distributed with mean equal to μ and variance equal to $\sigma_{\bar{x}}^2 = \sigma^2/n$. The approximation becomes more accurate as n becomes larger.

This result is important—it means that regardless of the shape of the population, the distribution of sample means will be normal if the sample is large enough. How large is large enough? If the distribution of the variable in the population is normal, the means of samples of size $n = 1$ will be normally distributed. If the distribution of the variable is symmetrical but not normal, very small samples will produce normal distributions. If the population distribution is highly skewed, larger samples will be needed. Fortunately, the normal distribution of the statistic occurs with samples of relatively small size, as Figure 11.6 indicates.

Confidence Interval Estimates

How does all this information help us make inferences about the population mean? It all ties together in the following way.

FIGURE 11.6   Distribution of Sample Means for Different Samples Sizes, Population Shapes

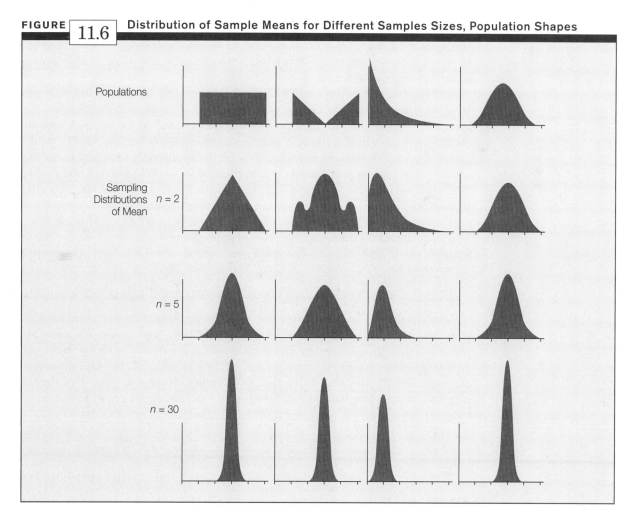

It is known that with any normal distribution, a specific percentage of all observations is within a certain number of standard deviations of the mean, for example, 95% of the values are within ±1.96 standard deviations of the mean. The distribution of sample means is normal if the Central-Limit Theorem holds. The mean of this sampling distribution is the population mean μ, and its standard deviation is given by the standard error of the mean, $\sigma_{\bar{x}}^2 = \sigma^2/n$. Therefore, it is true that:

- 68.26% of the sample means will be within $\pm 1\sigma_{\bar{x}}$ of the population mean.
- 95.45% of the sample means will be within $\pm 2\sigma_{\bar{x}}$ of the population mean.
- 99.73% of the sample means will be within $\pm 3\sigma_{\bar{x}}$ of the population mean.

In general, $\mu \pm z\sigma_{\bar{x}}$ will contain some certain proportion of all sample means, depending on the selected value of z. This expression can be rewritten as an inequality relation:

$$\mu - z\sigma_{\bar{x}} \leq \bar{x} \leq \mu + z\sigma_{\bar{x}} \tag{1}$$

which is held to be true a certain percentage of the time and which implies that the sample mean will be in the interval formed by adding and subtracting a certain number of standard deviations to the mean value of the distribution. This inequality can be translated to

$$\bar{x} - z\sigma_{\bar{x}} \leq \mu \leq \bar{x} + z\sigma_{\bar{x}} \tag{2}$$

If equation 1 is true, say, 95% of the time ($z = 1.96$), equation 2 is also true 95% of the time. When we make an inference on the basis of a single sample mean, we make use of equation 2.

It is important to note that equation 2 says nothing about the interval constructed from a particular sample as including the population mean. Rather, the interval addresses the sampling procedure. The interval around a single sample mean may or may not contain the true population mean. Our confidence in our inference rests on the property that 95% of all the intervals we could construct under that sampling plan would contain the true value. We trust or hope (or are "95% confident") that our sample is one of those 95 out of 100 that includes the true value (when $z = 1.96$).[7]

To illustrate this point, suppose the distribution of sample means of size $n = 2$ was normal, and say the sampling process yielded sample AB, in which the mean income was $29,000. The 95% confidence interval ($z = 1.96$) using equation 2 would then be ($\sigma_{\bar{x}} = \sqrt{\sigma_{\bar{x}}^2} = \sqrt{63,000,000}$) = 7937.25:

$$29,000 - 1.96(7937.25) \leq \mu \leq 29,000 + 1.96(7937.25) = 13,443 \leq \mu \leq 44,557$$

The confidence interval does not include the true (in this case, known) population value, and an inferential error would have been made. The example illustrates that after the sample has been drawn, it is a matter of fact whether the particular interval estimate covers the population mean. Table 11.4 illustrates the outcome for the first 10 of the 190 samples. Note that only 7 of the 10 intervals contain the true population mean. Confidence in the estimate arises

---

[7] This interpretation of a confidence interval is the classical statistics argument, which holds that the parameter is fixed in value. Thus, we do not interpret the statement probabilistically (i.e., "there is a 95% chance that the population mean is in our confidence interval"—wrong!), because a given interval *will* or *will not* contain the population parameter. Bayesian analysts adopt a different perspective. They combine judgment with sample information to produce values for the unknown parameter and then interpret the interval as a probability statement.

Confidence Intervals for First 10 Samples, Assuming the Distribution of Sample Means Was Normal

TABLE 11.4

Sample #	Identity	Mean	Lower Limit	Upper Limit	Confidence Interval True $\mu = 47,000$
1	AB	29,000	13,445	44,555	(_×_) ↓
2	AC	30,000	14,445	45,555	(_×_)
3	AD	31,000	15,445	46,555	(_×_)
4	AE	32,000	16,445	47,555	(_×_)
5	AF	33,000	17,445	48,555	(_×_)
6	AG	34,000	18,445	49,555	(_×_)
7	AH	35,000	19,445	50,555	(_×_)
8	AI	36,000	20,445	51,555	(_×_)
9	AJ	37,000	21,445	52,555	(_×_)
10	AK	38,000	22,445	53,555	(_×_)

because of the procedure, not because of a particular estimate. The procedure is one that with, say, a 95% confidence interval, if 100 samples were to be drawn, 95 of the confidence intervals would include the true population value.

Probability samples allow an estimate of the **precision** of the results in terms of how closely the estimates will tend to cluster around the true value. The greater the standard error of the statistic, the more variable, or less precise, the estimate.

If it disturbs you that the confidence level applies to the procedure and not to a particular sample result, you can take refuge in the fact that you can control the level of confidence with which the population value is estimated. Thus, if you do not wish to take the risk that you might have 1 of the 5 sample intervals in 100 that does not contain the population value, you might use a 99% confidence interval, in which the risk is that only 1 in 100 sample intervals does not contain the population mean. Further, if you are willing to increase the size of the sample, you can increase your confidence and at the same time increase the precision of the population value estimate (a topic explored in the next chapter).

Population Variance Unknown

There is one further complication. The confidence interval estimate made use of three values: μ, Z, and $\sigma_{\bar{x}}$. The mean $\bar{x}$ is computed from the sample, and z is specified to produce the desired level of confidence. But what about $\sigma_{\bar{x}}$? It is equal to $\sigma_{\bar{x}} = \sigma^2/\sqrt{n}$, and thus to calculate it, we need to know the standard deviation of the variable in the population. What do we do if σ is unknown? No problem. We can either use the value from a previous related marketing study, or, once the sample is selected and the information gathered, we can calculate the sample variance to estimate the population variance. The unbiased sample variance $\sigma^2 = s^2$ is calculated as

The equation for a standard error may save your life some day: $\sigma_{\bar{x}} = \sigma/\sqrt{n}$

$$s^2 = \frac{1}{n-1} \sum_{i=1}^{n} (X_i - \bar{x})^2$$

where $\bar{x}$ is the sample mean and n the sample size.[8] We compute the sample variance and use it to get the estimate of the standard error of the mean. When

[8] Division by *n*, the sample size, is more intuitive because it looks like an average (here, the average of the deviations squared). However, when the sample variance is defined with the "*n*" divisor, it produces a biased estimate. Thus, we use the unbiased estimate of the sample variance (based on *n* − 1).

the population variance, σ^2, is known, the standard error of the mean, $\sigma_{\bar{x}}$, is also known because $\sigma_{\bar{x}} = \sigma/\sqrt{n}$. When the population variance is unknown, the standard error of the mean can only be estimated. The estimate is given by $s_{\bar{x}}$, which equals $s/\sqrt{n}$, i.e., the sample standard deviation is substituted for the population standard deviation. Thus, if we draw sample AB, with its mean of 29,000,

$$s^2 = \frac{(28,000 - 29,000)^2 + (30,000 - 29,000)^2}{1} = 2,000,000$$

thus, $s = 1414$, $s_{\bar{x}} = s/\sqrt{n} = 1414/\sqrt{2} = 1000$, and the 95% confidence interval is now

$$29,000 - 1.96(1000) \leq \mu \leq 29,000 + 1.96(1000) = 27,040 \leq \mu \leq 30,960$$

which is somewhat smaller than before.[9]

Drawing the Simple Random Sample

Simple random samples are drawn using a table (hardcopy or in computer procedures like Excel) of random numbers.[10] Using a random number table involves the following sequence of steps. First, the elements of the parent population are numbered from 1 to N. Next, the numbers in the table are treated to have the same number of digits as N. With $N = 20$, two-digit numbers would be used; if N is between 100 and 999, three-digit numbers are required; and so on. Third, a starting point is determined randomly. We might simply open the table to some arbitrary place and point to a position on the page with our eyes closed. Since the numbers in a random number table are without order, it doesn't matter where we begin.[11] Finally, we proceed in some arbitrary direction (e.g., up, down, or across) and select those elements for the sample for which there is a match of serial number and random number.

To illustrate, consider the partial list of random numbers contained in Table 11.5. Since $N = 20$, we need to work with only two digits, and therefore we can use the entries in the table as is, instead of having to combine columns to produce numbers covering the range of serial numbers. Suppose that we had previously decided to read down and that our arbitrary start was in the 11th row, 4th column, specifically the number 77. This number is too high and would be discarded (our population elements are numbered only 1 to 20). The next two numbers would also be discarded, but the fourth entry, 02, would be used, because 2 corresponds to one of the serial numbers in the list, element B. The next five numbers would also be passed over as too large, but the number 05 would designate the inclusion of element E. Elements B and E would thus represent our sample of two.

An alternative strategy is to use a computer program to generate the random numbers. These algorithms are generally called "pseudo" random number

[9] The t-distribution would be used when σ was unknown; more on this in the chapter on hypothesis testing.
[10] The national draft during the Vietnam War using a lottery serves as an example of why tables or computers are better random number generators than "mechanical" devices like the aforementioned lottery ball machines. For that war, draft priorities were determined by drawing disks with birth dates stamped on them from a large container in full view of a TV audience. Unfortunately, the dates of the year had been poured into the bowl systematically, January first and December last. The bowl was then stirred vigorously, but still, December dates tended to be chosen first and January dates last. The procedure was later revised to produce a more random selection process. On a lighter note, there was an episode of the TV show *Monk* in which a lottery was fixed by painting the numbers of certain balls with metallic paint that would be magnetically attracted to equipment in the news center and therefore pop up with greater likelihood than nontreated balls.
[11] Note that one cannot discard a sample because it does not "look right."

TABLE **11.5**   **Abridged List of Random Numbers**

10 09 73 25 33	76 52 01 35 86	34 67 35 48 76	80 95 90 91 17	39 29 27 49 45
37 54 20 48 05	64 89 47 42 96	24 80 52 40 37	20 63 61 04 02	00 82 29 16 65
08 42 26 89 53	19 64 50 93 03	23 20 90 25 60	15 95 33 47 64	35 08 03 36 06
99 01 90 25 29	09 37 67 07 15	38 31 13 11 65	88 67 67 43 97	04 43 62 76 59
12 80 79 99 70	80 15 73 61 47	64 03 23 66 53	98 95 11 68 77	12 17 17 68 33
66 06 57 47 17	34 07 27 68 50	36 69 73 61 70	65 81 33 98 85	11 19 92 91 70
31 06 01 08 05	45 57 18 24 06	35 30 34 26 14	86 79 90 74 39	23 40 30 97 32
85 26 97 76 02	02 05 16 56 92	68 66 57 48 18	73 05 38 52 47	18 62 38 85 79
63 57 33 21 35	05 32 54 70 48	90 55 35 75 48	28 46 82 87 09	83 49 12 56 24
73 79 64 57 53	03 52 96 47 78	35 80 83 42 82	60 93 52 03 44	35 27 38 84 35
98 52 01 77 67	14 90 56 86 07	22 10 94 05 58	60 97 09 34 33	50 50 07 39 98
11 80 50 54 31	39 80 82 77 32	50 72 56 82 48	29 40 52 42 01	52 77 56 78 51
83 45 29 96 34	06 28 89 80 83	13 74 67 00 78	18 47 54 06 10	68 71 17 78 17
88 68 54 02 00	86 50 75 84 01	36 76 66 79 51	90 36 47 64 93	29 60 91 10 62
99 59 46 73 48	87 51 76 49 69	91 82 60 89 28	93 78 56 13 68	23 47 83 41 13
65 48 11 76 74	17 46 85 09 50	58 04 77 69 74	73 03 95 71 86	40 21 81 65 44
80 12 43 56 35	17 72 70 80 15	45 31 82 23 74	21 11 57 82 53	14 38 55 37 63
74 35 09 98 17	77 40 27 72 14	43 23 60 02 10	45 52 16 42 37	96 28 60 26 55
69 91 62 68 03	66 25 22 91 48	36 93 68 72 03	76 62 11 39 90	94 40 05 64 18
09 89 32 05 05	14 22 56 85 14	46 42 75 67 88	96 29 77 88 22	54 38 21 45 98
91 49 91 45 23	68 47 92 76 86	46 16 28 35 54	94 75 08 99 23	37 08 92 00 48
80 33 69 45 98	26 94 03 68 58	70 29 73 41 35	53 14 03 33 40	42 05 08 23 41
44 10 48 19 49	85 15 74 79 54	32 97 92 65 75	57 60 04 08 81	22 22 20 64 13
12 55 07 37 42	11 10 00 20 40	12 86 07 46 97	96 64 48 94 39	28 70 72 58 15
63 60 64 93 29	16 50 53 44 84	40 21 95 25 63	43 65 17 70 82	07 20 73 17 90
61 19 69 04 46	26 45 74 77 74	51 92 43 37 29	65 39 45 95 93	42 58 26 05 27
15 47 44 52 66	95 27 07 99 53	59 36 78 38 48	82 39 61 01 18	33 21 15 94 66
94 55 72 85 72	67 89 75 43 87	54 62 24 44 31	91 19 04 25 92	92 92 74 59 73
42 48 11 62 13	97 34 40 81 21	16 86 84 87 67	03 07 11 20 59	25 70 14 66 70
23 52 37 83 17	73 20 88 98 37	68 93 59 14 16	26 25 22 96 63	05 52 28 25 62
04 49 35 24 94	75 24 63 38 24	45 86 25 10 25	61 96 27 93 35	65 33 71 24 72
00 54 99 76 54	64 05 18 81 59	96 11 96 38 96	54 69 28 23 91	23 28 72 95 29
35 96 31 53 07	26 89 80 93 54	33 35 13 54 62	77 97 45 00 24	90 10 33 93 33
59 80 80 83 91	45 42 72 68 42	83 60 94 97 00	13 02 12 48 92	78 56 52 01 06
46 06 88 52 36	01 39 09 22 86	77 28 14 40 77	93 91 08 36 47	70 61 74 29 41
32 17 90 05 97	87 37 92 52 41	05 56 70 70 07	86 74 31 71 57	85 39 41 18 38
69 43 26 14 06	20 11 74 52 04	15 95 66 00 00	18 74 39 24 23	97 11 89 63 38
19 56 54 14 30	01 75 87 53 79	40 41 92 15 85	66 67 43 68 06	84 96 28 52 07
45 15 51 49 38	19 47 60 72 46	43 66 79 45 43	59 04 79 00 33	20 82 66 95 41
94 86 43 19 94	36 16 81 08 51	34 88 88 15 51	01 54 03 54 56	05 01 45 11 76
98 08 62 48 26	45 24 02 84 04	44 99 90 88 96	39 09 47 34 07	35 44 13 18 80
33 18 51 62 32	41 94 15 09 49	89 43 54 85 81	88 69 54 19 94	37 54 87 30 43
80 95 10 04 06	96 38 27 07 74	20 15 12 33 87	25 01 62 52 98	94 62 46 11 71
79 75 24 91 40	71 96 12 82 96	69 86 10 25 91	74 85 22 05 39	00 38 75 95 79
18 63 33 25 37	98 14 50 65 71	31 01 02 46 74	05 45 56 14 27	77 93 89 19 36
74 02 94 39 02	77 55 73 22 70	97 79 01 71 19	52 52 75 80 21	80 81 45 17 48
54 17 84 56 11	80 99 33 71 43	05 33 51 29 69	56 12 71 92 55	36 04 09 03 24
11 66 44 98 83	52 07 98 48 27	59 38 17 15 39	09 97 33 34 40	88 46 12 33 56
48 32 47 79 28	31 24 96 47 10	02 29 53 68 70	32 30 75 75 46	15 02 00 99 94
69 07 49 41 38	87 63 79 19 76	35 58 40 44 01	10 51 82 16 15	01 84 87 69 38

generators—after all, if a computer subroutine is generating the numbers, they are programmed, not random. But they're programmed to be as independent as possible (e.g., knowing a string of numbers does not help you predict subsequent numbers), hence appearing as random as possible.

On a final note, a simple random sample requires a numbered list of population elements, which means that the identity of each member of the target population must be known. For some populations this is no problem; e.g., if the study is to be conducted among *Fortune* magazine's list of the 500 largest corporations in the U.S., the list is readily available, and a simple random sample of these firms could be selected easily. For many other target populations, the list is harder to come by (e.g., all families living in a particular city).

Simple probability sampling is the most frequently used sampling scheme. But to give you a flavor for some alternatives, we show you two—stratified and cluster sampling.

Main types of *probability sampling*:

1. Simple probability sampling

2. Stratified sampling

3. Cluster sampling

Stratified Sampling

A stratified sample is a probability sample that is distinguished by these two steps:

1. The population is divided into *mutually exclusive and exhaustive* subsets.

2. A simple random sample of elements is chosen independently *from each* subset.

It is up to the marketer to choose the criterion or criteria used to create the groups. The subsets are called **strata** or subpopulations. Every population element is assigned to one and only one stratum and no population elements are omitted.

To illustrate, assume we divide our hypothetical population in Table 11.1 into two strata on the basis of educational level (you could use more than two strata if you wished). Suppose all those with a high school education or less are considered as one stratum and those with more education form another. Table 11.6 displays the results of this stratification procedure; elements A through J form what is labeled the first stratum and elements K through T form the second stratum.

Stage 2 in the process then requires that a simple random sample be drawn independently from each stratum. Suppose we wanted a final sample of size 2; we would select one element from each stratum. Within each stratum, the population elements are serially numbered from 1 to 10 like a simple

TABLE 11.6   Stratification of Hypothetical Population of Education

Stratum I Elements	Stratum II Elements
A	K
B	L
C	M
D	N
E	O
F	P
G	Q
H	R
I	S
J	T

probability sample, and a table of random numbers is consulted. The first number encountered between 1 and 10 designates the element from the first stratum. The element from the second stratum can be selected after another independent start or by continuing from the first randomly determined start. In either case it would again be designated by the first encounter with a number between 1 and 10.

Derived Population

Although only one sample of size 2 is selected, let us look at this derived population of all possible samples of size 2 for this sampling plan (see Table 11.7). Note that every possible combination of sample elements is no longer a possibility, since any combination of two elements within the same stratum is precluded. There are now only 100 possible combinations (not 190).

Sampling Distribution

Table 11.8 contains the classification of sample means by size, and Figure 11.7 displays the plot of this sample statistic. Note that in relation to Figure 11.5 (for simple random sampling), stratified sampling can produce a more concentrated distribution of estimates. This suggests one reason that we might choose a stratified sample: Stratified samples can produce sample statistics that are more precise (i.e., smaller error). With the stratification variable, there are fewer sample means that deviate widely from the population mean.

TABLE 11.7 **Derived Population of All Possible Samples of Size $n = 2$ with Stratified Selection**

K	Identity	Mean	k	Identity	Mean	k	Identity	Mean	k	Identity	Mean
1	AK	38,000	26	CP	45,000	51	FK	43,000	76	HP	50,000
2	AL	39,000	27	CQ	46,000	52	FL	44,000	77	HQ	51,000
3	AM	40,000	28	CR	47,000	53	FM	45,000	78	HR	52,000
4	AN	41,000	29	CS	48,000	54	FN	46,000	79	HS	53,000
5	AO	42,000	30	CT	49,000	55	FO	47,000	80	HT	54,000
6	AP	43,000	31	DK	41,000	56	FP	48,000	81	IK	46,000
7	AQ	44,000	32	DL	42,000	57	FQ	49,000	82	IL	47,000
8	AR	45,000	33	DM	43,000	58	FR	50,000	83	IM	48,000
9	AS	46,000	34	DN	44,000	59	FS	51,000	84	IN	49,000
10	AT	47,000	35	DO	45,000	60	FT	52,000	85	IO	50,000
11	BK	39,000	36	DP	46,000	61	GK	44,000	86	IP	51,000
12	BL	40,000	37	DQ	47,000	62	GL	45,000	87	IQ	52,000
13	BM	41,000	38	DR	48,000	63	GM	46,000	88	IR	53,000
14	BN	42,000	39	DS	49,000	64	GN	47,000	89	IS	54,000
15	BO	43,000	40	DT	50,000	65	GO	48,000	90	IT	55,000
16	BP	44,000	41	EK	42,000	66	GP	49,000	91	JK	47,000
17	BQ	45,000	42	EL	43,000	67	GQ	50,000	92	JL	48,000
18	BR	46,000	43	EM	44,000	68	GR	51,000	93	JM	49,000
19	BS	47,000	44	EN	45,000	69	GS	52,000	94	JN	50,000
20	BT	48,000	45	EO	46,000	70	GT	53,000	95	JO	51,000
21	CK	40,000	46	EP	47,000	71	HK	45,000	96	JP	52,000
22	CL	41,000	47	EQ	48,000	72	HL	46,000	97	JQ	53,000
23	CM	42,000	48	ER	49,000	73	IIM	47,000	98	JR	54,000
24	CN	43,000	49	ES	50,000	74	HN	48,000	99	JS	55,000
25	CO	44,000	50	ET	52,000	75	HO	49,000	100	JT	56,000

TABLE 11.8	Classification of Sample Means by Size with Stratified Sampling	
	Sample Mean	#Samples
	36,500–39,000	3
	39,500–42,000	12
	42,500–45,000	21
	45,500–48,000	28
	48,500–51,000	21
	51,500–54,000	12
	54,500–57,000	3

A second reason for drawing a stratified sample is to investigate some characteristic for particular subgroups. For example, by stratifying, we can guarantee representation in our sample of both those with a high school education or less and those with more education.

This feature can be extremely important when sampling from populations with rare segments. For example, the upper class represents only 3% of the total population, yet it might be an important segment to, say, a diamond ring manufacturer. It is often true of many populations in marketing that a small subset accounts for a large proportion of the behavior of interest (the so-called 80-20 rule, with 20% of the customers accounting for 80% of the purchases). Stratified sampling ensures representation from each subgroup.

Confidence Interval Estimate

In establishing a confidence interval with a simple random sample, we saw that we needed three things for $\bar{x} - zs_{\bar{x}} \leq \mu \leq \bar{x} + zs_{\bar{x}}$:

1. The confidence level, to select a z value

2. A sample mean $\bar{x}$

3. An estimate of the amount of sampling error, which was given by $s_{\bar{x}} = s/\sqrt{n}$

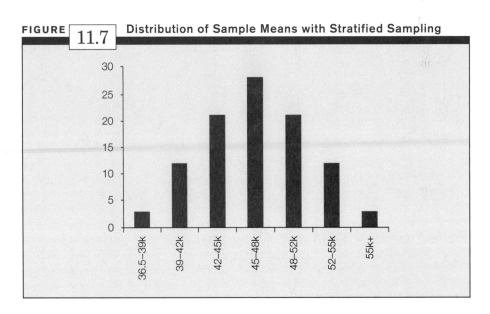

FIGURE 11.7   Distribution of Sample Means with Stratified Sampling

The same three quantities are required for making inferences with a stratified sample. The only difference in the procedure occurs in the way items 2 and 3 are generated. With stratified sampling, the sample estimate of the population mean and the standard error of estimate are determined by "appropriately weighting" the individual strata results.

What are the appropriate weights? They are related to the stratum population size relative to the total population size. Suppose two elements were sampled from each stratum, for a total sample of 4. In particular, suppose that B and E were randomly selected from the first stratum, and N and S from the second. Table 11.9 contains the sample means, sample variances, and estimated standard errors of estimate for each stratum, calculated exactly as before.

We first combine the strata sample means to produce an estimate of the population mean. The weights here are the relative proportions of the population in each of the strata, that is,

$$\bar{x}_{st} = \sum_{h=1}^{L} \frac{N_h}{N} \bar{x}_h \qquad (3)$$

where

N_h is the number of elements in the population in stratum h

N is the total size of the population

$\bar{x}_h$ is the sample mean for stratum h

$\bar{x}_{st}$ is the sample mean for a stratified sample

TABLE 11.9 **Sample Means, Sample Variances, and Estimated Standard Errors of Estimates for Each Stratum**

Stratum I

Element	Income
B	30,000
E	36,000

Mean:

$$\bar{x}_1 = \frac{1}{n_1} \sum_{i=1}^{n_1} X_i = \frac{30,000 + 36,000}{2} = 33,000$$

Variance:

$$s_1^2 = \frac{1}{n_1 - 1} \sum_{i=1}^{n_1} (X_i - \bar{x}_1)^2$$
$$= \frac{(30,000 - 33,000)^2 + (36,000 - 33,000)^2}{2 - 1}$$
$$= 18,000,000$$

Variance of estimate:

$$s_{\bar{x}_1}^2 = \frac{s_1^2}{n_1} = \frac{18,000,000}{2} = 9,000,000$$

Standard error of estimate:

$$s_{\bar{x}_1} = \sqrt{s_{\bar{x}_1}^2} = \sqrt{9,000,000} = 3000$$

Stratum II

Element	Income
N	54,000
S	64,000

Mean:

$$\bar{x}_2 = \frac{1}{n_2} \sum_{i=1}^{n_2} X_i = \frac{54,000 + 64,000}{2} = 59,000$$

Variance:

$$s_2^2 = \frac{1}{n_2 - 1} \sum_{i=1}^{n_2} (X_i - \bar{x}_2)^2$$
$$= \frac{(54,000 - 59,000)^2 + (64,000 - 59,000)^2}{2 - 1}$$
$$= 50,000,000$$

Variance of estimate:

$$s_{\bar{x}_2}^2 = \frac{s_2^2}{n_2} = \frac{50,000,000}{2} = 25,000,000$$

Standard error of estimate:

$$s_{\bar{x}_2} = \sqrt{s_{\bar{x}_2}^2} = \sqrt{25,000,000} = 5000$$

summed across all L strata. In the Table 11.9 example, $L = 2$; there are 10 elements in each stratum, 20 in all; and the overall point estimate of the population mean is

$$\bar{x}_{st} = \frac{N_1}{N}\bar{x}_1 + \frac{N_2}{N}\bar{x}_2 = \frac{10}{20}(33,000) + \frac{10}{20}(59,000) = 46,000$$

The relative sizes of the strata also factor into the standard error. The formula for the variance of the estimate is

$$s_{\bar{x}_{st}}^2 = \sum_{h=1}^{L} \left(\frac{N_h}{N}\right)^2 s_{\bar{x}_h}^2 \tag{4}$$

For the example

$$s_{\bar{x}_{st}}^2 = \left(\frac{N_1}{N}\right)^2 s_{\bar{x}_1}^2 + \left(\frac{N_2}{N}\right)^2 s_{\bar{x}_2}^2 = \left(\frac{10}{20}\right)^2 (9,000,000) + \left(\frac{10}{20}\right)^2 (25,000,000)$$

$$= 2,250,000 + 6,250,000 = 8,500,000$$

so that the standard error is

$$s_{\bar{x}_{st}} = \sqrt{8,500,000} = 2915.5$$

The 95% confidence interval for this sample would then be

$$\bar{x}_{st} - zs_{\bar{x}_{st}} \leq \mu \leq \bar{x}_{st} + zs_{\bar{x}_{st}}$$

$$46,000 - 1.96(2915.5) \leq \mu \leq 46,000 + 1.96(2915.5)$$

$$40,285 \leq \mu \leq 51,714$$

This interval is interpreted as before. The true mean may or may not be in the interval, but since 95 of 100 intervals constructed by this process contain the true mean, we are 95% confident that the true population mean income is between $40,285 and $51,714.

Increased Precision of Stratified Samples

We had mentioned that one reason to choose a stratified sample is that it reduces sampling error, or increases precision, and indeed, we see a narrower confidence interval. Consider equation 4 again. N and N_h are fixed. The only way for total sampling error to be reduced is for the variance of the estimate within each stratum to be made smaller. The variance of the estimate by strata, in turn, depends on the variability of the characteristic within the strata, because $s_{\bar{x}_h}^2 = s_h^2/n_h$, where s_h^2 is the sample variance within the hth stratum and n_h is the size of the sample selected from the hth stratum. Thus, the estimate of the mean can be made more precise to the extent that the population can be partitioned so that there is little variability within each stratum, i.e., each stratum is internally homogeneous.

Bases for Stratification

The investigator partitions the population according to one or more criteria that are expected to be related to the characteristic of interest. Thus, it was no accident that in the hypothetical example education was used to divide the population elements. As Table 11.1 indicates, there is a relation between these variables: the more years of school, the higher the income. Newspaper subscriptions, on the other hand, would have made a poor variable for partitioning, because there is no relation between paper subscriptions and income.

In addition, the standard error of estimate provides a clue to the number of strata that should be employed. Since the estimate depends only on variability within strata, the various strata should be made as homogeneous as possible. One way of doing this is to employ many, very small strata. There are practical limits, however, to the number of strata used in actual research studies, e.g., the creation of additional strata is often expensive in terms of sample design, data collection, and analysis.[12]

Proportionate stratified samples: proportional to population numbers

Disproportionate stratified samples: inversely proportional to population variances

Proportionate and Disproportionate Stratified Sampling

Once the decision is made to select a stratified sample, the researcher must decide whether it should be a proportionate or disproportionate stratified sample. With a **proportionate stratified sample**, the number of observations in the sample is in proportion to the relative number in the population. A stratum containing $1/5^{th}$ of all the population elements would account for $1/5^{th}$ of the total sample observations, and so on. Proportionate sampling was used in the example; each stratum contained ½ of the population and thus was sampled equally.

An alternative allocation scheme can produce still more efficient estimates. In **disproportionate stratified sampling**, if one group is known to be more heterogeneous in the population, we would sample more from it, to really nail down that estimate. If a group shows less variability in the population, we would take a smaller sample from that group—because they are similar, once we have sampled a few, we would pretty much know what the rest looked like (see Research Realities 11.1 for an ACNielsen example).

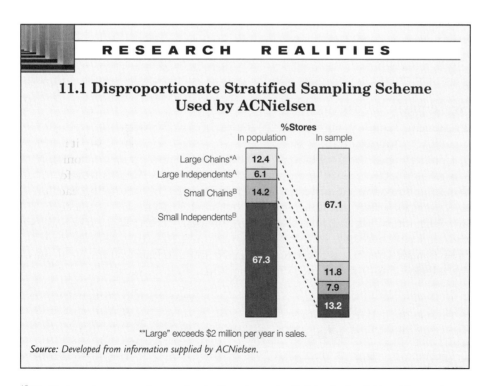

RESEARCH   REALITIES

11.1 Disproportionate Stratified Sampling Scheme Used by ACNielsen

*"Large" exceeds $2 million per year in sales.

Source: Developed from information supplied by ACNielsen.

One can sometimes anticipate the relative homogeneity likely to exist within a stratum on the basis of past studies and experience. Sometimes the investigator may have to rely on logic and intuition. For example, it might be expected that large retail stores would show greater variation in sales of some product than would small stores.

Cluster Sampling

Cluster sampling involves the following steps: (1) The parent population is divided into mutually exclusive and exhaustive subsets. (2) A random sample of the subsets is selected. If the investigator then uses all the population elements in the selected subsets for the sample, the procedure is one-stage cluster sampling. If a sample of elements is selected probabilistically from the selected subsets, the procedure is known as two-stage cluster sampling.

Note the similarities and differences between cluster sampling and stratified sampling. Both involve the division of the population into mutually exclusive and exhaustive subgroups, although the criteria used are different (described shortly). Then for stratified sampling, a sample of elements is selected from each subgroup, whereas with cluster sampling, one chooses a *sample of subgroups*.

Because one chooses a sample of subgroups with cluster sampling, it is important that each subgroup be representative of the population. At the extreme, if the distribution of the characteristic in each subgroup exactly parallels that for the population, one subgroup can tell all. Thus, in cluster sampling, the subgroups ideally should be as *heterogeneous* as possible.

How does cluster sampling compare to stratified sampling or simple probability sampling? **Statistical efficiency** is a way to compare sampling plans. One sampling plan is more statistically efficient than another if, for the same size sample, it produces a smaller standard error of estimate. Cluster samples are typically less efficient than stratified samples or simple random samples. Yet cluster sampling is probably the most widely used sampling procedure in large-scale field surveys because they can be more economically efficient.

Systematic Sampling

A systematic sample is an easy cluster sample. It involves selecting every k^{th} element after a random start.

Consider again the population of 20 individuals and suppose that a sample of 5 is to be selected from this population. Number the elements from 1 to 20. With 20 population elements and a sample size of 5, the sampling fraction is $n/N = 5/20 = 1/4$, meaning that one element in four will be selected, the sampling interval is 4. Thus, after a random start, every 4th element will be chosen, e.g., 1st, 5th, 9th, 13th, 17th, etc., or 2nd, 6th, 10th, 14th, 18th, etc.

Systematic sampling is one-stage cluster sampling, because all the elements in the selected cluster(s) are used. The subgroups or clusters are

Cluster I:	A, E, I, M, Q
Cluster II:	B, F, J, N, R
Cluster III:	C, G, K, O, S
Cluster IV:	D, H, L, P, T

The random start, of course, determines which of these clusters is used.

You can see how easy it is to draw a systematic sample. Further, given that the list is ordered by income, we are guaranteed representation from the low-income segment and the high-income segment.

There is a danger, however. If there is a natural periodicity in the list of elements, the systematic sample can produce estimates seriously in error. For example, suppose that we have the annual ticket sales of an airline by day and that we wish to analyze these sales in terms of length of trip. To analyze all 365 days may be prohibitively costly, but perhaps the research budget allows the investigation of 52 days of sales. A systematic sample of days using a sampling interval of 7 (365/52) would obviously produce some misleading conclusions, because the day's sales will reflect all Monday trips, Friday trips, or Sunday trips, for example.

Area Cluster Sampling

In every probability sampling plan discussed so far, the investigator needs a list of population elements in order to draw the sample. For many populations of interest, these detailed lists are unavailable or costly to construct. However, area cluster samples need only the list of population elements for the selected clusters.

Suppose that an investigator wished to measure certain characteristics of consultants, such as their earnings, attitudes toward the job, hours of travel, and so on. It would be extremely difficult (if not impossible) and certainly costly to develop an up-to-date roster listing each consultant. Yet such a list would be required for a simple random sample. A stratified sample would further require the investigator to possess knowledge about some additional characteristics of each person on the list (e.g., education, employer) so that the population could be divided into mutually exclusive and exhaustive subsets. With a cluster sample, on the other hand, one could use companies as sampling units. The investigator would generate a sample of business firms from the population of firms of interest. The business firms would be primary sampling units. The marketing researcher could then get a list of people working for each of the selected firms—a much more plausible assignment.

The same principle underlies **area sampling**. Current, accurate lists of population elements are rarely available. Directories of all those living in a city at a particular moment do not exist for many cities, and when they do, they are obsolete when published; people move, others die, and new households are constantly being formed. So what shall we do instead?

One-Stage Area Sampling

Suppose that the investigator is interested in estimating the amount of wine consumed per household in the city of Chicago and how consumption is related to family income. An accurate listing of all households is unavailable for the Chicago area. One approach to this problem is the following:

1. Choose a simple random sample of n city blocks from the population of N blocks.

2. Determine wine consumption and income for all households in the selected blocks, and generalize the sample relationships to the larger population.

The probability of any household being included in the sample can be calculated. It is given simply as n/N, because it equals the probability that the block on which it is located will be selected. Because the probabilities are known, the procedure is probability sampling. Here, though, blocks have been substituted for households when selecting primary sampling units. The list of blocks can be developed from city maps. Each block can be identified, and the existence of this universe of blocks permits the calculation of the necessary probabilities.

Because each household on the selected blocks is included in the sample, the procedure is one-stage area sampling. Note that the blocks divide the population into mutually exclusive and exhaustive subsets. Note further that the blocks do not serve very well as ideal subsets statistically for cluster samples; households on a given block can be expected to be somewhat similar with respect to their income and wine consumption, rather than heterogeneous as desired. On the other hand, the data-collection costs will be very low because of the concentration of households within each block.

Two-Stage Area Sampling

The distinguishing feature of the one-stage area sample is that all the households in the selected blocks (or other areas) are enumerated and studied. It is not necessary to employ all items in a selected cluster; the selected areas themselves can be sampled. We distinguish two types of two-stage sampling:

1. Simple, two-stage area sampling

2. Probability-proportional-to-size area sampling

With simple, two-stage area sampling, a certain proportion of 2nd-stage sampling units (e.g., households) is selected from each 1st-stage unit (e.g., blocks). Consider a universe of 100 blocks. Suppose that there are 20 households per block and that a sample of 80 households is required from this total population of 2,000 households. The overall sampling fraction is thus $80/2,000 = 1/25$. There are a number of ways by which the sample can be completed: by (1) selecting 10 blocks and 8 households per block, (2) selecting 8 blocks and 10 households per block, (3) selecting 20 blocks and 4 households per block, or (4) selecting 4 blocks and 20 households per block. The last alternative would, of course, be one-stage area sampling, whereas the first three would be two-stage area sampling.

The probability with which the blocks are selected is called the block or 1st-stage sampling fraction and is given as the ratio of n_B/N_B, where n_B and N_B are the number of blocks in the sample and in the population, respectively. For the first three schemes, the fractions would be, 1 in 10, 1 in 12.5, and 1 in 5. The probability with which the households are selected is the household or 2nd-stage sampling fraction. Since there must be a total of 80 households in the sample, the 2nd-stage sampling fraction differs for each alternative. The 2nd-stage sampling fraction is given as $n_{H/B}/N_{H/B}$, where $n_{H/B}$ and $N_{H/B}$ are the number of households per block in the sample and in the population. For sampling scheme 1, the household sampling fraction is calculated to be $8/20 = 2/5$, for scheme 2 it is $10/20 = 1/2$, and for scheme 3 it is $4/20 = 1/5$. Note that the product of the 1st-stage and 2nd-stage sampling fractions in each case equals the overall sampling fraction of $1/25$.

Which scheme would be preferable? Economies of data collection dictate that the second-stage sampling fraction should be high. This means that a great many households would be selected from each designated block, as with scheme 2. Statistical efficiency would dictate a small second-stage sampling fraction, because one can expect that the blocks would be relatively homogeneous, and thus it would be desirable to have very few households from any one block. Scheme 3 would be preferred on statistical grounds. Statistical sampling theory would suggest the balancing of these two criteria. There are formulas for this purpose that essentially reflect the cost of data collection and the variability of the characteristic within and between clusters.

| TABLE 11.10 | Illustration of Probability-Proportional-to-Size Sampling |

Block	#Households	Cumulative #Households
1	800	800
2	400	1200
3	200	1400
4	200	1600
5	100	1700
6	100	1800
7	100	1900
8	50	1950
9	25	1975
10	25	2000

Simple two-stage area sampling is quite effective when there are approximately the same number of 2nd-stage units per 1st-stage unit. When the 2nd-stage units are decidedly unequal, there can be bias in the estimate and probability-proportional-to-size sampling is the better choice.

Consider the data in Table 11.10, and suppose that a sample of 20 elements is to be selected from this population of 2,000 households. With **probability-proportional-to-size sampling**, a fixed number of 2nd-stage units is selected from each 1st-stage unit. After balancing economic and statistical considerations, suppose that the number of 2nd-stage units per 1st-stage unit is determined to be 10. Two 1st-stage units must be selected to produce a total sample of 20. The procedure gets its name from the way these 1st-stage units are selected. The probability of selection is variable because it depends on the size of the 1st-stage unit. In particular, a table of four-digit random numbers would be consulted. The first two numbers encountered between 1 and 2,000 are employed to indicate the blocks that will be used. All numbers between 1 and 800 indicate the inclusion of block 1, those from 801 to 1,200 indicate block 2, those from 1,201 to 1,400 indicate block 3, and so on.

The probability that any particular household will be included in the sample is equal, since the unequal 1st-stage selection probabilities are balanced by unequal 2nd-stage selection probabilities. Consider, for example, blocks 1 and 10, the two extremes. The 1st-stage selection probability for block 1 is $800/2,000 = 1/2.5$, since 800 of the permissible 2,000 random numbers correspond to block 1. In contrast, only 25 of the permissible random numbers (1,976 to 2,000) correspond to block 10, and thus the first-stage sampling fraction for block 10 is $25/2,000 = 1/80$. Because 10 households are selected from each block, the second-stage sampling fraction for block 1 is $10/800 = 1/80$, whereas for block 10 it is $10/25 = 1/2.5$. The products of the 1st- and 2nd-stage sampling thus compensate, since

$$\frac{800}{2000} \times \frac{10}{800} = \frac{25}{2000} \times \frac{10}{25}$$

which is also true for the remaining blocks. The size of each 1st-stage unit is easily obtained from census.gov.

Sampling gets trickier when collecting international data. Decisions must be made about coverage between countries, as well as likely markets and localities within countries. Most research budgets cannot afford thorough coverage, so choices are based on managerially driven questions (i.e., theory).

Summary

Sample design is a very detailed subject.[13] This chapter reviewed the basic types of samples that may be used to infer something about a population. A sample might be preferred to a census on grounds of cost or accuracy.

A practical procedure to use when drawing a sample includes the following steps:

1. Define the population.
2. Identify the sampling frame.
3. Select a sampling procedure.
4. Determine the sample size.
5. Select the sample elements.
6. Collect the data from the designated elements.

Probability samples are distinguished by the fact that every population element has a known, nonzero chance of being included in the sample. With nonprobability samples, the chance of inclusion is not calculable, because personal judgment is involved somewhere in the actual selection process. Thus, nonprobability samples do not allow the construction of the sampling distribution of the statistic in question. As a result, traditional tools of statistical inference are not legitimately employed with nonprobability samples. The basic types of nonprobability samples are convenience, judgment, and quota samples.

Simple random samples are probability samples in which each population element has an equal chance of being included and every combination of sample elements is just as likely as any other combination of n sample elements. Simple random samples were used to illustrate the basis of statistical inference, in which a parameter (a fixed characteristic of the population) is estimated from a statistic (a characteristic of a sample). The value of the statistic depends on the sample actually selected, since it varies from sample to sample. The derived population is the set of all possible distinguishable samples that could be drawn from a parent population under a given sampling plan, and the distribution of some sample statistic's values is the sampling distribution of the statistic. The concept of the sampling distribution is the cornerstone of statistical inference.

A stratified sample is a probability sample in which the parent population is divided into mutually exclusive and exhaustive subsets and a sample of elements is drawn from each subset. Stratified samples are typically the most statistically efficient (i.e., they have the smallest standard error of estimate), and they also allow the investigation of the characteristic of interest for particular subgroups within the population. The most statistically efficient stratified samples result when the strata are made as homogeneous as possible. Thus, variables expected to be correlated to the characteristic of interest, and whose values are known, are often employed when establishing the strata. In proportionate stratified sampling, the size of the sample taken from each stratum depends on the relative size of the stratum in the population, whereas with disproportionate stratified sampling, sample size depends on the variability within the stratum.

A cluster sample is a probability sample in which the parent population is divided into mutually exclusive and exhaustive subsets and then a random sample of subsets is selected. If each of the elements within the selected subsets is studied, it is one-stage cluster sampling; if the selected subsets are also subsampled, the procedure represents two-stage cluster sampling. Since only a sample of subsets is selected for analysis, statistical efficiency considerations suggest that the subsets be as heterogeneous as possible. A systematic sample is a form of cluster sample in which every k^{th} element is selected after a randomly determined start.

An area sample is an important type of cluster samples for large-scale studies. Area samples make use of one very desirable feature of cluster samples—one only needs the list of population elements for the selected clusters. By defining areas as clusters and then randomly selecting areas, the investigator needs to develop lists of population elements only for the selected areas. Even here the researcher can use dwelling units and select them systematically. Thus, area samples permit probability samples to be drawn when current lists of population elements are unavailable. In drawing area samples, the researcher attempts to balance statistical and economic considerations. Because small areas are basically homogeneous, statistical considerations suggest that a great many areas should be used. However, the economies of data collection dictate that few areas be used, and many observations collected within each area.

[13] For more on sampling, see Paul S. Levy and Stanley Lemeshow, *Sampling of Populations* (Wiley, 2008).

Questions

1. What is a census? What is a sample?
2. What is a convenience sample? What is a judgment sample?
3. Why is a quota sample a nonprobability sample?
4. What are the distinguishing features of a simple random sample?
5. Consider the estimation of a population mean. What is the relationship between the mean of the parent population and the mean of the derived population? Between the variance of the parent population and the variance of the derived population?
6. What role does the Central-Limit Theorem play in making inferences about a population mean?
7. What procedure is followed in constructing a confidence interval for a population mean when the population variance is known? When the population variance is unknown? What does such an interval mean?
8. How should a simple random sample be selected? Describe the procedure.
9. What is a stratified sample? How is a stratified sample selected?
10. What is a proportionate stratified sample? What is a disproportionate stratified sample? What must be known about the parent population to select each?
11. What is a cluster sample? How is a cluster sample selected?
12. What are the similarities and differences between a cluster sample and a stratified sample?

Applications and Problems

1. For each situation, identify the appropriate target population and sampling frame.
   a. The National Head Injury Foundation Inc. wants to test the effectiveness of a brochure soliciting volunteers for its local chapter in Indianapolis, Indiana.
   b. A regional manufacturer of yogurt selling primarily in the Pacific Northwest wants to test market three new flavors of yogurt.
   c. A national manufacturer wants to assess whether adequate inventories are being held by wholesalers in order to prevent shortages by retailers.
   d. A large wholesaler dealing in electronic office products in D.C. wants to evaluate dealer reaction to a new discount policy.
   e. The online branch of a men's casual clothing retailer wants to assess the satisfaction with a new credit and return policy.

2. The Gap wants to determine consumer preference for several varieties of t-shirts. Respondents will participate in a touch test—they will touch several different t-shirts and then state their preferences. Some aspects of the t-shirts that will be compared are armbands, neckbands, and shirt material. The marketing researcher conducting the study has recommended that the touch tests be conducted using mall intercepts.
   a. What problems, if any, do you see in trying to use the results of this study to estimate the population of consumers who buy t-shirts?
   b. Suggest an alternative to a mall intercept study for determining consumer preferences for t-shirts. Why is this a better method?

3. A leading film and electronics company wishes to investigate the market potential for a new kind of photo-imaging equipment. Because this is a completely new technology, the company believes that industry leaders might offer insights into the desires of customers and consumers. However, a list of industry leaders does not exist. Discuss possible methods of generating a sampling frame for the influential people in this high-tech industry.

4. The owners of a popular bed and breakfast inn in Kauai, Hawaii, noticed a decline in the number of tourists and length of stay during the past three years. An overview of industry trends indicated that the overall tourist trade was expanding and growing rapidly. The managers decided to conduct a study to determine people's attitudes toward the particular activities that were available at and around the inn. Because they wanted to cause the minimum amount of inconvenience to their guests, the owners devised the following plan. Interview request cards, which were available at the Chamber of Commerce office, the Visitor Information Center, and three of the more popular restaurants, indicated the nature of the study and encouraged visitors to participate. Visitors were asked to report to a separate room at either the Chamber of Commerce office or the Visitor Information Center. Personal interviews, lasting 20 minutes, were conducted at these locations.
   a. What type of sampling method was used?
   b. Critically evaluate the method used.

5. The makers of Spam (the weird meat, not the annoying e-mails) were planning to enter a new Asian market. Before the final decision about launching its product, management decided to test market the products in two cities. After reviewing the various cities in terms of external criteria, such as demographics, shopping characteristics, and so on, the research department settled on Yokohama and Hiroshima.
   a. What type of sampling method was used?
   b. Critically evaluate the method used.

6. A Credit Union chain in Philadelphia has witnessed a sharp increase in the number of branches it operates and in the company's gross sales and net profit margin in the past five years. Management plans to offer free retirement planning and consultation, a service for which other competing credit unions, banks, and brokerage firms charge a substantial price. To offset the increase in operating expenses, management plans to raise the rates on other services by 7%. Before introducing this new service and increasing rates, management decides to do a survey using customers as a sample and employing the method of quota sampling. Your assistance is required in planning the study.
   a. What variables would you suggest for the quotas? Why? List the variables with their respective levels.
   b. Management has kept close track of the demographic characteristics of customers during the five-year period and decides that these would be most relevant in identifying the sample elements to be used.

Variable	Level	%Customers
Age	0–15 years	5
	16–30 years	30
	31–45 years	30
	46–60 years	15
	61–75 years	15
	76 years+	5
Gender	Men	42
	Women	58
Income	$0–$9,999	10
	$10,000–$19,999	20
	$20,000–$29,999	30
	$30,000–$39,999	20
	$40,000+	20

   Based on these three quota variables, indicate the characteristics of a sample of 200 subjects.
   c. Discuss the possible sources of bias with the sampling method.

7. The following table lists the results of one question taken from a survey conducted for Joe's Bar and Grill. The Grill has recently undergone renovations, and with the new look, management has decided to change the menu. They are interested in knowing how well customers like the new menus.
   a. Calculate the mean, standard deviation, and confidence interval for menu preference assuming simple random sampling was used.

Respondent	Meal Eaten at Joe's Bar and Grill	Menu Preference on a 20-Point Scale
1	Breakfast	3
2	Breakfast	5
3	Breakfast	4
4	Breakfast	5
5	Breakfast	5
6	Lunch	10
7	Lunch	9
8	Lunch	8
9	Lunch	10
10	Lunch	9
11	Dinner	14
12	Dinner	15
13	Dinner	15
14	Dinner	14
15	Dinner	16

   b. Calculate the mean, standard deviation, and confidence interval for menu preference assuming stratified sampling based on the meal eaten was used (i.e., the strata being breakfast, lunch, and dinner customers). Assume that $N_i/N = 1/3$ for each stratum. How do the results compare with those you obtained with the previous sampling plan? Why?

8. The Nevada National Bank, headquartered in Las Vegas, has some 400,000 users of its credit card scattered throughout the state. The application forms for the credit card ask for the usual information about name, address, phone, income, education, and so on, that is typical of such applications. The bank is interested in determining if there is any relationship between the uses of the card and the socioeconomic characteristics of the user; e.g., is there a difference in the characteristics of those people who use the credit card for major purchases only (e.g., appliances) and those who use it for minor as well as major purchases?
   a. Identify the population and sampling frame that would be used by the bank.
   b. Indicate how you would draw a simple random sample from the sampling frame identified in part a.
   c. Indicate how you would draw a stratified sample from the sampling frame.
   d. Indicate how you would draw a cluster sample from the sampling frame.
   e. Which method would be preferred? Why?

9. Howdy Supermarkets is considering entering the Cleveland market. However, before doing so, management wishes to estimate the average square feet of selling space among potential competitors' stores to plan better the size of the proposed new outlet. A stratified sample of supermarkets in Cleveland produced the following results:

Size	Total# in City	#This Size in Sample	Mean Size (sq.ft.)	Std.Dev. (sq.ft.)
Small supermarkets	490	24	4,000	2,000
Medium supermarkets	280	14	27,000	4,000
Large supermarkets	40	2	60,000	5,000

a. Estimate the average-size supermarket in Cleveland. Show your calculations.
b. Develop a 95% confidence interval around this estimate. Show your calculations.
c. Was a proportionate or a disproportionate stratified sample design used in determining the number of sample observations for each stratum? Explain.

10. The manager of a local theater is interested in assessing customer satisfaction. The manager decides to distribute a survey to every 10th ticket purchaser.
a. What type of sampling is to be used?
b. Critically evaluate this method.

Determining Sample Size 12

Questions to Guide Your Learning:

Q1 How do we determine sample size to achieve a desired level of precision confidence?

Q2 How is this done when estimating a population mean vs. a population proportion?

In the previous chapter, we discussed sampling plans. In this chapter, we consider sample size. The researcher needs to determine the size of the sample required before collecting data. Often this estimation occurs at the research proposal stage, because sample size affects the cost of the research project.

The question of sample size is complex because it depends on the type of sample, the statistic in question, the homogeneity of the population, and the time, money, and personnel available for the study. We illustrate the basic statistical principles by determining sample size for simple random samples.

Before we get into those geeky details, though, let's look at the big picture. Sample size has to be big enough to satisfy two criteria—first, is it sufficient to make the results sound? Second, are the results convincing?

- For example, most of us think it's remarkable that a sample of only 300–400 voters can represent the likely political sentiment of the country, but statistically it's sufficient. But if the prediction were based on, say 50 citizens, who would believe the results?

- Same with marketing research—a survey of 45 customers might, under some conditions, be statistically sufficient, but are you going to want to stake a million-dollar decision, and your job, on such a small sample?

Basic Considerations

As you might imagine, the sampling distribution underlies the determination of sample size.[1] This distribution indicates how the sample estimates vary as a function of the sample, so the spread of the distribution indicates the error that may be associated with the estimate.

[1] Patrick Dattalo, *Determining Sample Size* (Oxford University Press, 2008).

For instance, the error associated with the estimation of a population mean by a sample mean is given by the standard error of the mean, $\sigma_{\bar{x}} = \sigma/\sqrt{n}$. The first factor to consider in estimating sample size, then, is the standard error.

A second consideration is the desired precision. Precision is the size of the confidence interval. For example, a researcher investigating mean income might want the sample estimate to be within $\pm\$1000$ of the true population value, which is a more precise estimate than $\pm\$5000$.

A third factor is the desired degree of confidence, e.g., 95% or 99%. Confidence and precision affect the required sample size in opposite ways—as confidence goes up, the width of the interval increases (or, precision decreases).

In a moment, we're going to take the equation for a confidence interval, turn it inside out, and solve for sample size. To help motivate this discussion, Figure 12.1 shows you how sample size and confidence levels affect the precision of research conclusions.

Sample Size Determination When Estimating Means

The relationships among the factors affecting sample size can be illustrated through an example. Consider a simple random sample to estimate the mean annual expenditures of visitors at a theme park on food and souvenirs. Recall that the Central-Limit Theorem suggests that the distribution of sample means will be normal for samples of reasonable size regardless of the distribution of expenditures in the population. Consider, then, the sampling distribution of sample means in Figure 12.2, and let's look at two cases: Case I, in which the population variance is known, and Case II, in which the population variance is unknown.

> When your boss resists paying for a big sample, remind him/her that with more data come more precision!

Case I: Population Variance Known

The population variance σ might be known from past studies, even though the average expenditures might be unknown. Given the relationship, $\sigma_{\bar{x}} = \sigma/\sqrt{n}$, we could derive the standard error of estimate, $\sigma_{\bar{x}}$.

Suppose that the decision maker desired the estimate to be within $\pm\$25$ of the true population value. Total precision is thus $50, and half precision (call it H) is $25.[2] Say the decision maker wishes to be 95% confident, then $z = 1.96$ (or roughly "2" to simplify the calculations).

Now we determine sample size. If we want our estimate to be no more than $25 removed from the true population value, we can simply equate the size of the specified half interval with the number of standard deviations to yield

$$H = z\sigma_{\bar{x}} = z\frac{\sigma}{\sqrt{n}} \tag{1}$$

This equation can be solved for n (H and z are specified, and σ is known from past studies):

$$n = \frac{z^2}{H^2}\sigma^2. \tag{2}$$

---

[2] We work with H instead of the full length of the interval because the normal curve is symmetrical around the true population mean, and it simplifies the calculations.

FIGURE **12.1**

Illustration of the Relationship between Sample Size, Confidence Levels, and Confidence Interval Precision (Narrowness)

Recall equation for confidence interval: $\bar{x} \pm z_\alpha \sigma_{\bar{x}}$ where: $\sigma_{\bar{x}} = \hat{\sigma}_x / \sqrt{n}$

Computation: 95% confidence, mean = 475 (say), sample standard deviation, $\hat{\sigma} = 100$:

n	95% confidence interval		interval width
5	$475 \pm 1.96\,(100/\sqrt{5})$	= 387.35 to 562.65	175.30
30	$475 \pm 1.96\,(100/\sqrt{30})$	= 439.22 to 510.78	71.56
100	$475 \pm 1.96\,(100/\sqrt{100})$	= 455.40 to 494.60	39.20
500	$475 \pm 1.96\,(100/\sqrt{500})$	= 466.23 to 483.76	17.53

What do those confidence interval widths look like? You'll need different levels of precision for different marketing research questions:

$\hat{\mu} = \bar{x} = 475$

By comparison, what if you wanted a 99% confidence interval? z changes from 1.96 to 2.58:

n	95% confidence interval		interval width
5	$475 \pm 2.58\,(100/\sqrt{5})$	= 359.62 to 590.38	230.76
30	$475 \pm 2.58\,(100/\sqrt{30})$	= 427.90 to 522.10	94.20
100	$475 \pm 2.58\,(100/\sqrt{100})$	= 449.20 to 500.80	51.60
500	$475 \pm 2.58\,(100/\sqrt{500})$	= 463.46 to 486.54	23.08

FIGURE 12.2   Sampling Distribution of Sample Means

Standard Deviation:

$$\sigma_{\bar{x}} = \frac{\sigma}{\sqrt{n}}$$

$\bar{x}$

$E(\bar{x}) = \mu$

To illustrate, suppose that the historic variation in expenditures on food and souvenirs as measured by σ was \$100. Then

$$n = \frac{(2)^2}{(25)^2}(100)^2$$

and $n = 64$. Thus, a relatively small sample needs to be taken to estimate the mean expenditure level when the population standard deviation is \$100 and the allowed precision is \$50.

If the estimate must be twice as precise (i.e., \$25 is the total width of the desired interval), then $H = 12.5$:

$$n = \frac{(2)^2}{(12.5)^2}(100)^2$$

and $n = 256$. Doubling the precision (cutting the total width of the interval in half) increased the required sample size by a factor of four. This is the trade-off between precision and sample size. Whenever precision is increased by a factor c, sample size is increased by a factor c^2. Thus, if the desired precision were \$10 instead of \$50—in other words, the estimate must be five times more precise ($c = 5$)—the sample size would be 1,600 instead of 64 ($c^2 = 25$).

One also pays dearly to increase the degree of confidence. For example, if one wished to be 99% confident in one's estimate rather than 95% confident, let's plug in $z = 3$ instead of 2 (with $H = 25$ and $\sigma = 100$):

$$n = \frac{(3)^2}{(25)^2}(100)^2$$

and $n = 144$, whereas $n = 64$ when $z = 2$. When z was increased by a factor of d ($d = 3/2$ here), sample size increased by a factor of d^2 ($d^2 = 9/4$ here).

In sum, you should be aware that there is a price to be paid for increased precision and confidence. We constantly strive for very precise estimates in which we can have a great deal of confidence, but we can see why we often learn to live with somewhat imprecise estimates.

Case II: Population Variance Unknown

What happens when the population variance is unknown, as is typically the case? As you might anticipate, the procedure is the same except that an estimated value of σ is used in place of the previously known value of σ.

Suppose that there were no past studies on which to base an estimate of σ. You could do a pilot study, a small, quick and dirty study to get a rough estimate. (See Research Realities 12.1 for helpful advice.)

A third possibility is to use the fact that for a normally distributed variable, the range of the variable is approximately equal to ±3 standard deviations. Thus, if you don't have an estimate of σ but you have an estimate of the range of variation, you can estimate the standard deviation by dividing by 6. To illustrate: Some theme park visitors might spend nearly nothing on souvenirs, others might visit several theme parks a year and buy a lot each time. Suppose that five days a year were considered typical of the upper limit, and food and souvenir expenses were calculated at $90 per day; the total dollar upper limit would be $450. The range would also be 450, and the estimated standard deviation would then be $450/6 = 75$.

With desired precision of ±$25 and a 95% confidence interval, the calculation of sample size is now

$$n = \frac{z^2}{H^2}s^2 = \frac{(2)^2}{(25)^2}(75)^2 = 36$$

A sample of size 36 would then be selected and the information collected. Suppose that these observations generated a sample mean, $\bar{x} = 35$, and a

RESEARCH   REALITIES

12.1 Estimating Variances When Using Rating Scales

Rating scales are bounded: On a five-point scale, for instance, responses cannot be less than 1 or greater than 5. This constraint leads to a relationship between the mean and the variance. For example, if a sample mean is 4.6 on a 5-point scale, there must be a large proportion of responses of 5, and it follows that the variance must be relatively small. On the other hand, if the mean is near 3.0, the variance can be greater. The nature of the relationship between the mean and the variance depends on the number of scale points and on the shape of the distribution of responses (e.g., approximately normal, or skewed, or uniformly spread among the scale values). By considering these factors, it is possible to estimate variances for use in calculating sample size requirements for a given number of scale points.

The table at the right lists ranges of variances likely to be encountered for various numbers of scale points. The low end of the range is the approximate variance when data values tend to be concentrated around some middle point of the scale, as in a normal distribution. The high end of the range is the variance that would be obtained if responses were uniformly spread across the scale points. Although it is possible to encounter distributions with larger variances than those listed (such as distributions with modes at both ends of the scale), such data are rare.

In most cases, data obtained using rating scales tend to be more uniformly spread out than in a normal distribution. Hence, to arrive at conservative sample-size estimates (that is, sample sizes that are at least large enough to accomplish the stated objectives), it is advisable to use a variance estimate at or near the high end of the range.

Number of Scale Points	Typical Range of Variances
4	0.7–1.3
5	1.2–2.0
6	2.0–3.0
7	2.5–4.0
10	3.0–7.0

Source: Research on Research *(synovate.com).*

sample standard deviation, $s_x = 60$. The confidence interval is then, as before, $\bar{x} \pm zs_{\bar{x}}$, or[3]

$$35 \pm 2\frac{s}{\sqrt{n}} = 35 \pm 2\frac{60}{\sqrt{36}} = 35 \pm 20, \quad \text{or} \quad 15 \leq \mu \leq 55$$

Note that the desired precision was ±\$25 and the obtained precision is ±\$20. The interval is narrower than planned (woohoo) because we overestimated the population standard deviation as judged by the sample standard deviation. If we had underestimated the standard deviation, the situation would have been reversed, and our confidence interval would have been wider.

Relative Precision

The preceding examples were all framed employing **absolute precision**. The estimates were to be within plus or minus so many units (e.g., dollars). It is also possible to frame the calculations of sample size employing **relative precision**. For example, if you require that an estimate is within ±10% of the mean, if the mean is 50, the interval will be from 45 to 55, whereas if the mean is 100, the interval will be from 90 to 110.

The calculation of sample size is no more complicated in the scenario of relative precision. The precision term H is simply replaced by the measure of relative precision:

Ethical Dilemma 12.1

Researchers in the lab of a regional food manufacturer recently developed a new dessert topping. This topping came in a variety of flavors and the manufacturer believed that the product had great promise. Management knew it would be necessary to convince the trade of its sales potential in order to get wholesalers and retailers to handle it, so they decided to test market the product in a couple of areas where they had strong distribution. It selected several stores with which it had a long working relationship to carry the product.

During the planned two-month test period, product sales did not begin to compare to sales of other dessert toppings. Feeling that such evidence would make it very difficult to gain distribution, the manufacturer decided to do two things: (1) run the test for a longer period, and (2) increase the number of accounts handling the test product. Four months later, the results were much more convincing and management felt more comfortable in approaching the trade with the test market results.

- Is it ok to conduct a test market in an area where one's reputation is especially strong?
- Do you need to report this fact to the trade so they can interpret the market response?
- Is it ethical to increase the size of the sample until one secures a result one wants? What if the argument for increasing sample size was that the product was so novel that two months simply was not enough time for consumers to become familiar with it?
- Would it have been more ethical to plan initially for a larger and longer test than to adjust the length and scope of the test on the basis of early results? Why or why not?

---

[3] Strictly speaking, we should use the t-distribution, since the population variance was unknown.

$$H = z\frac{\sigma}{\sqrt{n}}$$

becomes

$$r\mu = z\frac{\sigma}{\sqrt{n}}$$

where r is the measure of relative precision and μ is the population mean. Again, we simply solve for n. Divide both sides of the equation by $r\mu$ and multiply both sides by n^2 to yield

$$n = \frac{z^2\sigma^2}{r^2\mu^2} \tag{3}$$

There are sample size equations for absolute and relative estimation of means, and absolute and relative estimation of proportions.

The desired level of confidence is z, so z^2 is known, and r, the expressed level of precision is also known. The right-hand term, σ^2/μ^2, or $(\sigma/\mu)^2$, would entail making a judgment about the size of the population standard deviation relative to the size of the population mean. There might be past studies to guide the judgment. "What-if" scenarios (plugging in multiple likely values for σ and μ) are also helpful to see the range of what n is likely required to be.

Multiple Objectives

A study is rarely conducted to estimate a single parameter. It is much more typical for a study to involve multiple objectives. So, realistically, the researcher may be interested in both estimating the mean expenditures on food and souvenirs as well as the number of miles traveled in a year to the theme parks. Multiple means now need to be estimated. If each is to be estimated with 95% confidence and the desired absolute precision and estimated standard deviation are as given in Table 12.1, then you can see how the sample sizes also vary.

The different variables produce conflicting sample sizes; n could equal 36, 16, or 100, depending on the mean being estimated. The researcher must somehow reconcile these values to come up with a sample size suitable for the study as a whole. A conservative approach would be to choose $n = 100$, the largest value, to ensure that each variable is estimated with the required precision.

If the estimate of miles traveled were less critical than the others, then the use of a sample of size 100 would waste resources. Instead, focus on the variables that are most critical, and select a sample sufficient in size to estimate them with the required precision and confidence. The other variables would simply be estimated with a lower degree of confidence or less precision.

TABLE 12.1	Sample Size Needed to Estimate Each of Three Means		
	Variable		
	Expenditures on Food	Expenditures on Souvenirs	Miles Traveled
Confidence Level	95% ($z =1.96$)	95% ($z =1.96$)	95% ($z =1.96$)
Desired Precision	±$25	±$10	±100 miles
Estimated Standard Deviation	±$75	±$20	±500 miles
Required Sample Size	36	16	100

Sample Size Determination When Estimating Proportions

The examples considered previously all concern determining sample size to estimate means. The population proportion π is often another parameter of interest in marketing. Thus, we might be interested in determining the proportion of theme park visitors who are from out of state or who took at least one overnight trip, etc. The logic is the same, but the equations change slightly.

Absolute Precision

Let's start with what's different—the sampling distribution of the sample proportion. If the sample elements are independent, a reasonable assumption if the sample size is small relative to the population size, then the distribution of the sample proportion is the "binomial." When π is close to .5, or n is large, the binomial becomes indistinguishable from the normal;[4] thus, it is convenient to use the normal approximation when estimating sample size.

The distribution of sample proportions is centered around the population proportion (Figure 12.3), and the sample proportion is an unbiased estimate of the population proportion. The standard deviation of the normal distribution of sample proportions, i.e., the standard error of the proportion is $\sigma_p = \sqrt{\pi(1 - \pi)/n}$. Plugging σ_p into equation (1), we get

$$H = z\sigma_p \tag{4}$$

Substituting $\sqrt{\pi(1 - \pi)/n}$ for σ_p and solving for n yields

$$n = \frac{z^2}{H^2}\pi(1 - \pi) \tag{5}$$

Let's say that the researcher is interested in estimating the proportion of all travelers who took at least one overnight trip in the past year. The researcher

FIGURE 12.3   **Approximate Sampling Distribution of the Sample Proportion**

Standard Deviation:

$$\sigma_p = \sqrt{\frac{\pi(1 - \pi)}{n}}$$

$E(p) = \pi$

P

[4] The strict requirement is that $n\pi$ must be above a certain level if the normal curve is to provide a good approximation to the binomial. Some hold that $n\pi$ must be >5, or, even better, >10.

wants this estimate within ±2 percentage points, with 95% confidence in the result:

$$n = \frac{(2)^2}{(.02)^2} \pi(1 - \pi)$$

This equation contains two unknowns—the population proportion being estimated and the sample size—and is thus not solvable as it stands. To determine sample size, the researcher needs to estimate the population proportion. Yep! The researcher must estimate the very quantity the study is being designed to get at in order to determine sample size. Once again, you might use past studies or published data to generate an initial estimate. Alternately, you might conduct a pilot study or use informed judgment and a range of estimates to approximate the parameter.

Another "what-if" exercise is to run a worst-case scenario. For example, if it would be unacceptable to have a wide confidence interval, you can plug $\pi = .5$ into the equations since this value maximizes the standard error.[5] If in fact the standard error is smaller (π is less than or greater than .5), the real confidence interval will be narrower and contained in the more conservative estimate, the broader confidence interval based on $\pi = .5$.

Relative Precision

The estimation of sample size for relative precision of proportions is analogous to that for relative precision of means. For example, if the relative precision were ±10%, and if the sample proportion were .20, the interval would be .18 to .22; if the sample proportion were .30, the interval would be .27 to .33.

We use

$$r\pi = z\sigma_p = r\pi = z\sqrt{\frac{\pi(1 - \pi)}{n}}$$

where r is the specified relative precision. Solving for n, we obtain

$$n = \frac{z^2}{r^2} \frac{(1 - \pi)}{\pi} \tag{6}$$

Once again some initial estimate of the population proportion is needed. To illustrate, suppose that the population proportion was estimated to be .2, the level of confidence was 95% ($z = 2$), and the desired level of relative precision $r = .10$. Then

$$n = \frac{(2)^2}{(.10)^2} \frac{(.8)}{(.2)} = 1,600$$

After the information is collected from the sample respondents, $s_p = \sqrt{p(1 - p)/n}$ (not σ_p based on guesstimates of π) is used to calculate the confidence interval.

---

[5] Intuitively, the idea is that when $\pi = .5$, half of the population behaves one way and the other half the other way, so you would require more evidence for a valid inference than if the situation were more clear-cut and a substantial proportion all behaved in the same way.

Population Size and Sample Size

Note that the size of the population does not enter into the calculation of the size of sample. Except for one slight modification to be discussed shortly, it has no direct effect on the size of the sample. Why not?

When estimating a mean, if all population elements have exactly the same value of the characteristic, then a sample of $n = 1$ is all that is needed to determine the mean, regardless of whether there are 1,000, 10,000, or 100,000 elements in the population. The thing that affects the size of the sample is the *variability* in the population; the more variable the characteristic, the larger the sample needed to estimate it with some specified level of precision. This makes intuitive sense, and it can be seen in the formulas for determining sample size, $n = z^2\sigma^2/H^2$. Thus, population size affects sample size only indirectly through its impact on variability: The larger the population, the greater the potential for variation of the characteristic.

The slight modification alluded to earlier is the finite population correction. When the sample represents a large portion of the population, the assumption of independence between the sample elements may be no longer warranted, and the formulas must be altered accordingly. The formula for the standard error of the mean, $\sigma_{\bar{x}} = \sigma/\sqrt{n}$, would be adjusted to

$$\sigma_{\bar{x}} = \frac{\sigma}{\sqrt{n}} \sqrt{\frac{N - n}{N - 1}}$$

when the sample elements were not independent of one another, given this scenario of a sample size that is large relative to the population. The factor $(N - n)/(N - 1)$ is the finite population correction factor used when the estimated sample represents more than 5% of the population.[6]

Other Probability Sampling Plans

So far, the discussions of sample size have been based on simple random samples. There are formulas for determining sample size when other probability sampling plans are used. The formulas are more complex, but the same underlying principles apply.

The issue of sample size is compounded, however, by the fact that one now has a number of strata or a number of clusters with which to work. This means that one has to deal with within-strata variability and within- and between-cluster variability in calculating sample size, whereas with simple random sampling, only total population variability entered the picture.

Cost must also be equal. Cost did not enter directly into the calculation of sample size with simple random sampling, although it does affect sample size. Perhaps the costs of data collection with a sample of the calculated size would simply exceed the research budget, in which case cost would act to constrain sample size below that indicated by the formulas.

With stratified or cluster samples, cost exerts a direct impact. In calculating sample size, one has to allow for unequal costs per observation by strata or by cluster, and in implementing the sample size calculation, one has to have some initial estimate of these costs. The task then becomes one of balancing variability against costs and assessing their trade-offs.

---

[6] Ignoring the finite population correction results in overestimating the standard error of estimate.

Using Anticipated Cross Tabs to Determine Sample Size

Thus far, we have focused on the determination of sample size using only statistical principles, particularly the trade-off between confidence and precision. Another practical basis for determining sample size is the anticipated cross-classifications of the data.

Suppose that in our problem of estimating the proportion of all theme park visitors who took at least one overnight trip in the past year, we were also interested in assessing whether the likelihood of engaging in this behavior is somehow related to an individual's age and income. Suppose the age categories were <20, 20–29, 30–39, 40–49, and 50+, and the income categories were <$20,000, $20,000–$39,999, $40,000–$59,999, $60,000–$79,999, and $80,000+. We would estimate the proportions for each variable, but we should also recognize that the two variables are interrelated, in that increases in income are typically related to increases in age. To allow for this interdependence, we need to consider the effect of the two variables simultaneously. The way to do this is through a cross-classification table in which age and income jointly define the cells.[7]

Table 12.2 is a cross-classification table that could be used for this example. This dummy table is complete in all respects except for the numbers that actually go in each of the cells (to be determined by the actual data). In the table, 25 cells need estimation. It is unlikely that the decision maker is going to be comfortable with an estimate based on only a few cases. Yet even with a sample of, say, 500 travelers, there is only a potential of 20 cases per cell if the sample is evenly divided with respect to the age and income levels considered. Further, it is very unlikely that the sample would split this way, which would put the researcher in the awkward position of estimating the proportion in some cells with $n > 20$, and others on the basis of fewer than 20 cases.

Conversely, we can use the table to estimate sample size. First, compute the number of cells in the intended cross-classifications (e.g., 25 here). Then allow for the likely distribution of the variables and estimate the sample size so that the important cells can be estimated with a sufficient number of cases to inspire confidence in the results. For example, for the most critical cells, aim for 100+ observations, and 20–50 in the remaining cells. The researcher "builds up" the sample from the size of the cross-classification table with these considerations.

TABLE 12.2

 # and % of Theme Park Visitors Staying Overnight, as Function of Age and Income

	Age				
Income	<20	20–29	30–39	40–49	50+
<$20,000					
$20,000–$39,999					
$40,000–$59,999					
$60,000–$79,999					
$80,000+					

[7] We say more about analyzing cross-classification tables later in the book.

Ethical Dilemma 12.2

An account manager for an independent research agency believed that she had a good handle on her client's problem and major concerns. On the basis of this understanding, she had developed a set of dummy tables by which the client's concerns could be investigated. She had presented these to the client, the client accepted her recommendations, and they closed the meeting by discussing the size of the sample and how much the study would cost.

The account manager was experiencing some anxiety because she believed from the earlier discussions and some preliminary investigation that two of the seven hypotheses were especially promising. The sample size that was needed to investigate these two hypotheses was almost half of that needed to address the other hypotheses. The account manager was in a dilemma: should she take the safe route and recommend the larger sample size to the client and thereby ensure that all the tests could be completed, or should she recommend the smaller sample size and save the client some money.

- What would you recommend that the account manager do?
- Is it ethical for her to recommend the larger sample size when she is fairly certain that the smaller one will provide the answers the client needs? Is it ethical to do the reverse and recommend the smaller sample when there is some risk that the smaller sample will not adequately answer all the problems that the firm was hired to solve?
- What are the account manager's responsibilities to the client in a case like this?

RESEARCH REALITIES

12.2 Statistical Samples and Target Markets

Figure A contains secondary data, statistics on people who like to golf, classifying them by their age (using the census age categories). You could use data like these in a number of ways.

If you wanted golfers' opinions about a new golf shoe, you could do a "golf course intercept" with a simple probability sampling plan, and anticipate a sample with the ages of the respondents distributed much like that in the Figure. Indeed, if you were confident about the quality of the data in the figure, you could take this to be a rough estimate of the population, to use as a benchmark. You'd then compare your sample age distribution to this one, to judge whether your sample is representative of the golfing population.

If you were hoping to get more adoption of your golf shoe by younger golfers, you would look at these data and determine that you'd have to conduct a stratified sample, so as to increase the representation of the golfers younger than 44 years, even if your sample wasn't representative as a result.

The difference is statistical representativeness vs. targeting a nonrepresentative but demographically desired segment.

Figure A
#Rounds Played Annually by Golfer's Age

Source: From American Demographics, *June 2002, Copyright, Crain Communications Inc.*

(Continued)

Similarly, Figure B contains data on television audiences, for many stations, classifying them by three simple variables: the viewers' median age, the viewers' median income in thousands of dollars, and the percentage of the viewers who are male (each demographic presented separately per channel).

These data can also be used in a number of ways. We could estimate the sample size we would need to estimate the illusive female ESPN viewer (using the equation for proportions), or the apparently equally rare older MTV viewer (using the equation for means, as a rough approximation for these median data). We could use the equation for estimating sample size, plug in different values of "z" to represent different confidence levels, to determine the widths of the confidence intervals for, say, the age of the average ABC viewer compared with that of the CBS viewer. Are they different? The 95% confidence intervals, in both cases, will be narrower than the 99% confidence intervals. Wider intervals are more likely to overlap, which in turn would lead to the conclusion that the two stations attracted roughly the same age of viewers. Is that conclusion desirable? Would we prefer narrower intervals?

Figure B
TV Demographics

Source: From American Demographics, *June 2002, Copyright, Crain Communications Inc.*

This sort of analysis certainly works for any medium. Figure C contains radio listening preferences by the teen segment. You can see where you'd put your radio advertising budget if you wanted to attract these young consumers, top hits and hip-hop/rap stations. Would you program at R&B and alternative stations? Depends on what you want, depends on what you're marketing. Would you go to all news radio stations? Unlikely no matter what you're marketing.

All these examples show you secondary data in action. They present marketing research questions with the conjunction of marketing questions about targeted segments along with sampling questions (both the sampling schema as well as sampling size issues).

Figure C
Teen Radio Preferences

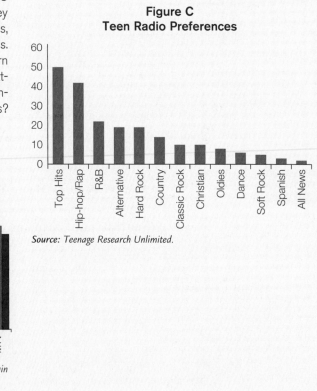

Source: Teenage Research Unlimited.

Don't forget what we said about the stages in the research process—they are very much related and a decision about one stage can affect the others, e.g., a decision about an analysis can have an important effect on the size of the sample required. Thus, think through the entire research problem, including how the data will be analyzed, before commencing the data-collection process.

Research Realities 12.2 pulls together information on sample size and sample plans. You can begin to see how the statistical questions about sampling plans and sample sizes relate to the marketing questions about target markets and audiences.

Summary

We reviewed the basic statistical principles involved in determining the size of a sample. The principles were used to develop confidence interval estimates for either a population mean or a population proportion using simple random samples. The examples demonstrated the influence of the sampling distribution of the statistic, the degree of confidence, and the level of precision on sample size. Both absolute and relative precision were discussed. The general conclusion is that sample size must be increased whenever population variability, degree of confidence, or the precision required of the estimate are increased.

Questions

1. In determining sample size, what factors must a marketing research consider?
2. When estimating a population mean, what is meant by absolute or relative precision?
3. What is the difference between degree of confidence and degree of precision?
4. If the population variance is known, how do you determine sample size (with some desired degree of precision and confidence)? When the population variance is unknown?
5. What effect would relaxing the absolute precision with which a population mean is estimated by 25% have on sample size? Decreasing confidence from 95% to 90% ($z = 1.64$)?
6. Suppose that one wants to estimate a population mean within $\pm10\%$ at the 95% level of confidence. How would one proceed and what quantities would one need to estimate?
7. Suppose you want to estimate a population proportion within ±3 percentage points at the 95% confidence. How would you proceed and what quantities would you need to estimate?
8. Suppose instead you want the estimate to be within $\pm3\%$ of the population value. What would be the procedure now and what quantities would you need to estimate?
9. What happens if the sample proportion is larger than the estimated population proportion used to determine sample size? If it is smaller? What value of the population proportion should be assumed if one wishes to take no chance that the generated interval will be larger than the desired interval?

Applications and Problems

1. A survey was being designed by the marketing research department of Conner Peripherals, Inc., a large ($2 billion plus) manufacturer of advanced electronic data storage for laptops. The general aim was to assess customer satisfaction with the drives. As part of this general objective, management wanted to measure the average maintenance expenditure per year per computer, the average number of malfunctions or breakdowns per year, and the length of service contracts purchased with new portable computers. Management wanted to be 95% confident in the results. Further, the magnitude of the error was not to exceed $\pm\$20$ for maintenance expenditures, ±1 malfunction, and ±3 months. The research department noted that although some individuals and businesses would spend nothing on maintenance expenditures per year, others might spend as much as $400. Also, although some computers would experience no breakdowns within a year, the maximum expected would be no more than three. Finally, although some computers might not be purchased with a service contract, others might be purchased with up to a 36-month contract.
   a. How large a sample would you recommend if each of the three variables is considered separately? Show all your calculations.
   b. What size sample would you recommend overall given that management thought that accurate knowledge of the expenditure on repairs was most important and the service contract length least important?
   c. The survey indicated that the average maintenance expenditure is $100 and the standard deviation is $60. Estimate the confidence interval for the population parameter μ. What can you say about the degree of precision?
2. The management of a major brewery wanted to determine the average number of ounces of beer

consumed per resident in the state of Washington. Past trends indicated that the variation in beer consumption (σ) was 4 ounces. A 95% confidence level is required, and the error is not to exceed $\pm 1/2$ ounce.

a. What sample size would you recommend? Show your calculations.

b. Management wanted an estimate twice as precise as the initial precision level and an increase in the level of confidence to 99%. What sample size would you recommend? Show your calculations. Comment on your results.

3. The director of a state park recreational center wanted to determine the average amount of money that each customer spent traveling to and from the park. On the basis of the findings, the director was planning on raising the entrance fee. The park director noted that visitors living near the center had no travel expenses but that visitors living in other parts of the state or out of state traveled upward of 250 miles and spent about 24 cents per mile. The director wanted to be 95% confident of the findings and did not want the error to exceed ± 50 cents.

a. What sample size should the park director use to determine the average travel expenditure? Show your calculations.

b. After the survey was conducted, the park director found that the average expenditure was $24.00 and the standard deviation was $15.00. Construct a 95% confidence interval. What can you say about the level of precision?

4. Pac-Trac Inc. is a large manufacturer of video games. The marketing research department is designing a survey to determine attitudes toward the products. In addition, the percentage of households owning video games and the average usage rate per week are to be determined. The research department wants to be 95% confident of the results and does not want the error to exceed ± 3 percentage points for video game ownership and ± 1 hour for average usage rate. Previous reports indicate that about 20% of the households own video games and that the average usage rate is 15 hours with a standard deviation of 5 hours.

a. What sample size would you recommend, assuming that only the percentage of households owning video games is to be determined? Show all your calculations.

b. What sample size would you recommend, assuming that only the average usage rate per week is to be determined? Show all your calculations.

c. What sample size would you recommend, assuming that both of the preceding variables are to be determined? Why?

d. After the survey was conducted, the results indicated that 30% of the households own video games and that the average usage rate is 13 hours (s.d. = 4). Compute the 95% confidence interval for the percentage of individuals owning video games. Is 95% ok?

e. Compute the 95% confidence interval for the average usage rate. Is 95% ok?

5. The local mass transit company in a southwest city of the United States recently started a campaign to encourage people to increase car pooling or use public transportation. To assess the effectiveness of the campaign, management wanted to do a survey to determine the proportion of people who had adopted the recommended energy-saving measures.

a. What sample size would you recommend if the error is not to exceed 65 percentage points and the confidence level is to be 90%? Show your calculations.

b. The survey indicated that the proportion adopting the measures was 20%. Estimate the 90% confidence interval. Is this level of precision ok?

6. A manufacturer wants to assess the taste preferences of children under age seven for its new brand of hot dogs versus its competitor's brand. They also want to assess the average number of hot dogs that a child under seven eats in a month. The director of marketing research wants to be 95% confident in the results of the study and does not want the error to exceed 1% on any of the estimates. The director believes that 75% of children under seven will prefer the new brand to the competitor's leading brand. Past research has shown that children eat approximately five hot dogs each month with a standard deviation of 1.

a. What sample size would you recommend, if only the percentage of kids under seven preferring the manufacturer's new brand of hot dogs is to be determined?

b. What sample size would you recommend, assuming that the average number of hot dogs consumed by a child under seven is to be determined?

c. The manufacturer decided to use a sample halfway between the two estimates. What is the consequence of doing so?

d. The actual results of the survey showed that 63% of children under seven prefer the manufacturer's new brand of hot dogs to the competitor's hot dogs. Compute the 95% confidence interval for this point estimate.

e. The actual results of the survey showed that a child under seven eats an average of seven hot dogs in a month with a sample standard deviation of 2. Compute the 95% confidence interval for this point estimate.

7. The transit system of a major metropolitan area was interested in determining the average number of miles a commuter drives to work. Past studies have shown that the variation (σ) in commuting distances was five miles. The managers of the transit system want to be 95% confident in the result and do not want the error to exceed .75 mile.

   a. What sample size would you recommend?

   b. The results of the survey showed that commuters actually drive an average of 20 miles to work with a standard deviation of 10. Compute the 95% confidence interval.

   c. Compute the 95% confidence interval if the mean was found to be 20 miles but the standard deviation was found to be 5 miles.

8. The owner of a local record store specializing in "alternative" music wanted to determine the average age of his customers. He estimated a 25-year range from his youngest customer to his oldest customer. He wanted to be 95% confident in the results of the survey, and he did not want the error to exceed nine months.

   a. What sample size would you recommend?

   b. The results of his survey indicated that the customers' average age is 35 with a standard deviation of 15. Construct a 95% confidence interval.

9. Tom Johnson, the owner of a local pizzeria, wanted to conduct a survey to find out local residents' favorite pizza toppings. However, he had only enough funds to have a sample of 100 local residents. Based on the sales of toppings in his pizzeria, Tom expected 40% of the residents to like pepperoni the best.

   a. If Tom wanted to be 95% confident in the results of this survey, what corresponding level of precision would he be able to achieve?

   b. If Tom instead wanted to not exceed an error rate of 5%, what corresponding level of confidence would he be able to achieve?

   c. Relate your results in parts a and b to the concept that one cannot increase both confidence and precision with a fixed sample size.

Field Procedures for Collecting the Data

13

Questions to Guide Your Learning:

Q1 What is "sampling error" vs. "nonsampling error"?

Q2 How can we minimize nonsampling errors?

The research process proceeds from sample design to the actual data collection. Data collection entails the use of some kind of field personnel operating either literally in the field or from an office (on the phone, via mail, e-mail or the Web). The field staff must be properly selected, trained, and monitored. This chapter gives you a perspective of what can go wrong when collecting data. An understanding of the various sources of error in data collection will enable you to evaluate the research project's strengths and limitations, so that it may serve as solid information for decision making.

Impact of Nonsampling Errors

Two types of errors arise in research studies: sampling errors and nonsampling errors. We've seen the first kind of errors in the chapters on sampling—there, we used a sampling distribution to see whether our observed statistic was similar to or different from the many possible samples that we might have obtained using the same sampling procedures. The statistic varies from sample to sample because we draw only part of the population in each case. Sampling error can be reduced (the distribution becomes more concentrated about the population parameter) by increasing sample size, because the sample statistic is more stable (equal across samples) when it is based on a larger number of observations (each sample has more data points in common). **Sampling error**, then, is the difference between our statistic and the values we'd expect over many repetitions of sampling.

Nonsampling errors reflect the many other kinds of error that arise in research, even when the survey is not based on a sample. They can be random or nonrandom. Random errors produce estimates that vary from the true value; sometimes above, sometimes below, but the average sample estimate will equal the population value. Nonrandom errors are more troublesome—they tend to produce mistakes only in one direction, biasing the sample value away from the population parameter, and we don't usually know in which direction; i.e., too high or too low. Nonsampling errors can occur due to errors in conception, logic, interpretation of responses, and statistics; errors in tabulation or coding; or errors in reporting the results.

Unlike sampling errors, we can't reduce nonsampling errors by increasing our sample size. In fact, nonsampling errors can increase with larger samples (thus, making them relatively more important as sample sizes get larger, since larger samples help reduce sampling error). Whereas sampling errors can be estimated, the magnitude and even direction of nonsampling errors is often unknown, e.g., it is difficult to answer the simple question, "Is our statistic an underestimation or overestimation of the parameter?" Finally, nonsampling errors usually increase the standard error of estimates and, therefore, the widths of confidence intervals. As Charlie Brown would say: Good grief!

Two common types of nonsampling errors—"no response" or poor responses—can wreak havoc with survey results. We try to reduce these errors by improving our research methods.

Bigger samples help sampling errors, but they don't fix nonsampling errors.

Types of Nonsampling Errors

Figure 13.1 lists types of nonsampling errors. **Nonobservation errors** means we've neglected parts of the survey population, e.g., they were accidentally not included or they did not respond. **Observation errors** occur when we get data from the sample but the information is inaccurate. With nonobservation errors, we usually know we have a problem of noncoverage or nonresponse, but with observation errors, we may not even be aware that a problem exists.

How do we estimate (the direction and magnitude of) possible data-collection errors? Studies have:

1. Relied on available, bias-free information, to serve as a validity check
2. Used split-run comparisons in which the respondent received different forms of the same questions, so that the person's consistency in responding could be measured
3. Measured the consistency of replies over time from the same respondent

These methods, while useful, cannot always be applied in marketing studies, and it becomes difficult to adjust the obtained information for response error. Instead, we usually take our data at face value. Thus, it is vital that researchers understand the sources of response bias so that they can better anticipate and prevent it.

FIGURE 13.1   Overview of Nonsampling Errors

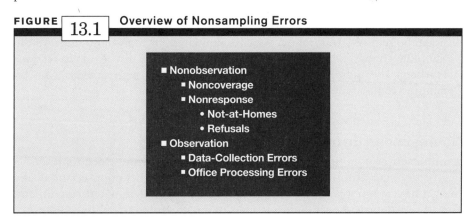

Noncoverage Errors

Noncoverage? Problem due to sampling frame. Spend the $ for a good list!

Noncoverage error is a sampling-frame problem. It means that our starting point, the sampling frame itself, doesn't include some elements of our target population. As a result, the probability that we will sample these units is zero. We can exclude a segment of the population deliberately, depending on our research question, e.g., we often survey only adults. But noncoverage means we've accidentally excluded a segment.

For instance, telephone directories are incomplete sampling frames, due to unlisted phone numbers, and the sampling frame of e-mail lists is still woefully inadequate. Or, consider that for mall-intercepts there is no list of population elements—only those people who shop in a particular mall have a chance of being included in the study, and their chances of being included depend on how much time they spend there. Given this sampling-frame problem, quota samples are often used in mall-intercept studies. Even so, nearly subconsciously, interviewers typically underselect in both the high- and low-income classes.

Noncoverage bias is *not* a problem in every survey. For some studies, clear, convenient, and complete sampling frames exist. For example, companies wanting to conduct a study among its loyalty card members should have little trouble with frame bias. The sampling frame is simply those with accounts.

Nevertheless, noncoverage bias is more likely than not, so we might ask: (1) How pervasive is it? (2) What can be done to reduce it? The first question can be addressed only by comparing the sample survey results with some outside criterion, i.e., a variable that can be established through an auxiliary quality check for some respondents, or from another reliable study, such as the population census.

The second issue, trying to lessen the effect of noncoverage is addressed by trying to improve the quality of the sampling frame, e.g., by taking the time to bring available city maps up to date, taking a sample to check the quality and representativeness of a mailing list with respect to a target population. Telephone surveys can be handled by random digit dialing.

If you know you have an imperfect sampling frame, you can weight subsample results to account for the imperfections. For example, in a study using a list of car registrations each contacted respondent might be asked, "How many cars do you own?" The response of someone who said two might be weighted ½, and someone who said three might be weighted ⅓.

While the precise adjustment procedures are technical, we note:

1. Noncoverage bias is a nonsampling error, so it is not dealt with in statistical formulas.

2. Noncoverage bias is not likely to be eliminated by increasing the sample size.

3. It can be of considerable magnitude.

4. It can be reduced, but not necessarily eliminated, by working to improve the sampling frame, and employing a sampling specialist to help reduce (through the sampling procedure) and adjust (through analysis) the remaining frame imperfections.

Nonresponse Errors

Another source of nonobservation bias is **nonresponse error**, which represents a failure to obtain information from the sample. It's hard to appreciate all the things that can go wrong with an attempt to contact a designated respondent. Figure 13.2 depicts the various outcomes of an attempted telephone contact.

FIGURE **13.2**   **Outcomes In Telephone Surveys**

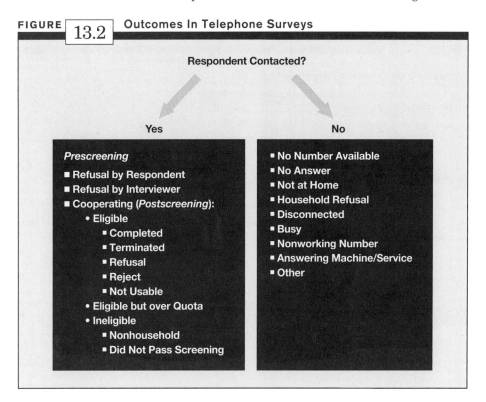

There is such a bewildering array of alternatives that even the calculation of a measure of the extent of the nonresponse problem becomes difficult. To try to assess the magnitude of nonresponse problems, a study was conducted by the Council of American Survey Research Organizations (CASRO).[1] They mailed questionnaires that displayed actual contact and response data from three phone surveys (a phone directory sample, a random-digit sample, and a list sample). Respondents (marketing researchers!) were asked to calculate the response, contact, completion, and refusal rates for each of the surveys. The results were rather different. Panel A of Table 13.1 displays the raw data from the phone directory sample. There was little agreement—using the same data, one organization computed the response rate as 12%, whereas another suggested it was 90%. Panel B displays the three most frequently used definitions, as well as the definitions producing the minimum and maximum response rates. Thus, there was little consensus industry-wide in methods of calculating rates of response and nonresponse. To improve this practice, CASRO developed a definition of response rate that the industry is supposed to embrace as the standard:

$$Response\ rate = \frac{\#completed\ interviews\ with\ responding\ units}{\#eligible\ responding\ units\ in\ the\ sample}$$

Nonresponse is a problem because it raises the question of whether the respondents are somehow different from those who didn't respond. Many studies have indicated that it is risky to assume that these groups are the same. The two main sources of nonresponse bias are not-at-homes and refusals.

---

[1] "On the Definition of Response Rates" www.casro.org.

| TABLE 13.1 | Response Rate Calculations for Telephone Directory Sample |

Panel A: Outcome of Telephone Call

A = Disconnected/nonworking telephone number	426
B = Household refusal	153
C = No answer, busy, not at home	1,757
D = Interviewer reject (language barrier, hard of hearing, ...)	187
E = Respondent refusal	711
F = Ineligible respondent	366
G = Termination by respondent	74
H = Completed interview	501
Total	4,175

Panel B: Most Frequent, Minimum, and Maximum Response Rates

Most frequent:

$$\frac{(B+D+E+F+G+H)}{All} = \frac{(153+187+711+366+74+501)}{4175} = 48\% \ (1)$$

$$\frac{(D+E+F+G+H)}{All} = \frac{(187+711+366+74+501)}{4175} = 44\% \ (2)$$

$$\frac{(H)}{All} = \frac{(501)}{4175} = 12\% \ (3)$$

Minimum: $\dfrac{(H)}{All} = \dfrac{(501)}{4175}$ = 12%

Maximum: $\dfrac{(E+F+G+H)}{(D+E+F+G+H)} = \dfrac{(711+366+74+501)}{(187+711+366+74+501)}$ = 90%

Source: "On the Definition of Response Rates" (published in 1982) and "CASRO Guidelines for Survey Research Quality" (revised in 1998). Council of American Survey Research Organizations, www.casro.org.

Not-at-Homes

Some respondents are inaccessible when the interviewer calls. There has been a long upward trend in this problem. The percentage of not-at-homes depends on the nature of the designated respondent and the time of the call. Seasonal variations occur, e.g., during the holidays, as do weekday-to-weekend variations, and so forth. To reduce the problem: For busy executives, make an appointment with the respondent. For consumers, computers redial.

One technique that is sometimes naïvely suggested for handling the not-at-homes is substituting the neighboring dwelling unit, or, in a phone survey, calling the next name on the list. This is a poor way of handling the not-at-home condition. All it does is substitute more at-homes for the population segment the researcher is in fact trying to reach, in effect aggravating the problem instead of solving it.

Interviewers can be compared with respect to their contact rate. The **contact rate (K)** is defined as the percentage of eligible assignments in which the interviewer makes contact with the designated respondent; essentially a measure of the interviewer's persistence:

$$K = \frac{\# \ eligible \ sample \ units \ contacted}{\# \ eligible \ sample \ units \ approached}$$

Ethical **Dilemma**   13.1

During the introduction in a telephone interview, interviewers introduce themselves, provide the research company's name, and then assure potential respondents that the client will be unable to link their responses back to them. However, the interviewer notes the respondents' first names and phone numbers on the completed survey so that the supervisor can randomly select a sample of questionnaires for verification. The possibility of a verification call is explained to the respondents.

Once the fieldwork has been completed, the research supplier bundles all the questionnaires and sends them to the client for coding, entry, and analysis. The questionnaires are sent with respondents' names and phone numbers attached.

- Is there a problem with providing names and phone numbers to the client company?
- If the client has signed a confidentiality agreement with the field company, is this problem avoided?

Interviewers with low contact rates can be checked to determine why. Perhaps they are operating in traditionally high not-at-home areas, such as high-income areas. Or, time of day may be a problem, with ineffective follow-up procedures. The field supervisor can help retrain the caller.

Researchers have suggested a statistical adjustment to lessen the effect of not-at-home nonresponse bias. Essentially, the responses from each informant are weighted by the inverse of their likelihood of being reached. For example, people who are usually not at home tend to be underrepresented in the survey, so their data are weighted more than respondents who say they're typically home and therefore reachable.

Refusals

In almost every study, some respondents refuse to participate. If contact is made, many people refuse to participate even before the interviewers completes their introductory words. Reasons include disinterest, inconvenient timing, concerns of privacy, and confusion between telemarketing and telephone calls for marketing research. The steep decline over the last decade of response rates (from 50–60% to about 20–25%) adds to the costs of these surveys. Research Realities 13.1 provides numbers representing contact rates and refusal rates per method of administration (phone, mall, Web).

The rate of refusals depends on the nature of the respondent, the topic of the research, the interviewer, etc. For example: (1) The culture can affect the refusal rate: e.g., in countries like Saudi Arabia, it is still nearly impossible to interview women. (2) The method used to collect the data makes a difference: Phone interviews yield slightly better response rates over mail questionnaires. (3) The research topic affects refusal rates: predictably those who respond are most interested in the topic. Nonresponse errors increase with the sensitivity of the information being sought. (4) People respond differently to different sponsors. (5) The interviewers themselves can have an important effect: Their approach, their manner, and their own demographic characteristics can affect a respondent's willingness to participate.

What can be done to enhance participation? There seem to be three available strategies. One, the initial response rate can be increased. Two, the impact of

RESEARCH   REALITIES

13.1 Response Rates

The Marketing Research Association has tracked participation rates in research studies and has analyzed these numbers per contact method (mra-net.org).

Modality of Survey	Contact Rate	Initial Refusal Rate	Survey Completion Rate
1) Telephone Overall	18%	33	26
Telephone RDD	10%	40	13
Telephone List	29%	24	45
Telephone B2B	19%	29	26
2) Mall/Central Location	38%	21	71
3) Internet Web Survey	34%	57	34

Note that the telephone lists appear to be beneficial; contact rates suggest they're not as inaccurate as you might think, and survey completions are strong.

The Mall serves as a workhorse for marketing research. You may be the sort of person who walks by those people with the clipboards saying, "Sorry," but many people stop. Once engaged in the interview, the completion rate is the strongest of all the techniques investigated. It's hard to walk away after agreeing to participate, and it's hard to say no to another person, in person.

The Web has strengths and weaknesses. It's quick and inexpensive, accessible to huge numbers of potential respondents, but the flipside is that it's anonymous and there is no social cost to quitting, upon seeing what the survey is about, or even in the middle of the survey.

For more information, also see: J. Michael Brick et al., "Nonresponse Bias in a Dual Frame Sample of Cell and Landline Numbers," *Public Opinion Quarterly*, 70 (5), 780–793; Robert M. Groves, "Nonresponse Rates and Nonresponse Bias in Household Surveys," *Public Opinion Quarterly*, 70 (5), 646–675; Scott Keeter et al., "Gauging the Impact of Growing Nonresponse on Estimates From a National RDD Telephone Survey," *Public Opinion Quarterly*, 70 (5), 759–779; Kurt Knapton and Steve Myers, "Demographics and Online Survey Response Rates," quirks.com; Linda Piekarski, "An Update on the State of 'Working Phone Rate,'" quirks.com.

refusals can be reduced through follow-up. Three, the obtained information can be extrapolated to allow for nonresponse.

Increasing Initial Response Rate

The nature of the respondent is beyond the researcher's control. The marketing problem dictates the target population, and this population is likely to contain households with different educational levels, income levels, cultural backgrounds, occupations, etc. We can try to sell respondents on the value of the research and the importance of their participation.[2] Advance notice may help. Some individuals refuse to participate because they do not wish to be identified with their responses, so a guarantee of confidentiality (if true) is often effective in calming such fears. Sometimes money or another incentive is offered.[3]

Nonresponse attributable to the sponsor can be overcome by hiding the sponsor, e.g., by hiring a professional research organization to conduct the field study. This is one reason companies with established, sophisticated research departments outsource some of their research.

[2] *Fortune* magazine recently conducted a survey and their introduction read, "Your name has been randomly chosen from a list of our subscribers to participate in an upcoming study for *Fortune* Magazine, conducted by XYZ, Inc." Standard, so far, but note their appeal: "Because you are part of a small, scientifically selected sample, your participation is essential to the accuracy of our study." Who could resist?

[3] Anja Goritz, "The Impact of Material Incentives on Response Quantity, Response Quality, Sample Composition, Survey Outcome, and Cost in Online Access Panels," *International Journal of Market Research*, 46 (3), 327–345.

Follow-up

Many of the circumstances surrounding a contact are temporary and change-able, so callbacks can reduce this problem. If a respondent declined participa-tion because he or she was busy or sick, a callback at a different time may be sufficient to secure cooperation. Thus, one means of reducing this source of bias is in the training of the field staff.

Perhaps little can be done regarding the research topic as a source of non-response bias, because it is dictated by the marketing problem to be solved. A sensitive research subject or one of little interest to the respondents is likely to elicit a high rate of refusals. Thus, the researcher needs to make the study as interesting as possible, e.g., avoiding those questions that are "interesting but not vital," with implications for the design of the survey instrument.

With mail and e-mail surveys, responses are frequently obtained with a 2nd or 3rd mailing to those who did not respond previously. Of course, follow-up re-quires identification of those not responding earlier, and respondents who know that they can be identified may refuse to participate. The alternative of sending each mailing to each designated sample member, without screening those who have responded previously, can be expensive for the research orga-nization and frustrating for the already cooperative respondents.

Adjusting the Results

If we could estimate the nonresponse bias, we could adjust the results accord-ingly. Suppose the problem was one of estimating the mean income for a certain population and responses were obtained from only a portion (p_r) of the desig-nated sample. The proportion not responding would be denoted p_{nr}. If $\bar{x}_r$ is the mean income of those responding and $\bar{x}_{nr}$ the mean income of those not re-sponding, then the overall mean would be

$$\bar{x} = p_r \bar{x}_r + p_{nr} \bar{x}_{nr}$$

This computation, of course, assumes that $\bar{x}_{nr}$ is known or at least can be estimated. An intensive follow-up of a sample of the nonrespondents is some-times used to generate this estimate for a crude adjustment of the initial results. Ignoring the initial nonresponse is equivalent to assuming that $\bar{x}_{nr}$ is equal to $\bar{x}_r$, which is usually incorrect.

A second type of adjustment involves keeping track of those responding to the initial contact, the first follow-up, the second follow-up, and so on. The mean of the variable is then calculated, and each subgroup is compared to determine whether any statistically significant differences emerge as a function of the difficulty experienced in making contact. If not, the variable mean for the nonrespondents is assumed to be equal to the mean for those responding. If a discernible trend is evident, the trend is extrapolated to allow for nonrespondents.

The preceding discussions all deal with *total* nonresponse. **Item nonresponse**, which can also be a problem, occurs when the respondent agrees to the total interview but refuses, or is unable, to answer some specific questions because of the content, form, or the amount of work required to produce the requested information.[4]

[4] See Gary S. Robertshaw and Norman E. Marr, "The Implications of Incomplete and Spurious Personal In-formation Disclosures for Direct Marketing Practice," *Database Marketing & Customer Strategy Management*, 13 (3), 186–197. For related respondent errors, see Scott D. Swain, Danny Weathers and Ronald W. Niedrich, "Assessing Three Sources of Misresponse to Reversed Likert Items," *Journal of Marketing Research*, 45 (1), 116–131.

We can distinguish between flagrant item nonresponse and isolated or sporadic nonresponse. If too many questions are left unanswered, the entire survey or interview becomes unusable. If only a few items are left unanswered, the respondent is included in the sample, and we use whatever data they did give us. In addition, the "don't know" and "no answers" can be treated as separate categories when reporting results.

Alternatively, the information from the missing item or items can sometimes be inferred from other information in the questionnaire.[5] If other questions on the questionnaire relate to the same issue, we check those data and formulate a consistent answer for the unanswered item. Regression is usually used where the missing item is treated as the criterion variable, and we attempt to predict that value from the respondent's other data. A simpler way of handling item non-response is to substitute for the missing data the average for that variable (based on the data of those who did respond to that item). Of course, in doing so, we are assuming that the nonrespondents are similar to those who answered the item.

Just as the contact rate can be used to compare and evaluate interviewers with respect to not-at-homes, at least two ratios have been suggested for comparing interviewers with respect to refusals: the **response rate R** and the **completeness rate C**. The response rate, discussed previously, equals the ratio of the {# of completed interviews with responding units} divided by the {# of eligible responding units in the sample}. The response rate reflects the interviewer's effectiveness at the door or on the phone. The completeness rate determines whether or not the response is complete. It is defined similarly but typically applies to the individual items in the study, such as the crucial or sensitive questions (e.g., a respondent's debt, etc.).

Field Errors

Field errors are by far the most prevalent type of observation error. They arise after the individual has agreed to participate in a study. Instead of cooperating fully, the individual refuses to answer specific questions, or provides a response that somehow differs from what is actually true or correct, errors that have been referred to as errors of omission and errors of commission. We discussed errors of omission (item nonresponse) in the last section. Now we turn to errors of commission, typically referred to as "response errors."

If you think about how complicated the response process actually is, you can see the many places where response errors can occur: Respondents first need to understand what is being asked. Second, the individual needs to engage in some cognitive processing to arrive at an answer, including retrieval of the pertinent attitudes, facts, or experiences, and the formulation of these cognitions into a response. Third, the person needs to evaluate the response in terms of its accuracy. Fourth, the respondent needs to evaluate the answer in terms of other human goals, even subconscious things like preserving one's self-image or attempting to please the interviewer. Finally, the participant needs to give the response that is the result of all this mental processing. Reaching the final step is the object of the survey process. Breakdowns can occur at any of the preceding steps resulting in an inaccurate answer—a response error.

Some data-collection errors arise due to the biases that both the interviewer and the interviewee bring to the marketing research interaction, as depicted in Figure 13.3. Each person brings certain background characteristics and psychological predispositions to the interview. Although some of the characteristics

---

[5] Patrick E. McKnight et al., *Missing Data* (Guilford, 2007).

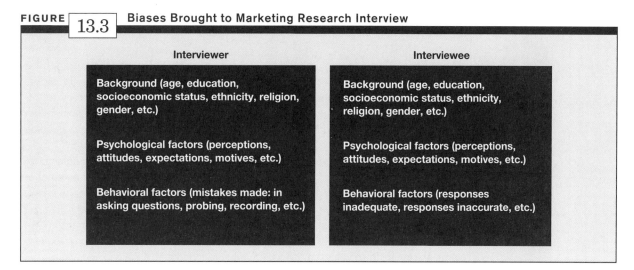

FIGURE 13.3   Biases Brought to Marketing Research Interview

Interviewer	Interviewee
Background (age, education, socioeconomic status, ethnicity, religion, gender, etc.)	Background (age, education, socioeconomic status, ethnicity, religion, gender, etc.)
Psychological factors (perceptions, attitudes, expectations, motives, etc.)	Psychological factors (perceptions, attitudes, expectations, motives, etc.)
Behavioral factors (mistakes made: in asking questions, probing, recording, etc.)	Behavioral factors (responses inadequate, responses inaccurate, etc.)

are readily observable, others are not. Yet both interviewer and interviewee form attitudes toward the other person on the basis of their initial perceptions. The interview is an interactive process, and both parties are important determinants of the process, perceiving and reacting to each other.

Background Factors

Better cooperation and more information are obtained when the backgrounds of the interviewer and respondent are similar than when they are different. This is particularly true for readily observable characteristics, such as ethnicity, age, and gender, but it also applies to characteristics such as social class and income. This suggests that it is productive to match the background characteristics of the interviewer and respondent as closely as possible, to enhance the probability of successful interviews.

There are often practical constraints, e.g., the interviewing profession attracts many part-time workers, such as students or school teachers, and these people probably do not represent a balanced demographic cross section of people. To minimize biases, we might compute a measure of interviewer variability while analyzing the results. Alternatively, we can modify interviewer schedules during a specific project to improve background matches. And recruiting could well be aimed at hiring interviewers with diverse demographic backgrounds, if other things are equal.

There are many types of interviewer bias. Sometimes a good, standardized survey makes better sense.

Psychological Factors

The interviewers themselves are human, and their opinions, perceptions, expectations, and attitudes affect the responses they receive. The primary way to control for these psychological factors is through training. We don't want these factors to affect interviewers' behavior during the interview, thereby contaminating the response.

As a result, most surveys are conducted using a rather rigid set of procedures that interviewers must follow. The instructions should be clear and should be written. Further, they should state the purpose of the study clearly. They should describe the materials to be used, such as questionnaires, maps, time forms, and so on. They should describe how each question should be asked, the kinds of answers that are acceptable, and the kinds and timing of probes that are to be used, if any. The

---

Ethical **Dilemma**   13.2

A well-known car agency needed to make a decision about whether to import a relatively unknown line of foreign cars to complement its domestic line. To aid its decision making, the agency contracted a research firm to conduct a study to determine potential consumer demand for this foreign car line. The results indicated that substantial awareness and interest existed, and consequently the decision was made to take on the new line.

To publicize the new line, a special preview was arranged for interested community members, such as local newspaper and radio people, executives in related automotive industries, filling station and repair shop owners, and leaders of men's and women's clubs. The agency's owners also wanted to invite the survey participants who had expressed an interest in the car; consequently, they asked the research firm to make known to them the respondents' names. The research firm refused to comply with this request, arguing that to do so would be a violation of the respondents' promised anonymity.

- Should the research firm comply with the agency's request?
- Does the car agency have the right to receive the participants' names since it has paid for the research?
- Would it have made a difference if the study had not been one to determine sales potential?
- What are some of the consequences of making the respondents' names known to the car agency?

---

instructions should also specify the number and identity of respondents that interviewers need to contact and the time constraints under which they will be operating. It is also important that the instructions are well organized and unambiguous.

The instructions must be clearly articulated, and it is even more important that interviewers understand and can follow them. Practice training sessions can be necessary. It might also be necessary to actually interview the interviewers with respect to study purposes and procedures. Finally, interviewers might also be required to complete the questionnaire to see if there is a relationship between the interviewers' answers and the answers they get when administering the questionnaire.

Behavioral Factors

The respondents' background, attitudes, expectations, and motives are also potentially biasing. Whether they actually introduce bias depends on how the interviewer and respondent interact. For example, even when the interviewing instructions and rules are rigid and the questionnaires relatively simple and structured, interviewers do not necessarily follow the rules. Interviewers might shorten questions or fail to follow up ambiguous answers, thereby introducing bias.

At least three interviewer behaviors lead to response bias: (1) errors in asking questions and in probing when additional information is required, (2) errors in recording the answer, and (3) errors due to cheating. The first problem is particularly acute with open-ended questions. No two interviewers are likely to use the same probes. Differences in answers, then, may be due to the probes rather than any "true" differences in the attitudes of the respondents.

The phrasing of questions can also introduce error. Interviewers sometimes reword the question to fit their perceptions of what the respondent is capable of understanding or in a way that incorporates their own opinions of what constitutes an appropriate answer. Even multiple-choice questions have potential for interviewer bias because interviewers sometimes emphasize one of the alternatives when stating the question. Slight changes in tone can change the meaning of the entire question.

One of an interviewer's main tasks is keeping the respondent interested and motivated. At the same time, the interviewer tries to record what the respondent is saying by dutifully writing down the person's answers. These dual, sometimes incompatible, responsibilities can also be a source of error. Interviewers may not correctly "hear" what the respondent is actually saying. Perhaps the respondent is inarticulate, or perhaps the interviewers are recording what they want to record. Lest we be too hard on interviewers, however, we need to recognize that their job is a difficult one. It demands a good deal of ingenuity, creativity, and dogged determination. Computer-driven surveys relieve some of these problems, but of course introduce others (e.g., a respondent cannot ask for clarification).

Finally, interviewer cheating can also be a source of response error. Cheating may range from the fabrication of a whole interview to one or two answers to make the response complete. Most commercial research firms validate 10–20% of the completed interviews through follow-up telephone calls or by sending postcards to a sample of "respondents" to verify that they have in fact been contacted.

As we've stated, it is more difficult to adjust for response errors than for nonresponse errors. Their direction and magnitude are unknown, because in order to estimate their effects, the true value must be known. The researcher's main hope lies in prevention rather than subsequent adjustment of the results. The various sources of errors themselves suggest preventives. For example, training can help reduce errors in asking questions and recording answers. Similarly, the way interviewers are selected, paid, and controlled could reduce cheating. Overall interviewer performance can be assessed by rating the quality of the work in terms of appropriate characteristics, such as costs, types of errors, ability to follow instructions, and so on.

Office Errors

Problems with nonsampling errors do not end with data collection. Errors arise in the editing, coding, tabulation, and analysis of the data. For the most part, these errors can be reduced, if not eliminated, through the exercise of proper controls in data processing. These questions are discussed in the next chapter.

Ethical Dilemma 13.3

"These new computer-voiced telephone surveys are wonderful!" your friend enthuses over lunch. "We don't have to pay telephone interviewers, so we can afford to have target numbers automatically redialed until someone answers. The public finds the computer's voice irritating and the whole notion of being interviewed by a machine rather humiliating, but we can overcome most people's reluctance to participate by repeatedly calling them until they give in and complete the questionnaire."

- Is it ethical to contact respondents repeatedly until they agree to participate in a research study? How many contacts are legitimate?
- If an industry is unable to constrain its members to behave ethically, should the government step in with regulations?
- If the public reacts against this kind of telephone survey, what are the results likely to be for researchers using traditional, more considerate telephone surveys?

Total Error Is Key

By now you can see that "total" error, rather than any single type of error, is key in designing good marketing research. Statistical theory indicates that large samples are much more likely to produce a statistic close to the population parameter being estimated than a small sample. However, that theory applies only to sampling error. Nonsampling error may increase because the larger sample requires more interviewers, which creates additional burdens in selection, training, and control. Further, nonsampling error is a much more insidious kind of error. We have attempted to highlight some of the more common sources of nonsampling error and suggest ways of dealing with them.

Table 13.2 summarizes the issues regarding nonsampling errors and how they can be reduced or controlled. You can use it as a checklist to evaluate the quality of research before making managerial decisions on the basis of the results.

TABLE 13.2 Overview of Nonsampling Errors and Some Methods for Handling Them

Type	Definition	Methods for Handling
Noncoverage	Failure to include some elements of the population in the sampling frame.	1. Improve basic sampling frame using other sources. 2. Reduce incidence by ignoring ineligibles on a list. 3. Adjust the results by appropriately weighting the subsample results.
Nonresponse	Failure to get data from some of the sample	
Not-at-homes	Designated respondent is not home when the interviewer calls.	1. Have interviewers make advance appointments. 2. Callback at another time. 3. Attempt to contact the designated respondent using another approach
Refusals	Respondent refuses to cooperate in the survey.	1. Convince respondents of the importance of their participation. 2. Provide advance notice that the survey is coming. 3. Guarantee anonymity. 4. Provide an incentive for participating. Hide sponsorship by using an independent research organization.
Field	Although the individual participates in the study, he or she refuses to answer specific questions or provides incorrect answers to them.	1. Match interviewer-respondent background characteristics. 2. Make sure interviewer instructions are clear and written down. 3. Conduct practice training sessions with interviewers.

(Continued)

		4. Have interviewers complete the questionnaire, examine the replies to check for relationship between these answers and their own answers.
		5. Verify a sample of each interviewer's interviews.
Office	Errors that arise when coding, tabulating, or analyzing the data	1. Use field edit to detect glaring omissions and inaccuracies in the data.
		2. Use a second edit in the office to handle data with incomplete answers, wrong answers, and answers that reflect a lack of interest.
		3. Use closed questions to simplify coding.
		4. When open-ended questions are used, divide the coding by questions, not by respondent data-collection forms.
		5. Have each coder code a sample of the other's work to ensure a consistent set of coding criteria is being employed.
		6. Prepare a code book that lists the codes for each variable and the categories included in each code.

Summary

This chapter concentrated on the data-collection phase of the research process. Researchers and consumers of research need to be aware of the many potential sources of error so that they can better evaluate research proposals and can place research results in a proper perspective. Researchers need an understanding of error sources so they can design studies with proper controls and allowances.

The main distinction is that between sampling error and nonsampling error. Sampling error represents the difference between the observed values of a variable and the long-run average of the observed values in repetitions of the measurement. Nonsampling errors include everything else. They may arise because of errors in conception, logic, analysis, data gathering, etc. They are divided into the two major categories: errors of nonobservation and errors of observation. Errors of nonobservation can, in turn, be divided into errors of noncoverage and errors of nonresponse. Errors of observation arise while collecting the data or while processing the information collected.

Noncoverage errors are essentially sampling frame problems. The list of population elements is rarely complete. Nonresponse errors reflect a failure to obtain information from certain elements of the population that were designated for inclusion in the sample. They can arise because the designated respondent was not at home or refused to participate. Empirical evidence indicates that the not-at-homes and the refusals differ from respondents, and thus a systematic bias is introduced when they are excluded.

The interviewer–interviewee interaction model was offered as a vehicle for conceptualizing the errors that can arise while collecting the data. This model presents the interview as an interactive process between interviewer and respondent. Each principal brings different background and psychological factors to the interview. These affect each person's behavior and the way he or she perceives the other's behavior.

Finally, office errors occur because of weaknesses in the procedures for editing, coding, tabulating, and analyzing the collected data. The research objective of minimization of total error was reiterated. Total error in conjunction with cost determines the value of any research effort.

Questions

1. Why is the distinction between sampling error and nonsampling error important?
2. What are noncoverage errors? Are they a problem with telephone surveys? Mail surveys? Personal interview studies? E-mail or Web questionnaires? How?
3. How can noncoverage bias be assessed? What can be done to reduce it?
4. What is nonresponse error? What are the basic types?
5. What can be done to reduce the incidence of not-at-homes in the final sample?
6. What is the contact rate? What role does it play in evaluating the results?
7. What are the typical reasons why designated respondents refuse to participate in a study? What can be done to reduce the incidence of refusals? Do refusals generally introduce random error or systematic biases into studies?
8. What is item nonresponse? How can you treat item nonresponse?
9. What are observation errors? What are the basic types of observation errors?
10. What does the interviewer–interviewee interaction model suggest with respect to the background and psychological characteristics of interviewers?
11. What types of interviewer behavior can lead to response bias?
12. Explain the statement, "Total error is key."

Applications and Problems

1. Discuss some potential problems with each of the following sampling frames. For each problem you list, indicate whether it would result in a noncoverage or overcoverage error.
   a. Phone book
   b. Mailing list
   c. E-mail list of students enrolled in your business school
   d. Maps
2. Sue Candleshoe, a manager of marketing research at a large over-the-counter drug manufacturer, wanted to investigate consumers' reactions to a recent poisoning scare in one of her brands. She needed the results quickly, but she was familiar with some of the faults of using a phone book for a sampling frame. Recommend another option that would allow Sue to get the results quickly by telephone but would not introduce as much bias as using a phone book.
3. Henry Brown owns a sailboat rental yard located in Sister Bay, Wisconsin. He has been considering altering the services that his business offers to customers. He would like to offer sailboards for rental as well as add a convenience store so that customers could picnic at the state park adjacent to his rental yard. Before making these changes, he has decided to administer a short questionnaire in the store to a random sample of customers. For a period of one month, clerks have been instructed to conduct personal interviews with every fourth customer. Henry gave specific instructions that on no account were customers to be harassed or offended. Identify the sources of noncoverage and nonresponse errors. Explain.
4. A major publisher of diverse magazines was interested in determining customer satisfaction with three of the company's leading publications: *Trend-Setter*, *BusWhiz*, and *CompuTech*. The three magazines dealt with women's fashions, business trends, and computer technology developments. Three sampling frames, consisting of lists of subscribers residing in New York, were formulated. Three random samples were to be chosen from these lists. Personal interviews were to be conducted. The publishing company had a regular pool of interviewers that it called on whenever interviews

were to be conducted. The interviewers had varying educational backgrounds, although 95% were high school graduates and the remaining 5% had some college education. In terms of age and gender, the range varied from 18 to 45 years, with 70% female and 30% male. The majority of interviewers were stay-at-home moms and students. Before conducting a survey, the company sent the necessary information in the mail and asked interviewers to indicate whether they were interested. The questionnaires, addresses, and other detailed information were then sent to those interviewers replying affirmatively. After the interviewer completed his or her quota of interviews, the replies were sent back to the company. The company then mailed the interviewer's remuneration.

a. Using the guidelines in 13.2, critically evaluate the selection, training, and instructions given to the field interviewers.

b. Using the interaction model, identify the major sources of bias that would affect the interviews.

C A S E S

CASE 4.1
Riverside County Humane Society (B)

Like a lot of nonprofits, Riverside County Humane Society (RCHS) is being expected to do more (services) with less (funding and donations). In an effort to halt further decline in the quality of its services and to provide better care for the pets at the center, the Membership Committee of the board of directors began making plans for a member/contributor drive. The organized drive was the first of its kind for the local chapter and the committee members wanted it to be as productive as possible.

As the plans began to evolve, the committee realized that the organization had only scattered bits and pieces of information about its current members. It did have a list of members and contributors for the last five years that had been compiled by the RCHS staff. In addition, it had access to the results of a survey that had been done by a staff member several years earlier that focused on member usage of shelter facilities and their opinions of shelter services and programs. However, the organization had only sparse knowledge of the profile of its typical member and contributor, why they belonged or contributed, how long they had been associated with the humane society, how the services of the humane society could be improved, and so on. The committee members believed information on these issues was important to the conduct of a successful membership drive, and thus they commissioned research to secure it.

Initial contacts with other humane society chapters and interviews with some RCHS staff and board members produced a number of hypotheses regarding who is likely to become a member or contributor, why, how much people are likely to give, and so on. The researchers are interested in examining these hypotheses through a mail survey sent to current members and contributors. (See Case 2.2, Riverside County Humane Society (A) for details.)

Sampling Plan

For the last five years, the RCHS had maintained a master list of members and contributors. Contributors were those who had sent a donation to RCHS but had not filled out an official form making them members, which essentially entitled them to receive RCHS's newsletter. The separate list of members contained all those who had expressed interest in membership and

who were receiving the newsletter. Both lists were alphabetical. The contributor list included the amount received from each person or business, but not the number of times the person or business had given during the last five years. The member list showed the number of years each organization or person had belonged.

For purposes of the study, all names of businesses or other organizations were deleted and a separate sample was taken from each list. Approximately 1,050 people were on the member list and 300 on the contributor list. The researchers decided to take 120 names from the member list and 50 from the contributor list. They identified those to be sent questionnaires by drawing two random numbers—3 and 5—using a random number table. They then sent questionnaires to the 3rd, 11th, 19th, and so on, person on the member list, and the 5th, 11th, 17th, and so on, person on the contributor list.

QUESTIONS

1. What is the sampling frame and is it a good frame for the target population?

2. What type of sample is being used?

3. Can you think of some ways in which the sample could be improved?

CASE 4.2
Sampling Lead-Users for New Products

The new, hot thing in testing new product concepts and product specifications is to bring in samples of "lead-users"—the customers who are "innovators" in terms of diffusion of innovation, or those who precede the "early adopters"—they're the earliest of adopters. The idea is that these customers are so highly involved in this product category that they're likely to encounter needs and desire benefits before the rest of the marketplace might even recognize that there's an issue or an unmet need. Their customer involvement is also so high that they're very likely to agree to be involved in beta testing products or giving their expert opinions about product design and the like.

QUESTIONS

1. What kind of information can you obtain from a "lead-user" sample?

2. Is this a probability sample? A cluster sample? A stratified sample? A convenience sample?

3. What limitations might there be to a lead-user sample?

CASE 4.3
Sampling from Your Loyalty Database

Cain is a holding company that publishes magazines. It has a large subscription database, across all its magazines. It wants to use this database to get feedback on some ideas about a new magazine, a new loyalty program, and a new pricing policy as it makes its periodicals available online.

Here's what they're thinking of doing. They have the entire database—that's their sampling frame. They're going to split the customers into "good ones" (subscribe to two or more magazines), "current customers" (subscribe to one), and "lapsed customers" (those who subscribed to one or more, more than six months ago but did not keep up their subscription).

Then, the database is huge and they only want a sample of 300 of each group (good/ current/ lapsed customers). So once the database is parsed into these three groups, they're going to take every 50th customer in the database until they have 300, then stop and go onto the next group.

QUESTIONS
1. What kind of sampling plan is this?

2. Evaluate the sampling plan.

CASE 4.4
International Differences in the Cost of Data

A multinational bank, MNB, was interested in measuring customer satisfaction with its consumer banking services and financial products. The managers at MNB Corporate differed in their opinions regarding the form of the optimal customer satisfaction study: survey, focus group, interview, and so on. So as a starting point, MNB commissioned bids from marketing research firms in the United States to describe how they would approach studying their U.S. banking customers. In particular, they asked the bidding firms to offer cost estimates, that is, how many customers could be sampled given the proposed budget of $15,000 for this research project using different techniques.

The bids covered a variety of research methods, which differed in their costs. They considered a personal interview method in which the customer would be intercepted in the bank and asked several questions regarding service and satisfaction. They compared that method to the costs of sending out mail surveys to current customers. Finally, they explored the efficiency of placing small, postcard-sized surveys at each teller station that the banking customer might pick up and complete and return at their leisure.

MNB gathered the marketing research firms' proposals to begin to make a decision of how the bank should approach its customers. In terms of outlay expenses, more postcards could be printed less expensively than surveys sent or interviewers staffing each of the local bank branches. However, in terms of response rates, somewhat fewer people turned down the personal interview than who returned the mail survey or postcard survey. Table 4.4.1 presents the comparative estimates

Table **4.4.1** The Estimates for the U.S. Samples	Interview	Mail Survey	Postcards
a. Research budget	$15,000	$15,000	$15,000
b. Cost per contact	$25	$2.50	$.25
c. Prospects reached*	2,400	6,000	60,000
d. Response rate	5%	3%	1.5%
e. Estimated net sample size (c × d)	120	180	900
f. Effective cost per capita (a/e)	$125.00	$83.33	$16.67

*For mail and postcard, c = a/b; for interviews, cost is $25 per hour, times a five-hour day, = $125 per day, for each interviewer. Each of 12 interviewers (spread across the area local bank branches) would spend two weeks (10 bank days) approaching and interviewing customers. Each interviewer on each day would target 20 bank customers, on average.

Table **4.4.2** The Projections for Indonesia	Interview	Mail Survey	Postcards
a. Research budget	$15,000	$15,000	$15,000
b. Cost per contact	$12*	$2.50	$.25
c. Prospects reached	5,000	6,000	60,000
d. Response rate	20%*	1.5%*	.5%
e. Estimated net sample size (c × d)	1,000	90	300
f. Effective cost per capita (a/e)	$15.00	$166.67	$50.00

*These estimates differ from those for conducting the research in the U.S. labor costs for interviewing are much less, propensities for customers to acquiesce and be interviewed are much greater, mail surveys are somewhat less efficient because CD-ROM databases on addresses are less accurate, and postcards are an unfamiliar format and are therefore rarely filled out. Given the changes in the interviewing parameters, if the project duration is still two weeks, 25 interviewers can be deployed, so 5,000 customers would be approached.

for the three different techniques. The table shows clearly that in the U.S., the postcard technique appears to be the most cost effective. Thus, the bank managers are considering implementing this research tool.

MNB's second concern is with a few of its satellite locations—in particular, the news from abroad is that the Indonesian banking customers are not happy—and MNB wants to understand what is going on. Its first assumption was that the bank should proceed with the postcard methodology to be able to compare the results in Indonesia to those from the States. However, they conducted some preliminary investigations and found the costs of the methods to be quite different. The bank plans to proceed with personal interviews in Indonesia. Consider Tables 4.4.1 and 4.4.2 and answer the questions that follow.

QUESTIONS

1. Under what conditions might it matter that one method is used in one country and another method is used in another?

2. What is the target population under investigation, both in the U.S. and in Indonesia? What are the differences between the sampling frames of each of the three techniques? What customers will each technique miss?

3. What other issues must the bank managers consider in addition to the cost efficiencies of the three methods?

CASE 4.5
Online Samples

You're working for a large pharmaceutical company on a brand management team, and your team is

responsible for building two initiatives. First, you're creating a Web site for social support—blogging by users and carriers to talk about their drug experiences but also how their disease impacts their lives, how they cope, things they've learned, just general, "we're here for you" kind of support. The second initiative is based on several pharma-firms' recent successes with flavors for children's medicines. Your drugs are for adults but you figure, if it works for kids, why not for adults too, so you're exploring the possible desire for several flavors (cherry, strawberry, piña colada, etc.).

Your team would like to get some good consumer data before proceeding, because each initiative would eventually require a good level of financial backing. You've got a beta version of the Web site developed, you're ready for potential-user feedback, and your chemists have created several flavors that are palatable, which your team is ready to test.

Your team meets with your boss and his boss. Your team has proposed a combination of marketing research methods, including a few focus groups, some online surveys, and some mall-intercepted interviews. Your boss is supportive, as you all knew he would be, from previous meetings, but he's keeping quiet because this meeting is the first during which the ideas are being presented to the big boss.

The big boss likes the focus group idea, doesn't really like the mall-intercept idea, but mostly wants results quickly ("yesterday!") and cheaply (ideally free—no line on the marketing budget). You all know he's exaggerating, but he's like that, and you know he's not exaggerating by much. So, he's pushing doing the testing of the Web site and the flavors via your online panel of past customers who have redeemed prescriptions for your drugs.

QUESTIONS

1. The online panel was, of course, part of your proposal. Shall you just "back down" and do what the big boss wants?

2. What are the characteristics of the e-panel likely to be?

3. What kind of information can you obtain from the online survey?

4. Will you be ready to launch both initiatives after conducting solely the online survey?

CASE 4.6
Sampling Gambling

Americans spend nearly $50 billion annually on gambling. That expenditure is more than three times the amount spent on going to the movies and theme parks, as alternative means of entertainment. State-run lotteries and casino games are the most popular legal games of chance.

Gambling traditionally held negative connotations, being associated with immoral or even criminal behavior. Critics worry that legalized gambling can encourage compulsive gamblers, that it may encourage people to gamble who can least afford to do so, and that casinos bring an undesirable element to the surrounding neighborhood.

Legalized gambling, however, especially in the form of state lotteries, has largely sanitized the image of gaming behavior. Among people who abstain from gambling, fewer people cite moral or religious objections, instead offering practical reasons: e.g. they don't want to spend the money, or they don't have the money to spend. Proponents claim casinos create jobs and provide revenue for education that would otherwise be raised by tax hikes.

Secondary data suggest that there is no particular demographic profile of a gambler—people of all walks of life (e.g. age and income) enjoy casinos and lotteries. Beyond demographics, the commonly held motivations appear to be a desire to win a large amount of money, and a quick and relatively inexpensive form of entertainment.

The heterogeneity of the demographics of gamblers and the homogeneity of their motives have left some casino managers perplexed as to how the consumer market might be segmented. One hypothesis, based on collective wisdom, is that novice gamblers tend to prefer slot machines because they are simple, whereas more experienced gamblers prefer games like blackjack, baccarat, and craps because they are more strategic in nature. Another frequent assumption is that people who buy lottery tickets are different from people who go to casinos, and that the two types of games satisfy different needs.

The Internet introduces yet another medium in which a consumer might gamble. Although the number of gamblers online are far fewer than those who frequent casinos or lotteries, and online gambling revenues are far less than nonelectronic games (approximately only $2 billion), the online gambling industry is expected to enjoy rapid growth.

If a gaming industry representative were to come to you and say, "I'd like to do some interviews. I want to know more about what kinds of games my casino visitors want me to provide. I want to know how much floor space to allot to slots versus blackjack tables. I want to know why they come to any casino, or my casino, rather than to the movies or something. Maybe I should just sell lottery tickets." How would you address the following issues?

QUESTIONS

1. What is the relevant population?

2. What would you recommend in terms of a sampling plan—would you intercept people in (or entering or exiting) casinos? Would you talk to people buying lottery tickets at convenience stores? Would you interview people strolling along in a shopping mall? What sampling frame does each of these locations presume?

3. If you wanted to verify the aforementioned assumptions (for example, that demographics do not matter, or that novice versus experienced gamblers have different game preferences), how would you modify your sampling plan?

4. How would you try to assess objectively whether there are moral or religious concerns against gambling? What kinds of sampling plans would you need to avoid, given the likelihood that they would shape your conclusions pro or con?

Data Analysis and Interpretation

Once data have been collected, the research process logically turns to analysis, which amounts to the search for meaning in the data. This translation and interpretation of data into information and meaning involves many questions and several steps:

Chapter 14 presents the idea of "preprocessing" the data–before analyses are run; e.g., from editing and coding, to "*cross-tabs.*"
- The Appendix to Chapter 14 presents the chi-square and log linear models.

Chapter 15 raises the questions that help us select the proper statistical analyses to conduct on the data.
- The Appendix to Chapter 15 presents a quick stats review, covering the logic of hypothesis testing, Type I and Type II errors, and the concept of power.

Chapter 16 presents procedures appropriate for examining differences (i.e., one-sample and two-sample t-tests).
- The Appendix to Chapter 16 extends the tests of differences to three or more groups, in the analysis of variance.

Chapter 17 examines associations between variables, such as correlations and regressions, for forecasting.

Chapter 18 introduces the multivariate techniques of discriminant analysis, factor analysis, cluster analysis, and multidimensional scaling.
- The Appendix to Chapter 18 continues with more fun multivariate techniques.

Preprocessing the Data, and Doing Cross-Tabs

14

Questions to Guide Your Learning:

Q1 What are the basic steps in *getting data ready* for analysis?

Q2 What are: coding, editing, and tabulation?

Q3 What information can we get from a *frequency table*?

Q4 What can I do with *nominal* data? What's a *Chi-square* goodness-of-fit test?

Q5 What can I do with *rank order* data? What's a *Kolmogorov-Smirnov* test?

Q6 What's a *cross-tab*? (I thought I already knew!)

Q7 What info can I get from a *contingency table?* What does *"conditional probability"* mean?

The purpose of analysis is to obtain meaning from the data. All previous steps in the research process have been undertaken to obtain the data in this search for meaning. In this chapter, we examine the preliminary analytical steps of editing, coding, and tabulation. We will create tables for the frequency distributions of variables, and look at the chi-square statistic.

Editing

The basic purpose of editing is to impose some minimum quality standards on the raw data. Editing involves the inspection and, if necessary, correction of each questionnaire or observation form. Inspection and correction are often done in two stages: the field edit and the central office edit.

The **field edit** is a preliminary edit, designed to detect the most glaring omissions and inaccuracies in the data. It is also useful in helping to control the field force and clear up its misunderstandings about procedures. For example, if the field staff is supposed to interview people, but all the questionnaires from one particular field agent have different markings, you'll know that person just gave the survey to the respondents to fill out themselves.

Ideally, the field edit is done by a field supervisor as soon as possible after the survey has been administered, so that problems can be corrected before the interviewing staff is disbanded and while the experience is still fresh in the interviewer's mind.

The field edit is followed by a **central office edit**, which involves more detailed scrutiny and correction of the completed returns. To ensure consistency, it is best if one individual handles all completed instruments. If this is impossible because of length and time considerations, the work can be divided, but the division should be by parts of the data-collection instruments rather than by respondents. That is, one editor would be concerned with editing "Part A," of all questionnaires, while the other would edit "Part B."

The central office has to decide how to handle incomplete answers, obviously wrong answers, and answers that reflect a lack of interest. Because such problems are more prevalent with questionnaires than with observational forms, we discuss these difficulties from that perspective, but the discussion applies to all types of data-collection forms.

It almost never happens that a study has all the returned questionnaires completely filled out. Some surveys have entire sections omitted; others reflect sporadic item nonresponse. The editor's decision on how to handle these incomplete questionnaires depends on the severity of the problem. Questionnaires that omit entire sections are obviously suspect, yet they should not automatically be thrown out. It might be, for example, that the omitted section is not relevant. The rest of this person's data would be usable in spite of the incomplete section. Alternatively, there might not be a logical justification for the large number of questions that went unanswered. In this case, the total reply would probably be thrown out, increasing the nonresponse rate for the study. Questionnaires containing only isolated instances of item nonresponse would be retained.

Careful editing of the questionnaire sometimes shows that an answer to a question is obviously incorrect. For example, respondents might be asked for the type of store in which they purchased a camera in one part of the questionnaire and the name of the store in another. If the person responded "department store" whereas the name of the store indicated a discount store, one of the answers is incorrect. The editor may be able to determine which from other information in the questionnaire. Alternatively, the editor may need to establish policies concerning which answer will be treated as correct, if either, when these inconsistencies or inaccuracies arise.

Indications that the completed questionnaire reflects a lack of interest on the part of the subject are sometimes subtle and sometimes obvious. For example, a subject who circled all 5s on a five-point scale for each of the 40 items in an attitude questionnaire in which some items were expressed negatively and some positively is obviously not taking the study very seriously. You would probably throw out such a response. If you're not sure, add a code to the survey so that you could run separate tabulations for both questionable instruments and obviously good questionnaires, to see if that makes any difference in the results and conclusions.

The preprocessing data mantra: editing, coding, tabulation!

Coding

Coding is the technical procedure by which raw data are transformed into symbols. The first step is specifying the categories or classes into which the responses are to be placed. There is no magic number of categories. Rather, the number depends on the research problem being investigated and the specific items used to generate the information.

Nevertheless, several rules for specifying the classes can be stated. First, the classes should be mutually exclusive and exhaustive. Every response should logically fall into one and only one category. Multiple responses are sometimes legitimate, e.g., if the question is, "When do you use whipped cream?" and the responses include "a dessert item," "an evening snack," and so on. But if a question asks the person's age, then only one age category is acceptable.

Coding scales is simple because the coding is established, for all practical purposes, when the data-collection instrument is designed (e.g., a seven-point scale results in data of 1s through 7s). Coding open-ended questions can be very difficult and time consuming, and is therefore more expensive. The coder has to determine appropriate categories on the basis of answers that are not always anticipated. Because of the freedom allowed to respondents, the responses can be so vague that they can be misclassified by coders in spite of the detailed instructions given to them.

When using several coders, it's best to have each coder focus on one or two questions, so they can get "good" at coding those questions, and provide consistency across the respondents' questionnaires. This approach is also more efficient because coders can learn the codes for their few questions without having to consult the codebook for every survey. Coders coding the same question can also double-check the others' work.

The second step in coding involves assigning code numbers to the classes. For example, gender might be assigned the letters M for male and F for female. Alternatively, the classes could be denoted by 1 and 2. Generally, it is better to use numbers than letters, because most data analysis is done by computer (e.g., Excel, add-ins, Sas, Spss, etc.). There are certain conventions when coding the data:

1. Use only numeric codes—not letters of the alphabet, special characters such as @, or blanks. Most statistical programs have difficulty manipulating anything but numbers.

2. Use standard codes for "No information." Thus, all "Don't know" responses, for any question on the survey, might be coded 8, "Blanks" as 9, and "Does not apply" as 0.

3. Give each respondent an identification number. This number need not, and typically does not, identify the respondent by name. The number simply ties the questionnaire to the coded data. This is often useful when data cleaning.

The final step in the coding process is to prepare a codebook. The codebook contains the general instructions indicating how each item of data was coded, so that the people conducting the data analysis can see what the people who were the coders did. The codebook lists the codes for each variable and the categories included in each code. It further indicates where the variable is located in the database.

Tabulation

Tabulation consists of counting the number of cases that fall into various categories. The tabulation may take the form of a simple tabulation or a cross-tabulation. **Simple tabulation** involves counting a single variable. It may be repeated for each variable in the study, but the tabulation keeps each variable separate. In **cross-tabulation**, two or more of the variables are treated simultaneously; the number of cases that have the joint characteristics are counted (e.g., the number of people who bought Campbell's soup at a Kroger store).

A number of important questions concerning the analysis of data can be illustrated using one-way tabulations. Let's work with the data in Table 14.1 as an example. The data were collected for a study focusing on car ownership.

Cross-tabs come soon!

One-Way Tabulation

One-way tabulations are useful in communicating the results of a study. In addition, they can be used for other purposes:

1. To determine the degree of item nonresponse

2. To locate blunders

TABLE 14.1   **Raw Data for Car Ownership Study**

	(1)	(2)	(3)	(4)	(5)	(6)	(7)	(8)	(9)	(10)	(11)
family ID	$income	# in family	educat. (yrs) hhold	region: North South	lifestyle Liberal Conserv.	#cars	car financed?	station wagon?	economy car?	van?	other car?
1001	26,800	3	12	N	L	1	N	N	N	Y	N
1002	17,400	4	12	N	L	1	N	N	N	N	Y
1003	14,300	2	10	N	L	1	N	N	N	N	Y
1004	35,400	4	9	N	L	1	N	N	N	N	Y
1005	24,000	3	8	N	L	1	N	N	N	N	Y
1006	17,200	2	12	N	L	1	N	N	Y	N	N
1007	27,000	4	12	N	L	1	N	N	N	N	Y
1008	16,900	3	10	N	L	1	N	N	N	N	Y
1009	26,700	2	12	N	L	1	N	N	N	N	Y
1010	13,800	4	6	N	C	1	Y	N	N	N	Y
1011	34,100	3	8	N	C	1	N	N	N	N	Y
1012	16,300	3	11	N	C	1	N	N	N	N	Y
1013	14,700	2	12	N	C	1	N	N	N	N	Y
1014	25,400	4	12	N	C	1	N	N	N	N	Y
1015	15,400	4	12	N	C	1	N	N	N	N	Y
1016	25,900	3	11	N	C	1	Y	N	N	N	Y
1017	36,300	3	12	N	C	1	N	N	N	N	Y
1018	27,400	2	12	N	C	2	N	N	N	N	Y
1019	17,300	2	12	N	C	1	N	N	N	N	Y
1020	13,700	3	8	N	C	1	N	N	N	N	Y
1021	26,100	2	12	N	C	1	N	N	Y	N	N
1022	16,300	4	12	N	C	1	Y	N	N	N	Y
1023	33,800	3	6	N	C	1	N	N	N	N	Y
1024	34,400	4	8	N	C	1	N	N	N	N	Y
1025	15,300	2	9	N	C	1	Y	N	N	N	Y
1026	35,900	3	12	N	C	1	N	N	N	N	Y
1027	15,100	4	12	S	L	1	N	N	N	Y	N
1028	17,200	2	12	S	L	1	N	N	N	N	N
1029	35,400	4	10	S	L	1	N	N	N	N	Y
1030	15,600	3	12	S	L	1	N	N	N	N	Y
1031	24,900	3	12	S	L	1	N	N	N	N	Y
1032	34,800	4	11	S	C	1	N	N	N	Y	N
1033	14,600	4	12	S	C	1	N	N	N	N	Y
1034	23,100	3	9	S	C	1	N	N	N	N	Y
1035	15,900	3	12	S	C	1	N	N	N	Y	N
1036	26,700	4	12	S	C	1	N	N	N	N	Y
1037	17,300	4	12	S	C	1	N	N	N	Y	N
1038	37,100	3	12	S	C	1	N	N	N	Y	N
1039	14,000	3	10	S	C	1	N	N	N	N	Y
1040	23,600	3	10	S	C	1	N	N	N	N	Y
1041	16,200	3	12	S	C	1	N	N	N	N	Y
1042	24,100	4	10	S	C	1	N	N	N	Y	N
1043	12,700	2	8	S	C	1	N	N	N	N	Y
1044	26,000	4	13	S	L	1	N	Y	N	N	N
1045	15,400	3	16	N	L	2	N	Y	Y	N	N
1046	16,900	4	16	N	L	1	N	N	N	N	Y
1047	23,800	6	10	S	C	1	Y	Y	N	N	N
1048	37,100	8	16	N	L	2	Y	N	Y	N	Y
1049	16,800	5	15	S	C	2	Y	N	N	N	Y

(Continued)

TABLE 14.1 Continued

	(1)	(2)	(3)	(4)	(5)	(6)	(7)	(8)	(9)	(10)	(11)
family ID	$income	# in family	educat. (yrs) hhold	region: North South	lifestyle Liberal Conserv.	#cars	car financed?	station wagon?	economy car?	van?	other car?
1050	22,900	5	8	N	L	1	N	Y	N	N	N
1051	13,700	6	8	N	L	1	Y	Y	N	N	N
1052	26,800	8	12	S	C	2	N	Y	N	N	Y
1053	16,100	8	12	N	L	2	N	Y	N	N	Y
1054	25,700	6	12	N	C	1	N	N	N	N	Y
1055	38,200	2	12	N	L	1	N	N	N	N	Y
1056	49,800	3	12	N	L	1	Y	N	N	N	Y
1057	60,400	4	12	N	L	1	Y	N	N	N	Y
1058	39,000	2	12	N	L	1	N	N	N	N	Y
1059	57,600	4	12	N	L	1	Y	N	N	N	Y
1060	42,000	3	12	N	L	1	N	N	N	N	Y
1061	38,600	3	12	N	L	1	N	N	N	Y	N
1062	66,400	4	12	N	L	2	Y	N	Y	N	Y
1063	71,200	2	12	N	L	1	Y	N	N	N	Y
1064	49,300	4	10	N	C	1	Y	N	N	N	Y
1065	37,700	4	10	N	C	1	Y	N	N	N	Y
1066	72,400	3	12	N	C	2	N	N	Y	N	Y
1067	88,700	3	12	N	C	1	N	N	N	Y	N
1068	44,200	2	12	S	L	1	Y	N	N	N	Y
1069	55,100	3	12	S	L	2	N	N	N	Y	Y
1070	73,300	4	12	S	L	1	N	N	N	Y	N
1071	80,200	2	12	S	L	1	Y	N	N	N	Y
1072	39,300	3	10	S	C	2	N	N	N	Y	Y
1073	48,200	4	12	S	C	1	N	N	N	N	Y
1074	57,800	2	12	S	C	1	Y	N	N	N	Y
1075	38,000	3	10	S	C	1	Y	N	N	Y	N
1076	81,300	4	16	N	L	1	N	Y	N	N	N
1077	96,900	4	16	N	L	2	N	N	N	N	Y
1078	44,700	3	14	N	L	1	N	N	N	N	Y
1079	107,300	3	17	N	L	1	N	N	N	N	Y
1080	38,100	2	13	N	L	2	Y	N	N	N	Y
1081	304,200	2	14	N	L	1	N	N	N	N	Y
1082	46,100	3	16	S	L	1	N	N	N	Y	N
1083	49,300	4	13	S	L	1	N	N	N	N	Y
1084	160,800	4	16	S	L	9	N	N	N	N	Y
1085	39,100	4	16	S	L	1	N	N	N	Y	N
1086	46,400	2	14	S	C	1	N	N	N	Y	N
1087	58,300	6	10	N	L	2	Y	N	N	N	Y
1088	47,800	5	10	S	L	2	Y	Y	N	N	Y
1089	58,000	7	8	N	L	2	Y	Y	N	N	Y
1090	69,600	9	12	N	L	2	Y	Y	N	N	Y
1091	44,200	11	12	N	L	2	N	N	Y	N	Y
1092	62,100	6	10	N	L	2	Y	Y	N	N	Y
1093	99,000	5	12	S	L	3	Y	N	Y	Y	Y
1094	53,300	6	12	S	L	2	N	Y	N	N	Y
1095	72,200	9	10	S	C	2	N	Y	N	Y	N
1096	64,700	7	12	S	C	2	Y	Y	N	Y	N
1097	77,300	6	16	N	L	2	Y	Y	Y	N	N
1098	116,900	10	18	N	L	3	Y	Y	Y	N	Y
1099	71,200	7	15	S	L	1	N	N	N	Y	N
1100	103,800	5	16	S	C	2	Y	Y	Y	N	N

3. To locate outliers (unusual observations)

4. To determine the empirical distribution of the variable in question

5. To calculate summary statistics

The first three of these are often referred to as "data cleaning."

Dealing with the **nonresponse** percentages is always aggravating. In fact, the degree of item nonresponse often serves as a useful indicator of the quality of the research. When it is excessive, it calls the whole research effort into question and suggests that a critical examination of the research objectives and procedures should be undertaken. When nonresponse is less extreme, it still demands that decisions be made with respect to what to do about the missing items before analyzing the data. There are several possibilities:

1. Leave the items blank and report that number as a separate category. This procedure works fine for simple one-way and cross-tabulations, but not as well for other statistical techniques.

2. "Case-wise deletion": If you're running a regression involving Q32, and some subjects didn't respond to that question, they would be deleted, temporarily, from that analysis. When you analyze a different set of variables, if those subjects responded to those questions, they would be back in the data set. When using this approach, you must continually report the number of cases on which the analysis is based, because the sample size is not constant across analyses. This approach also ignores the fact that a large proportion of missing data on any item might be insightful; it signals that respondents do not care very deeply about the issue being addressed by the question.

Ethical **Dilemma** 14.1

A manufacturer of aspirin had its marketing research department conduct a national survey among doctors to investigate what common household remedies doctors would be most likely to recommend when treating a patient with a cold. The question asked doctors to pick the one product they would most likely prescribe for their patients from among the choices Advil, Tylenol, aspirin, or none of the above. The distribution of responses was as follows:

Advil	100
Tylenol	100
Aspirin	200
None of the three	600
Total	1,000

The firm used the results of the survey as a basis for an extensive ad campaign that claimed: "In a national survey, doctors recommended aspirin two to one over Advil and Tylenol as the medicine they would most likely recommend to their patients suffering from colds."

- Is the firm's claim legitimate?
- Is it ethical for the firm to omit reporting the number of doctors that expressed no preference?
- What would be the fairest way to state the ad claim? Do you think stating the claim in this way would be as effective as stating it in the way the firm did?

3. Substitute values for the missing items. Typically, the substitution involves some measure of central tendency, such as the mean.

There is no single "right" answer for how missing items should be handled. The second option is the default in a lot of computing packages.

A **blunder** is an error—it can happen during editing, coding, or data entry. Consider the one-way tabulation of the number of cars owned per family in Table 14.2. A check of the original questionnaire indicates that the family having nine cars had, in fact, one car. The nine is a mistake. The simple one-way tabulation has revealed the error, and it can be easily corrected at this very early stage and it hadn't yet led to erroneous results in other analyses.

The sample size for the data displayed in Table 14.2 is 100, so the numbers are easy to convert to percentages. Percentages help communication. Note in Table 14.3, the percentages are presented to zero decimal places. Particularly with small samples, one has to be careful not to imply greater accuracy than the figures can support. Numbers also are easier to read when rounded off, and therefore probably have more impact to the manager reading the report. Occasionally, one decimal place might be used. The general rule in reporting percentages is: Unless decimals serve a special purpose, they should be omitted.

Sometimes the percentages also are presented in parentheses (see Table 14.4) immediately to the right or below the actual count entry in the table. Sometimes only the percentages are presented, and then it is imperative that the sample size (the total number of cases) is provided.

The third use of the one-way tabulation is to locate **outliers**. An outlier is not an error. It is an observation so different in magnitude from the rest of the data that the analyst chooses to treat it as a special case. This may mean eliminating the observation from the analysis or determining the specific factors that generated this unique observation.[1] Consider, for example, the tabulation of incomes contained in Table 14.4. The table indicates that there are only four families with incomes greater than $105,000, and Table 14.1 indicates that only

TABLE 14.2   Cars per Family

#Cars per Family	#Families
1	74
2	23
3	2
9	1

TABLE 14.3   Cars per Family, with Percentages

#Cars per Family	#Families	%Families
1	74	74
2	23	23
3	2	2
9	1	1

[1] Peter J. Huber and Elvezio M. Ronchetti, *Robust Statistics* (Wiley, 2009).

TABLE 14.4

Income Distribution of Respondents in Car Ownership Study

Income	#Families	%Families	Cumulative # Families	Cumulative % Families
< $15,000	8	(8.0)	8	(8.0)
$15,000–$24,900	25	(25.0)	33	(33.0)
$25,000–$34,900	15	(15.0)	48	(48.0)
$35,000–$44,900	18	(18.0)	66	(66.0)
$45,000–$54,900	8	(8.0)	74	(74.0)
$55,000–$64,900	8	(8.0)	82	(82.0)
$65,000–$74,900	7	(7.0)	89	(89.0)
$75,000–$84,900	3	(3.0)	92	(92.0)
$85,000–$94,900	1	(1.0)	93	(93.0)
$95,000–$104,900	3	(3.0)	96	(96.0)
$105,000+	4	(4.0)	100	(100.0)
Total #Families	100	(100.0)		

one family had an annual income greater than $161,000, namely, Number 1081, with an income of $304,200. It is not unreasonable for a family to have such an income, so the observation will be retained in the analyses, but it is clearly out of line with the rest of the sample and should probably be considered an outlier.

The fourth use of the one-way frequency tabulation is to determine the **empirical distribution** of the variable. Some researchers ignore the shape of the distribution and just go right to calculating summary statistics, such as the mean. That can be a serious mistake. Preferences for some products are bipolar, e.g., some people like "mild" salsa, and others like "hot" salsa. If you take an average, you might think you should roll out a new product that is "medium" salsa. Dumb! It's a good idea to get a feel for a variable's distribution before performing any analysis with it.

The distribution of a variable can be visualized through a **histogram**—a form of bar chart in which successive values of the variable are placed along the x-axis (abscissa), and the absolute frequency or relative frequency of occurrence of the values is indicated along the y-axis (ordinate). The histogram for the income data in Table 14.4 appears in Figure 14.1, with the incomes over $105,000 omitted because their inclusion would have required an undue extension of the income axis. It is readily apparent that the distribution of incomes is skewed to the right. The actual distribution can be compared to some theoretical distribution to determine whether the data are consistent with some *a priori* model.

Further insight into the empirical distribution of income can be derived by constructing the **frequency polygon**. The frequency polygon is obtained from the histogram by connecting the midpoints of the bars with straight lines. It is superimposed in Figure 14.1.

An alternative way of gaining insight is through the empirical **cumulative distribution function**. The number of observations with a value less than or equal to a specified quantity is determined—the cumulative frequencies are generated. Thus, in the right-hand column of Table 14.4, we see that there are eight families with incomes less than $15,000; 33 families (8 + 25) with incomes of $24,900 or less; and 48 families (8 + 25 + 15) with incomes of $34,900 or less. These cumulative frequencies are denoted along the ordinate in Figure 14.2, while the abscissa again contains incomes. The function is generated by

A picture is worth a megabyte of words!

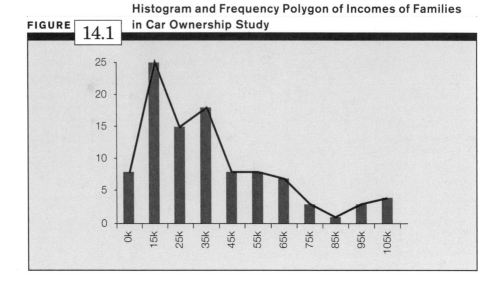

FIGURE 14.1

Histogram and Frequency Polygon of Incomes of Families in Car Ownership Study

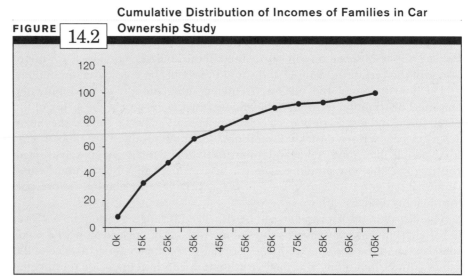

FIGURE 14.2

Cumulative Distribution of Incomes of Families in Car Ownership Study

connecting the points representing the given combinations of x's (values) and y's (cumulative frequencies) with straight lines.

The one-way tabulation is also useful in calculating other **summary** measures, such as the mode, mean, and standard deviation. The mode, or the most frequently occurring item, can be read directly from the one-way tabulation. Thus, Table 14.3 suggests that most families own one car. The mean, or "average" response, can be calculated from a one-way tabulation by weighting each value by its frequency of occurrence, summing these products, and dividing by the number of cases. The average number of cars per family given in the data in Table 14.3 would thus be estimated to be the following:

Value	Frequency	Value x Frequency
1	75	75
2	23	46
3	2	6
	100	127

or 127/100 = 1.27 cars per family.

The standard deviation provides a measure of spread in the data. It is calculated from the one-way tabulation by taking the deviation of each value from the mean and squaring these deviations. The squared deviations are then multiplied by the frequency with which each occurs, these products are summed, and then divided by sample size minus 1 to yield the sample variance. The square root is then the sample standard deviation. The calculation of the standard deviation is thus very similar to that for ungrouped data, except that each value is weighted by the frequency with which it occurs. The standard deviation for the data in Table 14.3 is thus calculated as follows:

Value	Value-Mean	(Value-Mean)^2	Frequency	Frequency Times Difference Squared
1	−.27	.0729	75	5.4675
2	.73	.5329	23	12.2567
3	1.73	2.9929	2	5.9858
				23.7100

yielding a variance of $23.7100/99 = .2395$ and a standard deviation of $\sqrt{.2395} = .4894$.

The one-way tabulation is also a communication vehicle for the results. All you have to do is look at Table 14.1 to see how much insight can be gathered about the variable and then compare that with the insight generated in the one-way tabulation contained in Table 14.4. When you realize that one-way tabulations also serve as the input to the histogram, frequency polygon, and empirical cumulative distribution function, and that they are also used to calculate summary statistics, you can see it's worth the time to study the tabulations to get a good feel for your data.

Goodness-of-Fit Chi-Square Test on One Variable

When we look at the distribution of income for the families in our car ownership sample, we might try to answer the question, "How representative is our sample?" (at least on this one demographic variable). The **chi-square** statistic can give us the answer. Suppose through the use of secondary data, like the U.S. Census, you were able to determine the income distribution for your target market (such as your metropolitan area and your particular head-of-household age focus). The car ownership income data from Table 14.4 are reproduced in the 2nd column of Table 14.5 for convenience, and the target percentages derived from the secondary data compose the 3rd column in Table 14.5. The question of representativeness is answered by comparing the data in the sample to the distribution that would be expected if the sample reflected the population.

We'll label the sample data "o" for "observed" frequency and "e" for the data you would "expect" if your sample were representative of the target population. Thus, the 2nd and 3rd columns are labeled o_i and e_i, denoting the **observed** number and **expected** number of observations that fall in the ith row for each of the r rows of income level. The chi-square is an easy spreadsheet computation. The differences between the observed and expected frequencies are computed $(o_i - e_i)$, and standardized by dividing by $\sqrt{e_i}$ (to compensate for the fact that a difference of, say, 5 is a proportionately smaller error where the base numbers are

TABLE 14.5	Car Ownership Data: One-Way Chi-Square on Income			
Income	o_i **#Families**	e_i = **Target Figures**	$\frac{(o_i - e_i)}{\sqrt{e_i}}$	$\frac{(o_i - e_i)^2}{e_i}$
< $15,000	8	22	−2.985	8.909
$15,000–$24,900	25	19	1.377	1.895
$25,000–$34,900	15	12	.866	.750
$35,000–$44,900	18	18	.000	.000
$45,000–$54,900	8	6	.816	.667
$55,000–$64,900	8	5	1.342	1.800
$65,000–$74,900	7	6	.408	.167
$75,000–$84,900	3	5	−.894	.800
$85,000–$94,900	1	5	−1.789	3.200
$95,000–$104,900	3	1.5	1.225	1.500
$105,000+	4	.5	4.950	24.500
Total #Families	100	100		χ^2 = 44.188

bigger, such as 22, than in the table where the numbers are smaller, e.g., 5 or 6). Square those pieces and sum them up, and the calculated χ^2 statistic is defined as follows:

$$\chi^2 = \sum_{i=1}^{r} \frac{(o_i - e_i)^2}{e_i}.$$

The chi-square for these data equals 44.188. By comparing it to a table of critical values, it can be interpreted as big (that is, the observed sample data do not follow the expected distribution) or small (the sample may be "off" from the target but the difference is attributable to sampling errors). Critical values for the χ^2 are available in many places (including a function in Excel); all you need is your alpha-level and you need to know the degrees of freedom, which in this case are computed as $(r - 1)$, i.e., the number of rows in the table minus 1.[2] The income table has 11 rows, and the critical χ^2 value for 10 degrees of freedom is 18.31. Our χ^2 value exceeds the critical value, so we reject the "null hypothesis" (that our sample resembles the population), and conclude that our sample is unlike the general population in terms of its distribution of incomes. (Does that matter? It depends on the research questions at hand.)

Standardized Residuals

It might seem that the 4th column in Table 14.5 was merely a "computational" worksheet column, en route to the final column to be summed, but it also contains valuable information. Whereas the χ^2 indicates, overall, whether the sample reflects the population, the numbers in the 4th column are called **standardized residuals**, and they indicate, for specific income brackets, whether the sample reflects the population or differs from it. Standardized residuals are interpretable like z-scores, in that if they exceed 1.96 in magnitude, they are significant.

In the income bracket of $35,000–44,900, our sample had exactly the same number of families as would be expected by the target population data.

Chi-square tells you, overall, is there a pattern.

Standardized residuals tell you, microscopically, cell-by-cell.

---

[2] FYI: The mean of the chi-square distribution is equal to the number of degrees of freedom v, and the variance is equal to $2v$. For large values of v, the chi-square distribution is approximately normally distributed.

Hence, the residual $(o_i - e_i)$ is zero. Less perfect matches are found in the other rows.

Many of the standardized residuals are positive, indicating that our sample contained more families with incomes in those categories than we would have predicted just knowing the population data. Conversely, the standardized residuals that are negative indicate that our sample contained fewer families with those incomes than we would have expected.

When the standardized residuals do not exceed 1.96, those differences, positive or negative, are attributable to sampling chance. When they exceed 1.96, they are considered "real" effects in the sample. For example, the -2.985 indicates that our sample included significantly fewer families with incomes less than \$15,000 than the target contains. On the high end of the income scale, the 4.950 indicates that the sample comprised significantly more families whose incomes exceed \$105,000 than characterizes the target population.

In total, we learn that our sample is somewhat more affluent than the target population. This difference must be factored into any subsequent projections about the rest of the data.

One-way chi-square statistics can be useful in numerous ways. This example used known population profile data as expected frequencies. The chi-square goodness-of-fit test can also help determine whether a sample seems to follow a particular form. For instance, if we want to use a statistical procedure that assumes our variable is normally distributed, we test that assumption. We would construct the sample frequency histogram to get the o_i's and compare them to the e_i's corresponding to the normally distributed counterpart to see whether we should proceed with the technique that requires normality.

There are numerous uses of the chi-square. For example, if the rows of a table represented manufacturers (e.g., Honda, Toyota, Ford, GM, Ferrari) or brands in a category (e.g., Gucci, Prada, Gap), the observed data may be market shares or sales in numbers of units, and the expected frequencies may be the comparable data on the previous selling quarter. Many types of "benchmark" data can be used as the expected frequencies against which to compare one's sample data.

Take another kind of example. Any time the marketer wants to know whether an observed pattern of frequencies corresponds to an "expected" pattern, the chi-square is appropriate. Suppose a cereal manufacturer knows that in the industry, the three standard sizes of cereal boxes—small, large, and family size—sell at different rates. For every small package, three large and two family size are also sold. Let's say the manufacturer conducts a market test to determine the relative frequencies of sales for one of their cereal lines.

Suppose that, in a test market over a one-week period, 1,200 boxes of the new cereal were sold and the distribution of sales by size was as follows:

Small	Large	Family	Total
240	575	385	1200

Are these data consistent with what is considered typical?

We'll compute the chi-square. We have the o_i, the observed number of cases falling in each of the three categories, and we need the e_i's, the expected number of cases for each category.

The null hypothesis would be that these sales would follow the typical distribution, of {small:large:family size} being {1:3:2}. The proportions are: $\pi_1 = 1/(1+3+2) = 1/6$, $\pi_2 = 3/6$, and $\pi_3 = 2/6$, so the expected sales would be: $e_1 = n\pi_1 = 1,200(1/6) = 200$ of the small size, $e_2 = n\pi_2 = 1{,}200(3/6) = 600$ of the large size, and $e_3 = n\pi_3 = 1{,}200(2/6) = 400$ of the family size. The χ^2 statistic is computed as:

$$\chi^2 = \frac{(240 - 200)^2}{200} + \frac{(575 - 600)^2}{600} + \frac{(385 - 400)^2}{400} = 9.60$$

The degrees of freedom is $v = k - 1 = 2$, and the tabled value of χ^2 for 2 df at $\alpha = .05$ is 5.99. Since the calculated value $\chi^2 = 9.60$ is larger, the conclusion is that the sample result would be unlikely to occur by chance alone. Rather, the preliminary market test results suggest that sales of this cereal line follows a different pattern than is typical. The null hypothesis of sales in the ratio of 1:3:2 is rejected.

A final application of the one-way chi-square is described in Research Realities 14.1. It's a versatile statistic.

Kolmogorov-Smirnov Test

The Kolmogorov-Smirnov test is similar to the chi-square in that it compares observed and expected frequencies to determine whether observed results are in accord with a stated null hypothesis. But the **Kolmogorov-Smirnov test** is appropriate for ordinal variables.

RESEARCH   REALITIES

14.1 It's a Conspiracy![3]

Mars Candy polled children to indicate their favorite colors, whereupon Mars introduced the new M&M color, blue. Subsequent investigation has indicated, however, that the blue M&M may appear less frequently in bags of these chocolates than its non-blue counterparts.

Conduct a study for yourself. Go out and purchase some M&M's, er, data. (Perhaps your dean will offer you research funds to study this phenomenon.) Count the number of each color, and sum those counts. If you found, say, 120 M&M's in the bag, how would you expect those 120 observations to be distributed over the six color categories; that is, what are the expected frequencies?

Compute the χ^2. Overall, what does it indicate? What do the standardized residuals tell you?

Do the answers change if you select Peanut M&M's instead of Plain? Peanut Butter? Almond? What special result do you find for the latter two?[4]

	o_i: Number of M&M's	e_i: Expected Number of M&M's	$\dfrac{(o_i - e_i)}{\sqrt{e_i}}$	$\dfrac{(o_i - e_i)^2}{e_i}$
Blue				
Brown				
Green				
Orange				
Red				
Yellow				
Total:				$\chi^2 =$

[3] Ronald D. Fricker, Jr., "The Mysterious Case of the Blue M&M's," *Chance* 9, 19–22.

[4] Statisticians distinguish between a "sampling zero," where you could have observations in that row, but you simply did not (e.g., your sample may have been too small), and a "structural zero," where it is not possible to obtain observations in that row. Which do you suppose the zeros are for, Peanut Butter and Almond orange M&M's?

Suppose a manufacturer of cosmetics is testing four different shades of a sparkly nail polish—pale pink, light pink, medium pink, and dark pink. The company has hired a marketing research firm to determine whether any distinct preference exists. If so, the company will manufacture only the preferred shades. Otherwise, it will have to market all shades.

If a sample of 100 yields 50 women who prefer the "pale" shade, 30 the "light," 15 the "medium," and 5 the "dark" shade, do these results indicate some kind of preference? The shading quality has an inherent ordering of light to dark, so the Kolmogorov-Smirnov test can be used to test the preference hypothesis. We specify the cumulative distribution function that would occur under the null hypothesis and compare that with the observed cumulative. The point at which the two functions show the maximum deviation is determined, and the value of this deviation is the test statistic.

The null hypothesis is that there is no preference, so it would be expected that 25% of the sample would like each shade. The cumulative distribution function resulting from this assumption is presented as the last column of Table 14.6.

Kolmogorov-Smirnov D is equal to the absolute value of the maximum deviation between the observed cumulative proportion and the theoretical cumulative proportion. For our data, $D = .80 - .50 = .30$. For $\alpha = .05$, the critical D for large samples is given by $(1.36/\sqrt{n})$, where n is the sample size. So our critical value is .136. Calculated D exceeds the critical value, and thus the null hypothesis of no preference among shades is rejected—the data indicate a statistically significant preference for the lighter shades.

Cross-Tabs

We now turn to the analysis of frequencies for variables studied two at a time. One variable in our investigation forms the rows of a table, another variable forms the columns. To continue with the car ownership example, we might tabulate "family size" crossed with "numbers of cars owned." The table entries represent the number of cases in our sample that have the joint characteristics of the row variable value (e.g., small vs. larger family) and the column variable value (e.g., few vs. many cars).

A cross-tabulation, better known as a "cross-tab," is easily the most widely used data analysis technique in marketing research—the "bread and butter" of marketers. Most marketing research studies go no further, and the studies that do use more sophisticated analytical methods still contain cross-tabs as an important component. Thus, the marketing researcher (analyst) and the

Cross-tabs are the heart of marketing research.

TABLE 14.6   Observed and Theoretical Cumulative Distributions of Nail Polish Color Preference

Shade	Observed Number	Observed Proportion	Observed Cumulative Proportion	Theoretical Proportion	Theoretical Cumulative Proportion
Pale Pink	50	.50	.50	.25	.25
Light Pink	30	.30	.80	.25	.50
Medium	15	.15	.95	.25	.75
Dark Pink	5	.05	1.00	.25	1.00

marketing manager (decision maker) both need to understand how cross-tabs are developed and interpreted.

Why are they so important? A cross-tab allows us to study relationships between variables. The variables for cross-tabs are either naturally nominal or ordinal, or they represent categorizations of continuous measures (e.g., categories of income or age).[5] Cross-tabs are also sometimes called "contingency tables" because we're looking at how one variable behaves contingent upon values of the other variable, e.g., are family size and car ownership independent of each other, or, instead, if you knew one (size of family), could you predict better than just guessing the other (number of cars)?

We start with a discussion of the kinds of relationships cross-tabs let us study. In the appendix, we present the chi-square test for a two-way table, and a discussion of log linear and logit models, tools often used to predict brand choices.

Contingent Relationships in Cross-Tabs

A number of important questions concerning the analysis of data can be illustrated using cross-tabulations. We'll work with the data on car ownership to answer the following questions:

- What characteristics distinguish families who own two or more cars from families who own one car (e.g., income)?

- What are the distinguishing characteristics of those who buy station wagons? Foreign economy cars? Vans?

- Are families who financed their automobile purchase different from those who did not?

Let's see if there is any relationship between the number of cars that a family owns and family income. To keep things simple, we'll use the median income in the population of $37,500 to split the sample into two groups—those with incomes above or below the average.

Table 14.7 presents the two-way classification of the sample families by income and number of cars. Looking at the marginal totals, we see that 75 families have one car or less, whereas 25 families have two cars or more. We also see that the sample is not unrepresentative of the population, at least as far as income is concerned: 54 families fall into the lower-than-average income group using the $37,500 cutoff.

Does the number of cars depend on income? Table 14.7 suggests yes—19 of the families owning two or more cars are in the upper-income group. We can

TABLE 14.7 Family Income and Number of Cars Family Owns

	#Cars		
Income	0 or 1	2+	Total
< $37,500	48	6	54
$37,500+	27	19	46
Total	75	25	100

[5] Relationships between pairs of continuous variables may be measured via correlations and regressions.

Ethical **Dilemma**   14.2

Sarah is very happy on the whole with the project that she has just completed for the Crumbly Cookie Company. Most of her hypotheses were supported by the survey data. Two hypotheses did not work out, but she thought that she would just leave them out of the report.
- Is it ethical to omit information that does not tally with your beliefs?
- Can valuable information be lost through the omission?

shed additional light on the relationship by computing percentages. Table 14.8 and Table 14.9 are mathematically equivalent to Table 14.7 but are based on percentages calculated in different directions: horizontally, or "row percentages" in Table 14.8 and vertically, or "column percentages" in Table 14.9.

Tables 14.8 and 14.9 contain quite different messages. Table 14.8 suggests that multiple-car ownership is affected by family income: 41% of the families with above-average incomes had two or more automobiles, but only 11% of the below-average-income families did. Table 14.9, on the other hand, suggests that 64% of those who owned one car had below-average incomes, whereas only 24% of those who owned two or more cars were below average in income. Does this mean that multiple-car ownership paves the way to higher income? Definitely not. Rather, it illustrates a fundamental rule of calculating percentages: Always calculate percentages in the direction of the causal factor, or across the effect factor. In this case, income is logically considered to be the cause, or independent variable, and multiple-car ownership to be the effect, or dependent variable. The percentages are correctly calculated, therefore, in the direction of income as in Table 14.8.

A useful way to think about the direction to calculate percentages is to conceptualize the problem in terms of **conditional probability**; the probability of one event occurring given that another event has occurred or will occur. Thus,

TABLE 14.8   Percentage Family Income by Number of Cars

	#Cars		
Income	0 or 1	2+	Total
< $37,500	89%	11%	100%
$37,500+	59%	41%	100%

TABLE 14.9   Family Income by Number of Cars, Column Percentage

	#Cars	
Income	0 or 1	2+
< $37,500	64%	24%
$37,500+	36%	76%
Total	100%	100%

the notion of the probability that the family has two or more cars given that they are high income makes sense, whereas the notion that the family is high income given that they have two or more cars does not.

This two-way cross-tab is just a start into the data. Consider the relationship between multiple-car ownership and size of family. Table 14.10 indicates the number of small and large families that possess two or more cars. Size of family is logically considered a cause of multiple-car ownership and not vice versa. Thus, the percentages would properly be computed in the direction of size of family or across number of cars. Table 14.11 presents these percentages and suggests that the number of cars a family owns is indeed affected by the size of the family—77% of the large families have two or more cars, whereas only 10% of the small families do.

So, does multiple-car ownership depend on family size or, as previously suggested, on family income? We need to simultaneously examine the effects of income and family size on likelihoods of multiple-car ownership. The two-way cross-tab needs to be partitioned into forming a three-way table of income, family size, and multiple-car ownership, as in Table 14.12.

Table 14.13 contains the percentages computed in the direction of income within each table. It looks like multiple-car ownership depends on both income and family size. For small families, 19% of those with above-average incomes have two or more cars, whereas only 4% of those with below-average incomes have

TABLE 14.10   Number of Cars and Size of Family

| Size of Family | #Cars | | Total |
	0 or 1	2+	
4 or less	70	8	78
5+	5	17	22
Total	75	25	100

TABLE 14.11   Number of Cars and Size of Family, Row Percentages

| Size of Family | #Cars | | Total |
	0 or 1	2+	
4 or less	90%	10%	100%
5+	23%	77%	100%

TABLE 14.12   Number of Cars by Income and Size of Family

| Income | 4 or less in family #Cars | | | 5 or more in family #Cars | | | Totals #Cars | | |
	0–1	2+	Total	0–1	2+	Total	0–1	2+	Total
< $37,500	44	2	46	4	4	8	48	6	54
$37,500+	26	6	32	1	13	14	27	19	46
Total	70	8	78	5	17	22	75	25	100

TABLE 14.13

Number of Cars by Income and Size of Family (Row % within Family Size)

Income	4 or less in family #Cars			5 or more in family #Cars			Totals #Cars		
	0–1	2+	Total	0-1	2+	Total	0–1	2+	Total
< $37,500	96%	4%	100%	50%	50%	100%	89%	11%	100%
$37,500+	81%	19%	100%	7%	93%	100%	59%	41%	100%

more than one automobile. For large families, 93% of the above-average-income and 50% of the below-average-income families have more than one vehicle.

The preceding comparisons highlight the effect of income on multiple-car ownership, holding family size constant. We could also compare the effect of family size on multiple-car ownership, holding income constant. We would find that each provides a partial explanation for multiple-car ownership.

The information in Tables 14.12 and 14.13 is there to be mined, but it could have been presented in a more revealing manner. Look specifically at the first row of the first section of Table 14.13, reproducing it as Table 14.14. One figure, 4%, is the percentage of small, below-average-income families that have two or more cars. The complementary percentage, 96%, represents those that have one automobile or none.

Table 14.15 shows the rest of the data in Table 14.13 treated in the same way. The entry in each case is the percentage of families in that category that own two or more automobiles. Table 14.15 conveys the same information as Table 14.13, but it delivers the message with greater clarity. The separate effect of income on multiple-car ownership, holding family size constant, can be determined by reading down the columns, while the effect of family size, holding income constant, can be determined by reading across the rows. Cool, yes? Omitting the complementary percentages has helped reveal the structure of the data.

TABLE 14.14

Car Ownership for Small, Below-Average-Income Families

Income	#Cars		Total
	0–1	2+	
< $37,500	96%	4%	100% (n = 46)

TABLE 14.15

Percentage of Families Owning 2+ Cars, by Income and Size of Family

Income	Size of Family		Total
	4 or less	5+	
< $37,500	4%	50%	11%
$37,500+	19%	93%	41%

Therefore, we'll use this format whenever we consider several explanatory variables simultaneously.

The original association between number of cars and family income reflected in Table 14.8 is called the **total** (or **zero order**) association between the variables. Table 14.15, which depicts the association between two variables within categories of family size, is called a conditional table that reveals the **conditional association** between the variables. Family size is a control variable here. Conditional tables that are developed on the basis of one control variable are called first-order conditional tables, and those developed using two control variables are called second-order conditional tables, etc.

Which variable has the greater effect on multiple-car ownership—income or family size? We can calculate the difference in proportions as a function of the level of the variable. Let's look at Table 14.8 for the effect of income on the probability of a family having multiple cars. The proportion of low-income families that have two or more cars is .11, whereas the proportion of high-income families is .41. The probability of having multiple cars is clearly different depending on the family's income, $(.41 - .11)$, high income increases the probability of having two or more cars by .30. Similarly in Table 14.11, the probability of multiple-car ownership is different depending on family size. Whereas .10 of the small families have multiple cars, .77 of the large families do. Thus, being a large family increases the probability of having two or more cars by .67 (i.e., $.77 - .10$) over small families.

To determine whether income or family size has the greater impact, the factors are considered simultaneously using a similar analysis. We draw the effect of income from Table 14.15. To determine income's effect, we hold family size constant, or we "control for" family size. So we must investigate the relationship between income and car ownership for small families and then again for large families. Among small families, having high income increases the probability of having multiple cars by .15 $(.19 - .04)$. Among large families, having high income increases the probability of having multiple cars by .43 $(.93 - .50)$ compared to low income. The size of the associations between income and multiple-car ownership are different for different family sizes. We conclude that there is a statistical interaction between the independent variables; to generate a single estimate of the effect of income on car ownership, an average of the separate effects needs to be computed. The weighted average takes into account the sizes of the groups: 78 small families and 22 large families, so the weights are .78 and .22. The weighted average is

$$.15(.78) + .43(.22) = .21$$

which suggests that, on average, high versus low income increases the probability of owning multiple cars by .21.

To investigate the effect of family size, we do the obverse, and hold income constant. We investigate the impact of family size on car ownership for low-income families, then for high-income families, and then generate a weighted average of the two results. Among low-income families, being large increases the probability of having multiple cars by .46 $(.50 - .04)$ compared to small families. Among high-income families, large size increases the probability by .74 $(.93 - .19)$ versus small size. There were 54 low-income and 46 high-income families, so the weighted calculation yields

$$.46(.54) + .74(.46) = .59$$

as the estimate of the impact of family size on multiple-car ownership.

Family size has a more pronounced effect on multiple-car ownership than does income. It increases the probability of having two or more cars by .59, whereas income increases it by .21.

Panel I: Initial Relationship Is Modified by the Introduction of a Third Variable

The previous example highlights an important application of cross-tabs—the use of an additional variable (family size) to refine an initial cross-tabulation (the relationship between car ownership and income). A number of conditions can occur when additional variables are introduced (see Table 14.16). As indicated in Panel IA, the two-way table may initially indicate the existence or nonexistence of a relationship between the variables, and the introduction of a third variable may refine that initial conclusion. We now offer examples in the rest of the table.

Case IB: Initial Relationship Is Spurious

In the automobile purchase study, it was expected that *van* ownership would be related to lifestyle—the hypothesis was that liberals would more likely own vans than would conservatives. Table 14.17 indicates that, contrary to expectation, conservatives are more apt than liberals to own vans, 24% vs.16%.

Is there a logical explanation for this unexpected finding? Let's add a third variable, region of the country, to the analysis. As Table 14.18 indicates, van ownership is not related to lifestyle, but instead depends on the location of residence. When region is held constant, there is no difference in van ownership between liberals and conservatives. Families living in the South are much more likely to own a van than are families who live in the northern states. It just so happens that people in the South tend to be more conservative in their lifestyle than people in the North. The original relationship is, therefore, said to be spurious.

TABLE 14.16   **Conditions That Can Arise with the Introduction of an Additional Variable into a Cross-Tabulation**

	With the Additional Variable	
Initial Conclusion	**Change Conclusion**	**Retain Conclusion**
Some Relationship	I	II
	A: Refine Explanation	
	B: Reveal Spurious Explanation	
	C: Provide Limiting Conditions	
No Relationship	III	IV

TABLE 14.17   **Van Ownership by Lifestyle**

	Own Van?		
Lifestyle	**Yes**	**No**	**Total**
Liberal	9 (16%)	46 (84%)	55 (100%)
Conservative	11 (24%)	34 (76%)	45 (100%)

TABLE 14.18   Van Ownership by Lifestyle and Region of Country

| Lifestyle | Region of Country | | Total |
	North	South	
Liberal	5%	41%	16%
Conservative	5%	43%	24%

We already know that region has a big effect and lifestyle very little, but we calculate the difference in proportions for each variable anyway, to demonstrate what is meant by a "main effect" without a statistical interaction. Consider first the zero-order association between van ownership and lifestyle contained in Table 14.17. Being conservative increases the probability of van ownership by .08 (.24 − .16) compared to being liberal. Yet Table 14.18 shows that this is a spurious effect due to region of the country, since it disappears when region is held constant. Among those living in the North, the partial association between van ownership and lifestyle is .00 (.05 − .05). For those in the South, there is a slightly higher probability of van ownership among conservatives, namely .02 (.43 − .41). This effect is so small that it can be attributed to rounding error or sampling error. Regardless of the region of the country in which the family resides, its political leaning has no effect on whether it owns a van.

Note that the effect of region is pronounced and consistent. Among liberal families, living in the South increases the probability of van ownership by .36 (.41 − .05) compared to living in the North. Among conservative families, living in the South increases the probability by .38 (.43 − .05). Within rounding error, the effect is the same for families with both philosophies, which means that there is no interaction among the two predictor variables. There is only a main effect of region on van ownership, and the best estimate of its size is given by either of these estimates or their average.

Case IC: Limiting Conditions Are Revealed

Does ownership of foreign economy cars depend on family size? Table 14.19 suggests that it does. Smaller families are less likely to own a foreign economy car than are larger families! Only 8% of the small families but 27% of the large families have such automobiles. Can this counterintuitive finding be accounted for?

Let's expand this cross classification by adding the number of cars variable. Table 14.20 presents the data, which indicate that it is only when large families have two or more cars that they own a foreign economy car. No large families with one car own such an automobile. The introduction of the third variable has revealed a condition that limits the effect of foreign economy car ownership—multiple-car ownership where large families are concerned.

TABLE 14.19   Import Economy Car Ownership by Family Size

| Size of Family | Own Import Economy Car? | | Total |
	Yes	No	
4 or fewer	6 (8%)	72 (92%)	78 (100%)
5+	6 (27%)	16 (73%)	22 (100%)

TABLE 14.20 Import Economy Car Ownership by Family Size and Number of Cars

| | Own Import Economy Car? | | |
Size of Family	Yes	No	Total
4 or fewer	4%	38%	8%
5+	0%	35%	27%

Panel II: Initial Conclusion of a Relationship Is Retained

Consider now the analysis of station wagon ownership. *A priori,* it would seem to be related to family size—larger families have a greater need for station wagons than smaller families. Table 14.21 suggests that larger families do display a higher propensity to own station wagons: 68% of the large families and only 4% of the small families own wagons.

Consider, however, whether income might also affect station wagon ownership. As Table 14.22 indicates, income has an effect beyond family size. As one goes from a small to a large family, the propensity to own a station wagon increases. With larger families, though, the increase is larger. From the other angle, if we focus solely on large families, there is an increase in station wagon ownership from below-average-income to above-average-income families. Thus, we retain the initial conclusion; large families display a greater tendency to purchase station wagons. Further, the effect of family size on station wagon ownership is larger than the effect of income.

Panel III: A Relationship Is Established with the Introduction of a Third Variable

Table 14.23 contains the cross-tab for financing crossed with education of the head of household. There is no relationship between education and this debt; the percentage of families is 30% in each case.

TABLE 14.21 Station Wagon Ownership by Family Size

| | Own Station Wagon? | | |
Size of Family	Yes	No	Total
4 or fewer	3 (4%)	75 (96%)	78 (100%)
5+	15 (68%)	7 (32%)	22 (100%)

TABLE 14.22 Station Wagon Ownership by Family Size and Income

| | Income | | |
Size of Family	< $37,500	$37,500+	Total
4 or fewer	4%	3%	4%
5+	63%	71%	68%

TABLE 14.23 Financed Car Purchase, by Education of Head of Household

| Education Level | Car Purchase Financed? | | Total |
	Yes	No	
H.S. or less	24 (30%)	56 (70%)	80 (100%)
Some College +	6 (30%)	14 (70%)	20 (100%)

Table 14.24 illustrates the situation when income is added to the analysis. For below-average-income families, the likelihood of financing increases with education. For above-average-income families, the financing decreases with education. The effect of education was obscured in the first analysis (in Table 14.23) because the effects canceled each other out. When income is also considered, the relationship of installment debt to education is in fact pronounced.

Panel IV: The Conclusion of No Relationship Is Retained with the Addition of a Third Variable

Table 14.25 starts to answer the question, "Is station wagon ownership affected by region of the country in which the family lives?" It looks like, no, station wagon ownership doesn't depend on region; 18% of the sample families living in both the North and the South are owners.

Let's look at the relationship when family size is taken into account. Table 14.26 shows again the percentages are constant across regions. The minor variation is due to rounding error. Small families display a low propensity to purchase station wagons, regardless of whether they live in the North or South. Large families have a higher propensity, and this, too, is independent of where they live. The original lack of relationship between station wagon ownership and region of residence is confirmed with the addition of the third variable, family size.

TABLE 14.24 Financed Car Purchase, by Education of Head of Household and Income

| Education Level | Income | | Total |
	< $37,500	$37,500+	
H.S. or less	12%	58%	30%
Some College +	40%	27%	30%

TABLE 14.25 Station Wagon Ownership by Region

| Region | Own Station Wagon? | | Total |
	Yes	No	
North	11 (18%)	49 (82%)	60 (100%)
South	7 (18%)	33 (82%)	40 (100%)

TABLE 14.26   Station Wagon Ownership by Region and Family Size

Region	Size of Family		Total
	4 or fewer	5+	
North	4%	69%	18%
South	3%	67%	18%

Summary Comments on Cross-Tabulation

The previous examples should highlight the tremendous usefulness of cross-tabulation as a tool in analysis. We have seen an application in which a third variable helped uncover a relationship not immediately discernible, as well as applications in which a third variable triggered the modification of conclusions drawn on the basis of a two-variable classification.

Why stop with three variables? Would the conclusion change with the addition of a fourth variable? A fifth? Indeed it might. In fact, the problem is that one never knows for sure when to stop introducing variables. The conclusion is always susceptible to change with the introduction of the "right" variable or variables. The researcher is always in the position of "inferring" that a relationship exists. Later research may demonstrate that the inference was incorrect, or perhaps "more complicated" than originally thought. This is why the accumulation of studies, rather than a single study, supporting a particular relationship is so vital to the advancement of knowledge.

Table 14.27 is an overview of the dilemma that the researcher faces. The true situation is unknown—if it were known, there would be no need to research it. The analyst may conclude that there is no relationship, or that there is some relationship between two or more variables when in fact there is none or there is some. Only one of these four possibilities in Table 14.27 necessarily corresponds to a correct conclusion—when the analyst concludes that there is no relationship and in fact there is none. Two of the other possibilities are incorrect, and one contains the possibility for error. Spurious noncorrelation results when the analyst concludes that there is no relationship when, in fact, there is. Spurious correlation occurs when the true state of affairs is one of no relationship among the variables, and the analyst concludes that one exists.

The opportunities for error are great, and this gives rise to a temptation to keep adding variables *ad infinitum*. Fortunately, the marketer is constrained by theory and by data. Theory is a constraint because certain tabulations simply do not make any sense. Data are a constraint in several ways. First, some variables might not have been measured. Once the analysis has begun, it's too late to say,

TABLE 14.27   The Researcher's Dilemma

Researcher's Conclusion	True Situation	
	No Relationship	Some Relationship
No Relationship	Correct decision	Spurious noncorrelation
Some Relationship	Spurious correlation	Correct decision if concluded relationship is of proper form

"If only we had collected information on variable X!" (Recall our urging you to create dummy tables before collecting data.) Second, unless the sample size is huge, the cell sizes can become extremely small in multidimensional tables. In our fairly simple example, the three-way table (income by family size by area of the country) had eight cells ($2 \times 2 \times 2$), yielding on average, only 12.5 cases per cell. This is clearly a small number on which to base any kind of conclusion. The problem would have been compounded with more variables (e.g., $2 \times 2 \times 2 \times 2$) and/or more levels of a variable (e.g., $3 \times 4 \times 5$).

Presenting Tabular Data

We certainly know how to analyze categorical (nominal and ordinal) data now! We've also seen some ways to present data to communicate your marketing point—we've seen a variety of two-way and three-way tables.

Alternatively, sometimes tabular results for commercial marketing-research studies are presented using "banners." A **banner** is a series of cross-tabulations between a criterion or dependent variable and several (sometimes many) explanatory variables in a single table on a single page. The dependent variable, or phenomenon to be explained, serves as the row variable. The predictor or explanatory variables serve as the column variables, with each category of these variables serving as a banner point. Table 14.28 shows what the banner format looks like for the car study. You can see why it is a flexible means of presentation—although only two explanatory variables are shown, income and family size, many more could be. The top line in each row of the table indicates the absolute number possessing the characteristic, whereas the second line indicates the percentage.

Banner tables allow a great amount of information to be conveyed in a very limited space, and their format makes it easy for nonresearch managers to understand the data. A difficulty with these tables is that they tend to hide relationships in which it is necessary to consider several variables simultaneously (e.g., the joint effect of income and family size on multiple-car ownership), consequently making it more difficult to probe alternative explanations for what is producing the results. They are an efficient form of data presentation, but they should not be considered as a substitute for careful cross-tabulation analysis.

TABLE 14.28   Banner Format for Car Ownership Data

	Total Sample	Income		Family Size	
		< $37,500	$37,500+	4 or fewer	5+
Total	100	54	46	78	22
	100	100	100	100	100
1	75	48	27	70	5
	75	89	59	90	23
2	23	6	17	8	15
	23	11	37	10	68
3	2	0	2	0	2
	2	0	4	0	9

Summary

This chapter reviewed the analysis functions of editing, coding, and tabulation. Editing involves the inspection and correction of each questionnaire or observation form. The field edit is aimed at correcting the most glaring omissions and inaccuracies while the field staff is still intact. The central office edit follows and involves a more careful scrutiny and correction of the completed data-collection instruments. In the central office edit, particular attention is given to such matters as incomplete answers, obviously wrong answers, and answers that reflect a lack of interest.

Coding is the procedure by which data are categorized. It involves the three-step process of (1) specifying the categories or classes into which the responses are to be placed, (2) assigning code numbers to the classes, and (3) preparing a codebook.

Tabulation consists of counting the number of cases that fall into the various categories. The simple, or one-way, tabulation involves the count for a single variable, whereas cross-tabulation involves counting the number of cases that have the characteristics described by two or more variables considered simultaneously. The one-way tabulation is useful for communicating the results of a study, and it can also be employed to locate blunders or errors, to determine the degree of item nonresponse, to locate outliers (observations very different in value from the rest), and to determine the empirical distribution of the variable in question. It also serves as basic input to the calculation of measures such as the mean, median,

and standard deviation, which provide a summary picture of the distribution of the variable.

The chi-square goodness-of-fit test is appropriate when a nominally scaled variable falls naturally into two or more categories and the analyst wants to determine whether the observed number of cases in each cell corresponds to the expected number. The Kolmogorov-Smirnov test is its ordinal counterpart.

Cross-tabulation is one of the more useful devices for studying the relationships among variables because the results are easily communicated. Further, cross-tabs can provide insight into the nature of a relationship, because the addition of one or more variables to a two-way cross-classification analysis is equivalent to holding each of the variables constant.

A useful method for determining the effect that one variable has on another variable in a cross-tab is to compute the difference in proportions with which the dependent variable occurs as a function of the levels of the independent variable. This can be done for zero-order tables as well as conditional tables of higher order. The higher order tables are used to remove the effects of other variables that might be influencing the dependent variable.

Finally, in commercial studies, tabular results are often presented using banners. Banners succinctly represent a series of cross-tabs between a dependent variable and several explanatory variables in a single table.

Questions

1. Distinguish among the preliminary data analysis steps of editing, coding, and tabulation.
2. What should you do with incomplete answers? Obviously wrong answers? Answers that reflect a lack of interest?
3. With how many digits should percentages be reported?
4. What is a histogram? A frequency polygon? What information do they provide?
5. What is the cumulative distribution function? Of what value is it?
6. How is the mean calculated from the one-way tabulation? The standard deviation?

7. What is the proper procedure for investigating the following hypotheses using cross-tabs?
   a. Consumption of Product X depends on a person's income.
   b. Consumption of Product X depends on a person's education.
   c. Consumption of Product X depends on both.
   d. How would you determine whether income or education had the greater effect on the consumption of Product X?
8. How do you explain the condition in which a two-way cross-tabulation of Variables X and Y revealed no relationship between X and Y but the introduction of Z revealed a definite relationship between X and Y?

Applications and Problems

1. A marketing research supplier has five employees in its coding department. The firm has just received 10,000 completed mail questionnaires. The survey contains 175 questions. How would you recommend that the company handle the editing and coding process? What would you instruct them to look for in the edit, and how would you recommend they handle each of these problems if found?

2. The WITT TV station was conducting research to develop programs that would be well received by the viewing audience and would be considered a dependable source of information. A two-part questionnaire was administered by personal interview to a panel of 3,000 respondents residing in the city of Chicago. The field and office edits were done simultaneously so that the deadline of May 1 could be met. A senior supervisor, Mr. Z, was placed in charge of the editing tasks and was assisted by two junior supervisors and two field workers. The two field workers were instructed to discard instruments that were illegible or incomplete. Both the junior supervisors were instructed to scrutinize 1,500 of the instruments each for incomplete answers, wrong answers, and responses that indicated a lack of interest. They were instructed to discard instruments that had greater than five incomplete or wrong answers (the questionnaire contained 30 questions). In addition, they were asked to use their judgment in assessing whether the respondent showed a lack of interest, in which case they should also discard the questionnaire.

   a. Critically evaluate the preceding editing tasks. Be specific.
   b. Make specific recommendations to Mr. D. Witt, the owner of the WITT TV station, about how the editing should be done.

3. Establish response categories and codes for the question, "What do you like about this new brand of cereal?"

4. Code the following responses using your categories and codes.
   a. "$1.50 is a reasonable price to pay for the cereal."
   b. "The raisins and nuts add a nice flavor."
   c. "The sizes of the packages are convenient."
   d. "I like the sugar coating on the cereal."
   e. "The container does not tear and fall apart easily."
   f. "My kids like the cartoons on the back of the package."
   g. "It is reasonably priced compared to other brands."
   h. "The package is attractive and easy to spot in the store."
   i. "I like the price; it is not so low that I doubt the quality and at the same time it is not so high as to be unaffordable."
   j. "The crispness and lightness of the cereal improve the taste."

5. A large manufacturer of electronic components for automobiles recently conducted a study to determine the average value of electronic components per automobile. Personal interviews were conducted with a random sample of 400 respondents. The following information was secured with respect to each subject's "main" vehicle when he or she had more than one.

Average Dollar Value of Electronic Equipment per Automobile

Dollar Value of Electronic Equipment	Number of Automobiles
Less than $50	35
$51 to $100	40
$101 to $150	55
$151 to $200	65
$201 to $250	65
$251 to $300	75
$301 to $350	40
$351 to $400	20
More than $401	5
Total # of automobiles	400

   a. Convert the preceding information into percentages.
   b. Compute the cumulative absolute frequencies, and then into relative frequencies.
   c. Prepare a histogram and frequency polygon with the average value of electronic equipment on the x-axis and the absolute frequency on the y-axis.
   d. Graph the empirical cumulative distribution function with the average value on the x-axis and the relative frequency on the y-axis.
   e. Locate the median, first sample quartile, and third sample quartile.
   f. Calculate the mean, standard deviation, and variance for the frequency distribution. (Hint: Use the midpoint of each class interval and multiply that by the appropriate frequency. For the interval starting at $401, assume the midpoint is 425.5.)

6. Moon Shine Company is a medium-sized manufacturer of shampoo. In recent years, the company has increased the number of product variations of Moon Shine shampoo from three to five to increase its market share. Management conducted a survey to compare sales of Moon Shine shampoo with sales of Sun Shine and Star Shine, the brand's two major competitors. A sample of 1,800 consumers indicated the following frequencies with respect to most recent shampoo purchased:

Shampoo	#Buying
Moon Shine	425
Sun Shine	1175
Star Shine	200
Total	1800

Past experience had indicated that three times as many households preferred Sun Shine to Moon Shine and that, in turn, twice as many households preferred Moon Shine to Star Shine. Management wants to determine if the historic tendency still holds, considering that Moon Shine Company has increased the range of shampoos available.

a. State the null and alternate hypotheses.

b. How many degrees of freedom are there?

c. What is the chi-square critical table value at the 5% level?

d. What is the calculated χ^2 value? Show all your calculations.

e. Should the null hypothesis be rejected or not? Explain.

7. A large financial institution wanted to know which options were most important to small businesses. The financial institution hypothesized that the options that businesses found to be important would vary as annual sales of the businesses varied. The financial organization set up a cross-tabulation to investigate if any changes in importance were occurring between the groups of businesses. The following table lists the number of businesses that reported each of the options as most important. Calculate the percentages. Interpret your calculations.

	Annual Sales	
Option	Under $2 million	$2 to $10 million
Checking account	50	30
Mutual fund	10	70
Savings account	40	50

8. A social organization was interested in determining if there were various demographic characteristics that might be related to people's propensity to contribute to charities. The organization was particularly interested in determining whether individuals over age 40 were more likely to contribute larger amounts than individuals under age 40. The average contribution in the population was $1,500, and this figure was used to divide the individuals in the sample into two groups, those who contributed more or less than average (see Table A).

In addition, the social organization wanted to know if contributions depended on income, age, or both. The median income in the population was $38,200, and this figure was used to split the sample into two groups (see Table B).

a. Does the amount of personal contribution depend on age? Generate the necessary tables to justify your answer.

b. Does contribution depend on age alone? Generate the tables to justify your answer.

c. Present the percentage of contributions that are more than $1,500 by age and income in tabular form. Interpret the table.

Table A: Personal Contribution and Age

	Age		
Contribution	$\leq$39	40+	Total
$\leq$$1500	79	50	129
$1500+	11	60	71
Total	90	110	200

Table B: Personal Contributions by Age and Income

	Income					
	< $38,200 Age		$38,200+ Age		Totals Age	
Contribution	$\leq$39	40+	$\leq$39	40+	$\leq$39	40+
$\leq$$1500	63	22	16	28	79	50
$1500+	7	18	4	42	11	60
Total	70	40	20	70	90	110

Appendix: Chi-Square and Related Indices for Cross-Tabs

14

Questions to Guide Your Learning:

Q1 What is a chi-square for cross-tabs?

Q2 What are contingency coefficients and the index of predictive association?

Q3 What are log linear models and logit models, and when would I use them?

Q4 What are the nonparametric tests: Spearman's rank correlation coefficient and the coefficient of concordance?

Now that we have a better appreciation for the kinds of relationships that might exist between two or more variables as depicted in a cross-tab, we need to follow-up these descriptive impressions with inferential tests. In Chapter 14, the chi-square test for a one-way tabulation was presented as a tool to enable the marketing researcher to determine whether the pattern observed in frequency data was "real," or was only random fluctuations due to sampling variability. Here too, we can proceed beyond descriptions of proportions in cross-tabs to find out whether various results reflected sample aberrations or real relationships between variables.

Hypotheses and Statistics to Test Them

For the chi-square on a two-way table, the null hypothesis is that there is no contingency between the two variables. We usually seek to reject that hypothesis in favor of supporting evidence for a relationship between the variables. Stated precisely, the null hypothesis for a two-way chi-square is this:

H_0: the row variable is independent of the column variable.

To say two variables are "independent" is also to say they show no association (which is analogous to saying they are not correlated). For example, if the two variables in Table 14A.1 are not related, then knowing the size of a family would not help predict the number of cars accurately—there is no contingent relationship. If asked to guess the number of cars in a household, one would use the distribution in the sample as a whole: The marginal frequencies of 75 versus 25 tell us the odds of having 0 or 1 car versus 2 or more cars are 3:1. Those proportions would be used as an estimate regardless of family size (i.e., for either row). The question is whether we can improve our prediction if we take into account family size. We should be able to, if there is a relationship between family size and car ownership.

TABLE **14A.1**	**Frequency Data on Car Ownership**		
	#Cars		
Family Size	**0–1**	**2+**	**Total**
4 or less	70	8	78
5+	5	17	22
Total	75	25	100

Chi-square tests whether the row and column variables are independent (unrelated).

The hypothesis to be tested states that the row variable, A (to use a generic label), is independent of the column variable, B. In Table 14A.1, A would be family size and B, the number of cars the family owns. For notation purposes, let:

A_1 = family of 4 or fewer members

A_2 = family of 5 or more members

B_1 = family owns 0 or 1 car

B_2 = family owns 2 or more cars

Recall from your basic statistics class that the probability of two events occurring jointly if those events are independent is simply the product of the likelihood of either occurring: $P(AB) = P(A) \times P(B)$. In the application to contingency tables, if variables A and B are indeed independent, then the probability of occurrence of the event A_1B_1 (a family with 4 or fewer members and 0 or 1 cars) is given as the product of the separate probabilities for A_1 and B_1:

$$P(A_1B_1) = P(A_1)P(B_1)$$

The probability $P(A_1)$ is given by the number of cases possessing the characteristic A_1, that is, n_{A1} (or the number of small families), over the total number of cases, n:

$$P(A_1) = \frac{n_{A_1}}{n} = \frac{78}{100}$$

Similarly, $P(B_1)$ is given by the number of cases having the characteristic B_1, or n_{B1} (the number of families having 0 or 1 car), over the total sample size. $P(B_1) = n_{B1}/n = 75/100$. The joint probability $P(A_1B_1)$ is:

$$P(A_1B_1) = P(A_1)P(B_1) = \left(\frac{78}{100}\right)\left(\frac{75}{100}\right)$$

Given a total of $n = 100$ cases, the number expected to fall in the cell A_1B_1, e_{11}, is given as the product of the total number of cases and the probability of any one of these cases falling into the A_1B_1 cell; that is,

$$e_{11} = nP(A_1B_1) = 100\left(\frac{78}{100}\right)\left(\frac{75}{100}\right)$$

Two of the n's cancel, so the formula for e_{11} simplifies to:

$$e_{11} = nP(A_1B_1) = nP(A_1)P(B_1) = n\frac{n_{A_1}}{n}\frac{n_{B_1}}{n} = \frac{n_{A_1}n_{B_1}}{n} = \frac{78 \times 75}{100}$$

Thus, to generate the expected frequencies for each cell, multiply the marginal frequencies and divide by the total. The expected frequencies appear in Table 14A.2.

TABLE 14A.2	Expected Frequencies on Car Ownership Data	
	#Cars	
Family Size	0–1	2+
4 or less	58.5	19.5
5+	16.5	5.5

The χ^2 value is calculated over the r rows and c columns, with o_{ij} and e_{ij} denoting the observed and expected number of observations in the $(i,j)^{th}$ cell:

$$\chi^2 = \sum_{i=1}^{r}\sum_{j=1}^{c}\frac{(o_{ij} - e_{ij})^2}{e_{ij}}$$

$$= \frac{(70 - 58.5)^2}{58.5} + \frac{(8 - 19.5)^2}{19.5} + \frac{(5 - 16.5)^2}{16.5} + \frac{(17 - 5.5)^2}{5.5}$$

$$= 2.261 + 6.782 + 8.015 + 24.046$$

$$= 41.104$$

The expected frequencies in any row sum to the marginal total so there are $(c - 1)$ degrees of freedom in a row (c is the number of columns). Similarly, the expected frequencies in a column must sum to the marginal total, thus there are $(r - 1)$ degrees of freedom per column (where r is the number of rows). Total degrees of freedom (df) in a two-way contingency table are $(r - 1)(c - 1)$.

In our problem, df = $(2 - 1)(2 - 1) = 1$. Using an $\alpha = .05$, the tabled critical value of χ^2 from the appendix in the back of the book is 3.84. The computed $\chi^2 = 41.104$ thus falls in the critical region. The null hypothesis (of independence) is rejected. Thus, we conclude that family size is a factor in determining number of cars purchased.

The chi-square test is one of the most widely used tests in marketing research.

Contingency Coefficient

The χ^2 contingency table test indicates whether two variables are independent, but it does not measure the strength of association when they are dependent. The contingency coefficient (C) can be used for this purpose. It is directly related to the χ^2 test, so it can be generated with little additional effort:

$$C = \sqrt{\frac{\chi^2}{n + \chi^2}}$$

Chi-square: are the variables related?

Contingency coefficient: how strong is the relationship?

where n is the sample size and χ^2 is calculated in the normal way.

The calculated χ^2 for the data just described is 41.104. The contingency coefficient is:

$$C = \sqrt{\frac{\chi^2}{n + \chi^2}} = \sqrt{\frac{41.104}{100 + 41.104}} = .540$$

Does this value indicate strong or weak association between the variables? We need to compare this value against its limits. When there is no association, the contingency coefficient is zero. When the variables are completely dependent or perfectly correlated, the upper limit is a function of the number of categories.

When the number of categories is the same for each variable (that is, $r = c$), the upper limit is: $\sqrt{(r-1)/r}$.

In the example, $r = c = 2$, so the maximum possible value for the contingency coefficient is .707. The calculated value, .540, is more than halfway between the limits of zero for no association and .707 for perfect association, suggesting that there is moderately strong association between size of family and number of cars purchased.

Index of Predictive Association

If we had a correlation coefficient, r, we would square it, r^2, to see how much variance in one variable is explained by the other. The index of predictive association does this for cross-tabs.

In the example of size of family vs. car ownership, there is one predictor variable, A (family size) and one criterion variable, B (number of cars in the household). Both variables have two classes: A_1 and A_2, and B_1 and B_2. Suppose we wish to predict the B classification of a family chosen at random—should we predict they'd fall into category B_1 (0 or 1 car), or B_2 (2 or more cars). If we have no knowledge of the family's classification on A, the best guess is to predict B_1, because 75% of all the observations fall in this category. On this basis, we would make 75% of all assignments correctly, since we would assign them all to B_1. (Of course, we would be wrong 25% of the time.) Suppose we know that the family is small (A_1)—the best guess is B_1, since 70 of 78 cases possessing A_1 fall in the B_1 classification. If the A classification is A_2 (the family is large), the best guess is B_2 (17 of 22 cases).

The index of predictive association, $\lambda_{B|A}$, measures the relative decrease in the probability of error by taking account of the A classification in predicting the B classification, over the error of prediction when the A classification is unknown. In the example, $\lambda_{B|A} = .48$. The errors in predicting the B classification are reduced by 48% by taking account of the A classification. The original classification error rate is 25%; these errors drop 12% (25% times .48 equals 12%; there would have been 25 misclassifications without knowing A, but with A, only 13 would be misclassified).

The index of predictive association varies from 0 to 1. It is zero if the A variable is of no help in predicting B. It is 1 if the knowledge of the A classification allows the B classification to be predicted perfectly. The index, predicting B from A, is calculated as follows. Let:

> Contingency coefficient is like a correlation.
> Index of predictive association is like regression.

$n_{.m}$ be the largest marginal frequency among the B classes, and

n_{am} be the largest frequency in the ath row of the table

Then:

$$\lambda_{B|A} = \frac{\sum\limits_{a} n_{am} - n_m}{n - n_m}$$

where $\sum\limits_{a} n_{am}$ is taken over all the A classes. For the example, $n = 100$. The largest marginal frequency among the B classes, $n_{.m}$, is 75, corresponding to 0 or 1 cars. If a family has 4 or fewer members, the largest frequency in the first row of the cross-classification table, n_{1m}, is 70; similarly, $n_{2m} = 17$. Thus, the index of predictive association is:

$$\lambda_{B|A} = \frac{(n_{1m} + n_{2m}) - n_m}{n - n_m} = \frac{(70 + 17) - 75}{100 - 75} = .48$$

We reduced the errors in predicting B from A, from 25 to 13, a 48% improvement. The enhanced predictive accuracy is substantial. (This result, that A

helps us understand B, is consistent with the chi-square test for independence on this contingency table, where we had rejected the notion of independence between the variables.)

These findings demonstrate the two important questions in association analysis. First, is there an association between the criterion and predictor variables, or are they independent? Second, if they are dependent, how much are predictions about the criterion variable improved by taking into account the important predictor variables? The chi-square test and contingency coefficient answer the first question, and the index of predictive association is used to answer the second. The distinction between these two questions is analogous to the difference between correlation and regression, which analogously seek linear association and prediction.

Log Linear Models

Log linear models extend the chi-square test to frequency tables of three or more variables.[1] For example, we might explore the relationship between family size, household income, and number of cars, as in Table 14A.3.

Recall that in the chi-square for two variables, the model of independence between A and the B was reflected in the equation for computing the expected frequencies:

$$e_{ij} = \frac{n_{A_i} n_{B_j}}{n}$$

This equation is multiplicative, which makes the calculus of optimization complicated. If we take the natural logarithm of both sides, the equation simplifies to a "linear" form (terms are added or subtracted) in the "log" scale—hence they are called "log linear" models:

$$\ell n(e_{ij}) = \ell n(n_{A_i}) + \ell n(n_{B_j}) - \ell n(n)$$

The first term on the right-hand side of the equation reflects the rows (A_i), the second term reflects the columns (B_j), and the third term, the total sample size.

To facilitate generalization to bigger tables and to more complex models, let us write the parameters simply as "u-terms":[2]

TABLE 14A.3   Car Ownership as a Function of Income and Family Size

A = family size	B = income	C = 0 or 1 car	2 or more
4 or fewer	< $37,500	44	2
	>$37,500	26	6
5 or more	< $37,500	4	4
	> $37,500	1	13

[1] See Stephen Fienberg, *The Analysis of Cross-Classified Categorical Data,* 2nd ed., (Springer, 2007). For related research, see Richard A. Briesch, Pradeep K. Chintagunta, and Edward J. Fox, "How Does Assortment Affect Grocery Store Choice?" *Journal of Marketing Research,* to appear; Timothy J. Gilbride, Greg M. Allenby, Geraldine Fennell, and Joel Huber, "Adjusting Choice Models to Better Predict Market Behavior," *Marketing Letters,* 16, 197–208; and Rakesh Niraj, V. Padmanabhan, and P. B. Seetharaman, "A Cross-Category Model of Households' Incidence and Quantity Decisions," *Marketing Science,* 27 (2), 225–235.
[2] With constraints, given the df or the fact that the estimates are centered on u, that $\sum_i u_{A(i)} = \sum_j u_{B(j)} = 0$.

$$\ell n(e_{ij}) = u + u_{A(i)} + u_{B(j)}$$

where

$$u = \frac{1}{rc}\sum_i \sum_j \ell n(e_{ij})$$

$$u_{A(i)} = \frac{1}{c}\sum_j \ell n(e_{ij}) - u$$

$$u_{B(j)} = \frac{1}{r}\sum_i \ell n(e_{ij}) - u.$$

> Log linear models: scary notation, but just an extension of cross-tabs.

The first term is an overall mean of the expected frequencies that looks unusual only because we are working in the natural log scale. The second two terms are also means (e.g., the sum over columns, j, divided by the number of columns) "centered around" (subtracting) the overall mean, u. The first term, u, is not typically of substantive interest, but the latter two, $u_{A(i)}$ and $u_{B(j)}$, reflect the differences among the rows (A), and those among the columns (B).

In Table 14A.2, variable A is family size, B is income, and C is the number of cars the family owns. We might wish to test whether there are significant associations between all pairs of variables, A and B, A and C, and B and C. We would write our model as follows:

$$\ell n(e_{ijk}) = u + u_{A(i)} + u_{B(j)} + u_{C(k)} + u_{AB(ij)} + u_{AC(ik)} + u_{BC(jk)}$$

with the first four terms estimated analogously to those in the equations above, and the last three terms which reflect the pairwise associations estimated as follows, for example:[3]

$$u_{12(ij)} = \frac{1}{k}\sum_k \ell n(e_{ijk}) - u_{1(i)} - u_{2(j)} - u$$

Suppose the model fit, but, say, the BC term was not significant (i.e., no relationship existed between income and number of cars); we might fit a model that is nested within the larger model, maintaining comparable fit, yet improved parsimony, for example:[4]

$$\ell n(e_{ijk}) = u + u_{A(i)} + u_{B(j)} + u_{C(k)} + u_{AB(ij)} + u_{AC(ik)}$$

In truth, in this particular example, it is not simply the case that we have three arbitrary variables and any of them might be related to any of the others. Rather, we have come to think of C, the number of cars, as the dependent variable that might be predicted once we know the family size, A, and the household income, B. Although the log linear models help us understand relationships among the variables, a "logit" model is used for prediction purposes.

---

[3] Both $u_{A(i)}$ and $u_{B(j)}$ are expressed as deviations around the u, thus: $\sum_i u_{AB(ij)} = \sum_j u_{AB(ij)} = 0$. As tables get bigger or models more complex, they cannot all be written in analytical form; the iterative proportional fitting or Newton-Raphson algorithm estimation procedures rely upon iterative convergence to solutions.

[4] The χ^2 may be computed, but usually we compute: $G^2 = 2\sum_{i=1}^{r}\sum_{j=1}^{c} o_{ij}\ell n(o_{ij}/e_{ij})$, a "badness of fit" index like χ^2 in that both get larger as the data and expected frequencies differ more, and both draw their critical values from chi-square tables, but G^2 has superior statistical properties.

Logits are really important in marketing research. They allow us to answer central marketing questions such as, "Will that household buy my product?" (i.e., the expected answer is yes or no) and "Which brand will that consumer choose?" (and the expected answer is one of a number of categories).

For our data, a logit model poses the question, "Are the odds of having 0 or 1 car vs. 2 or more cars different depending on the size and income of the family?" Imagine the model above stated for just the families with 0 or 1 cars ($C = 1$),

$$\ell n(e_{ij1}) = u + u_{A(i)} + u_{B(j)} + u_{C(1)} + u_{AB(ij)} + u_{AC(i1)} + u_{BC(j1)}$$

and comparing it to the model fit to the families that own 2 or more cars ($C = 2$):

$$\ell n(e_{ij2}) = u + u_{A(i)} + u_{B(j)} + u_{C(2)} + u_{AB(ij)} + u_{AC(i2)} + u_{BC(j2)}$$

We might compare the odds directly in a ratio, e_{ij1}/e_{ij2}, or again, given that it is easier to work in the log scale, we would examine the "log odds ratio," also called the "logit," as defined here:

$$\ell n(e_{ij1}/e_{ij2}) = \ell n(e_{ij1}) - \ell n(e_{ij2})$$
$$= u + u_{A(i)} + u_{B(j)} + u_{C(1)} + u_{AB(ij)} + u_{AC(i1)} + u_{BC(j1)}$$
$$- [u + u_{A(i)} + u_{B(j)} + u_{C(2)} + u_{AB(ij)} + u_{AC(i2)} + u_{BC(j2)}].$$

Note that several common terms cancel, and algebraically we are left with:

$$(u_{C(1)} - u_{C(2)}) + (u_{AC(i1)} - u_{AC(i2)}) + (u_{BC(j1)} - u_{BC(j2)})$$

Log linear models: correlations

Logit models: regression

In logit models, there are only two levels of the dependent variable (our variable C). And recall that the estimates sum to zero: $u_{C(1)} + u_{C(2)} = 0$. Thus, if $u_{C(1)}$ is some value such as .5, then $u_{C(2)}$ will equal $-.5$. Thus, the term $(u_{C(1)} - u_{C(2)})$ in the equation above may be restated as $(u_{C(1)} + u_{C(1)})$, or $2u_{C(1)}$. Thus, the equation above simplifies to:

$$2(u_{C(1)} + u_{AC(i1)} + u_{BC(j1)})$$

Now instead of seven terms in the model, there are only three, all of which involve the dependent variable, C; the first is a logit intercept, the second reflects the impact of A (family size) on C, and the third reflects the impact of B (household income) on C.

If we fit this logit model to the data in Table 14A.3, using a statistical computing package such as Sas or Spss, we obtain the following estimates:

$$\ell n(e_{ijk}) = -2.18 + 3.56(A_i) + 1.96(B_j)$$

Both predictors are significant (the printouts list standard errors of .73 and .72, respectively, for A and B; the parameter estimates in the equation, divided by their standard errors yield z-statistics of 4.88 and 2.72). Thus, both family size and household income are significant determinants in predicting the number of cars a family is likely to own.[5] Both parameters are positive, which indicates that as either predictor increases (larger family or greater income), the likelihood that the family owns 2 or more cars (compared with 0 or 1) increases.[6]

---

[5] Did we "know" this from the cross-tabs previously? Sort of. But now we know it "officially" via a statistical test.

[6] The models we have considered here require both the dependent variable and the predictors to be categorical. If some predictors are continuous, models called "logistic regressions" may be fit, using similar logic.

Nonparametric Measures of Association

We have been focusing on techniques and measures of association appropriate for nominal or ordinal data—cross-tabs, chi-square, contingency coefficient, index of predictive association, log linear, and logit models. There are also two indices that are appropriate only for the analysis of rank-order data—Spearman's rank-order correlation coefficient and the coefficient of concordance.

Spearman's Rank Correlation Coefficient

One of the best-known coefficients of association for rank-order data is Spearman's rank correlation coefficient, denoted r_s. The coefficient is appropriate when both variables are measured on an ordinal scale so that the sample elements may be ranked in two ordered series.

Suppose a company wished to determine whether there was an association between the overall performance of a distributor and the distributor's level of service. The company's management defined "overall performance" as a composite of measures of sales, market share, sales growth, and profit. The marketing research department developed an index of "service provided" based on customer complaints and compliments, service turnaround records, etc.

Table 14A.4 contains the ranks of the company's 15 distributors with respect to each of these performance criteria. We start by looking at the differences in ranks on each variable. Let X_i be the rank of the ith distributor in terms of service, and Y_i be the rank of the distributor with regard to overall performance. Let $d_i = X_i - Y_i$ be the difference in rankings. If the rankings on the two variables are exactly the same, each d_i will be zero. If there is some discrepancy in ranks, some of the d_i's will not be zero, and the greater the discrepancy, the larger some of the d_i's would be. The Spearman rank-order correlation coefficient is calculated as:

TABLE 14A.4   **Distributor Performance**

Distributor	Service Ranking X_i	Overall Performance Ranking Y_i	Ranking Difference $d_i = X_i - Y_i$	Difference Squared d_i^2
1	6	8	−2	4
2	2	4	−2	4
3	13	12	+1	1
4	1	2	−1	1
5	7	10	−3	9
6	4	5	−1	1
7	11	9	+2	4
8	15	13	+2	4
9	3	1	+2	4
10	9	6	+3	9
11	12	14	−2	4
12	5	3	+2	4
13	14	15	−1	1
14	8	7	+1	1
15	10	11	−1	1
				$\sum d_i^2 = 52$

$$r_s = 1 - \frac{6 \sum_{i=1}^{n} d_i^2}{n(n^2 - 1)}$$

In the example, $\sum_i d_i^2 = 52$, and $r_s = 1 - \frac{6(52)}{15(15^2 - 1)} = 1 - \frac{312}{3360} = .907$.

The null hypothesis is that there is no association between service level and overall performance, whereas the alternative hypothesis suggests there is a relationship. The null hypothesis that $\rho_s = 0$ can be tested by referring directly to tables of critical values of r_s or, when the sample size is greater than 10, by calculating the t statistic,

$$t = r_s \sqrt{\frac{n - 2}{1 - r_s^2}}$$

which is referred to a t-table for $n - 2$ degrees of freedom. Calculated t is:

$$t = .907 \sqrt{\frac{15 - 2}{1 - (.907)^2}} = 7.77$$

and critical t for $\alpha = .05$ and 13 degrees of freedom is 2.16. Calculated t exceeds critical t, and the null hypothesis of no relationship is rejected. Overall distributor performance is related to service level. The upper limit for the Spearman rank correlation coefficient is 1.0, since if there were perfect agreement in the ranks, $\sum d_i^2$ would be zero. Thus, the relationship is significant and relatively strong.

Coefficient of Concordance

In some cases, we want to analyze the association among three or more rankings of n objects or individuals. When there are k sets of rankings, we use Kendall's coefficient of concordance.

An example of the use of this index is in examining interjudge reliability. A computer equipment manufacturer was interested in evaluating its domestic sales branch managers. Many criteria could be used: sales from the branch office, sales in relation to the branch's potential, sales growth, and sales representative turnover are just a few. Management believed that different executives in the company would place different emphasis on the various criteria and that a consensus about how the criteria should be weighted would be hard to achieve. It was decided, therefore, that the VP in charge of marketing, the general sales manager, and the marketing research department should all attempt to rank the 10 branch managers from best to worst. Table 14A.5 contains these rankings. The company wished to determine whether there was agreement among these rankings.

The right-hand column of Table 14A.5 contains the sum of ranks assigned to each branch manager. If perfect agreement existed among the three rankings, the sum of ranks, R_i, for the top-rated branch manager would be $1 + 1 + 1 = k$, where $k = 3$. The second-rated branch manager would have sum of ranks $2 + 2 + 2 = 2k$, and the nth-rated branch manager would have sum of ranks $n + n + n = nk$. Thus, when there is perfect agreement among the k sets of rankings, the R_i would be k, $2k$, $3k, \ldots, nk$. If there is little agreement among the k rankings, the R_i would be roughly equal. Thus, the degree of agreement among the k rankings is measured by the variance of the n sums of ranks; the greater the agreement, the larger the variance in the n sums would be.

TABLE 14A.5 Branch Manager Rankings

Branch Manager	VP, Marketing	General Sale Manager	Marketing Research Dept.	Sum of Ranks, R_i
A	4	4	5	13
B	3	2	2	7
C	9	10	10	29
D	10	9	9	28
E	2	3	3	8
F	1	1	1	3
G	6	5	4	15
H	8	7	7	22
I	5	6	6	17
J	7	8	8	23

The **coefficient of concordance** (W) is a function of the variance in the sums of ranks. First, the sum of the R_i for each of the n rows is determined. Second, the average R_i, R, is calculated by dividing the sum of the R_i by the number of objects. Third, the sum of the squared deviations is determined; call this quantity s, where

$$s = \sum_i (R_i - \bar{R})^2$$

The coefficient of concordance finally is computed as:

$$W = \frac{s}{\frac{1}{12} k^2(n^3 - n)}$$

The denominator of the coefficient represents the maximum possible variation in sums of ranks if perfect agreement in the rankings were achieved. The numerator reflects the actual variation in ranks. The larger the ratio, the greater the agreement among the evaluations. For our data,

$$\bar{R} = \frac{(13 + 7 + \ldots + 23)}{10} = \frac{165}{10} = 16.5$$

$$s = (13 - 16.5)^2 + (7 - 16.5)^2 + \ldots + (23 - 16.5)^2 = 720.5$$

and

$$\left(\frac{1}{12}\right) k^2(n^3 - n) = \left(\frac{1}{12}\right)(3)^2(10^3 - 10) = 742.5$$

Thus,

$$W = \frac{720.5}{742.5} = .970$$

The significance of W can be examined by using special tables when the number of objects being ranked is small (when $n \leq 7$). When the sample size is larger, the coefficient of concordance is approximately chi-square distributed where $\chi^2 = k(n-1)W$ with $n-1$ degrees of freedom. The null hypothesis is that there is no agreement among the rankings, and the alternative hypothesis is that there is some agreement. For an assumed $\alpha = .05$, critical χ^2 for 9 degrees of freedom is 16.92, whereas calculated X^2 is:

$$X^2 = k(n-1)W = 3(9)(.970) = 26.2$$

Calculated X^2 exceeds critical χ^2, the null hypothesis of no agreement is rejected—there is indeed some agreement. Further, the agreement is good—the limits of W are .0 with no agreement and 1.0 with perfect agreement among the ranks. The calculated value of $W = .970$ suggests that although the agreement in the ranks is not perfect, it is certainly good. The marketing VP, general sales manager, and marketing research department applied essentially the same standards in ranking the branch managers.

Kendall has suggested that the best estimate of the true ranking of n objects is provided by the order of the various sums of ranks, R_i, when W is significant. Thus, the best estimate of the true ranking of the sales managers is that F is doing the best job, B the next best job, and C is doing the poorest job.

Summary

The chi-square statistic tests whether the associations spotted in cross-tabs are statistically reliable or more likely the result of sampling variability. Log linear models are a natural extension of the chi-square test to three- and higher-dimensional tables. The addition of variables naturally allows for more complex modeling.

Logit models are particularly important to the marketing researcher, because they allow the modeling of categorical dependent variables. Brand choice is categorical and predicting it is typically of great importance in many marketing decision systems.

The Spearman rank correlation coefficient and the coefficient of concordance are additional indices that can shed further light on associations between rank-order data.

Questions

1. What is the basic question at issue in a chi-square test on a two-way contingency table? What is the null hypothesis? How are the expected frequencies determined?
2. What is the contingency coefficient, and to what types of situations does it apply? How does one determine whether the association is "strong" or "weak"?
3. When is the index of predictive association used? What does $\lambda_{B|A} = .75$ mean?
4. How is a log linear model an extension of the χ^2?
5. If the data are ordinal and the analyst wishes to determine whether the observed frequencies correspond to some expected pattern, what statistical test is appropriate? How is it done?
6. When is the Spearman rank correlation coefficient used? How do you calculate and interpret it?
7. What is the coefficient of concordance? What is its rationale?

Applications and Problems

1. A large publishing house wants to determine if there is an association between newspaper publication choice and the education level of the customer. A random sample of 400 customers provided the data in Table A.
   a. State the null and alternate hypotheses.
   b. Generate the expected frequencies for each cell.
   c. Is there an association between newspaper publication choice and level of education at $\alpha = .05$? Show your calculations.
   d. What is the strength of association as measured by the contingency coefficient between education

level and newspaper choice? Show your calculations.

Table A: Education Level vs. Newspaper Choice: Observed Frequencies

| Newspaper Publication | Level of Education | | | |
	H.S.	Undergrad Degree	Graduate Degree	Total
A	75	45	5	125
B	35	10	30	75
C	50	35	10	95
D	65	35	5	105
Total	225	125	50	400

2. A marketing researcher from the publishing company in Problem 1 stated that the best estimate of newspaper choice by a customer chosen at random would be the A publication, since 31.25% (125 of 400) customers purchased this publication. The researcher further stated that 68.75% of the time the company would be wrong and decided to discard the previous study.

a. How could the predictive accuracy be improved? Show your calculations.

b. The index of predictive association is "more directly interpretable" than the contingency coefficient. Discuss.

Data Analysis—Basic Questions

15

Questions to Guide Your Learning:

Q1 What considerations underlie the choice of a statistical method to analyze data?

Q2 What are the main statistical methods useful for marketing researchers?

Q3 What are the implications of "levels of measurement" (nominal, ordinal, interval, ratio) for choice of statistical tools?

Q4 What is a univariate vs. multivariate analysis?

You've seen that data analysis begins with the preliminary steps of editing, coding, and tabulating. Those pre-processing procedures are important and common to all research studies. Some studies stop there, with tables and cross-tabs. Many involve additional analyses to answer in more detail the question, "What's going on in the data?" To extract more information and meaning from data, we need to know which statistical procedure is appropriate. This choice depends on qualities of the research problem and qualities of our particular data. This chapter highlights these considerations in the choice of methodology.

Choice of Analysis Technique: An Example

Assume that a study was completed by a consumer products firm that manufactures the dishwashing liquid Sheen.[1] The study was designed to determine consumers' perceptions of the gentleness of Sheen and its closest competitor, Glitter. A random sample of consumers was asked to rate each brand on a five-point mildness scale with the following descriptors, according to how they thought the brand affected their hands:

- Very rough (VR)
- Rough (R)
- Neither rough nor gentle (N)
- Mild (M)
- Very mild (VM)

Table 15.1 contains the responses from 10 consumers. The table also contains alternative ways of analyzing the data, and not all of them are appropriate, so some of their conclusions are wrong. We'll see that the conclusion depends on the method.

[1] Hey, it's not "glam," but this kind of thing is the brand manager's bread-and-butter.

TABLE 15.1 Consumers' Perceptions of Dishwashing Liquids

Respondent	Perception of VR R N M VM S	G	A −2 −1 0 1 2 S	G	B 1 2 3 4 5 S	G	C 5 4 3 2 1 S	G	D −1 0 1 S	G	E: Preferred Alternative
1	VM	VM	2	2	5	5	1	1	1	1	T[1]
2	M	VM	1	2	4	5	2	1	1	1	G
3	N	VM	0	2	3	5	3	1	0	1	G
4	M	VM	1	2	4	5	2	1	1	1	G
5	M	VM	1	2	4	5	2	1	1	1	G
6	M	VM	1	2	4	5	2	1	1	1	G
7	M	M	1	1	4	4	2	2	1	1	T[1]
8	M	R	1	21	4	2	2	4	1	21	S
9	N	R	0	21	3	2	3	4	0	21	S
10	N	M	0	1	3	4	3	2	0	1	G
Sums			8	12	38	42	22	18	7	6	
Averages			.9	1.2	3.8	4.2	2.2	1.8	.7	.6	

[1] A "T" in column E indicates a tie, in that both brands received the same rating.

There is no problem in most studies in deciding the question, "What ways *can* the analysis be done?" But there's a big problem in deciding the question, "How *should* the analysis be done?"

The methods reported in Table 15.1 vary according to how numeric values were assigned to the scale. For instance, underlying Method A is the assumption that mildness is desirable and roughness undesirable in dishwashing liquids. Thus, if the consumer believed that the dishwashing soap was very mild, that response received a positive score of +2. A response of "very rough" received a negative score of −2, and so on. The scores are totaled and averaged at the bottom of the table.

The averages for Method A show Sheen with an average of .8, and Glitter at 1.2. Both soaps are thus "mild." If we look at the differences between these averages and convert them to a percentage difference, with Sheen as the comparative yardstick, we find

$$\frac{\bar{x}_G - \bar{x}_S}{\bar{x}_s}(100) = \frac{1.2 - 0.8}{0.8}(100) = 50\%$$

and the conclusion is that Glitter is 50% milder on the hands. With Glitter as the basis of comparison, the result is:

$$\frac{\bar{x}_G - \bar{x}_S}{\bar{x}_s}(100) = \frac{1.2 - 0.8}{1.2}(100) = 33\%$$

and the conclusion is that Glitter is 33% milder on the hands. Similar calculations underlie each of the comparisons for Methods A through D. Methods B and C, for example, assign numbers to response categories similar to Method A, except that Method B uses all positive numbers (with "very mild" receiving a score of 5) and Method C reverses the scoring (so a score of 5 represents a "very rough" evaluation). Method D assigns negative values to "rough" evaluations and positive values to "mild" evaluations, but the "rough" and "very rough" evaluations receive the same score (−1), as do the "mild" and "very mild" evaluations (+1), so "rough" and "very rough" aren't distinguished by this approach (nor are "mild" vs. "very mild"). In contrast, Method E doesn't rely on average scores for all respondents but simply lists whichever alternative was rated higher by each respondent. The conclusions in Method E reflect the facts that Respondents 1 and 7 perceived Glitter and Sheen to be of equal mildness, 6 of 10 respondents perceived Glitter as milder, and 2 perceived Sheen as milder.

Table 15.2 offers simple analyses of each of these methods, trying to assess which of the two brands is milder. The right-hand column suggests a variety of conclusions, so we have to figure out which of these conflicting statements is correct, and why. The answer is Method E, and the reasons are what we illustrate in this chapter. A number of factors dictate the choice of analysis method, including the type of data, the research design, and the assumptions underlying the test statistic.

Before discussing these considerations, let's finish with these data. We'll show why the last statement is correct and, in the process, start to reveal some of the issues.

First, some researchers hold that the response categories reflect order, but not interval measurements. That is, even though "very rough" is rougher than "rough," the difference between "very rough" and "rough" is not the same as the difference between "rough" and "neither rough nor gentle." Further, as long as the order relationships are preserved on these data, the assignment of scale values is arbitrary, but the calculation of means is misleading. Thus, these researchers would argue that Methods A to D are inappropriate because the values were averaged.

Second, even if the data had interval properties, Methods A to D would still be incorrect for two reasons. First, the comparisons in Table 15.2 involve absolute

TABLE 15.2   Comparison of Dishwashing Liquids

Method	Base in Comparison	Calculations	Conclusion
A	Sheen	$\dfrac{\bar{x}_G - \bar{x}_S}{\bar{x}_s}(100) = \dfrac{1.2 - 0.8}{0.8}(100) = 50\%$	Glitter is 50% milder
	Glitter	$\dfrac{\bar{x}_G - \bar{x}_S}{\bar{x}_s}(100) = \dfrac{1.2 - 0.8}{1.2}(100) = 33\%$	Glitter is 33% milder
B	Sheen	$\dfrac{\bar{x}_G - \bar{x}_S}{\bar{x}_s}(100) = \dfrac{4.2 - 3.8}{3.8}(100) = 10.5\%$	Glitter is 11% milder
	Glitter	$\dfrac{\bar{x}_G - \bar{x}_S}{\bar{x}_s}(100) = \dfrac{4.2 - 3.8}{4.2}(100) = 9.5\%$	Glitter is 10% milder
C	Sheen	$\dfrac{\bar{x}_G - \bar{x}_S}{\bar{x}_s}(100) = \dfrac{2.2 - 1.8}{2.2}(100) = 18.2\%$	Glitter is 18% milder
	Glitter	$\dfrac{\bar{x}_G - \bar{x}_S}{\bar{x}_s}(100) = \dfrac{2.2 - 1.8}{1.8}(100) = 22.2\%$	Glitter is 22% milder
D	Sheen	$\dfrac{\bar{x}_G - \bar{x}_S}{\bar{x}_s}(100) = \dfrac{0.7 - 0.6}{0.7}(100) = 14.3\%$	Sheen is 14% milder
	Glitter	$\dfrac{\bar{x}_G - \bar{x}_S}{\bar{x}_s}(100) = \dfrac{0.7 - 0.6}{0.6}(100) = 16.7\%$	Sheen is 17% milder
E			60% of respondents thought Glitter was milder, 20% thought Sheen milder

magnitudes—each difference is compared to a mean, and the result is interpreted as a certain percentage of the mean. Such comparisons are inappropriate unless the variables have a natural zero. The comparisons involving Methods A through D would be meaningful, then, if the variables were on a ratio scale, but not when the zero position is arbitrary, as it is in these rating scales. Further, the evaluations of Sheen and Glitter are not independent and cannot be treated as such statistically. Instead, they represent multiple responses from the same individual. They are related or dependent samples, and the appropriate procedure involves an analysis of the difference in the evaluations per individual. Method E is the only procedure that correctly deals with these differences.

Third, the conclusion was that "60% of the people thought Glitter was milder on the hands." The question has not been raised about whether this is a statistically significant result. The question of significance involves the size of the sample used to generate the percentage. With our sample of only 10, the result is not significant, but if 60 out of 100 people thought that Glitter was milder on the hands than Sheen, the result would be statistically significant, even though the percentage preferring Glitter would remain the same. Sample size is an important barometer in determining whether a research finding is due to chance or whether it represents an underlying condition in the population.

Basic Considerations

The example has highlighted some of the considerations involved in the choice of analysis method. The appropriate technique depends on the type of data, the research design, and the assumptions underlying the test statistic and its related consideration, the power of the test.

Type of Data

When we were discussing the creation of questions for surveys, we talked about the differences between the **levels of measurement**—nominal, ordinal, interval, and ratio. We revisit those levels briefly here because they have clear implications for which statistics we can use on the data that arise from a survey. To understand the different implications, consider which transformations are permissible for variables measured on each of the levels.

Nominal

The nominal scale is used when categorizing objects. A letter or numeral is assigned to each category so that each number represents a distinct category. For instance, if we're coding gender, the numbers 1 and 2 (or 2&1, 0&1, etc.) serve equally as well as the letters M and F. The nominal scale remains undistorted with this "transformation," this substitution of the numbers. Thus, a "2" could be used to denote men and a "1" for women, or vice versa, without loss of information. With a nominal scale, the only permissible operation is counting, so the only measure of central tendency that is appropriate is the **mode**. In a sample of 60 men and 40 women, we cannot say that the "average gender is 1.4" (e.g., $.6 \times 1 + .4 \times 2$). All we can say is that there were more men in the sample than women, or that 60% of the sample was "male" regardless of whether we choose to call the category 1, 2, or M.

Ordinal

The ordinal scale represents a higher level of measurement because the numerals assigned reflect order as well. If we were to classify students into three

Now you see—"level of measurement" (nominal, ordinal, interval, ratio) is important because it helps determine which statistics you can use!

categories, such as good, average, and poor, we might call the categories A, B, and C, or we might use the numbers 1 = good, 2 = average, and 3 = poor, or even the reverse, in which good = 3 and poor = 1. The schemes are equally fine. The structure of an ordinal scale is undistorted by any substitution that preserves the order. The **median** and the **mode** are now both legitimate measures of central tendency. If 20 people ranked Product A 1st in comparison with Products B and C, whereas 10 ranked it 2nd and 5 ranked it 3rd, we could say that (1) the average (median) rank of Product A was one (with 35 subjects, the median is given by the 18th response when ranked from lowest to highest), and that (2) the modal rank was also one.

Interval

The assignment of numerals to objects using an interval scale conveys information about the magnitude of the differences between the objects. We can determine *how much more* one category is than another. We still cannot state that "A is five times larger than B," because the interval scale contains an arbitrary (not absolute) zero. An interval scale is undistorted under linear transformations; i. e., $y = b + cx$. The effect of this transformation is to shift the origin b units (moving the numbers up or down) and multiply the unit of measurement by c (stretching or shrinking the range on the scale), as in going from a Fahrenheit scale to Celsius. The mean, the median, and the mode are all appropriate measures of central tendency.

Ratio

The ratio scale has a natural zero point, so we can sensibly say that "A is twice as heavy" or "twice as tall as B." The ratio scale is undistorted under proportionate or scalar transformations; i.e., $y = cx$. The conversion of inches to centimeters is an example; c in this case would equal 2.54. All statistics appropriate for the interval scale are also appropriate for a ratio scale (i.e., **mean**, median, and mode). It's important to interpret numerical relationships properly, reflecting the properties of the measurement scale. Consider the following ad claim, like those you see on TV and in magazines:

New Lustre gets your clothes 20% brighter, you need 50% less detergent, and you can use water temperatures 30% lower than that required for old Lustre.

The "brighter" claim in this ad was probably based on consumers' subjective reactions to clothes washed with old Lustre. Consumers probably gave their perceptions on a "dingy" to "bright" rating scale. Suppose that a seven-point scale was used and that old Lustre received an average score of 5 and new Lustre got a 6; the 20% brighter claim would result from the calculation:

$$\frac{\bar{x}_{new} - \bar{x}_{old}}{\bar{x}_{old}}(100) = \frac{6 - 5}{5}(100) = 20\%$$

There is disagreement between people who insist that most marketing measurements, like these consumer ratings, reflect ordinal measurement vs. people who argue that such scales can be treated as interval measures. There is some evidence to support each position. On the one hand, even though a researcher develops scales to try to reflect equal increments, the scales aren't necessarily interpreted that way by the respondents. On the other hand, we can hope the patterns in data are largely robust (see Research Realities 15.1), and enhanced

RESEARCH   REALITIES

15.1 4-point? 5-point? Stability of Responses

Something that concerns marketing survey researchers is whether to offer "4 box" or "5 box" responses. The question is essentially whether respondents should be provided with a "don't know" or "no opinion" option.

Most researchers endorse that if a respondent doesn't know an answer or has no opinion, he or she should be allowed to state as much. Some researchers suggest that a neutral point, or "no opinion" answer, should not be provided, because most respondents are not likely to be exactly neutral on an issue, so they should be forced to take a stand, even if their preference is slight. Researchers who argue for including a neutral or "no opinion" category argue that forcing respondents to make a choice when their preferences are fuzzy or non-existent simply introduces response error into the results.

Market Facts ran a comparative study, asking 3,000 consumer about their purchase intention, for three different time frames, for several different product categories, whether they "definitely will buy" to "definitely would not buy" the product. Half the respondents were given the 4-point scales, the other half were given the 5-point scales that included the neutral point, "might or might not buy."

also largely comparable across the 4- vs. 5-point scales, within every category. The exception seems to be that in the absence of a "neutral" point (i.e., for the 4-point sample), the responses will tend to be more negative (to "probably not buy") vs. the fence-sitters in the five-point neutral category. Results are particularly "similar" if one collapses the "top two boxes," as is frequently done to demonstrate overall positive regard, i.e., "probably" or "definitely" will buy.

Purchase Intention in the next 30 days (new toothbrush, flashlight battery, electric light bulb):

Purchase Intention in the next 12 months (new car, microwave oven, vacation airline ticket):

Are there differences? Sort of. The 12-month chart looks remarkably stable (i.e., 4- vs. 5-point scales don't matter, the results are largely the same, except of course the middle category cannot have any data for the 4-point sample). The 30-day and 7-day charts are

Purchase Intention in the next 7 days (movie ticket, pudding or pie filling, frozen pizza):

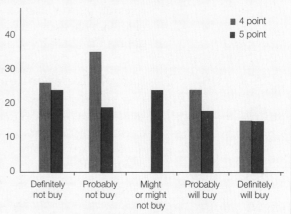

Source: "*Measuring Purchase Intent,*" Research on Research, *synovate. com. Also see Randall Thomas* "*Not Sure About 'Don't Know,'*" Quirks Marketing Research Review *(quirks.com).*

with larger samples. While the debate continues, a reasonably balanced argument suggests the following:

1. It is very safe, and certainly very useful, to treat the total score summed over a number of items as an interval scale.[2]

2. It is sometimes safe to treat individual items as interval scales, such as when specific steps have been taken to ensure the interval nature of the response categories.

3. It is always legitimate to treat the scale as ordinal when neither Condition 1 nor 2 is satisfied.

Suppose, on the other hand, that appropriate procedures were used, that the evaluation scale did reflect interval measurement, and that the calculation of means was appropriate. The "brighter" claim would still be in error, for the same reason that the temperature claim is also probably erroneous. More likely than not, the temperature claim would be based on the fact that whereas old Lustre required 200°F water to be effective, new Lustre requires only 140°F water; i.e., temperatures 30% lower, because:

$$\frac{200 - 140}{200}(100) = 30\%$$

The Fahrenheit scale is an interval scale (because it possesses an arbitrary zero) so the calculation of ratios on such scales is meaningless. To see the folly in this exercise, simply convert the 200°F and 140°F temperatures to their Celsius equivalents of 93.3°C and 60.0°C. Now you can use 36% lower temperatures with new Lustre.

Thus, only one of the three ad claims is probably legitimate—the claim that 50% less detergent is needed with new Lustre. The scale here is of the ratio variety—if one uses, say, ½ cup of new Lustre vs. 1 cup of old Lustre, then indeed one needs 50% less detergent.[3]

An understanding of the level of measurement underlying data is crucial to proper interpretation. Nominal, ordinal, interval, or ratio help determine which methods and statistics are meaningful for your data.

Research Design

A second consideration that affects the choice of analytical technique is the research design used to generate the data. The questions involve the dependency of observations, the number of observations per object, the number of groups being analyzed, and the control exercised over the variables of interest.

Sample Independence

Consider first the question of dependent or independent samples. Suppose that you were interested in determining the effectiveness of a recent mailing from a direct marketing campaign. Suppose that the measure of effectiveness was attitude toward a product, measured on an interval scale, and say the research design had been:

[2] For example, if questions 4, 5, and 6 on some survey all purport to measure consumer preference, it's not unusual, and for several reasons good practice, to create a new variable for each respondent in the database, called "preference" as a subscale, which is simply the average of the respondent's scores on questions 4–6.

[3] These claims of temperature *could* be supported with data if measures were made on a Kelvin scale, which possesses an absolute zero, and even the brightness claim would follow if measurements were made using an integrating sphere (which measures the amount of light reflected from an object placed in the sphere—black objects do not reflect any of the light directed at them, while white objects reflect 100% of the light directed into the sphere). The brightness claim does not follow, though, from the aggregation of consumer perceptions.

$$X \quad O_1$$
$$O_2$$

where O_1 represents the attitudes of those who received the targeted mailing and O_2 the attitudes of those who did not. In this case, the samples are independent. The O_2 measures do not depend on the O_1 measures. An appropriate test of significance would reflect the independence of the samples. In this case, the t-test for the difference in two means would be appropriate.[4]

If the research design had been:

$$O_1 \quad X \quad O_2$$

where there are again two sets of observations, O_1 and O_2, but now they're made on the same individuals, before and after receiving the mailing. The pre and post samples consist of the same individuals, so the measurements are not independent. The focus in the analysis is on the change in attitude per individual before and after exposure to the marketing exposure. The observations must be analyzed in pre/post pairs. A paired difference test for statistical significance should be used in this case.[5]

Number of Groups

Consider next the question of the number of groups being compared. Suppose that you were interested in the relative effectiveness of two different catalogs, so you run a controlled experiment in which some respondents receive one version, X_1, others get the other, X_2, and a third group receives neither. The design can be diagrammed:

$$X_1 \quad O_1$$
$$X_2 \quad O_2$$
$$O_3$$

There are three groups (two experimental and one control) whereas the previous design had two groups (one experimental and one control). The appropriate procedure is the analysis of variance.[6]

Ethical **Dilemma**   15.1

A beer producer conducted a study to determine whether consumers perceive an actual or a psychological difference in the taste of beer. As part of the experiment, each consumer was asked to taste three unmarked cans of beer and to order them according to preference. Although they were led to believe that the three cans of beer were different beers, the participants discovered when the beers were unmasked that the three cans were, in fact, the same beer. A fair proportion of participants had stated that the three beers tasted quite different.

- It is argued that such an experiment may induce stress in some participants inasmuch as it may lead them to doubt their competence as shoppers. Comment.
- Should the investigator offer some sort of psychic support (such as debriefing) upon completion of the experiment to counteract any possible negative effects?
- Under what conditions might debriefing be problematic?

---

[4] The t-test for the difference in means is discussed in Chapter 16.
[5] The paired difference statistical test is also discussed in Chapter 16.
[6] Analysis of variance is discussed in the appendix to Chapter 16.

Number of Variables

The number of measures per object also affects the choice of analytical procedure. In the direct marketing example, we had used "attitude toward the product" as the measure of effectiveness of the mailing, and we had contrasted the attitudes of the receivers with those of the nonreceivers. Suppose that we believe that the sales impact of the catalog must also be considered. We would now wish to contrast the two groups in terms of their attitude and also in terms of each group's sales. The design is still

$$X \quad O_1$$
$$O_2$$

but now O_1 and O_2 represent measures of both sales and attitudes.

One way to proceed would be to test for the differences in attitude, and then separately test for the differences in sales to the two groups. It's possible, though, for the two groups to differ only slightly on each criterion so that neither of the univariate tests detects a significant difference. Would we conclude that the mailing had no impact, even though the average attitude score and average sales were each slightly higher for the experimental group? Or do we conclude that the small, nonsignificant differences, taken together, indicate a real difference? It's also possible that each variable is significant but the results inconsistent; e.g., attitudes are more favorable in the control group but sales greater in the experimental group. Do we take the favorable and unfavorable results at their face value, or do we take the position that one of them represents a Type I error and in reality is attributable to chance?[7] To answer this question (and it becomes more difficult as the number of measures per object increases), we need to have some means of looking at groups on several characteristics simultaneously. This type of problem is handled using multivariate statistical procedures.[8]

Variable Control

Another important question in analysis involves the control of variables that can affect the result. Return to the design

$$X \quad O_1$$
$$O_2$$

in which the emphasis is on the differences in attitudes between the two groups. One variable that would certainly seem to determine attitudes is previous usage of the product. If so, in the experimental design, the analyst would like to control for prior usage to minimize its effect. A good way of doing this would be to make the experimental and control groups equal with respect to prior usage by matching, randomization, or some combination of these approaches. If this control procedure is followed, the t-test for analyzing the difference in two means can legitimately be employed. If the control is not affected but attitudes do depend on prior use of the product, the conclusions produced using the t-test will be in error to the extent that the two groups differ in their previous use of the product. One way to adjust for these differences is by allowing prior use to be a covariate—that is, by regressing attitudes on use and adjusting the attitude scores represented by O_1 and O_2 by the resulting regression equation. The adjusted scores for the experimental and control groups would then be compared.

[7] Type I error is discussed in the "quick stats review" appendix.
[8] See Chapter 18.

Assumptions Underlying Test Statistic

A final consideration in the choice of a statistical method is the set of assumptions supporting the various test statistics. As an example, let's look at the assumptions for the first test we saw, the t-test for the difference in two means.

Assume that the samples have been drawn independently of each other. Further, assume that the individuals composing the experimental group come from a population with unknown mean μ_1 and unknown variance σ_1^2, that those in the control group come from a population with unknown mean μ_2 and unknown variance σ_2^2, and that attitudes toward the product are normally distributed in each of these populations. Also assume that the variances of the two populations are equal—that is, $\sigma_1^2 = \sigma_2^2$; thus, a pooled estimator for the overall variance is used.[9] In sum, the assumptions are:

1. Independent samples
2. Normal distribution of the characteristic of interest in each population
3. Equal variances in the two populations

The t-test is more sensitive to the violations of some of these assumptions than others. For example, it works fine when the data aren't normal, but it's sensitive to violations of the equal-variance assumption.

Our point is to illustrate the fact that statistical tests depend on certain assumptions for their validity. If the assumptions are not met, sometimes they can be satisfied through a transformation on the data (e.g., change to log units). Sometimes a different test statistic should be chosen that relies on different assumptions, e.g., a distribution-free test.[10]

Overview of Statistical Procedures

This section provides an overview of the statistical techniques discussed in later chapters to help direct you to the sections that discuss the techniques appropriate for a given problem. Figure 15.1 illustrates the questions to be asked to determine the appropriate statistical technique. The questions are one of two varieties: First, how many variables are there (how many total variables, how many of those are classified as dependent variables to be predicted, etc.)? Second, what is the level of measurement (remember: nominal, ordinal, interval, ratio) of the variable(s)?

The first decision question in Figure 15.1 asks whether you're trying to predict a dependent variable or not. If yes, then if the dependent variable is continuous (interval or ratio-level scaled), you can compute a t-test, z-test, analysis of variance or regression, depending on the level of measurement of the predictor variables. If the dependent variable is categorical (nominal or ordinal), you could compute contingency coefficients, indices of predictive association, logits, or simple z-tests for proportions, if the predictor variable is nominal. When the predictor and dependent variables are both ordinal, the Spearman rank correlation coefficient is perfect. When the dependent variable is nominal, specifically group membership, and the predictors are continuous, discriminant analysis is appropriate.

If you're not trying to predict a particular variable, then the question becomes, "How many variables do you have?" If you're focusing on just one variable at a time, you can compute frequencies and percentages, chi-squares,

[9] The assumption of equality of variances is not mandatory, but when it does not hold, the "proper procedure" is shrouded in controversy. There is a vast statistical literature on this condition, known as the Behrens-Fisher problem.
[10] "Nonparametric tests" involve minimal assumptions. See Larry Wasserman, *All of Nonparametric Statistics* (Springer, 2007).

FIGURE 15.1   **Chart for Choosing among Statistical Tests**

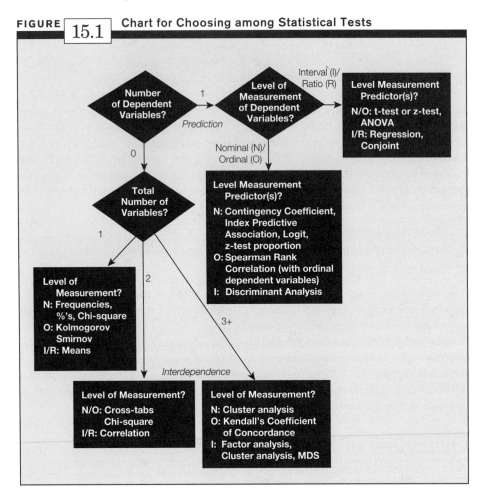

the Kolmogorov-Smirnov test, or just straightforward means, all depending on the level of measurement of the variable. The statistics listed thus far are considered **univariate**, because you're predicting one dependent variable or analyzing one variable.

If you have two or more variables, and none of them carries the special status of a dependent variable, you're not in the realm of "prediction," but in the realm of what's called the analysis of "interdependence," meaning simply, you're trying to figure out how two or more variables are somehow interrelated. If you have two variables, you can run cross-tabs and chi-squares if the variables are categorical, or correlations if the variables are continuous. If you have more than two variables, you're conducting a **multivariate** analysis. There are many useful multivariate techniques for the marketing research, most of which are discussed in later chapters.

Summary

We've discussed the basic considerations involved in choosing a statistical method to analyze the collected data. Scale of measurement, the research design, and the assumptions underlying the test statistic all affect this choice.

In terms of measurement theory, the origin of the numbers is important for the interpretation of the results. It makes a difference whether the level of measurement is nominal, ordinal, interval, or ratio.

Several questions in the research design affect choice of method, including the independence or dependence of the sample observations, the number of groups, the number of variables, and the control exercised over those variables likely to affect the results.

The role of each variable in the analysis and the level of measurement reflected by each variable interact to produce a complex classification scheme of statistical analytical techniques.

Questions

1. What basic considerations underlie the choice of a statistical test? Explain.

2. What are the basic levels of measurement? How does the type of data affect the choice of a statistical test?

Applications and Problems

1. Evaluate the following advertising claims. Do you think the claims are legitimate?
   a. "Con-Air gives you twice as much satisfaction while traveling—at a price 50% lower than other major airlines."
   b. "In blind taste tests, the majority of people preferred our beer twice as much as any other major brand of beer. Is it any wonder we sell 1.5 times more beer than our nearest competitor?"

2. Discuss whether the use of adjective rating scales reflects ordinal or interval measurement.

3. A large automobile manufacturer wanted to relate sales of its latest models by area to the demographic composition of each area as measured by such variables as average income, average size of household, average age of head of household, and so on.
   a. Is this dependence or interdependence analysis? Why?
   b. Are there any criterion or predictor variables? If so, what are they? Identify the level of measurement of each.

4. A survey asked users of a new deodorant product how satisfied they were with the product's performance using the following scale:

Very Satisfied	Satisfied	Neither Satisfied nor Dissatisfied	Dissatisfied	Very Dissatisfied
1	2	3	4	5

A research analyst noticed an interesting difference between male and female respondents. The mean satisfaction score for this product was 30% higher for women than men. Given the scale, is this a valid calculation? What are valid calculations? Can any comparison between men and women be made with these data?

5. On a product-tracking survey, the following three categories were used to capture consumers' knowledge and trial of different products: "Never heard of the product," "Heard of the product but have never bought the product," and "Have bought the product." These categories were coded 1, 3, 6. The research team leader changed the codes to 1, 2, 3 so that the scores reflected equal intervals. Explain why the team leader's correction is unnecessary and unwarranted.

6. With the introduction of grocery-store scanners, elaborate marketing experiments can be run in the field. For example, a company wanting to test the effects of a new advertising campaign on its breakfast cereal sales designed the following test to determine which campaign was the most effective. Six cities were chosen for this experiment. In three cities, viewers saw the new advertisement, and in the other three cities, viewers continued to see the traditional advertising campaign.
   a. Present the experimental design in diagrammatic form.
   b. What analysis technique would you recommend? What assumptions underlie the recommended test?
   c. Given the company's research objective, discuss alternative designs.

Appendix: Quick Stats Review

15

Questions to Guide Your Learning:

Q1 How do I frame a null hypothesis?

Q2 What is a "significance level"?

Q3 How is it related to a Type I error?

Q4 What is a Type II error? How is it related to power?

Q5 What is a one-tailed vs. a two-tailed significance test?

Many procedures discussed in the next few chapters test hypotheses, so we review some basic statistical concepts that underlie hypothesis testing in classical statistical theory. The best quantitative marketing research rests on these fundamental concepts.

Lest you think hypotheses are just for geeks, look at how specifically these hypotheses are frequently worded in popular business press magazines:

- "The most popular flight times will be 100% sold out, with more than 90% of the customers coming from the target segment."

- "Market share within the segment will exceed 80%."

- "Churn among targeted customers will decline from 11% to 3%."

- "Corporate discounts will decline from an average of $3500 to $0."

- "At least 85% of the senior executive segment will use the preflight meal service."

These are all extremely testable hypotheses, and upon learning the results, immediately implementable.

Null Hypothesis

A hypothesis may be rejected but can never be accepted except tentatively, because further evidence may prove it wrong. In other words, one rejects the hypothesis or does not reject the hypothesis on the basis of the evidence at hand. It is wrong to conclude, though, that since the hypothesis was not rejected, it can necessarily be accepted as valid or proven.

A simple example should illustrate the issue.[1] Let's say we're testing the "hypothesis" that "John Doe is a poor man." We

---

[1] We thank Dr. B. Venkatesh of The Burke Institute for suggesting this illustration of hypotheses.

observe that Doe dines in cheap restaurants, lives in a poor area in a run-down building, wears worn and tattered clothes, and so on. His behavior is consistent with that of a poor man, but we cannot "accept" the hypothesis that he is poor. It is possible that Doe may, in fact, be rich but cheap. We can continue gathering information about him, but for the moment we must decide not to reject the hypothesis. One single observation, for example if we were to learn that he has a six-figure bank account or that he owns 100,000 shares of some blue chip stock would allow the immediate rejection of the hypothesis, and support instead for the conclusion that "John Doe is rich."

Thus, in the absence of perfect information, which is the case when sampling, the best we can do is form hypotheses or conjectures about what is true. Further, our conclusions can be wrong, and thus there is always some probability of error in tentatively accepting any hypothesis. Statistical parlance holds that researchers commit a "Type I error" when they reject a true null hypothesis (and thereby find favor for the alternative); they commit a "Type II error" when they do not reject a false null hypothesis, which they should have, given that it is false. The null hypothesis is assumed to be true for the purpose of the statistical test. It's important to know that Type I errors can be specified to not exceed some specific amount (usually, $\leq .05$), but Type II errors are harder to control.[2]

The upshot is that we need to frame the null hypothesis in such a way that its rejection leads to the acceptance of the desired conclusion, the statement or condition that we wish to verify. For example, suppose that a firm was considering introducing a new product if it could achieve more than 10% of the market. The proper way to frame the hypotheses would be:

$$H_0 : \pi \leq .10$$

$$H_A : \pi > .10$$

If the evidence leads to the rejection of H_0, the researcher would then be able to "accept" the alternative (that the product could be expected to attract more than 10% of the market) and the product would be introduced, because statistically, such a result would have been unlikely to occur if the null were indeed true. If H_0 cannot be rejected, though, the product should not be introduced unless more evidence to the contrary becomes available. This particular example involves the use of a "one-tailed" statistical test; the alternate hypothesis is expressed directionally. There are plenty of research problems that warrant a "two-tailed" test. For example, the null might be that market share achieved by a line extension of Product X is no different from that achieved by the old formula, which was 10%. A two-tailed test would be:

$$H_0 : \pi = .10$$

$$H_A : \pi \neq .10$$

No direction (greater than or less than) is implied with the alternate hypothesis; the proportion is simply expressed as *not being equal* to .10.

The one-tailed test is preferred in marketing research when one outcome is preferred to another, e.g., greater market share, higher product quality, lower expenses, etc. In addition, when it is appropriate, the one-tailed test is more powerful statistically than the two-tailed alternative.

> Null hypothesis: e.g., no effect, no difference between groups…Hope to reject null

---

[2] We will have more to say about Type I and Type II errors shortly.

Types of Errors

The result of a statistical test on a null hypothesis is to reject it or not reject it. Two types of errors may occur. First, we might reject the null hypothesis when it is true. Second, we might not reject the null when we should have, i.e., it is false. These errors are termed **Type I error** and **Type II error** (or α error and β error, which are the probabilities associated with their occurrence).[3]

To illustrate each type of error, consider a legal analogy. Under U.S. criminal law, a person is innocent until proven guilty. Therefore, the judge and jury are always testing the hypothesis of innocence. The defendant may, in fact, be either innocent or guilty, but based on the evidence, the court may reach either verdict regardless of the true situation. Table 15A.1 displays the possibilities. If the defendant is innocent and the jury finds the person innocent, or if the defendant is guilty and the jury finds him or her guilty, the jury has made a correct decision. If, however, the defendant truly is innocent and the jury finds the person guilty, or if the defendant is guilty and the jury finds him or her not guilty, they have made an error. The jury must decide one way or the other, and thus the probabilities of the jury's decision must sum vertically to 1. If we let α represent the probability of incorrectly finding the person guilty when he or she is innocent, then $1 - \alpha$ must be the probability of correctly finding him or her not guilty. Similarly, β and $1 - \beta$ represent the probabilities of findings of innocence and guilt when the person is guilty. It should be clear that $\alpha + \beta$ is not equal to 1, although we'll see later that β must increase when α is reduced if other things remain the same. Because our society generally holds that finding an innocent person guilty is more serious than finding a guilty person not guilty, α error is reduced as much as possible in our legal system by requiring proof of guilt "beyond a reasonable doubt."[4]

Table 15A.2 contains the analogous research situation. Just as the defendant's true status is unknown to the jury, the true situation regarding the null hypothesis is unknown to the researcher. The researcher's dilemma parallels that of the jury in that he or she has limited information with which to work. Suppose that the null hypothesis is true. If the researcher concludes it is false, he or she has made a Type I error. The significance level associated with a statistical test indicates the probability with which this error may be made. Because sample information will always be somewhat incomplete, there will always be some α error. The only way it can be avoided is by never rejecting the null hypothesis (never finding anyone guilty, in the judicial analogy). The confidence level of a statistical test is $1 - \alpha$, and the more confident we want to be of a statistical result, the lower we must set α error. The power associated with a statistical test is

TABLE 15A.1 **Legal Analogy Illustrating Decision Error**

Verdict	True Situation: Defendant Is	
	Innocent	Guilty
Not Guilty	Correct decision: probability $= 1 - \alpha$	Error: probability $= \beta$
Guilty	Error: probability $= \alpha$	Correct decision: probability $= 1 - \beta$

[3] The two types of errors are not simply complementary, in that $\alpha + \beta \neq 1$.

[4] Most professions have some form of these concerns, e.g., medical diagnostic errors of "false positives" and "false negatives."

TABLE 15A.2 Types of Errors in Hypothesis Testing

Research Conclusions	True Situation: Null Hypothesis Is	
	True	**False**
Do not reject H_0	Correct decision: Confidence level probability $= 1 - \alpha$	Error: Type II, probability $= \beta$
Reject H_0	Error: Type I, Significance level probability $= \alpha$	Correct decision: Power of test probability $= 1 - \beta$

the probability of correctly rejecting a false null hypothesis. One-tailed tests are more powerful than two-tailed tests because, for the same α error, they are simply more likely to lead to a rejection of a false null hypothesis. β error represents the probability of not rejecting a false null hypothesis. There is no unique value associated with β error.

Procedure

Research Realities 15A.1 shows the typical steps that are followed in hypothesis testing. Suppose we're investigating the potential for a new product and the research involves the preferences of consumers. Perhaps, in the judgment of

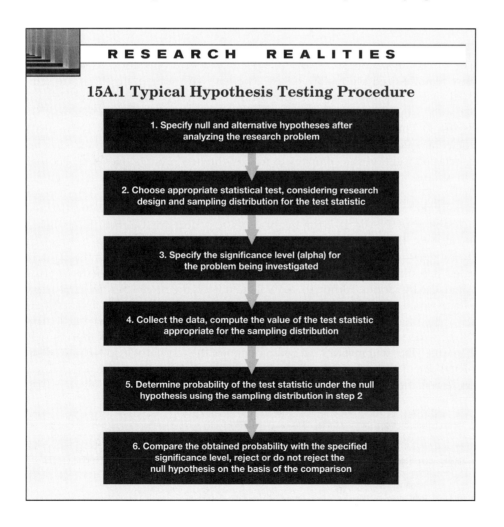

RESEARCH   REALITIES

15A.1 Typical Hypothesis Testing Procedure

1. Specify null and alternative hypotheses after analyzing the research problem

2. Choose appropriate statistical test, considering research design and sampling distribution for the test statistic

3. Specify the significance level (alpha) for the problem being investigated

4. Collect the data, compute the value of the test statistic appropriate for the sampling distribution

5. Determine probability of the test statistic under the null hypothesis using the sampling distribution in step 2

6. Compare the obtained probability with the specified significance level, reject or do not reject the null hypothesis on the basis of the comparison

management, the product should not be introduced unless at least 20% of the population could be expected to prefer it. 625 consumers were interviewed for their preferences.

Step 1. The null and alternate hypotheses would be:

$$H_0 : \pi \leq .20$$

$$H_A : \pi > .20$$

The hypotheses are framed so that if the null hypothesis is rejected, the product should be introduced.

Step 2. The appropriate sample statistic is the sample proportion, and the distribution of all possible sample proportions under the sampling plan is based on the assumption that the null hypothesis is true. The distribution of sample proportions is theoretically binomially distributed, but the large sample size permits the use of the normal approximation.[5] The z-test equals:

$$z = \frac{p - \pi}{\sigma_p}$$

where p is the sample proportion preferring the product and σ_p is the standard error of the proportion, or the standard deviation of the distribution of sample ps. In turn, σ_p equals:

$$\sqrt{\frac{\pi(1 - \pi)}{n}} = \sqrt{\frac{.20(.80)}{625}} = .016$$

where n is the sample size. Note this peculiarity of proportions. As soon as we have hypothesized a population value, we have said something about the standard error of the estimate. The proportion is the most clear-cut case of "known variance," since the variance is specified automatically with an assumed π.

Step 3. The researcher selects a significance level α. The α error is the probability of rejecting H_0—that is, concluding that $\pi > .2$, when in reality $\pi \leq .2$. This conclusion will lead the company to market the new product. However, because the venture will only be profitable if $\pi > .2$, a wrong decision to market would be financially unprofitable and possibly disastrous. The probability of Type I error should, therefore, be minimized as much as possible. We know however, that the probability of a Type II error increases as α is decreased, other things being equal. Type II error implies concluding that $\pi \leq .2$ when in fact $\pi > .2$, which in turn suggests that the company would table the decision to introduce the product when it could be profitable. The opportunity loss from making such an error could also be serious. Although, as explained later, the researcher does not know what β would be, he or she knows that α and β are related and that an extremely low value of a (say, $\alpha = .01$ or .001) might produce intolerable β errors. Therefore, the researcher decides on an α level of .05 as an acceptable compromise.[6]

Step 4. This step involves the computation of the test statistic, so it can be completed only after the data are collected. Suppose 140 of the 625 sample respondents preferred the product. The sample proportion is thus $p = 140/625 = .224$.

---

[5] The binomial tends toward the normal distribution for a fixed π as sample size increases. The effect is fastest when $\pi = .5$. As π departs from .5 in either direction, the normal approximation becomes less adequate, although it is generally held that the normal approximation may be used safely if the smaller of $n\pi$ or $n(1 - \pi)$ is 10 or more. If this condition is not satisfied, binomial probabilities can be calculated directly or found in tables. In the example, $n\pi = 625(.2) = 125$, and $n(1 - \pi) = 500$; thus, the normal approximation to binomial probabilities is adequate.

[6] We'll say more about α and its interpretation after we have introduced the notion of power.

The basic question is simple: "Is this value of p too large to have occurred by chance from a population with π assumed to be equal to .2?" or, in other words, "What is the probability of getting $p = .224$ when $\pi = .2$?"

$$z = \frac{p - \pi}{\sigma_p} = \frac{.224 - .20}{.0160} = 1.500$$

Step 5. The probability of occurrence of a z-value of 1.500 can be found from standard tabled values of areas under the normal curve. (See the appendix at the end of the book.) Figure 15A.1 shows the procedure. The shaded area between $-\infty$ and 1.500 equals .9332—this means that the area to the right of $z = 1.500$ is $1.000 - .9332$, or .0668. This is the probability of getting a z-value of 1.500 under a true situation of $\pi = .2$.

Step 6. Since the calculated probability of occurrence is higher than the specified significance level of $\alpha = .05$, the null hypothesis is not rejected. The product would not be introduced because, although the evidence is in the right direction, it is not sufficient to conclude beyond "any reasonable doubt" that $\pi > .2$. If the decision maker had been able to tolerate a 10% chance of committing a Type I error, the null hypothesis would have been rejected and the product marketed, since the probability of getting a sample $p = .224$ when the true $\pi = .2$ is, as we have seen, .0668.

Power

This example illustrates the importance of correctly specifying the risk of error. If a 10% chance of an α error were tolerable and the researcher specified $\alpha = .05$, a potentially profitable opportunity would have been foregone. The choice of the proper significance level involves weighing the costs associated with the two types of error.

The β error is not a constant. It is the probability of not rejecting a false null hypothesis, so this probability depends on the size of the difference between the true, but unknown, population value and the value assumed to be true under the null hypothesis. Other things being equal, we would prefer a test that minimizes such errors. And yet, since the power of a test equals $1 - \beta$, we prefer the test with the greatest power so that we have the best chance of rejecting a false null hypothesis. Our ability to do this depends on how false H_0 truly is. It could be just a little bit false or way off the mark, and the probability of an

FIGURE 15A.1   Probability of $z = 1.50$ with a One-Tailed Test

Area covered by arrow = .9332

$z = 1.50$

incorrect conclusion would certainly be higher in the first case. The difference between the assumed value under the null hypothesis and the true, but unknown, value is known as the **effect size**. As intuition suggests, large effects are easier to distinguish than small effects.

Consider again the following hypotheses:

$$H_0 : \pi \leq .20$$

$$H_A : \pi > .20$$

where $\sigma_p = .016$ and $\alpha = .05$, as before. Any calculated z-value greater than 1.645 causes us to reject this hypothesis, since this is the z-value that cuts off 5% of the normal curve. The z-value can be equated to the critical sample proportion through the formula

$$z = \frac{p - \pi}{\sigma_p} = \frac{p - .20}{.0160} = 1.645$$

or $p = .2263$. Thus, any sample proportion greater than p = .2263 will lead to the rejection of the null hypothesis that $\pi \leq .2$. This means that if 142 or more [.2263(625) = 141.4] of the sample respondents prefer the new product, the null hypothesis will be rejected and the product introduced, whereas if 141 or less of the sample respondents prefer it, the null hypothesis will not be rejected and the new product will not be introduced.

The likelihood of a sample proportion of $p = .2263$ is much greater for certain values of π than for others. Suppose, for instance, that the true but unknown value of π was .22. The sampling distribution of the sample proportions is still normal, but now it is centered around .22. The probability of obtaining the critical sample proportion $p = .2263$ under this condition is found from the normal curve table, where:[7]

$$z = \frac{p - \pi}{\sigma_p} = \frac{.2263 - .22}{.0166} = .380$$

The shaded area between $-\infty$ and $z = .380$ is given in the appendix as .6480, and thus the area to the right of $z = .380$ is equal to $1 - .6480 = .3520$ (see Panel B in Figure 15A.2). This is the probability that a value as large or larger than $p = .2263$ would be obtained if the true population proportion was $\pi = .22$. It is also the power of the test in that, if π is truly equal to .22, the null hypothesis is false and .3520 is the probability that the null will be rejected. Conversely, the probability that $p < .2263$ equals $1 - .3520 = .6480$, which is β error. The null hypothesis is false and yet the false null hypothesis is not rejected for any sample proportions p < .2263.

Suppose that the true population condition was $\pi = .21$ instead of $\pi = .22$, and the null hypothesis was again H_0: $\pi \leq .20$. Since the null hypothesis is less false in this second case, we would expect power to be lower and the risk of β error to be higher because the null hypothesis is less likely to be rejected. Let's see if that is indeed the case. The z-value corresponding to the critical p = .2263 is 1.000. Power given by the area to the right of $z = 1.000$ is .1587 (the β error is .8413), and so we get the expected result. (See Figure 15A.2, Panel C.)

Consider one final value, true $\pi = .25$. The null hypothesis of $\pi = .20$ would be way off the mark in this case, and we would expect only a small chance that it

[7] Note that σ_p is now $\sqrt{.22(.78)/625} = .0166$, because a different specification of p implies a different standard error of estimate.

FIGURE 15A.2

Computation of β Error and Power for Several Assumed True Population Proportions for the Hypothesis, $\pi \leq .20$

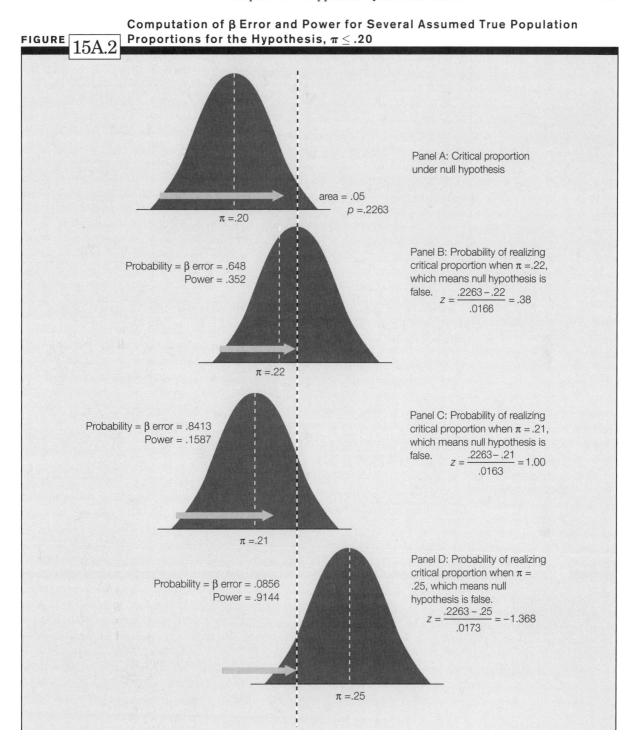

Panel A: Critical proportion under null hypothesis

area = .05
$p = .2263$

$\pi = .20$

Probability = β error = .648
Power = .352

Panel B: Probability of realizing critical proportion when $\pi = .22$, which means null hypothesis is false. $z = \dfrac{.2263 - .22}{.0166} = .38$

$\pi = .22$

Probability = β error = .8413
Power = .1587

Panel C: Probability of realizing critical proportion when $\pi = .21$, which means null hypothesis is false. $z = \dfrac{.2263 - .21}{.0163} = 1.00$

$\pi = .21$

Probability = β error = .0856
Power = .9144

Panel D: Probability of realizing critical proportion when $\pi = .25$, which means null hypothesis is false. $z = \dfrac{.2263 - .25}{.0173} = -1.368$

$\pi = .25$

would not be rejected and a Type II error would be committed. The calculations are displayed in Figure 15A.2, Panel D; $z = -1.368$, and the area to the right of $z = -1.368$ is .9144. The probability of β error is .0856, and the *a priori* expectation is confirmed.

TABLE 15A.3	β Error and Power for Different Assumed True Values of π and the Hypotheses $H_0: \pi \leq .20$ and $H_A: \pi > .20$	
Value of π	**Probability of Type II or β Error**	**Power of the Test: $1 - \beta$**
.20	$(.950) = 1 - \alpha$	$(.05) = \alpha$
.21	.8413	.1587
.22	.6480	.3520
.23	.4133	.5867
.24	.2133	.7867
.25	.0856	.9144
.26	.0273	.9727
.27	.0069	.9931
.28	.0014	.9986
.29	.0005	.9995
.30	.0000	1.0000

Table 15A.3 contains the power of the test for other selected population states, and Figure 15A.3 shows these values graphically. Figure 15A.3 is essentially the power curve for the hypothesis

$$H_0 : \pi \leq .20$$

$$H_0 : \pi > .20$$

and it confirms that the farther away the true π from the hypothesized value in the direction indicated by the alternate hypothesis, the higher the power. Note that power is not defined for the hypothesized value, because if the true value in fact equals the hypothesized value, a β error cannot be committed.

α = Type I error
β = Type II error
$1 - \beta$ = power

Because power is a function rather than a single value, the researcher attempting to balance Type I and Type II errors logically needs to ask how false the null hypothesis is likely to be and to establish the decision rule accordingly.

FIGURE 15A.3   Power Function for Data in Table 15A.3

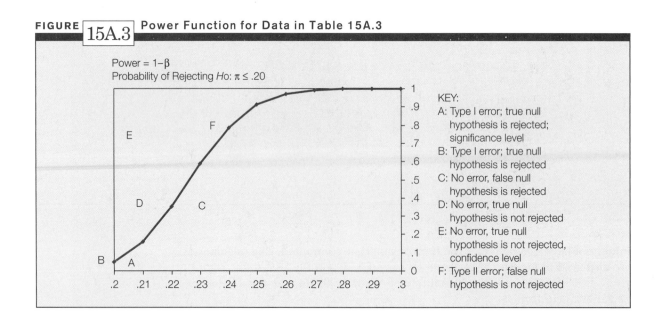

Power = $1-\beta$
Probability of Rejecting $Ho: \pi \leq .20$

KEY:
A: Type I error; true null hypothesis is rejected; significance level
B: Type I error; true null hypothesis is rejected
C: No error, false null hypothesis is rejected
D: No error, true null hypothesis is not rejected
E: No error, true null hypothesis is not rejected, confidence level
F: Type II error; false null hypothesis is not rejected

The way to control both errors within predetermined bounds for a given size effect is to vary the sample size. The need to specify all three items—α error (or degree of confidence), β error (or power), and the size of the effect it is necessary to detect—possibly explains why so many researchers content themselves with the specification of Type I or α error and allow β error to fall where it may. The failure to worry about the power of the statistical test represents one of the fundamental problems with the classical statistics hypothesis-testing approach as it is commonly practiced in marketing research. Moreover, Type II errors are often more costly than Type I errors.

Another common problem is the misinterpretation of what a "statistically significant result" really means.[8] A frequent misinterpretation is to view a p-value as the probability that the results occurred because of sampling error. Thus, $p = .05$ is (mistakenly) taken to mean that there is a probability of only .05 that the results were caused by chance and thus there must be something fundamental causing them. In actuality, a p-value of .05 means that *if* (and this is a big if) the null hypothesis is true as assumed, the odds are only 1 in 20 of getting a sample result as big or bigger than that which was observed. The p-value tells you the probability that you'd get the data you got, if the null hypothesis were true.

Another common misinterpretation is to equate statistical significance with practical significance. A difference can be of practical importance and not statistically significant if the power of the test is weak. Conversely, a result may be of no practical importance, even if highly significant, if the sample size is very large.

A third misinterpretation is to hold that the α or p-level chosen is in some way related to the probability that the research hypothesis captured in the alternative hypothesis is true. Typically, this probability is taken as the complement of the α level. Thus, a p-value of .05 is interpreted to mean that its complement, $1 - .05 = .95$, is the probability that the research hypothesis (the alternative) is true. Sometimes researchers say $p < .0001$ is "more significant" than $p < .05$, but this interpretation is incorrect. Significance is binary—a result is or is not significant.

The only logical conclusion that can be drawn when a null hypothesis is rejected at some predetermined p-level is that sampling error is an unlikely explanation of the results *given* that the null hypothesis is true. The null, as typically stated, holds that there is no relationship between two certain variables, say, or that the groups are equal with respect to some particular variable. Yet, we do not really believe that—we investigate the relationship between variables because we believe there is some association between them, or we contrast groups because we believe they are different with respect to some variable. Further, we can control our ability to reject the null hypothesis simply by the power we build into the statistical test, primarily through the size of the sample used to test it. If we ramped up our sample sizes to be big "enough," we would always reject the null.

Accordingly, be careful when interpreting results of hypothesis tests to not mislead yourself or others. Keep in mind both types of possible errors. Confidence intervals help avoid misinterpretations because they give more information about the results. A test of significance is just a yes-no situation: Either the sample result is statistically significant or it is not. In contrast, the confidence interval gives the yes-no answer, but also, by its width, a sense of the size of the effect in the data.

---

[8] See Iacobucci, "On p-values," *Journal of Consumer Research*, 32 (1), 6–11.

Summary

Many marketing research questions involve testing hypotheses. We took a look at the nature of the null hypothesis and its alternative. Type I and Type II errors were defined. The p-value and its proper interpretation were discussed. The power, or likelihood of finding significant results, was also presented.

Questions

1. Comment on the statement: "A hypothesis can never be accepted, only rejected." Is the statement true? Why or why not?
2. What is a Type I error? What is a Type II error? What is their relationship?
3. What is meant by statistical power?
4. What does it mean when the null hypothesis is rejected at the $\alpha = .10$ level?

Applications and Problems

1. Assume that the brand manager of a medium-sized manufacturer of consumer products decides to introduce a new brand of breakfast cereal if the company can initially acquire 1.5% of the market. The following hypotheses are to be tested:

$$H_0 : \pi \leq .015$$

$$H_a : \pi > .015$$

Explain and discuss the Type I and Type II errors that could occur while testing these hypotheses. What are the implications for the company?

2. Bentley Foods, Inc., a large manufacturer of frozen foods, has developed a new line of frozen pizza. Management has agreed to begin producing and marketing the new line if at least 15% of the population would prefer the pizza over other frozen pizzas currently available. To determine preferences, a sample of 1,000 consumers was obtained; 172 indicated that they would prefer the new product over existing brands.
   a. State the null and alternative hypotheses.
   b. Compute the standard error of the proportion.
   c. Calculate the z-statistic. What is the probability of obtaining this value of the z-statistic if the null hypothesis is true?
   d. The research manager for Bentley Foods is comfortable using the .05 significance level. Should the null hypothesis be rejected?
   e. At this significance level, what is the critical sample proportion?

3. A research team tested new batteries to see if they lasted significantly longer than the company's existing battery. Traditionally, all experiments have been run at $\alpha = .05$. After testing 100 old batteries as well as 100 new batteries, the mean life for the new battery was found to be greater than that of the old, at $\alpha = .05$ significance level; however, a new analyst became greatly excited when it was discovered that the difference was significant at $\alpha = .001$. He commented, "This product is much better than we thought; the difference is highly significant!"
   a. Is this a correct interpretation of the test results? Explain.
   b. Is it appropriate for the research team to announce that the difference in mean life is significant at $\alpha = .001$ instead of $\alpha = .05$?

Are My Groups the Same or Different?

16

Questions to Guide Your Learning:

Q1 What are the key statistics for testing differences?

Q2 How do I test a hypothesis I have about a mean? Two means?

Q3 Why does it matter whether I know the population variance or not, if I'm looking at means?

Q4 How do I compare proportions?

T his chapter presents statistical tests for examining differences. The difference of interest might be between your sample result and the expected population value, or it might be between two or more sample results. We focus on the parametric tests that are applicable when examining differences in means or proportions.

Hypotheses about One Mean

Many marketing research studies seek to make some statement about the population mean. The distribution of sample means is normal, with the mean equal to the population mean and the variance, $\sigma_{\bar{x}}^2$, equal to the population variance divided by the sample size $(\sigma_{\bar{x}}^2 = \sigma^2/n)$. The appropriate statistic for testing a hypothesis about a mean when the *population variance is known* is:

$$z = \frac{\bar{x} - \mu}{\sigma_{\bar{x}}}$$

where $\bar{x}$ is the sample mean, μ is the population mean, and $\sigma_{\bar{x}} = \sigma/\sqrt{n}$ is the standard error of the mean.

The z-statistic is appropriate if the sample comes from a normal population, or if the variable is not normally distributed in the population but the sample is large enough for the Central-Limit Theorem to be operative.

When the *population variance is unknown*, the standard error of the mean, $\sigma_{\bar{x}}$, is estimated by $s_{\bar{x}} = \frac{s}{\sqrt{n}}$, where s is the unbiased sample standard deviation:

$$\hat{\sigma} = s = \sqrt{\frac{\sum_{i=1}^{n}(X_i - \bar{x})^2}{n-1}}$$

The test statistic is $t = \dfrac{(\bar{x} - \mu)}{s_{\bar{x}}}$, which is t-distributed with $n-1$ degrees of freedom if the conditions for the t-test are satisfied. Those conditions are:

1. Is the distribution of the variable in the population normal or asymmetrical?
2. Is the sample size large or small?

If the variable of interest is normally distributed in the population, then the test statistic $\dfrac{(\bar{x} - \mu)}{s_{\bar{x}}}$ is t-distributed with $n - 1$ degrees of freedom. This is true whether the sample size is large or small. For small samples, we actually use t with n − 1 degrees of freedom when making an inference. Although t with $n - 1$ degrees of freedom is also the theoretically correct distribution for large n, the distribution approaches and becomes indistinguishable from the normal distribution for samples of 30 or more observations. The test statistic $\dfrac{(\bar{x} - \mu)}{s_{\bar{x}}}$ is therefore referred to a z-table when making inferences with large samples. Note, though, that we do this because the theoretically correct t-distribution (since σ is unknown) has become indistinguishable from the normal curve, and the latter is somewhat easier to use.

What if the population is not normally distributed and σ is unknown? If the distribution is symmetrical or displays only moderate skew, there is no problem. The t-test is quite robust to departures from normality. However, if the variable is highly skewed in the population, the appropriate procedure depends on the sample size. If the sample is small, the t-test is inappropriate. The variable must be transformed so that it is normal, or a distribution-free test must be used. If the sample is large, the normal curve could be used for making the inference, provided that the two following assumptions are satisfied:

1. The sample size is large enough so that the sample mean $\bar{x}$ is normally distributed because of the Central-Limit Theorem. The greater the asymmetry, the larger the sample must be to satisfy this assumption.
2. The sample standard deviation, s, is a close estimate of the population standard deviation σ. The greater the variability in the population, the larger the sample must be to justify this assumption.

Research Realities 16.1 summarizes the situation for making inferences about a mean for known and unknown σ and normally distributed and asymmetrical parent population distributions.

To illustrate the application of the t-test, consider a supermarket chain investigating the desirability of adding a new product to the shelves of its stores. Suppose that 100 units must be sold per week in each store for the item to be sufficiently profitable to warrant handling it in lieu of the many other products competing for the limited shelf space. The research department decides to investigate the item's turnover by putting it in a random sample of 10 stores for a limited period of time. The average sales per store per week are as shown in Table 16.1.

The variance of sales per store is unknown and has to be estimated, so the t-test is the correct parametric test if the distribution of sales is normal. The normality assumption seems reasonable in that the little sales evidence that is available does not indicate any real asymmetry, so let's assume that the normality assumption is satisfied.

RESEARCH   REALITIES

16.1 Testing Hypotheses about a Single Mean

Population distribution shape?	Sample size?	σ Known	σ Unknown
Distribution of variable in parent population is normal or symmetrical.	Small n	Use: $z = \dfrac{(\bar{x} - \mu)}{\sigma_{\bar{x}}}$	Use: $t = \dfrac{(\bar{x} - \mu)}{s_{\bar{x}}}$ where $s\bar{x} = s/\sqrt{n}$ and $s = \sqrt{\dfrac{\sum_{i=1}^{n}(X_i - \bar{x})^2}{n-1}}$ and refer to t-table for $n - 1$ degrees of freedom.
	Large n	Use: $z = \dfrac{(\bar{x} - \mu)}{\sigma_{\bar{x}}}$	Since the t-distribution approaches the normal as n increases, use: $z = \dfrac{(\bar{x} - \mu)}{s_{\bar{x}}}$ for $n > 30$.
Distribution of variable in parent population is asymmetrical.	Small n	There is no theory to support the parametric test. Either transform the variate so that it is normally distributed and then use the z-test, or use a distribution-free statistical test.	There is no theory to support the parametric test. Either transform the variate so that it is normally distributed and then use the t-test, or use a distribution-free statistical test.
	Large n	If the sample is large enough so that the Central-Limit Theorem is operative, use: $z = \dfrac{(\bar{x} - \mu)}{\sigma_{\bar{x}}}$.	If the sample is large enough so that the Central-Limit Theorem is operative and s is a close estimate of σ, use: $z = \dfrac{(\bar{x} - \mu)}{s_{\bar{x}}}$.

A one-tailed test is appropriate here, because it is only when the sales per store per week are at least 100 that the product will be introduced on a national scale. The hypotheses are:

$$H_0 : \mu \leq 100$$
$$H_A : \mu > 100$$

TABLE 16.1   Store Sales of Trial Products per Week

Store i	Sales X_i	Store	Sales X_i
1	86	6	93
2	97	7	132
3	114	8	116
4	108	9	105
5	123	10	120

From the data in Table 16.1,

$$\bar{x} = \frac{\sum\limits_{i=1}^{n} X_i}{n} = 109.4$$

and

$$s = \sqrt{\frac{\sum\limits_{i=1}^{n} (X_i - \bar{x})^2}{n-1}} = 14.40$$

The standard error of the mean $s_{\bar{x}} = \dfrac{s}{\sqrt{n}} = 4.55$. Calculations yield:

$$t = \frac{(\bar{x} - \mu)}{s_{\bar{x}}} = \frac{109.4 - 100}{4.55} = 2.07$$

The Scenarios:

Comparing one mean to *a priori* guess

• Variances known

• Variances unknown

Comparing two means

• Variances known

• Variances unknown

With a significance level of $\alpha = .05$, critical t with $v = n - 1 = 9$ degrees of freedom is 1.833 (see the t-table in Appendix C). We conclude that it is unlikely that the observed value would have occurred by chance if the sales per store in the population were really less than or equal to 100 units per week.

A confidence interval would give us some insight into the sales that might be expected if the product were introduced on a national scale. The formula is $\bar{x} \pm ts_{\bar{x}}$. For a 95% confidence interval and 9 degrees of freedom, $t = 1.833$, so the 95% confidence interval is $109.4 \pm (1.833)(4.55)$, or 109.4 ± 8.3, or, alternatively, $101.1 \le \mu \le 117.7$.

Suppose that the product had been placed in 50 stores and that the sample mean and standard deviation were the same; that is, $\bar{x} = 109.4$ and $s = 14.40$. The test statistic would be $z = 4.30$, which we would refer to a normal table given the larger sample size. Calculated z is greater than critical z, $z = 1.645$ for $\alpha = .05$, and, as expected, the same conclusion is warranted. The evidence is stronger now because of the larger sample of stores; the product could be expected to sell at a rate greater than 100 units per store per week. The confidence interval is $109.4 \pm (1.645)(2.04)$, or 109.4 ± 3.35, or $106.1 \le \mu \le 112.8$—a narrower interval, given the larger sample.

Hypotheses about Two Means

Consider testing a hypothesis about the difference between two population means. For example, when consumer expenditure surveys report that men who are 25–34 years old spend an average of $350.50 annually on clothing, vs. men who are 45–54 years old spending $461.60, are those means significantly different—do older men buy more in clothing, or more expensive clothing, than younger men, or is the difference not significant, and only due to sampling variability?

The methodology for testing a hypothesis about two means varies according to whether the samples are independent or related. We'll do both. Let's start by assuming that the samples are independent, and look at the three possible cases:

1. The two parent population variances are known.

2. The parent population variances are unknown but can be assumed equal.

3. The parent population variances are unknown and cannot be assumed equal.

Variances Are Known

Experience has shown that the population variance usually changes much more slowly than the population mean. This means that an "old" estimate of variance can often be used as the "known" population variance for studies that are being repeated. For example, if we check annually on the per capita soft-drink consumption of people living in different regions of the U.S., we could use last year's variance as the likely "known" variance for this year's study. Let's say we're trying to determine whether any differences exist between Northerners and Southerners in consumption of a new soft drink, called Spark. Past data indicate that per capita variation in the consumption of soft drinks is 10 ounces per day for Northerners and 14 ounces for Southerners as measured by the standard deviation, so we start with: $\sigma_N = 10$ and $\sigma_S = 14$.

The null hypothesis is that there is no difference between Northerners and Southerners in their consumption of Spark ($H_0 : \mu_N = \mu_S$), whereas the alternate hypothesis is that there is a difference ($H_a : \mu_N \neq \mu_S$). If $\bar{x}_N$ and $\bar{x}_S$, the sample means, are normally distributed, their sum or difference is also normal. The two sample means could be normally distributed because per capita consumption is normally distributed in each region or because the two samples are large enough that the Central-Limit Theorem helps us. In either case, the test statistic is:

$$z = \frac{(\bar{x}_1 - \bar{x}_2) - (\mu_1 - \mu_2)}{\sigma_{\bar{x}_1 - \bar{x}_2}}$$

where $\bar{x}_1$ is the sample mean for the first (Northern) sample; $\bar{x}_2$ is the sample mean for the second (Southern) sample; μ_1 and μ_2 are the unknown population means for the Northern and Southern samples; and $\sigma_{\bar{x}_1 - \bar{x}_2}$ is the standard error of estimate for the difference in means and is equal to $\sqrt{\sigma_{\bar{x}_1}^2 + \sigma_{\bar{x}_2}^2}$ where, in turn,

$$\sigma_{\bar{x}_1}^2 = \frac{\sigma_1^2}{n_1} \quad \text{and} \quad \sigma_{\bar{x}_2}^2 = \frac{\sigma_2^2}{n_1}$$

The "known" population variances are $\sigma_1^2 = (10)^2 = 100$ and $\sigma_2^2 = (14)^2 = 196$. Suppose we took a random sample of 100 Northerners and 100 Southerners, and found $\bar{x}_1 = 20$ oz. per day and $\bar{x}_2 = 25$. Is this a real difference in consumption rates? The standard error of estimate is

$$\sigma_{\bar{x}_1 - \bar{x}_2} = \sqrt{\frac{100}{100} + \frac{196}{100}} = \sqrt{2.96} = 1.72$$

and the calculated z is

$$z = \frac{(20 - 25) - (\mu_N - \mu_S)}{1.72} = \frac{-5 - 0}{1.72} = -2.906$$

Calculated z exceeds the critical tabled value of -1.96 for $\alpha = .05$, so we reject the null hypothesis. We conclude that there is a statistically significant difference in the per capita consumption of Spark by Northerners and Southerners.

The confidence interval for the difference in the two means is given by the formula

$$(\bar{x}_1 - \bar{x}_2) \pm z\sigma_{\bar{x}_1 - \bar{x}_2}$$

For a 95% confidence interval, $z = 1.96$, and the interval estimate of the difference in consumption of Spark by the two groups is $-5 \pm (1.96)(1.720) = -5 \pm 3.4$. Northerners on average are estimated to drink 1.6 to 8.4 ounces less of Spark per day than Southerners.

Variances Are Unknown

When the population variances are unknown, the standard error of the test statistic $\sigma_{\bar{x}_1 - \bar{x}_2}$ will be estimated. We'll start with:

$$s_1^2 = \frac{\sum_{i=1}^{n_1}(X_{i1} - \bar{x}_1)^2}{(n_1 - 1)} \text{ as an estimate of } \sigma_1^2$$

and

$$s_2^2 = \frac{\sum_{i=1}^{n_2}(X_{i2} - \bar{x}_2)^2}{(n_2 - 1)} \text{ as an estimate of } \sigma_2^2$$

The estimates of the standard error of the means become $s_{\bar{x}_1} = \frac{s_1}{\sqrt{n_1}}$ and $s_{\bar{x}_2} = \frac{s_2}{\sqrt{n_2}}$. The general estimate of $\sigma_{\bar{x}_1 - \bar{x}_2}$ is then:

$$\hat{\sigma}_{\bar{x}_1 - \bar{x}_2} = s_{\bar{x}_1 - \bar{x}_2} = \sqrt{\hat{\sigma}_{\bar{x}_1}^2 + \hat{\sigma}_{\bar{x}_2}^2} = \sqrt{s_{\bar{x}_1}^2 + s_{\bar{x}_2}^2} = \sqrt{\frac{\hat{\sigma}_1^2}{n_1} + \frac{\hat{\sigma}_2^2}{n_2}} = \sqrt{\frac{s_1^2}{n_1} + \frac{s_2^2}{n_2}}$$

If the two population variances *can be assumed to be equal,* a better estimate of the common population variance can be generated by *pooling* the samples to calculate:

$$s_p^2 = \frac{\sum_{i=1}^{n_1}(X_{i1} - \bar{x}_1)^2 + \sum_{i=1}^{n_2}(X_{i2} - \bar{x}_2)^2}{n_1 + n_2 - 2}$$

where s_p^2 is the pooled sample variance used to estimate the common population variance. In this case, the estimated standard error of the test statistic $s_{\bar{x}_1 - \bar{x}_2}$ simplifies to:

$$s_{\bar{x}_1 - \bar{x}_2} = \sqrt{s_p^2 \left(\frac{1}{n_1} + \frac{1}{n_2}\right)}$$

If the distribution of the variable in each population can further be assumed to be normal, the appropriate test statistic is

$$t = \frac{(\bar{x}_1 - \bar{x}_2) - (\mu_1 - \mu_2)}{s_{\bar{x}_1 - \bar{x}_2}}$$

which is t-distributed with $v = n_1 + n_2 - 2$ degrees of freedom.

For example, say a manufacturer of floor waxes has recently developed a new wax. The company is considering designs for two different containers for the wax, one plastic and one metal. The company decides to make the final determination on the basis of a limited sales test in which the plastic containers are introduced in a random sample of 10 stores and the metal containers are

TABLE 16.2	Store Sales of Floor Wax in Units

Store	Plastic Container	Metal Container	Store	Plastic Container	Metal Container
1	432	365	6	380	372
2	360	405	7	422	378
3	397	396	8	406	410
4	408	390	9	400	383
5	417	404	10	408	400

introduced in an *independent* random sample of 10 stores. The test results are contained in Table 16.2.

$$t = \frac{(403.0 - 390.3) - (0)}{8.15} = 1.56$$

This value is referred to a t-table for $v = n_1 + n_2 - 2 = 18$ degrees of freedom. The test is two-tailed because the null hypothesis is that the containers were equal; there was no *a priori* statement that one was expected to sell better than the other. For $\alpha = .05$ and 18 degrees of freedom, critical t = 2.101. (Look in the column headed $1 - \alpha = .975$ rather than .95 in the appendix, because this is a two-tailed test.) Calculated t is less than critical t, so the null hypothesis of no difference is not rejected. The sample data do not indicate that the plastic container could be expected to outsell the metal container in the total population, even though it did so in this limited experiment.

One of the assumptions underlying the previous procedure was that the variances in sales of the plastic and metal containers were equal in the population. The assumption could be checked using an F-test for the equality of variances, and indeed, the sample evidence does not contradict the assumption. If that assumption was not justified, then the pooling of variances would no longer be warranted, and the estimated standard error would be:

$$s_{\bar{x}_1 - \bar{x}_2} = \sqrt{\frac{s_1^2}{n_1} + \frac{s_2^2}{n_2}}$$

If the samples are both large so that s_1^2 and s_2^2 provide good estimates of their population variances σ_1^2 and σ_2^2, then a normal z-statistic can be used to examine the hypothesis.[1]

The preceding discussion assumed that the samples are independent and that the variable of interest is normally distributed in each of the parent populations. The normality assumption was again necessary to justify the use of the t-distribution. What happens if the variable is not normally distributed or the samples are not independent? The second half of Research Realities 16.2 summarizes the approach for nonnormal parent distributions for known and unknown σ, and the next section treats the case of dependent samples.

Now that you know how to test whether two groups are the same, or differ statistically significantly, take a look at Research Realities 16.3. You could apply

[1] If not, a question arises about how to treat this problem. One solution to this "Behrens-Fisher problem" creates df as a weighted average of the two samples' df (see the "Aspin-Welch test" in stats books).

RESEARCH   REALITIES

16.2 Testing Hypotheses about the Difference in Two Means

Population shape?	Sample size?	σ's Known	σ's Unknown
Distribution of variable in parent population is normal or symmetrical.	Small n	Use: $$z = \frac{(\bar{x}_1 - \bar{x}_2) - (\mu_1 - \mu_2)}{\sigma_{\bar{x}_1 - \bar{x}_2}}$$ Where $$\sigma_{\bar{x}_1 - \bar{x}_2} = \sqrt{\frac{\sigma_1^2}{n_1} + \frac{\sigma_2^2}{n_2}}$$	Can you assume $\sigma_1 = \sigma_2$? *If Yes:* Use pooled variance t-test where $$t = \frac{(\bar{x}_1 - \bar{x}_2) - (\mu_1 - \mu_2)}{s_{\bar{x}_1 - \bar{x}_2}}$$ and $$s_{\bar{x}_1 - \bar{x}_2} = \sqrt{\frac{\sum_{i=1}^{n_1}(X_{i1} - \bar{x}_1)^2 + \sum_{i=1}^{n_2}(X_{i2} - \bar{x}_2)^2}{n_1 + n_2 - 2}\left(\frac{1}{n_1} + \frac{1}{n_2}\right)}$$ with $(n_1 + n_2 - 2)$ degrees of freedom. *If No:* Approach is shrouded in controversy. Might use Aspin-Welch test.
	Large n	Use: $$z = \frac{(\bar{x}_1 - \bar{x}_2) - (\mu_1 - \mu_2)}{\sigma_{\bar{x}_1 - \bar{x}_2}}$$	Use: $$z = \frac{(\bar{x}_1 - \bar{x}_2) - (\mu_1 - \mu_2)}{s_{\bar{x}_1 - \bar{x}_2}}$$ and use pooled variance if variances can be assumed to be equal and unpooled variance if equality assumption is not warranted.
Distribution of variable in parent population is asymmetrical.	Small n	No theory to support the parametric test. Either transform the variates so that they are normally distributed and then use the z-test, or use a distribution-free statistical test.	No theory to support the parametric test. Either transform the variates so that they are normally distributed and then use the t-test, or use a distribution-free statistical test.
	Large n	If the individual samples are large enough so that the Central-Limit Theorem is operative for each separately, it will also apply to their sum or difference. Use: $$z = \frac{(\bar{x}_1 - \bar{x}_2) - (\mu_1 - \mu_2)}{\sigma_{\bar{x}_1 - \bar{x}_2}}$$	n_1 and n_2 must be large enough so that the Central-Limit Theorem applies to the sample means, so it can also be assumed to apply to their sum or difference. Use: $$z = \frac{(\bar{x}_1 - \bar{x}_2) - (\mu_1 - \mu_2)}{s_{\bar{x}_1 - \bar{x}_2}}$$ using a pooled variance if the unknown parent population variances are assumed equal and unpooled variance if the equality assumption is not warranted.

these tests for differences to see whether you detect international marketplace and demographic differences.[2]

---

[2] For example, see Manfred Schwaiger, Carsten Rennhak, Charles R. Taylor, and Hugh M. Cannon, "Can Comparative Advertising Be Effective in Germany? A Tale of Two Campaigns," *Journal of Advertising Research*, 41 (4), 2–13.

RESEARCH   REALITIES

16.3 Testing for International Marketplace Differences

These two figures depict some basic statistics on three countries: the U.S. and our northern and southern neighbors. The first panel presents a number of characteristics on which the three countries are fairly similar, compared with the second panel, which presents statistics on qualities where the countries vary more.

Tests for differences allow us to substantiate both claims. If we wanted to conclude that Canadians and Americans are similar (that is, "not statistically different") on things like education (the first set of bars), or energy consumption (the fourth set of bars), or if we sought to conclude whether the Mexican population was dispersed in urban vs. rural settings similarly to Canadians (the last set of bars), we would take the means for Canada and the U.S. on number of years of education and test via the t-test (since our standard deviation would be derived as an estimate from the sample). We'd then compare the U.S. and Canadian means on energy consumption. The Mexican-Canadian comparison involves proportions.

This panel of data includes the demographics that emphasize the countries' differences. The two-sample t-test could be used to test whether the number of tourist arrivals is the same in Canada and Mexico, and whether it is different from the numbers for the U.S. The Mexican numbers look different for youth (the first set of bars), employment of women (third set of bars), and car, phone, and television market penetration. If you have numbers like these, you're not supposed to "eye-ball" them and say, "gee, looks like the Mexican phone access is less." You have to support these claims statistically. In the appendix, you'll read about a method of analyzing the three groups simultaneously. Cool, huh?

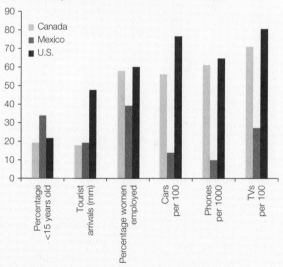

A Snapshot of North America: Some Differences

Source: Reprinted with permission from the May 2001 issue of American Demographics. Copyright, Crain Communications Inc. 2004.

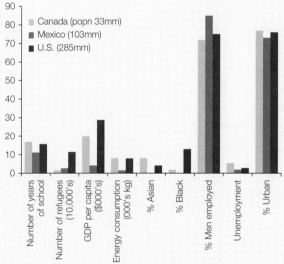

A Snapshot of North America: Similarities

Source: Reprinted with permission from the May 2001 issue of American Demographics. Copyright, Crain Communications Inc. 2004.

Samples Are Related

A manufacturer of camping equipment wanted to study consumer color preferences for a sleeping bag it had recently developed. The bag was of medium quality and price. Traditionally, the high-quality, high-priced sleeping bags used

New twist: are samples independent or related?

TABLE 16.3	Store Sales of Sleeping Bags	
Store	**Bright Colors**	**Earth Colors**
1	64	56
2	72	66
3	43	39
4	22	20
5	50	45

by serious campers and backpackers came in earth colors, such as green and brown. Previous research indicated that the low-quality, low-priced sleeping bags were frequently purchased for children, for use at slumber parties. The vivid colors were preferred by this market segment, with bright reds and oranges leading the way. Production capacity restrictions would not allow the company to produce both sets of colors. The company ran a test by offering both types of bags in a randomly selected sample of five stores. The sales per store are indicated in Table 16.3. Do the data present sufficient evidence to indicate a difference in the average sales for the different colored bags?

The appropriate procedure to address this question is the t-test for *related samples*.[3] We define a new variable d_i, where d_i is the difference between sales of the bright-colored bags and the earth-colored bags for the ith store. Thus:

$$d_1 = 64 - 56 = 8$$
$$d_2 = 72 - 66 = 6$$
$$d_3 = 43 - 39 = 4$$
$$d_4 = 22 - 20 = 2$$
$$d_5 = 50 - 45 = 5$$

Now calculate the mean difference:

$$\bar{d} = \frac{\sum\limits_{i=1}^{n} d_i}{n} = \frac{8 + 6 + 4 + 2 + 5}{5} = 5.0$$

and the standard error of that difference:

$$s_d = \sqrt{\frac{\sum\limits_{i=1}^{n_1} (d_i - \bar{d})^2}{(n-1)}} = \sqrt{\frac{20}{4}} = 2.24$$

The test statistic is

$$t = \frac{\bar{d} - D}{\left(\frac{s_d}{\sqrt{n}}\right)}$$

where D is the difference that is expected under the null hypothesis. Since there is no *a priori* reason why one color would be expected to sell better than the

[3] The t-test we've been using for the difference in means is *not appropriate* for this problem. That test requires (assumes) that the samples are independent. These samples are not—sales of bright-colored and earth-colored bags are definitely related, since they are both found in the same stores. This example differs from the floor wax example, in which the metal containers were placed in one sample of stores and the plastic containers were located in another. We need a procedure that takes into account the fact that the observations are related.

other, the appropriate null hypothesis is that there is no difference, whereas the alternate hypothesis is that there is:

$$H_0 : D = 0$$
$$H_0 : D \neq 0$$

Calculated t is:

$$t = \frac{5.0 - 0}{\left(\dfrac{2.24}{\sqrt{5}}\right)} = 5.0$$

This value is referred to a t-table for $v =$ (number of differences scores $- 1$) degrees of freedom; in this case, there are five paired differences, so $v = 4$. Critical t for $\alpha = .05$ is 2.776, so the hypothesis of no difference is rejected. The sample evidence indicates that the bright-colored sleeping bags are likely to outsell the earth-colored ones. This conclusion is consistent with a quick eye-balling of the data: the bright-colored sleeping bags outsold the earth-colored ones in each store. Finally, the 95% confidence interval is:

$$d \pm t(s_d/\sqrt{n})$$

or $5.0 \pm (2.776)(2.24/\sqrt{5}) = 5.0 \pm 2.8$, which suggests sales of the vivid-colored bags would be in the range of 2.2 to 7.8 bags greater per store on average.

Tests of differences on "related" samples arise frequently in marketing research. Often the setting is one of examining change. For example, one could pose the question, "Do 25–34 year old men spend significantly less on their clothing ($350.50) than on electronic equipment ($662.07), alcohol ($428.40), or apartment rental ($3505.05)?"

Hypotheses about Two Proportions

In this section, we illustrate the procedure for testing for the difference between two population proportions.[4] For example, there are significantly different views on the government's responsibility in health-care marketing issues, such as insurance coverage and affordable prescription drugs. Comparing segments based on gender, ethnicity, education, and age yield differences: e.g., 77% of women believe the government should provide health insurance coverage for more citizens, vs. 68% of men.

For the test of two proportions to be valid, the respective samples must be large enough so that the normal approximation (to the binomial distribution) can be used. This means that np and nq should be greater than 10 for each sample, where p is the proportion of "successes" and q is the proportion of "failures" in the sample, and n is the sample size.

Comparing two proportions, e.g., % satisfied customers in Singapore vs. Germany

To illustrate, consider a cosmetics manufacturer that was interested in comparing male college students and nonstudents in terms of their use of hair spray. Random samples of 100 male students and 100 male nonstudents in Austin, Texas, were selected, and their use of hair spray during the last three months was determined. Suppose that 30 students and 20 nonstudents had used hair spray within this period. Does this evidence indicate that a higher percentage of college students than nonstudents use hair spray?

---

[4] The tests for population proportions are logically considered with nominal data. Marketing examples abound: proportions of customers who "prefer A" vs. "prefer B"; "buy" vs. "do not buy"; are "brand loyal" vs. "not"; "sales reps meeting quota" vs. "not meeting quota."

We are interested in determining whether the two population proportions are different, so the null hypothesis is that they are the same:

$$H_0 : \pi_1 = \pi_2$$
$$H_0 : \pi_1 \neq \pi_2$$

where population 1 is the college students, and population 2 is the nonstudents. The sample proportions are $p_1 = .3$ and $p_2 = .2$, so $n_1 p_1 = 30$, $n_1 q_1 = 70$, $n_2 p_2 = 20$, $n_2 q_2 = 80$, and the normal approximation to the binomial distribution can be used. The test statistic is:

$$z = \frac{(p_1 - p_2) - (\pi_1 - \pi_2)}{\sigma_{p_1 - p_2}}$$

where $\sigma_{p_1 - p_2}$ is the standard error of the difference in the two sample proportions. What is $\sigma_{p_1 - p_2}$? For one sample, the variance of a single proportion is $\pi(1 - \pi)/n$, so the variance of the difference is:[5]

$$\sigma_{p_1 - p_2}^2 = \sigma_{p_1}^2 + \sigma_{p_2}^2 = \frac{\pi_1(1 - \pi_1)}{n_1} + \frac{\pi_2(1 - \pi_2)}{n_2}$$

Hence, the standard error is the square root:

$$\sigma_{p_1 - p_2} = \sqrt{\sigma_{p_1 - p_2}^2} = \sqrt{\left(\frac{\pi_1(1 - \pi_1)}{n_1} + \frac{\pi_2(1 - \pi_2)}{n_2} \right)}$$

Note that this term is given in terms of the two unknown population proportions π_1 and π_2. They're unknown, but we've assumed them to be equal (check the null), so we have a "natural" case of a *pooled variance* estimate. The term $s_{p_1 - p_2}^2$ is used to estimate $\sigma_{p_1 - p_2}^2$:

$$s_{p_1 - p_2}^2 = pq \left(\frac{1}{n_1} + \frac{1}{n_2} \right)$$

where

$$P = \frac{Total \ \# \ successes \ in \ the \ two \ samples}{Total \ \# \ observations \ in \ the \ two \ samples}$$

$$q = 1 - p$$

For the example,

$$p = \frac{30 + 20}{100 + 100} = \frac{50}{200} = .25$$

$$s_{p_1 - p_2}^2 = (.25)(.75) \left(\frac{1}{100} + \frac{1}{100} \right) = .00375$$

and $s_{p_1 - p_2} = .061$, calculated z is found to be

$$z = \frac{(.3 - .2) - (0)}{.061} = \frac{.1}{.061} = 1.64$$

---

[5] The variance of the sum (or difference) of two independent random variables is equal to the sum of the individual variances. Handy, huh?

RESEARCH   REALITIES

16.4 Examples of the Value in Testing Proportions

The following two figures focus on proportions, which could easily be tested using the z-test for two sample proportions presented in this chapter. In the coffee study, consumers were asked, "Do you think coffee has positive or negative health effects?" There are a number of ways to cut these data. You could compare the proportion of *coffee drinkers* who said "*positive*" to the proportion of *coffee drinkers* who said "*negative*" (the first two bars). (Even coffee drinkers acknowledge some detrimental effects of the drink.) You could compare the proportion of *coffee drinkers* who say "*positive*" (or "negative") to the proportion of people who *don't drink coffee* who said "*positive*" (or "negative"). (Hmm! More coffee drinkers think there are positive benefits, and fewer negative effects than non-coffee drinkers. Go figure!)

Gender can be tested, same with ethnicity. For age, the profiles (percentage who think positive vs. negative) look similar for the youngest groups (18–24 & 25–44 year olds), but around 45–54, opinions start changing, and the data are rather different among those 55 years and older.

In this chart, we have movie-going frequency. Consumers were theater-intercepted and asked, "How frequently do you go to the movies?"

____ Frequently (12 times a year or more)

____ Occasionally (2–11 times a year)

____ Infrequently (less than 2 times a year)

____ Never

You can see by this chart (and a z-test on proportions would confirm), that the most frequent movie goer is male (vs. female) and single (vs. married). The less frequent move goers (the three sets of four bars to the right) concur, by displaying the inverse pattern.

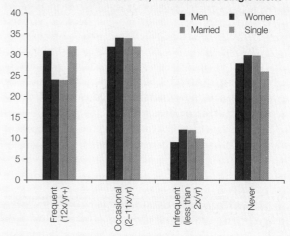

Who Goes to the Movies? Or, "Wanna Meet Single Men?"

Source of Data: MPA Worldwide Market Research.

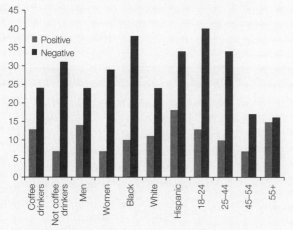

Java Has Positive or Negative Health Effects?

Source: Reprinted with permission from the May 2001 issue of American Demographics. *Copyright, Crain Communications Inc. 2004.*

whereas critical z = 1.96 for $\alpha = .05$. The sample evidence does not indicate that there is a difference in the proportion of college students and nonstudents using hair spray.

The 95% confidence interval calculated by the formula $(p_1 - p_2) \pm z(s_{p_1 - p_2})$, which is $(.3 - .2) \pm 1.96(.061) = .1 \pm .12$, yields a similar conclusion. The interval includes zero, suggesting that there is no difference in the proportions of guys who use hair spray in the two groups.

Comparing two proportions arises in a number of marketing research problems. Research Realities 16.4 gives you two ideas of how to apply these geeky equations to data to extract the marketing information you want.

Summary

Several statistical tests that are useful to marketing researchers for examining differences were discussed in this chapter. The "difference" might be between some sample result and some expected population value or between two sample results.

In testing a hypothesis about a single mean, the z-test is appropriate if the variance is known, whereas the t-test applies with unknown variance. A similar situation arises in the analysis of two means from independent samples. If the variances are known, the z-test is used. If the variances are unknown but assumed to be equal, a t-test using a pooled sample variance estimate applies. If the samples are related instead of independent, the t-test for paired differences is appropriate.

The test of the equality of proportions from two independent samples involves a natural pooling of the sample variances. The z-test is applicable.

Questions

1. What is the appropriate test statistic for making inferences about a population mean when the population variance is known? When the population variance is unknown? Suppose that the population variance is unknown, but the sample is large. What is the appropriate procedure then?
2. Suppose one is testing for the statistical significance of the observed difference between the sample means from two independent samples. What is the appropriate procedure when:
   a. known?
   b. unknown but can be assumed to be equal?
   c. unknown and cannot be assumed to be equal?
   d. What conditions must occur in each case regarding the distribution?
3. How do you test whether two parent population proportions differ?

Applications and Problems

1. A medium-sized manufacturer of paper products was planning to introduce a new line of tissues, hand towels, and toilet paper. However, management had stipulated that the new products should be introduced only if average monthly purchases per household were $2.50 or more. The product was market tested and the diaries of the 100 panel households living in the test market area were checked. They indicated that average monthly purchases were $3.10 per household with a standard deviation of $.50. Management is wondering what decision it should make and has asked for your recommendation.
   a. State the null and alternate hypotheses.
   b. Is the sample size considered large or small?
   c. Which test should be used? Why?

   d. At the 5% level of significance, would you reject the null hypothesis? Support your answer with the necessary calculations.
2. The president of a chain of department stores promised the managers of the various stores a bonus of 8% if the average monthly sales per store increased $300,000 or more. A random sample of 12 stores yielded the following sales increases:

Store	Sales Increase	Store	Sales Increase
1	$320,000	7	380,000
2	230,000	8	280,000
3	400,000	9	420,000
4	450,000	10	360,000
5	280,000	11	440,000
6	320,000	12	320,000

The president is wondering whether this random sample of stores indicates that the population of stores has reached the goal. (Assume that the population distribution is normal.)

a. State the null and alternate hypotheses.
b. Is the sample size considered small or large?
c. Which test should be used? Why?
d. Would you reject the null hypothesis at the 5% level of significance? Support your conclusion with the necessary calculations.

3. Travel Time Company, a large travel agency located in Baltimore, Maryland, wanted to study consumer preferences for its package tours to the East. For the past five years, Travel Time had offered two similarly priced package tours to the East that differed only in the places included in the tour. A random sample of five months' purchases from the past five years was selected. The number of consumers that purchased the tours during these five months is as follows:

Month	Packaged Tour I	Packaged Tour II
1	90	100
2	70	60
3	120	80
4	110	90
5	60	80

The management of Travel Time needs your assistance to determine whether there is a difference in preferences for the two tours.

a. State the null and alternate hypotheses.
b. What test would you use? Why?
c. What is the calculated value of the test statistic? Show your calculations.
d. What is the critical tabled value at the 5% significance level?
e. Would you reject the null hypothesis? Explain.
f. What can the management of Travel Time Company conclude about preferences for the two tours?

4. A manufacturer of exercise equipment for health clubs is interested in comparing usage of exercise equipment at health clubs by men and women. Random samples of 250 women and 250 men in Oklahoma City were selected and the usage of health club facilities was determined. The results indicated that 87 men and 51 women from the samples had been to a health club and had used exercise equipment at least once during the previous six weeks. The manufacturer is interested in determining whether this evidence indicates that a significantly higher percentage of men than women use exercise equipment at health clubs.

a. State the null and alternate hypotheses.
b. Which test would you use? Why?
c. Calculate the test statistic. Show all your calculations.
d. Assuming that $\alpha = .05$, can you conclude that a higher proportion of men use exercise equipment at health clubs? Since the discovery that a larger proportion of women than men use such equipment would be just as important a finding, use a two-tailed test.
e. Construct a 90% confidence interval for the difference between the proportion of men and the proportion of women using exercise equipment at health clubs. What conclusions can you draw from the confidence interval?

5. The Spazi Italian food company is considering introducing a new extra-spicy spaghetti sauce. Before introducing the new sauce, however, the company wants to test it against its major competitor's spicy sauce. In a mall test, shoppers were stopped at random and asked to taste the two sauces. Shoppers were then asked to rate the sauces on a scale of 1 to 10, with 1 being awful and 10 being excellent. The table that follows shows the ratings given to the two sauces by 10 shoppers:

Shopper	Spazi's Sauce	Other Sauce	Shopper	Spazi's Sauce	Other Sauce
1	1	7	6	8	10
2	7	10	7	10	7
3	5	7	8	2	8
4	6	10	9	3	8
5	2	9	10	9	10

a. What is the appropriate test to use for analyzing these scores? Explain.
b. At $\alpha = .05$, is there a significant difference in ratings for these two sauces?
c. Is this an appropriate design to use for this situation? Explain. What are alternative designs that may be more appropriate for this situation?
d. After looking at Spazi's scores, do you think that additional research is warranted? Why?

Appendix: Analysis of Variance

Questions to Guide Your Learning:

Q1 What is the analysis of variance, a.k.a., ANOVA?

Q2 How do these concepts enter in: between-variation vs. within-variation?

I n this appendix, we turn to the **analysis of variance (ANOVA)**. You'll see that ANOVA is an extension of the t-test in two ways. First, where the t-tests enable us to compare a sample mean to a population mean, or two sample means to each other, ANOVA lets us compare means that result from three or more groups. Second, in a two-sample t-test, there is only one predictor variable that defines the group membership, e.g., men vs. women, brand A loyalists vs. those for brand B, or consider even the "plastic vs. metal containers" example that we used before and will use again. In ANOVA, two or more factors can define the groups and help us understand the data. For example, we might divide our data into the groups: male vs. female crossed with brand A loyal vs. B loyal. We look at both of these qualities of the analysis of variance.

We begin with the example from Chapter 16, on plastic vs. metal containers because the data are familiar to you (either that or we're really into packaging). There are only two means (plastic, metal), so normally, we actually wouldn't conduct an ANOVA—we'd do a two-sample t-test, as we did in Chapter 16. However, we'll work on the two-group example to present the basics, then we'll extend it.

Let's define the data point, X_{ij} = the ith observation on the jth treatment or group. There are two treatments in the example: $j = 1$ refers to plastic containers and $j = 2$ to metal containers. For each treatment there are 10 stores. Thus, for the first treatment $X_{11} = 432$, $X_{21} = 360$, ..., $X_{10,1} = 408$ and for the second treatment $X_{12} = 365$, $X_{22} = 405$, and $X_{10,2} = 400$.

n_j = the number of observations in the jth treatment; $n_1 = 10$ and $n_2 = 10$.

n = the total number of observations in all treatments combined: $n_1 + n_2 = 20$.

$\bar{x}_{.j}$ = the mean of the jth treatment $(j = 1,2)$:

$$\bar{x}_{.j} = \frac{\sum_{i=1}^{n_j} X_{ij}}{n}$$

Thus,

$$\bar{x}_{.1} = \frac{432 + 360 + \ldots + 408}{10} = 403.0$$

and

$$\bar{x}_{.2} = \frac{365 + 405 + \ldots + 400}{10} = 390.3$$

$\bar{x}_{..}$ = the grand mean of all n observations:

$$\bar{x}_{..} = \frac{\sum_{j=1}^{2} \sum_{i=1}^{n_j} X_{ij}}{n} = \frac{432 + \ldots + 408 + 365 + \ldots + 400}{20} = 396.7$$

Any given data point (sales figures, here) will likely deviate from the overall mean, $\bar{x}_{..}$, just as any data show variability. In ANOVA, we're interested in the extent to which the difference between the data point X_{ij} and the grand mean, $\bar{x}_{..}$, may be attributable to the fact that it is a plastic or metal container (i.e., $\bar{x}_{.1}$ and $\bar{x}_{.2}$ may differ somewhat from each other, and therefore from $\bar{x}_{..}$), vs. the fact that there will simply be natural variation in the sales of each type of container within any given store (i.e., the X_{i1}'s will vary around $\bar{x}_{.1}$, and the X_{i2}'s will vary around $\bar{x}_{.2}$). Conceptually,

$$(X_{ij} - \bar{x}_{..}) = (\bar{x}_{.j} - \bar{x}_{..}) + (X_{ij} - \bar{x}_{.j})$$

The first difference on the right-hand side is called a treatment or between-group difference, and the second is called a within-group difference.

Total variability = between + within

The basic idea underlying the analysis of variance is that the population variance can be estimated from the sample in several ways, and comparisons among these estimates can tell us a great deal about the population. The null hypothesis is that the two population means are equal; $\mu_1 = \mu_2$. If the null hypothesis is true, then, except for sampling error, the following three estimates of the population variance should be equal:

1. The **total variation**, computed by comparing each of the 20 sales figures with the grand mean
2. The **between-group variation**, computed by comparing each of the two treatment means with the grand mean
3. The **within-group variation**, computed by comparing each of the individual sales figures with the mean of its own group

If, however, the hypothesis is not true and there is a difference in the means, then while we expect some inevitable within-group variation (essentially sampling error), we'd expect to see a good sized between-group variation.

These three separate estimates of the population variation are computed in the following way for k groups.

1. **Total variation—sum of squares total SS_T:**

$$SS_T = \sum_{j=1}^{k} \sum_{i=1}^{n_j} (X_{ij} - \bar{x}_{..})^2$$
$$= (432 - 396.7)^2 + \ldots + (408 - 396.7)^2$$
$$+ (365 - 396.7)^2 + \ldots + (400 - 396.7)^2$$

The difference between *each observation* and the *grand mean* is determined; the differences are squared and then summed.

2. **Between-group variation—sum of squares between groups SS_B:**

$$SS_B = \sum_{j=1}^{k} n_j (\bar{x}_{\cdot j} - \bar{x}_{..})^2$$
$$= 10(403.0 - 396.7)^2 + 10(390.3 - 396.7)^2$$

The difference between each *group mean* and the *overall mean* is determined, the difference is squared, each squared difference is weighted by the number of observations making up the group, and the results are summed.[1]

3. **Within-group variation—sum of squares within groups SS_W:**

$$SS_W = \sum_{j=1}^{k} \sum_{i=1}^{n_j} (X_{ij} - \bar{x}_{\cdot j})^2$$
$$= (432 - 403.0)^2 + \ldots + (408 - 403.0)^2$$
$$+ (365 - 390.3)^2 + \ldots + (400 - 390.3)^2$$

The difference between *each observation* and its *group mean* is determined, and then the differences are squared and then summed.

SS_T measures the overall variation of the n observations. The more variable the n observations are, the larger the SS_T. SS_B reflects the total variability of the means. The more similar the groups are (i.e., the closer the k groups' means), the smaller SS_B becomes. If they differ a lot, SS_B will be large. SS_W measures the amount of variation within each group. If there is little variation among the observations making up a group, SS_W is small. These sources of variability sum: $SS_T = SS_B + SS_W$.

We divide each of these sums of squares by their appropriate degrees of freedom, to obtain a "mean square" (i.e., MS_B, MS_W) and these MS's are unbiased estimates of the population variance. If the null hypothesis (of no difference among population means) is true, they are all estimates of the same variance and should not differ more than we'd expect by chance. If the variance between groups (MS_B) is significantly greater than the variance within groups (MS_W), then we reject the null.

In other words, we can view the variance within groups as a measure of the amount of variation in sales of containers that may be expected on the basis of chance. It is the *error variance* or *chance variance*. The between-group variance reflects error variance *plus* any group-to-group differences due to differences in popularity of the two containers. If the between-group variance is significantly larger than the within-group variance, the difference may be attributed to group-to-group variation, and the hypothesis of equality of means is discredited.

---

[1] Alternatively, SS_B can be written: $SS_B = \sum_{j=1}^{k} \sum_{i=1}^{n_j} (\bar{x}_{\cdot j} - \bar{x}_{..})^2$.

So we need the degrees of freedom. The total number of degrees of freedom is equal to $n - 1$; we begin with n data points and there is only a single constraint $\bar{x}_{..}$ in the computation of SS_T. For the within-group sum of squares, there are n observations and k constraints, one constraint for each treatment mean. Hence, the degrees of freedom for the within-group sum of squares equals $k(n_j - 1) = n - k$. There are k values, one corresponding to each treatment mean, in the calculation of SS_B, and there is one constraint imposed by $\bar{x}_{..}$; hence, the degrees of freedom for the between-group sum of squares is $k - 1$.

The separate estimates of the population variance, i.e., the mean squares are:

$$MS_T = \frac{SS_T}{df_T} = \frac{SS_T}{n-1}$$

$$MS_B = \frac{SS_B}{df_B} = \frac{SS_B}{k-1}$$

$$MS_W = \frac{SS_W}{df_W} = \frac{SS_W}{n-k}$$

The mean squares computed from the sample data are estimates of the true mean squares. The expected population values are:

$$E(MW_W) = \sigma^2 = \text{Error variance or chance variance}$$

and

$$E(MW_B) = \sigma^2 + \text{Treatment effect}$$

The ratio $E(MS_B)/E(MS_W)$ equals 1 if there is no treatment effect. It is greater than 1 if there is a difference in the sample means. We use the sample mean squares to estimate this ratio:

$$F = \frac{MS_B}{MS_W}$$

which follows the F-distribution. The F-distribution depends on two degrees of freedom: one corresponding to the mean square in the numerator $(k - 1)$ and one corresponding to the mean square in the denominator $(n - k)$. For the plastic and metal container sales data, these degrees of freedom are 1 and 18. Using $\alpha = .05$, critical F is 4.41 (see the f-distribution model in Appendix D).

ANOVA goes beyond t: more than 2 groups

The results are compiled in Table 16A.1 in an "analysis-of-variance table." The calculated F value is 2.43, which is less than the critical F, so not surprisingly (we know these data), the sample evidence is not sufficient to reject the hypothesis of the equality of the two means.[2]

The plastic and metal containers example is the simplest type of what is known as a **completely randomized design**. The distinguishing feature of this design is that experimental treatments are assigned to the stores on a random basis. In this case, the container types were assigned to the stores at random, with no attempt to match stores or make them equal in any way. We assign the stores randomly to conditions to form groups that are roughly equivalent initially, so that if there are differences in sales, the sales may be attributable to the container differences.

ANOVA goes beyond t: more than 1 factor

[2] A random variable that is t-distributed with v degrees of freedom, when squared corresponds to an F with 1 and v df; that is, $t^2 = F$, and if $t \sim t_v$, then $t^2 \sim F_{1,v}$. For our data, $v_1 = k - 1 = 1$, $F_{1,18} = t_{18}^2 = (1.56)^2 = 2.43$.

TABLE 16A.1 Analysis of Variance of Sales of Plastic vs. Metal Containers

Source of Variation	Sum of Squares	Degrees of Freedom	Mean Square	F-Ratio
Between group	806.5	1	806.5	2.43
Within group	5978.1	18	332.1	
Total	6784.6	19		

We can make our previous model statement of "between" vs. "within" terms more precise. The model for a completely randomized design is:

$$X_{ij} = \mu + \tau_j + \varepsilon_{ij}$$

where any data point, X_{ij}, consists of three components: the overall mean μ; the effect of the jth treatment, τ_j; and the random error associated with the ith observation in the jth treatment group, ε_{ij}. The null hypothesis of equality of population means is equivalent to the hypothesis that the treatment effects are all zero, i.e., $\mu_1 = \mu_2$ implies that $\tau_1 = \mu_1 - \mu_2 = 0$. The alternate hypothesis, when there are k treatments, is that at least one of the treatment effects is not zero, equivalent to the statement that at least one mean differs from the others:

$H_0 : \tau_j = 0$ for all $j = 1,..., k$

$H_a : \tau_j \neq 0$ for at least one j where $j = 1,..., k$

The assumptions underlying the model and the test are (1) the samples are independent, (2) the variable is normally distributed, and (3) the variance is the same for each treatment. The last assumption is necessary to justify the pooling of variances and, in this respect, is also similar to the t-test for two means.

Randomized Blocks

You can appreciate the difficulty that can arise in the preceding situation if, by chance, the stores selected to handle one type of container were, say, systematically larger than the stores chosen to distribute the other type. If a significant difference had been observed, it could have been because the plastic container was sold in the large stores, which have greater sales potential simply because they have more traffic, i.e., having nothing to do with any real preference for plastic containers.

If there is a source of extraneous variation that could potentially distort the results of an experiment, we can use a **randomized-block design**. This design involves the grouping of "similar" test units into blocks and the random assignment of treatments to test units in each block. The test units are matched on the expected extraneous source of variation (e.g., store size in the container example). The hope is that the units within each block will be more alike than units selected completely at random. Since the differences between blocks can be taken into account in the variance analysis, the error mean square should be smaller than it would be if a completely randomized design had been used. The test should be more efficient.

Suppose we're choosing among three possible sales training programs to enhance the effectiveness of our sales force of 500 reps. Before choosing a program and rolling it out on a big scale, management wants a trial run on a sample of 30 sales reps. We know the reps differ in sales ability, so we decide to match the sales reps in terms of their ability (using their past sales as the matching criterion). We create 10 blocks, with 3 sales reps within a block who have roughly equal sales records.

The sales by these 30 reps, who have undergone training in one of the programs A, B, or C, are measured and presented in Table 16A.2. The randomized-block model is:[3]

$$X_{ij} = \mu + \tau_j + \beta_i + \varepsilon_{ij}$$

where

X_{ij} is the ith observation (i^{th} block) on the jth treatment

μ is the overall mean

τ_j is the effect attributable to the jth treatment or training program, $j = 1,2,\ldots, k$

β_i is the effect attributable to the ith block or ability level, $i = 1,2,\ldots, r$

ϵ_i is the random error associated with the ith observation on the jth treatment

The assumptions are that a random sample is drawn from each of the kr (k treatments times r blocks) populations; X is normally distributed in each of the kr populations; the variance of each is the same; and the block and treatment effects are additive. Except for the last assumption, these are the same assumptions that were made in the completely randomized design. But now there are kr populations, whereas there were k populations with the completely randomized design.

Let $j = 1$ be training program A, $j = 2$ program B, and $j = 3$ program C. The average sales are:

$$\bar{x}_{.1} = \frac{\sum\limits_{i=1}^{r} X_{i1}}{r} = \frac{42 + 36 + \ldots + 38}{10} = 39.3$$

$$\bar{x}_{.2} = \frac{\sum\limits_{i=1}^{r} X_{i2}}{r} = \frac{51 + 35 + \ldots + 36}{10} = 43.7$$

$$\bar{x}_{.3} = \frac{\sum\limits_{i=1}^{r} X_{i3}}{r} = \frac{43 + 36 + \ldots + 35}{10} = 40.4$$

TABLE 16A.2   Sales Generated by 3 Different Training Programs ($000's)

Block	Program: A	B	C	Block	Program: A	B	C
1	42	51	43	6	29	35	30
2	36	35	36	7	52	50	54
3	40	52	44	8	46	49	44
4	38	47	42	9	40	44	40
5	32	38	36	10	38	36	35

[3] The example is also an illustration of a "mixed" model, with the treatments being "fixed" (only these three programs are of interest) and the sales reps being "random."

And the overall mean is

$$\bar{x}_{..} = \frac{1}{n}\sum_{j=1}^{k}\sum_{i=1}^{r} X_{ij} = \frac{(42+\ldots+38) + (51+\ldots+36) + (43+\ldots+35)}{30} = 41.1$$

In addition to the total, treatment, and error sum of squares, we must now compute the sum of squares corresponding to blocks. The block means are:

$$\bar{x}_{i.} = \frac{\sum_{j=1}^{k} X_{ij}}{k}$$

for the ith block. Thus, for the first block, $i = 1$,

$$\bar{x}_{1.} = \frac{\sum_{j=1}^{k} X_{1j}}{k} = \frac{(42 + 51 + 43)}{3} = 45.3$$

The remaining block means, calculated similarly, follow:

$\bar{x}_{2.} = 35.7$	$\bar{x}_{5.} = 35.3$	$\bar{x}_{8.} = 46.3$
$\bar{x}_{3.} = 45.3$	$\bar{x}_{6.} = 31.3$	$\bar{x}_{9.} = 41.3$
$\bar{x}_{4.} = 42.3$	$\bar{x}_{7.} = 52.0$	$\bar{x}_{10.} = 36.3$

The sums of squares are:

$$SS_T = \sum_{j=1}^{k}\sum_{i=1}^{r}(X_{ij} - \bar{x}_{..})^2$$
$$= (42 - 41.4)^2 + (36 - 41.1)^2 + \ldots + (35 - 41.1)^2$$
$$= 1333.5$$

$$SS_{TR} = \sum_{j=1}^{k} r(\bar{x}_{.j} - \bar{x}_{..})^2$$
$$= 10(39.3 - 41.1)^2 + 10(43.7 - 41.1)^2 + 10(40.4 - 41.1)^2$$
$$= 104.9$$

$$SS_B = \sum_{i=1}^{r} k(\bar{x}_{i.} - \bar{x}_{..})^2$$
$$= 3(45.3 - 41.1)^2 + 3(35.7 - 41.1)^2 + \ldots + 3(36.3 - 41.1)^2$$
$$= 1093.5$$

$$SS_E = SS_T - SS_{TR} - SS_B$$
$$= 1333.5 - 104.9 - 1093.5$$
$$= 135.1$$

The randomized-block model posits any sample response as the sum of four additive factors: (1) the overall mean, (2) the effect of the jth treatment, (3) the effect of the ith block, and (4) the error term. Table 16A.3 is the analysis-of-variance table for this model. There are now two F-ratios of interest—one corresponding to blocks and one for treatments. Calculated F for the treatment mean square is 6.98; critical F for $\alpha = .05$ and $v_1 = 2$ and $v_2 = 18$ is 3.55. Calculated F exceeds critical F, and the null hypothesis of equal means is rejected.

TABLE 16A.3

Analysis of Variance of Randomized-Block Design Investigating Sales Programs

Source of Variation	Sum of Squares	Degrees of Freedom	Mean Square	F-Ratio
Blocks	1093.5	$(r - 1) = 9$	121.50	16.18
Treatments	104.9	$(k - 1) = 2$	52.45	6.98
Error	135.1	$(r - 1)(k - 1) = 18$	7.51	
Total	1333.5	$rk - 1 = 29$		

There is a difference in the effectiveness of at least one of the training programs. Program B, in particular, produces significantly better sales.[4]

Calculated F for the block effect is 16.18. Critical F for $\alpha = .05$ and $v_1 = 9$ and $v_2 = 18$ is 2.46. Since calculated F exceeds critical F, the block variation is statistically significant. This means that the grouping of sales representatives according to ability before assigning the treatment was effective; it eliminated a source of variation in the results. The randomized-block design was more efficient than a completely randomized design would have been.

The randomized-block design allowed us to test the treatment factor (training program), while controlling for an extraneous factor (sales ability). There are many more kinds of experimental designs. A "Latin-Square" design allows us to test for a treatment, while controlling for two extraneous factors (e.g., sales ability *and* size of sales territory). An important and frequently used experimental design is the "factorial," discussed next.

Factorial Designs

We promised at the beginning of the chapter to show you two ways that the analysis of variance is an extension of a two-group t-test. We have now seen how the ANOVA may be used with three (or more) groups. We also stated that it can be used to investigate the effects of two or more factors in the same experiment. The factorial design is an experiment in which we've varied more than one factor. For instance, it might be desirable to investigate the sales impact of the shape of the packaging, in addition to whether the container is metal or plastic. Suppose two shapes, cylindrical and rectangular, were being considered for the containers. Package shape and package type would both be called factors, and we'd use a **factorial design**.

There are three very good reasons to use a factorial design. First, we can study the interaction of the factors. The plastic container might sell better as cylinders, whereas the metal container might sell better in rectangular box shapes. An interaction can only be investigated if the factors are considered simultaneously. Second, a factorial design is efficient—if two separate experiments were conducted (one to study the effect of container type and another to study the effect of container shape), some data would yield information about either piece of the puzzle. But by combining the two factors in one experiment, all the observations bear on both factors, so factorials are said to be more "economical." Third, the conclusions reached have broader application, since each factor is studied with varying combinations of the other factors. This result is much more useful (multiple factors or considerations are more like the real world) than it would be if everything else had been held constant.

[4] If the null hypothesis is rejected, "contrasts" are run to determine which means are statistically significantly different.

The factorial design may be used with any of the single-factor designs previously discussed—completely randomized, randomized block, etc. The underlying model changes, as does the analysis-of-variance table, but the principle remains the same. Let's look at a factorial version of a completely randomized design.

Consider again our sales reps. Suppose management is thinking of the three training programs again, but also the frequency with which the sales reps contact their leads. We'll call the frequency factor "A," which takes on the values "high" and "low" (frequent and infrequent would be defined precisely depending on the particular industry, product purchase cycle rates, etc.). The three training programs are now called B_1, B_2, and B_3. We have a 2×3 factorial experiment in which each of the two levels of A occurs with each of the three levels of B to yield six treatment conditions. Suppose that the treatments were randomly assigned to each of five sales representatives. Thus, there would be five replications for each treatment.

	Training Program		
Contact Frequency	**B_1**	**B_2**	**B_3**
A_1	$A_1\,B_1$	$A_1\,B_2$	$A_1\,B_3$
A_2	$A_2\,B_1$	$A_2\,B_2$	$A_2\,B_3$

Suppose that the results were as contained in Table 16A.4. Let:

α_i = the effect of the ith level of the A factor (contact frequency), $i = 1,\ldots, a$

β_j = the effect of the jth level of the B factor (training received), $j = 1,\ldots, b$

$(\alpha\beta)_{ij}$ = the effect of the ith level of the A factor and j^{th} level of the B factor

X_{ijk} = the kth observation on the ith level of the A factor and the jth level of the B factor

μ = the grand mean

ε_{ijk} = the error associated with the kth observation on the ith level of A and j^{th} level of B

TABLE 16A.4   **Sales Generated by Various Personal and Telephone Call Plans**

Telephone Call Plan	Personal Call Plan			Total	Mean
	B_1	**B_2**	**B_3**		
A_1	42	51	43		
	40	52	44		
	52	50	54	691	46.1
	46	49	44		
	40	44	40		
A_2	36	35	36		
	38	47	42		
	32	38	36	543	36.2
	29	35	30		
	38	36	35		
Total	393	437	404	1234	41.1
Mean	39.3	43.7	40.4		
Cell	$A_1\,B_1$	$A_1\,B_2$	$A_1\,B_3$	$A_2\,B_1$	$A_2\,B_2$	$A_2\,B_3$
Total	220	246	225	173	191	179
Mean	44.0	49.2	45.0	34.6	38.2	35.8

The underlying model for this completely randomized design suggests that any observation X_{ijk} can be written as the sum of the grand mean, treatment effects, and an error term:

$$X_{ijk} = \mu + \alpha_i + \beta_j + (\alpha\beta)_{ij} + \varepsilon_{ijk}$$

Total variability =
Contact variation
+ training variation
+ contact*training interaction
+ within

The assumptions are the same as for a completely randomized design except there are now $a{\times}b$ populations, whereas in the completely randomized design there were k populations—one for each treatment. Otherwise, though, we still assume that the distribution of the variable in each of the populations is normal and that the populations have the same variance.

There are three main hypotheses, all of which essentially state that the treatment effects are zero (the cell means are equal). The alternate hypotheses are that at least some of the cell means differ. The hypotheses can be written as follows:

$H_0^{(A)} : \alpha_i = 0$

$H_A^{(A)} : \alpha_i \neq 0$ for some α_i, or, not all $\alpha_i = 0$

$H_0^{(B)} : \beta_j = 0$

$H_A^{(B)} : \beta_j \neq 0$ for some β_j, or, not all $\beta_j = 0$

$H_0^{(AB)} : (\alpha\beta)_{ij} = 0$

$H_A^{(AB)} : (\alpha\beta)_{ij} \neq 0$ for some i or j (or, not all $(\alpha\beta)_{ij} = 0$).

The first two hypotheses state that there are no differences caused, respectively, by the levels of the A and B factors; the third says that the effects caused by Factors A and B are additive. To test these hypotheses, the following sums of squares are needed ($n = 5$ replications):

$$SS_T = \sum_{i=1}^{a}\sum_{j=1}^{b}\sum_{k=1}^{n}(X_{ijk} - \bar{x}_{...})^2$$
$$= (42 - 41.1)^2 + (40 - 41.1)^2 + \ldots + (35 - 41.1)^2$$
$$= 1333.5$$

$$SS_{TR} = n\sum_{i=1}^{a}\sum_{j=1}^{b}(\bar{x}_{ij.} - \bar{x}_{...})^2$$
$$= 5[(44.0 - 41.1)^2 + (49.2 - 41.1)^2 + (45.0 - 41.1)^2(34.6 - 41.1)^2 + (38.2 - 41.1)^2 + (35.8 - 41.1)^2]$$
$$= 839.9$$

$$SS_A = bn\sum_{i=1}^{a}(\bar{x}_{i..} - \bar{x}_{...})^2$$
$$= 3(5)[(46.1 - 41.1)^2 + (36.2 - 41.1)^2] = 735.1$$

$$SS_B = an\sum_{i=1}^{b}(\bar{x}_{.j.} - \bar{x}_{...})^2$$
$$= 2(5)[(39.3 - 41.1)^2 + (43.7 - 41.1)^2 + (40.4 - 41.1)^2] = 104.8$$

$$SS_{AB} = SS_{TR} - SS_A - SS_B$$
$$= 839.9 - 735.1 - 104.8 = 0.0$$

$$SS_E t = SS_T - SS_{TR}$$
$$= 1333.5 - 839.9 = 493.6$$

Analysis of Variance Table for 2×3 Factorial Experiment of Telephone and Personal Call Plans

TABLE **16A.5**

Source of Variation	Sum of Squares	Degrees of Freedom	Mean Square	F Ratio
A (telephone)	735.1	$(a - 1) = 1$	735.1	35.86
B (personal)	104.8	$(b - 1) = 2$	52.4	2.56
A × B (interaction)	.0	$(a - 1)(b - 1) = 2$	.0	.00
Error	493.6	$ab(n - 1) = 24$	20.5	
Total	1333.5	$abn - 1 = 29$		

Table 16A.5 contains the various mean squares and F-ratios. For the interaction term, the calculated F is zero. Critical F for $\alpha = .05$ and $v_1 = 2$, $v_2 = 24$ is 3.40. Calculated F is less than critical F, and the null hypothesis is not rejected—there is no special combination of frequency and training that yields better or worse sales results.

Consider next the effectiveness of the training—calculated F is again less than critical F, and the null hypothesis of equality of means is not rejected. The data do not indicate any difference in the effectiveness of the three training programs.

Consider finally the frequency of contract: Calculated F is 35.86, and critical F for $v_1 = 1$, $v_2 = 24$ and $\alpha = .05$ is 4.26. Since calculated F exceeds critical F, the null hypothesis is rejected. There is a difference in effectiveness of the two frequencies. An examination of the cell means in Table 16A.4 indicates that A1 ("frequent") is much better than A2 ("infrequent"). If the company were to make a change, this would be the strategy to adopt.

If the interaction term had tested significantly, we would not have bothered to check for the significance of the A and B factors by themselves. Rather, we would have looked for the best combination of frequency and training, because a significant interaction term would have indicated that the effects were not additive; a significant interaction term would have implied that the effects of A were different for some levels of B, or vice versa.

Summary

The analysis of variance, ANOVA, is the statistical extension of a t-test. The generalization is in two directions: 1) ANOVA allows us to model three or more groups simultaneously, and 2) the groups may be defined on two or more factors. There are many types of experimental designs, the completely randomized design, the randomized-block design, and the factorial design being the preeminent tools of marketing researchers.

Questions

1. What is the basic idea underlying the analysis-of-variance procedure? In general, how are these sources of variation computed? What is the basic statistic used to test for the differences among means in analysis of variance?

2. When is a randomized-block design used?

3. When is a factorial design appropriate?

Applications and Problems

1. Mr. LePew, the advertising manager of a medium-sized manufacturer of rug and room deodorizers, has developed three preliminary advertising campaigns for the company's line of deodorizers. The three campaigns are tested in an independent sample of 24 cities across the U.S., and the sales in each city are monitored. (Note: (1) Cities are randomly assigned to each treatment or campaign, and (2) the 24 cities are comparable in terms of various socio-economic and demographic variables.) The results of this test market are as follows:

Sales ($000's)

City	Ad 1	City	Ad 2	City	Ad 3
1	10	9	9	17	12
2	6	10	7	18	10
3	8	11	6	19	8
4	12	12	10	20	13
5	6	13	6	21	11
6	8	14	4	22	10
7	9	15	5	23	9
8	7	16	5	24	7

Mr. LePew wants to determine if sales differ as a result of the three advertising campaigns. He requires your assistance in analyzing the preceding information.

a. State the null and alternate hypotheses.
b. What statistical test is appropriate in this situation? Identify the assumptions underlying the test of the hypotheses.
c. Compute the grand mean and the mean of the jth treatment ($j = 1, 2, 3$). Show your calculations.
d. Compute the total variation (the sum of squares total). Show your calculations.
e. Compute the between-group variation (sum of squares between groups). Show your calculations.
f. Compute the within-group variation (sum of squares within groups). Show your calculations.
g. What are the degrees of freedom associated with each of these sums of squares?
h. Compute the mean squares associated with each of the sums of squares. Show your calculations.
i. Complete the following analysis-of-variance table.
j. Discuss your findings on the basis of preceding calculations. (Note: Assume that $\alpha = .05$ to find the critical F value.)

Source of Variation	Sum of Squares	Degrees of Freedom	Mean Square	F Ratio
Between-group				
Within-group				
Total				

2. A major business school is considering different training approaches for its executive MBA students. For a particular intro course, the question is how best to offer the learning experience: the traditional lecture format vs. a group discussion format, and simultaneously a traditional text vs. online Web resource materials.

A simple experiment is conducted using 20 new executive students. Using a factorial design, the 20 managers were randomly assigned to one of four training groups: lecture and standard text, discussion and text, lecture and Web materials, discussion and Web.

At the conclusion of the course, the managers were given a comprehensive test to determine how much of the material each retained from the coursework. The training coordinator plans to use this information to determine how the new course should be implemented in the future. The test scores for each of the participants are as follows:

Group 1: Lecture-Textbook	Group 2: Discussion-Text	Group 3: Lecture-Web	Group 4: Discussion-Web
62	74	84	94
78	86	72	84
86	76	72	88
64	88	66	78
70	84	88	86

a. State the null and alternate hypotheses.
b. Complete the following table:

Source of Variation	Sum of Squares	Degrees of Freedom	Mean Square	F Ratio
A (instruction format)				
B (instruction materials)				
A×B (interaction)				
Error				
Total				

c. What recommendations can you make based on the findings of the experiment? (Note: Assume that $\alpha = .05$ to find the critical F value.)

What are the underlying assumptions for the ANOVA model? Which assumption is necessary to allow the pooling of variances? What happens if this assumption is violated and the variances are still pooled?

3. A beverage company is testing different point-of-purchase displays. The marketing manager selects 12 stores in a market area and assigns them at random to the following treatment conditions: control group (no change in display), end-of-aisle display, and store shelf flyer with tear-away coupon. The manager will measure the sales occurring in each treatment condition and analyze the figures using ANOVA. The sales for each store are shown in the following table:

Control Stores (no change)	Experimental Group 1 (end of aisle display)	Experimental Group 2 (shelf display with coupon)
6	18	7
14	11	11
19	20	18
17	23	10

a. List the sources of variation for this test and their degrees of freedom.

b. Considering the underlying assumptions for ANOVA, which of these assumptions may be violated? Is there a more appropriate design for this experiment? Discuss the advantages and disadvantages of your proposed design.

c. Assume all assumptions and perform a one-way analysis of variance. What is the calculated F statistic? At $\alpha = .05$, can we reject the null hypothesis of no difference in sales between the treatment groups?

Are These Variables Related?

17

Questions to Guide Your Learning:

Q1 How do I interpret the various outputs of a regression?

Q2 What's the difference between correlation and regression?

Q3 What is an intercept? A slope?

Q4 What is multicollinearity, and should I be concerned?

In the previous chapters, we focused on data analysis techniques that have the goal of testing the significance of differences, e.g., the difference between a sample and a population, or between two or more samples. In many other circumstances, the marketing researcher has a different question: to determine whether there is any **association** between two or more variables. If there is, how strong are the relationships, and what is the nature of the relationship?

We try to **predict** the value of one variable, such as the consumption of a specific product by a household, on the basis of one or more other variables, such as the family's income and number of kids in the household. Prediction, or **forecasting**, is a crucial element of business planning and marketing strategy. The expectation is that some aspects of a consumer or marketplace can serve as predictors or leading indicators of consumer or market behavior. If we can understand the antecedents (e.g., consumers' attitudes), we can understand, predict, and perhaps even change the consequences (the consumers' purchase behaviors).

The variable being predicted is called the **dependent variable**, or criterion variable. The variables that are the predictors are called the **independent variables**.

Simple Regression and Correlation Analysis

Regression and correlation analysis are terms referring to techniques for studying the relationship between two or more variables. The two terms are often used interchangeably, but the purposes are different. Correlation analysis involves measuring the closeness of the relationship or joint variation between two variables at a time. Regression analysis refers to the techniques used to derive an equation that relates the criterion variable to one or more predictor variables. Regression models the criterion

If a business report is talking "prediction" or "forecasting," odds are (99:1), it's a regression.

variable when one or more predictor variables are held fixed, e.g., is it the case that households with high incomes and few kids are more likely to purchase luxury vacations than households with less income and more kids?[1] It is perfectly legitimate to measure the closeness of the relationship between variables (i.e., compute a correlation) without deriving an estimating equation (i.e., conduct a regression). Similarly, one can perform a regression analysis without investigating the correlation. It is common to do both.

We'll start with correlation analysis, first clarifying the distinction between correlation and causation. The use of the terms dependent (criterion) and independent (predictor) variables to describe the measures in correlation analysis stems from the mathematical functional relationship between the variates, not from a logic that one variable is dependent on another in a causal sense. Nothing in correlation analysis, or any other mathematical procedure, can be used to establish causality. All these procedures can do is measure the nature and degree of association or covariation between variables. Statements of causality must be based on theories and knowledge about the phenomena under investigation, not the mathematics.

Simple Regression

Correlation:
"Is *X* correlated with *Y*?" is the same question as "Is *Y* correlated with *X*?"

Regression:
"Is *X* useful in predicting *Y*?" is NOT the same as "Is *Y* useful in predicting *X*?"

Consider an example of a national manufacturer of a sonic toothbrush, Shine. The firm is interested in investigating the effectiveness of its marketing efforts. The company uses regional wholesalers to distribute Shine and supplements its efforts with company sales representatives and TV advertising. It intends to use annual territory sales as its measure of effectiveness. These data and information on the number of sales reps serving a territory are readily available in company records. The other characteristics—TV ad spots and wholesaler efficiency—are more difficult to determine. Obtaining information on TV advertising in a territory requires analysis of advertising schedules and a study of area coverage by channel to determine which areas each broadcast is reaching. Wholesaler efficiency requires rating the wholesalers on a number of criteria and aggregating the ratings into an overall measure of wholesaler efficiency, where 4 = outstanding, 3 = good, 2 = average, and 1 = poor. Because of the time and expense required to generate these advertising and distribution characteristics, the company has decided to carry out its analysis employing only a sample of its sales territories. The data for a simple random sample of 40 territories are contained in Table 17.1.

The effect of each of the marketing-mix variables on sales can be investigated in several ways. One way is simply to plot sales as a function of each of the variables. Figure 17.1 contains these "scatter diagrams." Panel A suggests that sales increase as the number of TV spots per month increases. Panel B suggests that sales increase as the number of sales reps in a territory increases. Panel C suggests there is little relationship between sales and wholesaler efficiency.

Panels A and B further suggest that the relationship between sales and each of the predictor variables could be adequately captured with a straight line. One way to generate these relationships would be to "eyeball" it—draw a straight line through the points in the graphs. Such a line would represent the average value of the criterion variable, sales, for given values of either of the predictor

---

[1] The regression model theoretically applies to fixed levels of predictor variables (*X*s), but it can apply when the *X*s are random, if certain conditions are satisfied, see Thomas P. Ryan, *Modern Regression Methods* (Wiley, 2008).

TABLE 17.1   Territory Data for Shine

Territory	Sales ($000's) Y	Advertising (TV spots per month) X_1	# Sales Reps X_2	Wholesaler Efficiency Index X_3
005	260.3	5	3	4
019	286.1	7	5	2
033	279.4	6	3	3
039	410.8	9	4	4
061	438.2	12	6	1
082	315.3	8	3	4
091	565.1	11	7	3
101	570.0	16	8	2
115	426.1	13	4	3
118	315.0	7	3	4
133	403.6	10	6	1
149	220.5	4	4	1
162	343.6	9	4	3
164	644.6	17	8	4
178	520.4	19	7	2
187	329.5	9	3	2
189	426.0	11	6	4
205	343.2	8	3	3
222	450.4	13	5	4
237	421.8	14	5	2
242	245.6	7	4	4
251	503.3	16	6	3
260	375.7	9	5	3
266	265.5	5	3	3
279	620.6	18	6	4
298	450.5	18	5	3
306	270.1	5	3	2
332	368.0	7	6	2
347	556.1	12	7	1
358	570.0	13	6	4
362	318.5	8	4	3
370	260.2	6	3	2
391	667.0	16	8	2
408	618.3	19	8	2
412	525.3	17	7	4
430	332.2	10	4	3
442	393.2	12	5	3
467	283.5	8	3	3
471	376.2	10	5	4
488	481.8	12	5	2

variables: TV spots, or number of sales reps. One could then enter the graph with, say, the number of TV spots in a territory and read off the average level of sales expected in the territory. The difficulty with the graphic approach is that two analysts might generate slightly different lines to describe the relationship, and then the question would be which line is right—which one fits the data better.

FIGURE 17.1   **Scatter Diagrams of Sales vs. Marketing-Mix Variables**

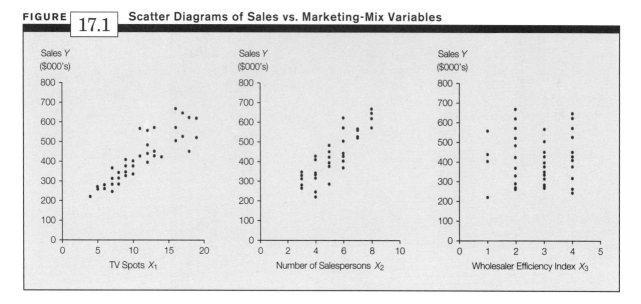

An alternative approach is more objective, to mathematically fit a line to the data. The general equation of a straight line is $Y = \alpha + \beta X$, where α is the Y intercept (the value we predict for Y if $X = 0$) and β is the slope coefficient (how much we predict Y to change as a function of X changing 1 unit).

As written, the model is a deterministic model. When a value of the predictor variable is substituted in the equation with specified α and β, a unique value for Y is predicted with no allowance for error. Yet, when investigating customer behavior (e.g., psychological and economic variables), there is rarely, if ever, zero error. Thus, we tweak the model slightly to allow for this error. We now call this a probabilistic model:

$$Y_i = \alpha_1 + \beta_1 X_{i1} + \varepsilon_i$$

where

Y_i is the level of sales in the ith territory

X_{i1} is the level of advertising in the ith territory

e_i is the error associated with the ith observation

The error term represents all kinds of "noise," such as our failure to include in the model all possible determining factors of sales, the fact that there is an unpredictable element in human behavior, and the condition that there are errors of measurement. The probabilistic model says that for a given X_i value, we predict the "average" value of Y. Individual values will fluctuate above and below this average.

The solution for finding the line of "best fit" for this model requires that we make some assumptions about the distribution of the error term. We will find the line of best fit defined to be the one that minimizes the sum of the deviations squared about the line (the least-squares solution). Consider Figure 17.2, and suppose that the line drawn in the figure is the estimated equation. We use a caret (or hat, a "^") to indicate an estimated value, the error for the ith observation is the difference between the actual Y value, Y_i, and the estimated Y value, $\widehat{Y}_i$; that is, $e_i = Y_i - \widehat{Y}_i$. The least-squares solution is based on the

FIGURE 17.2   Relationship Between Y and X_1 in the Probabilistic Model

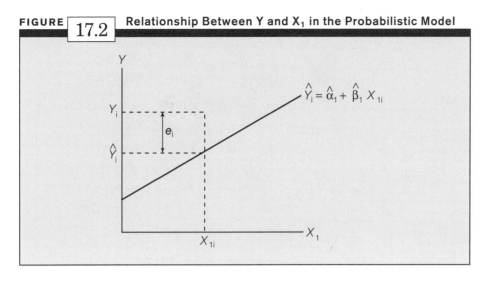

principle that the sum of these squared errors should be made as small as possible; that is,

$$\sum_{i=1}^{n} \varepsilon_i^2$$

should be minimized. The sample estimates $\widehat{\alpha}_1$ and $\widehat{\beta}_1$ of the true population parameters α_1 and β_1 are determined so that this condition is satisfied.

Three simplifying assumptions are made about the error term in the least-squares solution:

1. The mean or average value of the disturbance term is zero.
2. The variance of the error term is constant and independent of the values of the predictors.
3. The values of the error term are independent of one another.

Given these assumptions, the sample estimates of the intercept and slope population parameters, α and β in the general case are:

$$\widehat{\alpha} = y - \widehat{\beta}\,\overline{x}$$

$$\widehat{\beta} = \frac{n\sum_{i=1}^{n}(X_i - x)(Y_i - y)}{nS_x^2} = \frac{n\sum_{i=1}^{n}X_i Y_i - \left(\sum_{i=1}^{n}X_i\right)\left(\sum_{i=1}^{n}Y_i\right)}{n\left(\sum_{i=1}^{n}X_i^2\right) - \left(\sum_{i=1}^{n}X_i\right)}$$

where

$$y = \frac{1}{n}\sum_{i=1}^{n}Y_i$$

$$x = \frac{1}{n}\sum_{i=1}^{n}X_i$$

Thus, one needs various sums, sums of squares, and sums of cross products to generate the least-squares estimates.

To predict sales Y from the number of TV spots per month X_1, use the data provided in Table 17.1 to confirm these pieces of the computations:

$$\sum_{i=1}^{40} Y_i = 260.3 + 286.1 + ... + 481.8 = 16,451.5$$

$$\sum_{i=1}^{40} X_{i1} = (5 + 7 + ... + 12) = 436.0$$

$$\sum_{i=1}^{40} X_{i1}Y_i = 5(260.3) + 7(286.1) + ... + 12(481.8) = 197,634$$

$$\sum_{i=1}^{40} X_{i1}^2 = (5)^2 + (7)^2 + ... + (12)^2 = 5476$$

$$y = \frac{16451.5}{40} = 411.3$$

$$x = \frac{436}{40} = 10.9$$

Therefore:

$$\widehat{\beta} = \frac{n\sum_{i=1}^{n} X_i Y_i - \left(\sum_{i=1}^{n} X_i\right)\left(\sum_{i=1}^{n} Y_i\right)}{n\left(\sum_{i=1}^{n} X_i^2\right) - \left(\sum_{i=1}^{n} X_i\right)} = \frac{40(197,634) - (436)(16,541.5)}{40(5476) - (436)^2} = 25.3$$

$$\widehat{\alpha} = y - \widehat{\beta}_1 x_1 = 411.3 - (25.3)(10.9) = 135.4$$

The regression equation is plotted in Figure 17.3. The slope of the line is given by β_1. The value 25.3 of $\widehat{\beta}_1$ suggests that, for every unit increase in TV spots, sales increase by \$25,300. The estimate is vital information that helps determine whether advertising expense is worth the estimated return. The estimate of the intercept parameter is $\widehat{\alpha}_1 = 135.4$; this value indicates where the line crosses the Y axis because it represents the estimated value of Y when the predictor variable equals zero.

Standard Error of Estimate

The line seems to fit the points fairly well, but Figure 17.3 shows that some deviation still occurs in the points about the line. The size of these deviations measures the accuracy of the prediction, or the goodness of the fit of the line. We compute a measure of the variation of the points around the line in much the same way as we compute a standard deviation. Call the variance of these random error ε_i's σ_ε^2 or $\sigma_{Y/X}^2$. When the population variance σ^2 is unknown, an unbiased estimate is given by:

$$\widehat{s}^2 = \frac{\sum_{i=1}^{n}(X_i - x)^2}{n-1}$$

FIGURE 17.3   **Plot of Equation Relating Sales to TV Spots**

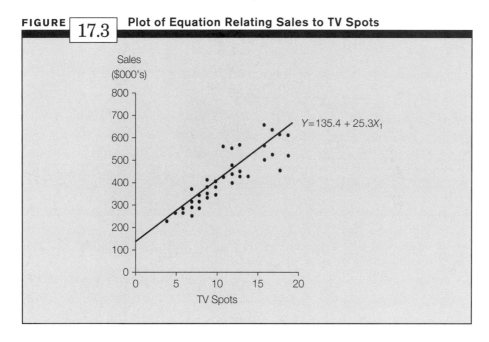

Similarly, let $s^2_{Y/X}$ be an unbiased estimate of $\sigma^2_{Y/X}$:

$$s^2_{Y/X} = \frac{\sum_{i=1}^{n} e_i^2}{n-2} = \frac{\sum_{i=1}^{n} (Y_i - \widehat{Y}_i)^2}{n-2}$$

where Y_i and $\widehat{Y}_i$ are the observed and estimated values of Y for the ith observation. The square root, $s_{Y/X}$, is called the standard error of estimate.

The interpretation of the standard error of estimate parallels that for any standard deviation. Consider some value for X_{i1}. The standard error of estimate means that for any value of TV spots X_{i1}, Y_i (sales) tends to be distributed about the corresponding $\widehat{Y}_i$ value—the point on the line—with a standard deviation equal to the standard error of estimate. Note that the variation about the line is the same throughout the entire length of the line. The point on the line changes with X_{i1}, but the distribution of Y_i values around the line does not. Figure 17.4 depicts the situation under the assumption that the error term is rectangularly distributed, for example.

The smaller the standard error of estimate, the better the line fits the data (the closer the data points lie to the line). For the line relating sales to TV spots, it is $s_{Y/X} = 59.6$ (we'll see shortly how to assess that number as large or small).

Inferences about the Slope Coefficient

To answer the question about whether the slope coefficient, $\widehat{\beta}_1 = 25.3$, is significantly greater than zero (i.e., is the effect of advertising on sales "real" or just due to chance) requires an additional assumption—namely, that the errors are normally distributed.[2] If the ε_i are normally distributed, then $\widehat{\beta}_1$ is also normally distributed. In other words, if we were to take repeated samples from our population and calculate a $\widehat{\beta}_1$ for each sample, the distribution of these estimates

[2] Regardless of the distribution of the error term, the least-squares estimators of the population parameters are "blue," i.e., **b**est, **l**inear, **u**nbiased **e**stimators of the true population parameters. But if we wish to make statistical inferences about the regression coefficients, we must assume normally distributed errors.

FIGURE 17.4   **Rectangular Distribution of Error Term**

would be normal and centered on the true population parameter β_1. The variance of the distribution of $\widehat{\beta}_1$ s is equal to:

$$\sigma^2_{\widehat{\beta}_1} = \frac{\sigma^2_{Y/X}}{\sum\limits_{i=1}^{n} (X_{i1} - x_1)^2}$$

The population value $\sigma^2_{Y/X}$ is unknown, so $\sigma^2_{\widehat{\beta}_1}$ has to be estimated, but we substitute the standard error of estimate $s_{Y/X}$ for $\sigma_{Y/X}$:

$$s^2_{\widehat{\beta}_1} = \frac{s^2_{Y/X}}{\sum\limits_{i=1}^{n} (X_{i1} - x_1)^2}$$

The null hypothesis is that "no linear relationship exists between the variables," whereas the alternate hypothesis is that a linear relationship does exist:

$$H_0 : \beta_1 = 0$$
$$H_0 : \beta_1 \neq 0$$

The test statistic, $t = (\widehat{\beta}_1 - \beta_1)/s_{\widehat{\beta}1}$, is distributed t with $n - 2$ degrees of freedom. In the example,

$$s^2_{\widehat{\beta}_1} = \frac{59.6}{723.6} = 4.91$$

$$s_{\widehat{\beta}_1} = \sqrt{4.91} = 2.22$$

$$t = \frac{(25.3 - 0)}{2.22} = 11.4$$

For a .05 level of significance, the tabled t-value for $n - 2 = 38$ df is 2.02. Our calculated t exceeds that, so we reject the null hypothesis. We conclude that $\widehat{\beta}_1$ is sufficiently different from zero to warrant the assumption of a linear relationship between sales and TV spots.[3]

---

[3] This conclusion does not mean that the true relationship between sales and TV spots is necessarily linear, only that the evidence indicates that Y (sales) changes as X_1 (TV spots) changes and that we may obtain a better prediction of Y using X_1 and the linear equation than if we simply ignored X_1 (e.g., perhaps the relationship between X_1 and Y is linear only in the range of the number of TV spots we measured).

What if we do not reject the null? β_1 is the slope of the line over the range of our observations and it indicates the linear change in Y for a one-unit change in X_1. If we do not reject the null hypothesis that β_1 equals zero, it does not mean that Y and X_1 are unrelated. There are two possibilities. First, we may simply be committing a Type II error by not rejecting a false null hypothesis. Second, it is possible that Y and X_1 might be related in some curvilinear manner, and we have simply chosen the wrong model to describe the situation.

Prediction of Y

Having established that the regression is not attributable to chance, we use it to predict sales from given values of the number of TV spots. Two cases must be considered:

1. Predicting the average value of Y for a given X_1

2. Predicting an individual value of Y for a given X_1

For a given X_1 value, say, X_{01}, the Y value predicted by the regression equation is the average value of Y given X_1. Thus, in a territory with 10 TV spots per month, the expected sales $\widehat{Y}_0$ are:

$$\widehat{Y}_0 = \widehat{\alpha}_1 + \widehat{\beta}_1 X_{01} = 135.4 + 25.3(10) = 388.4$$

This is an unbiased estimate of the true average value of expected sales when there are indeed 10 TV spots per month in a territory. Individual territory sales may, of course, be above or below the average. $\widehat{Y}_0$ may not exactly equal Y_0, the population mean it is estimating for the given X_1 value, so it would seem useful to place bounds of error on the estimate.

To determine the bounds of error, it is necessary to know the variance of the distribution of Y_0 given X_{01}. This variance is estimated as:

$$s^2_{\widehat{Y}_0/X_{01}} = s^2_{Y/X_1} \left(\frac{1}{n} + \frac{(X_{01} - x_1)^2}{\displaystyle\sum_{i=1}^{n} (X_{i1} - x_1)^2} \right)$$

Note that this variance depends on the particular X_1 value in question. When X_1 equals its mean, the variance is smallest, because $(X_{01} - x_1)$ then equals zero. As X_1 moves away from the mean, the variance increases. For 10 TV spots per day,

$$s^2_{\widehat{Y}_0/X_{01}} = (59.6)^2 \left(\frac{1}{40} + \frac{(10 - 10.9)^2}{723.6} \right) = 92.8$$

The confidence interval for the estimate is given by

$$\widehat{Y}_0 \pm t s_{\widehat{Y}_0/X_{01}}$$

where t is the tabled t-value on $n - 2$ df. For a .05 level of significance and 38 df, $t = 2.02$. Thus, the confidence interval for the average value of sales when there are 10 TV spots per month is:

$$388.4 \pm 2.02\sqrt{92.8} = 388.4 \pm 19.5$$

Although this equation enables us to predict the average level of sales for all sales territories with 10 TV spots per month, we might also want to predict the sales that could be expected in some particular territory. This prediction contains an additional element of error, the amount by which the particular territory deviates from the average. The error in predicting a specific value is larger than that for predicting the average value. Specifically, it equals:

$$s_{Y_0/X_{01}}^2 = s_{Y/X_1}^2 \left(1 + \frac{1}{n} + \frac{(X_{01} - x_1)^2}{\sum_{i=1}^{n} (X_{i1} - x_1)^2} \right)$$

where the caret is removed from Y_0 to indicate that we are now talking about a specific value of Y_0 rather than an average value. Note that $s_{Y_0/X_{01}}^2$ also equals $s_{Y_0/X_{01}}^2 + s_{Y/X_1}^2$. This alternate expression shows why the confidence interval is wider when the prediction involves a specific value of Y_0 instead of the average value. The second term in this expression, s_{Y/X_1}^2, represents the estimated amount by which the particular value deviates from the average value. For 10 TV spots per month,

$$s_{Y_0/X_{01}}^2 = (59.6)^2 \left(1 + \frac{1}{40} + \frac{(10 - 10.9)^2}{723.6} \right) = 3645$$

and the confidence interval is

$$Y_0 \pm t s_{Y_0/X_{01}} = 388.4 \pm 2.02\sqrt{3645} = 388.4 \pm 122.0$$

Note that the bounds of error are much wider when a particular Y value is being predicted.

Even though the regression equation can be used to develop predictions about the average value of *Y* for a given *X*, you should be careful when doing any prediction. It is particularly risky to predict outside of the range of values on which the equation was developed (i.e., "extrapolation"). Check Research Realities 17.1 for Mark Twain's view on the matter!

RESEARCH   REALITIES

17.1 Life on the Mississippi—742 Years from Now

Mark Twain may not have been a statistician, and he may not have had the aid of a computer, but he knew enough about the tricks numbers can play to write this little spoof for those who would predict "logical" outcomes based on past data.

"In the space of one hundred and seventy-six years the Lower Mississippi has shortened itself two hundred and forty-two miles. This is an average of a trifle over one mile and a third per year. Therefore, any calm person, who is not blind or idiotic, can see that in the Old Oölitic Silurian Period, just a million years ago next November, the Lower Mississippi River was upward of one million three hundred thousand miles long, and stuck out over the Gulf of Mexico like a fishing-rod. And by the same token any person can see that seven hundred and forty-two years from now the Lower Mississippi will be only a mile and three-quarters long, and Cairo and New Orleans will have joined their streets together, and be plodding comfortably along under a single mayor and a mutual board of aldermen. There is something fascinating about science. One gets such wholesale returns of conjecture out of such a trifling investment of fact."

Source: Mark Twain, Life on the Mississippi.

Correlation Coefficient

So far, we have been concerned with whether X and Y are related. Suppose that we also wanted to know the *strength of their linear relationship.*

For the correlation model, we assume X_i to be a random variable also. That is, a respondent yields both an X_i and a Y_i value. In addition, we assume that the observations come from a bivariate normal distribution, which implies that the X and Y variables are also univariately normally distributed.

We draw a sample of n observations from a bivariate normal distribution. Let ρ represent the strength of the linear association between the two variables in the population and r is the sample estimate.

Assume that the sample of n observations yielded the scatter of points shown in Figure 17.5. Now consider the division of the figure into the four quadrants formed by erecting perpendicular axes at x and y. Take any point P with co-ordinates (X_i, Y_i) and define the deviations:

$$x_i = X_i - x$$
$$y_i = Y_i - y$$

where the small letters indicate deviations around a mean. In Figure 17.5, we see that the product $x_i y_i$ is:

- Positive for all points in Quadrant I
- Negative for all points in Quadrant II
- Positive for all points in Quadrant III
- Negative for all points in Quadrant IV

Hence, the quantity $\sum x_i y_i$ will reflect the linear association between X and Y, because:

- If the association is positive, most of the data points will lie in Quadrants I and III, and $\sum x_i y_i$ will be positive.
- If the association is negative, most of the data points will lie in Quadrants II and IV, and $\sum x_i y_i$ will be negative.
- If no relation exists between X and Y, the points will be scattered over all four quadrants and $\sum x_i y_i$ will be near zero.

FIGURE 17.5   Scatter of Points for Sample of n Observations

These intuitions based on $\sum x_i y_i$ are fine, but we don't use it exactly in the calculations—it has to be corrected for sample size and the units of measurement for the variables (e.g., changing feet to meters). When we make these adjustments, the result is the **Pearson product-moment correlation coefficient:**

$$r = \frac{\sum_{i=1}^{n}(X_i - x)(Y_i - y)}{n s_X s_Y} = \frac{\sum_{i=1}^{n} x_i y_i}{n s_X s_Y}$$

where s_X is the standard deviation of the X variable and s_Y is that for Y. The correlation coefficient computed from the sample data is an estimate of the parent population parameter ρ, and we will use r to test hypotheses about ρ. (Note the identity in the numerator of this equation for r and the earlier equation for β_1.)

The product-moment coefficient of correlation may vary from -1.0 to $+1.0$. Perfect positive correlation, where an increase in X determines exactly an increase in Y, yields a coefficient of $+1.0$. Perfect negative correlation, where an increase in X determines exactly a decrease in Y, yields a coefficient of -1.0. Figure 17.6 depicts these situations and others to illustrate the size of the correlation coefficient associated with a particular degree of scatter.

The square of the correlation is the **coefficient of determination**. It is equal to:

$$r^2 = 1 - \frac{s_{Y/X}^2}{s_Y^2}$$

In the absence of the predictor variable, our best estimate of the criterion variable is the sample mean, $\bar{y}$. If low variability in sales from territory to territory exists, the sample mean is a good estimate of the expected sales in any territory. It is a poor estimate though, if there is high variability. Thus, the variance in sales s_Y^2 is a measure of the "badness" of such an estimating procedure. Bringing the predictor X into the model might improve the estimates (if the equation fits

FIGURE 17.6   **Sample Scatter Diagrams and Their Correlation Coefficients**

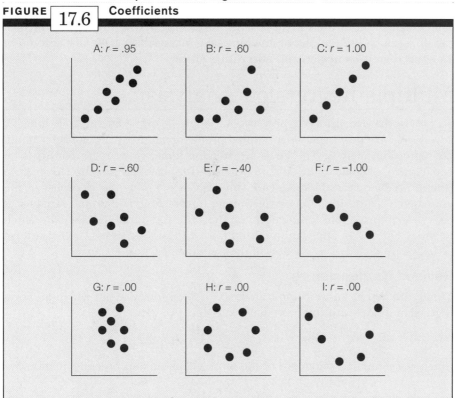

the data). Since the $s^2_{Y/X}$ measures the scatter of the points around the regression line, $s^2_{Y/X}$ can be considered a measure of the "badness" of an estimating procedure that takes account of X. We can compare these measures to see whether our knowledge of X helps us predict Y more accurately.

Specifically, if $s^2_{Y/X}$ is small relative to s^2_Y, then X can be said to have substantially improved the predictions of the criterion variable. Conversely, if $s^2_{Y/X}$ is approximately equal to s^2_Y, then X can be considered not to have helped improve the predictions of Y. Thus, the ratio $s^2_{Y/X}/s^2_Y$ can be considered to be the ratio of variation left unexplained by the regression line divided by the total variation:

$$r^2 = 1 - \frac{(unexplained\ variation)}{(total\ variation)}$$

The right side of the equation can be combined in a single fraction to yield:

$$r^2 = \frac{(total\ variation - unexplained\ variation)}{(total\ variation)}$$

Total variation minus unexplained variation leaves "explained variation," or the variation in Y that is accounted for or explained by X. Thus, the coefficient of determination is interpreted as:

$$r^2 = \frac{(explained\ variation)}{(total\ variation)}$$

where "total variation" means the variance in Y. For the sales and TV spot example, $r^2 = .77$. This means that 77% of the variation in sales across territories can be explained by the variation in TV advertising across territories. Thus, we can do a (much) better job of estimating sales in a territory if we take account of TV spots than if we neglect this advertising effort.

Multiple-Regression Analysis

So far, we have considered only two variables in our analysis: sales and TV advertising. We now bring in additional predictor variables and consider multiple-regression analysis. The goals are still the same; we want to construct an equation to estimate values of the criterion variable, but now we do so from several predictor variables. And we still wish to measure the closeness of the estimated relationship. Our objective in introducing additional variables is basic—to improve our predictions of the criterion variable.[4] (See Research Realities 17.2 for an application of multiple regression to assess CEO salaries—actual vs. predicted as a function of their companies' performances.)

Revised Nomenclature

Things are getting more complicated, so we need to revise our notation. For a regression model with three predictor variables, we write

$$Y = \alpha + \beta_1 X_1 + \beta_2 X_2 + \beta_3 X_3 + \varepsilon$$

Simple Regression:

$y = fn(x)$

Multiple Regression:

$y = fn(x_1, x_2, x_3, \ldots)$

Easy!

which is a simplified statement of the more elaborate and precise equation:

$$Y_{(123)} = \alpha_{(123)} + \beta_{Y1.23} X_1 + \beta_{Y2.13} X_2 + \beta_{Y3.12} X_3 + \varepsilon_{(123)}$$

In this more precise system:

- $Y_{(123)}$ is the value of Y estimated from the regression equation, in which Y is the criterion variable and X_1, X_2, and X_3 are the predictor variables.

- $\alpha_{(123)}$ is the intercept parameter in the multiple-regression equation.

- $\beta_{Y1.23}$ is the coefficient of X_1 in the regression equation. It is called the **coefficient of partial (or net) regression**. Note the two subscripts to the left of the decimal point—the first identifies the criterion variable, and the second identifies the predictor variable of which this β value is the coefficient. There are always two primary subscripts. The subscripts to the right of the decimal point indicate which other predictor variables are in the regression equation. $\beta_{Y1.23}$ is called the **partial regression coefficient** because it reflects the impact of X_1 on Y, having partialled out, or statistically controlled for, X_2 and X_3.

- $\varepsilon_{(123)}$ is the error associated with the prediction of Y when X_1, X_2, and X_3 are the predictor variables.

[4] For examples, see Rick L. Andrews, Imran S. Currim, Peter Leeflang, and Jooseop Lim, "Estimating the SCAN·PRO Model of Store Sales," *International Journal of Research in Marketing*, 25, 22–33; Yuxin Chen and Sha Yang, "Estimating Disaggregate Models Using Aggregate Data via Augmentation of Individual Choice," *Journal of Marketing Research*, 44, 613–621; Peter Ebbes, Michel Wedel, Ulf Bockenholt, and Ton Steememan, "Solving and Testing for Regressor-Error Independence When No Instrumental Variables are Available," *Quantitative Marketing and Economics*, 3, 365–392; Ajay Kalra, Mengze Shi, and Kannan Srinivasan, "Sales-force Compensation Scheme and Consumer Inferences," *Management Science*, 49 (5), 655–672; Yunchuan Frank Liu and Z. Zhang, "The Benefits of Personalized Pricing in a Channel," *Marketing Science*, 25 (1), 97–105; Vicki G. Morwitz, Joel Steckel, and Alok Gupta, "When do Purchase Intentions Predict Sales?" *International Journal of Forecasting*, 23 (3), 347–364; Raghunath S. Rao, Rajesh K. Chandy, and Jaideep C. Prabhu, "The Fruits of Legitimacy: Why Some New Ventures Gain More from Innovation that Others," *Journal of Marketing*, 72, 58–75; and Hong Yuan and A. Krishna, "Pricing of Mall Services in the Presence of Sales Leakage," *Journal of Retailing*, 84, 95–117.

RESEARCH   REALITIES

17.2 Regression and CEO Compensation

Business periodicals frequently publish charts of CEO pay, along with indicators of corporate performance. The following data were sampled from Jerry Useem's "CEO Pay" *Fortune,* but *Forbes* ("What the Boss Makes") and *Business Week* ("Executive Pay") publish their own versions.

Use the corporate performance indicators (sales in millions of dollars, and return on earning) to predict the CEO salary and bonus package (in thousands of dollars). After obtaining the regression coefficient estimates, plug the actual company performance numbers into the equation to obtain the predicted CEO salary figures.

a. Which CEOs are overcompensated? Which are undervalued?

b. If you were one of the CEOs identified as having been overcompensated, how might you argue that a regression model has limitations in this application?

Everybody's being rated. Here are analogous (pay and performance) statistics on baseball's "best hitters." Run the predictions, and see who is a good "value" vs. who is overpaid. Who should renegotiate? Who should keep quiet?

Player	At Bats	Total Bases	Salary (000's)
Bonds	403	322	$15,000
Thome	480	325	11,167
Ramirez	436	282	17,185
Giles	497	309	8,563
Rodriguez	624	389	22,000
Walker	477	287	12,667
Guerrero	614	364	11,500
Giambi	560	335	11,429
Ordonez	590	352	9,000
Helton	553	319	10,600
Sosa	556	330	16,875
Palmeiro	546	312	9,000

Company	Total Compensation in Millions	Shareholder Return
Apple Computer	$78.1	−34.6%
Honeywell	68.5	−27.3
Cisco Systems	54.8	−27.7
Lucent Technologies	38.2	−75.4
Tenet Healthcare	35.0	−58.1
Hancock Financial Services	34.3	−31.7
Sun Microsystems	31.7	−74.7
Abbott Laboratories	30.4	−26.7
American Intl. Group	29.2	−26.9
Alcoa	24.8	−34.6
Schering-Plough	24.4	−36.4
Wyeth	22.2	−37.9

It is common practice to use the simpler notation, e.g., β_2, but the more elaborate notation, $\beta_{Y2.13}$, helps us remember to interpret the solution precisely.

Multicollinearity Assumption

The assumptions that we made about the error term for simple regression model also apply to multiple regression. In addition, for multiple regression, we require another assumption—that the predictor variables not be correlated among themselves. When the data result from a survey rather than an experiment, this assumption is often violated because many variables of interest in marketing vary together (e.g., higher incomes typically correlate with higher education levels). **Multicollinearity** is said to be present in a multiple-regression problem when the predictor variables are correlated among themselves. We'll return to this issue.

Coefficients of Partial Regression

Let's say we want to model sales as a function of TV spots, as before, but also number of sales reps. We could run a simple regression using sales reps to predict sales, as we did using TV spots to predict sales. Alternatively, we could consider the simultaneous influence of TV spots and number of sales reps on sales using multiple-regression analysis. If we assume that that is indeed the research problem, the regression model would be written

$$Y_{(12)} = \alpha_{(12)} + \beta_{Y1.2}X_1 + \beta_{Y2.1}X_2 + \varepsilon_{(12)}$$

indicating that the criterion variable, sales in a territory, is predicted by two variables, X_1 (TV spots per month) and X_2 (number of sales reps).

The parameters are estimated from sample data using least-squares procedures via computer. For this problem, the equation turns out to be:

$$\widehat{Y}_{(12)} = \widehat{\alpha}_{(12)} + \widehat{\beta}_{Y1.2}X_1 + \widehat{\beta}_{Y2.1}X_2 = 69.3 + 14.2X_1 + 37.5X_2$$

This regression equation may be used to estimate the level of sales expected in a territory, given the number of TV spots and number of sales reps in the territory. Like any other least-squares equation, this line (actually it's a plane in this case because three dimensions are involved) fits the points in such a way that the sum of the deviations about the line is zero. In other words, if sales for each of the 40 sales territories were to be estimated from this equation, the positive and negative deviations about the line would exactly balance.

The level at which the plane intercepts the Y axis is given by $\widehat{\alpha}_{(12)} = 69.3$. Assuming that the multicollinearity assumption is satisfied, the coefficients of partial regression $\widehat{\beta}_{Y1.2}$ and $\widehat{\beta}_{Y2.1}$, can be interpreted as the average change in the criterion variable associated with a unit change in the appropriate predictor variable *while holding the other predictor variable constant.* Thus, assuming that there is no multicollinearity, $\widehat{\beta}_{Y1.2} = 14.2$ indicates that on the average, an increase of $14,200 in sales can be expected with each additional TV spot in the territory if the number of sales representatives is not changed. Similarly, $\widehat{\beta}_{Y2.1} = 37.5$ suggests that each additional sales representative in a territory can be expected to produce $37,500 in sales, on the average, if the number of TV spots is held constant.

In simple regression, we tested the significance of the slope coefficient using the t-test. The calculated t was 11.4 for the sales–TV spot relationship. The significance of the regression could also have been checked with an F-test. In the case of a two-variable regression, calculated F is equal to calculated t squared: $F = t^2 = (11.4)^2 = 130.6$. In general, calculated F is equal to the ratio of the "mean square due to regression" to the "mean square due to residuals." In simple regression, the calculated F value would be referred to an F-table for 1 and $n - 2$ degrees of freedom. The conclusion would be exactly equivalent to that derived by testing the significance of the slope coefficient employing the t-test with $n - 2$ df.

In the multiple-regression case, the significance of the overall regression is examined using an F-test. The appropriate degrees of freedom are k and $n - k - 1$, where there are k predictor variables. Critical F for 2 and $40 - 2 - 1 = 37$ degrees of freedom and a .05 level of significance is 3.25. Calculated F for the regression we just ran, relating sales to TV spots and sales reps, is 128.1. Since calculated F exceeds critical F, the null hypothesis of "no relationship" is rejected. A statistically significant linear relationship exists between sales and the predictor variables (number of TV spots and number of sales reps).

Now that we know the overall function is significant, the slope coefficients for each separate predictor can also be tested to see whether they significantly contribute to the prediction. A t-test is used, and the validity of the procedure is highly dependent on whether there exists multicollinearity in the data. If the data are highly multicollinear, there is a tendency to commit Type II errors (i.e., many of the predictor variables will be judged as not being related to the criterion variable when in fact they are). It is even possible to have a high R^2 value and to conclude that the overall regression is statistically significant with none of the coefficients being significant. The difficulty with the t-tests for the significance of the individual slope coefficients arises because the standard error of estimate of the least-squares coefficients, s_{b_i}, increases as the dependence among the predictor variables increases. And, of course, as the denominator of calculated t gets larger, t itself decreases, occasioning the conclusion of no relationship between the criterion variable and the predictor variable in question.

Is multicollinearity a problem in our example? Consider again the simple regression of sales on TV spots; β_1 was equal to 25.3. Thus, when the number of sales representatives in a territory was not considered, the average change in sales associated with an additional TV spot was $25,300. Yet when the number of sales representatives was considered, the average change in sales associated with an additional TV spot was $14,200 ($\widehat{\beta}_{Y1.2} = 14.2$). Part of the sales effect that we were attributing to TV spots was in fact due to the number of sales representatives in the territory. We were thus overstating the effect of the TV advertising because of the way decisions have historically been made in the company. Specifically, those territories with the greater number of sales reps also received more TV advertising support (or vice versa). Perhaps this was logical, because they contained a larger target market. Nevertheless, the fact that the two predictor variables are not independent (the correlation between TV spots and #sales reps is $r = .78$) has caused a violation of the assumption of independent predictors. Multicollinearity is present within this data set.

A multicollinear condition reduces the efficiency of the estimates for the regression parameters: the amount of information about the effect of each predictor variable on the criterion variable declines as the correlation among the predictor variables increases. In Figure 17.7, it is assumed that a perfect linear relationship exists between the two predictor variables, TV spots and number of sales reps, and also that a strong linear relationship exists between the criterion variable sales and TV spots. Consider the change in sales from $75,000 to $100,000. This change is associated with a change in the number of TV spots from three to four. This change in TV spots is also associated with a change in the number of sales reps from four to five. What is the effect of a TV spot on sales? Can we say it is $100 - 75 = 25$, or $25,000? No. Historically a sales representative has been added to a territory whenever the number of TV spots has been increased by one (or vice versa). The number of TV spots and sales representatives varies in direct proportion, and it is impossible to distinguish their separate influences on sales (their influence when the other predictor variable is truly held constant).

Very little meaning can be attached to regression coefficients when multicollinearity is present, as in our example. The "normal" interpretation of the

FIGURE 17.7

Hypothetical Relationship Between Sales and TV Spots and Between TV Spots and Number of Sales Representatives

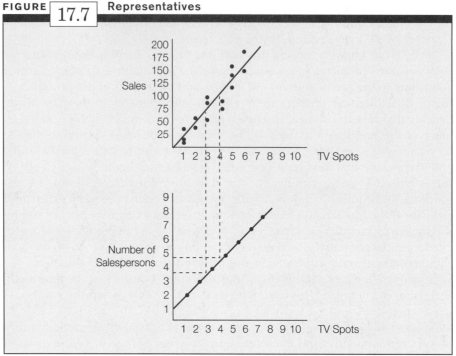

regression coefficient as "the average change in the criterion variable associated with a unit change in the appropriate predictor variable while holding the other predictor variables constant" does not hold. The equation may still be used for prediction, however, e.g., to predict sales in the various territories for given levels of TV spots and number of sales reps, assuming that conditions are stable. The partial-regression coefficients should not be used, though, as the basis for making marketing strategy decisions when significant multicollinearity is present.[5]

Coefficients of Multiple Correlation and Determination

In simple regression, the measure of the strength or closeness of the relationship between the criterion and predictor variables is very important (recall the correlation, r, and its square, the coefficient of multiple determination). In multiple regression, there are analogous coefficients.

The coefficient of multiple correlation is formally denoted by $R_{Y.123}$, where the first subscript identifies the criterion variable and the next subscripts identify the predictor variables. The **coefficient of multiple determination** is denoted by $R^2_{Y.123}$ or R^2. It represents the proportion of variation in the criterion variable that is accounted for by the predictor variables. In the investigation of the relationship between sales and TV spots and #sales reps, $R^2_{Y.12} = .874$. This means

---

[5] Another interpretation danger is that it is reasonable to assume that both the #sales reps serving a territory and the #TV spots per month were determined on the basis of territorial potential. If this is the case, the implied causality is reversed or at least confused; instead of the #sales reps and #TV spots determining sales, (potential) sales determine the former quantities, and they in turn could be expected to affect realized sales. If this scenario holds, the coefficient-estimating procedure needs to take into account the two-way "causation" among the variables via the estimation of simultaneous equation systems.

that 87.4% of the variation in sales is associated with variation in TV spots and #sales reps. The new sales reps variable has improved the fit of the regression line; 87.4% of the variation in sales is accounted for by the two-predictor variable model, whereas only 77.5% had been accounted for previously by the one-predictor model. The square root of this quantity, $R_{Y.12} = .935$, is the coefficient of multiple correlation. (While r ranges from -1.0 to $+1.0$, and r^2 from .0 to 1.0, both R and R^2 range from .0 to 1.0.)

Coefficients of Partial Correlation

Two additional quantities must be considered when interpreting the results of a multiple-regression analysis that are not present in simple-regression analysis: the coefficient of partial correlation and its square, the coefficient of partial determination.

In simple regression, when we relate sales Y to TV spots X_1, we write the coefficient of simple determination as:

$$r_{Y.1}^2 = 1 - \frac{(unexplained\ variation)}{(total\ variation)} = 1 - \frac{s_{Y.1}^2}{s_Y^2}$$

where the unexplained variation is given by the square of standard error of estimate, $s_{Y.1}^2$, and total variation, by the variance in the criterion variable s_Y^2.

For multiple regression with two predictor variables, X_1 and X_2, we denote the standard error of estimate by $s_{Y.12}$ and its square by $s_{Y.12}^2$. The standard error of estimate measures the variation still remaining in the criterion variable Y after the two predictor variables X_1 and X_2 have been taken into account. Since $s_{Y.1}^2$ measures the variation in the criterion variable that remains after the first predictor variable has been taken into account, the ratio $s_{Y.12}^2/s_{Y.1}^2$ can be interpreted as measuring the relative degree to which the association among the three variables Y, X_1, and X_2 provides information about Y over and above that provided by the association between the criterion variable and the first predictor variable alone. In other words, the ratio $s_{Y.12}^2/s_{Y.1}^2$ measures the relative degree to which X_2 adds to the knowledge about Y after X_1 has already been fully utilized. The ratio is the basis for the **coefficient of partial determination**, which in the sales (Y) versus TV spots (X_1) and number of sales representatives (X_2) example is:

$$r_{Y2.1}^2 = 1 - \frac{s_{Y.1}^2}{s_Y^2} = 1 - \frac{(45.2)^2}{(59.6)^2} = 1 - .576 = .424$$

This result means that 42.4% of the variation in sales, not associated with TV spots, is incrementally associated with the number of sales reps. Alternatively, the errors made in estimating sales from TV spots are, as measured by the variance, reduced by 42.4% when the sales reps variable X_2 is added to X_1 as an additional predictor. The square root of the coefficient of partial determination is the **coefficient of partial correlation**.

Our example had two predictors. Thus, we defined the coefficient of partial determination for the number of sales representatives X_2 as $r_{Y2.1}^2$. We could similarly define a coefficient of partial determination for TV spots. It would be denoted as $r_{Y1.2}^2$, and it would represent the percentage of the variation in sales not associated with X_2 that is incrementally associated with X_1; this latter coefficient would show the incremental contribution of X_1 after the association between Y and X_2 had already been considered.

When there are more than two predictors, we can define many more coefficients of partial determination. If we had three predictor variables, we could calculate $r_{Y2.1}$, $r_{Y3.1}$, $r_{Y1.2}$, $r_{Y3.2}$, $r_{Y1.3}$, and $r_{Y2.3}$. We could also calculate $r_{Y1.23}$, $r_{Y2.13}$, and $r_{Y3.12}$.

Summary

This chapter examined the question of association or covariation between variables when one of the variables is considered a criterion variable. Simple regression and correlation analysis are the primary statistical devices for analyzing the association between a single predictor and a single criterion variable. This model allows the estimation of a functional equation relating the variables, as well as an estimate of the strength of the association between them. Some of the more useful outputs from a simple-regression analysis are the following:

1. The functional equation, which allows the prediction of the criterion variable for assumed values of the predictor variable

2. The standard error of estimate, which provides an absolute measure of the lack of fit of the equation to the data

3. The coefficient of determination, which provides a relative assessment of the goodness of fit of the equation

4. The slope coefficient, which indicates how much the criterion variable changes, on the average, per unit of change in the predictor variable

The regression model is readily extended to incorporate multiple predictor variables to estimate the criterion variable. If the predictor variables are not correlated among themselves, each partial regression coefficient indicates the average change in the criterion variable per unit change in the predictor variable in question, holding the other predictor variables constant. If the predictor variables are correlated among themselves, little substantive meaning can be attached to the slope coefficients, although the regression equation often can be used successfully for prediction. The coefficient of multiple determination measures the proportion of the variation in the dependent variable explained by all the predictor variables. The coefficient of partial determination measures the relative degree to which a given variable adds to our knowledge of the criterion variable over and above the other predictor variables.

Questions

1. What is the distinction between statistical tests for group differences and tests to investigate association?

2. What is the difference between regression analysis and correlation analysis?

3. What assumptions are made about the error term in the least-squares solution to the regression problem? When the analyst wishes to make an inference about a regression population parameter, what additional assumption is necessary?

4. What is the standard error of estimate?

5. Suppose that an analyst wished to make an inference about the slope coefficient in a regression model. What is the appropriate procedure? What does it mean if the null hypothesis is rejected? If it is not rejected?

6. What is the correlation coefficient, and what does it measure? What is the coefficient of determination, and what does it measure?

Applications and Problems

1. The quality of public school education has become a major political issue. In many states, dissatisfied parents vote for school-choice legislation that allows them to use public money to send their children to the school they deem most appropriate. Under some school-choice legislation, parents can even choose to send their children to private schools and pay only the difference between the amount charged by the private school and the amount it would have cost to send the child to a public school.

One local school district in which parents were calling for school-choice reform hired a marketing research company to assess customer satisfaction and relate this satisfaction to demographic variables. The school district had hypothesized that satisfaction was related to income levels, with those earning more money being more dissatisfied with the public school system. The research company found that income explained only 10% of the total variance in school satisfaction; thus, the company stated that no relationship existed between income and school satisfaction. Given the analysis described, is this a valid conclusion for the research company to make? Why?

2. A cereal manufacturer believes that there is an association between cereal sales and the number of facings the cereal has on each store's shelves. Eight stores were surveyed to test this hypothesis. The data are as follows:

Facings	Sales
5	45
6	50
6	52
7	53
5	44
7	57
6	49
8	56

a. Is there an association between shelf facings and sales?
b. Is it appropriate to state that increased shelf facings produce additional sales?
c. What other variables may help predict cereal sales?

3. The Brite-Lite Bottling Company, which provides glass bottles to various soft-drink manufacturers, has the following information pertaining to the number of cases per shipment, size of cartons, and the corresponding transportation cost:

#Cases per Shipment (00's)	Size of Carton (cubic inches)	Transportation Costs ($)
15	12	200
22	16	260
35	20	310
43	24	360
58	28	420
65	32	480
73	36	540
82	40	630
85	44	710
98	48	730

The marketing manager is interested in the relationship between the number of cases per shipment and the transportation costs. You're supposed to help with the regression.

a. Plot the transportation costs as a function of the number of cases per shipment.
b. Interpret the scatter diagram.
c. Calculate the coefficients $\widehat{\alpha}$ and $\widehat{\beta}$, develop the regression equation, and interpret the coefficients.
d. Calculate the standard error of estimate and interpret it.
e. Compute the t-value with $n - 2$ degrees of freedom with the use of the following formula for the square root of the variance of the distribution of βs:

$$s_{\widehat{\beta}_1} = \sqrt{\frac{s^2_{Y/X}}{\sum_{i=1}^{10}(X_i - x)^2}}$$

$$t = \frac{\widehat{\beta}_1 - \beta_1}{s_{\widehat{\beta}_1}}$$

where β is assumed to be zero under the null hypothesis of no relationship; that is,

$$H_0 : \beta_1 = 0$$
$$H_0 : \beta_1 \neq 0$$

f. What is the tabled t-value at a .05 significance level?
g. What can you conclude about the relationship between transportation costs and number of cases shipped?
h. The marketing manager wants to estimate the transportation costs for 18 cases.
   i. Use the regression model to derive the average value of Y_0.
   ii. Provide a confidence interval for the estimate.

4. Using the same data, imagine that the marketing manager of Brite-Lite Company wants to determine if there is an association between the size of carton and the transportation cost per shipment. (The company follows a policy of including the same-sized cartons for any particular shipment.) Refer to the previous question for information on the transportation costs per shipment and size of carton.

a. Calculate the correlation coefficient and interpret it.
b. Determine the coefficient of determination and interpret it.

5. Working with the Brite-Lite data, suppose that the marketing manager wants to see a multiple-regression analysis with number of cartons per shipment and size of cartons as predictor variables and transportation costs as the criterion variable. The marketing researcher has devised the following regression equation:

$$\widehat{Y} = \widehat{\alpha}_{(12)} + \widehat{\beta}_{Y1.2} X_1 + \widehat{\beta}_{Y2.1} X_2$$
$$= -41.44 - 3.95 X_1 + 24.44 X_2$$

where X_1 is the number of cartons per shipment and X_2 is the size of the carton.
a. Interpret $\widehat{\alpha}_{(12)}$, $\widehat{\beta}_{Y1.2}$, and $\widehat{\beta}_{Y2.1}$.
b. Is multiple regression appropriate in this situation? If yes, why? If no, why not?

6. Carol Lynne and K. C. Lee are leaders of a popular local country and western band. Each week from late spring to early fall, the band played an outdoor concert at a different park located in the city. Advertising for the concerts consisted of handbills posted around the city on public billboards, at supermarkets, and so on. During some weeks, Carol, K. C., and the other band members were able to distribute many handbills; during other weeks, fewer were distributed. Similarly, many people attended some concerts, and only a few attended others. At the end of the summer, the band wanted to know if there were any relationship between the number of handbills that were distributed and the number of people attending its concerts. Following are the approximate number of handbills distributed each week along with the number of people attending that week's concert:

# Handbills	# People
900	625
550	400
750	450
300	200
600	500
1000	650
400	375
325	350
675	400
200	200
500	500
150	125
500	300
700	550
600	400

a. Develop and interpret a scatter diagram showing the number of people as a function of the number of handbills.
b. Calculate $\widehat{\alpha}$ and $\widehat{\beta}$, and fit a regression equation using a statistical software package.
c. Interpret $\widehat{\alpha}$ and $\widehat{\beta}$. Be specific.
d. What is the standard error of estimate, and what is its interpretation in this situation?
e. What is the t-value associated with $\widehat{\beta}$? Is this value significant at the .05 level? If so, what can be concluded about the relationship between the number of handbills distributed and the number of people attending the concerts?
f. How much of the variance in the number of people attending the concerts can be explained by the number of handbills delivered?
g. What are some other factors that might be included in a multiple-regression model to explain the number of people attending the concerts?

Appendix: Conjoint Analysis

17

Questions to Guide Your Learning:

Q1 What is a variable transformation?

Q2 What is a dummy variable?

Q3 What is a conjoint analysis? How does this method help us study consumer "trade-offs"?

Q4 How do I run a conjoint analysis: What kind of data are needed, and how do I do it?

In this appendix, we focus on conjoint analysis. A number of conjoint approaches have been offered, but consistently the best-performing technique is regression-based. Hence, following our discussion of regression, we look at the machinery of a conjoint. The trick is running regressions with dummy variables. We get to dummy variables shortly, and conjoint after that, but we start with "transformations" as a more general issue.

Variable Transformations

Simple or multiple regressions should really always be called "simple linear regression" and "multiple linear regression," because each models linear relationships among variables. The scope of the regression model and its applicability may be expanded by transforming variables.

A variable transformation is simply a change in the scale in which the given variable is expressed. Consider the model

$$Y = \alpha X_1^{\beta_1} X_2^{\beta_2} X_3^{\beta_3} \varepsilon$$

in which the relationships are assumed to be multiplicative. At first glance, it would seem impossible to estimate the parameters α, β_1, β_2, β_3 using our normal least-squares procedures. However, consider the model

$$W = \ell n(Y) = \alpha' + \beta_1 Z_1 + \beta_2 Z_2 + \beta_3 Z_3 + \varepsilon'$$

This model is linear, so it can be fitted by the standard least-squares procedures, and it is exactly equivalent to our multiplicative model if we simply let:

$$
\begin{aligned}
W &= \ell n(Y) \\
\alpha' &= \ell n(\alpha) \\
Z_1 &= \ell n(X_1) \\
Z_2 &= \ell n(X_2) \\
Z_3 &= \ell n(X_3) \\
\varepsilon' &= \ell n(\varepsilon)
\end{aligned}
$$

Thus, we have converted a nonlinear model to a linear model using variable transformations. To solve for the parameters of our multiplicative model, we simply:

1. Take the natural log of Y and each of the Xs
2. Solve the resulting equation by the normal least-squares procedures
3. Take the antilog of α' (raise e to α' power) to derive an estimate of α
4. Read the values of the β_i, because they are the same in both models

This transformation involved both the criterion and predictor variables. It is also possible to change either, but not both. Exponential and logarithmic transformations are very useful, because they relax the constraints imposed by the assumptions that the relationship between the criterion variable and the predictor variables is linear and additive, and that the errors are homoscedastic (constant for all values of the predictors).

In the next section, we discuss dummy variables. They offer another form of transformation, to allow for nonlinearities, and nominal or ordinal variables in regression.

Dummy Variables

The analysis of the sales data from the previous chapter is not complete. No attention was given to the effect of distribution on sales, as measured by the wholesaler efficiency index. One way of considering the effect of wholesaler efficiency on sales is to introduce the index directly; i.e., the X_3 value for each observation is simply the value recorded in the last column of the dataset. Letting X_3 represent the wholesaler efficiency index, the multiple-regression equation is:

$$Y = \alpha + \beta_1 X_1 + \beta_2 X_2 + \beta_3 X_3 + \varepsilon$$

The least-squares estimate of β_3 in this equation turns out to be $\widehat{\beta}_3 = 11.5$. If the predictor variables are independent, this beta means that the estimated average change in sales is $11,500 for each unit change in the wholesaler efficiency index. Thus, a fair distributor could be expected to sell $11,500 more on the average than a poor one; a good one could be expected to average $11,500 more than a fair one; and an excellent one could be expected to sell $11,500 more on the average than a good one. The sales increments are assumed to be constant for each change in wholesaler rating. The implication is that the wholesaler efficiency index is an interval-scaled variable and that the difference between a poor and a fair wholesaler is the same as the difference between a fair one and a good one. You might not be comfortable with this assumption for rating scales.

An alternative way of proceeding is to convert the rating index into a set of dummy variables, that is, binary variables. A binary variable takes on one of two values, 0 or 1. They are very flexible; they can provide a numerical representation for attributes or characteristics that are not essentially quantitative. For example, one could introduce gender into a regression equation using the dummy variable X_i, where

$X_i = 0$ if the person is female

$X_i = 1$ if the person is male

The technique is readily extended to handle multichotomous as well as dichotomous classifications. For instance, suppose that one wanted to introduce the variable social class into a regression equation, and there were three distinct class levels: upper, middle, and lower class. This could be handled using two dummy variables, say, X_1 and X_2, where

	X_1	X_2
• if a person belongs to the upper class	1	0
• if a person belongs to the middle class	0	1
• if a person belongs to the lower class	0	0

Given that alternative coding schemes could be used (e.g., X_1 to denote middle class and X_2 to denote lower class), it is important that the interpretation be tied back to the coding of the variables. A classification with m categories is unambiguous when represented by a set of $m - 1$ binary variables; an mth dummy variable is superfluous.

Suppose that we were to employ three dummy variables to represent the four-category wholesaler efficiency index in the sales model and that

	X_3	X_4	X_5
• if a wholesaler is poor	0	0	0
• if a wholesaler is fair	1	0	0
• if a wholesaler is good	0	1	0
• if a wholesaler is excellent	0	0	1

The regression model is:

$$Y = \alpha + \beta_1 X_1 + \beta_2 X_2 + \beta_3 X_3 + \beta_4 X_4 + \beta_5 X_5 + \varepsilon$$

The least-squares estimates of the wholesaler efficiency parameters are:

$$\widehat{\beta_3} = 9.2 \qquad \widehat{\beta_4} = 20.3 \qquad \widehat{\beta_5} = 33.3$$

These coefficients indicate that on the average, a fair wholesaler could be expected to sell \$9,200 more than a poor one, a good wholesaler could be expected to sell \$20,300 more than a poor one, and an excellent wholesaler could sell \$33,300 more than a poor one. Note that all these coefficients are interpreted relative to the baseline which has the codes of {0, 0, 0} ("poor" in this case).

The coefficient differences tell us about the difference in sales effectiveness. The estimated difference in expected sales from a good wholesaler and a fair wholesaler is $\widehat{\beta_4} - \widehat{\beta_3} = 20.3 - 9.2 = 11.1$ (that is, \$11,100). Similarly, an excellent wholesaler could be expected on the average to sell $\widehat{\beta_5} - \widehat{\beta_4} = 33.3 - 20.3 = 13.0$ (i.e., \$13,000) more than a good one.

The use of dummy variables indicates that the relationship between sales and the wholesaler efficiency index is not linear as was assumed when the index was introduced as a single interval-scaled variable. Instead of an across-the-board increase of \$11,500 with each rating change, the respective increases are 9.2 (\$9,200) from poor to fair, 11.1 (\$11,100) from fair to good, and 13.0 (\$13,000) from good to excellent.

Conjoint Analysis

A very special implementation of a dummy variable regression is conjoint analysis, or conjoint measurement. Consumers make judgments about preferences among products or brands, where the products or brands they're responding to represent some systematic combinations of attributes. The goal is to determine the features that respondents most prefer. Consumers might use such attributes as miles per gallon, seating capacity, price, length of warranty, and so on, in making judgments about which automobile they prefer. Yet, if asked to do so directly, many respondents find it difficult to state which attributes they were thinking about and how they were combining them to form overall judgments. Rather than trying to obtain a sense of which attributes are important directly from consumers' self-reports, consumers are simply asked for their preferences and their value systems are inferred from those choices.

RESEARCH   REALITIES

17A.1 Conjoint Analysis in Marketing Research

Conjoint analysis is extremely popular in marketing research. The data are easy to get and it's easy to run the analyses. Conjoint analysis is frequently applied in new product design:

• Lands' End may be the first apparel retailer to have used conjoint analysis. They presented six pairs of outfits to customers, asking which of each pair was preferred. From these data were derived combinations of features personally customized to each respondent's preferences, e.g., button-down, cotton vs. wool sweaters, color, price, etc. The intention clearly is to enhance the customer's satisfaction, including ease of Web transactions.[1]

• The EZPass transponder toll system between New York and New Jersey was designed to optimize drivers' satisfaction via a conjoint study. Combinations of price, lane usage, whether the tags would be transferable across vehicles within a household, etc., were evaluated by 3,369 commuters via RDD. The overall conjoint results demonstrated which features should be emphasized (number of lanes) and which could be de-emphasized in the design of the electronic toll system (tag transference across vehicles).[2]

• Researchers studied parents' willingness to pay for their children to be vaccinated with one of the three new products. Product profiles varied by "type of infection covered," "duration of coverage," and "price," producing 18 combinations in all for examination.[3]

Conjoint analysis is also big in marketing pricing studies:

• It's difficult to obtain data on price sensitivities on regular surveys. When asked what price we're willing to pay for some product, we all choose the lowest possibility offered. In conjoint however, whereas our preferences might begin with low prices, the advantage of studying "trade-offs" means that at some point, we must either pay more to get more, or continue to pay less but also get less.[4]

Conjoint analysis has also been used in segmentation:

• Segments of "green" customers attach greater benefit to environmentally friendly products, for some purchases to the point of being price insensitive, compared with "less green" customers who do not value the green or energy-saving attributes as much.

[1] David Lipke, "Product by Design," *American Demographics,* adage.com.

[2] Terry G. Vavra, Paul E. Green, and Abba M. Krieger, "Evaluating EZPass: Using Conjoint Analysis to Assess Consumer Response to a New Tollway Technology," *Marketing Research,* 11, 5–13.

[3] Claudine Sapede and Isabelle Girod, "Willingness of Adults in Europe to Pay for a New Vaccine," *International Journal of Market Research* 44, 463–476.

[4] Kamel Jedidi and John Zhang, "Augmenting Conjoint Analysis to Estimate Consumer Reservation Price," *Management Science,* 48, 1350–1368; Tulin Erdem, Joffre Swait, and Jordan Louviere, "The Impact of Brand Credibility on Consumer Price Sensitivity," *International Journal of Research in Marketing,* 19, 1–19.

The word conjoint has to do with the notion that the relative values of things **con**sidered **joint**ly can be measured when they might not be measurable if taken one at a time. Typically, respondents would be asked to order the stimuli (products, brands, etc.) from most to least desirable. In doing so, the consumer implies the relative value of the features that comprise the various stimuli. The conjoint analysis assigns values to the levels of each of the attributes that describe consumer's opinions. Research Realities 17A.1 offers a sampling of the questions marketing researchers have answered using conjoint techniques.

Example

Suppose that we are considering introducing a new coffee maker and wish to assess how consumers evaluate the following levels of each of these product attributes:

- Capacity—4, 8, and 10 cups
- Price—$28, $32, and $38
- Brewing time—3, 6, 9, and 12 minutes

Conjoint analysis allows us to study how consumers make trade-offs.

For all three of these attributes, most consumers would probably prefer either the most or least of each property—the largest capacity maker, the shortest brewing time, at the lowest price. Unfortunately, life is not that simple. The larger coffee maker costs more to manufacture; faster brewing means a larger heating element for the same pot capacity, which also raises the cost; a larger-capacity maker with no change in the heating element requires increased brewing time. In sum, a consumer is going to have to **trade-off** some of one feature to obtain more of another. The manufacturer is interested in determining how consumers value these specific attributes. Is low price most valued, or are consumers willing to pay a higher price to secure some of the other features? At what price should the coffee maker go to market, and with what other attributes?

To answer these questions, we would form all possible combinations of these product attributes, 36 combinations in all, and describe each coffee maker on an index card or a separate computer screen. We would then ask a respondent to order these product descriptions from least desirable (rank = 1) to most desirable (rank = 36), with higher numbers reflecting greater preference. Suppose that the ordering contained in Table 17A.1 resulted from this process.

Note that, as we anticipated, the respondent preferred least the $38 maker with 4-cup capacity and 12-minute brewing time (rank = 1) and preferred most the 10-cup maker with 3-minute brewing time priced at $28 (rank = 36). If the respondent cannot have his/her 1st choice, she/he is willing to "suffer" with a longer brewing time to get the 10-cup maker for $28 (rank = 35). The consumer

TABLE 17A.1   Respondent Ordering of Product Descriptions

Brewing Time (minutes)	Capacity: 4 cups			8 cups			10 cups		
	Price $28	$32	$38	$28	$32	$38	$28	$32	$38
3 mins	17	15	6	30	26	24	36	34	28
6 mins	16	12	5	29	25	22	35	33	27
9 mins	9	8	3	21	20	8	32	31	23
12 mins	4	2	1	14	13	7	19	18	11

is not willing to suffer too much, though, as reflected by the 3rd choice (rank = 34). Rather, the consumer is willing to pay a little more to secure the faster 3-minute brewing time rather than having to endure an even slower 9-minute brewing time, in effect, showing a willingness to trade-off price for brewing time.

The conjoint analysis attempts to answer these questions: What are the individual's utilities for price, brewing time, and pot capacity in determining preferences and choices?

Procedure

Several analytical procedures have been used to run a conjoint analysis. Yet dummy variable regressions increasingly are being used to estimate the components of a conjoint analysis. The consumer's preferences (e.g., the judgments of 1 through 36) would form the dependent variable, and dummy variables representing the attributes (such as price) would comprise the predictors. The advantages of the dummy variable regression approach include:

• The wide availability of regression software

• The wide understanding and accessibility of regression as a model

• Demonstrable robustness and comparable results of the dummy variable approach compared to alternative, more sophisticated approaches

To demonstrate, suppose we create dummy variables for each of the attributes:

X_1 = 1 if brewing time = 6 minutes (otherwise, X_1 = 0),

X_2 = 1 if brewing time = 9 minutes

X_3 = 1 if brewing time = 12 minutes

Y_1 = 1 if capacity = 8 cups

Y_2 = 1 if capacity = 10 cups

Z_1 = 1 if price = $32

Z_2 = 1 if price = $38

and fit a regression model to the preference judgments:

$$\text{Predicted preference} = \beta_1 X_1 + \beta_2 X_2 + \beta_3 X_3 + \beta_4 Y_1 + \beta_5 Y_2 + \beta_6 Z_1 + \beta_7 Z_2$$

The beta weights reflect the consumer's "utilities" of the attributes.[5] If an attribute did not matter, the beta estimate would be zero (i.e., changing the feature would have no impact on the predicted preference rating). The larger the beta, the more utility the attribute has—the more the consumer cares about it.

For example, fitting a regression to the data in Table 17A.1 yields the following estimates:

$$\text{Predicted preference} = -0.06 X_1 - 0.28 X_2 - 0.59 X_3 + 0.53 Y_1 + 0.86 Y_2 - 0.09 Z_1 - 0.36 Z_2$$

That is, we have obtained the following utilities for each level of these attributes:

Brewing Time		Capacity		Price	
3 minutes	0	4 cups	0	$28	0
6 minutes	−.06	8 cups	.53	$32	20.09
9 minutes	−.28	10 cups	.86	$38	20.36
12 minutes	−.59				

---

[5] They're also called "part-worths," sort of meaning, how much is this part (component such as price) worth?

Most often, a simple additive function is used so that the utility of any combination of features is simply the sum of the utilities of the attribute levels making up the combination. Thus, a 10-cup, 9-minute brewing time, $32 pot would have a utility of .49 (.49 = .86 − .28 − .09). The utilities for each of the other alternatives are shown in Table 17A.2.

These utilities may be plotted against the original judgments to see how well the estimated utilities anticipate the consumer's overall preferences. A measure of the goodness of prediction can be obtained by computing the correlation between the original judgments (the data in Table 17A.1) and the predicted utilities (the values in Table 17A.2). For these data, the utilities have captured the preference structure of the consumer very well, $r = .99$.

In addition, the utility estimates themselves may be plotted to examine whether the relationships between the levels of each attribute and the utility consumers place on the levels are linear or nonmonotonic. The utility estimates for capacity and price look approximately linear: more cups are better than fewer, and less expensive is better than more expensive. Brewing time is slightly quadratic—as waiting time increases, utility drops off faster; thus, a seemingly benign decision to go to market with a brewing time of 12 minutes versus 9 will lose more potential customers than the analogous decision of going to market with 9 minutes versus 6.

> Conjoint analysis tells us what *features* matter most and what *level* of each feature is most (and least) desired.

The relative importance of each of these attributes can be understood by examining the range of utilities between the highest- and lowest-rated levels of the attribute. The rationale is that, if all levels of, say, price have the same utility to an individual, then we would say that price is unimportant to the person or that the person was price insensitive. Conversely, if different levels of price produce widely differing utilities, the individual is sensitive to the levels, implying the attribute is important. In interpreting these importance values, one has to remain cognizant that they depend on the range of the attributes used to structure the stimuli. Thus, if price levels of $28, $38, and $48 were used instead of $28, $32, and $38, the differences in utilities for the various price levels would have been greater, suggesting that price was relatively more important to the individual than other attributes. Given the attribute levels used, capacity is most important and price is least important to the subject.

The real payoff from conjoint analysis comes from the fact that one can use the results to identify the optimal levels and importance of each attribute in structuring a new-product offering. Further, by aggregating consumers who have similar preferences or utility functions, products can be designed that come closer to satisfying particular market segments. Thus, conjoint analysis is quite useful at the concept-evaluation stage of the product-development process.

TABLE 17A.2 Utilities for Feature Combinations

| Brewing Time (minutes) | Capacity: 4 cups | | | 8 cups | | | 10 cups | | |
	Price $28	$32	$38	$28	$32	$38	$28	$32	$38
3 mins	.00	−.09	−.36	.53	.44	.17	.86	.77	.50
6 mins	−.06	−.15	−.42	.47	.38	.11	.80	.71	.44
9 mins	−.28	−.37	−.64	.25	.16	−.11	.58	.49	.22
12 mins	−.59	−.68	−.95	−.06	−.15	−.42	.27	.18	−.09

Key Decisions

The example illustrates a conjoint analysis study, but it is a simple example and does not convey a proper appreciation for the many decisions analysts typically have to make to conduct a conjoint study. Figure 17A.1 highlights the more critical decision points.

Select Attributes

The first step in the process involves deciding on the attributes to be used when constructing the stimuli. When choosing, marketers should be guided by the principles that the attributes used should be both actionable and important to individuals. Actionable attributes are those that the company can do something about; that is, it has the technology or resources to make the changes that might be indicated by consumer preferences.

Important attributes are those that actually affect consumer choice, as determined by managerial judgment or exploratory research. In any single conjoint study, only a handful of all the attributes that could be used are used, so it is important that they be selected with care. When the number of attributes that need to be varied exceed reasonable limits with respect to data-collection problems, a series of conjoint studies can be conducted. The number of attributes actually used in a typical conjoint analysis study averages six or seven.

Determine Attribute Levels

Step 2 involves specifying the actual levels for each attribute. The number of levels for each attribute has a direct bearing on the number of stimuli respondents will be asked to judge and consequently the burden placed on each consumer. In general, we like to minimize that burden (both for the goodwill toward that consumer as well as to try to maintain data quality). At the same time, we like to end up with good estimates of the utility of each attribute level. Our ability to generate good estimates requires that the number of stimuli be relatively large

FIGURE 17A.1 **Key Decisions When Conducting a Conjoint Analysis**

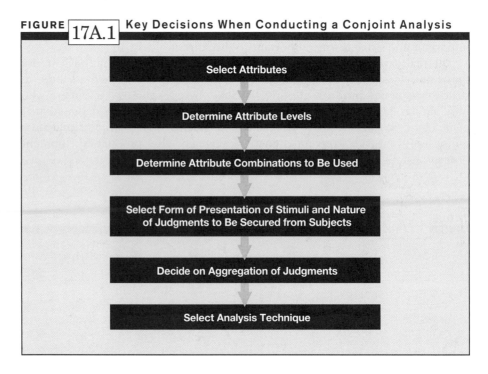

Select Attributes

Determine Attribute Levels

Determine Attribute Combinations to Be Used

Select Form of Presentation of Stimuli and Nature of Judgments to Be Secured from Subjects

Decide on Aggregation of Judgments

Select Analysis Technique

versus the number of parameters that need to be estimated, and the number of parameters in turn depends on the preference model being embraced.

In addition, we must face the question, "Is the model linear in the sense that more or less of the attribute can be expected to be most desired, or nonlinear in some way?" Most subjects may prefer the lowest price or the highest quality when choosing a ballpoint pen, suggesting a linear relationship between their utilities and the attribute levels. At the same time, many may prefer a medium point to a fine or broad point, suggesting that a nonlinear relationship may be appropriate. The nonlinear model requires estimating more parameters than the linear model.

When creating stimuli for a conjoint judgment task, marketers also need to be aware that there is a relationship between the number of levels used to measure an attribute and the inferred importance of the attribute to the respondent. Specifically, the empirical evidence suggests that the more levels one uses for an attribute, the more important the attribute is going to appear in the conjoint. Although analysts might want to include more levels for those attributes expected to produce nonlinear versus linear utility functions, they also need to be aware of the erroneous conclusion this can produce about the importance of each of the attributes.

Another factor that affects the choice of attribute levels is their effect on consumer choice. Using levels that are similar to those in existence increases respondents' believability in the task and the validity of their preference judgments. Using attribute levels outside the range normally encountered decreases the believability of the task for respondents but can increase the accuracy by which the parameters can be estimated statistically. Similarly, decreasing the intercorrelations among the attributes being varied (such as by combining a very low price with very high quality) decreases the believability of the options for respondents but also increases the accuracy with which the parameters can be estimated. The general recommendation seems to be to make the ranges for the various attributes somewhat larger than what is normally found but not so large as to make the options unbelievable.

Determine Attribute Combinations

The third major decision is deciding on the specific combinations of attributes that will be used—that is, what the full set of stimuli will look like. In our example, only three attributes were considered, but the respondent was required to make 36 judgments. Since the number of possible combinations is given by the product of the number of levels of the attributes, one can readily appreciate what happens to the judgment task if the number of attributes or the number of levels for any attribute is increased. Can we reasonably expect a respondent, for example, to provide meaningful judgments if there are five attributes at three levels each (not an unusual case) requiring $3 \times 3 \times 3 \times 3 \times 3 = 3^5 = 243$ rank-order judgments? In such a situation, analysts might be tempted to reduce the number of attributes that are varied (e.g., 3^5) or the number of levels (2^5) at which attributes are set. An alternative scheme is to use only select combinations of the attributes. For example, it is possible to use orthogonal designs to select a subset of the total number of stimuli if the analyst is willing to assume that there are no interactions among the attributes (e.g., that a person's utility for various width tips on a ballpoint pen is independent of the utility for prices).

The example used the "full-profile" approach to collect the judgments—all possible combinations of each of the attributes resulted in its own stimulus. One

FIGURE 17A.2 **Pair-wise Approach to Data Collection in Conjoint Analysis**

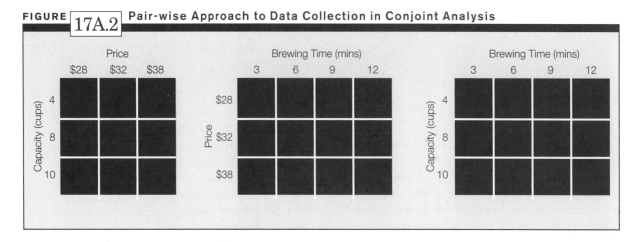

can simplify the judgment task by using a trade-off matrix to structure the stimuli instead of the full-profile approach.[6] The trade-off matrix, or pair-wise procedure, treats two attributes at a time but considers all possible pairs. Thus, in the example, the subject would be asked to indicate preference between each combination of brewing time and price, brewing time and capacity, and price and capacity by independently completing each of the matrices contained in Figure 17A.2.

It is typically easier for subjects to supply pair-wise judgments than full-profile judgments. On the other hand, typically, more pair-wise judgments are required, and one runs a danger of missing some important trade-offs among attributes when the pair-wise approach to data collection is used. There can also be a potential loss in realism when only two attributes are considered at a time, because respondents are then forced to make some implicit assumptions about the levels of the other attributes not explicitly varied. The full-profile approach tends to be more popular than the pair-wise approach in practice.

Another approach uses paired comparisons. An advantage of the paired-comparison approach is that it allows one to check how consistent respondents are in their judgments. Thus, unmotivated or uninterested respondents (those whose answers display a great deal of inconsistency, which suggests that the respondents are not taking the task seriously) can be removed from the analysis. Respondents simply indicate which stimulus in each pair they prefer and by how much. Figure 17A.3, for example, depicts one pair of coffee makers.

Increasingly, any of these data-collection approaches are being administered via computer, which has several advantages:

• The judgments requested from a respondent can be made individual-specific, with different attributes and attribute levels used for each consumer/segment. Thus, respondents can be interviewed in detail about only those attribute

[6] Joel Huber, "What We Have Learned from 20 Years in Conjoint Research," sawtoothsoftware.com. Conjoint analysis continues to be vigorously researched; see Anocha Aribarg and Natasha Zhang Foutz, "Category-Based Screening in Choice of Complementary Products," *Journal of Marketing Research,* to appear; Richard R. Batsell and John B. Elmer, "How to Use Market-Based Pricing to Forecast Consumer Purchase Decisions," *Journal of Pricing Management,* 1 (2), 5–15; Bernhard Baumgartner and Winfried J. Steiner, "Are Consumers Heterogeneous in Their Preferences for Odd and Even Prices?," *International Journal of Research in Marketing,* 24, 312–323; Min Ding, "An Incentive-Aligned Mechanism for Conjoint Analysis," *Journal of Marketing Research,* 44 (3), 214–223; Raghuram Iyengar, Kamel Jedidi, and Rajeev Kohli, "A Conjoint Approach to Multipart Pricing," *Journal of Marketing Research,* 45 (2), 195–210; Bart Vermeulen, Peter Goos, and Martina Vandebroek, "Models and Optimal Designs for Conjoint Choice Experiments Including a No-Choice Option," *International Journal of Research in Marketing,* 25, 94–103. For related research, see Rebecca W. Hamilton and Joydeep Srivastava, "When 2 + 2 Is Not the Same as 1 + 3," *Journal of Marketing Research,* 45 (3), 450–461.

FIGURE 17A.3 Computer-Administered Paired-Comparison Choice

levels that would be acceptable to them and about only those attributes that they regard as important.

- The number of judgments required from an individual can be reduced because the parameters can be estimated iteratively, as soon as a sufficient number of judgments are obtained. Additional questions posed to a respondent can be structured to provide the most incremental information, taking into account what has already been estimated about the respondent's utilities.

- Results can be shown to respondents immediately at the end of the exercise. They can be given the opportunity to comment on how realistically the estimates seem to mirror their preferences. The results can also be given to management more quickly.

Select Form of Presentation of Stimuli and Nature of Judgments

Step 4 in the process involves selecting the form of presentation of the stimuli and the nature of the judgments to be collected from subjects. The full-profile approach has used variations and combinations of three basic approaches—verbal description, paragraph description, and pictorial representation. Verbal description relies on presenting the cues in list form, typically one stimulus per screen, much as was assumed in the coffee-maker example. Paragraph description operates just as the name implies; a paragraph is used to describe each stimulus. Pictorial description relies on some kind of visual prop or three-dimensional model. When visual aids are used, they are typically used in combination with verbal descriptions.

Related to the issue of the form of presentation of the stimuli is the issue of the nature of the judgments that will be secured from respondents. The two most common approaches measure respondents' preferences for each alternative or their intention to buy each alternative. In the earliest applications of conjoint analysis, respondents were asked to rank-order the alternatives according to preference or intention to buy, but rating scales have recently become more popular. Ranks are easy to use for consumers, easy to administer, and keep the judgment task as close as possible to a consumer's behavior while actually shopping. Those using rating scales believe that they are less time consuming, more convenient for respondents to use, and easier to analyze. The nature of the task is different in the two schemes. When the rank-order method is used, consumers are asked to make relative judgments with respect to their preference for one alternative over another. When the rating method is used, the judgments are typically made independently—consumers are asked to indicate their degree of liking of each stimulus by rating their preference or intention-to-buy as each alternative is presented.

Decide on Aggregation of Judgments

Step 5 involves deciding if the responses from individual consumers will be aggregated and, if so, how? Although it is possible to derive the utilities for each level of each attribute at the individual level, much as we did in the example, individual-level results are difficult for marketing managers to use for developing marketing strategy. The other extreme is to pool the results across all consumers and then to estimate one overall utility function. This option fails to recognize any heterogeneity in preference that might exist among respondents, which in turn reduces the predictive power of the model.

The middle ground is to form segments or groups of respondents in such a way that the model has both predictive power and clear marketing-strategy implications for managers. The question, of course, is how these groups should be formed. Typically, segments are formed that are homogeneous with respect to the benefits that the respondents want from the product or service. Operationally, this goal translates into estimating utilities for the individual-level models and then clustering respondents into groups that are homogeneous with respect to the utilities assigned to the various levels of the individual attributes.

An attractive feature of conjoint analysis is that it allows market share predictions for selected product alternatives. For example, a common choice rule is the "1st-choice rule," which assumes that, if the consumer had been shopping, he or she would choose to buy the object that he or she had rated highest in terms of preference. Given the estimated utilities for each level of each attribute, the marketer can predict which of several product options being considered is likely to appeal most to respondents and what may also be the share of preference for each of the other options. The utilities can also be linked with consumers' personal characteristics, e.g., do high-income households have a higher utility for after-sale service than low-income households?

Select Analysis Technique

Step 6 in the execution of a conjoint analysis study involves selecting the technique by which the input data will be analyzed. The choice depends in part on the type of preference model embraced and the method that was used to secure the input judgments. When linear or nonlinear models are hypothesized to capture preference, a parameter estimation model like regression can be used to estimate the functions.

General Comments

Conjoint analysis addresses vital marketing questions in product design, and the technique is not restricted to product evaluations. It can be used whenever one is making a choice among multiattribute alternatives. With multiattribute alternatives, the consumer typically does not have the option of having more of everything that is desirable and less of everything that is not desirable. Instead, most decisions involve trading off part of something in order to get more of something else. Conjoint analysis attempts to mirror the trade-offs a consumer is willing to make. The modeling is rather straightforward, and the payoff (the results) is highly informative, making conjoint among the more popular of marketing research tools. It is most often used for product design and concept evaluation, in applications such as airlines, credit cards, pantyhose, and pharmaceuticals. Conjoint studies are also used regularly in pricing decisions, market segmentation questions, or advertising decisions. Finally, conjoint analysis has been used to evaluate vendors, determine the rewards that a sales force values, and determine consumer preferences for attributes of health organizations, and the list goes on.[7]

Summary

Variable transformations increase the scope of regression models, because they allow certain nonlinear relationships to be considered. Dummy or binary variables allow the introduction of nominal variables in the regression equation.

Conjoint analysis may be viewed as a special application of dummy variable regression, and it is an extremely powerful marketing tool for the planning of product development.

Questions

1. What is a variable transformation? Why is it employed?
2. What is a dummy variable? When is it used? How is it interpreted?

3. What is conjoint analysis? When is it used? How do you run one?

Applications and Problems

1. The management of HotSiteTravel Company decided to introduce new vacation packages. However, management was uncertain about the price and destination to introduce. The marketing research department decided to use conjoint analysis to determine the level of each attribute that would come closest to satisfying consumers. The following levels of each of the product attributes were used:

| Price: | $499/week | $799/week | $1299/week |
| Destination: | Cancun | Miami | San Diego |

A respondent's rank ordering of the various product descriptions are noted here (1 is least preferred, 9 is most preferred):

| | Destination | | |
Price	Cancun	Miami	San Diego
$499	4	1	2
$799	6	5	3
$1299	9	8	7

---

[7] For more on conjoint programs (for both data collection and analysis), see sawtoothsoftware.com, spss.com, and dssresearch.com/library/conjoint. For more research, see Qing Liu, Thomas Otter, and Greg M. Allenby, "Investigating Endogeneity Bias in Marketing," *Marketing Science*, 26 (5), 642–650; and Raj Sethuraman, Roger Kerin, and William Cron, "A Field Study Comparing Online and Offline Data Collection Methods for Identifying Product Attribute Preferences Using Conjoint Analysis," *Journal of Business Research*, 58 (2), 602–610.

The regression assigned the following utilities:

Price	Utility	Destination	Utility
$499	0	Cancun	.6
$799	.43	Miami	.2
$1299	1.03	San Diego	.1

a. Calculate the utilities for all 9 travel package combinations.

b. Plot the original input judgments against the derived utilities from (a). Discuss your findings.

c. How might you characterize a segment that prefers the $499 price? The $1299 price?

d. Would you expect a linear utility function for price? For destination?

2. Imagine you've completed your recruiting, and you have six job offers from which to choose: Job A is on the West Coast and it pays $200,000; B is on the West Coast paying $50,000; C is in the Midwest paying $200,000; D is in the Midwest paying $50,000; E is East Coast at $200,000; and F is East Coast at $50,000.

a. Which job do you prefer? If you cannot take your first choice job, what attribute are you willing to trade-off for the other?

b. If you compare your answers to your friends', do you think salary preferences will tend to be linear? Will location?

Multivariate Data Analysis

18

Questions to Guide Your Learning:

Q1 How are multivariate statistical methods useful?

Q2 What information can a discriminant analysis provide?

Q3 How might a factor analysis help me develop surveys?

Q4 How might I use cluster analysis to assist in a market segmentation study?

Q5 How does multidimensional scaling yield perceptual maps?

I n this chapter, we present the four most popular multivariate statistical techniques for marketing researchers:

1. Discriminant analysis
2. Factor analysis
3. Cluster analysis
4. Multidimensional scaling

We introduce each technique by describing the kinds of problems the method is ideal to solve. We describe the logic underlying each analysis and how to interpret the results.

Discriminant Analysis

Many marketing problems involve the investigation of group differences. Two or more groups are compared and the question is: do the groups differ, and if so, how. For example, we might be interested in determining the characteristics that differentiate the following:

• Light and heavy users of a product
• Purchasers of our brand and those of competing brands
• Good, mediocre, and poor sales representatives
• Good and poor loan risks

Suppose the groups were to be compared along demographic-socioeconomic lines. We might calculate the mean income, age, and education level to determine the profiles for each group. We could compare the groups on one variable at a time, to become more familiar with the data, and form hypotheses about how the groups are different. However, such a univariate analysis would not indicate the relative importance of each variable. Furthermore, the variables are likely to be at least somewhat correlated, so the tests of each variable not independent.

Suppose that we were investigating the characteristics that distinguish light from heavy investors of our mutual funds. If the groups differed on mean income levels, it is also likely that they would show a difference in educational level, because these two variables are fairly highly correlated. Yet if we were interested in segmenting the market using income and education, we would want to use the total effect of both variables in combination, not their separate effects. Further, we would be interested in determining which of the variables was more important or had the greater impact (e.g., like comparing the size of betas in multiple regression).

Discriminant analysis is a method of constructing a linear combination of the variables (i.e., a weighted sum) in such a way that this newly created variable optimally discriminates among the groups. We can then assess how the groups differ with respect to this new score, and we can look at the weights assigned to each of the variables to understand their relative importance.

When two groups are being compared, one linear combination, or discriminant function, results. When the technique is applied to the analysis of three or more groups (e.g., light, medium, and heavy users), several discriminant functions can result.

Two-Group Case

We begin with the simple case of two groups. Consider the following example. A pharmaceuticals firm that relied upon a large sales force conducted a "new account" sales contest among its salespeople to try to increase the number of distributors handling the firm's products. The contest ran for three months. Each salesperson was assigned a quota for the number of new accounts he or she was expected to generate in that period. The quotas were determined by the sales analysis department, which had historic data on the penetration of different industry segments and the number of accounts of each type that were not current customers in each sales territory. All salespeople who had 15 or more new accounts placed an order during the contest period received an all-expense-paid vacation for two to Hawaii. Salespeople who had at least five new accounts received an HDTV. Those converting fewer than five new accounts received nothing. As it turned out, 15 salespeople won the grand prize, another 15 the consolation prize, and a third of the salespeople won nothing.

The sales analysis department wanted to know what sales activities made a difference in terms of whether a salesperson was a prize winner or not. To demonstrate a two-group discriminant analysis, we will look at what activities had the greatest impact on whether a salesperson won a grand prize vs. a consolation prize (we'll compare all three groups later).

Table 18.1 contains the data that the sales analysis department collected on the new account activities. Figure 18.1 contains a plot of two of the variables, and it depicts who the grand prize winners and consolation prize winners are. In general, the "percentage of calls with advance appointments" and "total number of calls" were positively related to success; the more of these activities, the more likely the salesperson was to be a grand prize winner than a consolation prize winner. There were exceptions, though. Some consolation prize winners made more calls on new accounts than did grand prize winners. Similarly, some grand prize winners made fewer advance appointments than did consolation prize winners. Overall, however, the grand prize winners made more calls, and did so with appointments.

The graphical approach is intuitively insightful, but it has its limitations. First, it is time consuming to construct all the graphs that might be useful. Even with

Discriminant Analysis: Salespeople's New Account Activities

TABLE **18.1**

Grand Prize Winner (W)	# Calls New Accounts X_1	% with Advance Appointments X_2	Calls to Prospects X_3	# New Accounts Visited X_4
1 RMB	130	62	148	42
2 ALB	122	70	186	44
3 BCC	89	68	171	32
4 JJC	104	58	135	40
5 EDC	116	40	160	36
6 WPD	100	65	151	30
7 RHH	85	66	183	42
8 BEK	113	59	130	25
9 DAK	108	52	163	41
10 JJN	116	48	154	48
11 MYS	99	57	188	32
12 PJS	78	70	190	40
13 CET	106	61	157	38
14 LLV	94	58	173	29
15 LMW	98	64	137	36
Mean	103.9	59.9	161.7	37.0
Consolation Prize Winner (C)				
1 JGB	105	39	155	45
2 RAB	86	60	140	33
3 HAF	64	48	132	36
4 PPD	104	36	119	29
5 BCE	102	53	143	41
6 ASG	73	62	128	30
7 WLH	94	51	152	36
8 LHL	59	64	130	28
9 RJL	84	31	102	32
10 WFM	91	47	96	35
11 JRP	83	40	87	30
12 EJS	95	42	114	28
13 VES	68	52	123	26
14 HMT	101	51	98	24
15 BMT	89	39	117	33
Mean	86.5	47.7	122.4	32.4
Unsuccessful Salespeople (U)				
1 RBB	80	23	69	32
2 GEB	47	42	74	33
3 ADC	26	37	132	20
4 JFC	94	24	68	26
5 LDE	57	32	94	23
6 JFH	38	41	83	28
7 JCH	29	52	96	22
8 RPF	48	24	73	26
9 APL	57	36	82	28
10 HAL	39	37	98	21
11 ERM	51	38	117	24
12 WRR	40	42	112	22

(Continued)

TABLE 18.1 Continued				
Unsuccessful Salespeople (U)	# Calls New Accounts X_1	% with Advance Appointments X_2	Calls to Prospects X_3	# New Accounts Visited X_4
13 JTS	64	21	67	29
14 JMV	35	32	78	25
15 HEY	51	29	81	26
Mean	50.4	34.0	88.3	25.7
Overall Mean	80.3	47.2	124.1	31.7

only four variables, there are six possible pairs to graph,[1] and higher dimensional graphs become difficult to interpret. We need a mechanism to assess the effect of each factor, taking into account the factors' partially overlapping information.

Determining the Coefficients

To differentiate the two groups, we build an index that separates them on the basis of their measured characteristics. The index is a linear combination of four components: number of calls on new accounts X_1, percentage of calls with advance appointments X_2, telephone calls made to prospects X_3, and number of new accounts visited X_4:

$$Y = v_1 X_1 + v_2 X_2 + v_3 X_3 + v_4 X_4$$

where v_1, v_2, v_3, and v_4 are the weights indicating the importance of each X in helping us distinguish the prize winning groups. The equation is called a linear combination—we're "combining" the information contained in the four X variables to create a single new score, Y. The equation is "linear" because once the Xs are multiplied by their importance weights, the terms are simply added together (or subtracted, with no terms such as $X_1 X_2$).

FIGURE 18.1   Scatter Plot on Sales Force Data

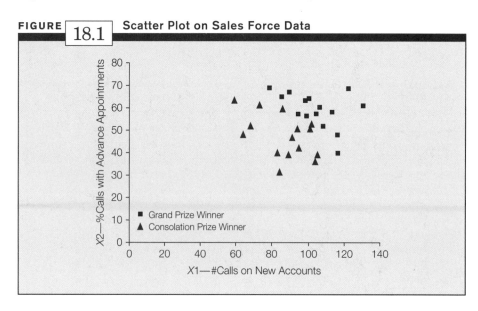

---

[1] The number of possible two-way graphs for m variables is given by the standard combinatorial formula:
$$\binom{m}{2} = \frac{m!}{(m-2)!2!} = \frac{m(m-1)}{2}.$$

Given values for v_1 through v_4, we can calculate a Y or index score for each of the 30 prize winners. The question is how to derive values for the weights, v_1 through v_4?

In discriminant analysis, the weights are derived so that the variation in Y scores (i.e., the new index) between the two groups is as large as possible, while the variation in Y scores within the groups is as small as possible. That is, the ratio of "between-group differences" to "within-group differences" is maximized.

To keep this simple, consider for the moment only X_1 (# calls on new accounts) and X_2 (# calls with advance appointments). Given values for v_1 and v_2, we would calculate a Y score for each of the 30 prize winners using the linear combination:

$$Y = v_1 X_1 + v_2 X_2$$

It turns out that the values for v_1 and v_2 that maximize the ratio of the between-group to within-group variation with respect to the new index scores are $v_1 = .064$ and $v_2 = .106$:

$$Y = .064 X_1 + .106 X_2$$

We can calculate each salesperson's score on the new index, and we can graph the model, because most algebraic concepts (e.g., a linear combination of variables) have geometric counterparts (e.g., a new axis in the plot). In Figure 18.1, we draw the axis from the origin to the coordinates (.064, .106), which are the v-weights.[2] Figure 18.2 contains the new axis that represents the linear combination. (Note the axis does not necessarily go through the scatterplot, as we expect for regression lines.) Take each person's data point and "project" it onto the new axis; that is, draw a line from each data point to the axis in such a way that the line drawn is perpendicular to the axis. These projections represent the Y scores that we have computed using the discriminant analysis equation. What had been a two-dimensional scatterplot (X_1 versus X_2) is now simplified to a frequency distribution on the one-dimensional line (Y).

Once all the data points have been projected onto the discriminant axis, note that most of the consolation prize winners are lower on the new dimension than most of the grand prize winners. The distinction is not perfect (there is some overlap), but given that the v-weights were determined in a way to optimally separate the groups, there are no other v-weights, or no other orientation of that axis in the plot, that could yield better discrimination between the groups.[3]

We can now use Y, the index score from the discriminant analysis model, to classify each salesperson as a grand prize winner or a consolation prize winner. If the salesperson's index score is closer to the mean of the grand prize winners' index scores, we would classify him or her as a grand prize winner, and vice versa.

---

[2] The plot is scaled from 0 to 140 on X_1 and 0 to 80 on X_2, so it is more convenient to draw the line from the origin to a multiple of the v-weights, e.g., to the coordinates (64, 106).

[3] Once the axis is drawn, there is also a relationship between the (algebraic) *correlations* among $\{X_1, X_2, Y\}$, and the (geometric) *cosines* of angles between X_1 and X_2 and the new axis, Y. For example, if X is horizontal, and Y is vertical, we would say they're perpendicular (90 degree angle, cosine = 0). The variables associated with those placements would be: $\{1,0\}$ and $\{0,1\}$, and we'd also say they were uncorrelated. If X is horizontal, and Y was right on top of it, both variables would be $\{1,0\}$, they'd be correlated $r = 1.0$, and we'd say they are multicollinear (0 degree angle between them, cosine = 1). If X is horizontal $\{1,0\}$ and Y is horizontal but $\{-1,0\}$, they'd be opposites, correlated $r = -1.0$ (angle is 180 degrees, cosine = -1). In our example, take each weight, say, v_1 for X_1 (.064), divide by the square root of the sum of the squared v-weights, and this is the cosine of the angle between X_1 and the new axis: $(.064)^2 + (.106)^2 = .015$, and $\sqrt{.015} = .122$. Since $.064/.122 = .525$, the angle θ between the X_1 and the new discriminant axis is given by $\cos \theta = .525$, or $\theta = 58°$. Cool, huh?

FIGURE 18.2   Discriminant Analysis Plot with New Axis

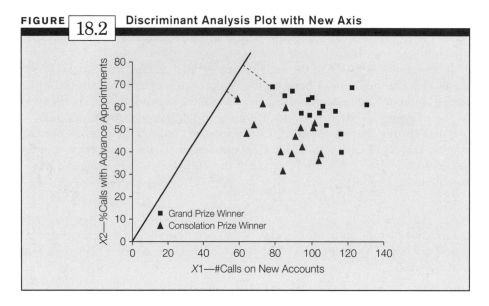

Now let's proceed to the more complex, four-variable problem. The discriminant weights are $v_1 = .058$, $v_2 = .063$, $v_3 = .034$, and $v_4 = -.032$, so the linear combination that maximally differentiates between the groups is:[4]

$$Y = .058X_1 + .063X_2 + .034X_3 - .032X_4$$

The function presents the weights to be applied to X_1 through X_4 so that the distribution of Y scores show the largest separation (or, distinguish most clearly) between grand prize and consolation prize winners (compared to any other possible linear combination that could have been formed). These Y scores are known as discriminant scores, and they are presented for our sample in Table 18.2. You can see that the discriminant scores of grand prize winners are similar in magnitude, as are those of consolation prize winners, and that the two sets of scores are different from each other. The members within the groups are as much alike as possible on these generated scores, and the groups themselves are as different as possible.

With this analysis, we have taken a four-variable problem and reduced it to a much simpler, univariate problem by forming a linear combination of $X_1 - X_4$ to get one Y. We need to compare only the Ys rather than all four Xs. Further, we know that the groups are as different as possible with respect to these Ys. But how does that help us understand how grand prize winners differ from consolation prize winners in terms of their new account activities? Further, how does that help the sales analysis department isolate the factors that were most critical to salespeople's success? We need to:

1. Interpret the discriminant function Y.

2. Use it to classify individuals in groups.

Interpreting the Discriminant Function

First, we must verify that the discriminant function is statistically significant. (If the function is not significant, we shouldn't interpret the function—it's

---

[4] The weights are given by the eigenvector in the solution of the equation: $(W^{-1}B - \lambda I)v = 0$, where W is the pooled within-sample covariance matrix and B is the between-group, sum-of-squares, and cross-products matrix.

TABLE 18.2

Discriminant Analysis Example: Calculated Discriminant Scores for Grand Prize and Consolation Prize Winners Using the Discriminant Function: $Y = .058X_1 + .063X_2 + .034X_3 - .032X_4$

Grand Prize Winner (W)	# Calls New Accounts X_1	% with Advance Appointments X_2	Calls to Prospects X_3	# New Accounts Visited X_4	Y
1 RMB	130	62	148	42	15.2
2 ALB	122	70	186	44	16.5
3 BCC	89	68	171	32	14.3
4 JJC	104	58	135	40	13.0
5 EDC	116	40	160	36	13.6
6 WPD	100	65	151	30	14.1
7 RHH	85	66	183	42	14.0
8 BEK	113	59	130	25	13.9
9 DAK	108	52	163	41	13.8
10 JJN	116	48	154	48	13.5
11 MYS	99	57	188	32	14.8
12 PJS	78	70	190	40	14.2
13 CET	106	61	157	38	14.2
14 LLV	94	58	173	29	14.1
15 LMW	98	64	137	36	13.3
Mean	103.9	59.9	161.7	37.0	
Consolation Prize Winner (C)					
1 JGB	105	39	155	45	12.4
2 RAB	86	60	140	33	12.5
3 HAF	64	48	132	36	10.1
4 PPD	104	36	119	29	11.4
5 BCE	102	53	143	41	12.8
6 ASG	73	62	128	30	11.6
7 WLH	94	51	152	36	12.7
8 LHL	59	64	130	28	11.0
9 RJL	84	31	102	32	9.3
10 WFM	91	47	96	35	10.4
11 JRP	83	40	87	30	9.4
12 EJS	95	42	114	28	11.2
13 VES	68	52	123	26	10.6
14 HMT	101	51	98	24	11.7
15 BMT	89	39	117	33	10.6
Mean	86.5	47.7	122.4	32.4	

meaningless because the estimates differ only due to sampling error.) Most statistical computing packages routinely print F-statistics, and in our example, the discriminant function is statistically significant, so the interpretation of the function can proceed.

Discriminant Coefficients

Discriminant coefficients are interpreted in much the same way as regression coefficients, in that each coefficient reflects the relative contribution of a unit change of each of the independent variables on the discriminant function. A small coefficient means that a one-unit change in that particular variable produces a small change in the discriminant function score, and a larger coefficient, a larger change in Y.

Also like regression coefficients, discriminant coefficients are affected by the scale of the independent variables, i.e., the original function $Y = .058X_1 + .063X_2 + .034X_3 - .032X_4$ contains the weights to be applied to the variables in raw-score scales. This scaling means that if the unit of measurement for one of the variables changes (e.g., measure variable X_2 as a proportion rather than as a percentage), the discriminant function also changes. To remove these arbitrary scale-of-measurement effects, we standardize the discriminant weights before trying to compare the variables' contributions. We multiply each raw score weight v_k by the standard deviation of variable k. Call v_k^* the standardized weight, then:

$$v_k^* = v_k s_k$$

where s_k is the pooled (across samples) standard deviation of the kth variable. Considering our grand and consolation prize winners, we pool over only the two prize groups, to obtain the pooled sample standard deviations for the four variables: $s_1 = 16.76$, $s_2 = 10.89$, $s_3 = 28.16$, and $s_4 = 6.33$. Therefore:

$$v_1^* = v_1 s_1 = .058(16.76) = .972$$
$$v_2^* = v_2 s_2 = .063(10.89) = .686$$
$$v_3^* = v_3 s_3 = .034(28.16) = .957$$
$$v_4^* = v_4 s_4 = -.032(6.33) = -.203$$

Standardize the weights before interpreting the relative importance of variables.

With the standardized weights all being on the same "scale," we can compare their sizes to determine the relative contribution of the variables. They indicate that the variables "number of calls on new accounts" (X_1) and "telephone calls made to prospects" (X_3) are the most important and that "number of new accounts visited" (X_4) is the least important in differentiating grand prize from consolation prize winners. Further, variables X_1 through X_3 exert a positive effect but in contrast, X_4 has a negative impact on the likelihood of being a grand prize winner.

Discriminant Loadings

A third method for assessing the importance of the variables in discriminating between groups is to study the discriminant loadings. These values are the correlations between each variable (X_1 through X_4) in turn with the discriminant score (Y). These correlations are as follows:

Between Y and X_1: .627

Between Y and X_2: .679

Between Y and X_3: .847

Between Y and X_4: .441

The loadings suggest that variable X_3 (telephone calls made to prospects) is the most important, and variable X_4 (number of new accounts visited) is the least. (The difference in the ordering of the variables, compared to the standardized weights, is due to the correlations among the predictors.) As with any correlation coefficient, the squared discriminant loadings (r^2) indicate the amount of variance that the discriminant score (Y) shares with the variable (X).

In sum, three quantities are typically used to assess the relative importance of variables in discriminating between groups:

1. The mean differences of the groups on each variable

2. The standardized discriminant function coefficients

3. The discriminant loadings

All three produce similar conclusions when little correlation exists among the predictors. When multicollinearity is a problem, their conclusions will differ, and the same caveats that apply when interpreting coefficients in regression apply here.

Classifying Individuals Using the Discriminant Function

To assist in interpretation, we could also calculate the discriminant score for each group. To do this, we insert the mean values of the variables for each group into the discriminant function equation. For the grand prize winners, the means were: $\bar{x}_1 = 103.9$, $\bar{x}_2 = 59.9$, $\bar{x}_3 = 161.7$, and $\bar{x}_4 = 37.0$, so the mean discriminant score for grand prize winners, $\bar{Y}_W$, is:

See if the model works—use the scores to predict classifications.

$$\begin{aligned} \bar{Y}_W &= v_1\bar{x}_1 + v_2\bar{x}_2 + v_3\bar{x}_3 + v_4\bar{x}_4 \\ &= .058(103.9) + .063(59.9) + .034(161.7) - .032(37.0) = 14.2 \end{aligned}$$

For consolation prize winners, $\bar{x}_1 = 86.5$, $\bar{x}_2 = 47.7$, $\bar{x}_3 = 122.4$, and $\bar{x}_4 = 32.4$, and the mean discriminant score, $\bar{Y}_C$, is calculated to be:

$$\bar{Y}_C = .058(86.5) + .063(47.7) + .034(122.4) - .032(32.4) = 11.2$$

On average, grand prize winners have higher discriminant scores on Y than consolation prize winners (alternatively, we could average the discriminant scores in Table 18.2 in each group).

We have established that the discriminant function provides statistically reliable differentiation for these data. Now let's see whether it provides meaningful and practical differentiation between the two groups. We use the discriminant function to classify each salesperson into the "grand prize" or "consolation prize" groups (as if we didn't know their actual group membership). We then compare the prediction with the individual's known actual classification to see if the function provides meaningful discrimination to accurately guess each individual's prize status. We use the simple decision rule: If a salesperson's discriminant score is closer to the mean score for grand prize winners than for consolation prize winners, we will classify the salesperson as a grand prize winner.

An alternative equivalent procedure is to compute the score that divides the mean discriminant scores. This "cutting score" is then used to assign objects to groups in the following way: If the individual's score is above the cutting score, classify the salesperson as a grand prize winner; if it is below, classify the salesperson as a consolation prize winner. When the groups are equal in size, the cutting score, Y_{cs}, is given as the simple average of the mean discriminant scores for the groups; i.e., by the calculation $Y_{cs} = (\bar{Y}_W + \bar{Y}_C)/2 = (14.2 + 11.2)/2 = 12.7$. When the groups are not equal, the formula needs to be modified to take the size of each group into account. The appropriate formula is then

$$Y_{cs} = \frac{(n_2\bar{Y}_1 + n_1\bar{Y}_2)}{(n_1 + n_2)}$$

where $\bar{Y}_1$ and $\bar{Y}_2$ are the mean discriminant scores and n_1 and n_2 the sizes of Groups 1 and 2, respectively.

Either decision rule essentially finds the group most similar to the individual. The resulting predicted classifications are presented in the right-hand column of Table 18.3. Table 18.4 contains the predicted classifications as the columns, and the known, actual classifications as the rows. We can use this table to assess the accuracy of the predictive classification decision rule. The entries on the

Discriminant Analysis Example: Predicted Group Membership Using the Simple Classification Rule

TABLE 18.3

| Grand Prize Winners (W) | Discriminant Score Y_i | Differences from Mean of | | Predicted Group Membership |
		First Group $Y_i - \overline{Y}_W =$ $Y_i - 14.2$	Second Group $Y_i - \overline{Y}_C =$ $Y_i - 11.2$	
1	15.2	1.0	4.0	W
2	16.5	2.3	5.3	W
3	14.3	.1	3.1	W
4	13.0	21.2	1.8	W
5	13.6	20.6	2.4	W
6	14.1	20.1	2.9	W
7	14.0	20.2	2.8	W
8	13.9	20.3	2.7	W
9	13.8	20.4	2.6	W
10	13.5	20.7	2.3	W
11	14.8	.6	3.6	W
12	14.2	.0	3.0	W
13	14.2	.0	3.0	W
14	14.1	20.1	2.9	W
15	13.3	20.9	2.1	W
Consolation Prize Winners (C)				
1	12.4	21.8	1.2	C
2	12.5	21.7	1.3	C
3	10.1	24.1	21.1	C
4	11.4	22.8	.2	C
5	12.8	21.4	1.6	W
6	11.6	22.6	.4	C
7	12.7	21.5	1.5	W[1]
8	11.0	23.2	20.2	C
9	9.3	24.9	21.9	C
10	10.4	23.8	20.8	C
11	9.4	24.8	21.8	C
12	11.2	23.0	.0	C
13	10.6	23.6	20.6	C
14	11.7	22.5	.5	C
15	10.6	23.6	20.6	C

[1] The assignments were actually carried out using more significant digits in the calculations of discriminant scores. While the calculations to one decimal place suggest this case is equidistant from the two group means, it actually is slightly closer to the mean for the grand prize winners.

Discriminant Analysis Example: Matrix of Actual vs. Predicted Group Membership

TABLE 18.4

| Actual Classification | Predicted Classification | | Total |
	Grand Prize Winner	Consolation Prize Winner	
Grand Prize Winner	15	0	15
Consolation Prize Winner	2	13	15

diagonal represent the hit rate, or the proportion of people who have been correctly classified, P_{cc}:

$$P_{cc} = (15 + 13)/(30) = 28/30 = .933$$

Approximately 93% of the salespeople are correctly classified as grand prize or consolation prize winners on the basis of their new account activities.

Assessing Classification Accuracy

How good is that hit rate? The sample sizes were equal, thus chance would be 50%, so 93% sounds very good. What if the two groups were not equal in size—suppose that in a sample of 100 salespeople, 20 won grand prizes and 80 won consolation prizes (e.g., perhaps the sales contest requirements were changed). Useful criteria to evaluate hit rates include: the maximum chance criterion and the proportional chance criterion.

The maximum chance criterion holds that any object chosen at random should be classified as belonging to the larger group, because that will maximize the proportion of cases correctly classified. In the 80-20 example, we would classify everybody as a consolation prize winner, because that would make 80% of the classifications correct.

This classification rule is not very helpful from a marketing viewpoint, though, because we wish to identify the two types of winners. We would like to classify some salespeople as grand prize winners and thereby improve upon the *a priori* odds. In such instances, we use the proportional chance criterion, C_{pro}, as the standard of evaluation:

$$C_{pro} = \alpha^2 + (1 - \alpha)^2$$

where

α = the proportion of individuals in Group 1

$(1 - \alpha)$ = the proportion of individuals in Group 2

For 20 grand prize winners (Group 1) and 80 consolation prize winners (Group 2), this index equals $C_{pro} = .2^2 + (.8)^2 = .68$. If we use a discriminant function and get a classification accuracy of, say, 85%, that hit rate would look good compared to chance alone ($C_{pro} = .68$), but not so impressive against the maximum chance criterion (.80).[5]

Before leaving the "two-group discriminant" case … a couple of comments. First, given that the same data used to develop the discriminant model are also used to test the model, there is an upward bias—the hit rate is somewhat overstated. The criterion used to fit the model generates an equation that is derived to be statistically optimal, so ideally, the actual predictive accuracy of the model should be tested on a new sample of data. However, it is costly and time consuming to collect more data, so what is often done is to split the original sample of observations into two subsamples. One subsample is the "analysis sample" and it is used to develop the equation, while the other is the "holdout sample" and it is used to examine how well the equation predicts group membership.

Second, the particular decision rule we used to classify grand prize and consolation prize winners minimize the costs of misclassification (that is, it will be optimal) when: (1) the costs of misclassifying a grand prize winner as a consolation prize winner, and vice versa, are equal; (2) the *a priori* probabilities of

---

[5] When the two groups are equal in size, as they are in the original example, the proportional chance criterion equals the maximum chance criterion (that is, $C_{pro} = .5^2 + (1 - .5)^2 = .25 + .25 = .5$).

winning each prize are equal; and (3) the distribution of the variables in the two populations is multivariate normal with equal and known covariance matrices.

Three-Group Case

Let's now consider discriminant analysis for $k \geq 3$ groups. The biggest change that occurs when we move beyond two groups is that there can be more than one discriminant function.[6] When there are k groups and p variables, the maximum number of discriminant functions are given by the following rules:

- If there are more variables p than groups k (the typical case), there will be at most $k - 1$ discriminant functions.

- If the number of variables p is less than the number of groups k, there will be no more than p discriminant functions.

In either case, the number of statistically significant discriminant functions is usually less than the maximum number possible. It depends on whether the extracted functions provide "meaningful differentiation" among the objects forming the groups.

Consider again the example of salespeople, but this time, let's look at all three groups (grand prize winners, consolation prize winners, and salespeople who won nothing). The number of groups ($k = 3$) is less than the number of variables ($p = 4$), so the number of discriminant functions that can be derived is $k - 1 = 2$.

The two discriminant functions turn out to be

$$Y_1 = .064X_1 + .079X_2 + .027X_3 - .002X_4$$
$$Y_2 = 2.036X_1 - .037X_2 + .041X_3 - .003X_4$$

The functions have the following interpretation: Of all the linear combinations of the four variables that could be developed, the first function provides maximum separation among the three groups. Then, given the first linear combination, the second function provides maximum separation among all possible linear combinations that were uncorrelated with (i.e., so as not to be redundant) the first set of scores ($r_{Y1,Y2} = 0$).

Classifying Respondents

We check the statistical significance of these functions before trying to use them to classify salespeople, and find that only the first function is significant. Thus, we develop a classification rule that depends only on it. The rule is an extension of the one previously described; we assign salespeople to the group closest to their discriminant score. To do so, we need to know the mean discriminant scores for each group. They are generated by substituting the means of the four variables for each group in the discriminant function:

Grand prize winner:	$\overline{Y}_W = .064(103.9) + .079(59.9) + .027(161.7)$ $-.002(37.0) = 15.67$
Consolation prize winner:	$\overline{Y}_C = .064(86.5) + .079(47.7) + .027(122.4)$ $-.002(32.4) = 12.54$
Unsuccessful salesperson:	$\overline{Y}_U = .064(50.4) + .079(34.0) + .027(88.3)$ $-.002(25.7) = 9.58$

---

[6] There are two variations when there are more than two groups: the *classical* approach generates one classification function for each group that maximizes the likelihood of correct classifications of the members of the group. It produces $g(g - 1)/2$ discriminant functions (where g is the number of groups) to separate each pair of groups. The *simultaneous* approach (also known as the canonical approach) is emphasized here.

The cutting scores $(15.67 + 12.54)/2 = 14.11$ and $(12.54 + 9.58)/2 = 11.06$ bisect the difference in mean scores between grand prize and consolation prize winners, and between consolation prize winners and unsuccessful salespeople. Thus, any salesperson with a score less than 11.06 would be considered an unsuccessful contest competitor, those with discriminant scores greater than 14.11 would be considered grand prize winners. Those with scores between 11.06 and 14.11 would be considered consolation prize winners. The scores and predicted classifications are contained in Table 18.5. Table 18.6 contains the matrix of predicted versus actual classifications. The performance of this procedure is quite good; the hit rate says 91.1% of the salespeople are predicted correctly, against the chance criterion of 33%. The incorrect predictions involve consolation prize winners (two of whom are predicted to be grand prize winners and two of whom are predicted to be unsuccessful in the sales contest), so we might say that, perhaps not surprisingly, the function is particularly effective in discriminating between the extremes: the grand prize winners and those who did not win anything.

TABLE 18.5

Discriminant Scores for Each Salesperson and Predicted Group Membership Using the Function $Y = .064X_1 + .079X_2 + .027X_3 - .002X_4$

Person	Score	Prediction[1]	Person	Score	Prediction	Person	Score	Prediction
1 RMB	17.25	W	1 JGB	14.00	C	1 RBB	8.80	U
2 ALB	18.40	W	2 RAB	14.06	C	2 GEB	8.32	U
3 BCC	15.73	W	3 HAF	11.47	C	3 ADC	8.18	U
4 JJC	14.91	W	4 PPD	12.74	C	4 JFC	9.76	U
5 EDC	14.94	W	5 BCE	14.60	W	5 LDE	8.73	U
6 WPD	15.66	W	6 ASG	13.06	C	6 JFH	7.92	U
7 RHH	15.63	W	7 WLH	14.18	W	7 JCH	8.58	U
8 BEK	15.45	W	8 LHL	12.38	C	8 RPF	6.94	U
9 DAK	15.45	W	9 RJL	10.59	U	9 APL	8.71	U
10 JJN	15.39	W	10 WFM	12.14	C	10 HAL	8.08	U
11 MYS	15.97	W	11 JRP	10.83	U	11 ERM	9.45	U
12 PJS	15.69	W	12 EJS	12.50	C	12 WRR	8.93	U
13 CET	15.88	W	13 VES	11.81	C	13 JTS	7.56	U
14 LLV	15.32	W	14 HMT	13.17	C	14 JMV	6.88	U
15 LMW	15.06	W	15 BMT	11.95	C	15 HEY	7.75	U

[1] W, grand prize winners; C, consolation prize winners; U, unsuccessful salespeople.

TABLE 18.6

Discriminant Analysis Example: Matrix of Actual vs. Predicted Group Membership

Actual Classification	Predicted Classification			
	Grand Prize Winner	Consolation Prize Winner	Unsuccessful Salesperson	Total
Grand Prize Winner	15	0	0	15
Consolation Prize Winner	2	11	2	15
Unsuccessful Salesperson	0	0	15	15

Key Variables

To determine the key new-account activities that differentiated salespeople's performance, we transform the v_k coefficients to their standardized counterparts, to equate the "units" so we can compare the impact of the variables. The standardized weights are:

$$v_1^* = v_1 s_1 = .064(15.91) = 1.018$$
$$v_2^* = v_2 s_2 = .079(8.97) = .709$$
$$v_3^* = v_3 s_3 = .027(19.99) = .540$$
$$v_4^* = v_4 s_4 = -.002(5.37) = -.011$$

Number of calls on new accounts, X_1, is the most important variable in differentiating among the levels of success in the sales contest, whereas the number of new accounts visited, X_4, is the least important. However, there is some correlation among the predictors so the relative importance of each predictor should be interpreted with a degree of caution.

Marketing Applications of Discriminant Analysis

Discriminant analysis has been used for a variety of marketing problems, including:

- Determining characteristics that distinguish the listening audiences of radio stations

- Differentiating among segments of automobile buyers

- Predicting adopters and nonadopters of new products

- Relating purchase behavior to advertising exposure

Also see Research Realities 18.1.

The main "take away" on the question, "When do I use discriminant analysis?" is this: Discriminant analysis is applicable when the marketing researcher has data on customers who fall into groups, and the information on the customers can be used to understand how the groups differ.

RESEARCH   REALITIES

18.1 A Global Application of Discriminant Analysis

Why do some international firms enjoy success in the U.S. while others do not? Marketing researchers conducted a telephone survey of nearly 100 marketing vice presidents or presidents of international (European or Japanese) industrial products firms that had established a manufacturing presence in the U.S. during the last 30 years.

Firms were considered "successful" if they had achieved at least 5% market share in the U.S., and were classified as "underachieving" with less. The results of a discriminant analysis revealed the main ingredients of the successful firms to be:

- A larger percentage of senior managers in the U.S. firm who were U.S. nationals

- A greater commitment to research and development

- A willingness to tailor product design to local taste

Other factors that were tested did not matter; neither mode of entry into the U.S. (acquiring or building a facility) nor competitive pricing were predictive in discriminating between successful firms and unsuccessful ones.

Sources: Zoher E. Shipchandler and James S. Moore, "Factors Influencing Foreign Firm Performance in the U.S. Market," American Business Review 18, 62–68.

Factor Analysis

Factor analysis is different from discriminant analysis in that it doesn't try to predict one variable (such as group membership in discriminant analysis) by other variables. Techniques like factor analysis are referred to as tools for "interdependence analysis." All the variables have equal status, and none is singled out for special treatment as a dependent variable. These models pose different variations on the question, "How are these p variables interrelated?"

Factor analysis addresses a number of goals. One of its goals is usually referred to as "data reduction." Factor analysis simplifies data analysis by taking advantage of the correlations among p variables—extracting that overlapping information and reducing the problem down to just a few core "factors." For example, Table 18.7 shows two sets of correlations among $p = 9$ variables. The correlations in Panel A suggest that the nine variables might be reduced down to 2 factors. Variables 1–4 seem to go together, as do variables 5–9 (the correlations between the variables in each set are relatively high). The two sets seem to behave differently, though, because the correlations between 1–4 and 5–9 are rather low. (If all the correlations were high, we would use only one factor.) In contrast, Panel B suggests that three factors underlie the nine variables; i.e., variables 1–3, 4–6, and 7–9 covary.

To conduct a factor analysis, we need to translate that conceptual understanding of factor analysis into a mathematical model. Mathematically, a factor is a linear combination of variables, chosen to capture the "essence" of the data.

Consider a company with a large sales force (pharmaceuticals, insurance, cosmetics, machine parts suppliers, automobile dealerships, etc.). Suppose the

TABLE 18.7   **Factor Analysis Example: Two Hypothetical Sets of Correlations among 9 Variables**

Panel A (Probably Two Factors):

Variable	1	2	3	4	5	6	7	8	9
1	1.00								
2	.96	1.00							
3	.94	.88	1.00						
4	.91	.95	.89	1.00					
5	.05	.09	.08	.10	1.00				
6	.12	.04	.03	.11	.92	1.00			
7	.07	.14	.06	.03	.86	.91	1.00		
8	.10	.12	.08	.04	.94	.95	.88	1.00	
9	.08	.11	.06	.13	.97	.87	.91	.90	1.00

Panel B (Probably Three Factors):

Variable	1	2	3	4	5	6	7	8	9
1	1.00								
2	.92	1.00							
3	.95	.98	1.00						
4	.07	.13	.02	1.00					
5	.09	.05	.11	.95	1.00				
6	.06	.09	.07	.90	.89	1.00			
7	.10	.08	.10	.08	.14	.10	1.00		
8	.05	.07	.09	.09	.06	.12	.94	1.00	
9	.13	.04	.08	.13	.09	.06	.91	.92	1.00

company is interested in isolating the personality traits that lead to successful sales. There are many ways to measure the performance of a salesperson, e.g., sales growth, profitability of sales, new account sales, etc. The company wants its salespeople to be good at all these things, not just one, so looking at any single measure would seem inadequate. On the other hand, salespeople who are good at generating sales of one kind are often also good at generating sales of another; i.e., we'd expect these three performance measures to be correlated. Table 18.8 contains data for a sample of 50 sales reps. (To compensate for differences in sales territory, these measures were converted to an index where 100 indicates "average.")

TABLE 18.8

Factor Analysis Example: Sales Performance Data for Sample of Sales Representatives

Sales Rep	Sales Growth X_1	Sales Profitability X_2	New Account Sales X_3
1	93.0	96.0	97.8
2	88.8	91.8	96.8
3	95.0	100.3	99.0
4	101.3	103.8	106.8
5	102.0	107.8	103.0
6	95.8	97.5	99.3
7	95.5	99.5	99.0
8	110.8	122.0	115.3
9	102.8	108.3	103.8
10	106.8	120.5	102.0
11	103.3	109.8	104.0
12	99.5	111.8	100.3
13	103.5	112.5	107.0
14	99.5	105.5	102.3
15	100.0	107.0	102.8
16	81.5	93.5	95.0
17	101.3	105.3	102.8
18	103.3	110.8	103.5
19	95.3	104.3	103.0
20	99.5	105.3	106.3
21	88.5	95.3	95.8
22	99.3	115.0	104.3
23	87.5	92.5	95.8
24	105.3	114.0	105.3
25	107.0	121.0	109.0
26	93.3	102.0	97.8
27	106.8	118.0	107.3
28	106.8	120.0	104.8
29	92.3	90.8	99.8
30	106.3	121.0	104.5
31	106.0	119.5	110.5
32	88.3	92.8	96.8
33	96.0	103.3	100.5
34	94.3	94.5	99.0
35	106.5	121.5	110.5
36	106.5	115.5	107.0
37	92.0	99.5	103.5
38	102.0	99.8	103.3
39	108.3	122.3	108.5

Sales Rep	Sales Growth X_1	Sales Profitability X_2	New Account Sales X_3
40	106.8	119.0	106.8
41	102.5	109.3	103.8
42	92.5	102.5	99.3
43	102.8	113.8	106.8
44	83.3	87.3	96.3
45	94.8	101.8	99.8
46	103.5	112.0	110.8
47	89.5	96.0	97.3
48	84.3	89.8	94.3
49	104.3	109.5	106.5
50	106.0	118.5	105.0

Summarizing Data

If the purpose in factor analysis is to summarize the important information contained in the data by a fewer number of factors, the question is, "What is 'important information'?" Two kinds of information are typically highlighted: the variance of each variable (variability across customers), and the correlation between variables (covariation of variables across customers).[7]

Table 18.9 contains the pairs of correlations among the variables, and Table 18.10 is the "loadings" matrix that results from performing a principal components analysis (PCA) on the data. The loadings matrix is one of the key outputs in factor analyses, so let's interpret those.

TABLE 18.9   Factor Analysis: Simple Pair-Wise Correlations among the Performance Measures

	X_1	X_2	X_3
X_1	1.000		
X_2	.926	1.000	
X_3	.884	.843	1.000

TABLE 18.10   Factor Analysis: Factor Loading Matrix

Variable	Factor		
	F_1	F_2	F_3
X_1	.976	.083	−.203
X_2	.961	.232	.151
X_3	.945	−.321	.056
Sum of Squares	2.769	.164	.067

[7] Most factor analyses are run using standardized variables because in many problems, the raw variables reflect different units of measurement. By standardizing the variables (to mean zero and unit standard deviation), the effect of measurement is removed. The researcher need not actually standardize the variables—the first step of a factor analysis in statistical computing packages is to compute the matrix of correlations among the variables you specify. Recall the equation for a correlation between two variables X and Y: $r_{xy} = \sum_{i=1}^{n} \frac{(X_i - \bar{x})(Y_i - \bar{y})}{n s_X s_Y}$. In this equation, the data X_i and Y_i are adjusted to standard scores when the means are subtracted and the standard deviations divided.

Factor Loadings

The individual entries are the correlations between the variables (rows) and the factors (columns). For example, .976 (the entry in the 1st row and 1st column) represents the correlation between the 1st variable and the 1st factor; .083 is the correlation between the 1st variable and the 2nd factor; .961 the correlation between the 2nd variable and 1st factor, and so on. These correlations are called factor loadings. When we examine the table of loadings, we find that all three variables correlate highly with (we'd say "load heavily on") Factor F_1.

These numbers are correlations, so if we square them, we obtain the proportion of variation in the variable that is accounted for by the factor. Thus,

$$.976^2 = .952$$
$$.961^2 = .924$$
$$.945^2 = .894$$

are the proportions of variance in variables 1, 2, and 3, respectively, accounted for by the first factor. Thus, with just a single factor, we have very nearly represented the entire variance of each of the three variables (the 1's on the diagonal in the correlation matrix in Table 18.9).

We might also check to see how well our single factor captures the correlations among the three variables. To represent the covariability of two variables, we multiply the factor loadings of the two variables (two different rows), one factor at a time, and then sum up the products over the factors. Say we wanted to see how well the model predicted the value for the correlation between variables 1 and 2, r_{12}. We multiply the respective column entries of rows 1 and 2 of Table 18.10 and add the products:

$$(.976)(.961) + (.083)(.232) + (-.203)(.151) = .926$$

In this case, we reproduce exactly the original correlation, r_{12}, between variables 1 and 2 displayed in Table 18.9. The general formula is:

$$r_{jt} = \sum_{k=1}^{3} a_{jk} a_{tk}$$

where j and t denote the original variables, k denotes the factor, and a_{jk} is the loading or correlation between the jth variable and k^{th} factor (the jth row and k^{th} column of Table 18.10). Although we have fit our data well, note that in doing so, we have not achieved the parsimonious goal of "data reduction"—we began with three variables, and we now have three factors.[8] We usually extract fewer factors than we had variables to begin with.

What happens when fewer factors are used? The model no longer reproduces the pair-wise correlations exactly; rather, they are only estimated, however, the estimates are often quite good. The estimate is given by the same formula, but now we sum from 1 to m, where m denotes the number of factors being considered ($m < p$). For one-factor ($m = 1$), the estimated correlation between variables 1 and 2 ($j = 1$, $t = 2$) is:

$$\widehat{r}_{12} = \sum_{k=1}^{m} a_{1k} a_{2k} = (.976)(.961) = .937$$

---

[8] Any set of correlations can be reproduced exactly if the number of factors equals the number of variables.

This estimate is close to the true value of .926. The other estimates are also quite good: $\hat{r}_{13} = (.973)(.945) = .922$ and $\hat{r}_{23} = (.961)(.945) = .908$, compared to the actual values of .884 and .843.

Communalities

This example, showing the results for the extremes of one versus three factors, demonstrates the natural tension in factor analysis—the more factors that are extracted, the better the data are represented. However, the fewer the factors extracted, the easier it is to work with the results, interpret them, and communicate them.[9] Is one factor sufficient, or is more than one factor needed to summarize the data adequately? To answer this question, it is helpful to realize that in a principal components solution, the m newly formed components are uncorrelated. This means that the proportion of variance accounted for by m factors is simply the sum of the proportions accounted for by each factor. Take two factors, for example. The proportion of the variation in each variable accounted for by a two-factor solution is:

Variable 1: $(.976)^2 + (.083)^2 = .959$

Variable 2: $(.961)^2 + (.232)^2 = .977$

Variable 3: $(.945)^2 + (321)^2 = .997$

These values, which express the proportion of the variance of the variables extracted by m factors, are called the **communalities** of the variables and are typically denoted as h_j^2 (for variable j). Thus, we see that two factors account for 95.9% $(=h_1^2)$ of the variation in X_1, 97.7% $(=h_2^2)$ of the variation in X_2, and 99.7% $(=h_3^2)$ of the variation in X_3. The two-factor model does a remarkable job in accounting for the variability within the data. Variable 1 is most poorly captured, but even for it, 95.9% of its total variability is captured by the first two principal components. How do we know what percentage is enough? How many factors should we retain?

The column totals in Table 18.10 can assist the analyst in making a decision. Given that the row/column entries represent the correlations between the variables and the factors, and their squares represent the proportions of variation in each variable explained by the factor, the sum of the squares in a column provides a measure of the amount of variation accounted for by that factor. Take factor/column 1, for example:

$$(.976)^2 + (.961)^2 + (.945)^2 = 2.769$$

is the column total. The three variables are all standardized to unit variance (recall we started with a correlation matrix, 1's on the diagonal, in Table 18.9), so the total variance equals 3. Thus, the proportion of total variance that is accounted for by the first factor is 2.769/3 = 92.3%. The first two factors account for $(2.769 + .164)/3 = .978$, or 97.8% of the total variance. The second factor accounts for 5.5% of the total variance in the three variables. In the interest of scientific parsimony, it would seem that a one-factor solution would suffice; the addition of the second factor provides only a small gain in explained variation. (The argument is one of diminishing returns—does the second factor explain enough additional variance that it is worth retaining it?)

---

[9] The trade-off is found in most statistical modeling. For example, in multiple regression, prediction is better—the R higher—with more predictors. However, the model is easier to understand, and easier to express to marketing research clients, with fewer predictors.

Conceptual Basis of Principal Components Analysis (PCA)

The objective of a PCA is to transform a set of interrelated variables into a set of uncorrelated linear combinations of these variables. Each linear combination (or component) accounts for a decreasing proportion of the variance in the original variables, subject to the condition that each linear combination is uncorrelated (geometrically at right angles) to all previous linear combinations.

The physical analogy of a watermelon should help in understanding the conceptual basis of PCA. The watermelon has three basic dimensions; call them length, width, and height, and conceive of them as being at right angles to one another. Further, let length always refer to the longest dimension, width to the next longest dimension that is perpendicular to the length axis, and height to the axis perpendicular to the length and width axes. Now, the total size of the watermelon can be indicated by specifying its length, width, and height. Would fewer dimensions provide a reasonably accurate estimate of its size? It all depends on the shape of the watermelon. Suppose that the watermelon was oddly shaped, very long and narrow, much like a cigar. Then its size would be fairly accurately indicated by simply specifying only its length (you wouldn't need the other dimensions really). If the melon were long and wide but rather flat, like a somewhat deflated football, two dimensions would be needed to accurately portray its size. Finally, if it were your good old-fashioned, normal watermelon—long, wide, and high—all three dimensions would be needed to describe its size.

The principal components correspond to the axes of the watermelon in this three-dimensional problem. Now return to the sales performance data. Each sales rep has three scores, one for each of the performance criteria. The scores could thus be plotted in 3D space (the coordinates being the reported values for X_1, X_2, and X_3). The task in PCA is to produce a set of uncorrelated composite scores that measure what the variables have in common, trying to do so getting as much "bang for the buck" (accounting for the most variance in the first component).

The 1st component corresponds to the principal axis of the ellipsoid in three space (the length of the watermelon). Of all the linear combinations that could be formed, it explains the maximum variation contained in all the original variables. Whether it adequately captures the information contained in the data depends on the shape of the concentration of the swarm of points. If the 3D scatterplot of the data results in a cigar-shaped figure, one factor is enough.

If not, more than one factor is needed to summarize the data. The 2nd principal component would be chosen so that it accounts for the maximum variation left unexplained (i.e., uncorrelated with the first, or the width of the watermelon begins at a right angle to the length). Thus, a PCA reveals how several measures can be combined and reduced down to a single measure. If the variation accounted for by each additional component is substantial, that indicates several components are needed to adequately model the data.

Determining the Number of Factors

One of the more important decisions in factor analysis is determining the number of factors necessary to account for the variation in the data. For the sales performance data, the determination is fairly straightforward. Recall the 1st component explains 92% of the variance, and the 2nd, only 5% more. Thus, we conclude that one component effectively summarizes the data.

Sometimes more components are required. To illustrate, let's look at some data from a study on the images of various department stores. The data were collected using the semantic differential scales in Figure 18.3.[10] Table 18.11 shows the correlations among these items. A PCA was conducted, and the amount of variation accounted for by each factor is presented in Table 18.12.

A number of rules have been advanced for deciding how many factors to retain for a factor analytic solution. Two of the most popular are (1) latent roots and (2) the scree test. The latent roots criterion holds that the amount of variation explained by each factor must be greater than 1. The rationale is that the variation in each variable is 1.0 after the variable has been standardized, and a factor should account for at least that much variation to be considered useful from a data summarization perspective. Since there are two factors with latent roots greater than 1, the latent roots criterion would suggest a two-factor solution for the department-store image data.

The scree test plots the latent roots against the number of factors, in their order of extraction, as in Figure 18.4. Note how the curve drops sharply at first and then levels off as it approaches the horizontal axis. This is often the case in such plots, and the method actually gets its name because of the resemblance of

FIGURE 18.3   Items Used to Measure Department Store Image

1. Convenient place to shop	__ : __ : __ : __ : __ : __ : __	Inconvenient place to shop
2. Fast checkout	__ : __ : __ : __ : __ : __ : __	Slow checkout
3. Store is clean	__ : __ : __ : __ : __ : __ : __	Store is dirty
4. Store not well organized	__ : __ : __ : __ : __ : __ : __	Store is well organized
5. Store is messy, cluttered	__ : __ : __ : __ : __ : __ : __	Store is neat, uncluttered
6. Convenient store hours	__ : __ : __ : __ : __ : __ : __	Inconvenient store hours
7. Far from home or work	__ : __ : __ : __ : __ : __ : __	Store is close to home, or work
8. Store has bad atmosphere	__ : __ : __ : __ : __ : __ : __	Store has good atmosphere
9. Attractive decor inside	__ : __ : __ : __ : __ : __ : __	Unattractive decor inside
10. Store is spacious	__ : __ : __ : __ : __ : __ : __	Store is crowded

TABLE 18.11   Factor Analysis: Correlations among Items in Department Store Image Survey

	X_1	X_2	X_3	X_4	X_5	X_6	X_7	X_8	X_9	X_{10}
X_1	1.00									
X_2	.79	1.00								
X_3	.41	.32	1.00							
X_4	.26	.21	.80	1.00						
X_5	.12	.20	.76	.75	1.00					
X_6	.89	.90	.34	.30	.11	1.00				
X_7	.87	.83	.40	.28	.23	.78	1.00			
X_8	.37	.31	.82	.78	.74	.30	.29	1.00		
X_9	.32	.35	.78	.81	.77	.39	.26	.82	1.00	
X_{10}	.18	.23	.72	.80	.83	.16	.17	.78	.77	1.00

[10] The negative descriptor sometimes appears on the left and sometimes on the right, so the scoring was reversed for those variables where the negative descriptor appeared on the right so that higher scores consistently reflect more desirable amounts of the property. For a seven-point scale, you create new item = 8 − old item to get the reversal.

TABLE 18.12   Factor Analysis: Amount of Variance Explained Per Factor

Factor	Variance Explained
1	5.725
2	2.761
3	.366
4	.357
5	.243
6	.212
7	.132
8	.123
9	.079
10	.001

the plot to a side view of a mountain. The high value(s) at the left-top represents the peak of the mountain, the drop in values represents the mountain face, and at the foot of the mountain, there is a fairly straight line approaching horizontal, where rocks that have fallen off the mountain have piled up. The pile of rocks is called scree. The last "real" factor is considered to be that point before the scree begins. In the example, the scree or straight line begins at Factor 3; thus, the scree plot criterion suggests that a two-factor solution is sufficient to capture the store image data.

Factor analysis is extremely useful in survey development.

How much of the total variation in the data is explained by the two-factor solution? The total variance of the 10 variables when standardized is 10. The first component accounts for $5.725/10 = 57.3\%$, and the second component accounts for $2.761/10 = 27.6\%$. The two components together account for 84.9%

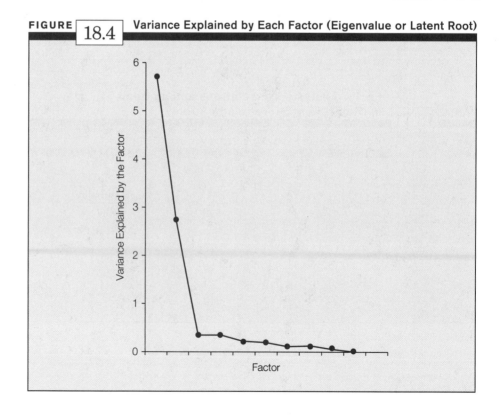

FIGURE 18.4   Variance Explained by Each Factor (Eigenvalue or Latent Root)

of the total variation in the 10 variables. (Note that the potential third factor would explain only an additional 3.66% of the variance, an amount not deemed worthy to pursue—it is just noise.)

In addition to examining how much variance among the 10 variables is explained by the 2 factors, we can also investigate the communalities of each of the separate variables, as we did for the previous example; i.e., how much of the variation in each variable is accounted for by the two-factor solution? The loadings matrix is contained in Table 18.13, and the communalities are in the right-hand column (recall, square each loading and add the results across factors). Thus, for variable 1, the communality is $(.633)^2 + (.707)^2 = .900$. The information contained in each of the variables is captured rather nicely by the two-factor solution. Variable 5 is most poorly captured, but even so, 81.8% of its variation is reflected by the first two components.[11]

Substantive Interpretation

The purposes of factor analysis are actually two: data reduction, as we've seen, but also substantive interpretation. After we find a small set of factors that summarizes the important information contained in a larger set of variables, we then wish to understand those factors.

In our principal components examples, we've seen the utility of data reduction, but we haven't said much yet about interpretation. For interpretation, we wish to identify the construct(s) that underlie the observed variables. Figure 18.5 depicts the model where two factors are assumed to have given rise to the five measures. Recall from your basic statistics class that "correlation does not imply causation": X_1 and X_2 may be correlated because X_1 causes X_2, X_2 causes X_1, or some other cause is common to both X_1 and X_2. The factor analysis model posits the last scenario—that a common factor gives rise to both X_1 and X_2, thereby producing the observed correlation between the variables. The idea is that these variables share a factor in common that reflects some underlying, unobserved construct(s).

For the sales performance data, where one factor effectively summarizes the data, the substantive interpretation is straightforward. A factor score can be calculated for each sales representative using this "general performance" factor, and the sales representatives can then be ranked according to these factor

TABLE 18.13

Factor Analysis: Unrotated Principal Components Matrix for Department Store Image Data

Variable	Factor 1	Factor 2	Communality
1	.633	.707	.900
2	.621	.695	.869
3	.872	−.241	.819
4	.833	−.366	.828
5	.774	−.469	.818
6	.626	.719	.908
7	.619	.683	.850
8	.859	−.303	.829

[11] Taking $p = 10$ variables down to two factors is a good example of the idea of "data reduction," or making the analysis more parsimonious. It's even more impressive when 20 or 100 variables are simplified down to two or three or five factors.

FIGURE 18.5   Search for Substantive Interpretation in a Factor Analysis Solution

scores. The "best" performing sales representative will have the highest score and the "worst" sales representative the lowest score.

Rarely is a factor solution so tidy—even the store image data are slightly more complex. In these more complicated situations (when there are two or more factors), it is useful to "rotate" the initial factor solution to facilitate substantive interpretation.

Rotating the Factors

What are the factors in the store image data? An interpretation based on the loadings in Table 18.13 is somewhat obscure. All 10 variables load on the first factor. Variables 1, 2, 6, and 7 also have high positive loadings on the second factor. Figure 18.6 shows a plot of the loadings (using the two factors as the axes and the loadings as coordinates). Variables 1, 2, 6, and 7 occupy the same general location, and variables 3, 4, 5, 8, 9, and 10 also occupy the same general two-space location. If we rotate the original factor axes to a new orientation, it may facilitate interpretation of the factors.

Several alternatives have been proposed by which the new linear combinations can be formed. Just about all these methods attempt to produce loadings that are close to either 0 or 1, because such loadings show more clearly what things go together and, in this sense, are more interpretable. When a variable is uncorrelated with a factor (that is, the loading is near zero, or less than .3 in magnitude), we can dismiss the variable as not being useful in interpreting the factor. Conversely, when a variable is more highly correlated (the loading is nearer 1, or, say, greater than .5), we rely on that variable to help us interpret and understand the factor.

Both orthogonal and oblique rotations have been proposed. Orthogonal rotations preserve the right angles that exist among the factor axes. Oblique rotations do not, which means that the factors themselves can be correlated.[12]

---

[12] Use "promax" programmed in Sas and Spss.

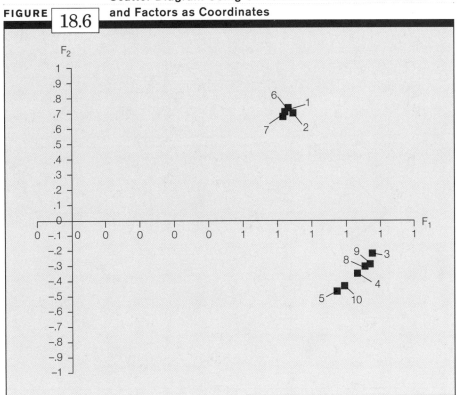

FIGURE 18.6

Scatter Diagram Using Correlations Between Variables and Factors as Coordinates

Figure 18.7 displays the "varimax" orthogonal rotation of the original axes. Varimax attempts to simplify the factor loadings by forcing them to be near 0 or 1. Varimax is a robust and simple procedure that typically enhances the interpretability of factors, and it is consequently the most popular orthogonal rotation scheme. In the figure, the original axes are labeled F_1 and F_2, and the rotated axes are labeled F_1' and F_2'.

Note that each of the new axes seems to be purer than the original axes. That is, whereas the variables had high loadings—as represented by the magnitude of the vertical projections—on both of the original factor axes, they seem to have high loadings on either one or the other of the new axes, but not both. Table 18.14 presents the "rotated factor loadings," which are the magnitudes of these vertical projections, or the correlations of the variables with the new factors.

Naming the Factors

What are these factors? We'll name the factors according to which variables go with each factor.

1. Begin with the first variable and first factor in the rotated factor-loading matrix and move horizontally from left to right looking for the highest loading. Circle that loading. Repeat this procedure for each of the other variables in turn.

2. Examine each of the circled loadings and assess its "significance." The significance of any loading can be judged using either statistical or practical criteria. Statistical criteria mean that the loading is statistically significant at some specified alpha level, typically .05. This means that for samples of fewer

FIGURE 18.7   Scatter Diagram after Orthogonal Rotation of Axes

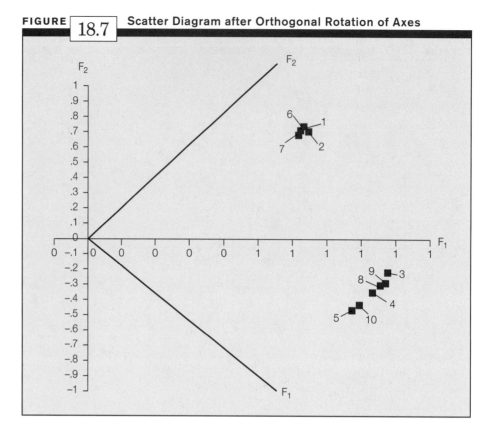

than 100, the loading would have to be greater than .30 to be considered statistically significant (and means that the factor accounts for at least 9% of the variation in the variable).

3. Underline the other significant loadings using the criteria decided on in Step 2.

4. Examine the loading matrix and identify all those variables that do not have significant loadings on any factor. Every variable is expected to load on some

TABLE 18.14   Factor-Loading Matrix for Department Store Image Data after Orthogonal Rotation of Two Principal Components Using Varimax

Variable	Factor 1	Factor 2	Communality
1	.150	.937	.900
2	.147	.920	.869
3	.864	.269	.819
4	.899	.142	.828
5	.904	.024	.818
6	.138	.943	.908
7	.151	.909	.850
8	.886	.209	.829
9	.887	.221	.835
10	.910	.045	.831
Eigenvalue	4.859	3.628	

factor, but if there is a variable that does not, you can either (1) interpret the solution as it is and simply ignore those variables without any large loading, or (2) critically evaluate each of the variables that do not load significantly on any factor; specifically, if a variable is of minor importance to the study's objective and it has a low communality index, you might eliminate the variable and derive a new factor solution.

5. Focus on the significant loadings, and attempt to name the factors on the basis of what the variables that load on a given factor seem to have in common. Variables that have significant loadings on more than one factor complicate the naming task and are also candidates for elimination, depending on the purpose of the study as well as on whether the mixed pattern of loadings makes sense or indicates there are fundamental problems with the variable or item.

It turns out that when these steps are applied to the loadings in Table 18.14, each variable loads significantly on one and only one factor: variables 3, 4, 5, 8, 9, and 10 load only on Factor 1, and variables 1, 2, 6, and 7 load only on Factor 2. If you read the survey items, their content suggests that Factor 1 is a "store atmosphere" factor; e.g., is the store clean, organized, spacious, and in general has a nice atmosphere. Factor 2 reflects whether the store is a convenient place to shop because of its hours, its location, and the speed of the checkouts. Therefore, we would probably want to call it a "convenience" factor. Instead of describing differences in department stores using the 10 original variables, considerable economy is gained by describing these differences in terms of the two derived factors. For these data, we have achieved "data reduction" and "substantive interpretation."

Note that the rotation of a factor solution is conducted for one reason only— to facilitate the isolation and identification of the factors underlying a set of observed variables. The rotation does not help explain additional variance. If two factors were originally needed to capture the important information in the data, two factors will also be needed after the rotation, if information is not to be discarded. To see this, one simply has to compare Tables 18.13 and 18.14. The communalities for each variable are the same before or after rotation. The contribution of each factor in accounting for the variation in each variable has changed, but the total explained variation has not. For variable 1, the communality before rotation was $(.633)^2 + (.707)^2 = .900$, and after rotation it is $(.150)^2 + (.937)^2 = .900$, but before rotation the 2nd factor accounted for 50.0% and after rotation it accounts for 87.8%. The contributions of the factors have been altered, but no additional variation has been accounted for (nor has any been lost). The same holds true for the contribution of factors to total explained variation (i.e., not just variable-by-variable). The total variance explained remains constant, but the contribution of variance explained is reapportioned across factors. Initially, the contribution of the 1st factor was $5.725/10 = 57.3\%$ and the 2nd was $2.761/10 = 27.6\%$, for a total of 84.9%. After rotation, the contribution of the 1st factor is $4.859/10 = 48.6\%$ and the 2nd is $3.628/10 = 36.3\%$.

The Key Decisions

We stated that factor analysis represents a body of techniques for studying the interrelation among a set of variables. The method used to analyze both the sales performance data and the store image data was based on the "principal components model," which posits:

$$z_j = W_{j1}F_1 + W_{j2}F_2 + \ldots + W_{jm}F_m, j = 1, 2, \ldots, p$$

This model assumes that any of the p performance variables could be perfectly described by a set of m common components. Factor analysts argue that this model can be enhanced. In particular, we might suspect that it is unreasonable to expect all the variance of a variable to be summarized by common factors only; a fraction may be "unique." For example, although income and assets are both manifestations of the underlying trait of "being rich," they are not the same.

What are the differences and implications? The classic factor model is:

$$z_1 = W_{11}F_1 + W_{12}F_2 + \ldots + W_{1m}F_m + d_1 V_1$$
$$z_2 = W_{21}F_1 + W_{22}F_2 + \ldots + W_{2m}F_m + d_2 V_2$$
$$\ldots$$
$$z_p = W_{p1}F_1 + W_{p2}F_2 + \ldots + W_{pm}F_m + d_p V_p$$

This model looks similar to the principal components model, except for the additional $d_j V_j$ terms. In this model, each variable is described linearly in terms of m common factors and a factor unique to the particular observed variable.

The distinction between the classical factor analysis model and the principal components model can be best appreciated by again referring to the sales performance data. We saw that if we had used all three principal components and their loadings, we were able to reproduce exactly the correlation matrix, including the 1's in the diagonal. By comparison, for the classical factor model, we care more about the correlations between variables (the off-diagonal elements in a correlation matrix) than any variable's variance (the diagonal values). The correlations between variables are reproduced by means of the common factors alone (i.e., what do the variables have in "common"). The variances for each variable (i.e., the 1's in the diagonal of the correlation matrix) are achieved using the common factors and the unique factors together. Another way to think about it is to replace the 1's in the correlation matrix with numbers approximating the communalities (what the variable has in common with other variables). Of course, this raises the question of how these communalities are to be estimated.

Generating Communality Estimates

The most popular approach to estimating communalities uses multiple regression. Each variable is regressed on all of the other variables in the analysis, in turn, to get the resulting R^2's. The diagonal of the correlation matrix is replaced by these squared multiple correlations before the correlation matrix is factor analyzed. This technique has been demonstrated to work well; it is widely available and often the default in the major statistical computing packages.

Decision Items

A number of decisions enter into a factor analysis. Figure 18.8 outlines the sequence of issues that arise. Let's briefly review the essential questions that need to be addressed at each stage in the process.

1. Should factor analysis be applied to the data?

   a. Factor analysis does not work well if any, or certainly if many, of the variables are binary. Rating scales generally work fine.

   b. One might examine the correlation matrix to determine whether a factor analysis is likely to prove fruitful. Factor analysis is concerned with the homogeneity of items, which means that some of the values in the

FIGURE 18.8   Key Decisions When Factor Analyzing Data

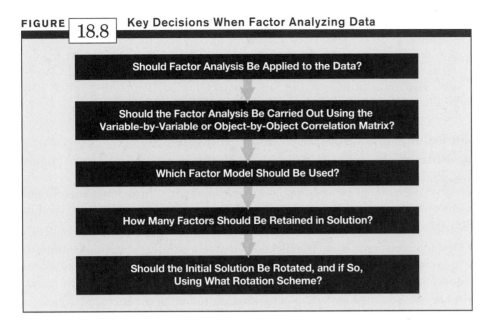

Should Factor Analysis Be Applied to the Data?

Should the Factor Analysis Be Carried Out Using the Variable-by-Variable or Object-by-Object Correlation Matrix?

Which Factor Model Should Be Used?

How Many Factors Should Be Retained in Solution?

Should the Initial Solution Be Rotated, and if So, Using What Rotation Scheme?

correlation matrix should be large, i.e., they go together. A pattern of low correlations throughout the matrix indicates a heterogeneous set of items, probably inappropriate for factoring. A related diagnostic involves plotting the eigenvalues. The plot should indicate a sharp break. If the plot results in a continuous, unbroken line, factoring may be inappropriate. (These conditions often go together.)

2. Typically, a factor analysis is carried out on a variable-by-variable correlation matrix because most studies aim at determining which variables go together. However, the object-by-object (e.g., consumer-by-consumer) matrix can also be analyzed.

3. Which factor model would be used? We discussed the principal components model and the factor model, in which 1's and communalities are placed in the diagonal of the correlation matrix before it is analyzed.

4. How many factors should be retained in the solution? We discussed the latent roots and scree criteria, which generally work well.

   a. When too few factors are retained and rotated, the output can be difficult to interpret—the variance in each variable is forced on too few factors, resulting in a number of midsize loadings rather than loadings near 0 and 1.

   b. When too many factors are retained and rotated, some factors come out capturing the variance of a single variable or, at most, two variables. This result is counter to the whole notion underlying factor analysis, which suggests that a factor is a latent construct reflecting what a number of observed variables have in *common* (a "factor" with a single variable loading on it seems not to have identified variables with anything in common).

   c. In general, the evidence suggests that over-factoring by extracting one or two extra factors has fewer severe consequences than does taking too few factors.

5. Should the initial solution be rotated, and if so, using what rotation scheme? Often, different rotation schemes largely converge in what they reflect about the data. However, even if they highlight slightly different properties in the

data, it is useful to keep in mind that all rotations are equivalent from a statistical point of view. They differ only in how they distribute the variation accounted for across the factors, which, of course, is what is used to name the factors. Thus, performing several rotations and examining the results to see which rotation produced the "most interpretable" structure is often very productive.

Marketing Applications of Factor Analysis

In marketing, factor analysis historically has been used to name the factors captured by the measures, as we've illustrated, as well as to "purify" scale items in survey refinement by isolating and then eliminating those items that do not seem to belong with the rest of the items. Factor analysis has also been used in lifestyle and psychographic research problems to:[13]

- Develop consumer profiles reflecting people's attitudes, activities, interests, opinions, perceptions, and preferences to better predict their consumption and purchase behavior
- Ascertain key attributes that determine customer preferences for products (e.g., brand equity studies), or organizations
- Assess a company's image
- Isolate the dimensions of print ads that most affect readership
- Develop measure of job satisfaction in B-to-B contexts
- Screen variables before running regressions to reduce the problem of multicollinearity.

The bottom line on when to use factor analysis is this: Factor analysis is useful when a survey contains multiple correlated measures that may be measuring a common underlying construct. Factor analysis extracts few factors from many variables and yet retains most of the "important information." As a result, it helps the marketing researcher simplify the task at hand.

Cluster Analysis

There are lots of marketing questions that revolve around classifying objects. Very often the objects to be classified are customers—if you hear "segmentation," you should think "cluster analysis." A firm segmenting its market is seeking to group potential customers into homogeneous groups that are large enough to be profitably cultivated. The segmentation base could involve many characteristics, including socioeconomic, psychological, and buyer behavior variables. Cluster analysis helps the marketing researcher identify natural groupings of the customers even with complex multivariate data. To segment customers using only one or two variables would be an oversimplification, but how should the multiple variables be combined? Cluster analysis techniques assign objects to groups so that there is as much similarity within groups, and difference between groups, as possible.[14]

Segmentation? Probably was a cluster analysis!

[13] For an example, see Kenneth P. Gwinner, Stephen W. Brown, Mary Jo Bitner, and Ajith Kumar, "Service Customization Through Employee Adaptiveness," *Journal of Service Research,* 8 (2), 131–148.

[14] Recall that for discriminant analysis, there were *a priori* groups, and we were trying to understand the group differences using variables measured on the individuals in those groups. For cluster analysis, we have the obverse problem; we are trying to use information on consumers to form groups.

An important use of cluster analysis is identifying aggregates of consumers who behave similarly. By determining the areas where they live and the demographics of those areas from census data, geodemographic segments of the population can be formed. Research Realities 18.2, for example, lists some features of subgroups in the Claritas Prizm system. We tend to live near people who are similar to us, and at the same time, our clusters can be found in several geographic locations. For example, the "Towns and Gowns" lifestyle, which includes disproportionately high rentals of foreign videos and use of online services, and low usage of coupons and drycleaners, is similar whether the clustered customers are in Berkeley, Boulder, or Gainesville.

Another application for cluster analysis is test markets. Test markets require two cities that are similar so that when one serves as the test market and the other as a control, we can attribute any sales differences to our marketing tweaks. But how do you determine which cities are alike? To keep things simple, say we cared about only two city characteristics—population and median income. We standardize the variables to equate their scales of measurement, such as in Table 18.15.

RESEARCH   REALITIES

18.2 Characteristics of Selected Subgroups in Prizm Lifestyle Clusters

Major Group	Subgroups[1]	Demographic Description	Lifestyle, Media, Financial Preferences
Suburban Elite	• Blue-Blood Estates • Money and Brains • **Furs & Station**	New-money families in suburbs, upwardly mobile white collar, college grads, age 35–54	Own family laptop(s), all-news radio, 31 stock transactions/yr
Affluentials	• **Pools & Patios** • Two More Rungs • Young Influentials	Upper-middle income, two-income empty nesters, age 45–64, in upscale suburbs	Foreign cruise, epicurean magazines $5,000 + mutual funds
Greenbelt Families	• Young Suburbia • **Blue-Chip Blues**	Upper-middle income, traditional suburban families, age 25–44, mixed white/blue collar, single-family houses	Go fishing, watch headline news, interest-bearing checking accounts
Urban Gentry	• Urban Gold Coast • Bohemian Mix • Black Enterprise • **New Beginnings**	Lower-middle income families and singles, age 25–34, low-level white collar and clerical	Jog/run, have first mortgage
Exurban Boom	• God's Country • **New Homesteader** • Towns & Gowns	Lower-middle income, town-dwelling, young families, age 18–34, some college, blue/white collar	Ride motorcycles, nostalgia radio, veterans life insurance
Suburban Elders	• **Levittown, USA** • Gray Power • Rank and File	Middle-income, suburban, (older couples) age 55–65, tract housing, two income, high school education	Belong to a union, golden oldies radio, Christmas Club account

[1] The **bold** subgroup is the largest subgroup in its major group. For more information, see Prizm Lifestyle Cluster System (Claritas.com).

Cluster Analysis Example: Key Characteristics
TABLE | **18.15** | **of Cities to Be Grouped (In Standardized Units)**

City	Income X_1	Population X_2
A	1.14	1.72
B	−1.25	−1.17
C	1.62	.89
D	1.64	1.35
E	.55	.10
F	−.94	−1.25
G	.89	1.32
H	−.87	−.63
I	−.44	−.07
J	.08	−.55
K	−.18	.62
L	−1.29	−.86
M	−1.07	−1.38
N	−.09	.02
O	.21	−.11

A simple, subjective way of grouping objects is to plot the results and make a visual assignment. Figure 18.9 uses the variables of income and population as axes. The scatterplot suggests that there are three distinct clusters in the data:

• Cluster 1, consisting of Cities {A, C, D, G}
• Cluster 2, consisting of Cities {E, I, J, K, N, O}
• Cluster 3, consisting of Cities {B, F, H, L, M}

The visual assignment procedure worked in this example because there were only two variables and the natural groupings were pretty clear. However, the

Cluster Analysis Example: 2-Dimensional Plot of City
FIGURE | **18.9** | **Characteristics**

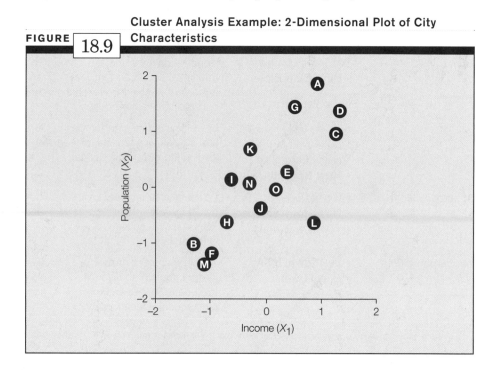

cities might be grouped on many characteristics, and it would be useful to have a way of incorporating the higher dimensionality. Further, it would be useful to have a more objective means of forming the clusters, using indices of "similarity" or "likeness."

Euclidean Distance to Measure Similarity

One measure that captures the closeness of two objects in a scatterplot is the **Euclidean distance** between the points. In the 2D figure, the distance between cities A and C is calculated:

$$d_{A,C} = \sqrt{(X_{C1} - X_{A1})^2 + (X_{C2} - X_{A2})^2}$$

where X_{C1} represents the coordinate of city C on the 1st dimension, median income. This distance is:

$$d_{A,C} = \sqrt{(1.62 - 1.14)^2 + (.89 - 1.72)^2} = .959$$

If, in addition to having income and population variables on the cities, we also had a variable that captured, say, literacy rates, we would effectively have a 3-dimensional problem. The Euclidian distance is easily extended:

$$d_{A,C} = \sqrt{(X_{C1} - X_{A1})^2 + (X_{C2} - X_{A2})^2 + (X_{C3} - X_{A3})^2}$$

and generally, for any two objects, i and j:

$$d_{ij} = \sqrt{\sum_{k=1}^{3} (X_{ik} - X_{jk})^2}$$

(The generalization to n dimensions to account for n characteristics would mean the sum goes from $k = 1$ to n.)

The "distance" between all 15 cities is presented in Table 18.16. (These Euclidean distances capture psychological dissimilarity or distance; not geographical distances between cities.) Note that distance is an inverse measure of similarity because the larger the distance, the farther apart the objects. For these 15 cities, there are $15(14)/2 = 105$ distances in the matrix; in general for n objects, there are $n(n-1)/2$ distances. How can we use these distances to find clusters?

Clustering Methods

A number of clustering methods exist for forming groups of objects. There are "linkage" and "nodal" procedures, and variations within each method. The objective underlying each method is the same—to assign objects to groups so that there will be as much similarity within groups and as much difference between groups as possible. The different methods can produce widely divergent results for the same data, and none of the methods is as yet accepted as the "best" under all circumstances. The marketing researcher must, therefore, be familiar with the various methods to choose the one that is most compatible with the research project's goals.

Single Linkage

Single-linkage computer programs operate in the following way: First, the similarity values are arrayed from most to least similar. Then, those objects with the

| TABLE 18.16 | Distance Between Cities I and J in 2-Space | | | | | | | | | | | | | |

| | | 1 A | 2 B | 3 C | 4 D | 5 E | 6 F | 7 G | 8 H | 9 I | 10 J | 11 K | 12 L | 13 M | 14 N | 15 O |
i=	j=															
1	A	.000														
2	B	3.750	.000													
3	C	.959	3.533	.000												
4	D	.622	3.834	.460	.000											
5	E	1.724	2.203	1.330	1.658	.000										
6	F	3.626	.320	3.337	3.663	2.011	.000									
7	G	.472	3.283	.847	.751	1.266	3.155	.000								
8	H	3.092	.660	2.917	3.197	1.597	.624	2.627	.000							
9	I	2.388	1.366	2.273	2.518	1.004	1.282	1.924	.706	.000						
10	J	2.505	1.467	2.108	2.458	.802	1.237	2.038	.953	.708	.000					
11	K	1.718	2.085	1.820	1.961	.896	2.019	1.279	1.428	.737	1.199	.000				
12	L	3.544	.313	3.396	3.670	2.075	.524	3.083	.479	1.160	1.405	1.850	.000			
13	M	3.807	.277	3.520	3.847	2.194	.184	3.336	.776	1.454	1.418	2.189	.565	.000		
14	N	2.098	1.662	1.919	2.182	.645	1.528	1.628	1.015	.361	.595	.607	1.488	1.709	.000	
15	O	2.053	1.804	1.729	2.044	.400	1.619	1.583	1.199	.651	.459	.828	1.677	1.803	.327	.000

highest similarity (or smallest distance) are clustered together. Two objects might come together to form a cluster, or an object might join an already formed cluster. Then the next most similar items are clustered, etc. The threshold of how similar two objects must be before being joined is systematically lowered, and the union of objects at each similarity value is recorded. The union of two objects (i.e., the admission of an object into a cluster, or the merging of two clusters) is by the criterion of a "single linkage." This means that if the similarity level in question is, say, .20, a single link of an object at that level with any member of a cluster would enable the object to join the cluster. Similarly, any pair of objects (one in each of two clusters) related at the criterion level will make their clusters join.

Let's begin, for example, with all the similarity values less than 1.000 in Table 18.16. When arrayed from most similar to least similar, the tabulation in Table 18.17 results. The highest reported similarity value (or the smallest distance) is

| TABLE 18.17 | All Distances Less than 1.00 Arrayed in Increasing Order of Dissimilarity | | | | |

Distance Level	City Pairs	Distance Level	City Pairs	Distance Level	City Pairs
.184	FM	.524	FL	.737	IK
.277	BM	.565	LM	.751	DG
.313	BL	.595	JN	.776	HM
.320	BF	.607	KN	.802	EJ
.327	NO	.622	AD	.828	KO
.361	IN	.624	FH	.847	CG
.400	EO	.645	EN	.896	EK
.459	JO	.651	IO	.953	HJ
.460	CD	.660	BH	.959	AC
.472	AG	.706	HI		
.479	HL	.708	IJ		

.184, the distance between F and M. Starting at a distance of zero, the first computer iteration would be to this value, and objects F and M would be joined to form a cluster. The next table entry is .277, the distance between objects B and M. Consider what happens at this second computer iteration value.

Since M has already been joined to F at the first iteration, the situation can be diagrammed as follows:

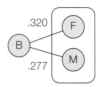

Will B be allowed to join the cluster consisting of the elements F and M? The answer is yes under the criterion of single linkage. Even though the distance from B to F is higher than the cutoff threshold of .2 (it's .320), that doesn't matter under the criterion of single linkage. Rather, the one link between B and M that satisfies the criterion value is sufficient to allow B to join F and M to form the larger group BFM.

The next iteration would be to the similarity value .313, representing the distance between B and L. Would L be allowed to join the group BFM at this iteration value? Again, the answer would be yes under the criterion of single linkage (even though the distances between F and L (.524), and L and M (.565) are both greater than the criterion value at this iteration (.313)).

Next, since BFL and M are already joined, nothing further happens at the similarity value .320 (for B and F). At the value .327, N joins O, and I joins this new pair at the iteration value .361 to form the larger group INO. E and J are subsequently admitted to this cluster of objects at the iteration values .400 and .459, respectively.

The process continues to cluster together objects until, after the 15th iteration corresponding to a distance of .607, the situation looks like this:

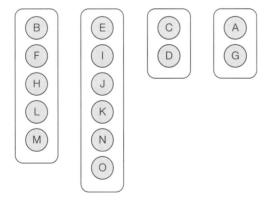

At this point, none of the variables is still in a cluster by itself.

When do the clusters themselves join to form larger groupings? According to the criterion of single linkage, the clusters join when the distance between any pair of objects in the distinct clusters equals the iteration distance value. Consider, for example, the situation between Clusters 3 and 4, which can be diagrammed as follows:

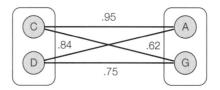

At an iteration value of .622, Cluster 3 will be joined with Cluster 4, because the single bond between A and D satisfies the criterion.

Note that although the clusters are joined because of the single link between two members of the respective clusters, some of the members within the newly formed cluster are much farther removed (or very different) from one another; e.g., the distance from A to C is .959 and the distance from C to G is .847, approximately 1.5 times larger than the merging distance. Single linkage thus frequently produces *chaining*, that is, long, straggling groups, yielding solutions that are not particularly helpful to the researcher.

Cluster analysis results are often presented in the form of a dendrogram, a "tree" figure that indicates the groups of objects formed at various similarity (distance) levels. The dendrogram for the city data employing the single linkage method is shown in Figure 18.10.

Objects A through O are shown at the top. As we saw, the class FM forms first (d_{FM} .184); B is admitted to this cluster at a distance iteration value of .277; and so on. These unions and the values at which they occur (called the fusion coefficient) are shown on the horizontal axis in the figure. What are the natural groupings in the data? It depends on what similarity level you're using. At a distance level of .50, there are five separate classes, reading from left to right:

- Group 1—CD
- Group 2—AG
- Group 3—INOEJ
- Group 4—K
- Group 5—FMBLH

FIGURE 18.10   **Dendrogram of City Data Using Single Linkage Clustering**

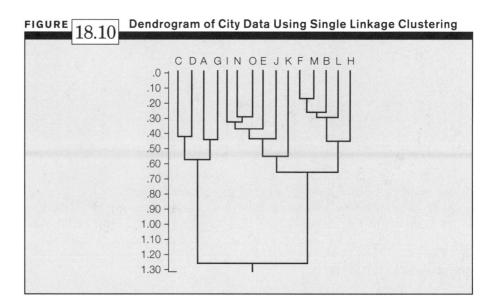

If instead a distance level of .65 is to be used, there are three clusters:

• Group 1—CDAG

• Group 2—INOEJK

• Group 3—FMBLH

Finally, if one selects a distance level of .80, there are only two groups:

• Group 1—CDAG

• Group 2—INOEJKFMBLH

Many researchers would probably select a cutoff distance of .65, because the 2D portrayal of the data suggests that there are three natural groupings. With p variables, the decision concerning the proper cutoff value must be made without such a visual referent, making the decision much more difficult.

If the researcher simply needed two cities that were very much alike, he or she might use a stringent criterion level, such as .35 to obtain groups with quite homogeneous cities (in this example, one group consisting of the cities N and O and the other group consisting of F, M, B, and L). If a larger number of test-market cities were necessary, he or she would relax the requirement on the similarity coefficient, e.g., .65, which would produce the three groups listed above: {CDAG}, {INOEJK}, {FMBLH}.

An alternative way of deciding the number of clusters is to plot the number of clusters against the fusion coefficients. Note, for example, that at a value of .184 in the figure, where objects F and M join, there are 14 groups. At the value of .277, where objects F, M, and B join, there are 13 groups, and so on. These fusion values and number of groups serve as the coordinates for the two points farthest to the left in Figure 18.11.

The idea is to use a fusion plot in much the same way as the plot of eigen-values is used in factor analysis. The researcher looks for large jumps in the

FIGURE 18.11   Plot of Number of Clusters vs. Fusion Coefficient

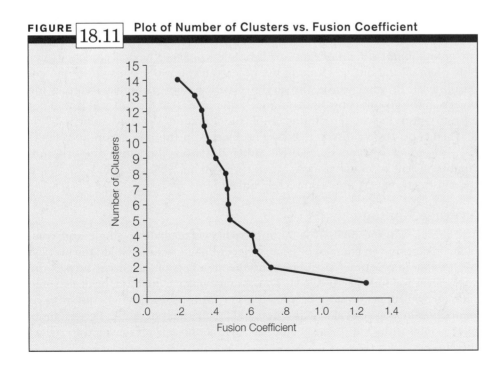

fusion coefficient, indicating that two relatively dissimilar clusters have been merged, which suggests that the number of clusters before the merger is the most probable solution. Alternatively, the researcher can look to see where the curve flattens out, which suggests that no new information is portrayed by the subsequent mergers of the clusters that would follow. Note that in Figure 18.11 the curve flattens at two points, once when going from five to four clusters and once when going from two clusters to one, implying that five or two clusters exist in the data. The incremental change in the fusion coefficient also suggests either five or two clusters are in the data, since there is a substantial jump in the value of the coefficient between five and four and between two and one clusters. As the example indicates, these rules of thumb for determining the number of clusters can be helpful, but they sometimes produce ambiguous results.

Complete Linkage

In the complete-linkage clustering method, an object joining a cluster at a certain similarity coefficient must be that close or closer to every member of the cluster. Thus, unlike the previous technique, a single bond with just one member of the cluster would not be sufficient to effect the juncture. This condition is rigorous, with groups forming only when the criterion level is lowered considerably. As a result, complete linkage has a tendency to produce very tight, compact clusters. The clusters are so well-defined that complete link clustering is one of the more useful and popular of clustering techniques.

Consider the group of cities ADGC. This group will eventually form under the complete linkage criterion, but consider how. The respective distances are:

	A	C	D	G
A	.000			
C	.959	.000		
D	.622	.460	.000	
G	.472	.847	.751	.000

At a value of .460, objects C and D join, and at .472, A and G join. When will the two groups join? Under the criterion of complete linkage, they will come together only when all the linkages among the objects in the two groups satisfy the criterion level. In other words, the largest distance (most dissimilar) among the objects in the groups controls the union. This means that the two groups will not join to form the larger cluster until the iteration distance value .959 is reached. This largest distance, between object A in the one group and object C in the other, ensures that all the other distances also satisfy the criterion (that is, if .959 is "close enough," then surely so are .622, .847, and .751), and the clustered objects are "completely linked."

Average Linkage

The average-linkage method is an approach intermediate to single and complete linkage. As the name implies, an object will join a cluster when the average of all similarities between the object and the members of the cluster surpass the given level for linkage to occur. The average-linkage method involves some simple calculations: As soon as a new cluster forms, these average distances or similarities must be calculated and updated for the next iteration. For example, once C joins with D at the level .460, the matrix above is recalculated to reflect the cluster:

	A	CD	G
A	.000		
CD	.7905	.000	
G	.472	.799	.000

where .7905 = (.959 + .622)/2 and .799 = (.847 + .751)/2, the average of A with C and D, and the average of G with C and D. You can see from this smaller 3 × 3 matrix, in the next step, A would join G at the .472 level. The matrix of similarities is again updated:

	AG	CD
AG	.000	
CD	.7948	.000

where .7948 = (.7905 + .7990)/2, the average of CD with A and with G. These computations may not seem like much, especially for our small example of 15 (and here, 4) objects, but remember that cluster analysis is frequently used to segment customers—sometimes hundreds of thousands of them.

Although more computer-intensive in terms of calculations, empirical evidence indicates that the average-linkage method generally works well. For example, in simulation studies where there are known cluster configurations, average link recovers the results cleanly. It seems to exhibit the advantage of complete link (fairly tight clusters) without the disadvantage of the very rigorous criterion that all objects must be sufficiently similar. Because it performs so well empirically, it is probably the most popular of the cluster linkage techniques.

The linkage methods are all considered hierarchical clustering methods; if objects C and D cluster together when there are five clusters, they will also be together in the same cluster, perhaps with additional objects, when there are four clusters, and so on. The dendrogram captures the resulting hierarchy—an object cannot break out of a cluster once it has been subsumed into the cluster.

Nodal Methods

Another class of clustering method involves selecting an object that serves as the focal object, or "node" for a cluster. The remaining objects are then allocated to each cluster on the basis of their similarity to the focal object(s). The basic operation of the nodal methods is illustrated by the following scheme:

- Choose objects that have the least similarity or greatest distance between each other.

- Consider these two objects as extreme nodes, and allocate all remaining objects to one or the other cluster based on their similarity to those extreme nodes.

- Split the two resulting clusters in the same way. Continue the process until the collection of objects is split into its original members.

In the city example, Cities D and M are most dissimilar (d_{DM} = 3.847), and thus they would be considered as the nodes for the two clusters. Each of the remaining objects would then be allocated to each cluster on the basis of the shortest distance to either D or M. Thus, the first iteration would form these clusters:

- Group 1—DACEGK

- Group 2—MBFHIJLNO

Next, in Group 1, the least similar cities are D and K ($d_{DK} = 1.961$), so they would be considered new nodes, and the remaining objects in Group 1 would be allocated to each of the new clusters on the basis of their distances to these new nodes. Those new groups would be:

- Group 1A—DACG
- Group 1B—KE

Similarly, Group 2 would be divided (using B and J as new nodes) to yield:

- Group 2A—BFHLM
- Group 2B—JINO

At each stage, the cluster analyst could check to see if the resulting subgroups should be retained, or combined back together, based on, say, some average measure of similarity between the objects within and among subgroups.

An alternative nodal clustering method employs a "prime" node. The prime node is the most "prototypical" object—the object that has characteristics closest to the average for all the objects. Because the data have been standardized, the average median income and average population for the 15 cities are zero. City N is most typical (its values on both variables are closest to zero, the standardized mean), so it would be considered the prime node, and the clustering begins around it. Cities are added to this cluster one at a time. After each addition, a measure of the resulting homogeneity of the cluster is determined. When the measure of homogeneity (e.g., the average-within-cluster distance) takes a large jump in value, the "natural" limits of the cluster are considered to have been exceeded, and the last object added to the cluster is removed. The proper solution would be the previous stage in the iterative clustering.

After this primary cluster is determined, it is removed from the analysis. A new prototype object is determined from the remaining objects, and the process is repeated. The procedure continues until all the objects have joined clusters or until only a few isolated objects remain. (They could be left alone, or they could be attached to the clusters that they fit best.) The nodal methods are also known as "iterative partitioning methods" because of the way they work; they begin with some initial partition of the data and subsequently change these assignments.

Initial partitions are chosen in other ways as well. An alternative is to specify "seed points" by picking certain objects to serve as group centroids or even to randomly assign objects to one of a prespecified number of clusters (e.g., three). Regardless of how the initial assignment of objects to groups is determined, the next step is to calculate the centroids (group means) of each cluster and then to reallocate each data point to the nearest cluster. After all reassignments are made, the centroids of the new clusters are computed, and the process is repeated until no reassignments occur. Thus, iterative partitioning methods make more than one pass through the data, which usually results in good solutions, even if the initial partition was rough.

Currently, the most popular partitioning method is the "k-means" approach, which requires that the number of clusters, k, be specified in advance and that k starting points be determined by selecting certain objects to serve as nodes (purposively or randomly). In the first pass through the data, each object is assigned to one of the k starting points according to which starting point it is most similar or closest to. Then (1) the mean or centroid for each group is calculated and (2) the objects are reassigned on the basis of the mean to which they are closest. These two steps are repeated until no objects are reclassified. Research Realities 18.3 visually demonstrates the operation of the k-means approach.

R E S E A R C H   R E A L I T I E S

18.3 Operation of k-Means Cluster Analysis

Suppose that the two swarms of data depicted as circles in Figure A were two clusters of points in a two-dimensional plot awaiting discovery. If we want to find the two-cluster solution, we first pick two starting points. As a random choice, suppose that the starting points are at the A and B in the point swarm on the right.

FIGURE 18.A

We measure the distance of each point to the starting points A and B, classifying each data point into the group associated with the closer of those two. In Figure B, each point is identified with a circle or triangle, depending on whether it is closer to A or B.

FIGURE 18.B

Only the lower right side of the right-hand swarm in Figure B is closer to B than A. Now we compute the averages, or "centers of gravity" of all the circle data points and all the triangle data points. We indicate those by labels A and B in Figure C.

FIGURE 18.C

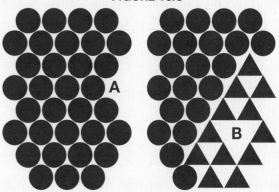

In Figure D we have reclassified each point according to whether it is closer to the new A or the B.

FIGURE 18.D

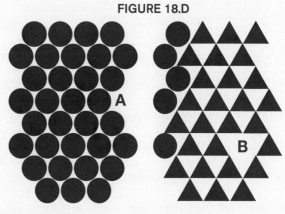

Notice that only a few points in the right-hand swarm are still closer to the A than to the B. Again, we compute the averages of the points now classified as

(Continued)

circles and those classified as triangles, indicating those positions by A and B in Figure E.

FIGURE 18.E

With one more iteration through the data, all points on the left would be identified as circles and all on the right as triangles, so the continuation of this process would result in no further reclassification of points. In real data, this process would have converged even more quickly if our starting points had not been chosen so poorly. For example, if one point had been in the swarm on the left and the other in the swarm on the right, convergence might have been immediate. On the other hand, whereas the example suggests k-means can recover quickly from a poor specification of starting points, that is not always true—it depends on how clearly separated the groups are.

Source: "*Convergent Cluster Analysis System (CCA),*" *(sawtoothsoftware.com).*

Key Decisions

The discussion so far may suggest that to use cluster analysis, there is only one decision to be made: namely, which clustering method to use. *Au contraire.* A cluster analysis requires making decisions at each of the four stages depicted in Figure 18.12.

Select and Code Attributes

Stage 1 focuses on the related questions, "Which attributes will we use to generate the clusters?" and "How will these attributes be coded?" The example assumed that income and population were the most important variables in finding similar cities. These variables are both ratio-scaled, and no additional coding (other than standardization) was necessary before generating Euclidean distances to assess similarity. However, had we changed the city characteristics used to define similarity, the clusters might well have changed.

FIGURE 18.12 **Key Decisions When Cluster Analyzing Data**

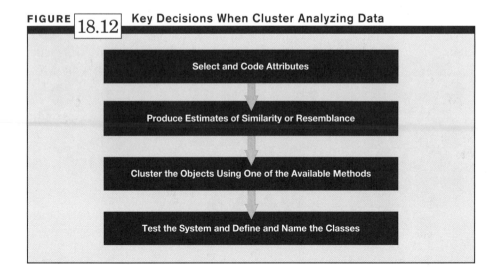

The literature does not provide a great deal of guidance with regard to selecting attributes. Yet the choice of variables used to cluster the objects is one of the most critical decisions analysts make. The best advice seems to be to choose those variables that make sense conceptually rather than using any and all variables simply because they are available.

When coding the attributes, it is necessary to keep their basic nature in mind. Some of them may be continuous in nature (e.g., income), whereas others may be categorical (e.g., geography). For example, we could have created a dummy variable to represent whether a city was in the southern or northern U.S.

The basic problem is to select the variables that represent the concept of similarity for the given study. Ideally, some theory or assumptions based on prior brand knowledge would provide the basis for a rational choice of the variables to be used. The importance of using theory to guide the choice of variables should not be underestimated. Naïve empiricism (i.e., include as many variables as possible and see what comes out) always produces muddy results.

Produce Estimates of Similarity or Resemblance

The estimates of similarity (used to specify the closeness of the objects) also depend on the level of measurement of the attributes. In our example, both income and population were ratio-scaled, so it was natural to define similarity computing Euclidean distance. But say you wish to cluster people into similar groups for a market segmentation study, where a number of variables would be nominally or ordinally scaled (e.g., marital status, religious preference, stage in the life cycle). What kind of similarity index should be used as input to the cluster algorithm? Are they to be binary (0 = absence, 1 = presence of an attribute), or matching coefficients (e.g., two customers are more similar if they both subscribe to *Sports Illustrated*), or are the coefficients to reflect categories (e.g., someone in the household subscribes to theater, opera, or orchestra series performances), and so on?

If the input measures reflect cardinal measurement (i.e., whole numbers), the basic decision is whether to use a distance function or a correlation coefficient to capture resemblance. If the researcher chooses a distance function, should it be Euclidean distance, as in the example, or should it be city-block distance, or Mahalanobis distance? Euclidean distance is the most popular, yet it is not "scale invariant." That is, the relative ordering of the objects in terms of their similarity can be affected by a simple change in the scale by which one or more of the variables are measured. For example, we could measure income in dollars or in thousands of dollars and that can affect the ordering of the similarity coefficients if the data are not first standardized (to mean zero and standard deviation one). In general, we want similarity coefficients that are not sensitive to the units of measurement. Standardization is one way to equate units, but it carries its own costs, e.g., it can reduce the differences between groups on the variables that may well be the best discriminators of group differences. The best advice seems to be: If the variables' measurement scales are roughly of the same magnitude, it might be best not to standardize them. If the variables are measured on widely differing units, standardization is needed to prevent the variables measured in larger units from dominating the cluster solution.

What if the data are dichotomous or multichotomous? Usually a "matching coefficient" is used. A matching coefficient represents the number of qualities that two objects share. However, this simple notion begs the question of what kind of matches should count: Positive matches? Negative matches? Both kinds?

To illustrate the dilemma, consider the data for three objects contained in Panel A of Table 18.18. Each object has been measured on 10 attributes; a 1 indicates that the object possesses the attribute and a 0 indicates that it does not. The attributes could represent any number of features of the objects. Suppose that the attributes indicate which of 10 magazines these three people read, and we wish to calculate the similarity of reading habits for each of the people-pairs AB, AC, and BC. A 1–1 indicates that both people read the magazine—a positive match; a 0–0 indicates that neither person reads that particular magazine—that's a negative match; a 1–0 means that the first person reads it but the second does not, whereas a 0–1 indicates the opposite, implying a mismatch in reading habits. Panel B of Table 18.18 summarizes the information contained in Panel A concerning the number of positive matches, negative matches, and mismatches for each of the three pairs.

Panel C of Table 18.18 illustrates the computation of several popular similarity coefficients. Formula C1 expresses similarity as a function of the ratio of

TABLE 18.18   Some Alternative Similarity Coefficients

A. Attributes Possessed by Each Object

Object	Attributes									
	1	2	3	4	5	6	7	8	9	10
A	1	0	0	0	1	0	0	1	1	1
B	0	1	0	0	1	0	0	1	0	0
C	0	0	1	0	0	1	0	1	1	0

B. Summary of the # of Positive Matches, Negative Matches, and Mismatches

	Object Pairs		
	AB	AC	BC
# positive matches (a)	2	2	1
# negative matches (b)	4	3	4
# mismatches (c)	4	5	5

C. Similarity of the Various Pairs Using Alternative Similarity Coefficients

Coefficient	Object Pair	Value
C1. $\dfrac{a}{(a+b+c)}$	AB	.200
	AC	.200
	BC	.100
C2. $\dfrac{a}{(a+b)}$	AB	.333
	AC	.400
	BC	.250
C3. $\dfrac{a}{(a+c)}$	AB	.333
	AC	.286
	BC	.167
C4. $\dfrac{(a+c)}{(a+b+c)}$	AB	.600
	AC	.700
	BC	.600
C5. $\dfrac{c}{(a+b)}$	AB	.667
	AC	1.000
	BC	1.000

{# positive matches} versus {the total # of attributes on which the objects were measured}. Formula C2 also emphasizes positive matches, but it is based on the ratio of {# positive matches} to {# of total matches, both positive and negative}. Mismatches do not explicitly count in C2. Formula C3 compares {# positive matches} to {# positive matches plus # mismatches}; it de-emphasizes negative matches while considering mismatches. Formula C4 also considers mismatches; it compares {# positive matches plus # mismatches} to {the total # comparisons made between the objects}. Formula C5 looks at {# features on which the objects are different} versus {# on which they are the same}.

The essential difference among the formulas is how they handle the different kinds of matches and the mismatches. A case could be made for any one of them when deciding which people have more similar reading habits. We could argue that it's the magazines that two people both read that determines whether they have similar reading habits, so we should choose a coefficient that emphasizes positive matches. Alternatively, we could argue that it's important to note that neither one reads, say, *Sports Illustrated*, which means we should choose an index that emphasizes negative matches as well. Or, we could argue that because one of the respondents reads *Sports Illustrated* whereas the other doesn't indicates something important about the similarity of their reading habits, and we would therefore want to give some weight to mismatches, though perhaps not as much as to positive or negative matches.

The important thing to note about these five coefficients is that they produce different orderings in terms of the similarity of the three objects. Coefficient C1 indicates that object pairs AB and AC are the most similar. Coefficient C2 suggests that object pair AC is more similar than AB, and that, in turn, is more similar than BC. A different ordering of similarity is produced by coefficient C3, etc. There is no answer as to which emphasis is inherently correct—it depends on the objectives of the marketing research study.

The most popular of the five coefficients highlighted in Table 18.18 are coefficients C1 and C3. Coefficient C1 is known as the **simple matching coefficient**, and C3 is called **Jaccards' coefficient**. Both emphasize the importance of positive matches.

A different kind of measurement problem arises if some variables are interval- or ratio-scaled whereas others are categorical. Should the continuous variables be converted to categorical variables so that a matching coefficient can be calculated? If they aren't categorized, how are the two types of measures to be combined?

Gower's coefficient of similarity to the rescue!—it's capable of handling binary (e.g., gender), multicategory (e.g., religious preference), and quantitative (e.g., age) characteristics:

$$S_{ij} = \frac{\sum_{k=1}^{m} w_k s_{ijk}}{\sum_{k=1}^{m} w_k}$$

where S_{ij} is the similarity of objects i and j, s_{ijk} is the similarity of objects i and j on the kth characteristic, with m characteristics in all. The value s_{ijk} must be ≥ 0 and ≤ 1. With qualitative characters, it is 1 when there is a match and 0 with a mismatch. With quantitative characters, $s_{ijk} = (|X_{ik} - X_{jk}|/R_k)$, where X_{ik} and X_{jk} are the values of attribute k for the ith and j^{th} objects, and R_k is the range of character k in the sample, w_k is the weight attached to the kth attribute.

The coefficient allows you to specify which of the two types of matches count with respect to any attribute. You simply set w_k to 1 if the comparison counts and

0 if not. Further, the coefficient allows you to weight some attributes more than others. For example, in Panel A of Table 18.18, say the first five attributes represent readership of business magazines and the last five refer to general-interest magazines such as *Time* and *Newsweek*. If we are trying to cluster executives in terms of their reading of business literature, we might want to weight the positive matches more than the negative ones. The situation can be diagrammed as follows:

Attribute

Object	1	2	3	4	5	6	7	8	9	10
A	1	0	0	0	1	0	0	1	1	1
B	0	1	0	0	1	0	0	1	0	0
S_{ijk}	0	0	1	1	1	1	1	1	0	0
w_k	2	2	2	2	2	1	1	1	1	1

The overall similarity of executives A and B is:

$$S_{AB} = \frac{2(0) + 2(0) + 2(1) + 2(1) + 2(1) + 1(1) + 1(1) + 1(1) + 1(0) + 1(0)}{2 + 2 + 2 + 2 + 2 + 1 + 1 + 1 + 1 + 1} = \frac{9}{15} = .600$$

To illustrate the computation of Gower's coefficient for quantitative characteristics, consider the city data again. For City A, income has a value of 1.14 and population a value of 1.72. For City E, income has a value of .55 and population a value of .10. The range of population values across all cases is 3.10, and the range for income values is 2.93. The similarity of objects $A(i = 1)$ and $E(j = 5)$ in terms of income $(k = 1)$ would be $s_{151} = (|1.14 - .55|/2.93) = .201$, whereas in terms of population $(k = 2)$ it would be $s_{152} = (|1.72 - .10|/3.10) = .526$. Assuming that we wanted to weight income and population equally, the overall similarity of objects A and E would be:

$$S_{AE} = \frac{1(.201) + 1(.526)}{1 + 1} = .364$$

As these two example illustrate, Gower's coefficient offers a great deal of flexibility in generating similarity values, which is one of the primary reasons for its popularity.

Cluster the Objects Using One of the Available Methods

Computer simulations have been used to compare the "performance" of different clustering methods—each is tested to see how well it can recover known configurations. The hierarchical methods work fairly well, but tend to have problems when the data contain a high level of error. One problem is that what appear to be trivial decisions made early in the clustering tend to have large effects on the final outcome because only one pass is made through the data. The multiple-pass partitioning methods work best, particularly k-means. However, this method's performance depends on the use of fairly accurate starting points. Thus, be careful when basing decisions on interpretations of cluster analysis output.

Recognize that the different methods are variants but share the same aim. Thus, they're not mutually exclusive alternatives but complementary procedures to get at the same objective, and sometimes they can be used in combination. For example, one way of getting the seed points for a k-means approach is to use average linkage and the resulting dendrogram to determine both the number of clusters and which objects to use as the starting points for each cluster.

Test the System and Define and Name the Clusters

Suppose we've derived a set of clusters. Now the question is: What do they mean?

First we test whether the results offer a reasonable summary of the data—is the solution consistent with the input similarities (whether correlation or distance matrix)? Suppose we got a dendrogram from one of the linkage cluster methods. For each pair of objects, we could read the fusion coefficient (also known as the *cophenetic value,* or the *amalgamation coefficient*) from the dendrogram. If the dendrogram represented perfectly all the information in the similarity matrix, the fusion value for each pair of objects would exactly equal the input similarity value. Compare the actual distances between objects F, M, and H (from the distance matrix in Table 18.16) with the distances where the objects joined the cluster (read from the dendrogram):

Object Pair	Actual Distance	Distance When Joined
FM	.184	.184
FH	.624	.479
MH	.776	.479

A similar comparison can be made for each of the other 225 pairs of objects, and then some measure of goodness of fit (e.g., a correlation) between the actual values with the obtained values can be calculated.

Methodologists also recommend a cross-validation test of the reliability of the cluster solution across data sets. That is, the data are split into at least two subsets, and the question is whether the same clusters are produced when the different portions of the data set are analyzed.

Still another test of the usefulness of the cluster solution is to perform significance tests comparing the clusters on variables that were not used to generate the cluster solution. For example, we could compare our 15 cities in terms of the average age of the population. Those cities in the same cluster should be similar, or approximately equal in terms of average age, whereas those cities in different clusters should be different.

If the resulting clusters are acceptable, the marketing research must then describe and name them. The cluster's description typically centers on those variables that determine membership in a given class vs. membership in other classes. The task of naming clusters is often a fun, creative one for marketers (recall the labels of "Pools & Patios," "Young Suburbia," "New Homesteaders," etc.).

Marketing Applications of Cluster Analysis

We've emphasized two pervasive and important marketing problems that cluster analysis is frequently called upon to address: 1) segmenting customers and 2) forming homogeneous groups of cities in preparation for test marketing.

The applications of cluster analysis in marketing continue to increase, such as:

- Sorting households' demand patterns for electricity
- Grouping TV programs into similar types on the basis of viewers' reports
- Grouping other media in terms of the similarity of their audience appeal
- Finding homogeneous census tracts, e.g., for consumer and political purposes
- Grouping brands and products on the basis of how similar to competitors' products they are perceived to be, thus how likely they are to serve as substitutes
- Determining spheres of opinion leadership in word-of-mouth networks
- Assessing the similarity of countries and cultures in world markets

R E S E A R C H   R E A L I T I E S

18.4 Recommendation Agents = Cluster Analysis

A booming use of cluster analysis is the online recommendation agent. When you visit Amazon, Netflix, etc., and a list of books, movies, music, or other products are suggested to you, where do these recommendations come from?

Internet providers store huge matrices (100,000s of customers as rows and their inventory of SKUs as columns). When consumer j purchases book k, the jth, k^{th} element in the matrix becomes a "1" rather than the previous "0." Two consumers are indexed as similar if they have purchased a number of SKUs in common. Once a consumer has been identified as similar to a segment of other customers, the segment's portfolio of purchase histories become sources of recommendations.

Sources: Dawn Iacobucci, Phipps Arabie, and Anand Bodapati, "Recommendation Agents on the Internet," Journal of Interactive Marketing *14, 2–11. Also see Anand Bodapati, "Recommendation Systems with Purchase Data,"* Journal of Marketing Research, *45 (1), 77–93; and Girish N. Punj and Robert Moore, "Smart Versus Knowledgeable Online Recommendation Agents,"* Journal of Interactive Marketing *21 (4), 46–60.*

Also see Research Realities 18.4. The question, "When do I use cluster analysis?" is easily answered. Cluster analysis is an extremely useful statistical tool to help the marketing researcher identify groups of similar things; e.g., brands, products, and, most frequently, people in segmentation studies.[15]

Multidimensional Scaling and Perceptual Mapping

Multidimensional scaling (MDS) has been used primarily to capture consumers' perceptions of brands through the creation of perceptual maps. MDS is a technique to measure and represent people's perceptions about various objects—products, brands, stores, etc. In its constant quest for a differential advantage, an organization must correctly position its products against competitive offerings. To do this, managers need to identify the following:

- The number of dimensions consumers use to distinguish products and the competition
- The names of these dimensions
- The positioning of existing products along these dimensions
- The location where consumers prefer a product to be on the dimensions

One way managers can grasp the positioning of their brand versus competing brands is through the study of perceptual maps. In these maps, each product or brand occupies a specific point on the map. Brands that are similar lie close together, and those that are different are farther apart.

Research Realities 18.5 depicts the perceived competitive situation between Hallmark and Wal-Mart as they ready themselves for the big Christmas shopping season. Consumers' perceptions of different retailers' Christmas themes are mapped, e.g., some stores emphasize convenience, others a more religious tone.

[15] For a nice overview, see Jon R. Kettenring, "The Practice of Cluster Analysis," *Journal of Classification,* 23, 3–30. Also see Wayne S. DeSarbo, Duncan Fong, J. Liechty, and K. Saxton, "A Hierarchical Bayesian Procedure for Two-Mode Cluster Analysis," *Psychometrika,* 31, 5417–5572.

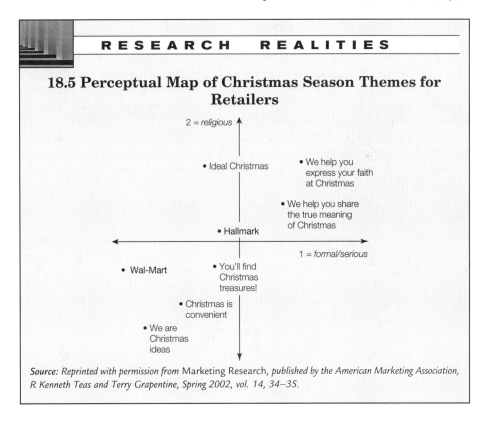

18.5 Perceptual Map of Christmas Season Themes for Retailers

Source: Reprinted with permission from Marketing Research, *published by the American Marketing Association, R Kenneth Teas and Terry Grapentine, Spring 2002, vol. 14, 34–35.*

The first dimension was labeled "formal/serious" and the second dimension captured the variability of the stores' "religious" appeal.

Perceptual maps can be created in several ways. As Figure 18.13 indicates, they can be created using *attribute-based* or *non-attribute-based* approaches. The attribute-based approach works with data obtained from the popular sort of survey item where a consumer rates an object (e.g., their satisfaction with their stay at a hotel) on several attributes (e.g., value, friendliness of staff, ease of check-in/out, room ambience, etc.). We discuss the attribute-based MDS approach shortly; we begin with the non-attribute-based approach.

MDS = Perceptual mapping!

FIGURE 18.13   Alternative Approaches to the Development of Perceptual Maps

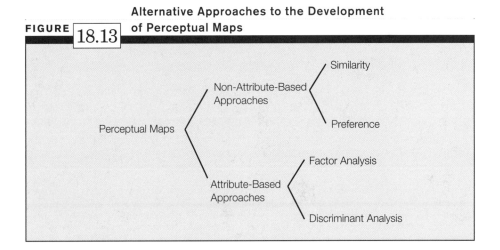

The "non-attribute-based" approach to MDS requires different data. Customers are asked to make judgments about the **similarities** among objects (e.g., Marriott vs. Hyatt vs. Four Seasons). Are the objects all alike? All dissimilar? Just how close are they perceived to be in psychological space? The notion of psychological proximity plays a central role in the technique of multidimensional scaling, and the technique is sometimes referred to as the analysis of proximities data.[16]

When making these similarity judgments, people are free to use the characteristics that matter most to them. The marketer uses the MDS model to place the brands in a multidimensional space in which the number of dimensions corresponds to the number of characteristics the individual used in forming the judgments.

Example Problem

Suppose we want to develop a perceptual map for cameras. Label the brands or camera models A through J. We would ask consumers to report their perceptions of the similarities among the 10 cameras by asking them to judge all possible pairs of cameras—45 pairs in all. There are a number of ways we can collect the data; say we conduct a mall intercept, bringing volunteers into our lab (a small office rented in the mall). We would prepare a set of 45 cards, where each card has a picture or a description of each pair of cameras. We would ask the consumer to rank the cards by increasing dissimilarity of the camera pairs using whatever criteria he or she normally uses to distinguish cameras. The individual could be instructed to sort the cards into four piles with the piles labeled extremely similar, somewhat similar, somewhat dissimilar, and extremely dissimilar. After placing each of the 45 cards in one of the piles, the individual is then asked to order those within each pile from most similar to least similar. Alternatively, we might send participants to our Web site where we display on screen the 10 cameras, one at a time. Then we cycle through presenting the 45 pairs, asking the consumer to judge the similarity of each pair on a nine-point scale (1 = "very similar cameras" to 9 = "very different cameras").[17] Either route, suppose Table 18.19 resulted from this process. The table indicates that the

TABLE 18.19   Respondent Similarity Judgments for Cameras

Camera	A	B	C	D	E	F	G	H	I	J
A										
B	28									
C	5	29								
D	24	21	17							
E	32	1	26	18						
F	37	3	34	25	4					
G	31	36	22	7	35	41				
H	27	43	20	13	42	45	9			
I	16	40	23	12	39	44	10	6		
J	7	30	2	15	33	38	19	14	11	

[16] Psychological proximity is defined as the psychological distance perceived between two objects, or between a person's preference for an object, resulting in the scaling of similarities and preferences, respectively.

[17] "Nonmetric" MDS takes ordinal input data (the ranks) and, using monotonic regressions, derives the map. "Metric" models take rating scale data as input (interval-level, like the rating scale) and relate the model-derived distances to the input dissimilarity judgments through a more restrictive, linear relationship.

respondent perceived Cameras B and E as the most similar, Cameras C and J as the next most similar, and Cameras F and H as the least similar.

Given the data in the table, at least three questions arise:

1. How many dimensions underlie this respondent's judgments about the similarity-dissimilarity of the 10 cameras?

2. What does the configuration—the map—look like? Which cameras are perceived as most similar and which are perceived as most dissimilar when they are all considered simultaneously?

3. What attributes are being used by this consumer in making his or her judgments?

MDS can answer these questions.

Conceptual Operation of Computer Programs

Many programs can perform a multidimensional scaling analysis. The programs operate by finding the best "fit" in several dimensions, where quality of fit is determined by how well the distance between the points matches the input judgments. Thus, if the distances between the points in a 2D configuration, say, when ordered for smallest to largest perfectly matched the order of the input judgments of similarity, the fit would be perfect. To the extent the ordering of the distances is inconsistent with the judged similarities, the fit is imperfect.

The programs start with an arbitrary configuration in each of several dimensions (1-D, 2-D, 3-D, etc.). Given the arbitrary configuration, they move the points around in systematic fashion using a series of iterations to improve the fit until that is no longer possible, at which time they stop and report how good or bad the fit is.

The number of dimensions that are appropriate for one's data and that should be interpreted and communicated is determined by looking at the quality of fit in each dimension, recognizing that it is easier to get a better fit in more dimensions because there is more latitude in how the points can be moved. The basic aim is to find the lowest dimensionality in which the fit is good, that is, where the distances between the objects match the similarity judgments.

Example Solution

Figure 18.14 displays the computer-determined two-space solution for the rank-order data of Table 18.19. As the figure shows, the cameras are fairly heterogeneous, although Cameras B, E, and F appear similar to the respondent, and Cameras A, C, and J seem to form another cluster. One can immediately see how a picture like this could help a firm or product manager quickly identify the company's or product's major competitors, as well as how the picture could be used to formulate a repositioning strategy.

Why two dimensions? The basic objective in MDS is to find the lowest dimensional solution in which there is good correspondence between the input judgments and the distances between the objects. As suggested, the lower space solutions rarely provide a perfect fit—some differences will exist between the plotted distances and the judged similarities. Thus, one can compute a measure of the lack of fit for each dimension. The lower the lack-of-fit index, the better the computer configuration matches the original configuration.

Different MDS programs report different lack-of-fit indices. The particular configuration displayed in Figure 18.14 was developed using Kruskal's "stress"

FIGURE 18.14   **Multidimensional Scaling Map of Similarity Judgments**

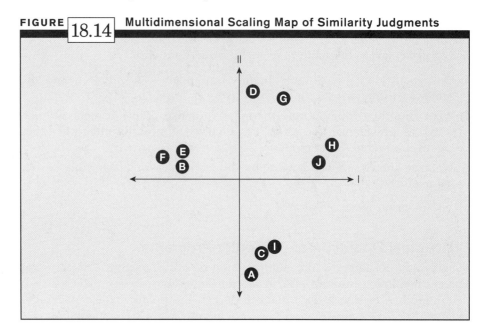

for its lack-of-fit index.[18] Figure 18.15 displays the plot of the stress value as a function of the number of dimensions that represent the solution. The fit in 1-D is fair-to-poor using Kruskal's evaluations:

Stress	Goodness of Fit
.200	Poor
.100	Fair
.050	Good
.025	Excellent
.000	Perfect

The fit in 2-D appears adequate enough to conclude that the 2-D solution is appropriate. The stress value of .019 is excellent, and there is an elbow in the stress function. The elbow indicates that goodness of fit substantially improves with an increase in the number of dimensions from 1 to 2, but improves only slightly as the number of dimensions is increased to 3 or 4. Thus, the 2-D solution is parsimonious (the objective of simplicity and minimum dimensionality), and it reproduces the original rankings as efficiently as do the 3- and 4-space solutions.[19]

Once we have the dimensions, our next task is to name them.[20] Several approaches can be used. First, the individual can be asked to evaluate the objects

[18] Kruskal's "stress" is the most commonly used measure for lack of fit (J. B. Kruskal, "Multidimensional Scaling by Optimizing Goodness of Fit to a Nonmetric Hypothesis," *Psychometrika* 29, 1–27).

[19] The stress plot should remind you of the scree plot in factor analysis, or the fusion coefficient plot in cluster analysis. These plots are used to help determine the number of dimensions to retain in the model. The diagnostic sought is the "break" or "elbow" in the curve. In factor analysis, a "variance explained" (or "goodness" of fit) index is being plotted, hence the number of factors to retain is the number that precedes the break (1 in this case), because the next small number indicates that little is improved with the additional factor. In contrast, for MDS, "stress" (a badness-of-fit index) is plotted, so the number of dimensions to keep is the number that follows the break (2 in the figure), because that additional dimension reduces the badness of fit to something reasonable.

[20] This task is analogous to naming factors in factor analysis. In factor analysis, we examine the variables that load (correlate) high on a factor to infer what that factor is capturing. In MDS, we compare the brands at the left-most and right-most of the map (and then, top versus bottom, and so on) to try to determine what they have in common and how they differ, in order to deduce a sensible name for the dimension.

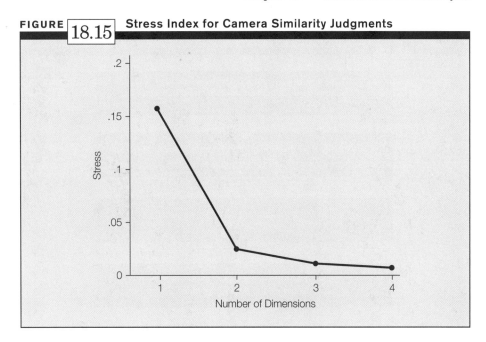

FIGURE 18.15   Stress Index for Camera Similarity Judgments

(here, the cameras) in terms of several attributes, such as digital, brand name, value, automatic focus, and so on. The researcher correlates the attributes for each object with the coordinates for each object. Another approach is to have the manager interpret the dimensions using his or her own experience and the visual configuration of points. Still a third approach is to attempt to relate the dimensions to physical characteristics of the cameras, such as physical size or price.

Suppose that the dimensions were named using one of these schemes, and that dimension 1 turned out to be a "good value" dimension whereas dimension 2 turned out to be an "easy to use" dimension. Suppose also that you are the manager for Brand J. The perceptual map in Figure 18.14 indicates that your brand is perceived as being difficult to use and only an average value by our single respondent. If a large enough number of respondents felt this way, and you are suffering market share problems, it might behoove you to examine how value, and especially ease-of-use, can be increased.

We have been focusing (cameras, get it?) on the placement of the objects in the map, but we can also put consumers' preferences into the same geometric space. An individual's "ideal" camera is a hypothetical camera possessing just the perfect combination of the two attributes, ease of use and value. Consumers' ideal points are located from the preference data that they supply. For preferences, the objective is to locate the ideal point so that the distance between the customer's ideal and each of the objects corresponds as closely as possible to the stated preferences for the objects.

Key Decisions

We have presented the conceptual underpinnings of MDS; let's review the analytical decisions that must be made (see Figure 18.16). First, specify the set of products or brands that will be considered. Although they will be partly determined by the purpose of the study, they will not be completely specified by it, and analysts will have some discretion in choosing products or brands to use.

FIGURE 18.16   **Key Decisions When Conducting a Multidimensional Scaling Analysis**

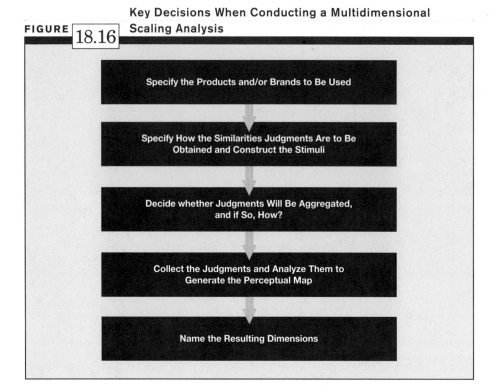

When exercising this discretion, analysts need to recognize that the dimensions that appear in the perceptual map are a direct function of the stimulus set that was used to collect the judgments. For example, suppose that a study was being conducted to determine respondents' perceptions of various soft drinks. If no diet soft drinks were included in the stimulus set, this very important dimension would not appear in the results. Thus, in designing an MDS, it is important to consider the range of perceived similarity of the objects in the set. To avoid missing an important dimension, marketers may be tempted to include every conceivable product or brand in the stimulus set. This strategy, though, can place such a burden on respondents (task tedium) that their answers may become errorful and meaningless.

The burden on respondents depends partly on the number of judgments each has to make and partly on the difficulty of each judgment. Both of these issues, in turn, depend on how the similarity judgments are obtained. Under each alternative are two main alternatives and a number of options. The two major options are "direct" or "indirect" similarity judgments, two terms that are relatively self-explanatory. The direct methods rely on data-collection mechanisms in which respondents compare stimuli using whatever criteria they desire and, on the basis of that comparison, state which of the stimuli are most similar, least similar, and so on (as we have been discussing). The indirect methods operate differently—these are the "attribute-based" approaches that we describe in the section that follows.

The third decision to make is whether the judgments of individual respondents will be aggregated so that group perceptual maps or individual maps will be generated. The problem with individual maps is that they would be numerous, even for a modest sample size (e.g., 100 MDS maps, one for each sample member), so it becomes difficult for the marketing manager to use to develop marketing strategy. Managers typically look at marketing planning questions in terms of segments, not individuals. Yet, as soon as the segment issue is raised, the question becomes one of deciding how the individual judgments will be aggregated. Is it likely that individuals used the same number of criteria when evaluating the various brands? Even if they used the same number, are the criteria themselves likely to be the same? If they are not, what criteria should be used to group respondents? One popular algorithm allows everyone to weight the dimensions differently when forming their judgments. So, in the cameras example, "value" would be weighted more for some people, and "ease of use" would be more important to others.

Step 4 involves the actual collection of the judgments and their processing. The last decision involves labeling the dimensions, a task that needs to be done rigorously and objectively to be persuasive to management.

Attribute-Based Approaches

The attribute-based approaches obtain "indirect" measures of customers' perceptions of similarities between objects. Instead of asking for a direct rating of similarity, for which respondents select their own criteria to compare the alternatives, they are asked to make the standard ratings of brands on a number of attributes (or check which brands possess which attributes, etc.). The attributes rating scales (e.g., semantic differential or Likert scales) are chosen by the marketers, prespecifying the features or criteria for the respondents.

For example, rather than asking, "How similar are cameras A and B?" we would ask, for example, "How easy to use is camera A?" "How easy to use is camera B?" "How good is the value of camera A?" and "How good is the value of camera B?" A measure of similarity is then calculated for each pair of brands (usually the correlation between the ratings of the brands). These derived similarity indices are subsequently analyzed to get the map. One advantage of the attribute-based approaches to the development of perceptual maps is that they do make the naming of dimensions easier. They also seem to be easier for respondents to use.

Comparison of Approaches

The advantages of the attribute-based versus the non-attribute-based approaches to multidimensional scaling analysis are summarized in Table 18.20. Most of the non-attribute-based applications in marketing use similarity judgments. Similarity measurement has the advantage of not depending on a predefined attribute set. This is a two-edged sword. Although it allows respondents to use only those dimensions that they normally use in making judgments among objects, it creates difficulties in naming the dimensions. Further, different consumers can use different dimensions, and one then has to grapple with how best to combine consumers when forming maps. Constructing a separate map for each individual is prohibitively costly. Aggregating all the responses and then developing one map distorts reality because it implies a homogeneity in perceptions that probably does not exist.

In contrast, the attribute-based approaches presume that the list of attributes the consumers rated is relatively complete. They assume that a person's perception or evaluation of a stimulus is some combination of the individual's reactions to the attributes being rated. Yet people may not perceive or evaluate objects in terms of underlying attributes, but holistically, not decomposable in terms of separate attributes. Or, the marketer may simply overlook the inclusion of an attribute that the customer considers important.

Comparison of the Non-Attribute- and Attribute-Based Approaches for Developing Perceptual Maps

TABLE 18.20

Technique	Respondent Measures	Advantages	Disadvantages
Non-attribute-based similarity judgments	Judged similarity of products or brands	+Doesn't depend on pre-defined attribute set +Allows respondent to use their normal criteria when judging objects +Perception of whole may not be simply the sum of the perception of the parts	−Difficult to name dimensions −Difficult to determine if, and how, judgments of individuals should be combined −Criteria respondents use depend on stimuli being compared −Requires special programs −Provides oversimplified view of perceptions when few objects are not used
Attribute-based discriminant or factor analysis	Ratings on products or brands on prespecified attributes	+Facilitates naming the dimensions +Easier to cluster respondents into groups with similar perceptions +Easy to use +Programs readily available	−Requires a relatively complete set of attributes −Rests on assumption that overall perception of a stimulus brand is made of the individuals' reactions to the attributed being rated

Regardless of the approach taken, the appeal of multidimensional scaling analysis lies in the maps produced by the technique. MDS is well-suited for:

- Strategic competitive analysis
- The evaluation of advertisements
- Test marketing
- Store image research
- Brand-switching research

In sum, the answer to the question, "When do I use multidimensional scaling?" is basically: Whenever you wish to obtain a map of customer perceptions and preferences. These maps can be used to provide insight into some very basic questions about markets, including the following:[21]

1. The salient product attributes perceived by buyers in the market

2. The combination of attributes buyers most prefer

3. The products that are seen as substitutes and those that are differentiated from one another

4. The viable segments that exist in a market

5. The opportunities and unserved segments in a market that can support a new-product venture

[21] For more on MDS, see J. Douglas Carroll and Phipps Arabie, "Multidimensional Scaling," in Michael Birnbaum (ed.), *Measurement, Judgment, and Decision Making* (Academic Press), pp. 179–250. Also see Wayne S. DeSarbo, Rajdeep Grewal, and Crystal J. Scott, "A Clusterwise Bilinear Multidimensional Scaling Methodology for Simultaneous Segmentation and Positioning Analyses," *Journal of Marketing Research*, 45 (4), 280–292 and Romana Khan, Peer Orazem, and Daniel Otto, "Deriving Empirical Definitions of Spatial Labor Markets," *Journal of Regional Science*, 41, 735–756.

Summary

Multivariate techniques are those that involve the analysis of multiple (p) measures. They're particularly useful in marketing research because every consumption decision is based on many variables.

Discriminant analysis treats p measures in a dependency relationship (some variables are used to predict another). Discriminant analysis shows the relationship between a dichotomous or multichotomous criterion variable and a set of p predictor variables. The emphasis is on determining the variables that are most important in discriminating among the objects falling into the various classes of the criterion variable. With a number of predictor variables and a multichotomous criterion variable, several discriminant functions may be derived. The discriminant function or functions can also be used to predict the classification of new objects.

Factor analysis examines the interdependence among all p variables. The emphasis is on isolating the factors that are common to the interrelated observed variables to summarize the important information in the data and assist in interpreting it. The initial factor solution and the choice of the number of factors to be retained are key in accomplishing the first task, whereas the rotation of the initial solution is important for accomplishing the latter.

Cluster analysis searches for the natural groupings among objects described by p variables. It places together the objects that are similar in terms of the p variables. Their similarity is properly captured with a coefficient reflecting the scale of measurement that underlies the variables. The analyst has many choices in this regard, as well as with respect to the clustering algorithm that will be used to generate the groupings.

Multidimensional scaling is a technique to obtain perceptual maps. The input data are typically direct similarity judgments that reflect comparisons between pairs of objects like brands. The MDS model seeks to represent the objects as points in a map so that similar objects are close in space, and different objects are farther apart in space. The number of dimensions is determined by examining stress indices, and the labeling of the dimensions can be subjective or can be assisted through the use of additional ratings data and regression.

Questions

1. When do you use a discriminant function—what can it tell you?
2. What is the purpose of factor analysis. What do factor loadings tell you?
3. What can a cluster analysis tell you?
4. What kind of data are required for an MDS? How do you interpret the dimensions?

Applications and Problems

1. The management of a large chain of grocery stores is thinking about opening several chains, "south of the border," in Mexico. The manager wants to determine how national-brand shoppers and private-label shoppers differ with respect to income and the size of household. Personal interviews with a random sample of national-brand shoppers and private-label shoppers generated the following data:

National-Brand Shoppers	Annual Income ($000s) X_1	Household size (#persons) X_2	Private-Label Shoppers	Annual Income ($000s) X_1	Household size (#persons) X_2
1	16.8	3	1	17.3	4
2	21.4	2	2	15.4	3
3	17.3	4	3	14.3	4
4	18.4	1	4	14.5	5
5	23.2	2	5	17.4	2
6	21.1	5	6	16.7	6
7	14.5	4	7	13.9	7
8	18.9	1	8	12.4	7
9	17.8	2	9	15.3	6
10	19.3	1	10	13.3	4

A discriminant analysis of the data resulted in the following discriminant function:

$$Y = .333X_1 - .315X_2$$

a. What criterion was satisfied in deriving these weights?
b. Use the discriminant function to derive the discriminant scores (Y) for each shopper.
c. What do the discriminant scores indicate?
d. Compute the pooled standard deviation for X_1 and X_2.
e. Convert the original weights of the discriminant function to standardized weights.
f. Interpret the discriminant function by evaluating the standardized weights.
g. Compute the mean values of the variables for each group.
h. Compute the mean discriminant scores for each group. Interpret them.
i. Compute the cutting score.
j. For each shopper (i), next to the discriminant score (Y_i), compute $Y_i - \overline{Y}_1$ and $Y_i - \overline{Y}_2$. Determine which difference is smaller for each shopper, and in so doing, predict their group membership.
k. Create the table of predicted versus actual classifications. Compute the hit rate or the proportion correctly classified. Assess the goodness of the hit rate by computing the proportional chance criterion. Interpret your results.
l. Suppose that management wanted to classify two individuals according to whether they were national-brand shoppers or private-label shoppers. The characteristics are as follows:

Individual I	Individual II
ii. X_1—annual income, $18,300	X_1—annual income, $21,000
iii. X_2—household size, four persons	X_2—household size, seven persons

m. How should management classify these individuals? Show your calculations.

2. Prefertronics, Inc. is a medium-sized manufacturer of electronic toys. The vice president of sales has asked Bill Jurkowski, a product manager, to conduct a marketing research study to determine the key attributes that contribute to consumer preferences for the firm's products. Jurkowski had interviewers conduct personal interviews with a random sample of 100 customers. The respondents were asked to rate Prefertronics' toys on four attributes (expensive–inexpensive, safe–unsafe, educational–uneducational, and good quality–

poor quality) using a seven-point semantic differential scale. Jurkowski conducted a principal components analysis with the standardized scores, which resulted in the following factor-loading matrix. Jurkowski needs your help in analyzing this information.
The factor-loading matrix was as follows:

Factors

Variable	1	2	3	4
X_1	.812	.567	.121	.070
X_2	.532	−.743	.321	.249
X_3	.708	−.640	.205	.217
X_4	.773	.630	.018	.078

where
X_1 = expensive–inexpensive
X_2 = safe–unsafe
X_3 = educational–uneducational
X_4 = good quality–poor quality

a. What are the individual row/column entries called, and what do they indicate?
b. What does the entry in the 2nd row and 1st column indicate?
c. What is the proportion of variation in each of the four variables that is accounted for by Factor 1? Show your calculations.
d. What is the proportion of variation in each of the four variables that is accounted for by Factor 2? Show your calculations.
e. The following table is a partially completed correlation matrix derived from the preceding factor-loading matrix. Complete the original correlation matrix using all four of the factors. Hint: Use the formula $r_{jt} = \sum_k a_{jk} a_{ik}$.

Simple Pair-Wise Correlations among the Attributes (computed from four factors)

	X_1	X_2	X_3	X_4
X_1	1.000			
X_2	.067	1.000		
X_3			1.000	
X_4			.165	1.000

f. For comparison, complete the following correlation matrix using only the first and second factors to estimate the correlations. Comment on your results.

Simple Pair-Wise Correlations among the Attributes (computed from two factors)

	X_1	X_2	X_3	X_4
X_1	1.000			
X_2		1.000		
X_3			1.000	
X_4				1.000

g. Compute the proportion of the total variation in the data that is accounted for by each of the four factors. Show your calculations. Comment on your results.

h. On the basis of the preceding computations, discuss how well the variability and covariability of the variables was reproduced by two factors compared to four factors.

i. Construct a scatter diagram using the correlations between the variables and the first and second factors as coordinates of the points.

j. On the basis of the scatter diagram, would you recommend that the factors be rotated? If yes, why? If no, why not?

k. Assume that the factors were rotated. Provide an interpretation of the factors.

l. Assume that the original factor solution was rotated. Explain the following statement: "The contribution of each factor in accounting for the variation in the respective variables has changed; however, the total variation accounted for by the factors has remained constant."

3. Adstar, Inc. is a large advertising agency located in New York City. The marketing research manager wants to identify the market segments for one of the agency's clients, a manufacturer of caffeine-free soft drinks, so that an effective advertising campaign can be developed. The manufacturer believes that the product would appeal to high-income families with large households. The marketing research manager has collected information from a probability sample of 500 regular purchasers of the caffeine-free soft drink. The manager has decided to use cluster analysis but is not familiar with the technique. Information pertaining to a sample of 10 regular purchasers is given to you. The following table contains the standardized scores for income and household size for the sample of 10 respondents.

**Avgerage Ratings on Attributes
(in standardized units)**

Respondents	Income X_1	Household Size X_2
1	−2.75	−2.50
2	3.00	3.00
3	2.50	2.75
4	−1.75	−2.25
5	4.00	3.50
6	−3.50	−2.75
7	2.75	3.25
8	−2.25	−2.50
9	3.50	2.50
10	−3.00	−3.25

a. Plot the individual scores in two dimensions using the two variables as axes. What does the plot suggest?

b. Determine the similarity of each pair of respondents by computing the Euclidean distance between them.

c. Use the single-linkage clustering method to develop the clusters. Consider the similarity values less than 1.00 (from part b), and array the distances from most similar to least similar.

d. What clusters exist after the 4th iteration (distance levels of approximately .70)?

e. What clusters exist after the 8th iteration (distance levels of approx. 1.12)?

f. Construct a dendrogram for similarity values up to approx. .56. Interpret the dendrogram.

g. Suppose that the complete linkage method of clustering is used; indicate at what distance level the results will be the same as part e.

4. Crystal Clear Beverage Company, a medium-sized manufacturer of bottled water, wanted to expand its line of clear beverages with the introduction of a clear cola. Five major brands served the market. The marketing research department decided to use multidimensional scaling to determine the viable opportunities in the market. Perceptions of the similarities among the five brands resulted in the following similarity judgments.

Respondent Similarity Judgments

Brand:	A	B	C	D	E
A					
B	5				
C	9	1			
D	10	2	6		
E	8	7	4	3	

The coordinates of the brands (determined by the computer model) in two-space for the preceding rank-order data are as follows:

	Dimension 1	Dimension 2
A	−.80	.30
B	−.60	.25
C	−.75	−.20
D	−.50	−.18
E	−.60	−.39
Ideal	−.55	.50

a. Plot the brands and the ideal point.

b. How are the distances between the objects ordered? The stress value, as a function of the number of dimensions employed, is shown in the following table:

# Dimensions	Stress
1	.110
2	.105
3	.100
4	.095

c. Plot the stress values.

d. Do you think that the similarity judgments between the brands can be captured by one dimension? Give three reasons to support your decision.

e. The marketing research department has identified dimension 2 as "price." How would you advise management to position its brand?

Appendix: More Multivariate Statistical Techniques

18

Questions to Guide Your Learning:

Q1 What is a correspondence analysis?

Q2 What kinds of questions can structural equations models answer?

Q3 What are neural networks?

Q4 What are social networks?

Multivariate models are constantly proliferating—some methods come and go whereas others prove to be sufficiently useful to the marketing researcher that they are adopted and demonstrate staying power. In this appendix, we describe four techniques—correspondence analysis, structural equations modeling, neural networks, and social networks—that are relatively recent developments, but so useful that they should be added to your analytical repertoire.

Correspondence Analysis

Correspondence Analysis (CA) produces results that look much like MDS. A perceptual map is obtained in which the interpoint distances are interpreted to represent the similarities between the objects (e.g., brands).

CA differs from MDS in two ways. First, the data requirements are flexible: The data can be rating scales (as in MDS) or frequencies (e.g., number of consumers who checked a brand as their favorite from a list). Second, in addition to the map containing points representing objects, CA also allows points to represent attributes of those objects and attributes of the respondents.

For example, Figure 18A.1 contains the results of a correspondence analysis in which marketing researchers were studying the character of Web sites as a marketing tool, compared to traditional media. The various media (e.g., Web, radio, telemarketing) were the objects; they are plotted close together if they were perceived to be similar, as per MDS. In addition, there are attributes of the media plotted (do they stimulate emotions, is there strong audience involvement), as well as attributes of the respondents (segment age groups, favorite beers).

The points representing the attributes of the media help interpret the configuration and the dimensions; the closer one of the media is to one of the attribute ratings, the more that attribute is descriptive of that medium. For example, Web sites share two qualities of telemarketing: Both cost relatively little to

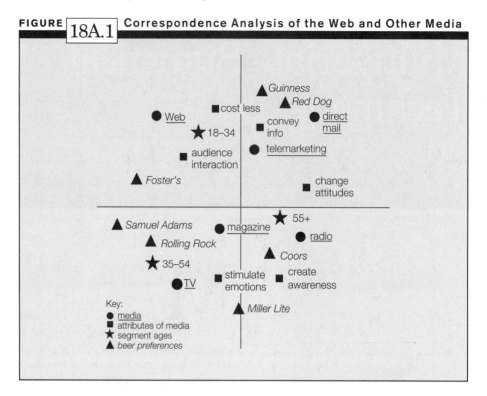

FIGURE **18A.1** **Correspondence Analysis of the Web and Other Media**

reach their target markets, and both involve interactions with the target audience members. Both of these media are different from TV and radio in being more about conveying information and less about stimulating emotions, creating awareness, or attempting to change attitudes.

The points representing the attributes of people can help segment consumers, and richly illustrate their lifestyles and the images that are likely to appeal to them when trying to reach them. For example, the youngest segment enjoys the Web, and drinks Foster's, Guinness, and Red Dog. The oldest segment in the sample enjoys radio and magazines and prefers Coors.

The essential objective of correspondence analysis is to represent everything as a Euclidean distance—the similarities between the objects, the extent to which different attributes describe those objects, and the segments of consumers that prefer those objects. The same distance formula is used as in cluster analysis or MDS (for $k = 2$ dimensions):

$$d_{ij} = \sqrt{\sum_{k=1}^{2} (X_{ik} - X_{jk})^2}$$

where d_{ij} represents the distances between any two points in the map. For MDS, the distances would be computed among six objects—the six media. For CA, the distances are computed among 22 entities: the 6 media, the 6 attributes, the 3 segment age groups, and the 7 beer brands. References to learn more about correspondence analysis abound, and procedures for fitting the CA model are increasingly accessible in statistical computing packages (e.g., SAS, SPSS).[1]

---

[1] For a nice example, see David B. Whitlark and Scott M. Smith, "Pick and Choose," *Marketing Research*, 9–14, marketingpower.com.

Structural Equations Models

A structural equations model (SEM) is like a multiple regression in that several variables are used to predict another variable. SEMs are more complex, however, in that they may comprise many layers of variables and their interrelationships. Thus, a variable that is predicted by one set of variables may in turn help predict yet another. Variables that are predicted are known as dependent variables (as in regression) or endogenous variables. Variables that are used to predict others are referred to as exogenous variables.

A structural equations model for customer loyalty is depicted in Figure 18A.2. Ultimately, the marketing researchers wish to understand loyalty, which they posit as a direct function of brand equity and customer satisfaction. In turn, they expect brand equity to be a function of advertising, brand awareness, and image or price. In an indirect manner, then, loyalty is a function of advertising, brand awareness, and image—through brand equity.

If we were to try to fit the model in Figure 18A.2 via regression, we would state the following direct relationships and run five regressions:

loyalty = b_1 brand equity + b_2 customer satisfaction

brand equity = c_1 advertising + c_2 brand awareness + c_3 image/price

customer satisfaction = d_1 image/price + d_2 quality

brand awareness = e_1 advertising + e_2 distribution

image/price = f_1 advertising + f_2 distribution + f_3 quality

The advantage of SEM over running a series of regressions is that these components of the larger model are fit simultaneously, so the researcher can test at once all the interrelationships, and direct and indirect paths, statistically controlling for all the others.

FIGURE 18A.2   Structural Equations Model of Customer Loyalty

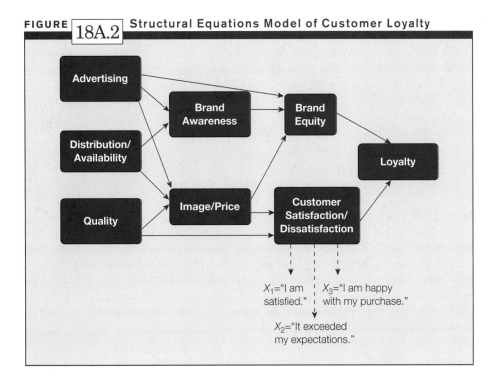

In the example, as these equations indicate, no variables are used to predict advertising, distribution, or quality, so they compose the set of exogenous variables. The others are endogenous. Brand awareness, brand equity, image/price, and customer satisfaction may also be referred to as mediators, in that they establish indirect links from some variables to others.

Another advantage of SEM over regression is that it uses factor analysis to take advantage of the correlations among variables tapping a common construct. In the figure, this element of SEM is depicted only for the construct of customer satisfaction (to keep the figure simple). There it is noted that customer satisfaction was measured by three indicator variables, X_1 ("I am satisfied"), X_2 ("It exceeded my expectations"), and X_3 ("I am happy with my purchase"). If these three variables had been used to predict loyalty, without first acknowledging that they share an underlying construct, their intercorrelations would have caused problematic multicollinearity. In SEM, their intercorrelations are first leveraged advantageously to identify the underlying factors, then the factors are used to predict the other endogenous constructs.[2]

Neural Networks

Neural networks derive from models of expert systems, where the "neural" descriptor captures the idea that these models are rough analogs of the brain. Each neuron in the brain receives inputs from other neurons, which it combines in some manner to create a resulting output signal that it subsequently passes along to other neurons. Regardless of the model's origin, or whether researchers currently believe that a network model truly describes neural functioning, network techniques have exploded as powerful and flexible analytical tools.

In their use as statistical tools, neural networks are composed of three types of layers: an input layer, an output layer, and a hidden layer. To explain neural networks in terms of regression, we would say the input layer consists of the predictor variables and the output layer, the dependent variable. Neural networks modelers call the variables nodes.

As an example, consider the network model depicted in Figure 18A.3. In this figure, the marketing researchers are using neural nets to assist them in their go/no-go decision in launching a product line in China. There are three input nodes: how the concept tested, how it fared at in-home use testing, and the marketing department's forecasts of market share.

The hidden layer is also composed of nodes. They are functions that translate the inputs into the output. The inputs to one hidden node are weighted and combined and then sent along to the next layer. The neural net in Figure 18A.3 would be like a regression if the following conditions were true: (1) There was no second, hidden node (labeled "function 2"), or links to or from it; and (2) the weights going from the three input layer nodes to the hidden layer node were betas and the combination was linear. This neural net is more complicated than a regression because of that second hidden node. Furthermore, neural nets are different from regressions because the combining function may be nonlinear. For example, market share is a continuous input (more is better) and it needs to get translated into the go/no-go step-function decision.

[2] Software for SEMs include Lisrel (ssicentral.com) and Calis (in Sas) and Amos (in Spss). For a nice example, see Devon S. Johnson, "Beyond Trial: Consumer Assimilation of Electronic Channels," *Journal of Interactive Marketing* 22 (2), 28–44.

FIGURE 18A.3 **Neural Networks Model of Product Introduction**

In addition, neural network modelers speak of a network model learning the relationship among the variables. What learning means for an algorithm is convergence and cross-validation. Specifically, a "training" data set is introduced to the neural network model, which seeks to optimize the model predictions to fit the data by trying weights and functions, and updating iteratively to improve the fit. Then, when the weights and nodal functions have been estimated on the training data, the hold-out sample of data is input to see how well the model fits in the cross-validation, which is used to further refine the model parameters and specifications.

Neural nets are gaining popularity because they are so flexible and very few assumptions are made about the data. The only challenge is that these techniques require large databases, but given the pervasiveness of large databases (e.g., for CRM), even this is not a problem.[3]

Social Networks

Social networks and neural networks have little in common. Social network techniques facilitate the description of relationships between actors. In marketing, actors can be organizations, departments within organizations, or consumers, as in word-of-mouth networks.[4]

Consider the network depicted in Figure 18A.4. This network shows the flow of information among four marketing representatives of a high-tech firm, three engineers, and two computer scientists. The actors in the network are depicted by the labels, "M1" (1st marketer), M2 (2nd marketer), E1 (1st engineer), and so on.

The communication relationships that exist among these nine actors are depicted by the arrows linking them. Note that most of the communications are represented by bidirectional arrows, meaning that the flow of information goes in both directions. However, a few arrows are unidirectional, representing that

---

[3] See Lars Gronholdt and Anne Martensen, "Analyzing Customer Satisfaction Data: A Comparison of Regression and Artificial Neural Networks," *International Journal of Market Research* 47 (2), 121–130.

[4] E.g., Douglas Bowman and Das Narayandas, "Managing Customer-Initiated Contacts with Manufacturers," *Journal of Marketing Research* 38, 281–297; Aric Rindfleisch and Christine Moorman, "The Acquisition and Utilization of Information in New Product Alliances," *Journal of Marketing* 65, 1–18; James Ward and Amy Ostrom, "Complaining to the Masses," *Journal of Consumer Research*, 33 (2), 220–230.

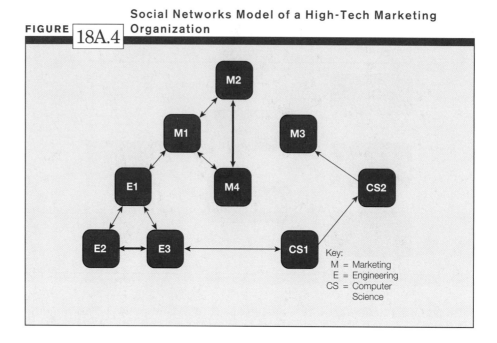

FIGURE 18A.4 **Social Networks Model of a High-Tech Marketing Organization**

CS1 (or CS2) shares information with CS2 (or M3), but information is not returned reciprocally. These asymmetric ties may be sensible if, say, CS2 worked for CS1, and CS1 was merely keeping CS2 informed of the firm's developments. Note also that the "strength of ties" can be captured with, say, the bold lines between M2 and M4, and between E2 and E3. These bold lines indicate that the communication ties in these two dyads are even stronger than those among the other people in the network.

Network data may be collected in a variety of ways. Each of these nine people might be asked, "How often do you talk with employee X about your work projects?" where each of the eight remaining network members' names would appear as "X" in turn. The relation might be asked more specifically, "How often do you ask for advice from X?" or "How often do you share data with X?" The relation might convey content beyond communication, for example, "How much do you respect X?" "Would your position in the company be enhanced if X were laid off in a downsizing?" or "Do you and your family socialize with X and X's family?" and so forth. Data might also be observational, for example, noting the number of e-mails in the company system that are sent from M1 to M2 and back again. Network researchers have also clocked social interaction time (e.g., around the water cooler, or visits by one person to another's office).

The diagrams of network connections are often very enlightening. For example, this figure might indicate some problem for M3, a marketing person who gets information only through CS2, and not as a function of communication with others in the marketing department.

Beyond the graphs, it is also important to analyze them more systematically. The relationship between actors i and j is recorded in a matrix, where the (i^{th}, j^{th}) element is a "1" if actor i sends an e-mail, say, to j, and "0" if not, and the (j^{th}, i^{th}) element in the matrix is a "1" if actor j sends an e-mail to actor i, and "0" if not. These matrices are then analyzed to identify certain qualities of the relationship structures. For example, actors E3 and CS1, and E1 and M1 would be considered actors with high "centrality," because if their respective links were broken, communication would not flow throughout the entire network. For information to pass from M4 to M3, say, these two particular links must remain intact. The centrality of an actor is one indication of the actor's importance in the network—without these key actors, the structure of the network would change substantially. If, on the other hand, actor M2 or E2 were removed from the network, the flow of communication would remain largely unchanged—other actors would make up for their loss, so these are "less central" actors in the network.

Subgroups are also a focus of network analysis. The members M1, M2, and M4, and the engineers form two "cliques," groups of actors who are all inter-connected amongst themselves. Cliques can be beneficial, as in this setting of sharing information. Cliques in other applications can be troublesome, for ex-ample, as in coalition formation and negotiation disputes. Whether a quality of a network (centrality, cliques, etc.) is good or bad depends on the setting and the content of the relationships being represented in the network.

C A S E S

CASE 5.1
CTM Productions (B)[1]

CTM Productions, formerly Children's Theatre of Madison, was formed in 1965 to "produce theater of the highest quality." CTM's mission is to ensure that the theatre's efforts are inclusive of the entire family. For CTM to fulfill its role in the community, the organization must identify its present audience in terms of demographic, psychographic, and media-exposure characteristics.

The research team decided to study the audience of CTM's production To Kill a Mockingbird. The study had three major objectives: (1) to develop an audience profile, including demographic and media-exposure data; (2) to provide a framework and data-collection instrument for future marketing research; and (3) to supply a list of potential season subscribers.

CTM had never undertaken marketing research prior to this study, so internal secondary information about previous audiences did not exist. External secondary information provided guidance as to the types of questions to be asked in a survey and the appropriate phrasing of these questions. The questionnaire was shown previously, in CTM Productions (A).

CTM's volunteer ushers distributed the survey at each of the 15 performances of To Kill a Mockingbird. The number of completed surveys for each show varied with the size of the audience for that show. A total of 1,016 usable surveys were collected during the course of the study. The research team wants to analyze the data to understand the profile of CTM audiences in general as well as how the audience profiles vary among different performances of the same production.

QUESTIONS

1. Discuss the implications for CTM's marketing team if there are significant differences in the demographic profiles of those people attending the afternoon versus the evening shows.

2. Generate a priori hypotheses about the demographic profiles for the To Kill a Mockingbird performances. Identify the cross-tabulations necessary to test your hypotheses. Explain why these particular cross-tabulations are necessary.

3. Using the data, run one-way tabulations on these data. Discuss the general findings from these tabulations.

4. Run the cross-tabulations that you chose. What recommendations would you make to CTM based on these tables? Are the recommendations actionable? Explain.

5. What are the limitations of these profiles? Explain.

CASE 5.2
E-Food and the Online Grocery Competition (C)[2]

Ashley Sims, the MBA student who is thinking about starting an online grocery, has some click-stream data to analyze. She recruited 10 volunteers for her study as they left a local retail grocery store. At a mutually convenient time, each participant came to the local library and sat before Sims's computer, where they were told to try using the system as if they were really going to shop for groceries. Upon completion, Sims asked them what they thought of the whole process. Figure 5.2.1 contains click-streams from four of these consumers.

QUESTIONS

1. What do you learn upon examination of the click-streams? How does consumer 1 think? Consumer 2? Consumer 3? What do you suppose is going on with consumer 4?

2. Could you reproduce the layout of the screens—where the various buttons (for example, "sort by price," "sort by nutritional value") are located, using these data? (Keep in mind that a boxed area on which a user clicks takes up several spaces in all directions, and that most users' clicks are not precisely in the center of the buttons.)

3. What do you suppose long time intervals between clicks mean? What assumptions are you making?

4. What recommendations would you make to Sims about designing her online grocery software, based on what these click-stream data suggest?

[1] The contributions of Sara L. Pitterle to this case are gratefully acknowledged.

[2] Click-stream data available online at our Web site.

Figure **5.2.1**	**Click-Stream Data from Online Grocery Consumers**

Consumer 1: ,11:29:42:03; 50:49; welcome scrn. ,11:31:05:23; 50:19; search scrn. ,11:31:48:10; 49:47; i5 'coke'. ,11:32:52:00; 85:31; sort-by-size. ,11:34:02:03; 84:61; sort-by-nutrition. ,11:37:12:59; 83:77; sort-by-price. ,11:37:44:09; 83:76; sort-by-price. ,11:38:29:42; 85:44; sort-by-brand. ,11:40:33:13; 90:81; buy-2,cocacola, 6-12zcans,$2.99,notonsale. ,11:41:47:53; 10:13; returntosearch. ,11:42:42:52; 50:49; i5 'pretzels'. ,11:42:57:12; 50:50; o5 'notfound'. ,11:43:14:51; 50:49; i5'pretzels'. ,11:43:22:33; 84:49; noinput. ,11:43:42:03; 84:45; sort-by-brand. ,11:44:12:15; 92:67; buy-1,roldgold, 15oz, $1.99,onsale. ,11:44:47:13; 10:15; returntosearch. ,11:46:02:02; 50:51; i5'snickers'. ,11:46:24:03; 85:31; sort-by-size. ,11:46:54:12; 89:85; buy-3,bigsnickers,3.7oz,$.95,notonsale. ,11:47:41:42; 95:05; checkout.

Consumer 2: ,14:39:12:13; 50:47 welcome scrn. ,14:39:28:23; 50:42; personal-list. ,14:40:10:49; 10:89; i5'2'. ,14:40:52:38; 90:88; buy-2,lettuce,head,$1.39,notonsale. ,14:41:22:53; 11:86; i5'1'. ,14:41:42:07; 89:86; buy-1,deanskimmilk,.5gal,$2.09, notonsale. ,14:42:09:10; 11:82; i5'3'. ,14:42:29:42; 90:81; buy-3,lrgdelicapples,$1.29/lb,notonsale. ,14:43:13:13; 10:60; i5'1'. ,14:43:19:53; 91:61; buy-1,ryebread,slcd,1lb,$2.29,notonsale. ,14:44:14:42; 94:06; checkout.

Consumer 3: ,08:23:09:42; 50:49; welcome scrn. ,08:23:17:43; 50:20; search scrn. ,08:23:58:10; 50:49; i5'mustard'. ,08:24:11:01; 85:75; sort-by-price. ,08:24:52:53; 89:61; buy-1,smlFrnchylwmustard,8oz.,$.95,onsale. ,08:25:27:23; 09:10; returntosearch. ,08:26:32:00; 50:48; i5 'buns'. ,08:27:11:12; 10:15; returntosearch. ,08:27:49:21; 49:50; i5'hotdog buns'. ,08:29:18:51; 90:05; buy-1,htdgbuns,8ct,$2.19,onsale. ,08:33:11:12; 94:05; checkout.

Consumer 4: ,16:53:22:01; 50:50; welcome scrn. ,16:55:31:55; 50:49; welcome scrn. ,16:57:44:19; 50:62; browse. ,17:02:22:50; 95:95; helpscroll. ,17:13:42:33; 14:75; browse-frozen. ,17:17:59:22; 35:65; browse-icecream. ,17:23:45:49; 94:91; noinput. ,17:24:18:09:42; 94:95; helpscroll. ,17:30:10:27; 76:15; browse-icespecialties. ,17:32:41:03; 94:96; helpscroll. ,17:35:12:02; 50:90; i5 'buy 1 icecream'. ,17:37:07:42; 50:10; o5 'cannotexec'. ,17:39:50:15; 95:06; checkout.

*The full click-stream data are online at our Web site. The format of the data contains the essential information: Each click is stored between "," and ".". The first piece of information depicted in the click-stream data unit is the PC internal time recorder in hours, minutes, seconds, and 60ths of seconds. The second piece of information is the location on the screen upon which the user clicked. The pixel coordinates offer the most precise measurement of location, but for ease of interpretation, those coordinates have been translated to units ranging from 0 to 100, with the first coordinate denoting the relative placement of the click from left (0) to right (100), and the second coordinate denoting bottom (0) to top (100) of the screen. The final piece of information is the http, the exact location in internet space of where the click sends the user. For the purposes of this analysis, the data have already been preprocessed, so as to interpret those Internet locations. For example, rather than an apparently meaningless-looking location of www.onlinefood.com/1445.html, the data are represented as: softdrink/CocaCola/sort-size-by-value (that is, the "onlinefood.com" is constant since all these clicks are in its subdomain, and the content of the html is provided). In the content stream, o = output (something the computer displays) and i = input (something the user enters).

CASE 5.3
Internet Advertising and Your Brain (B)

Recall your responsibilities as the key marketing person for a relatively new Internet company that offers travel packages for "extreme sports." Given that the majority of customers are young men, and that young men are disproportionately online, it was thought that purchasing Internet banner ads at popular sites would be a cost-efficient way of encouraging these thrill-seekers and potential buyers to click through your banner ad at the host site, sending them onto your site to, it was hoped, learn about and eventually purchase an extreme sports vacation adventure.

As marketing guru, you had created two ads, a "beauty" ad (colorful and big on graphics) and an "info" ad (less splashy, more writing, and detail). You tested both of these ads in a left-screen position and a right-screen position. Your research led you to expect that the beauty ad might do better at the left, so as to be processed by the right-brain hemisphere, which handles

pictures better. Analogously, the info ad might do better at the right, to be processed by the left brain, which deals with verbal, detailed information better.

You've obtained the click-through data from your banner advertisement Web hosts, in proportion to the traffic to their site who did not click through your banner onto your site. The results are presented below in an analysis of variance table format. Some of the information is missing—you need to fill it in before answering the questions that follow. (The critical F-value for each test is 4.00.)

The incomplete analysis of variance table of results follows:

Source	SS	df	MS	F	
Banner Type	18.4	1	?	?	?
Banner Placement	13.3	1	?	?	?
Type x Placement	?	1	?	?	?
Error	670.1	?	?	?	?
Total	756.0	99	?	?	?

The mean number of click-throughs for each combination of ad banner type (beauty or info) and ad banner placement (left or right) are as follows:

Banner Placement	Banner Type		Marginal Means
	Beauty	Info	
Right	152.5	175.4	163.9
Left	182.5	144.6	163.5
Marginal Means	167.5	160.0	

QUESTIONS

1. Fill in the analysis of variance table of results.

2. What effects are "significant" (that is, can you reject the null hypothesis)? What is going on in these data?

3. Which banner type (beauty/info) and which banner location (left/right) would you choose? Why? Can you make the choices (type and location) independently?

4. Were your initial guesses about the beauty/info and left/right combinations correct?

5. What strategic questions might supplement your interpretation of the data?

CASE 5.4
A Picture Is Worth a Megabyte of Words: Census Data and Trends in Lifestyle Purchases

Although it is always dangerous to make generalizations about people and their consumption behaviors, it is helpful to the marketer to have an aggregate sense of what people tend to buy as a function of some of their demographic characteristics. For example, household expenditures on furniture might be higher for younger people as they begin to set up house, and decline as the house is established. With a fact like this in hand, and extrapolations of the likely sizes and timing of baby-booms and baby-busts, a furniture manufacturer could use this trend information to project market sizes, and to modify the product line (for example, bean bag chairs for college students, finer wood and upholstered furniture for older, wealthier consumers).

The data that follow were extracted from the Bureau of Labor Statistics and reflect expenditures on various goods and services categories, broken down by the census age groups. Within each purchase category (the columns), the data have been calibrated so that a score of "100" means the age group (the row) spends about the average on that category. Numbers that exceed 100 mean that the age group spends more on that category of purchases than the other age groups, and numbers that are less than 100 mean that age group spends less than other age groups. For example, people younger than 25 years old and those 65 years old or older spend less on food; people between the ages of 35–44 and 45–54 spend more. People aged 25–34 and 55–64 spend about the "average." Use these data to answer the questions that follow.

QUESTIONS

1. If you wanted to know whether expenditures on furniture and computers were correlated, why might the actual computation of a correlation coefficient be inappropriate, or at least not very compelling?

2. Plot these data with the age categories as the horizontal axis, and the different columns as profiles depicting the peaks and valleys of expenditures with age.
   a. Plot total spending by age and overlay that plot with the plots of food by age and women's apparel by age. What is the pattern of spending on these apparent basic necessities?
   b. Overlay the plots for furniture, computers, and health care by age. Generally speaking, what are your target age groups if you are Scandinavian Design? Dell? A hospital network or health and life insurance company?
   c. Overlay the plot for entertainment expenditures by age with the plot for travel by age. How do we tend to amuse ourselves as younger versus older people?
   d. Finally, use whichever variables interest you and whatever plotting format you think will lend insight to creatively discover any other phenomenon in the data.

Age (in years)	Total Spending	Food	Women's Apparel	Furniture	Computers	Health Care	Entertainment	Travel
<25	59	74	62	55	60	30	62	47
25–34	99	101	85	105	98	67	109	81
35–44	129	134	119	147	119	96	141	98
45–54	130	128	145	126	161	111	123	143
55–64	105	101	120	107	103	122	95	136
65–74	77	69	87	64	55	149	73	102
75+	50	39	49	19	15	141	26	53

CASE 5.5
CountryCable: Customer Satisfaction Survey Data[3]

CountryCable is a television cable service that focuses on people who live in small towns. The ability to provide good cable service is more challenging when the technology infrastructure is more basic in the outlying areas. Basically, these companies provide "cable" through an electronic combination of actual cable and satellite dishes. The company wants to know how their customers think they're doing, and what are the most important areas for improvement.

Two months ago, the survey shown in Figure 5.5.1 was enclosed with the cable subscriber's bill. The particular market sampled was thought to be representative of any other small town segment that the company serves. This particular market comprises 12,500 subscribers.

Within one month to six weeks, the data came back from 75 subscribers, and these data are shown in Figure 5.5.2. Surveys came back from 23 other

Figure **5.5.1**	Customer Satisfaction Survey

Please tell us how satisfied you are with your CABLE TELEVISION SERVICE:

1) My cable TV service is priced reasonably.

    Strongly Disagree 1 2 3 4 5 6 7 Strongly Agree

2) I get good value for the TV shows I can watch for the price I pay.

    Strongly Disagree 1 2 3 4 5 6 7 Strongly Agree

3) The variety of programs is

    Very Poor 1 2 3 4 5 6 7 Really Great

4) There are ___ kinds of TV shows I can watch

    Not many 1 2 3 4 5 6 7 Very many

5) My service has been reliable.

    Strongly Disagree 1 2 3 4 5 6 7 Strongly Agree

6) The cable's always working.

    Strongly Disagree 1 2 3 4 5 6 7 Strongly Agree

7) Are you: ___ Male ___ Female

8) Overall, I'm satisfied with my cable TV service:

    Strongly Disagree 1 2 3 4 5 6 7 Strongly Agree

[3] Data are available online in an Excel file, ready for analysis.

Figure **5.5.2**	Customer Satisfaction Survey Data

Obs	q1	q2	q3	q4	q5	q6	q7	q8
1	3	4	7	6	6	5	1	6
2	7	6	5	5	6	6	2	5
3	4	3	4	4	4	5	1	2
4	1	4	6	5	5	2	2	5
5	6	4	1	4	3	4	1	4
6	4	4	6	7	5	5	2	5
7	4	4	3	2	5	5	2	3
8	3	3	2	5	4	2	1	4
9	5	5	3	2	3	3	1	2
10	3	4	5	3	6	6	1	6
11	7	6	7	6	5	3	2	5
12	5	7	4	7	6	4	2	7
13	5	7	2	7	7	5	1	6
14	4	1	4	3	3	5	2	6
15	4	5	6	6	4	5	1	5
16	4	5	4	1	2	3	2	1
17	4	6	6	7	4	3	2	6
18	3	7	7	5	5	5	2	7
19	5	4	3	5	4	7	1	4
20	3	1	4	6	2	2	2	1
21	4	5	6	6	4	5	1	7

(continued)

Obs	q1	q2	q3	q4	q5	q6	q7	q8
22	6	5	3	4	4	3	2	5
23	2	5	7	6	4	5	1	6
24	4	3	1	1	4	4	1	3
25	4	5	7	1	1	3	1	3
26	3	3	3	2	3	5	1	4
27	2	5	5	4	3	3	1	3
28	5	5	5	6	5	4	2	5
29	4	5	6	6	6	5	1	5
30	7	7	5	3	7	7	2	3
31	6	6	2	1	1	1	1	2
32	4	6	4	1	6	7	1	5
33	2	4	4	1	5	5	2	2
34	4	5	2	6	5	4	2	5
35	5	4	2	4	5	6	2	3
36	4	6	6	3	5	5	2	7
37	4	5	6	5	4	3	2	5
38	5	5	2	4	4	4	1	7
39	5	2	7	4	4	4	1	1
40	4	5	4	4	6	4	1	4
41	4	3	4	4	3	5	2	4
42	6	5	1	3	3	4	2	2
43	1	1	5	5	3	3	1	3
44	4	6	1	1	3	2	1	4
45	4	5	3	6	7	6	2	7
46	5	7	7	7	6	5	1	7
47	2	2	4	4	3	3	1	2
48	5	2	3	2	2	1	2	1
49	3	5	6	2	3	4	1	7
50	1	2	4	4	5	6	1	1
51	7	6	5	4	5	5	2	6
52	1	1	2	4	2	4	1	3
53	5	5	4	4	6	6	1	7
54	6	5	7	6	4	7	1	5
55	6	4	4	6	6	5	2	4
56	7	6	6	6	7	7	2	5
57	6	6	6	7	6	4	2	6
58	2	2	4	2	7	7	2	4
59	2	4	7	5	3	4	2	7
60	2	3	5	2	1	3	1	4
61	4	5	5	4	6	5	1	4
62	3	4	3	3	4	1	2	3
63	5	6	5	2	5	5	1	6
64	4	6	1	4	4	2	1	5
65	3	3	7	6	3	2	2	4
66	2	1	5	5	5	6	1	2
67	4	5	7	5	4	5	2	3
68	5	6	6	5	7	5	2	5
69	7	6	4	5	3	2	1	5
70	7	6	4	6	7	6	1	4
71	4	4	5	4	4	5	1	6
72	5	5	7	6	4	4	2	4
73	2	1	5	6	4	3	1	3
74	5	4	5	7	7	7	2	6
75	2	5	3	4	5	4	1	6

subscribing households, but the surveys were unusable, e.g., they were filled out incorrectly (more than one number circled, or no numbers circled, but the customer vented his or her feelings by writing all over the survey, etc.).

The coding of these data is straightforward. Questions 1–6 and 8 are seven-point rating scales, and these correspond to the numbers in the database. Question 7 is gender, and the codes are "1" for the men and "2" for the women.

QUESTIONS

1. What are the marketing questions for CountryCable? What are CountryCable's research questions? What do CountryCable's hypotheses appear to be?

2. According to the data, how satisfied are these customers?

3. In the data, what attributes appear to drive satisfaction?

4. Conceptually, are there any questions that appear to be reliability checks for any other question? What are the correlations between such pairs of items?

5. If you try to use Q1–Q7 to predict the overall judgment of satisfaction, Q8, what problems might you encounter? For example, is multicollinearity likely going to be a problem? (Check the correlations among the variables. Is there an R^2 that is significant but the individual predictors are not? Does one survey item predict significantly when another survey item that looks highly related does not?) Could you form scales, say, by averaging the two "variety" questions, and using that average as a single predictor, replacing the two individual items? (Would those two items have to be correlated?) Could you apply this strategy anywhere else? Does this help clarify the data analyses?

6. The cable company thinks it has to communicate differently to men and women. What do the data say on this point?

7. If the company is concerned with weak performance on satisfaction, what do these data suggest it should focus on to regain customers' loyalty, or do the data suggest the customers are already happy?

8. Do you think CountryCable would have addressed all their questions? If you were to (re)design this study, what would you do differently? Sampling? Questionnaire design?

CASE 5.6
Teeth-Whitening Conjoint Study

A new product entry to service our collective vanity is the whitening agents we may apply to our teeth. Colgate and Crest have their paints and strips available already in the marketplace. A large pharmaceuticals firm knows it would be trivial to develop a competitor product. Further, it has channels of distribution available for ready access to consumers. In addition, it is confident of its own image to assure a high quality perception that should contribute to immediate positive brand equity.

Thus, it is considering variants on such a teeth-whitening agent to offer to the market. To finalize the product's attributes, it conducted a conjoint study. The firm put the current products in the middle of a focus group table and ran 6 focus groups, composed of 8–12 members of the general consumer public, 2 in Atlanta (1 was for "heavy coffee drinkers" in particular), 1 in Denver, 1 in L.A., 1 in Minneapolis, and 1 in Tampa. The participants passed the products around, opened them up, smelled them and tasted and felt them. Blow-ups of several recent print ads were displayed on the walls around the table.

After discussing the merits of such products, the experience with or possible interest in trying these products, the moderator passed around a 7-page survey. The first 6 pages were the conjoint task. The final page asked participants to answer questions about themselves (age, gender, frequency of dental visits, etc.). The conjoint task is where we focus our attention.

Figure 5.6.1 has two pages of the 7-page survey. The marketing researchers are investigating the following experimental conjoint design: the form of the whitening agent application (gel, strips, or paint), a price point ($3.49, $2.19, $1.99), and the taste (regular, mint, or cherry). Finally, the last consideration is whether a celebrity spokesperson is featured in the advertisement, or just a picture of the product's packaging (which features a big white tooth, a toothbrush, etc.). This design is a 3 (form) × 3 (price) × 3 (taste) × 2 (ad) factorial. Hence, there are $3 \times 3 \times 3 \times 2 = 54$ possible combinations that the participants had to rate. Each page of the survey contained nine of the combinations. The pages that are not featured in Figure 5.6.1 are those for the "regular" and "cherry" taste, but otherwise those pages look the same as the ones you see for "mint."

Each profile of feature combinations has a rating scale at the very bottom, and the participants are supposed to indicate the extent to which they like that particular bundle of attributes. The ratings for each person were analyzed via conjoint, using dummy variables:

$$\widehat{Y}_{preference-rating} = \widehat{b}_0 + \widehat{b}_1 D_{strips} + \widehat{b}_2 D_{paint}$$
$$+ \ \widehat{b}_3 D_{med-price} + \widehat{b}_4 D_{low-price} + \widehat{b}_5 D_{mint}$$
$$+ \ \widehat{b}_6 D_{cherry} + \widehat{b}_7 D_{no-spokesperson}$$

Figure 5.6.2 contains the results of this conjoint. Compared to gel, paint is a bit preferred, and strips are greatly preferred. The medium price is considered better than the high price, but the cheapest price isn't better still (perhaps people were concerned that quality would fall off if the product were priced too cheaply). The mint taste is thought to be better than the regular taste, and the cherry taste is even better than the mint. The ads were preferred when they didn't have a celebrity in them.

QUESTIONS

1. What should the firm do? Do you have all the data you need to answer this question?
   a. If not, what else do you wish to know?
   b. If these data are faulty, how would you rerun any part of the study?
   c. If so, what should the firm do?

2. Perhaps you don't have all the data you'd like. Nevertheless, in the real world, sometimes this is all you have. No more time or money to conduct more research. What would you do? Launch? Not launch? Why? Any other options?

CASE 5.7
Sports Marketing and Television Programming

When you sit down to watch TV, how do you decide what channel to watch? ESPN has conducted some media research that suggests 75% of TV viewers just flip on their "favorite channel" first. The next most popular strategies are: "turn to the specific show you are tuning in to watch" (40%), and "check the listings" (40%). There are some people who "randomly surf" (30%) and some whose entertainment destiny is determined by another ("someone else decides" gets 15%).

Figure 5.6.1   Part of the Conjoint Survey on Teeth-Whitening Agents

Teeth Whitener A		Teeth Whitener B		Teeth Whitener C	
Gel $3.49 Mint		Strips $3.49 Mint		Paint $3.49 Mint	
Like Least 1 2 3 4 5 6 7 Like Most		Like Least 1 2 3 4 5 6 7 Like Most		Like Least 1 2 3 4 5 6 7 Like Most	

Teeth Whitener D	Teeth Whitener E	Teeth Whitener F
Gel $2.19 Mint	Strips $2.19 Mint	Paint $2.19 Mint
Like Least 1 2 3 4 5 6 7 Like Most	Like Least 1 2 3 4 5 6 7 Like Most	Like Least 1 2 3 4 5 6 7 Like Most

Teeth Whitener G	Teeth Whitener H	Teeth Whitener I
Gel $1.99 Mint	Strips $1.99 Mint	Paint $1.99 Mint
Like Least 1 2 3 4 5 6 7 Like Most	Like Least 1 2 3 4 5 6 7 Like Most	Like Least 1 2 3 4 5 6 7 Like Most

Teeth Whitener J	Teeth Whitener K	Teeth Whitener L
Gel $3.49 Mint	Strips $3.49 Mint	Paint $3.49 Mint
Like Least 1 2 3 4 5 6 7 Like Most	Like Least 1 2 3 4 5 6 7 Like Most	Like Least 1 2 3 4 5 6 7 Like Most

Teeth Whitener M	Teeth Whitener N	Teeth Whitener O
Gel $2.19 Mint	Strips $2.19 Mint	Paint $2.19 Mint
Like Least 1 2 3 4 5 6 7 Like Most	Like Least 1 2 3 4 5 6 7 Like Most	Like Least 1 2 3 4 5 6 7 Like Most

Teeth Whitener P	Teeth Whitener Q	Teeth Whitener R
Gel $1.99 Mint	Strips $1.99 Mint	Paint $1.99 Mint
Like Least 1 2 3 4 5 6 7 Like Most	Like Least 1 2 3 4 5 6 7 Like Most	Like Least 1 2 3 4 5 6 7 Like Most

The first choice, a favorite station, dominates the others. This finding suggests that people are more "station loyal" than "specific TV show loyal." It also suggests that a TV channel needs to be concerned with its brand popularity.

ESPN knows its primary segment is men (any guy over 18). Sports and News are the only two genres where 50% of men say they "watch as often as possible." Figure 5.7.1 shows simple descriptive statistics on top-of-mind mentions of favorite TV

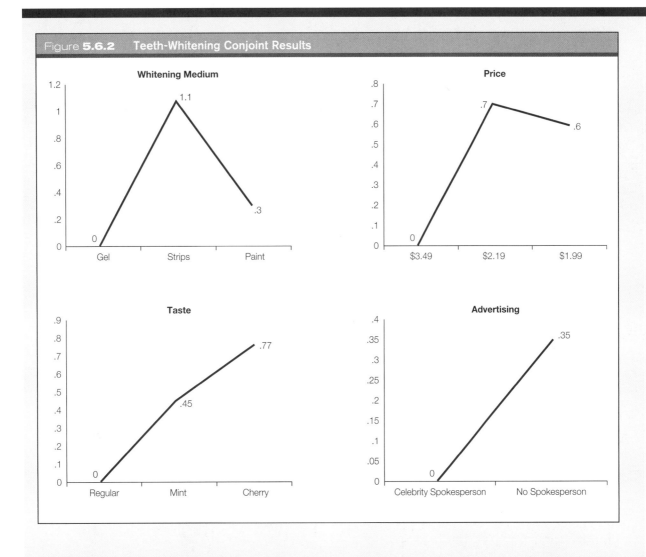

Figure **5.6.2**   Teeth-Whitening Conjoint Results

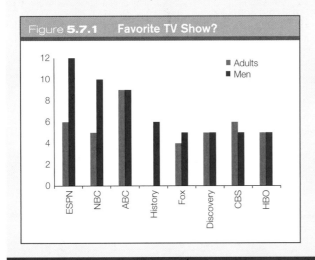

Figure **5.7.1**   Favorite TV Show?

networks. ESPN clearly dominates, and it is followed by NBC, ABC, the History Channel, and others. Figure 5.7.2 shows that the strong popularity of ESPN is stable. The figure lists only the top 3, and the "popularity" is even more impressive when you factor in that most households receive on average more than 85 stations.

To get a sense of the "strengths and weaknesses" or relative positioning of the popular stations, a sample of viewers were asked to rate a selection of networks on characteristics such as: informative, helps me relax, likeable, talks to me, witty, high quality, trustworthy, respects its audience, unique, etc. These attribute ratings were factor analyzed and the factors described the channels as providing:

Figure **5.7.2**   **Stability of Popularity of ESPN among Men**

6. Should ESPN be concerned with these other strongly branded stations?

7. Should ESPN advertise on the History Channel?

8. How might you modify the study if you were to run a similar one?

9. Were the attributes that were selected somehow loaded in ESPN's favor?

10. Where should you draw a sample?

11. To what population of customers could you generalize the findings?

Source: Based loosely on Artie Bulgrin, "Television Network Branding in a Digital Environment" ESPN, Inc., Research Report.

- Integrity and information
- Relevance and involvement
- Entertainment and fun

TV channels that scored well on the first factor, "integrity and information," included the History Channel and Discovery. The "relevant and involvement" channels included ESPN, Discovery, History, and HBO. The "entertaining and fun" stations included HBO, NBC, and ESPN.

Now what? We're coming to the close of the book—you know a lot about marketing and marketing research. You know how to translate a marketing question into a marketing research one. You know about sampling, study design, and data analysis. You should be able to easily contemplate the following questions.

QUESTIONS

1. How could ESPN use this information?

2. What was learned (e.g., you could have guessed that men compose the likely target audience)?

3. Would your interpretation of the findings differ if you knew that the sample was a stratified "ESPN viewers" sample or a simple probability random sample?

4. Would you characterize ESPN as having strong brand equity?

5. How does this research inform other channels as brands?

CASE 5.8
Repositioning a Brand

A small, regional airline carrier, which we'll call *East-2-West,* was looking to reposition its brand. The philosophy of this company had been as a high-end service provider, with no distinction between business and coach classes, offering good food and complimentary beverages of any kind. The airline's target customer was mostly men, based locally, 25–50 years old.

The airline had a 90:10 business to leisure ratio of travelers as its current customer base. It had greater than 75% of its customers satisfied, or at least reporting on surveys that they would "probably" or "definitely" fly East-2-West again. Over the years, customers told the airline they wanted convenient schedules, nonstop flights, good prices, and a frequent flyer program as their main criteria to stay with this airline rather than flying with a competitor.

The airlines industry is a notoriously tough business, and when the economy softens, it only gets tougher. Margins are narrow, the service provision is seen as a commodity, etc.

In this environment, East-2-West was looking into whether it could create a new, low-fare carrier for the growing customer segment seeking value. In particular, it wondered whether it could create such a service repositioning that would still be consistent with its image.

East-2-West commissioned some marketing research. The marketing researchers interviewed both customers who were loyal to the airline and those who had flown on the airline but preferred other airlines. The qualitative results are summarized here.

East-2-West was described in the interview data as:

- Comfortable, Roomy
- Excellent Service
- Business Oriented
- Attentive
- Convenient

The customers who were loyal to East-2-West also characterized the airline as friendly and reliable. The interviewers also asked the two segments for words that did not describe the airline. These included:

- Competitive
- Elegant
- Warm
- Classic
- On Time
- Efficient

To supplement these qualitative data, the perceptual map in Figure 5.8.1 was also drawn. This map was the result of customer surveys. In the surveys, customers were asked to describe both East-2-West, as well as other carriers.

QUESTIONS

Discuss East-2-West's goals and results, covering topics such as:

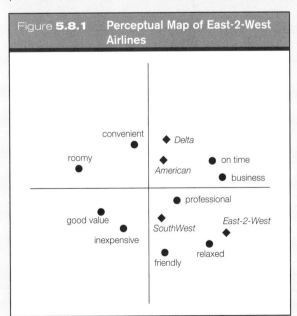

Figure **5.8.1** **Perceptual Map of East-2-West Airlines**

1. Are the company's goals good ones for the economic and competitive environment?

2. Are the goals consistent with the company's traditional strengths?

3. Will there be customer confusion with this repositioning?

4. What problems do you foresee that East-2-West apparently didn't in terms of its new positioning?

5. Can you use the qualitative or perceptual map data to substantiate your answers to any of these questions?

6. Turning to the perceptual map, how would you characterize the dimensions? Are the results consistent with the qualitative data? According to the map, if East-2-West is successful in its repositioning, what competition might it confront?

7. What additional data would you want before repositioning an airline?

CASE 5.9
Conjoint—Brand & Pricing

Ford is working on creating a "next generation" hybrid car. Initial market offerings were well-received, but the novelty has worn off, and the next set of buyers will only buy these cars if there are no sacrifices to be made while simultaneously feeling good about helping the environment. Some people buy cars based on price points, others for reliability (whereby brand name usually serves as a proxy, along with *Consumer Reports* kinds of data), and still others like all the bells and whistles. Hybrids are not smart cars when many bells and whistles are added (they start consuming too much energy, regardless of the kind of energy, e.g., having implications for distance between charges, etc.).

Ford gets a large marketing research company to run a conjoint study for them. You have a friend interning there, and he's got questions for you. The conjoint study basically explored "brand," "price," and "MP3 player."

- For brand, Ford figured they had the respect of some consumers, but not all, so they might launch the car "anonymously" with the brand name "Eco" (for ecological, economical, etc.).

- For price, the price points they're starting with are $22,000 and $29,000. Depending on the results at

Figure **5.9.1**   Study Design for the Brand/Pricing Conjoint Hybrid Car Project

A Ford hybrid MP3, $22,000

B Eco hybrid MP3, $22,000

C Ford hybrid $22,000

D Eco hybrid $29,000

E Eco hybrid $22,000

F Ford hybrid $29,000

G Eco hybrid MP3, $29,000

H Ford hybrid MP3, $29,000

Figure **5.9.2**   Excel Template for Brand/Pricing Conjoint

Car	Brand	BrandDV	Price	PriceDV	MP3?	MP3DV	Your Rating	Avg*
A	Ford	1	22	0	y	1	—	80.1
B	Eco	0	22	0	y	1	—	95.2
C	Ford	1	22	0	n	0	—	26.7
D	Eco	0	29	1	n	0	—	25.2
E	Eco	0	22	0	n	0	—	35.3
F	Ford	1	29	1	n	0	—	24.7
G	Eco	0	29	1	y	1	—	90.3
H	Ford	1	29	1	y	1	—	75.7

*Mean rating, over $N = 750$ consumers: 0 = "I would never buy this" to 100 = "I think this is great and I would very much like to buy it."

these price points, they might explore others down the road (e.g., $26k, $32k, etc.).

• Finally, regarding the MP3 player, building in a compatible player slot was the only bell or whistle that Ford was confident that they could provide economically, at least among the perks they thought consumers might want.

The design of the stimuli is in Figure 5.9.1, and the data are in Figure 5.9.2. Help your friend do the conjoint.

QUESTIONS

1. To really get a feel for what's going on, complete the task yourself. Look at the eight cars, and rate them on the 0 ("I would never buy this") to 100 ("I want to go out and buy this right now!") scale. Add your judgments to the "your data" spaces.

2. Analyze your data in Excel (if you use Sas, Spss, XLStat, great, but even in Excel, go to "more functions," "statistical," and use "Linest"). Do the results make sense to you?

3. Analyze the customer data that your friend's marketing research firm collected. What recommendations would you tell your friend to make to Ford?

CASE 5.10
Segmentation Study

You're responsible for frozen meals at your CPG firm. Your firm is large and highly successful—a world leader.

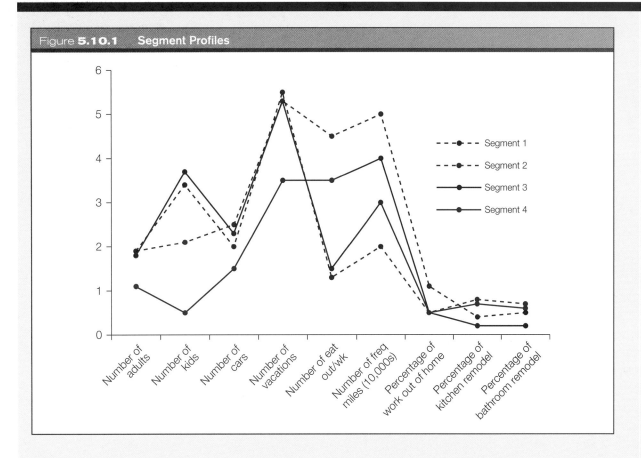

Figure **5.10.1**   **Segment Profiles**

They have many marketing research firms with whom they have alliances or on whom they've relied for studies in the past. One of those firms has completed a segmentation study for your team, which is considering a number of directions for expansion. Possible line extensions include a diverse "ethnic" line (Mexican foods, Thai foods, etc.), a "healthy eats" line (low sugar and fat content, etc.), and a "convenient but tastes good" line (primarily for families who have more children than spare time).

The basic segmentation profiles are presented in Figure 5.10.1. The oft-relied-upon marketing research firm is convinced it has four segments, and thinks it should advise you to pursue segments 1, 2, and 4.

QUESTIONS

1. First, what do you make of the segmentation findings?

2. Second, do you agree with the segments to target?

The Research Report

## part 6

This closing section of the book consists of one chapter and an epilogue.

Chapter 19 discusses one of the most important parts of the entire research process, the research report. The research report often becomes the standard by which the research effort is assessed. The epilogue ties together the parts of the research process, reinforcing the points made earlier: that the steps in the research process are highly interrelated and that a decision made at one stage has implications for the others as well.

The Research Report

19

Questions to Guide Your Learning:

Q1 What should a research report look like?

Q2 How can I improve my writing and my presentation skills?

Q3 What different purposes might different kinds of graphs serve?

Creating useful reports requires considerable skill and attention to detail. Regardless of the sophistication displayed in other portions of the research process, the project is a failure if the research report fails. The research steps determine the content, and the research report provides the form. Given that the report is all that many executives see of the project, it becomes the yardstick for evaluation. The writer must ensure that the report informs without misinforming.

The report must tell readers what they need and wish to know. Typically, executives are interested in results and must be convinced of the usefulness of the findings. They wish to act on the report, but they must also recognize the caveats entailed in the results. Thus, the researcher must convey these limitations and details of the methods.

To enhance this communication, we discuss four concepts: (1) the criteria by which research reports are evaluated, (2) the parts and forms of the written research report, (3) the oral report, and (4) some graphic means of presenting the results.

Criteria of Research Reports

Research reports are evaluated by one fundamental criterion—communication with the reader. The reader is the reason that the report is prepared, so it must be tailor-made for the reader(s), keeping in mind their technical sophistication, interest in the subject area, and the use they will make of it.

The technical sophistication of the readers determines their capacity for understanding methodological decisions, such as experimental design, measures, sampling plan, analysis technique, etc. Readers with little technical sophistication will probably be overwhelmed (and annoyed) by the use of unexplained technical jargon. Researchers must be particularly sensitive to this, because, being technical people and taking much jargon for granted, they may fail to realize that they are using technical language and terms. Executives higher in the organization usually want only the proverbial "executive summary"—results, but not a discussion of how the results were obtained. Other executives want considerable information on the research methods used in the study and the statistical results, but not the researcher's conclusions and recommendations.

The report writer's difficulties in tailoring the report are often compounded by the existence of several audiences. The marketing vice president might have a different technical capacity and level of interest than the manager responsible for the product discussed in the report. This problem sometimes requires the preparation of several reports, although usually the conflicting demands are satisfied with one report that contains both technical and nontechnical sections for different readers.

Give details if readers are technical; otherwise, keep it simple.

Writing Criteria

To be effective, a report should be complete, accurate, clear, and concise:

1. A report is *complete* when it provides all the information readers need in language they understand. This means that the writer must continually ask whether every question in the original assignment has been addressed. What alternatives were examined? What was found? The report must include necessary definitions and explanations but they must be succinct. The length of a report should be proportional to its contribution. Report writers tend not to waste collected information, but too much information may be distracting. If the report is big, it may discourage readers from even attempting to digest its contents. In general, the amount of detail should be proportionate to the amount of direct control users can exercise over the areas under discussion.

2. A report must be *accurate* and careful in discussing the data and offering logical reasoning. Table 19.1 illustrates some examples of sources of inaccuracy in reports.

3. *Clarity* is probably violated more than any other principle of good writing. Clear and logical thinking and precise expression produce clarity. When the underlying logic is fuzzy or the presentation imprecise, readers have difficulty understanding what they read. To be *clear,* the organization of the report should follow an outline of major points. Tell the reader where you are going and then do what you said you were going to do. Use short paragraphs and short sentences. Don't mumble; once you have decided what to say, come out and say it. Choose your words carefully. (See Research Realities 19.1.) Don't expect to get it right the first time; expect to revise, and when doing so, try to reduce the length. That forces you to simplify and remove the clutter. Constantly ask yourself, "What am I trying to say?" (you'll be surprised at how often you don't know). Strip your sentences of all adverbs and adjectives. Let the verbs and nouns do the work.

4. A report must also be *concise.* The writer must be selective about what is included, and avoid trying to impress the reader with all that has been found. If something does not pertain directly to the subject, it should be omitted. Concise writing is effective because it makes maximum use of every word—no word or phrase can be removed without destroying the whole composition.

Reading your draft aloud helps identify sections that should be pruned or rewritten.

1. Title page
2. Table of contents
3. Executive summary
   a. Introduction
   b. Results
   c. Conclusions
   d. Recommendations
4. Introduction
5. Body
   a. Methodology
   b. Results
   c. Limitations
6. Conclusions and recommendations
7. Appendix
   a. Copies of data-collection forms
   b. Statistics details, n, etc.
   c. Tables not included in the body
   d. Bibliography

Form of the Report

There is no single, acceptable organization for a report, but the following format is fairly standard, yet flexible. We discuss each element in turn.

TABLE 19.1   Examples of Inaccuracy in Report Writing

A. Simple Errors in Addition or Subtraction

"In the United States, 14% of the population has an elementary school education or less, 51% has attended or graduated from high school, and 16% has attended college."

- An oversight such as this (14 + 51 + 16 do not equal 100%) can be easily corrected by the author, but not so easily by the reader because he or she may not know if one or more of the percentage values is incorrect or if a category might have been left out of the tally (e.g., grad school).

B. Confusion Between Percentages and Percentage Points

"The company's profits as a percentage of sales were 6.0% in 1995 and 8.0% in 2000. Therefore, they increased only 2.0% in five years."

- In this example, the increase is, of course, 2.0 percentage points, or 33%.

C. Inaccuracy Caused by Grammatical Errors

"The reduction in the government's price supports for dairy products has reduced farm income $600 million to $800 million per year."

- To express a range, the author should have written: "The reduction in the government's price supports for dairy products has reduced farm income by between $600 million and $800 million per year."

D. Confused Terminology Resulting in Fallacious Conclusion

"The Jones's household and annual income increased from $30,000 to $60,000 over the past ten years, thereby doubling the family's purchasing power."

- Although the Jones's household annual income may have doubled in the 10 years, the family's purchasing power probably did not. It may have declined, given that the cost of living, as measured by the consumer price index, increased over the same period. It may have increased, given that discretionary income from $60K is much greater than that from $30K once basic needs are paid.

Title Page

The title page indicates the subject of the report, the name of the organization for which the report is made, the name of the organization submitting it, and the date.

R E S E A R C H   R E A L I T I E S

19.1 Choose Words Well

- Use short words, not long words that mean the same thing, e.g., "use" not "utilize."

- Avoid jargon, e.g., "provide incentives," not "incentivize"; and "conclusion," not "net net."

- Write simply and naturally—the way you talk, e.g., "The important point is," not "Importantly"; and

"There are four reasons," not "The reasons are fourfold."

- Cut redundancies, e.g., "study," not "study in depth"; or "The plan," not "The advance plan."

Table of Contents

The table of contents lists, in order of appearance, the divisions and subdivisions of the report with page references. In short reports, the table of contents may simply contain the main headings. It should include lists of tables and figures and their page numbers.

Executive Summary

The executive summary is the heart and core of the report. Many executives read only this summary. Others read more, but they use the summary as a guide to see what else they'll read.

The true summary is not an abstract of the whole report in which everything is restated in condensed form; neither is it a simple restatement of the subject, nor a brief statement of the significant results and conclusions. A true summary gives the high points of the entire body of the report. Properly written, the summary saves busy executives' time without sacrificing their understanding.

The introduction in the summary provides the reader with minimal background to appreciate the study's results, conclusions, and recommendations. It should state who authorized the research and for what purpose. It should explicitly outline the problem(s) or hypotheses that guided the research. The key findings should be presented.

Conclusions and recommendations are not the same. A conclusion is an opinion based on the results. A recommendation is a suggestion for appropriate future action. Conclusions should be included in the summary section. The writer is in a better position to base conclusions on the evidence than are the readers, being more familiar with the methods used to generate and analyze the data.

Recommendations are another matter. Some managers simply prefer to determine the appropriate courses of action themselves and do not want the writer to offer recommendations. Others hold that the writer, being closest to the research, is in the best position to suggest a course of action. Increasingly, marketing researchers are being asked to interpret the findings in terms of what they mean to the business and to make recommendations as to appropriate courses of action. You will probably know what is expected of you (or ask). If in doubt, provide your recommendations. The reader can always ignore them.

A good test of a summary is self-sufficiency—can it stand on its own, or does it collapse without the full report?

Introduction

The introduction provides background information that readers need to appreciate the rest of the report. Its length and detail depend on the readers' familiarity with the subject, the approach to it, and the treatment of it. As a rule, a report with wide distribution requires more extensive introduction than a report for a narrow audience.

The introduction defines terms. For instance, in a study of market penetration of a new product, the introduction might be used to define the market and discuss which products and companies were considered "competitors" in projecting the new product's market share.

The introduction may provide pertinent history. What similar studies have been conducted? What findings did they produce? What circumstances precipitated the present study? How were its scope and emphasis determined?

The introduction should state the specific objectives of the research. If the project is part of a larger, overall project, this should be mentioned. Each of the subproblems or hypotheses should be explicitly stated. After reading the introduction, readers should know exactly what the report concerns and what it omits.

Body

The details of the research are contained in the body of the report. This includes details of method, results, and limitations.

A challenge in report writing is knowing how much detail to go into when presenting the research methods. Sufficient information must be presented so that readers can appreciate the research design, data-collection methods, sample procedures, and analyses that were used without being overwhelmed. However, technical jargon, which is often a succinct way of communicating a complex idea, should be omitted, because many readers will not understand it.

Readers must be told whether the design was exploratory, descriptive, or causal, as well as why the particular design was chosen. What are its merits in terms of the problem at hand? Readers should also be told whether the results are based on secondary or primary data. If primary, were they based on observation or questionnaire? And if the latter, were the questionnaires administered in person or by mail, e-mail, or telephone? Again, it is important to mention why the particular method was chosen. What were its perceived advantages over alternative schemes? This may mean briefly discussing the perceived weaknesses of the other data-collection schemes that were considered.

Sampling is a technical subject, and the writer cannot hope to convey all the nuances. A reader needs to understand at least three things pertaining to the sample: what was done, how it was done, and why was it done. For example:

1. How was the population defined? What were the geographical, age, gender, or other bounds?

2. What sampling units were used? Business organizations or business executives? Households, or individuals within a household? Why were these sampling units chosen?

3. How was the list of sampling units generated? Did this produce any weaknesses? Why was this method used?

4. Were any difficulties experienced in contacting designated sample elements? How were these difficulties overcome, and was bias introduced in the process?

5. How was the sample actually selected? How large a sample was selected?

It is useful to discuss the method in general before detailing the results. Thus, if statistical significance was established through chi-square analysis, the writer might provide the general rationale and calculation procedure for the chi-square statistic, as well as the assumptions surrounding this test and how well the data supported the assumptions.

The findings of the study comprise the bulk of the report, with supporting tables and figures. The results need to address the specific problems posed, and they must be presented with some logical structure. The first requirement suggests that information that is interesting but irrelevant to the specific problems guiding the research be omitted. The second requirement suggests that the tables and figures should not be a random collection but should reflect some sensible ordering, e.g., perhaps organized by subproblem, geographic region, time, or other criterion that structured the investigation. Tables and figures should be used liberally when presenting results. Tables in the appendix are complex and detailed, but the tables in the body of the report should be simple summaries of focused information. Brief verbal summaries of each table show the reader to the main patterns and exceptions.

There is no such thing as a "perfect" study; every study has its limitations. The researcher knows the limitations and does not hide them from the readers. A frank admission of the study's limitations can actually increase rather than

Ethical Dilemma 19.1

As a member of an independent research team, it is your job to write the final report for a client. One of your colleagues whispers to you in passing, "Make it sound very technical. Lots of long words and jargon—you know the sort of thing. We want to make it clear that we earned our money on this one."
- Is it ethical to obscure the substance of a report beneath complex language?
- Will some clients be impressed by words that they do not fully understand?

diminish (as is sometimes feared) the readers' opinion of the quality of the research. If some limitations are not stated and readers discover them, they may begin to question the whole report and assume a much more skeptical, critical posture than they would if the limitations were explicitly stated. Stating them also allows the writer to discuss whether the limitations might bias the results.

For example, the sources of nonsampling error and the suspected direction of their biases should be discussed. Readers should be informed about how far the results can be generalized. To what populations can they be expected to apply? If the study was done in Miami, readers should be warned not to generalize the results to the southern states or to all the states. The writer should provide the proper caveats for readers.

Conclusions and Recommendations

The results precipitate the conclusions and recommendations. There should be a conclusion for each study objective. Researchers need to be careful that the conclusions drawn reflect an unbiased interpretation of the data.

Researchers' recommendations should follow the conclusions. In developing recommendations, focus on the value of the information that has been gathered, and interpret this information in terms of what it means for the business. One of the best ways to do this is by offering specific recommendations as to the appropriate courses of action, and reasons why. Although not all managers want the researcher's recommendations, many do, and the researcher needs to be prepared to offer and support them.

Appendix

The appendix contains material that is too complex, detailed, specialized, or not absolutely necessary for the text. The appendix typically contains as an exhibit a copy of the questionnaire used to collect the data. It may also contain maps used to draw the sample, or detailed calculations used to determine sample size. The appendix may include calculations of test statistics and often includes detailed tables from which the summary tables in the body of the report are generated. The appendix is read by only the most technically competent and interested reader, so material shouldn't appear in the appendix if its omission from the body of the report would create gaps in the presentation. Table 19.2 serves as a checklist of items to include in reports.

The Oral Report

In addition to the written report, most marketing research investigations require one or more oral reports. They may also require interim progress reports. They almost always require a formal oral report at the conclusion of the study. The

TABLE 19.2   Checklist for Evaluating Research Reports

A. **Origin: What Is Behind the Research**
  ✓ Does the report identify the firms or departments that initiated and paid for the research?
  ✓ Is there a statement of the research purpose that says what it was meant to accomplish?
  ✓ Are the organizations that designed and conducted the research identified?

B. **Design: The Concept and the Plan**
  ✓ Is there a full, nontechnical description of the research design?
  ✓ Is the design consistent with the stated purpose for which the research was conducted?
  ✓ Does it address questions that respondents are capable of answering?
  ✓ Is there a precise statement of the population represented?
  ✓ Does the report clearly describe the method of sample selection?
  ✓ Are copies of questionnaire forms and other study materials available in the appendix?

C. **Execution: Collecting and Handling the Information**
  ✓ Does the report describe the data-collection and data-processing procedures?

D. **Stability: Sample Size and Reliability**
  ✓ Was the sample large enough to provide stable findings?
  ✓ Are sampling error limits shown if they can be computed?
  ✓ Are any possible nonsampling errors described?

E. **Applicability: Generalizing the Findings**
  ✓ Does the report specify when the data were collected?
  ✓ Is it clear who is underrepresented by the research, or not represented at all?
  ✓ If the research has limited application, is there a statement covering who or what it represents and the times or conditions under which it applies?

F. **Meaning: Interpretations and Conclusions**
  ✓ Are the measurements described in simple and direct language?
  ✓ Are the actual findings differentiated from the interpretation of the findings?
  ✓ Have the research findings been interpreted rigorously and objectively?

G. **Candor: Open Reporting and Disclosure**
  ✓ Is there a full disclosure of how the research was done?
  ✓ Has the research been fairly presented?

principles surrounding the preparation and delivery of the oral report parallel those for the written report. Presenters need to realize that many listeners will not truly understand the technical ramifications involved in research and will not be able to judge whether the research done is "quality research." However, they can judge whether the research was presented in a professional, confidence-inspiring manner or in a disorganized, uninformed one. A quality presentation can disguise poor research, but quality research cannot improve a poor presentation.

Preparing the Oral Report

The first imperative is to know the audience: its technical level of sophistication and members' involvement in the project. In general, it is better to err on the side of too little technical detail than too much. Executives want to hear and see what the information means to them as marketing managers, e.g., what do the data suggest in terms of marketing actions? They can ask for the necessary clarification about the technical details if they want it.

The flow of the presentation usually follows one of two popular forms. Both begin by stating the general purpose of the study and its specific objectives. They differ in terms of when the conclusions are introduced. In the most popular structure, the conclusions are introduced after all the evidence supporting a particular course of action is presented. By progressively disclosing the facts, the presenter is building a logical case in sequential fashion.

The alternative structure involves presenting the conclusions immediately after the purpose and main objectives. The structure tends to involve managers immediately in the findings. It not only gets them thinking about what actions are called for given the results but also sensitizes them to paying attention to the evidence supporting the conclusions. It places them in the desirable position of wanting to evaluate the strength of the evidence supporting an action, because they know beforehand the conclusions that were drawn from it.

The structure used depends on the corporate culture as well as the presenter's own comfort level. In either case, the evidence supporting the conclusions must be presented systematically, and the conclusions drawn must be consistent with the evidence.

A third important consideration for effective delivery of the oral report is the use of appropriate visual aids. PowerPoint presentations, flip charts, transparencies, and whiteboards can all be used, depending on the size of the group and the physical facilities of the meeting room. Finally, make sure your visuals can be read easily by those in the back of the room (see Table 19.3).

> If you're presenting using technology, don't count on it. Bring backups (e.g., simple transparencies).

Delivering the Oral Report

Honor the time limit set for the meeting. Use only a portion of the time set aside for the formal presentation, no more than a third to a half. At the same time, don't rush the presentation of the information, so plan not to present too many

Ethical Dilemma 19.2

A colleague confides in you: "I've just run a survey for a restaurant owner who is planning to open a catering service for parties, weddings, and the like. He wanted to know the best way to advertise the new service. In the questionnaire, I asked respondents where they would expect to see ads for catering facilities, and the most common source was the newspaper. I now realize that my question only established where people usually see ads, not where they would like to see them. All we know is where other caterers advertise! Yet I'm sure my client will interpret my findings as meaning that the newspaper is the most effective media vehicle. Should I make the limitations of the research explicit?"

- What are the costs of making the limitations of the research explicit?
- What are the costs of not doing so?
- Isn't promoting the correct use of the research one of your prime obligations?

TABLE **19.3**   **Tips for Preparing Effective Presentation Visuals**

1. Keep it simple.
2. One minute per visual. One main point. Few words.
3. Bring copies of slides to hand out to the audience before your presentation.
4. Number your pages to facilitate questions and discussion.
5. BIG font!
6. Build complexity. If you have a complicated concept to communicate, start with the ground level and use three or four slides to complete the picture.

slides (details can be prepared on "back-up slides" anticipating certain questions). Remember that the audience is hearing it for the first time. Reserve the remaining time for questions and discussion. One of the unique benefits of the oral presentation is that it allows interaction. Use this benefit to advantage to clear up points of confusion and to highlight points deserving special emphasis.

Keep the presentation simple and uncluttered so that the audience does not have to mentally backtrack to think about what has been said. When writing out the presentation, choose simple words and sentences that are naturally spoken and expressed in your usual vocabulary.

Graphic Presentation of the Results

The old adage that "a picture is worth a thousand words" is equally true for business reports. Text and tables can be used to present quantitative information, but graphs can often serve that purpose better. There are three basic kinds of graphics: charts that show *how much,* maps that show *where,* and diagrams that show *how.* Charts are generally the most useful of the three types for research reports, and diagrams the least. The following sections discuss a few of the more common chart types and maps.[1]

Pie Chart

Probably one of the more familiar charts—the **pie chart** is simply a circle divided into sections, with each section representing a portion of the total. The sections

Ethical **Dilemma** 19.3

You are writing the final report for top management to make the case that your new advertising campaign has increased sales dramatically in trial areas. Your conceptual arguments on behalf of the new campaign are very convincing, but although there has been a consistent rise in sales in trial areas, the bar charts look rather disappointing: 61,500 units the first month, 61,670 units the next, 61,820 the next…the increase is barely visible! Then you notice how much more exciting your results would look if the y-axis were broken above the origin so that the plots started at 50,000 units.
- Where does salesmanship stop and deception start?

---

[1] See Nicholas H. Lurie and Charlotte H. Mason, "Visual Representation: Implication for Decision Making," *Journal of Marketing*, 71 (1), 160–177.

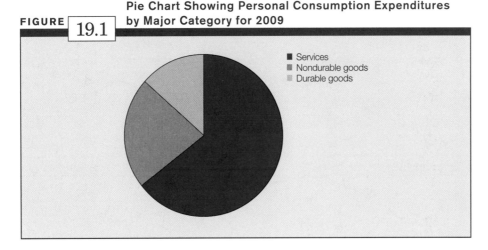

19.1

Pie Chart Showing Personal Consumption Expenditures by Major Category for 2009

are presented as part of a whole, so the pie chart is particularly effective for depicting relative size or emphasizing comparisons. For example, Figure 19.1 shows the breakdown of personal consumption expenditures by major category for 2009. The conclusion is obvious: Expenditures for services account for the largest proportion of total consumption expenditures. Further, expenditures for services and nondurable goods completely dwarf expenditures for durable goods.

Figure 19.1 has three slices, and the interpretation is obvious. With finer consumption classes, a greater number of sections would have been required, and although more information would have been conveyed, emphasis would have been lost. As a rule of thumb, no more than six slices should be generated; the division of the pie should start at the 12 o'clock position; and the sections should be arrayed clockwise in decreasing order of magnitude.

Line Chart

The line chart is a two-dimensional chart that is particularly useful in depicting dynamic relationships, such as time-series fluctuations of one or more series. For example, Figure 19.2 shows the sales of domestic and imported cars during the period 1996–2009.

The line chart is probably the most commonly used chart. It is typically constructed with the x-axis representing time and the y-axis representing values of the variables. Each line representing different variables should be distinctive in color or form (e.g., dots and dashes in suitable combinations) and explained in a legend.

Bar Chart

The bar chart has many variations. Figure 19.3 is a bar chart that shows personal consumption expenditures by major category at a single point in time. It expresses the same relative information as Figure 19.1, but also reveals the magnitudes. Figure 19.4 shows a "grouped" bar chart for the automobile sales data, where one set of bars represents the domestic sales, and the other set of bars, the imports. Both are represented per year.

One of the trickiest things to know is how to represent the data you've got. Research Realities 19.2 takes some data that looks overwhelming at first, then breaks it down into informative and understandable chunks of information.

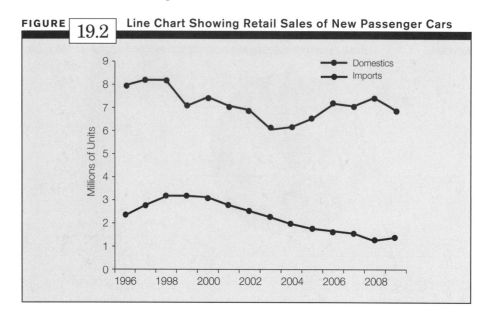

FIGURE 19.2   Line Chart Showing Retail Sales of New Passenger Cars

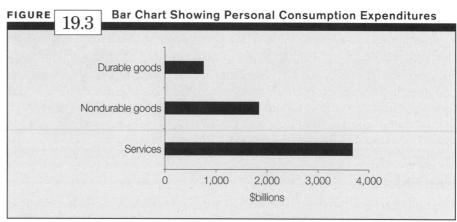

FIGURE 19.3   Bar Chart Showing Personal Consumption Expenditures

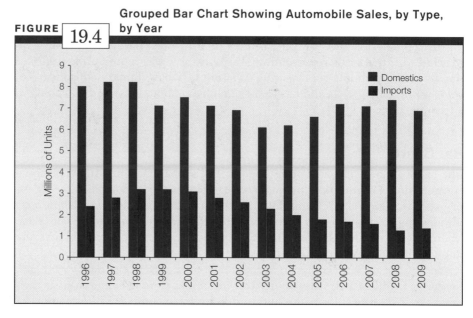

FIGURE 19.4   Grouped Bar Chart Showing Automobile Sales, by Type, by Year

Maps

Maps focus attention on geographic areas. Data maps are especially suited to the presentation of rates, ratios, and frequency-distribution data by areas. In constructing data maps, the quantity of interest is broken into groups, and shading or color is used to display the numerical group in which each area belongs. In general, it is helpful to keep the group intervals approximately equal and to use a limited number of shadings, 4–7 and certainly no more than 10. Map figures can be useful in comparing performance between markets, or within markets over time, e.g., to gauge the degree of success of recent marketing mix implementation.

A picture is worth a megabyte of words.

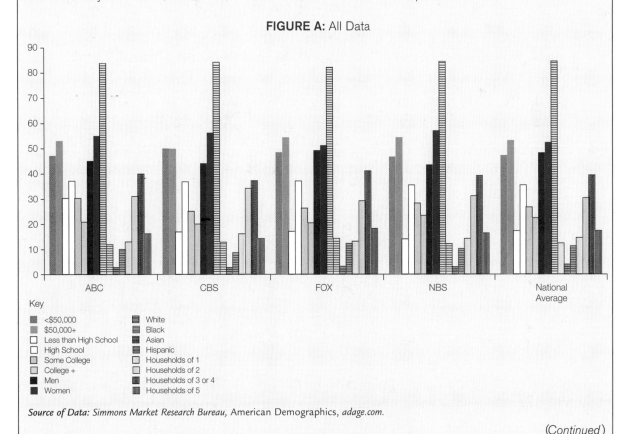

RESEARCH REALITIES

19.2 Demographic Profile of TV Viewers

Television ratings and their break-down per audience characteristics is extremely critical, e.g., to advertisers who seek to ensure their budgets are being spent against their targeted customers. The following data show basic demographic data on viewers for the three traditional major networks, ABC, CBS, and NBC and Fox, as well as reporting the national statistics for a basis of comparison.

If this chart were to appear in a marketing research report, or a business magazine, it would not be effective. It is too complicated to digest, and therefore it would have no impact on the reader.

FIGURE A: All Data

Source of Data: Simmons Market Research Bureau, American Demographics, adage.com.

(Continued)

Some levels of the variables seem superfluous. If we know the % of male viewers, can we not figure out the percentage of female viewers? If income is divided only into two rough categories (less than and greater than $50,000), can't we delete one of these categories and focus on the other? We even selected out two levels of education. This simplification is done for the chart below. However, ethnicity and household size cannot be further simplified (unless we knew the particular focus of the marketing research). Thus, while improved, this chart has only four fewer bars, and it's still overwhelming.

FIGURE B: Selectivity on Variable Level

Why must we view all demographics simultaneously? This chart focuses on race and is easier to read. The large number for the White category dominates, however, and overwhelms the differences among the other categories...

So, let's temporarily set aside the numbers for the White category, to allow the slight but discernible patterns among the minority ethnicities to come through. This chart is the first that allows us to translate "data" into "information." We can see that Blacks gravitate

FIGURE C1: Focus on Demographic: Ethnicity

FIGURE C2: Focus on Demographic: Minority Ethnicity

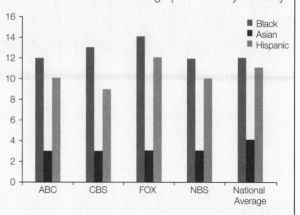

more toward Fox and CBS. Asians aren't served well by any of these TV stations. Hispanics are like Blacks in preferring Fox, but unlike Blacks in not preferring CBS.

So, use the information. If your products are targeted toward Blacks, where do you spend your TV advertising dollars? Hispanics? Asians?

FIGURE C3: Focus on Demographic: Gender

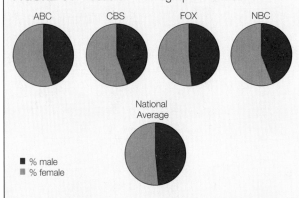

FIGURE C4: Focus on Demographic: Income

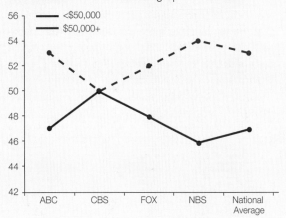

Which network is winning the hearts and minds of the male or female viewers? What pattern would be desirable?

• If you're an EDLP retailer, which stations get your ad dollars?

• If you're selling Beemers, where does your ad $ go?

Summary

The research report was discussed. Four points were emphasized: the criteria for evaluating research reports, the elements of a written research report, the delivery of an oral report, and the graphic presentation of results.

The fundamental criterion for the development of every research report is communication with the audience. The readers' interests, capabilities, and circumstances determine what goes in the report, what is left out, and how the information is presented. The other criteria that need to be kept in mind in preparing the report include: completeness, accuracy, clarity, and conciseness.

A report includes: title page, table of contents, summary, introduction, body, conclusions and recommendations, and appendix. An oral report begins by stating the general purpose of the study and the specific objectives. The remainder of the presentation needs to systematically build on the evidence so that logical conclusions are drawn.

Graphic presentation is often the best way to communicate those findings that require emphasis. Three main forms are the pie chart, the line chart, and the bar chart.

Questions

1. What is meant by the report criteria of completeness, accuracy, clarity, and conciseness?
2. On the one hand, research reports should be complete. On the other hand, they should be concise. Are these two objectives incompatible? If so, how do you reconcile them?
3. What is the essential content of each of the following parts of the research report?
   a. Title page
   b. Table of contents
   c. Executive summary
   d. Introduction
   e. Body
   f. Conclusions and recommendations
   g. Appendix
4. What are the key considerations in preparing an oral report?

Applications and Problems

1. Many marketing research professionals would argue that the summary is the most important part of the research report. Describe the information that should be contained in the summary and why it is so important.

2. Discuss the difference between conclusions and recommendations in research reports.

Marketing research can be approached in several ways. The perspective used in this book is primarily a project emphasis.

We focused on the definition of a problem and the research needed to answer it. We separated each step of the research process into logical components so that we could highlight the research design issues that arise at each stage. Yet we pointed out that these steps are highly interrelated, and a decision made at one stage has implications for the others as well. To remind us how this integration functions, the research process and some of the key decisions that must be made are reviewed in this epilogue.

A research project should not be conceived as the end in itself. Projects arise because managerial problems need solving. The problems themselves may concern the identification of market opportunities, the evaluation of alternative courses of action, or control of marketing operations. These activities are the essence of the managerial function, so the research activity can also be viewed from the broader perspective of the firm's marketing intelligence system.

Marketing research was defined as the function that links the consumer, customer, and public to the marketer through information—information used to identify and define marketing opportunities and problems; to generate, refine, and evaluate marketing actions; to monitor marketing performance; and to improve our understanding of marketing as a process. Addressing these issues involves the systematic gathering, recording, and analyzing of data. These tasks are logically viewed as a sequence called the research process, consisting of the following steps:

1. Formulate the problem.
2. Determine the research design.
3. Design data-collection methods and forms.
4. Design the sample and collect the data.
5. Analyze and interpret the data.
6. Prepare the research report.

The decision problem logically comes first. It dictates the research problem and the design of the project. However, the transition from *problem* to *project* is not an automatic one. There is a good deal of iteration from problem specification to tentative research design to problem respecification to modified research design and back again. This is natural, and one of the researcher's more important roles involves helping define and redefine the problem so that it can be researched and so that it answers the decision maker's problem. This task can be formidable, because it requires a clear specification of objectives, alternatives, and environmental constraints and influences. The decision maker may not readily provide these, and it is up to the researcher to dig them out in order to design effective research.

Sometimes research is not necessary. If the decision maker's views are so strongly held that no amount of information might change them, the research will be wasted. It is up to the researcher to determine this before, rather than after, conducting the research. Asking "what if" questions can be diagnostic: What if consumer reaction to the product concept is very favorable? What if it is unfavorable? What if it is only slightly favorable? If the decision maker indicates that the same decision will be made in each case, there are other objectives that have not been explicitly stated. Every research project should have one or more objectives, and one should not proceed to other steps in the process until these can be explicitly stated.

It is also important to ask whether the contemplated benefits of the research exceed the expected costs. It is a mistake to assume that simply because something might change as a result of the research, the research is called for. It may be that the likelihood of finding something that might warrant a change in the decision is so remote that the research still would be wasted. Researchers constantly need to ask: Why should this research be conducted? What could we learn that we do not already know? Will the expected benefits from the research exceed its costs? If the answers indicate research, then the question logically turns to: What kind?

If the problem cannot be formulated as some specific "if-then" relationship, exploratory research is in order. The primary purpose of exploratory research is to gather ideas and insights. The output of an exploratory study will not be answers but more specific questions or statements of tentative relationships. The search for insights demands a flexible research design. Structured questionnaires or probability sampling plans are not used in exploratory research, because the emphasis is not on gathering summary statistics. The personal interview is much more appropriate than the telephone interview, and that, in turn, is more appropriate than a mail survey, to allow for unstructured questions. Interviewees are chosen because they can provide the desired information; thus, a convenience or judgment sample is acceptable here, whereas it would be completely out of place in descriptive or causal research. Focus groups are an extremely useful and popular means for gaining important insights.

When the exploratory effort has generated one or more specific hypotheses to be investigated, the next research thrust would logically be descriptive or causal research. The design actually selected depends on the conviction with which the tentative explanation is held to be the explanation, and the feasibility and cost of conducting an experiment. Though experiments typically provide more convincing proof of causal relationships, they also usually cost more than descriptive designs. This fact is one reason descriptive designs are the most commonly employed type in marketing research.

Whereas exploratory designs are flexible, descriptive designs are structured. They generally employ structured questionnaires or scales because these forms provide advantages in coding and tabulating. In descriptive designs, the emphasis is on generating an accurate picture of the relationships among variables. Probability sampling plans are optimal if one seeks to generalize back to the broader population. Descriptive studies typically rely heavily on cross-tabs or other means of investigating the association among variables, such as regression analysis, although the emphasis can also be on the search for differences. The great majority of descriptive studies are cross-sectional, although some do use longitudinal information.

Experiments are the best means for making inferences about cause-and-effect relationships, because, if designed properly, they provide the most compelling evidence about concomitant variation, time order of occurrence of variables, and elimination of other factors. A key feature of the experiment is that the researcher is able to control who will be exposed to the experimental stimulus (the presumed cause). This assignment of participants to conditions allows the researcher to establish the prior equality of groups by randomization, which in turn allows the adjustment of the results to eliminate many contaminating influences.

The emphasis in experiments is on testing a specific relationship, so causal designs demand a clear specification of what is to be measured and how it is to be measured. Structured data-collection instruments should be used, and, though structured questionnaires and scales are often employed, experiments can also be used to collect observational data, with the result of typically more objective, accurate information. The major thrust in the analysis of experimental results is a test for differences between those exposed to the experimental stimulus and those not exposed; t-tests and the analysis of variance procedures are most often used.

This brief summary should remind the reader how intimately the marketing research steps are interrelated. Note how the basic nature of the research design implies a number of choices in terms of the structure of the data-collection form, design of the sample, and collection and analysis of the data. A decision about appropriate research design does not completely determine the latter considerations, of course, but definitely suggests their basic qualities. The marketing researcher still has to determine the specific format, e.g., is the structured questionnaire to be disguised or undisguised; is the probability sample to be simple, stratified, or cluster; how large a sample is needed, etc. The marketing researcher has to balance the various sources of error so that the overall total error can be diminished.

Marketing research can be quite complicated. When done well, it is extremely useful and valuable to the manager who wishes to make important decisions. Marketing research can also be fun!

We hope this text has given you sufficient overview that whether your career takes you close to marketing research questions or you work with marketing research results in a broader managerial scope, you'll understand how to obtain the information you need. We also sincerely hope that in addition to your having a greater appreciation for marketing research information, the text provides sufficient details to serve as a resource throughout your career.

Best wishes!

Cumulative Probabilities for the Standard Normal Distribution

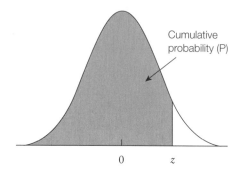

Cumulative probability (P)

0   z

Entries in the table give the area under the curve to the left of the z value. For example, for $z = 1.25$ the cumulative probability is .8944.

z	.00	.01	.02	.03	.04	.05	.06	.07	.08	.09
.0	.5000	.5040a	.5080	.5120	.5160	.5199	.5239	.5279	.5319	.5359
.1	.5398	.5438a	.5478	.5517	.5557	.5596	.5636	.5675	.5714	.5753
.2	.5793	.5832a	.5871	.5910	.5948	.5987	.6026	.6064	.6103	.6141
.3	.6179	.6217a	.6255	.6293	.6331	.6368	.6406	.6443	.6480	.6517
.4	.6554	.6591a	.6628	.6664	.6700	.6736	.6772	.6808	.6844	.6879
.5	.6915	.6950a	.6985	.7019	.7054	.7088	.7123	.7157	.7190	.7224
.6	.7257	.7291a	.7324	.7357	.7389	.7422	.7454	.7486	.7517	.7549
.7	.7580	.7611a	.7642	.7673	.7704	.7734	.7764	.7794	.7823	.7852
.8	.7881	.7910a	.7939	.7967	.7995	.8023	.8051	.8078	.8106	.8133
.9	.8159	.8186a	.8212	.8238	.8264	.8289	.8315	.8340	.8365	.8389
1.0	.8413	.8438a	.8461	.8485	.8508	.8531	.8554	.8577	.8599	.8621
1.1	.8643	.8665a	.8686	.8708	.8729	.8749	.8770	.8790	.8810	.8830
1.2	.8849	.8869a	.8888	.8907	.8925	.8944	.8962	.8980	.8997	.9015
1.3	.9032	.9049a	.9066	.9082	.9099	.9115	.9131	.9147	.9162	.9177
1.4	.9192	.9207a	.9222	.9236	.9251	.9265	.9279	.9292	.9306	.9319
1.5	.9332	.9345a	.9357	.9370	.9382	.9394	.9406	.9418	.9429	.9441
1.6	.9452	.9463a	.9474	.9484	.9495	.9505	.9515	.9525	.9535	.9545
1.7	.9554	.9564a	.9573	.9582	.9591	.9599	.9608	.9616	.9625	.9633
1.8	.9641	.9649a	.9656	.9664	.9671	.9678	.9686	.9693	.9699	.9706
1.9	.9713	.9719a	.9726	.9732	.9738	.9744	.9750	.9756	.9761	.9767
2.0	.9772	.9778a	.9783	.9788	.9793	.9798	.9803	.9808	.9812	.9817
2.1	.9821	.9826a	.9830	.9834	.9838	.9842	.9846	.9850	.9854	.9857
2.2	.9861	.9864a	.9868	.9871	.9875	.9878	.9881	.9884	.9887	.9890
2.3	.9893	.9896a	.9898	.9901	.9904	.9906	.9909	.9911	.9913	.9913
2.4	.9918	.9920a	.9922	.9925	.9927	.9929	.9931	.9932	.9934	.9936
2.5	.9938	.9940a	.9941	.9943	.9945	.9946	.9948	.9949	.9951	.9952
2.6	.9953	.9955a	.9956	.9957	.9959	.9960	.9961	.9962	.9963	.9964
2.7	.9965	.9966a	.9967	.9968	.9969	.9970	.9971	.9972	.9973	.9974
2.8	.9974	.9975a	.9976	.9977	.9977	.9978	.9979	.9979	.9980	.9981
2.9	.9981	.9982a	.9982	.9983	.9984	.9984	.9985	.9985	.9986	.9986
3.0	.9986	.9987a	.9987	.9988	.9988	.9989	.9989	.9989	.9990	.9990

Critical Values of χ^2

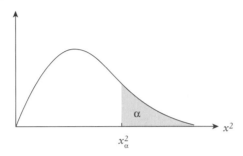

Degrees of Freedom	$\chi^2_{.995}$	$\chi^2_{.990}$	$\chi^2_{.975}$	$\chi^2_{.950}$	$\chi^2_{.900}$
1	0.0000	0.0002	0.0010	0.0039	0.0158
2	0.0100	0.0201	0.0506	0.1026	0.2107
3	0.0717	0.1148	0.2158	0.3518	0.5844
4	0.2070	0.2971	0.4844	0.7107	1.0636
5	0.4117	0.5543	0.8312	1.1455	1.6103
6	0.6757	0.8721	1.2373	1.6354	2.2041
7	0.9893	1.2390	1.6899	2.1673	2.8331
8	1.3444	1.6465	2.1797	2.7326	3.4895
9	1.7349	2.0879	2.7004	3.3251	4.1682
10	2.1559	2.5582	3.2470	3.9403	4.8652
11	2.6032	3.0535	3.8157	4.5748	5.5778
12	3.0738	3.5706	4.4038	5.2260	6.3038
13	3.5650	4.1069	5.0088	5.8919	7.0415
14	4.0747	4.6604	5.6287	6.5706	7.7895
15	4.6009	5.2293	6.2621	7.2609	8.5468
16	5.1422	5.8122	6.9077	7.9616	9.3122
17	5.6972	6.4078	7.5642	8.6718	10.0852
18	6.2648	7.0149	8.2307	9.3905	10.8649
19	6.8440	7.6327	8.9065	10.1170	11.6509
20	7.4338	8.2604	9.5908	10.8508	12.4426
21	8.0337	8.8972	10.2829	11.5913	13.2396
22	8.6427	9.5425	10.9823	12.3380	14.0415
23	9.2604	10.1957	11.6886	13.0905	14.8480
24	9.8862	10.8564	12.4012	13.8484	15.6587
25	10.5197	11.5240	13.1197	14.6114	16.4734
26	11.1602	12.1981	13.8439	15.3792	17.2919
27	11.8076	12.8785	14.5734	16.1514	18.1139
28	12.4613	13.5647	15.3079	16.9279	18.9392
29	13.1211	14.2565	16.0471	17.7084	19.7677
30	13.7867	14.9535	16.7908	18.4927	20.5992
40	20.7065	22.1643	24.4330	26.5093	29.0505
50	27.9907	29.7067	32.3574	34.7643	37.6886
60	35.5345	37.4849	40.4817	43.1880	46.4589
70	43.2752	45.4417	48.7576	51.7393	55.3289
80	51.1719	53.5401	57.1532	60.3915	64.2778
90	59.1963	61.7541	65.6466	69.1260	73.2911
100	67.3276	70.0649	74.2219	77.9295	82.3581

Critical Values of χ^2 *(continued)*

Degrees of Freedom	$\chi^2_{.100}$	$\chi^2_{.050}$	$\chi^2_{.025}$	$\chi^2_{.010}$	$\chi^2_{.005}$
1	2.7055	3.8415	5.0239	6.6349	7.8794
2	4.6052	5.9915	7.3778	9.2103	10.5966
3	6.2514	7.8147	9.3484	11.3449	12.8382
4	7.7794	9.4877	11.1433	13.2767	14.8603
5	9.2364	11.0705	12.8325	15.0863	16.7496
6	10.6446	12.5916	14.4494	16.8119	18.5476
7	12.0170	14.0671	16.0128	18.4753	20.2777
8	13.3616	15.5073	17.5345	20.0902	21.9550
9	14.6837	16.9190	19.0228	21.6660	23.5894
10	15.9872	18.3070	20.4832	23.2093	25.1882
11	17.2750	19.6751	21.9200	24.7250	26.7568
12	18.5493	21.0261	23.3367	26.2170	28.2995
13	19.8119	22.3620	24.7356	27.6882	29.8195
14	21.0641	23.6848	26.1189	29.1412	31.3193
15	22.3071	24.9958	27.4884	30.5779	32.8013
16	23.5418	26.2962	28.8454	31.9999	34.2672
17	24.7690	27.5871	30.1910	33.4087	35.7185
18	25.9894	28.8693	31.5264	34.8053	37.1565
19	27.2036	30.1435	32.8523	36.1909	38.5823
20	28.4120	31.4104	34.1696	37.5662	39.9968
21	29.6151	32.6706	35.4789	38.9322	41.4011
22	30.8133	33.9244	36.7807	40.2894	42.7957
23	32.0069	35.1725	38.0756	41.6384	44.1813
24	33.1962	36.4150	39.3641	42.9798	45.5585
25	34.3816	37.6525	40.6465	44.3141	46.9279
26	35.5632	38.8851	41.9232	45.6417	48.2899
27	36.7412	40.1133	43.1945	46.9629	49.6449
28	37.9159	41.3371	44.4608	48.2782	50.9934
29	39.0875	42.5570	45.7223	49.5879	52.3356
30	40.2560	43.7730	46.9792	50.8922	53.6720
40	51.8051	55.7585	59.3417	63.6907	66.7660
50	63.1671	67.5048	71.4202	76.1539	79.4900
60	74.3970	79.0819	83.2977	88.3794	91.9517
70	85.5270	90.5312	95.0232	100.4252	04.2149
80	96.5782	101.8795	106.6286	112.3288	116.3211
90	107.5650	113.1453	118.1359	124.1163	128.2989
100	118.4980	124.3421	129.5612	135.8067	140.1695

Critical Values of t

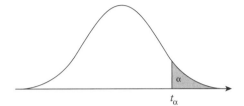

Degrees of Freedom	$t_{.100}$	$t_{.050}$	$t_{.025}$	$t_{.010}$	$t_{.005}$
1	3.078	6.314	12.706	31.821	63.657
2	1.886	2.920	4.303	6.965	9.925
3	1.638	2.353	3.182	4.541	5.841
4	1.533	2.132	2.776	3.747	4.604
5	1.476	2.015	2.571	3.365	4.032
6	1.440	1.943	2.447	3.143	3.707
7	1.415	1.895	2.365	2.998	3.499
8	1.397	1.860	2.306	2.896	3.355
9	1.383	1.833	2.262	2.821	3.250
10	1.372	1.812	2.228	2.764	3.169
11	1.363	1.796	2.201	2.718	3.106
12	1.356	1.782	2.179	2.681	3.055
13	1.350	1.771	2.160	2.650	3.012
14	1.345	1.761	2.145	2.624	2.977
15	1.341	1.753	2.131	2.602	2.947
16	1.337	1.746	2.120	2.583	2.921
17	1.333	1.740	2.110	2.567	2.898
18	1.330	1.734	2.101	2.552	2.878
19	1.328	1.729	2.093	2.539	2.861
20	1.325	1.725	2.086	2.528	2.845
21	1.323	1.721	2.080	2.518	2.831
22	1.321	1.717	2.074	2.508	2.819
23	1.319	1.714	2.069	2.500	2.807
24	1.318	1.711	2.064	2.492	2.797
25	1.316	1.708	2.060	2.485	2.787
26	1.315	1.706	2.056	2.479	2.779
27	1.314	1.703	2.052	2.473	2.771
28	1.313	1.701	2.048	2.467	2.763
29	1.311	1.699	2.045	2.462	2.756
30	1.310	1.697	2.042	2.457	2.750
35	1.306	1.690	2.030	2.438	2.724
40	1.303	1.684	2.021	2.423	2.704
50	1.299	1.676	2.009	2.403	2.678
60	1.296	1.671	2.000	2.390	2.660
120	1.289	1.658	1.980	2.358	2.617
∞	1.282	1.645	1.960	2.326	2.576

Percentage Points of the F Distribution. $\alpha = .05$

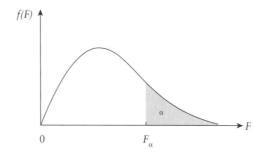

Numerator Degrees of Freedom

v_1/v_2	1	2	3	4	5	6	7	8	9
1	161.4	199.5	215.7	224.6	230.2	234.0	236.8	238.9	240.5
2	18.51	19.00	19.16	19.25	19.30	19.33	19.35	19.37	19.38
3	10.13	9.55	9.28	9.12	9.01	8.94	8.89	8.85	8.81
4	7.71	6.94	6.59	6.39	6.26	6.16	6.09	6.04	6.00
5	6.61	5.79	5.41	5.19	5.05	4.95	4.88	4.82	4.77
6	5.99	5.14	4.76	4.53	4.39	4.28	4.21	4.15	4.10
7	5.59	4.74	4.35	4.12	3.97	3.87	3.79	3.73	3.68
8	5.32	4.46	4.07	3.84	3.69	3.58	3.50	3.44	3.39
9	5.12	4.26	3.86	3.63	3.48	3.37	3.29	3.23	3.18
10	4.96	4.10	3.71	3.48	3.33	3.22	3.14	3.07	3.02
11	4.84	3.98	3.59	3.36	3.20	3.09	3.01	2.95	2.90
12	4.75	3.89	3.49	3.26	3.11	3.00	2.91	2.85	2.80
13	4.67	3.81	3.41	3.18	3.03	2.92	2.83	2.77	2.71
14	4.60	3.74	3.34	3.11	2.96	2.85	2.76	2.70	2.65
15	4.54	3.68	3.29	3.06	2.90	2.79	2.71	2.64	2.59
16	4.49	3.63	3.24	3.01	2.85	2.74	2.66	2.59	2.54
17	4.45	3.59	3.20	2.96	2.81	2.70	2.61	2.55	2.49
18	4.41	3.55	3.16	2.93	2.77	2.66	2.58	2.51	2.46
19	4.38	3.52	3.13	2.90	2.74	2.63	2.54	2.48	2.42
20	4.35	3.49	3.10	2.87	2.71	2.60	2.51	2.45	2.39
21	4.32	3.47	3.07	2.84	2.68	2.57	2.49	2.42	2.37
22	4.30	3.44	3.05	2.82	2.66	2.55	2.46	2.40	2.34
23	4.28	3.42	3.03	2.80	2.64	2.53	2.44	2.37	2.32
24	4.26	3.40	3.01	2.78	2.62	2.51	2.42	2.36	2.30
25	4.24	3.39	2.99	2.76	2.60	2.49	2.40	2.34	2.28
26	4.23	3.37	2.98	2.74	2.59	2.47	2.39	2.32	2.27
27	4.21	3.35	2.96	2.73	2.57	2.46	2.37	2.31	2.25
28	4.20	3.34	2.95	2.71	2.56	2.45	2.36	2.29	2.24
29	4.18	3.33	2.93	2.70	2.55	2.43	2.35	2.28	2.22
30	4.17	3.32	2.92	2.69	2.53	2.42	2.33	2.27	2.21
40	4.08	3.23	2.84	2.61	2.45	2.34	2.25	2.18	2.12
60	4.00	3.15	2.76	2.53	2.37	2.25	2.17	2.10	2.04
120	3.92	3.07	2.68	2.45	2.29	2.18	2.09	2.02	1.96
∞	3.84	3.00	2.60	2.37	2.21	2.10	2.01	1.94	1.88

Denominator Degrees of Freedom

Percentage Points of the *F* Distribution. α = .05 *(continued)*

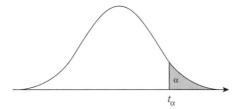

t_α

				Numerator Degrees of Freedom						
v_1/v_2	10	12	15	20	24	30	40	60	120	∞
1	241.9	243.9	245.9	248.0	249.1	250.1	251.1	252.2	253.3	254.3
2	19.40	19.41	19.43	19.45	19.45	19.46	19.47	19.48	19.49	19.50
3	8.79	8.74	8.70	8.66	8.64	8.62	8.59	8.57	8.55	8.53
4	5.96	5.91	5.86	5.80	5.77	5.75	5.72	5.69	5.66	5.63
5	4.74	4.68	4.62	4.56	4.53	4.50	4.46	4.43	4.40	4.37
6	4.06	4.00	3.94	3.87	3.84	3.81	3.77	3.74	3.70	3.67
7	3.64	3.57	3.51	3.44	3.41	3.38	3.34	3.30	3.27	3.23
8	3.35	3.28	3.22	3.15	3.12	3.08	3.04	3.01	2.97	2.93
9	3.14	3.07	3.01	2.94	2.90	2.86	2.83	2.79	2.75	2.71
10	2.98	2.91	2.85	2.77	2.74	2.70	2.66	2.62	2.58	2.54
11	2.85	2.79	2.72	2.65	2.61	2.57	2.53	2.49	2.45	2.40
12	2.75	2.69	2.62	2.54	2.51	2.47	2.43	2.38	2.34	2.30
13	2.67	2.60	2.53	2.46	2.42	2.38	2.34	2.30	2.25	2.21
14	2.60	2.53	2.46	2.39	2.35	2.31	2.27	2.22	2.18	2.13
15	2.54	2.48	2.40	2.33	2.29	2.25	2.20	2.16	2.11	2.07
16	2.49	2.42	2.35	2.28	2.24	2.19	2.15	2.11	2.06	2.01
17	2.45	2.38	2.31	2.23	2.19	2.15	2.10	2.06	2.01	1.96
18	2.41	2.34	2.27	2.19	2.15	2.11	2.06	2.02	1.97	1.92
19	2.38	2.31	2.23	2.16	2.11	2.07	2.03	1.98	1.93	1.88
20	2.35	2.28	2.20	2.12	2.08	2.04	1.99	1.95	1.90	1.84
21	2.32	2.25	2.18	2.10	2.05	2.01	1.96	1.92	1.87	1.81
22	2.30	2.23	2.15	2.07	2.03	1.98	1.94	1.89	1.84	1.78
23	2.27	2.20	2.13	2.05	2.01	1.96	1.91	1.86	1.81	1.76
24	2.25	2.18	2.11	2.03	1.98	1.94	1.89	1.84	1.79	1.73
25	2.24	2.16	2.09	2.01	1.96	1.92	1.87	1.82	1.77	1.71
26	2.22	2.15	2.07	1.99	1.95	1.90	1.85	1.80	1.75	1.69
27	2.20	2.13	2.06	1.97	1.93	1.88	1.84	1.79	1.73	1.67
28	2.19	2.12	2.04	1.96	1.91	1.87	1.82	1.77	1.71	1.65
29	2.18	2.10	2.03	1.94	1.90	1.85	1.81	1.75	1.70	1.64
30	2.16	2.09	2.01	1.93	1.89	1.84	1.79	1.74	1.68	1.62
40	2.08	2.00	1.92	1.84	1.79	1.74	1.69	1.64	1.58	1.51
60	1.99	1.92	1.84	1.75	1.70	1.65	1.59	1.53	1.47	1.39
120	1.91	1.83	1.75	1.66	1.61	1.55	1.50	1.43	1.35	1.25
∞	1.83	1.75	1.67	1.57	1.52	1.46	1.39	1.32	1.22	1.00

Denominator Degrees of Freedom

Percentage Points of the F Distribution. $\alpha = .01$

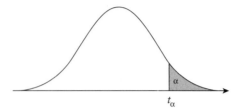

Numerator Degrees of Freedom

v_1/v_2	1	2	3	4	5	6	7	8	9
1	4052	4999	5404	5624	5764	5859	5928	5981	6022
2	98.50	99.00	99.16	99.25	99.30	99.33	99.36	99.38	99.39
3	34.12	30.82	29.46	28.71	28.24	27.91	27.67	27.49	27.34
4	21.20	18.00	16.69	15.98	15.52	15.21	14.98	14.80	14.66
5	16.26	13.27	12.06	11.39	10.97	10.67	10.46	10.29	10.16
6	13.75	10.92	9.78	9.15	8.75	8.47	8.26	8.10	7.98
7	12.25	9.55	8.45	7.85	7.46	7.19	6.99	6.84	6.72
8	11.26	8.65	7.59	7.01	6.63	6.37	6.18	6.03	5.91
9	10.56	8.02	6.99	6.42	6.06	5.80	5.61	5.47	5.35
10	10.04	7.56	6.55	5.99	5.64	5.39	5.20	5.06	4.94
11	9.65	7.21	6.22	5.67	5.32	5.07	4.89	4.74	4.63
12	9.33	6.93	5.95	5.41	5.06	4.82	4.64	4.50	4.39
13	9.07	6.70	5.74	5.21	4.86	4.62	4.44	4.30	4.19
14	8.86	6.51	5.56	5.04	4.69	4.46	4.28	4.14	4.03
15	8.68	6.36	5.42	4.89	4.56	4.32	4.14	4.00	3.89
16	8.53	6.23	5.29	4.77	4.44	4.20	4.03	3.89	3.78
17	8.40	6.11	5.19	4.67	4.34	4.10	3.93	3.79	3.68
18	8.29	6.01	5.09	4.58	4.25	4.01	3.84	3.71	3.60
19	8.18	5.93	5.01	4.50	4.17	3.94	3.77	3.63	3.52
20	8.10	5.85	4.94	4.43	4.10	3.87	3.70	3.56	3.46
21	8.02	5.78	4.87	4.37	4.04	3.81	3.64	3.51	3.40
22	7.95	5.72	4.82	4.31	3.99	3.76	3.59	3.45	3.35
23	7.88	5.66	4.76	4.26	3.94	3.71	3.54	3.41	3.30
24	7.82	5.61	4.72	4.22	3.90	3.67	3.50	3.36	3.26
25	7.77	5.57	4.68	4.18	3.85	3.63	3.46	3.32	3.22
26	7.72	5.53	4.64	4.14	3.82	3.59	3.42	3.29	3.18
27	7.68	5.49	4.60	4.11	3.78	3.56	3.39	3.26	3.15
28	7.64	5.45	4.57	4.07	3.75	3.53	3.36	3.23	3.12
29	7.60	5.42	4.54	4.04	3.73	3.50	3.33	3.20	3.09
30	7.56	5.39	4.51	4.02	3.70	3.47	3.30	3.17	3.07
40	7.31	5.18	4.31	3.83	3.51	3.29	3.12	2.99	2.89
60	7.08	4.98	4.13	3.65	3.34	3.12	2.95	2.82	2.72
120	6.85	4.79	3.95	3.48	3.17	2.96	2.79	2.66	2.56
∞	6.63	4.61	3.78	3.32	3.02	2.80	2.64	2.51	2.41

Denominator Degrees of Freedom

Percentage Points of the *F* Distribution. $\alpha = .01$ *(continued)*

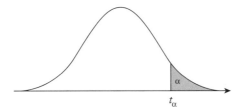

t_α

Numerator Degrees of Freedom

v_1/v_2	10	12	15	20	24	30	40	60	120	∞
1	6056.	6107.	6157.	6209.	6234.	6260.	6286.	6313.	6340.	6366.
2	99.40	99.42	99.43	99.45	99.46	99.47	99.48	99.48	99.49	99.50
3	27.23	27.05	26.87	26.69	26.60	26.50	26.41	26.32	26.22	26.13
4	14.55	14.37	14.20	14.02	13.93	13.84	13.75	13.65	13.56	13.46
5	10.05	9.89	9.72	9.55	9.47	9.38	9.29	9.20	9.11	9.02
6	7.87	7.72	7.56	7.40	7.31	7.23	7.14	7.06	6.97	6.88
7	6.62	6.47	6.31	6.16	6.07	5.99	5.91	5.82	5.74	5.65
8	5.81	5.67	5.52	5.36	5.28	5.20	5.12	5.03	4.95	4.86
9	5.26	5.11	4.96	4.81	4.73	4.65	4.57	4.48	4.40	4.31
10	4.85	4.71	4.56	4.41	4.33	4.25	4.17	4.08	4.00	3.91
11	4.54	4.40	4.25	4.10	4.02	3.94	3.86	3.78	3.69	3.60
12	4.30	4.16	4.01	3.86	3.78	3.70	3.62	3.54	3.45	3.36
13	4.10	3.96	3.82	3.66	3.59	3.51	3.43	3.34	3.25	3.17
14	3.94	3.80	3.66	3.51	3.43	3.35	3.27	3.18	3.09	3.00
15	3.80	3.67	3.52	3.37	3.29	3.21	3.13	3.05	2.96	2.87
16	3.69	3.55	3.41	3.26	3.18	3.10	3.02	2.93	2.84	2.75
17	3.59	3.46	3.31	3.16	3.08	3.00	2.92	2.83	2.75	2.65
18	3.51	3.37	3.23	3.08	3.00	2.92	2.84	2.75	2.66	2.57
19	3.43	3.30	3.15	3.00	2.92	2.84	2.76	2.67	2.58	2.49
20	3.37	3.23	3.09	2.94	2.86	2.78	2.69	2.61	2.52	2.42
21	3.31	3.17	3.03	2.88	2.80	2.72	2.64	2.55	2.46	2.36
22	3.26	3.12	2.98	2.83	2.75	2.67	2.58	2.50	2.40	2.31
23	3.21	3.07	2.93	2.78	2.70	2.62	2.54	2.45	2.35	2.26
24	3.17	3.03	2.89	2.74	2.66	2.58	2.49	2.40	2.31	2.21
25	3.13	2.99	2.85	2.70	2.62	2.54	2.45	2.36	2.27	2.17
26	3.09	2.96	2.81	2.66	2.58	2.50	2.42	2.33	2.23	2.13
27	3.06	2.93	2.78	2.63	2.55	2.47	2.38	2.29	2.20	2.10
28	3.03	2.90	2.75	2.60	2.52	2.44	2.35	2.26	2.17	2.06
29	3.00	2.87	2.73	2.57	2.49	2.41	2.33	2.23	2.14	2.03
30	2.98	2.84	2.70	2.55	2.47	2.39	2.30	2.21	2.11	2.01
40	2.80	2.66	2.52	2.37	2.29	2.20	2.11	2.02	1.92	1.80
60	2.63	2.50	2.35	2.20	2.12	2.03	1.94	1.84	1.73	1.60
120	2.47	2.34	2.19	2.03	1.95	1.86	1.76	1.66	1.53	1.38
∞	2.32	2.18	2.04	1.88	1.79	1.70	1.59	1.47	1.32	1.00

Denominator Degrees of Freedom

A

absolute precision Degree of precision in an estimate of a parameter expressed as within plus or minus so many units.

accuracy Criterion used to evaluate a research report according to whether the reasoning in the report is logical and the information correct.

administrative control Term applied to studies relying on questionnaires and referring to the speed, cost, and control of the replies afforded by the mode of administration.

analysis of cases Intensive study of selected examples of the phenomenon of interest.

analysis of variance (ANOVA) Statistical test used with interval data to determine if two or more samples came from populations with equal means.

area sampling Form of cluster sampling in which areas (e.g., census tracts, blocks) serve as the primary sampling units. The population is divided into mutually exclusive and exhaustive areas using maps, and a random sample of areas is selected. If all the households in the selected areas are used in the study, it is one-stage area sampling. If the areas themselves are subsampled with respect to households, the procedure is two-stage area sampling.

attitudes/opinions Some preference, liking, or conviction regarding a specific object or idea; a predisposition to act.

awareness/knowledge Insight into or understanding of facts about some object or phenomenon.

B

banner A series of cross-tabulations between a criterion, or dependent, variable and several explanatory variables in a single table.

bar chart Chart in which the lengths of the bars show relative amounts of variables or objects.

Bayes' rule Formal mechanism for revising prior probabilities in the light of new information.

Bayesian probability Probability based on a person's subjective or personal judgments and experience.

behavior What respondents have done or are doing.

benchmarking The comparison of one's data (e.g., customers' reception of service quality) to an industry standard, or best-practices.

brain wave research Research technique that assesses the stimuli that participants find arousing or interesting by using electrodes fitted to their head that monitor the electrical impulses emitted by the brain.

branching questions A technique used to direct respondents to different places in a questionnaire based on their response to the question at hand.

brand-switching matrix Two-way table that indicates which brands a sample of people purchased in one period and which brands they purchased in a subsequent period, thus highlighting the switches occurring between brands as well as the number of persons that purchased the same brand in both periods.

C

causal research Research design in which the major emphasis is on determining a cause-and-effect relationship.

census A complete canvass of a population.

Central-Limit Theorem Theorem that holds that if simple random samples of size n are drawn from a parent population with mean μ and variance σ^2, then when n is large, the sample mean will be approximately normally distributed with the mean equal to μ and variance equal to σ^2/n. The approximation becomes more accurate as n becomes larger.

central office edit Thorough and exacting scrutiny and correction of completed data-collection forms, including a decision about what to do with the data.

chi-square goodness-of-fit test Statistical test to determine whether some observed pattern of frequencies corresponds to an expected pattern.

clarity Criterion used to evaluate a research report: *Is the phrasing in the report precise?*

classical probability Probability determined by the relative frequency with which an event occurs when an experiment is repeated under controlled conditions.

cluster analysis Body of techniques concerned with developing natural groupings of objects based on the relationships of the p variables describing the objects.

cluster sample A probability sample distinguished by a two-step procedure in which (1) the parent population is divided into mutually exclusive and exhaustive subsets, and (2) a random sample of subsets is selected. If the investigator then uses all population elements in the selected subsets for the sample, the procedure is one-stage cluster sampling; if a sample of elements is selected probabilistically from the subsets, the procedure is two-stage cluster sampling.

codebook A document that describes each variable, gives it a code name, and identifies its location in the record.

coding Technical procedure by which data are categorized; it involves specifying the alternative categories or classes into which the responses are to be placed and assigning code numbers to the classes.

coefficient alpha A statistic that summarizes the extent to which a set of items making up a measure intercorrelate, or go together.

coefficient of concordance Statistic used with ordinal data to measure the extent of association among two or more variables.

coefficient of determination Term used in regression analysis to refer to the relative proportion of the total variation in the criterion variable that can be explained or accounted for by the fitted regression equation.

coefficient of multiple correlation In multiple-regression analysis, the square root of the coefficient of multiple determination.

coefficient of multiple determination In multiple-regression analysis, the proportion of variation in the criterion variable that is accounted for by the covariation in the predictor variables.

coefficient of partial correlation In multiple-regression analysis, the square root of the coefficient of partial determination.

coefficient of partial determination Quantity that results from a multiple-regression analysis that indicates the proportion of variation in the criterion variable not accounted for by the earlier variables that is accounted for by adding a new variable into the regression equation.

coefficient of partial (or net) regression Quantity resulting from a regression that indicates the average change in the criterion variable per unit change in a predictor variable, *holding all other predictor variables constant;* the interpretation applies only when the predictor variables are independent, as required for a valid application of the multiple-regression model.

cohort The aggregate of individuals who experience the same event within the same time interval.

communality Quantity resulting from a factor analysis that expresses the proportion of the variance of a variable extracted by *m* factors, where *m* can vary from 1 to the total number of variables; the communalities help determine how many factors should be retained in a solution.

communication Method of data collection involving questioning of respondents to secure the desired information using a data-collection instrument called a questionnaire.

comparative rating scale Scale requiring participants to make their ratings as a series of relative judgments or comparisons rather than as independent assessments.

completely randomized design Experimental design in which the experimental treatments are assigned to the test units completely at random.

completeness Criterion used to evaluate a research report: *Does the report provide all the information readers need in a language they understand?*

completeness rate (C) Measure used to evaluate and compare interviewers in terms of their ability to obtain needed information from contacted respondents; the completeness rate measures the proportion of complete contacts by an interviewer.

computer-assisted interviewing (CAI) The conducting of surveys using computers to manage the sequence of questions in which the answers are recorded electronically through the use of a keyboard.

conciseness Criterion used to evaluate a research report: *Is the writing in the report crisp and direct?*

conditional association Association existing between two variables when the levels of one or more other variables are considered in the analysis; other variables are called control variables.

conditional probability Probability that Event A will occur when it is known whether another Event B has occurred.

confusion matrix Device used in discriminant analysis to assess the adequacy of the discriminant function; it's a cross-classification table, in which the variables of cross classification are the actual group membership categories and the predicted group membership categories, and the entries are the number of observations falling into each cell.

conjoint analysis Technique in which respondents' utilities or valuations of attributes are inferred from the preferences they express for various combinations of these attributes.

constant sum method A type of comparative rating scale in which an individual is instructed to divide a sum (e.g., 100 points) among two or more attributes on the basis of their importance to him or her.

Construct, or constitutive or conceptual definition Definition in which a given construct is defined in terms of other constructs in the set, sometimes in the form of an equation that expresses the relationship among them.

construct validity Approach to validating a measure by determining what construct, concept, or trait the instrument is in fact measuring.

contact rate (*K*) Measure used to evaluate and compare the effectiveness of interviewers in making contact with designated respondents. K = number of sample units contacted/total number of sample units approached.

content validity Approach to validating a measure by determining the adequacy with which the domain of the characteristic is captured by the measure; sometimes called face validity.

contingency coefficient Statistic used to measure the extent of association between two nominally scaled attributes.

contingency table Statistical test employing the X^2 statistic that is used to determine whether the variables in a cross-classification analysis are independent.

controlled test market A market in which an entire marketing test program is conducted by an outside service; also called a forced distribution test market.

convenience sample Nonprobability sample, sometimes called an accidental sample, because those included in the sample enter by accident, in that they just happen to be where the study is being conducted when it is being conducted.

convergent validity Confirmation of the existence of a construct determined by the correlations exhibited by independent measures of the construct.

cophenetic value Level at which a pair of objects or classes are linked in cluster analyses.

correlation analysis Statistical technique used to measure the closeness of the linear relationship between two or more interval scaled variables.

cross-sectional study Investigation involving a sample of elements selected from the population of interest at a single point in time.

cross-tabulation Count of the number of cases that fall into each of several categories when the categories are based on two or more variables considered simultaneously.

cumulative distribution function Function that shows the number of cases having a value less than or equal to a specified quantity; the function is generated by connecting the points representing the combinations of Xs (values) and Ys (cumulative frequencies) with straight lines.

cutting score Term used in discriminant analysis to indicate the score that divides the groups; if the object's score is above the cutting score, the object is assigned to one group, whereas if its score is below the cutting score, it is assigned to the other group.

D

data system The part of a decision support system that includes the processes used to capture and the methods used to store data coming from a number of external and internal sources.

decision support system (DSS) A coordinated collection of data, system tools, and techniques with supporting software and hardware by which an organization gathers and interprets relevant information from business and the environment and turns it into a basis for marketing action.

decision tree Decision flow diagram in which the problem is structured in chronological order, typically with small squares indicating decision forks and small circles indicating chance forks.

dendrogram Treelike device employed to interpret the output of a cluster analysis that indicates the groups of objects forming at various similarity levels.

deontology An ethical or moral reasoning framework that focuses on the welfare of the individual and that uses means, intentions, and features of the act itself in judging its ethicality; sometimes referred to as the rights or entitlements model.

depth interview Unstructured personal interview in which the interviewer attempts to get respondents to talk freely and to express their true feelings.

derived population Population of all possible distinguishable samples that could be drawn from a parent population under a specific sampling plan.

descriptive research Research design in which the major emphasis is on determining the frequency with which something occurs or the extent to which two variables covary.

dialog system The part of a decision support system that permits users to explore the databases by employing the system models to produce reports that satisfy their particular information needs; also called language systems.

dichotomous question Fixed-alternative question in which respondents are asked to indicate which of two alternative responses most closely corresponds to their position on a topic.

discriminant analysis Statistical technique employed to model the relationship between a dichotomous or multichotomous criterion variable and a set of p predictor variables.

discriminant validity Criterion imposed on a measure of a construct requiring that it not correlate too highly with measures from which it is supposed to differ.

disguise Amount of knowledge about the purpose of a study communicated to the respondent by the data-collection method. An undisguised questionnaire is one in which the purpose of the research is obvious from the questions posed, whereas a disguised questionnaire attempts to hide the purpose of the study.

disproportionate stratified sampling Stratified sample in which the individual strata or subsets are sampled in relation to both their size and their variability; strata exhibiting more variability are sampled more than proportionately to their relative size, whereas those that are very homogeneous are sampled less than proportionately.

domain sampling model A measurement model that holds that the true score of a characteristic is obtained when all the items in the domain are used to capture it. Only a sample of items is typically used, so a primary source of measurement error is the inadequate sampling of the domain of relevant items; to the extent that the sample of items correlates with true scores, it is good.

double-barreled question A question that calls for two responses and thereby creates confusion for the respondent.

dummy table Table that contains a title and headings to denote the categories to be used for each variable making up the table to categorize the data when they are collected.

dummy (or binary) variable Variable that is given one of two values, 0 or 1, and that is used to provide a numerical representation for attributes or characteristics that are not essentially quantitative.

E

editing Inspection and correction, if necessary, of each questionnaire or observation form.

electronic test market Market or geographic area in which a firm tracks purchases made by specific households that are part of its panel, using identification cards held by panel members and the electronic recording using scanners of the products they purchase.

element Term used in sampling to refer to the objects on which measurements are to be taken, such as individuals, households, business firms, or other institutions.

equal-appearing intervals Self-report technique for attitude measurement in which consumers are asked to indicate those statements in a larger list of statements (typically 20 to 22) with which they agree and disagree; their attitude scores are the average score of the scale values of the statements with which they agree.

equivalence Measure of reliability applied to both single instruments and measurement situations. When applied to instruments, the equivalence measure of reliability is the internal consistency or internal homogeneity of the set of items forming the scale; when applied to measurement situations, the equivalence measure of reliability focuses on whether different observers or different instruments used to measure the same individuals or objects at the same point in time yield consistent results.

ethics A concern with the development of moral standards by which situations can be judged; applies to all situations in which there can be actual or potential harm of any kind (e.g., economic, physical, or mental) to an individual or group.

expected value Value resulting from multiplying each consequence by the probability of that consequence occurring and summing the products.

expected value of perfect information Difference between the expected value under certainty and the expected value of the optimal act under uncertainty.

expected value of a research procedure Value determined by multiplying the probability of obtaining the kth research result by the expected value of the preferred decision given the kth research result and summing the products.

expected value under certainty Value derived by multiplying the consequence associated with the optimal act under each possible state of nature by the probability associated with that state of nature and summing the products.

experience survey Interviews with people knowledgeable about the general topic being investigated.

experiment Scientific investigation in which an investigator manipulates and controls one or more independent variables and observes the dependent variable for variation concomitant to the manipulation of the independent variables.

experimental design Research investigation in which the investigator has direct control over at least one independent variable and manipulates at least one independent variable.

experimental mortality Experimental condition in which test units are lost during the course of an experiment.

exploratory research Research design in which the major emphasis is on gaining ideas and insights; particularly helpful in breaking broad, vague problem statements into smaller, more precise subproblem statements.

external data Data that originate outside the organization for which the research is being done.

external validity One criterion by which an experiment is evaluated; the extent to which the observed experimental effect can be generalized to other populations and settings.

eye camera Camera used to study eye movements while the participant reads advertising copy.

F

factor Linear combination of variables.

factor analysis Body of techniques concerned with the study of interrelationships among a set of variables, none of which is given the special status of a criterion variable.

factor loading Quantity that results from a factor analysis and that indicates the correlation between a variable and a factor.

factorial design Experimental design used when the effects of two or more variables are being studied simultaneously; each level of each factor is used with each level of each other factor.

field edit Preliminary edit, typically conducted by a field supervisor, designed to detect the most glaring

omissions and inaccuracies in a completed data-collection instrument.

field error Nonsampling error that arises during the actual collection of the data.

field experiment Research study in a realistic situation in which one or more independent variables are manipulated by the experimenter under as carefully controlled conditions as the situation will permit.

field survey Survey research conducted in realistic situations (e.g., shopping mall, home).

fixed-alternative questions Questions in which the responses are limited to stated alternatives.

fixed sample Sample for which size is determined *a priori* and needed information is collected from the designated elements.

focus group Personal interview conducted among a small number of individuals simultaneously; the interview relies more on group discussion than on directed questions to generate data.

frequency polygon Figure obtained from a histogram by connecting the midpoints of the bars of the histogram with straight lines.

full profile An approach to collecting respondents' judgments in a conjoint analysis in which each stimulus is made up of a combination of each of the attributes.

funnel approach An approach to question sequencing that gets its name from its shape, starting with broad questions and progressively narrowing the scope.

fusion coefficients In linkage cluster analysis, the numerical values at which various cases merge to form clusters; also called amalgamation coefficients, can be read from dendrograms.

G

galvanometer Device used to measure the emotion induced by exposure to a particular stimulus by recording changes in the electrical resistance of the skin associated with the minute degree of sweating that accompanies emotional arousal; in marketing research, the stimulus is often specific advertising copy.

geodemography The availability of demographic consumer behavior and lifestyle data by arbitrary geographic boundaries that are typically quite small.

goodness of fit Statistical test employing X^2 to determine whether some observed pattern of frequencies corresponds to an expected pattern. *See also* chi-square goodness-of-fit test.

graphic rating scale Scale in which individuals indicate their ratings of an attribute by placing a check at the appropriate point on a line that runs from one extreme of the attribute to the other.

H

halo effect Problem arising in data collection when there is carryover from one judgment to another.

histogram Form of bar chart on which the values of the variable are placed along the x-axis, or abscissa, and the absolute frequency or relative frequency of occurrence of the values is indicated along the y-axis, or ordinate.

history Specific events external to an experiment but occurring at the same time that may affect the criterion or response variable.

hit rate Measure used to assess the results of a discriminant analysis by measuring the proportion of the objects that were correctly classified by the discriminant function(s) in the group to which they actually belong.

hypothesis A statement that specifies how two or more measurable variables are related.

I

implicit alternative An alternative answer to a question that is not expressed in the options.

implied assumption A problem that occurs when a question is not framed to explicitly state the consequences; thus,

it elicits different responses from individuals who assume different consequences.

incidence The percentage of the general population that satisfies the criteria defining the target population.

index of predictive association A statistic used to measure the extent of association between two nominally scaled attributes.

information control Term applied to studies using questionnaires and concerning the amount and accuracy of the information that can be obtained from respondents.

instrument variation Any and all changes in the measuring device used in an experiment that might account for differences in two or more measurements.

intention Anticipated or planned future behavior.

interdependence analysis Problem in multivariate analysis to determine the relationship of a set of variables among themselves; no one variate is selected as special in the sense of the dependent variable.

internal data Data that originate within the organization for which the research is being done.

internal validity One criterion by which an experiment is evaluated; the criterion focuses on obtaining evidence demonstrating that the variation in the criterion variable was the result of exposure to the treatment or experimental variable.

interval scale Measurement in which the assigned numbers legitimately allow the comparison of the size of the differences among and between members.

interviewer–interviewee interaction model Model that attempts to describe how an interviewer and a respondent could be expected to respond to each other during the course of an interview; it is helpful in suggesting techniques by which response errors can be potentially reduced.

item nonresponse Source of nonsampling error that arises when a respondent agrees to an interview but refuses or is unable to answer specific questions.

itemized rating scale Scale in which individuals must indicate their ratings of an attribute or object by selecting one from among a limited number of categories that best describes their attitude toward the attribute or object.

J

judgment sample Nonprobability sample that is often called a purposive sample; the sample elements are handpicked because they are expected to serve the research purpose.

K

k-means One of the nodal or partitioning methods for cluster analysis; the technique revolves around the selection of k starting points and the assignment of each element to the starting point to which it is most similar. After all points are assigned, the mean or centroid for each group is determined. Then the objects are reassigned on the basis of which mean they are closest to, and the process of computing new centroids and reassigning points is repeated until no objects are reclassified.

Kolmogorov–Smirnov test Statistical test employed with ordinal data to determine whether some observed pattern of frequencies corresponds to some expected pattern; also tests whether two independent samples have been drawn from the same population or from populations with the same distribution.

L

laboratory experiment Research investigation in which investigators create a situation with exact conditions in order to control some variables and manipulate others.

Latin-square design Experimental design in which (1) the number of categories for each extraneous variable we wish to control is equal to the number of treatments, and (2) each treatment is randomly assigned to categories according to a specific pattern. The Latin-square design is appropriate when two extraneous factors are to be explicitly controlled.

leading question A question framed to give the respondent a clue about how he or she should answer.

line chart Two-dimensional chart constructed on graph paper in which the x-axis represents one variable (typically time) and the y-axis represents another variable.

literature search Search of statistics, trade journal articles, other articles, magazines, newspapers, and books for data or insight into the problem at hand.

longitudinal study Investigation involving a fixed sample of elements that is measured repeatedly through time.

M

mail questionnaire Questionnaire administered by mail to designated respondents with an accompanying cover letter to be returned by mail by the participant to the research organization.

mall intercept A method of data collection in which interviewers in a shopping mall stop a sample of those passing by to ask them if they would be willing to participate in a research study; those who agree are typically taken to any interviewing facility that has been set up in the mall, where the interview is conducted.

market test Controlled experiment, done in a limited but carefully selected sector of the marketplace; its aim is to predict the sales or profit consequences, either in absolute or relative terms, of one or more proposed marketing actions.

marketing information system (MIS) Set of procedures and methods for the regular, planned collection, analysis, and presentation of information for use in making marketing decisions.

marketing research Function linking the consumer to the marketer through information used to identify and define marketing opportunities and problems; to generate, refine, and evaluate marketing actions; to monitor marketing performance; and to improve understanding of marketing as a process.

maturation Processes operating within the test units in an experiment as a function of the passage of time *per se*.

maximum chance criterion Decision rule used in discriminant analysis to develop a comparison yardstick for assessing the predictive accuracy of the discriminant function: the maximum chance criterion holds that an object chosen at random should be classified as belonging to the largest size group.

MDS *See* multidimensional scaling (MDS).

measurement Rules for assigning numbers to objects to represent quantities of attributes.

method variance The variation in scores attributable to the method of data collection.

model system The part of a decision support system that includes all the routines that allow the user to manipulate the data in order to conduct the kind of analysis the individual desires.

motive Need, want, drive, wish, desire, or impulse, or any inner state that energizes, activates, or moves and that directs or channels behavior toward goals.

multichotomous question Fixed-alternative question in which respondents are asked to choose the alternative that most closely corresponds to their position on the topic.

multicollinearity Condition said to be present in a multiple-regression analysis when the predictor variables are not independent as required but are correlated among themselves.

multidimensional scaling (MDS) Approach to measurement in which people's perceptions of the similarity of objects and their preferences among the objects are measured, and these relationships are plotted in a multidimensional space.

multivariate Problem of analysis in which there are two or more measures of each of *n* sample objects, and the variables are to be analyzed simultaneously.

N

nominal scale Measurement in which numbers are simply assigned to objects or classes of objects solely for the purpose of identification.

noncoverage error Nonsampling error that arises because of a failure to include some units or entire sections of the defined survey population in the actual sampling frame.

nonobservation error Nonsampling error that arises because of nonresponse from some elements designated for inclusion in the sample.

nonparametric tests Class of statistical tests, also known as distribution-free tests, that are applicable when the data reflect nominal or ordinal measurement, or when the data reflect interval measurement but the assumptions required for the appropriate parametric test are not satisfied.

nonprobability sample Sample that relies on personal judgment somewhere in the element-selection process and therefore prohibits estimating the probability that any population element will be included in the sample. *See also* quota sample.

nonresponse error Nonsampling error that represents a failure to obtain information from some elements of the population that were selected and designated for the sample.

nonsampling errors Errors that arise in research that are not due to sampling; nonsampling errors can occur because of errors in conception, logic, misinterpretation of replies, statistics, and arithmetic; errors in tabulating or coding; or errors in reporting the results.

not-at-home Source of nonsampling error that arises when replies are not obtained from some designated sampling units because the respondents are not at home when the interviewer calls.

O

observation Method of data collection in which the situation of interest is watched and the relevant facts, actions, or behaviors are recorded.

observation error Nonsampling error that arises because inaccurate information is obtained from the sample elements or because errors are introduced in processing the data or in reporting the findings.

office error Nonsampling error that arises in the processing of the data because of errors in editing, coding, entering, tabulating, or some other part of the analysis.

omnibus panel Panel in which the information collected from the participating panel members varies from study to study.

open-ended question Question characterized by the condition that respondents are free to reply in their own words rather than being limited to choosing from among a set of alternatives.

operational definition Definition of a construct that describes the operations to be carried out in order for the construct to be measured empirically.

ordinal scale Measurement in which numbers are assigned to data on the basis of some order (e.g., more than, greater than) of the objects.

outlier Observation so different in magnitude from the rest of the observations that the analyst chooses to treat it as a special case.

overcoverage error Nonsampling error that arises because of the duplication of elements in the list of sampling units.

P

paired comparison A data-collection procedure in which respondents indicate which item in each pair of items is preferred; when used in conjoint analysis, the items in each pair represent predetermined combinations of attributes.

pair-wise procedure Method by which pairs of stimuli (e.g., print ads, brands)

are presented to be compared, as when asking consumers, "Which do you prefer?"

panel (omnibus) Fixed sample of respondents who are measured repeatedly over time but on variables that change from measurement to measurement.

panel (true) Fixed sample of respondents who are measured repeatedly over time with respect to the same variables.

parameter Fixed characteristic or measure of a parent or target population.

parametric tests Class of statistical tests used when the variable(s) is (are) measured on at least an interval scale.

part-worth function Function that describes the relationship between the perceived utilities associated with various levels of an attribute and the objective or physical levels of the attributes (e.g., utilities associated with various prices).

payoff table Table containing three elements: alternatives, states of nature, and consequences of each alternative under each state of nature.

people meter A device used to measure when a TV is on, to what channel it is tuned, and who in the household is watching it. Each member in a household is assigned a viewing number, which the individual is supposed to enter into the people meter whenever the set is turned on, the channel is switched, or the person enters or leaves the room.

performance of objective tasks Method of assessing attitudes that rests on the presumption that a person's performance of a specific assigned task (e.g., memorizing a number of facts) depends on the person's attitude.

personal interview Direct, face-to-face conversation between a representative of the research organization (the interviewer) and a respondent, or interviewee.

personal (or subjective) probability *See* Bayesian probability.

personality Normal patterns of behavior exhibited by an individual; the attributes, traits, and mannerisms

that distinguish one individual from another.

physiological reaction technique Method of assessing attitudes in which the researcher, by electrical or mechanical means, monitors the individual's response to the controlled introduction of some stimuli.

pictogram Bar chart in which pictures represent amounts, say, piles of dollars for income, pictures of cars for automobile production, people in a row for population.

pie chart Circle, representing a total quantity, divided into sectors, with each sector showing the size of the segment in relation to that total.

plus-one sampling Technique used in studies employing telephone interviews in which a single randomly determined digit is added to numbers selected from the telephone directory.

population *See* target population.

power Function associated with a statistical test indicating the probability of correctly rejecting a false null hypothesis.

pragmatic validity Approach to validation of a measure based on the usefulness of the measuring instrument as a predictor of some other characteristic or behavior of the individual; it is sometimes called predictive validity or criterion-related validity.

precision Desired size of the estimating interval when the problem is one of estimating a population parameter; the notion of degree of precision is useful in determining sample size.

pre-test Use of a questionnaire (or observation form) on a trial basis in a small pilot study to determine how well the questionnaire (observation form) works.

primary data Information collected specifically for the purpose of the investigation at hand.

primary source Originating source of secondary data.

probability-proportional-to-size sampling Form of cluster sampling in which a fixed number of second-stage units is selected from each first-stage cluster. The probabilities associated with the selection of each cluster are variable because they are related to the relative sizes of each cluster.

probability sample Sample in which each population element has a known, nonzero chance of being included in the sample.

projective technique A method of questioning respondents using a vague stimulus that respondents are asked to describe, expand on, or build a structure around; the basic assumption is that an individual's organization of the relatively unstructured stimulus is indicative of the person's basic perceptions of the phenomenon and reactions to it.

proportional chance criterion Decision rule used in discriminant analysis to develop a comparison yardstick for assessing the predictive accuracy of the discriminant function; the proportional chance criterion compares the percentage of objects likely to be classified correctly by chance alone to the model's algorithm.

proportionate stratified sampling Stratified sample in which the number of observations in the total sample is allocated among the strata in proportion to the relative number of elements in each stratum in the population.

psychographic analysis Technique that investigates how people live, what interests them, and what they like; it is also called lifestyle or *AIO* analysis, because it relies on a number of statements about a person's *A*ctivities, *I*nterests, and *O*pinions.

Q-sort technique General methodology for gathering data and processing the collected information. The participants are assigned the task of sorting various statements by placing a specific number of statements in each sorting category; the emphases are on determining the relative ranking of stimuli by individuals and deriving clusters of individuals who display similar preference orderings of stimuli.

quota sample Nonprobability sample chosen in such a way that the

proportion of sample elements possessing a certain characteristic is approximately the same as the proportion of the elements with the characteristic in the population; each field worker is assigned a quota that specifies the characteristics of the people he or she is to contact.

random-digit dialing (RDD) Technique used in studies employing telephone interviews in which the numbers to be called are randomly generated.

random error Error in measurement due to the transient aspects of the person or measurement situation.

randomized-block design Experimental design in which (1) the test units are divided into blocks or homogeneous groups using some external criterion, and (2) the objects in each block are randomly assigned to treatment conditions. The randomized-block design is typically employed when there is one extraneous influence to be explicitly controlled.

randomized-response model Interviewing technique in which potentially embarrassing and relatively innocuous questions are paired, and the question the respondent answers is randomly determined.

ratio scale Measurement that has a natural or absolute zero and that therefore allows the comparison of absolute magnitudes of the numbers.

recall loss A type of error caused by a respondent forgetting that an event happened at all.

refusals Nonsampling error that arises because some designated respondents refuse to participate in the study.

regression analysis Statistical technique used to derive an equation that relates a single criterion variable to one or more predictor variables.

relative precision Degree of precision desired in an estimate of a parameter as expressed relative to the level of the estimate of the parameter.

reliability Similarity of results provided by independent but comparable

measures of the same object, trait, or construct.

research design Framework or plan for a study that guides the collection and analysis of the data.

research process Sequence of steps in the design and implementation of a research study, including problem formulation, determination of sources of information and research design, determination of data-collection method and design of data-collection forms, design of the sample and collection of the data, analysis and interpretation of the data, and the research report.

response latency The amount of time a respondent deliberates before answering a question.

response rate (R) Measure used to evaluate and compare interviewers in terms of their ability to induce contacted respondents to participate in the study; R = number of interviews/ number of contacts.

S

sample Selection of a subset of elements from a larger group of objects.

sample survey Cross-sectional study in which the sample is selected to be representative of the target population and in which the emphasis is on the generation of summary statistics such as averages and percentages; also called a field survey.

sampling control Term applied to studies relying on questionnaires and concerning the researcher's dual abilities to direct the inquiry to a designated respondent and to secure the desired cooperation from that respondent.

sampling distribution Distribution of values of some statistic calculated for each possible distinguishable sample that could be drawn from a parent population under a specific sampling plan.

sampling error Difference between the observed values of a variable and the long-run average of the observed values in repetitions of the measurement.

sampling frame List of sampling units from which a sample will be drawn; the list could consist of geographic areas, institutions, individuals, or other units.

sampling units Nonoverlapping collections of elements from the population.

scanner Electronic device that automatically reads imprinted Universal Product Codes (UPC) as the product is pulled across the scanner, looks up the price in an attached computer, and instantly prints the price of the item on the cash register tape.

secondary data Statistics not gathered for the immediate study at hand but for some other purpose.

secondary source Source of secondary data that did not originate the data but secured them from another source.

selection bias Contaminating influence in an experiment occurring when there is no way of certifying that groups of test units were equivalent at some previous time.

self-report Method of assessing attitudes in which individuals are asked directly for their beliefs about or feelings toward an object or class of objects.

semantic differential Self-report technique for attitude measurement in which people are asked to check which cell between a set of bipolar adjectives or phrases best describes their feelings toward the object.

sentence completion Questionnaire containing a number of sentences that consumers are directed to complete with the first words that come to mind.

sequence bias Distortion in the answers to some questions on a questionnaire because the replies are not independently arrived at but are conditioned by responses to other questions; problem is particularly acute in mail questionnaires because the respondent can see the whole questionnaire.

sequential sample Sample formed on the basis of a series of successive decisions. If the evidence is not conclusive after a small sample is taken, more observations are taken; if still inconclusive after these additional observations, still more observations are taken. At each stage, a decision is made about whether more information should be collected or whether the evidence is sufficient to draw a conclusion.

simple random sample Probability sample in which each population element has a known and equal chance of being included in the sample and in which every combination of n population elements is a sample possibility and is just as likely to occur as any other combination of n units.

simple tabulation Count of the number of cases that fall into each category when the categories are based on one variable.

simulated test marketing Test marketing done by firms in shopping malls or consumers' homes as a prelude to a full-scale marketing test for the product.

snake diagram Diagram (so called because of its shape) that connects with straight lines the average responses to a series of semantic differential statements, thereby depicting the profile of the object or objects being evaluated; also called profile plot.

snowball sample Judgment sample that relies on the researcher's ability to locate an initial set of respondents with the desired characteristics; these individuals are then used as informants to identify still others with the desired characteristics.

Spearman's rank correlation coefficient (r_s) A statistic employed with ordinal data to measure the extent of association between two variables.

split ballot A technique used to combat response bias in which one phrasing is used for a question in one-half of the questionnaires whereas an alternative phrasing is used in the other one-half of the questionnaires.

spurious correlation Condition that arises when there is no relationship between two variables but the analyst concludes that a relationship exists.

spurious noncorrelation Condition that arises when the analyst concludes that there is no relationship between two variables but, in fact, there is.

stability A technique for assessing the reliability of a measure by measuring the same objects or individuals at two different points in time and then correlating the scores; the procedure is known as test–retest reliability assessment.

standard error of estimate Term used in regression analysis to refer to the absolute amount of variation in the criterion variable that is left unexplained or unaccounted for by the fitted regression equation.

standard test market A market in which companies sell their products through normal distribution channels.

Stapel scale Self-report technique for attitude measurement in which respondents are asked to indicate how accurately each of a number of statements describes the object of interest.

statistic Characteristic or measure of a sample.

statistical efficiency Measure used to compare sampling plans; one sampling plan is said to be superior (more statistically efficient) to another if, for the same size sample, it produces a smaller standard error of estimate.

statistical regression Tendency of extreme cases of a phenomenon to move toward a more central position during the course of an experiment.

storytelling Questionnaire method of data collection relying on a picture stimulus such as a cartoon, photograph, or drawing about which the consumer is asked to tell a story.

stratified sample Probability sample that is distinguished by the two-step procedure in which (1) the parent population is divided into mutually exclusive and exhaustive subsets, and (2) a simple random sample of elements is chosen independently from each group or subset.

stratum chart Set of line charts in which quantities are aggregated or a total is disaggregated so that the distance between two lines represents the amount of some variable.

stress Measure of the "badness of fit" of a configuration determined by multidimensional scaling analysis when compared to the original input data.

structure Degree of standardization imposed on the data-collection instrument. A highly structured questionnaire is one in which the questions to be asked and the responses permitted are completely predetermined; a highly unstructured questionnaire is one in which the questions are only loosely predetermined and respondents are free to respond in their own words and in any way they see fit.

summated ratings Self-report technique for attitude measurement in which people are asked to indicate their degree of agreement or disagreement with each of a number of statements; a person's attitude score is the total obtained by summing the scale values assigned to each category checked.

syndicated research Information collected on a regular basis that is then sold to interested clients (e.g., Nielsen Retail Index).

systematic error Error in measurement that is also known as constant error, since it affects the measurement in a systematic way.

systematic sample Probability sample in which every 8th element in the population is designated for inclusion in the sample after a random start.

T

tabulation Procedure by which the number of cases that fall into each of a number of categories are counted.

tachistoscope Device that provides the researcher timing control over a visual stimulus; in marketing research, the visual stimulus is often a specific advertisement.

target population Totality of cases that conforms to some designated specifications.

teleology An ethical or moral reasoning framework that focuses on the net consequences that an action may have. If the net benefits minus all costs are positive, the act is morally acceptable; if the net result is negative, the act is not morally acceptable.

telephone interview Telephone conversation between a representative of the research organization, the interviewer, and a respondent or interviewee.

telescoping error A type of error resulting from the fact that most people remember an event as having occurred more recently than in fact is the case.

testing effect Contaminating effect in an experiment occurring because the process of experimentation itself affected the observed response. The main testing effect refers to the impact of a prior observation on a later observation, whereas the interactive testing effect refers to the condition when a prior measurement affects the test unit's response to the experimental variable.

Thematic Apperception Test (TAT) Copyrighted series of pictures about which the consumer is asked to tell stories.

total association Association existing between the variables without regard to the levels of any other variables; also called the zero-order association between the variables.

trade-off matrix A method of structuring the stimuli that respondents evaluate in a conjoint analysis that treats two attributes at a time but considers all possible pairs; also known as the pair-wise procedure.

turnover table *See* brand-switching matrix.

Type I error Rejection of a null hypothesis when it is true; also known as α error.

Type II error Failure to reject a null hypothesis when it is false; also known as β error.

U

unbiased Used to describe a statistic when the average value of the statistic equals the population parameter it is supposed to estimate.

univariate Problem of analysis in which there is a single measurement on each of n sample objects or there are several measurements on each of the n observations, but each variable is to be analyzed in isolation.

utilitarianism The most well-known branch of teleological ethics; the utilitarian perspective holds that the correct course of action is the one that promotes the greatest good for the greatest number and that all acts for which the net benefits exceed the net costs are morally acceptable.

V

validity Term applied to measuring instruments reflecting the extent to which differences in scores on the measurement reflect true differences among individuals, groups, or situations in the characteristic that it seeks to measure, or reflect true differences in the same individual, group, or situation from one occasion to another, rather than constant or random errors.

variable transformation Change in scale in which a variable is expressed.

varimax Angle-preserving rotation of a factor-analytic solution done to facilitate substantive interpretation of the factors.

voice-pitch analysis Type of analysis that examines changes in the relative frequency of the human voice that accompany emotional arousal.

W

word association Questionnaire containing a list of words to which respondents are instructed to reply with the first word that comes to mind.

Z

zero-order association *See* total association.

A

Absolute precision, 317–318, 319–320
Accuracy
    of classification, 487
    in primary data collection, 188
    problems of, 146–148
ACNielsen. *See* Nielsen Group
Activities, interests, and opinions (AIO)
inventories, 178–179
Adjusting the results for nonresponse
errors, 335–336
Administrative control of questionnaires,
197–201
Advertising
    consumer awareness and knowledge
    of, 182–183
    measuring exposure and effectiveness
    of, 164–170
    multimedia services, 167–168
    print media, 166–167
    television and radio, 164–166
Advertising Agency's Datebook, 129–130
Affiliations information, online sources of,
155–156
After-only with control group design,
115–116
AIO. *See* Activities, interests, and opinions
(AIO) inventories
Ambiguous words, 217–219
American Marketing Association (AMA), 44
    definition of marketing research, 5
Analysis of cases, 62–63
Analysis of variance (ANOVA), 428–432
Arbitron, 89, 90
Area cluster sampling, 305
Associations as source of secondary
data, 153
Attitude measurement
    attitude-scaling procedures, 236
    choice of scales, 247
    classification and assessment of error,
    254–256
    comparative rating scales, 246–247
    equal-appearing intervals, 237–239
    graphic rating scales, 244–246
    importance judgments, 244
    Likert method of summated ratings,
    239–241
    observation of behavior, 236–237
    performance of an objective task, 237
    physiological reactions, 237
    reliability of, 258–260
    scales of, 233–235
    scaling of psychological attributes,
    235–247
    self-report scales, 236, 237–247
    semantic differential, 241–242
    Stapel, 242–244

    validity of, 256–258
    variations in scores, 253–254
Attitudes
    defined, 232
    primary data of, 180–182
Audits, 75
    store audits, 161
Awareness and knowledge, primary data
of, 182–183

B

Banners, 374
Bar charts, 568–569
Before-after with control group design,
113–114
Behavior
    behavioral factors in field errors,
    338–339
    observation of, 236–237
    primary data of, 184–186
BehaviorScan, 162–164
Benchmarking, 62–63
Between-group variation, 429, 430
Bias
    noncoverage, 330
    in personal interviews, 337
    selection,110–111
    See also Errors
Big Brothers of Fairfax County, 48
Blunders, 356
    See also Errors
BMW, 63
Branching questions, 221
Brand Association Maps, 138–139
Brand loyalty, 90–93
Brand name, choosing a, 50–51
Brand name/trade name information,
online sources of, 156
Brand switching, 90–93
Brand-switching matrix, 91, 92
Business information
    online sources, 156
    as source of secondary data, 153

C

CA. *See* Correspondence analysis (CA)
Cases, analysis of, 62–63
Case studies
    Advertising Agency's Datebook,
    129–130
    Bakhill Foods, 130–132
    Big Brothers of Fairfax County, 48

    Brand Association Maps, 138–139
    Choosing a brand name, 50–51
    Comparing Ads Against a Databank,
    270–271
    Conjoint—Brand and Pricing,
    553–554
    Countrycable: Customer Satisfaction
    Survey Data, 547–548
    Critiquing Questionnaires, 274–279
    CTM Productions, 268–270, 544
    Customer Relationship Manager,
    133–135
    E-Food and the online grocery
    competition, 49–50, 263–264,
    544–545
    Ethnography in Practice: The Case of
    ESPN Zone, Chicago, 135–138
    Extending a travel brand, 54–55
    Flowers 4U, 48–49
    HotStuff Computer Software,
    127–129
    International Differences in the Cost of
    Data, 345–346
    Internet Advertising and Your Brain,
    132–133, 545–546
    Measuring Magazines, 271–273
    Moving consumers from awareness to
    loyalty, 51–52
    Online Samples, 346–347
    A Picture is Worth a Megabyte of Words,
    546–547
    Premium Pizza Inc., 264–268
    Qualitative data from open-ended
    survey items: a service quality example,
    52–54
    Repositioning a Brand, 552–553
    Riverside County Humane Society,
    127, 344
    Sampling from Your Loyalty Database,
    345
    Sampling Gambling, 347
    Sampling Lead-Users for New Products,
    344–345
    Secondary Data on Health from CDC,
    273–274
    Segmentation Study, 554–555
    Sports Marketing and Television
    Programming, 549–552
    Teeth-Whitening Conjoint Study, 549,
    550–551
Causality
    concept of, 99
    concomitant variation, 99–102, 118
    and correlation, 442
    and descriptive research, 118–119
    elimination of other possible causal
    factors, 103, 118

and exploratory research, 118–119
role of the evidence in, 103–105
time order of occurrence of variables, 102–103, 118
Causal research
defined, 59, 60
questionnaires for, 204
Census, 282
Census data, 155, 173–174
categorizing ethnicity in, 145–146
information from population census, 143
Central-limit theorem, 293
Central office edit, 350–351
CEO compensation and multiple-regression analysis, 455
Chief Information Officer (CIO), 27
Children, scales for, 247
China, marketing research in, 10
Chi-square, 378–388
goodness-of-fit, 359–362
standardized residuals, 360–362
Choosing a brand name, 50–51
Claritas Inc, 158, 159
Prizm Lifestyle Cluster System, 506–507
Classification accuracy, 487
Classification of respondents, 488–489
Cluster analysis, 26, 506–524
clustering methods, 510–516
clustering the objects, 522
Euclidean distance to measure similarity, 509–510
key decisions in, 516–523
k-means, 517–518
linkage methods. See Linkage methods in cluster analysis
marketing applications of, 523
nodal methods, 515–516
production of estimates of similarity or resemblance, 519–522
selecting and coding attributes, 517–519
testing the system, 522–523
uses of, 506–508, 524
Cluster profile, sample, 159
Cluster samples, 285, 304–307
area cluster sampling, 305
cost factors for, 321
one-stage area sampling, 305–306
systematic sampling, 304–305
two-stage area sampling, 306–307
Coding, 32, 79–81, 351–352
Coefficient of concordance, 386–388
Coefficient of determination, 452
Coefficient of multiple correlation, 458–459
Coefficient of multiple determination, 458–459
Coefficient of partial correlation, 459–460
Coefficient of partial regression, 454, 456–458
Coefficients, determining, 480–482
Cohort analysis, 94–95
Communalities, 495

Communication method of primary data collection
advantages and disadvantages of, 186–188
objectivity and accuracy in, 188
questionnaires. See Questionnaires
speed and cost of, 187–188
versatility of, 186–187
Communication with decision makers, 34–37, 38, 45
Company information, 174
online sources, 155, 156
Comparative rating scales, 246–247
Comparing Ads Against a Databank, 270–271
Competitors, data on, 21
Completely randomized design, 431
Completeness rate, 336
Computer-aided interviewing (CAI), 195–197
Computerized Adaptive Telephone Interviewing (CATI), 195, 196
Computer programs for multidimensional scaling (MDS), 527
Concomitant variation, 99–102, 118
Concurrent validity, 256
Conditional association, 368
Confidence interval, 314
Confidence interval estimates, 293–295, 300–302
Conjoint analysis, 463–475
Conjoint—Brand and Pricing, 553–554
Constant sum scaling method, 246
Construct validity, 257–258
Consumer information, 174–175
Consumer Mail Panel (CMP), 170
Consumer Price Index (CPI), 287
Contact rate, 332
Content validity, 256–257
Contingency coefficient, 380–381
Convenience samples, 285, 286
Convergent validity, 258
Cooperation for questionnaires, 193
Correlation analysis, 441–442
See also Regression analysis
Correlation coefficient, 451–454
Correspondence analysis (CA), 537–538
Cost
as advantage of secondary data, 143–144, 150–151
of primary data collection, 187–188
Council of American Survey Research Organizations (CASRO), 331, 332
Countrycable: Customer Satisfaction Survey Data, 547–548
Cover letters of questionnaires, 221–222
Criterion-related validity. See Predictive validity
Critical values of t, 579
Critical values of χ^2, 577–578
Critiquing Questionnaires, 274–279
Cross-cultural differences. See Cultural differences
Cross-sectional analysis, 86, 93–95
cohort analysis, 94–95

Cross-tabulation, 352, 363–374
conclusion of no relationship is retained with addition of third variable, 372
contingent relationships in, 364–373
introduction of a third variable, 369–371
relationship established with third variable, 371–372
retaining initial conclusion of relationship, 371
summary comments on, 373–374
CTM Productions, 268–270, 544
Cultural differences, 37–38
cross-cultural information, 175–176
in marketing research, 206
in response styles, 255–256
Cumulative distribution function, 357
Cumulative probabilities, 576
Customer information module, 20–21
Customer management software, 26
Customer profiles, 156–158
Customer Relationship Manager, 133–135
Customer relationships management (CRM), 18, 19

D

Dashboards, 23
Data, 20–22, 24
on competitors, 21
customer information module, 20–21
government data, 21
industry information, 21
sales forecasts, 21
See also Primary data; Secondary data
Data analysis
assumptions underlying test statistic, 399
choice of technique, 390–393
coding, 32, 351–352
editing, 32, 350–351
multivariate analysis. See Multivariate analysis
and research design, 396–398
steps in, 32
tabulation. See Tabulation
and type of data, 393–396
See also Datamining
Databases
datamining, 25–27
size of, 21–22
Data collection
method and forms, 31, 32
nonsampling errors. See Nonsampling errors
primary data. See Primary data
questionnaires. See Questionnaires
secondary data. See Secondary data
Data mining, 25–27, 150
Day-after recall (DAR), 182
DecisionEdge, 26
Decision makers, 34–37
Decision problems translating to research problems, 37–38

Decision support system (DSS), 18–25
    components of, 20–24
    data, 20–22
    design of, 18–20
    interfaces, 22–23
    models, 22
Demographic and socioeconomic
characteristics, primary data of, 177–178
Dependent variables, 441
Depth interviews, 68–69
Derived population
    in simple random samples,
    288–289, 290
    in stratified samples, 299
Descriptive research
    and causality, 118–119
    classification of, 86
    cross-sectional analysis. See Cross-
    sectional analysis
    defined, 59, 60
    longitudinal analysis. See Longitudinal
    analysis
    questionnaires for, 204
    uses of, 84–86
Determining the coefficients, 480–482
Dialog systems, 22–23
Diary panels, 158–161
Dichotomous questions, 214–216
Direct mailing, 26
Discriminant analysis, 477–490
    and international markets, 490
    marketing applications of, 490
    three-group case. See Three-group
    case, discriminant analysis of
    two-group case. See Two-group case,
    discriminant analysis of
Discriminant coefficients, 483–484
Discriminant function, 482–483, 485–487
Discriminant loadings, 484–485
Discriminant validity, 258
Disguise
    in observation method of data
    collection, 201
    in questionnaires, 188, 190, 205
Disproportionate stratified samples,
303–304
Double-barreled questions, 220
Dummy tables, 85
Dummy variables, 464–465
Dun's Business Locator, 156–157

E

Economic information, 175
    online sources, 156
Editing, 32, 350–351
    central office edit, 350–351
    field edit, 350
EEGs, 79
Effect size, 408
E-Food and the online grocery competition,
49–50, 263–264, 544–545

Electronic test markets, 120
Elimination of other possible causal
factors, 103, 118
E-mail surveys. See Online surveys
Empirical distribution, 357
Employment opportunities in marketing
research, 13–15
Enterprise Miner, 26
Equal-appearing intervals, 237–239
Equivalence, 259–260
Errors
    classification and assessment of,
    254–256
    of estimate, 446–447
    field. See Field errors
    nonsampling. See Nonsampling errors
    random, 254, 328
    sampling, 328–329
    systematic, 254
    telescoping errors, 209–210
    Type I error, 404–405
    Type II error, 404–405
    See also Accuracy
ESPN Zone, 135–138
Estimate, standard error of, 446–447
Estimates in questionnaires, 219–220
Ethnography, 75–76, 77
Ethnography in Practice: The Case of ESPN
Zone, Chicago, 135–138
Euclidean distance, 509–510
Evidence of causality, 103–105
    See also Causality
Experience surveys, 62
Experimental designs
    common notations describing,
    107–108
    extraneous variables. See Extraneous
    variables
    pre-experimental designs, 111–113
    quasi-experimental designs, 116–118
    true experimental designs, 113–116
    vs. nonexperimental designs,
    118–119
Experimental mortality as extraneous
variable, 111
Experiments
    as evidence of causality, 103–105
    field, 105–107
    internal and external validity, 107
    laboratory, 105, 106–107
    problems with, 119–120
    See also Test marketing
Exploratory research
    analysis of cases, 62–63
    and causality, 118–119
    defined, 58–59, 60
    experience surveys, 62
    literature searches, 62
    and qualitative data, 61
    questionnaires for, 205
    types of, 61–63
    uses of, 60–61
Ex post facto research, 118
Extending a travel brand, 54–55

External secondary data, 151–156
External validity, 107
Extraneous variables
    experimental mortality, 111
    history, 108–109
    instrument variation, 109–110
    maturation, 109
    pre-experimental designs, 111–113
    quasi-experimental designs, 116–118
    selection bias, 110–111
    statistical regression, 110
    testing effect, 109
    true experimental designs, 113–116
Eye camera, 78

F

Factor analysis, 491–506
    key decisions in, 503–506
    marketing applications of, 506
    substantive interpretation. See
    Substantive interpretation in factor
    analysis
    summarizing data. See Summarizing
    data in factor analysis
Factorial designs, 435–438
Factor loadings, 494–495
Farmers Insurance, 26
Fax surveys, 191
    administrative control of, 197–201
    advantages and disadvantages of, 200
    sampling control for, 192
Field edit, 350
Field errors, 336–339
    background factors, 337
    behavioral factors, 338–339
Field experiments, 105–107
    validity of, 107
    vs. laboratory experiments, 106–107
Field studies for observational method, 74,
75–77
Fixed-alternative questions, 189,
212–216
Fixed samples, 285
Flowers 4U, 48–49
FMRIs, 79
Focus groups, 63–67
    limits of, 61, 67
    moderators, 63, 65–66
    multiple groups, 64–65
    new trends in, 67
    online, 3, 67
    participants in, 64
    post-session activities, 66–67
    purposes of, 63
    tips for successful, 67
    a typical session, 66
    vs. depth interviews, 68–69
Follow-ups, 335
Forecasting, 441
Four-group six-study design, 114–115
Frequency polygon, 357
Funnel approach, 220

G

Galvanometer, 78
General business information, online sources of, 156
Generalizations in questionnaires, 219–220
General Mills, 41, 43
General Motors, 26
Gillette Company, 29, 30
Globalization, 7, 37–38
    See also International markets
Goodness-of-fit chi-square test, 359–362
Government contract information, online sources of, 156
Government data, 21
Gower's coefficient of similarity, 521
Graphic presentation in research reports, 566–571
Graphic rating scales, 244–246
Graphics, 23
Groups, number of, 397

H

Histogram, 357
History as extraneous variable, 108–109
Homescan Service, 164, 165
HotStuff Computer Software, 127–129
Hypotheses, 60
    about one mean, 413–416
    about two means, 416–423
    about two proportions, 423–426
    errors, 404–405
    null, 402–411
    power in, 407–411
    statistics to test, 378–382
    steps in testing, 405–407

I

Implicit assumptions, 219
Independent variables, 441
Index of predictive association, 381–382
Industry information, 21
    online sources, 155
Information control for questionnaires, 194–197
Information Resources Inc. (IRI), 12
    BehaviorScan, 162–164
Instrument variation as extraneous variable, 109–110
Intelligent Miner, 26
Intentions, primary data of, 184, 185
Interactive testing effect on extraneous variable, 109
Interfaces, 22–23, 24
Internal secondary data, 148–151
Internal validity, 107
International and cross-cultural information, 175–176
International Differences in the Cost of Data, 345–346

International markets
    and discriminant analysis, 490
    marketing research for, 7
    testing for differences, 421
    See also Cultural differences; Globalization
Internet Advertising and Your Brain, 132–133, 545–546
Interval scales, 235, 236, 243–244, 394
Interviews
    depth. *See* Depth interviews
    and extraneous variables, 109–110
    personal. *See* Personal interviews
    telephone. *See* Telephone interviews
Item nonresponse, 216, 335

J

Jaccards' coefficient, 521
Japan, marketing research in, 12–13
Job titles and responsibilities, 14, 27
Judgment samples, 285, 286–287

K

Key informant surveys. *See* Experience surveys
K-means, 517–518
Knowledge, primary data of, 182–183
Kodak, 12
Kolmogorov-Smirnov test, 362–363

L

Laboratory experiments, 105
    for observational method, 74, 77–78
    validity of, 107
    vs. field experiments, 106–107
Laddering, 69
Land O'Lakes, 45
Leading questions, 219
Letters of the alphabet, perceptions of, 103, 104
Levels of measurement, 393–396
Lifestyle characteristics, primary data of, 178–182
Likert method of summated ratings, 239–241
Line charts, 567–568
Linkage methods in cluster analysis
    average linkage, 514–515
    complete linkage, 514
    single linkage, 510–514
Literature searches, 62
Log linear models, 382–384
Longitudinal analysis, 86–93
    brand loyalty and brand switching, 90–93
    examples of, 86–88
    panels, 89
Loyalty, brand. *See* Brand loyalty
Loyalty programs, 27
    as sources of secondary data, 149

M

Mail panels, 170
Mail questionnaires, 191
    advantages and disadvantages of, 200
    cover letters for, 221–222
    example of, 207–208
    getting cooperation for, 193
    information control for, 195
    sampling control for, 192
Main testing effect on extraneous variable, 109
Mall intercept, 191
Maps in research reports, 569
Market information, 174–175
Marketing information system (MIS), 18–25
    components of, 20–24
    data, 20–22
    design of, 18–20
    interfaces, 22–23
    models, 22
Marketing managers. *See* Decision makers
Marketing mix, 4
Marketing research
    choosing a research supplier, 44–45
    definition of, 5
    employment opportunities in, 13–15
    examples of, 2–3
    and globalization, 7
    job titles and responsibilities, 14, 27
    justification of, 42–44
    organization of, 11–13
    producers of, 7–11
    role of, 3–7
Marketing research projects, 18, 24–25
Marketing research studies as sources of secondary data, 150
Market share, measuring, 158–164
    diary panels, 158–161
    scanners, 161–164
    store audits, 161
Market tests. *See* Test marketing
Massively parallel processing (MPP), 25
Matching, 111
Maturation as extraneous variable, 109
MDS. *See* Multidimensional scaling (MDS)
Mean, 394
Measurement
    of attitudes. *See* Attitude measurement
    classification and assessment of error, 254–256
    defined, 234
    reliability of, 258–260
    validity of, 254–256, 256–258
    variations in, 253–254
Measurement error, 216
Measuring advertising exposure and effectiveness, 164–170
Measuring Magazines, 271–273
Mediamark Research, 167–170
Media Metrix Inc., 12
Median, 394
Membership clubs as sources of secondary data, 149

Mergers information
    online sources, 155–156
Miller Lite, 37
Minute Maid Company, 39–40
Mode, 393, 394
Models, 22, 24
Moderators, 63, 65–66
Motivation, primary data of, 184
Motivation research, 190
Moving consumers from awareness to loyalty, 51–52
Multichotomous questions, 212–214, 216
Multicollinearity assumption, 455–456
Multidimensional scaling (MDS), 524–532
    attribute-based approaches, 531
    comparison of approaches, 531–532
    computer programs for, 527
    example problem, 526–527
    example solution, 527–529
    key decisions in, 529–531
Multimedia services, 167–168
Multiple-choice questions, 212–214
Multiple-regression analysis, 454–460
    and CEO compensation, 455
    coefficients of multiple correlation and determination, 458–459
    coefficients of partial correlation, 459–460
    coefficients of partial regression, 454, 456–458
    multicollinearity assumption, 455–456
    revised nomenclature, 454–455
Multivariate analysis, 400
    cluster analysis. See Cluster analysis
    correspondence analysis (CA), 537–538
    discriminant analysis. See Discriminant analysis
    factor analysis. See Factor analysis
    multidimensional scaling. See Multidimensional scaling (MDS)
    neural networks, 540–541
    social networks, 541–543
    structural equations models (SEM), 539–540

N

National Purchase Diary (NPD), 8, 12, 89, 158–161
NCR Corporation, 25
Neural networks, 540–541
NFO Research Inc., 170
Nickelodeon, 89, 91
Nielsen Group, 8, 12, 89
    disproportionate stratified sampling scheme, 303
    Homescan Service, 164, 165
    SCANTRACK, 161
    Television Index, 164–166
Nominal scales, 234, 236, 393
Noncoverage errors, 330

Nonexperimental designs vs. experimental designs, 118–119
Nonobservation errors, 329–336
    noncoverage errors, 330
    nonresponse errors, 330–336
Nonparametric measures of association, 385–388
Non-probability samples, 285, 286–287
    convenience, 285, 286
    judgment, 285, 286–287
    quota, 285, 287
Nonresponse errors, 330–336
    adjusting the results, 335–336
    degree of, 365–366
    follow-up, 335
    increasing initial response rate, 334
    not-at-homes, 332–333
    refusals, 333–334
Nonsampling errors
    field errors, 336–339
    impact of, 328–329
    methods of handling, 340–341
    noncoverage errors, 330
    nonobservation errors, 329–336
    nonresponse errors, 330–336
    observation errors, 329, 336–339
    types of, 329–339
North American Industry Classification System (NAICS), 156, 157
Not-at-homes, 332–333
NPD Group. See National Purchase Diary (NPD)
Null hypothesis, 402–411

O

Objectivity in primary data collection, 188
Observational methods, 72–79
    examples of, 74
    field studies, 74, 75–77
    Hi-Tech Mechanical Measures, 78–79
    lab studies, 74, 77–78
    uses of, 74–75
Observation errors, 329, 336–339
    field errors, 336–339
    office errors, 339
Observation method of primary data collection
    advantages and disadvantages of, 186–188
    disguised vs. undisguised, 201
    forms for, 224–228
    objectivity and accuracy in, 188
    speed and cost of, 187–188
    structured vs. unstructured, 201
    versatility of, 186–187
Observation of behavior, 236–237
Omnibus panels, 89
One-group pre-test-post-test design, 112
One-shot case studies, 112
One-stage area sampling, 305–306
One-way tabulation, 352–359
Online communities, 2, 3
Online computer searches, 154–156

Online ethnography, 77
Online focus groups, 3, 67
Online marketing research companies, 12
Online panels, 89, 199
Online Samples, 346–347
Online shopping as source of secondary data, 149
Online surveys, 191
    administrative control of, 197–201
    advantages and disadvantages of, 198, 200
    getting cooperation for, 193
    graphic rating scales for, 244–246
    guidelines for, 223
    information control for, 195
    sampling control for, 192
Open-ended questions, 212
Opening questions, 220
Operational definitions, 251, 252
Opinions, primary data of, 180–182
    See also Attitudes
Oral research reports, 563–566
Ordinal scales, 234–235, 236, 243–244, 393–394
Outliers, 356–357
Ownership information, online sources of, 155–156

P

Panels, 89
    advantages of, 92
    brand loyalty and brand switching, 90–93
    diary, 158–161
    disadvantages of, 92–93
    mail, 170
    mall vs. e-panels, 199
    omnibus panels, 89
    online panels, 89
    true panels, 89, 90–93
Parameters, 288
Parent population in simple random samples, 288
Parker Pen Company, 89
Partial regression coefficient, 454
PCA. See Principal Components Analysis (PCA)
Percentage points of the F distribution, 580–583
Perceptual mapping. See Multidimensional scaling (MDS)
Personal interviews
    administrative control of, 197–201
    advantages and disadvantages of, 200
    bias in, 337
    computer-aided interviewing (CAI), 195–197
    defined, 191
    getting cooperation for, 193
    information control for, 194–195
    sampling control for, 192–193
Picture is Worth a Megabyte of Words, A, 546–547

Pie charts, 566–567
Planned change, 34
Population mean, 289–292
Population proportions, 423–426
Population size and sample size, 321
Population variance, 295–296
    hypothesis testing, 413–423
    sample size estimates, 313–317
Power in hypotheses, 407–411
Precision
    absolute, 317–318, 319–320
    relative, 317–318, 320
    of stratified samples, 302
Prediction, 441
Prediction of Y, 449–450
Predictive association, index of, 381–382
Predictive validity, 256
Pre-experimental designs, 111–113
Premium Pizza Inc., 264–268
Pre-testing questionnaires, 223–224
Primary data, 31
    of attitudes and opinions, 180–182
    of awareness and knowledge,
    182–183
    of behavior, 184–186
    communication method of collection.
    See Communication method of primary
    data collection
    defined, 142
    of demographic and socioeconomic
    characteristics, 177–178
    of intentions, 184, 185
    of motivation, 184
    observation method of collection. See
    Observation method of primary data
    collection
    of psychological and lifestyle
    characteristics, 178–182
    questionnaires. See Questionnaires
    types of, 177–186
Primary source, 147
Principal Components Analysis (PCA),
495–496
Print media, 166–167
Prizm Lifestyle Cluster System, 506–507
Probability-proportional-to-size
sampling, 307
Probability samples, 285, 287–307
    cluster. See Cluster samples
    simple random. See Simple random
    samples
    stratified. See Stratified samples
Problem formulation, 29–30, 34–35
Product sales, measuring, 158–164
    diary panels, 158–161
    scanners, 161–164
    store audits, 161
Program strategy, 29
Projective techniques, 69–72, 190
    sentence completion, 70–71
    storytelling, 72, 73
    word association, 70
Projects, marketing research. See Marketing
research projects

Project strategy, 29
Promotional mailing, 26
Proportionate stratified samples, 303–304
Proportions, population. See Population
proportions
Psychological and lifestyle characteristics,
primary data of, 178–182
Psychological attributes, scaling of,
235–247
Psychological factors in field errors,
337–338
Pupilometrics, 78

Q

Quadrant analysis, 244–245
Qualitative data from open-ended survey
items: a service quality example, 52–54
Qualitative research methods
    coding, 79–81
    depth interviews, 68–69
    and exploratory research, 61
    focus groups. See Focus groups
    observational methods. See
    Observational methods
    projective techniques. See Projective
    techniques
Quasi-experimental designs, 116–118
Questionnaire design
    form of response, 212–216
    individual question content, 208–211
    length, 223
    method of administration, 205–208
    physical characteristics, 221–223
    pre-testing, 223–224
    question sequence, 220–221
    sample of mail questionnaire,
    207–208
    specification of information sought,
    204–205
    steps in, 205, 225–226
    using scales for responses,
    212–214, 216
    wording in, 216–220
Questionnaires
    administration methods for, 191–201
    administrative control of, 197–201
    design of. See Questionnaire design
    disguise in, 188, 190, 205
    editing of. See Editing
    getting cooperation for, 193
    information control for, 194–197
    pre-testing, 223–224
    sampling control, 192–193
    structured-disguised questionnaires,
    190–191
    structured-undisguised questionnaires,
    188–189
    structure of, 188, 190, 205
    unstructured-disguised
    questionnaires, 190
    unstructured-undisguised
    questionnaires, 189–190

Questions
    branching, 221
    dichotomous, 214–216
    double-barreled, 220
    fixed-alternative, 189, 212–216
    individual question content, 208–211
    leading, 219
    multichotomous, 212–214, 216
    multiple-choice, 212–214
    open-ended, 212
    opening, 220
    sensitive, 210–211, 221
    sequence of, 220–221
    using scales for responses,
    212–214, 216
    wording of, 216–220
Quota samples, 285, 287

R

R. L. Polk and Co., 157–158
Radio advertising, 166
Radio Frequency Identification (RFID)
tags, 2–3
Random digit dialing (RDD), 192
Random errors, 254, 328
Randomization, 111, 113
Randomized blocks, 432–438
Randomized response model, 211
Rating scales, estimating variances when
using, 316
Ratio scales, 235, 236, 394–396
Recall loss, 210
Refusals, 333–334
Regression analysis, 26
    correlation coefficient, 451–454
    multiple-regression analysis. See
    Multiple-regression analysis
    prediction of Y, 449–450
    simple regression analysis, 441–454
    slope coefficient, 447–449
    standard error of estimate, 446–447
Relative precision, 317–318, 320
Reliability of measurement, 258–260
Repositioning a Brand, 552–553
Research design
    causal research. See Causal research
    defined, 58
    descriptive research. See Descriptive
    research
    exploratory research. See Exploratory
    research
    relationships between types, 59
    as second step in research process,
    30–31
    types of, 58–60
Research problems, decision problems
translating to, 37–38
Research process, 29–42
    decision makers, 34–37
    problem formulation, 29–30, 34–35
    research proposal, 38–42
    steps in, 29–33

Research proposal, 38–42
Research reports
    appendix, 563
    bar charts, 568–569
    body of, 561–563
    checklist for evaluating, 564
    conclusions and recommendations, 563
    criteria of, 558–563
    examples of inaccuracy in, 560
    executive summary, 561
    form of, 559–563
    graphic presentations, 566–571
    introduction, 561
    line charts, 567–568
    maps in, 569
    oral reports, 563–566
    pie charts, 566–567
    preparation of, 32
    table of contents, 560–561
    title page, 560
    writing criteria, 559
Research suppliers, choosing, 44–45
Resemblance, production of estimates of, 519–522
Response errors. See Field errors
Response latency, 78–79
Response rates, 334, 336
    increasing initial, 334
    for telephone interviews, 331–332
    See also Nonresponse errors
Responses, stability of, 395
Retail industry, marketing research for, 2
Return on Investment (ROI), 3, 18, 19
Riverside County Humane Society, 127, 344
ROI. See Return on Investment (ROI)
Roper Starch Readership Service, 166–167
Rorschach ink blot test, 72
Rubbermaid, 34

S

Sales forecasts, 21
Sales invoices, 149
Samples
    design of, 31–32
    fixed, 285
    independence of, 396–397
    non-probability samples. See Non-probability samples
    probability samples. See Probability samples
    sequential, 285
    steps in drawing, 283–285
    target population, 282, 283–284
    types of, 285
Sample size, 285
    basic considerations for, 312–313
    cost factors for, 321
    decisions regarding, 32
    and multiple objectives, 318
    and population size, 321

precision in determining, 317–318, 319–320
    relationship between confidence levels and confidence interval precision, 314
    using anticipated cross tabs to determine, 322–324
    when estimating means, 313–318
    when estimating proportions, 319–320
Sample surveys. See Cross-sectional analysis
Sampling control for questionnaires, 192–193
Sampling distribution, 291, 299–300
Sampling errors, 328–329
Sampling frame, 31, 284, 330
Sampling from Your Loyalty Database, 345
Sampling Gambling, 347
Sampling Lead-Users for New Products, 344–345
Scales
    for attitude measurement, 233–235
    choice of, 247
    comparative rating, 246–247
    equal-appearing intervals, 237–239
    graphic rating, 244–246
    interval, 235, 236, 243–244, 394
    Likert method of summated ratings, 239–241
    nominal, 234, 236, 393
    ordinal, 234–235, 236, 243–244, 393–394
    rating, 316
    ratio, 235, 236, 394–396
    scaling of psychological attributes, 235–247
    self-report, 236, 237–247
    semantic differential, 241–242
    Stapel, 242–244
    use in questionnaires, 212–214, 216
Scanners, 161–164
SCANTRACK, 161
Seasonality as extraneous variable, 108
Secondary data, 30
    advantages of, 143–144
    census data, 173–174
    company information, 174
    defined, 142
    disadvantages of, 144–148
    economic and statistical information, 175
    external, 151–156
    internal, 148–151
    international and cross-cultural information, 175–176
    market and consumer information, 174–175
    online computer searches, 154–156
    problems of accuracy, 146–148
    problems of fit, 144–146
    standardized marketing information services. See Standardized marketing information services
    types of, 148–156
    using, 142–148

Secondary Data on Health from CDC, 273–274
Secondary source
    defined, 147
    of secondary data, 147–148
    The Statistical Abstract of the United States, 147
Segmentation Study, 554–555
Selection bias as extraneous variable, 110–111
Self-report scales, 236, 237–247
SEM. See Structural equations models (SEM)
Semantic differential scales, 241–242
Sensitive questions, 210–211, 221
Sentence completion, 70–71
Sequence of questions, 220–221
Sequential ordering, 102
Sequential samples, 285
Serendipity, 34, 66
Service quality example, 52–54
Similarity, 525
Similarity, production of estimates of, 519–522
Simmons Media/Marketing Service, 167, 168–169
Simple matching coefficient, 521
Simple random samples, 285, 287–298
    central-limit theorem, 293
    confidence interval estimates, 293–295
    derived population, 288–289, 290
    drawing, 296–298
    parent population, 288
    population variance, 295–296
    sample mean versus population mean, 289–292
Simple regression analysis, 441–454
Simple tabulation, 352
Simulated test market (STM), 122
Simulations, 24
    computer, 77–78
Single-source data, 162
Slope coefficient, 447–449
Snowball sample, 287
Social networks, 2, 3, 541–543
Socioeconomic characteristics, primary data of, 177–178
Spearman's rank correlation coefficient, 385–386
Speed. See Time
Sports Marketing and Television Programming, 549–552
Stability, 259
Standard error of estimate, 446–447
Standardized marketing information services, 156–170
    customer profiles, 156–158
    customized measurements, 170
    mail panels, 170
    measuring product sales and market share, 158–164
Standardized residuals, 360–362
Standard test markets, 120
Stapel scale, 242–244
Static-group comparison, 112–113

Statistic
  defined, 288
  unbiased, 289
  Statistical Abstract of the United States, The, 147
Statistical information, 175
Statistical regression as extraneous variable, 110
STM. *See* Simulated test market (STM)
Store audits, 161
Storytelling, 72, 73
Stratified samples, 285, 298–304
  bases for stratification, 302–303
  confidence interval estimate, 300–302
  cost factors for, 321
  derived population, 299
  increased precision of, 302
  proportionate and disproportionate, 303–304
  sampling distribution, 299–300
Structural equations models (SEM), 539–540
Structure
  in observation method of data collection, 201
  in questionnaires, 188, 190, 205
Structured-disguised questionnaires, 190–191
Structured-undisguised questionnaires, 188–189
Substantive interpretation in factor analysis, 499–503
  naming the factors, 502–503
  rotating the factors, 500–502
Summarizing data in factor analysis, 493–499
  communalities, 495
  conceptual basis of Principal Components Analysis (PCA), 495–496
  determining the number of factors, 496–499
  factor loadings, 494–495
Summary, 358
Summated ratings, 239–241
Survey Research Center, University of Michigan, 184
Surveys
  e-mail. *See* Online surveys
  experience, 62
  fax. *See* Fax surveys
  telephone. *See* Telephone interviews
  See also Questionnaires
Symmetric multiprocessing (SMP), 25
Systematic errors, 254
Systematic sampling, 304–305

T

Tabulation, 32, 352–359
  cross. *See* Cross-tabulation of data, 32
  one-way, 352–359

presenting tabular data, 374
  simple, 352
Target markets and statistical samples, 323–324
Target population, 282, 283–284
Teeth-Whitening Conjoint Study, 549, 550–551
Telephone interviews, 191
  administrative control of, 197–201
  advantages and disadvantages of, 200
  Computerized Adaptive Telephone Interviewing (CATI), 195, 196
  getting cooperation for, 193
  information control for, 195
  outcomes in, 331
  practices, 194
  random digit dialing (RDD), 192
  response rates for, 331–332
  sampling control for, 192
Telescoping errors, 209–210
Television advertising, 164–166
Testing effect on extraneous variable, 109
Test marketing
  growth of, 119
  problems with, 119–120
  types of, 120–122
  use of cluster analysis, 507
Thematic Apperception Test (TAT), 72
Thought units, 80
Three-group case, discriminant analysis of, 488–490
  classifying respondents, 488–489
  key variables, 489–490
Time
  as advantage of secondary data, 143–144
  considerations in primary data collection, 187–188
Time order of occurrence of variables, 102–103
Time-series experiment, 116–118
TiVo, 164
Total association, 368
Total variation, 429, 430
True experimental designs, 113–116
True panels, 89, 90–93
Two-group case, discriminant analysis of, 478–487
  assessing classification accuracy, 487
  classifying individuals using the discriminant function, 485–487
  determining the coefficients, 480–482
  discriminant coefficients, 483–484
  discriminant loadings, 484–485
  interpreting the discriminant function, 482–483
Two-stage area sampling, 306–307
Type I error, 404–405
Type II error, 404–405

U

Unanticipated change, 34
Unbiased statistic, 289
Univariate statistics, 400
Universal Product Codes (UPCs), 161–162
Unstructured-disguised questionnaires, 190
UPCs. *See* Universal Product Codes (UPCs)

V

Validity, 107
  construct, 257–258
  content, 256–257
  of measurement, 254–256, 256–258
  predictive, 256
VALS. *See* Value and Lifestyles (VALS) inventories
Value and Lifestyles (VALS) inventories, 179, 180, 181–182
Variables
  control of, 398
  dependent, 441
  dummy, 464–465
  extraneous. *See* Extraneous variables
  independent, 441
  number of, 398
  See also Multivariate analysis
Variable transformations, 463–464
Variance, analysis. *See* Analysis of variance (ANOVA)
Variance, population. *See* Population variance
Versatility of primary data collection, 186–187
Virtual reality, 77–78
Voice pitch analysis, 79

W

Wal-Mart, 25
Web surveys. *See* Online surveys
Within-group variation, 429, 430
Word association, 70
Wording of questions, 216–220

X

Xerox, 35, 62

Y

Youth market, 147

Z

Zero order association, 368

A

Abrams, Bill, 75n
Adiguzel, Feray, 224n
Albaum, Gerald, 215
Allenby, Greg M., 382n, 475n
Anderson, Eugene W., 22n
Andrews, Rick L., 454n
Angrosino, Michael, 201n
Ansari, Asim, 88n
Arabie, Phipps, 524, 532n
Aribarg, Anocha, 472n
Arora, Neeraj, 116n
Atkinson, Paul A., 75n

B

Bachmann, Duane P., 199
Bao, Yeqing, 215
Batsell, Richard R., 472n
Baumgartner, Bernhard, 472n
Baumgartner, Hans, 90n, 256
Bearden, William, 178n
Berndt, Ernst R., 123
Bitner, Mary Jo, 506n
Bockenholt, Ulf, 454n
Bodapati, Anand, 524
Borghini, Stefania, 75n
Bowman, Douglas, 541n
Boyle, Gregory J., 70n
Bradburn, Norman M., 218
Bradlow, Eric T., 2n, 94n
Briesch, Richard A., 382n
Bronner, Fred, 197n
Brown, Stephen W., 506n
Bruner, Gordon C., 178n
Buckley, Nick, 2n
Bucklin, Randolph E., 89n, 157n

C

Campbell, Donald T., 116n
Cannon, Hugh, 162n, 420n
Carman, James, 67n
Carroll, J. Douglas, 532n
Chandy, Rajesh K., 454n
Chen, Qimei, 257n
Chen, Yuxin, 454n
Chintagunta, Pradeep K., 382n
Cho, Young Ilk, 256
Christen, Markus, 116n
Churchill, Gilbert A., Jr, 247
Clancy, Kevin J., 122n
Clark, Robert, 193n
Coelho, Pedro S., 215
Colby, Deborah, 3n

Conan Doyle, Arthur, 103n
Cooke, Mick, 2n
Coulter, Robin A., 256
Cron, William, 475n
Crowley, Ed, 24n
Currim, Imran S., 454n

D

Datallo, Patrick, 312n
de Jong, Martijn G., 256
DelVecchio, Devon, 116n
DeSarbo, Wayne S., 523n, 532n
Deutskens, Elisabeth, 197n
Diamond, Nina, 75n
Dineen, Brian R., 116n
Ding, Min, 472n
Dolen, Willemijn, 67n
Dommeyer, Curt J., 199
Donohue, Julie M., 123
Du, Rex Y., 94n
Dube, Jean-Pierre, 162n
Duhachek, Adam, 135n
Durante, Richard, 76
Dutta, Shantanu, 116n

E

Ebbes, Peter, 454n
Edelstein, Herb, 19
Elberse, Anita, 88n
Elfrink, John, 199
Elmer, John B., 472n
Erdem, Tulin, 466n
Escalas, Jennifer E., 71n
Esteves, Susana P., 215
Etzel, Michael J., 252

F

Fader, Peter S., 2n, 19, 94n
Farr, Marc, 157n
Faulkner, Margaret, 123
Feeham, Michael, 76
Fennell, Geraldine, 382n
Fienberg, Fred, 79n, 382n
Fong, Duncan, 523n
Forman, Chris, 149n
Foutz, Natasha Zhang, 472n
Fowler, Floyd J., 193n

Fox, Edward J., 382n
Fox, Jean-Paul, 256
Frees, Edward W., 90n
Fricker, Ronald D., Jr., 362n

G

Ganesan, Shankar, 90n
Gardyn, Rebecca, 79n
Gaski, John F., 252
Germain, Richard, 87
Ghose, Anindya, 149n
Gilbert, Jennifer, 79n
Gilbride, Timothy J., 382n
Girod, Isabelle, 466n
Goldfarb, Avi, 149n
Gonul, Fusun F., 116n
Gonzales-Benito, Javier, 157n
Gonzales-Benito, Oscar, 157n
Goos, Peter, 472n
Goritz, Anja, 334n
Graham, Hugh, 237n
Grapentine, Terry A., 525
Grecco, Chris, 206n
Green, Paul E., 466n
Greenleaf, Eric, 256
Gregory, James R., 13n
Grewal, Rajdeep, 532n
Gronholdt, Lars, 541n
Gupta, Alok, 454n
Gupta, Sachin, 162n
Gupta, Sunil, 88n
Gutchess, Angela H., 79n
Gwinner, Kenneth P., 506n

H

Hamilton, Kate, 64
Hamilton, Rebecca W., 472n
Hanssens, Dominique M., 287n
Hardie, Bruce G. S., 19
Hayes, Constance L., 25n
Heijden, Peter G. M. van der, 211n
Henderson, Naomi R., 64
Henderson, Pamela W., 221n
Henderson, Ty, 116n
Hensel, Paul, 178n
Hershberger, Edmund, 13n
Hitchon, Jacqueline C., 127n, 264n
Hofstede, Frenkel Ter, 116n
Hogg, Alan, 199
Holton, Lisa, 76
Hox, Joop J., 211n

Huber, Joel, 382n, 472n
Huber, Mark W., 22n
Huber, Peter J., 356n
Hui, Sam, 2n

I

Iacobucci, Dawn, 23, 411n, 524
Iyengar, Raghuram, 88n, 472n

J

James, Karen, 178n
Jank, Wolfgang, 157n
Jarvis, Cheryl Burke, 116n
Javalgi, Rajshekhar, 7n
Jedidi, Kamel, 466n, 472n
Jerath, Kinshuk, 19
Johnson, Devon S., 540n
Johnson, Timothy, 256
Jones, Catherine, 157n
Jong, Ad de, 197n

K

Kalra, Ajay, 454n
Kalyanam, Kirthi, 123
Kamakura, Wagner, 94n
Kannan, P. K., 157n
Kavaliunas, John, 146
Kennedy, Rachel, 123
Kerin, Roger, 475n
Kettenring, Jon R., 523n
Khan, Romana, 532n
King, Hal, 206n
Kivetz, Ran, 149n
Klink, Richard R., 116n
Kobayashi, Kazuo, 13n
Kohli, Rajeev, 472n
Kozinets, Robert V., 75n, 77
Krieg, Peter, 122n
Krieger, Abba M., 466n
Krishna, A., 162n, 454n
Krushkal, J. B., 528n
Kuijlen, Ton, 197n
Kulesa, Patrick, 256
Kumar, Ajith, 506n

L

Lacey, Russell, 71n
Lach, Jennifer, 26n
Lattin, James, 149n
Lauring, Stephen, 45
Lee, Barton, 10
Lee, Julie Ann, 179n
Leeflang, Peter, 454n
Leichty, John C., 88n

Lemeshow, Stanley, 308n
Lensvelt-Mulders, Gerty J. L. M., 211n
Lepkowski, James M., 193n
Levy, Paul S., 308n
Levy, Sidney, 73
Lewis, Michael, 149n
Li, Shibo, 88n
Liechty, J., 523n
Likert, Rensis, 239n
Lim, Jooseop, 454n
Linn, Susan, 91
Lipke, David, 466n
Liu, Qing, 475n
Liu, Yunchuan Frank, 454n
Llc, Isr, 256
Lohmeyer, Lori, 119n
Louviere, Jordan, 179n, 466n
Lurie, Nicholas, 566n
Lynch, John G., Jr., 209n

M

Maas, Cora J. M., 211n
MacElroy, Bill, 223
Malter, Alan J., 90n
Mariampolski, Hy, 76
Marlowe, David, 64
Marr, Norman E., 335n
Martensen, Anne, 541n
Masanis, Todd, 123
Mason, Charlotte H., 566n
McElgunn, Jim, 119n
McGovern, Gail, 149n
McGrath, Mary Ann, 75n
McGraw, A. Peter, 209n
McIntyre, Shelby, 123
McKnight, Patrick E., 336n
Mellers, Barbara A., 209n
Michaud, Andrea, 191
Miller, Jeff, 199
Mittal, Vikas, 22n
Montgomery, Alan L., 88n
Moon, Youngme, 149n
Moore, James S., 490
Moore, Robert, 524
Moorman, Christine, 90n, 541n
Morgan, Neil A., 22n
Moriarty, Eleanor, 199
Morrison, Donald G., 89n
Morwitz, Vicki G., 454n
Moscardo, Gianna, 179
Moses, Elissa, 182
Mourali, Mehdi, 257n
Mukherji, Prokriti, 116n
Muniz, Albert, 75n

N

Narayandas, Das, 541n
Neff, Jack, 88, 287n
Netemeyer, Richard, 178n

Netzer, Oded, 149n
Niedrich, Ronald W., 239n, 335n
Nijs, Vincent, 88n
Niraj, Rakesh, 382n
Novak, Thomas P., 90n
Nyeck, Simon, 257n

O

Okazaki, Shintaro, 195n
Orazem, Peer, 532n
Osgood, Charles E., 241n
Ostrom, Amy, 541n
Otter, Thomas, 475n
Otto, Daniel, 532n

P

Padmanabhan, V., 382n
Pauwels, Koen, 88n, 89n
Payne, Stanley L., 218
Peter, J Paul, 247
Pitterle, Sara L., 544n
Polk, Thad A., 79n
Pons, Frank, 257n
Prabhu, Jaideep C., 454n
Prelac, Drazen, 209n
Price, Linda L., 256
Punj, Girish N., 524

R

Rajiv, Surendra, 116n
Rao, Raghunath S., 454n
Reid, Donna J., 67n
Reid, Fraser J. M., 67n
Rennhak, Carsten, 420n
Rindfleisch, Aric, 90n, 541n
Ritov, Ilana, 209n
Rivers, Drew, 215
Robertshaw, Gary S., 335n
Roddy, Clive, 70n
Rodgers, Shelly, 257n
Rogers, Robert D., 215
Ronchetti, Elvezio M., 356n
Rook, Dennis, 63n
Roster, Catherine, 215
Ruyter, Do de, 67n
Ruyter, Ko de, 197n
Ryals, Lynette, 123
Ryan, Thomas P., 107n, 442n

S

Sahami, Mehran, 26n
Saklani, Soumya, 10
Sapede, Claudine, 466n
Sarvary, Miklos, 116n
Saxton, K., 523n

Schor, Juliet B., 91
Schwaiger, Manfred, 420n
Schweidel, David A., 94n
Scott, Crystal J., 532n
Seetharaman, P. B., 382n
Segal, Madhav, 13n
Seshasainam, Preethika, 149n
Sethuraman, Raj, 475n
Shandasani, Prem, 63n
Shao, Alan T., 215
Sharma, Subhash, 178n
Shavitt, Sharon, 256
Sherry, John F., 75n
Shi, Mengze, 454n
Shipchandler, Zoher E., 490
Siddarth, S., 89n, 157n
Silva-Rosso, Jorge M., 157n
Slotegraaf, Rebecca, 89n
Smith, J. Alexander, 162n
Smith, Scott M., 538n
Soutar, Geoffrey N., 179n
Spears, Nancy, 87
Srinivasan, Kannan, 88n, 454n
Srinivasan, Shuba, 88n
Srinivasan, V., 149n
Srivastava, Ashok, 26n
Srivastava, Joydeep, 472n
Stanek, Larry P., 40
Stanley, Julian, 116n
Steckel, Joel, 454n
Steel, David, 193n
Steememan, Ton, 454n
Steenkamp, Jan Benedict, 90n, 256
Steiner, Winfried J., 472n
Stewart, David W., 7n, 63n
Strizhakova, Yuliya, 256
Suci, George J., 241n
Sudman, Seymour, 92n, 218
Swain, Scott, 239n, 335n

Swait, Joffre, 466n
Synodinos, Nicolaos E., 13n

T

Tannenbaum, Percy H., 241n
Tatterson, David, 10
Taylor, Charles R., 420n
Teas, R. Kenneth, 525
Thomas, Randall, 395
Twain, Mark, 450

U

Underhill, Paco, 2n, 74n
Urminsky, Oleg, 149n

V

Vandebroek, Martina, 472n
Vavra, Terry G., 466n
Vazzana, Gary, 199
Vence, Deborah, 7n, 19, 143, 201
Venkatesh, B., 402
Vermeulen, Bart, 472n
Villanueva, Julian, 287n
Viswanathan, Madhu, 257n

W

Wansink, Brian, 92n, 218
Ward, James, 541n
Wardlaw, Jessica, 157n

Wasseman, Todd, 119n
Wasserman, Larry, 399n
Weathers, Danny, 239n, 335n
Wedel, Michel, 224n, 454n
Wells, Leigh, 19
Wells, William D., 257n
Wentz, Laurel, 146
Wetzels, Martin, 197n
Whitlark, David B., 538n
Williams, David, 162n
Wilson, Hugh, 123
Wolf, Marianne, 122n
Wolf, Sharon, 76
Wyner, Gordon, 7n

Y

Yang, Sha, 454n
Yoo, Shijin, 287n
Yoon, Carolyn, 79n
Young, Robert B., 7n
Yu, Julie H., 215
Yuan, Hong, 454n

Z

Zaltman, Gerald, 71n
Zaltman, Lindsay H., 71n
Zauberman, Gal, 209n
Zeisel, Hans, 100n, 101n
Zhang, Jie, 162n
Zhang, John, 466n
Zhang, Z., 454n
Zheng, Yuhuang, 149n